A History of Goblins

Matt King

A History of Goblins

palgrave
macmillan

Matt King
Department of History
University of South Florida
Tampa, USA

ISBN 978-3-032-01062-9   ISBN 978-3-032-01063-6   (eBook)
https://doi.org/10.1007/978-3-032-01063-6

Cover illustration: © past art / Alamy, designed by eStudioCalamar

This Palgrave Macmillan imprint is published by the registered company Springer Nature Switzerland AG.
The registered company address is: Gewerbestrasse 11, 6330 Cham, Switzerland

If disposing of this product, please recycle the paper.

For Meara, who supported me as I went full Goblin Mode despite her being pregnant with our little goblin.

And for Octavia, the aforementioned little goblin.

Acknowledgments

I could not have written this book without the support of an incredible group of colleagues, librarians, archivists, administrators, friends, and family. I am grateful to my colleagues at the University of South Florida (USF) for providing guidance on various aspects of this project. Nicole Discenza and Anne Latowsky assisted with translations of Middle English and Old French texts (respectively). Amy Rust, Brian Connolly, and Mako Nozu directed me to relevant sources related to their areas of expertise. The members of the USF Humanities Institute Faculty Writing Support Group (Jeni Knight, Emily Jones, Liz Ricketts-Jones, and Kyle Burke) held me accountable to deadlines and gave invaluable comments on multiple chapter drafts. Funding from USF Research & Innovation, Humanities Institute, and Department of History allowed me to travel and access paid databases for this book.

I am also indebted to the scholars and subject area experts who were kind enough to respond to an email from a stranger asking about them about goblins: Michael Ostling, Jessica Hemming, Mikki Brock, Krin Gabbard, Eric Lott, JanBart Hendriksen, Scott Bruce, Selena Fox, George Franklin, Riven Lake, Ben Kowalsky-Grahek, Morgan Daimler, Steve Jackson, and Brad Eden. Our correspondence has strengthened this work and exposed me to avenues of scholarship that I otherwise would not have encountered. I want to give special thanks to Ron James and Simon Young for providing generous feedback on my project and a draft of its introduction. Carla Suhr was kind enough, too, to search her corpus of witchcraft pamphlets for mentions of goblins. I am also grateful to the editorial team at the journal *Folklore* for allowing me to use portions of my 2024 article

"Taxonomizing Goblins from Folklore to Fiction" (Volume 135, Issue 1) across the chapters of this book (copyright held by the Folklore Society). It is accessible here: https://doi.org/10.1080/0015587X.2023.2259727. To anyone that I forgot to include in these above lists, I apologize profusely.

Librarians, archivists, and curators are the unsung heroes of this book. I cannot imagine a work of this scope without access to digital resources that cross institutional and political borders. I would like to thank those that organize and maintain these invaluable repositories, including the staff at (in no particular order) the British Library, Getty Museum, University of Maine, Florida State University, University of South Florida, Oxford University, Cambridge University, Library of Congress, Clemson University, University of Michigan, Harvard University, University of California Santa Barbara, Penn State University, National Library of Medicine, Brigham Young University, University of Glasgow, University of Edinburgh, Metropolitan Museum of Art, and Johns Hopkins University. I want to especially thank Kathryn Mercer and the staff at the Taranaki Research Centre (Te Pua Wānanga o Taranaki) for opening their doors to me and providing me with access to resources related to the Goblin Forest. I wish my section on this magnificent landscape could have been longer—but who knows, it might end up being an article project in the future! The staff at USF, especially ILL-miracle-worker Sandra Law, were also instrumental in helping me navigate our university's Byzantine bureaucracy and obtain research-related resources.

I owe a particular debt of gratitude to those who work to preserve our history and culture without compensation by scanning, uploading, and archiving media on the Internet Archive, Project Gutenberg, and Wikimedia (among other repositories). The preservation of this public domain content at the grassroots level is inspiring and has immeasurably enriched this book. I know virtually nothing about these people beyond the usernames they provide in metadata for these digitized sources, but I want them to know that their work is deeply appreciated. The team behind Zotero also deserves praise for their commitment to helping scholars organize their work through their development of free, open-source software.

I am grateful to Carly Silver at Palgrave for seeing something of value in this project when it was still in its early stages and working with me to see it over the finish line. My initial drafts of this book's introduction were (to put it lightly) in a rough spot as I fluctuated between wanting to write a pop history and a more academic title. Carly's assistance steered me (rightly) to the latter and has led me to produce a much better book. The anonymous peer reviewers of my book proposal and manuscript also provided fantastic feedback that strengthened its argument and direction; if I knew who you were, I would thank you! All mistakes within this book are my own.

Finally, I wish to thank my network of family and friends for their support in the process of writing this history. My parents (Matt and Karen) and sister (Stephanie) provided useful commentary on a handful of chapter drafts. My incredible partner, Meara, has been a pillar of support during both good days and more goblin-y days. I could not have written this book without her love and care.

Associate Professor, Department of History   Matt King
University of South Florida
Tampa, USA

CONTENTS

List of Figures

xvi   LIST OF FIGURES

LIST OF TABLES

CHAPTER 1

Introduction to *A History of Goblins*

It is hard to find a place devoid of goblins. They have stalked the corners of our Earth and fantasy universes in countless variations since the Middle Ages—and the goblins you might encounter today reflect this rich history. Practitioners of modern paganism can provide you with guidelines for contacting goblins, though these creatures might range in disposition from the friendly household helper to the mischievous trickster. Goblins can be found in different kinds of natural landscapes, from the rocky spires of Goblin Valley State Park in Utah to the moss-covered trees of New Zealand's Goblin Forest. You can find goblins working the day shift at Gringotts Wizarding Bank in the *Harry Potter* series and waiting to ambush unwary travelers in the pixelated universe of *The Elder Scrolls Online*. Internet forums dedicated to the Goblincore aesthetic are filled with images of fungi, frogs, moss, and other underappreciated oddities of the natural world that embody its titular inspiration. Those with a particular attachment to this imagery sometimes call themselves "practicing goblins." You can even manifest your inner Goblin Mode by channeling the living-among-your-filth-and-rejecting-societal-norms attitude that so perfectly reflected the messiness of the end of Covid-era lockdowns that it was Oxford Dictionaries' 2022 Word of the Year.

The many variations of goblins you can find today are the result of a fascinating history dating back to the Middle Ages through which people have crafted their own interpretations of what could fittingly be given the

M. King, *A History of Goblins*, https://doi.org/10.1007/978-3-032-01063-6_1

"goblin" label: preternatural creatures of many dispositions, demons, people, wildlife, natural landscapes, genres of stories, and aesthetic standards. Our earliest records of goblins come from the pens of medieval clerics who were perennially occupied with the issue of salvation. They worried that demonic goblins or a demon named Goblin could seduce the Christian faithful into sin. In the era of the Reformation, however, Protestant theologians concluded that goblins were either Catholic follies or baseless superstitions perpetuated (primarily) by uneducated women. Although some urban elites agreed with this sentiment, countless others saw these entities as very real parts of their world whose fleeting interactions with humans helped to explain the otherwise unexplainable. In this poorly documented morass of oral traditions, goblins were usually a generic category of creature that lived in an elusive Fairyland alongside elves, ghosts, hobgoblins, and fairies—all of which could be used interchangeably. Underneath these blurry classifications, though, was an underlying association of the goblin with the abnormal and irregular such that the word could pejoratively describe harmful legislation, Catholic doctrine, and people with atypical appearance (as perceived by any given author).

In the nineteenth century, scholars in the British Isles catalogued goblins alongside other folkloric creatures so that they could be compared across ethnicities and national borders. In these studies, goblins were most often used to designate wide categories of preternatural creatures, but some saw the goblin and hobgoblin as a distinctly English household entity comparable to a range of other creatures from European traditions. Colonial administrators and missionaries operating in the Global South, however, showed little concern for these distinctions. Instead, they used the ubiquitous goblin to label countless creatures from the Japanese *tanuki* to the West African *iwin*. Such designators were less important to these authors than the "civilizing" mission at the heart of their colonial activities, especially conversion to Christianity. Fairy tale compilations of the 1800s based on European folklore used the goblin as a broad designator, too, though it also became increasingly associated with a particular kind of diminutive, grotesque, and masculine troglodyte. Authors emphasized these attributes using language of unnatural freakery—and sometimes even applied the goblin label to humans with physical disabilities or oddities. Language of scientific racism contributed to the labeling of the "pygmies" of Central Africa as goblin-like and as the ancestors of the original European fairies.

By the beginning of the twentieth century, goblins had taken on many forms. The monumental popularity of J.R.R. Tolkien's Middle-earth corpus, however, has had an outsized influence on perceptions of goblins as a specific kind of fantastical creature: short, dark-skinned, cave-dwelling, malevolent, crafty, eminently killable humanoids that serve as foils to parties of heroic adventurers in neo-medieval fantasy universes of lightness/good against darkness/evil. Gary Gygax drew heavily on these motifs in early iterations of his tabletop game, *Dungeons & Dragons* (*D&D*). As low-level antagonists, goblins were cannon fodder for groups of (primarily) young men looking to fulfill their heroic fantasies against foes with unambiguous combat statistics and abilities. Countless works of fantasy media broadly depict goblins along these lines, though it would be a mistake to see such iterations as uncontested. Since the 1980s, some creators have rejected these Tolkienian tropes and the racialism undergirding them. Instead, they have portrayed goblins as sympathetic and bestowed positive characteristics on these creatures inspired by earlier motifs: crafting new technologies, slipping between enemy lines as spies, and upcycling goods found in dungeons. In children's literature of the twenty-first century, too, goblins often serve as misunderstood creatures, strange in appearance but well meaning at heart, whose presence shows the harm that comes from stereotyping those who are different.

This rehabilitation of goblins has perhaps reached its inevitable conclusion in the 2020s. The viral phenomena of Goblincore and Goblin Mode use their titular inspiration as an avatar for two different kinds of resistance to societal norms in the curated age of social media. Their popularity shows that the goblin—ugly, weird, peculiar, misunderstood, and ubiquitous—is widely perceived as a fitting creature to embody appearances and behaviors outside the realm of the acceptable. To be a goblin is to be transgressive; to be transgressive is appropriate when societal expectations are so absurd. Goblins, which for so long were depicted as crude mimicries for a given group's vision of what is right or normal, have thus become an acceptable label or even identity for people to bestow on themselves.

This history is as much a work about goblins as it is the people and societies that crafted them. Such an expansive undertaking has required a mountain of historical evidence and modern scholarship to craft. It is to these sources that we now turn.

SCOPE AND SOURCES

The question that looms largest in the framing of this history is what should be considered a goblin. Should it be restricted to those things specifically called goblins? Or should it envelop creatures or ideas with shared characteristics like the hob, brownie, fairy, pixie, *sidhe*, *Tylwyth Teg*, *huldufölk*, *álfar*, *tengu*, *yōkai*, *skrzat*, *kobold*, and *duende* (to name a few)? The latter approach, I think, would be an important academic endeavor of comparative folklore and cultural history. It would also be a mammoth undertaking that could easily span dozens of volumes and require a breadth of expertise far beyond the reach of any single scholar. For this book, then, my definition of a goblin is strictly lexical and intentionally restricting. I consider demons, preternatural creatures, humans, objects, and ideas that people have explicitly called goblins, including spelling variations and derived words like "hobgoblin." I do not presume an implicit definition of what a goblin looks like or how it ought to behave. Instead, I build a history of goblins from the many ways in which the lexeme has been deployed.[1]

This book, then, is a history of the word "goblin" and its derivations. The breadth of even this approach, which is limiting by design, is imposing. For hundreds of years, the goblin was often a generic marker for demons or preternatural creatures interchangeable with (among other creatures) ghosts, elves, hobgoblins, spirits, and fairies in the English language—and countless others outside of Anglophone traditions.[2] It was a versatile lexeme across genres and contexts. Lewis Carroll, for example, when considering titles for the book that became *Alice's Adventures in*

---

[1] In his study of Icelandic trolls, Jakobsson similarly encourages readers to "refrain from imagining that they know precisely what a troll is." They do "not constitute a race or species," and the conflation of trolls with witches, ghosts, vampires, demons, possessed animals, and mountain dwellers makes taxonomic classification futile. Ármann Jakobsson, *The Troll Inside You: Paranormal Activity in the Medieval North* (Santa Barbara: Punctum Books, 2017), 18.

[2] Noel Williams argues as much: "So the relation between supernatural name and putative referent is a loose one, such that the form of the word may vary whilst the referent remains constant (in some sense), or the referent may vary for a word of fixed form, or both may vary.... Nor is fairy either unique or distinct from other names such as elf, pixy, puck, and goblin. It has no precisely specifiable form, but shades into forms such as *frairies*, *ferrishers*, and *fairfolk*." Noel Williams, "The Semantics of the Word Fairy: Making Meaning Out of Thin Air," in *The Good People: New Fairylore Essays*, ed. Peter Narváez (Lexington: University Press of Kentucky, 1991), 471.

Wonderland (1865), wrote out potential options that included both *Alice's Doings in Elf-Land* and *Alice Among the Goblins*.[3] In the late nineteenth and early twentieth centuries, too, some folklorists categorized preternatural entities from within and outside Anglophone Britain as members of "Goblindom," which indicates the wide umbrella of what these creatures could be. The label was pejoratively applied to ludicrous ideas, atypical landscapes, and people with physical disabilities (all of which were contingent upon the normative eye of a given author). The proliferation of goblins in fantasy literature and media has only expanded this scope of interpretations.

This history of the word "goblin" inherently favors English-language source materials, though I consider other linguistic traditions and scholarship surrounding them as relevant, from the Welsh *coblyn* to the German *kobold* to the Japanese *goburin* (ゴブリン). Hovering around this history, too, are the evolving circumstances in which other preternatural creatures and ideas associated with goblins were invoked, especially elves and fairies. Although I am unable to write parallel histories of these intertwining lexemes in a single monograph, I have tried to make comparisons between them as they intersect. My approach to the history of the goblin therefore has substantial limitations from its definitional outset. As additional difficulties and ambiguities arise in this book, I consider them (most frequently in footnotes), and I devote some of the conclusion to a discussion of possible paths for future research. Indeed, I hope this narrative, however restrictive, provides a workable case study and point of comparison for studies of preternatural creatures and their derivations across historical contexts.

Limitations notwithstanding, this lexical approach to the history of the goblin has certain advantages, especially relating to the issue of classification. Scholars have long struggled with how to categorize the creatures of folk traditions and their many derivations. The magisterial *Standard Dictionary of Folklore, Mythology, and Legend* (1949) provides one definition of the goblin rooted in the French tradition of the domestic spirit:

> A household spirit who plays the same role in French folklore as the Scotch and English brownies, bogles, and boggarts, the German kobolds, etc. He is very helpful around the house but also of capricious and erratic temper,

[3] Lewis Carroll and Roger Lancelyn Green, *The Selected Letters of Lewis Carroll* (London: Palgrave Macmillan, 1989), 29.

mischievous and prankish, given to rapping on walls and doors, moving furniture in the night, breaking dishes, banging pots and pans around, snatching bedclothes off sleepers, etc. Food is left out for the goblin, and often doors are left open for him, just as for all household spirits of this kind in other parts of Europe. Goblins frequent homes where the wine is plentiful and the children pretty. They bring the children dainty tidbits but also punish them when they disobey their mothers. They are fond of horses and often ride them in the night, but also often tangle their manes. The recommended way to get rid of a goblin (if he becomes more of a nuisance than a help) is to sprinkle flaxseed on the floor. He is such a good housekeeper that he will be obliged to pick it up, but after a while he will get tired and go away.[4]

Compare this definition with the simpler one provided by eminent folklorist Katharine Briggs in her 1976 encyclopedia. She considers goblins "a general name for evil and malicious spirits, usually small and grotesque in appearance."[5] W.A. Senior, meanwhile, sidesteps issues of classifications entirely by describing goblins as a "convenient monster to bend, spindle, fold, or mutilate to serve their multiple and multifarious purposes, and that's why we still don't know what one is. At least I don't."[6] The latest iteration of the *Oxford English Dictionary* admirably attempts to hybridize these many ideas from folklore with other contexts:

[4] Maria Leach and Jerome Fried, eds., *Standard Dictionary of Folklore, Mythology, and Legend*, vol. I (New York: Funk & Wagnalls, 1949), 457.

[5] The remainder of this definition briefly notes the more benevolent nature of the hobgoblin (except to Puritans) and the similarities between the "highland FUATH," the French *gobelin*, and the English goblin. Katharine Briggs, *An Encyclopedia of Fairies: Hobgoblins, Brownies, Bogies, and Other Supernatural Creatures* (New York: Pantheon Books, 1976), 194. To be fair, Briggs acknowledged the impossibility of providing discrete, coherent, definitions of these creatures. She was operating, too, in a rich tradition of scholars attempting to classify the inhabitants of Fairyland. Hunt, for example, divided the members of the "fairy family" of Cornwall into five "clearly distinguishable" categories. Robert Hunt, *Popular Romances of the West of England, Or, The Drolls, Traditions and Superstitions of Old Cornwall*, vol. 1 (London: John Camden Hotten, 1865), 65.

[6] W.A. Senior, "Goblins," *Journal of the Fantastic in the Arts* 13, no. 2 (2002): 113. Lysaght approaches the issue of classification with more flexibility in her pioneering study on the banshee. Recognizing variations in name across Ireland, she considers beings associated with announcing recent deaths or ones about to occur. This flexibility is, in part, due to the more focused nature of her archive. Patricia Lysaght, *The Banshee: The Irish Death Messenger* (Boulder: Robert Rinehart Publishers, 1986).

(1) A small, ugly, gnome-like creature of folklore, fairy tales, and fantasy fiction; in early use considered as malevolent or demonic, in later use often as merely mischievous. Sometimes more generally: any imaginary being invoked to frighten children. Cf. hobgoblin. Goblins are often associated with the stealing of children and the stealing and hoarding of gold. They are frequently believed to live in caves, and are now often depicted as green-skinned.

(2) *Figurative.* A source or cause of evil or harm; a malign or destructive influence.[7]

To be sure, all of these definitions envelop a substantial strand of the goblins considered in this history. But they are also either restrictive (*Standard Dictionary*/Briggs/*OED*) such that they exclude some groups specifically called "goblins," or so broad (Senior) that they strip the lexeme of any specificity.[8] For the latter, it is unclear what distinguishes the goblin from virtually any other preternatural creature or monster. For the former, it is unclear how some folkloric iterations of the goblin slot into their definitions. When we encounter the occasional beautiful goblin, how does that creature fit? What about the benevolent and merry goblin? What about the goblin that haunted a particular structure or environment? What about people who considered werewolves and will-o'-the-wisps to be subsumed into the broad category of goblins?

Eschewing a descriptive definition of the goblin allows for a more holistic consideration of the many variations of this lexeme. It allows us to cross from the worlds of demonology and folklore into the many other genres in which goblins materialized, each of which necessarily built off earlier interpretations. We do not need to "lump" or "split" goblins, nor do we need to classify them as "social" or "solitary" creatures, nor do we need to

---

[7] "Goblin, n.1," in *Oxford English Dictionary* (New York: Oxford University Press, March 2022), https://www.oed.com/view/Entry/79613. Future entries for the current iteration of the *OED* will be simplified as *OED*, "[Headword]."

[8] Sometimes, these definitions can lead creatures to be labeled as goblins when they are never named as such. Ostling argues that Pippi Longstocking, for example, has "many standard definitional characteristics of the goblin," but that no one has treated her as one. Michael Ostling, "Introduction: Where've All the Good People Gone?," in *Fairies, Demons, and Nature Spirits: "Small Gods" at the Margins of Christendom*, ed. Michael Ostling (New York: Palgrave Macmillan, 2017), 7.

seek a singular "etic" classification informed by their functions.[9] The word itself is the object of analysis in all its messy diversity, both within and outside of folklore. This is not to say, however, that the word "goblin" is so amorphous and ambiguous as to be devoid of meaning.[10] Even if the goblin was conflated with other creatures and ideas across its history (and even if its naming conventions were less important than the cultural "niches" it occupied) the word still meant something to those who wrote, uttered, or visualized it.[11] To borrow from Michael Ostling and Richard Forest:

[9] On these categories, see Michael Ostling and Richard Forest, "'Goblins, Owles and Sprites': Discerning Early-Modern English Preternatural Beings through Collocational Analysis," *Religion* 44, no. 4 (2014): 548–49; Simon Young and Davide Ermacora, "Introducing the Social Supernatural," in *The Exeter Companion to Fairies, Nereids, Trolls and Other Social Supernatural Beings: European Traditions*, Simon Young and Davide Ermacora, eds. (Exeter: University of Exeter Press, 2024), 4–7. Indeed, as Young argues (here in the context of Cornish folklore), even though folklorists inevitably classify, it is ultimately a "futility," and our classifications are mere "epistemological tools to better understand an amorphous, flowing and yet poorly documented reality" that ought not to be confused with "reality itself." Simon Young, "Against Taxonomy: The Fairy Families of Cornwall," *Cornish Studies* 21, no. 1 (2013): 223–37.

[10] Lewis Spence wrestled with this idea in the 1940s, arguing that the fairy "cannot basically be separated from the ghost, the goblin, or the demon" but that it has "in the course of ages, assumed characteristics which in a secondary sense distinguish it sufficiently from all of these to permit the scientific observer, and to some extent the peasant or the savage, to rank it as a separate variety of spirit, if not as a distinct species. From which it will be manifest that I regard the plea for the identity of all spiritual beings as slightly over-strained." Lewis Spence, *British Fairy Origins* (London: Watts & Co., 1946), 55.

[11] Here, I agree with Francis Young that "folkloric beings can change almost unrecognisably over time, and names thus serve as a poor guide to their nature." The goal of this book, though, is not to search for a singular nature of the goblin, but rather to consider the many ways in which that name has changed over time—both within and outside folkloric contexts. Francis Young, *Twilight of the Godlings: The Shadowy Beginnings of Britain's Supernatural Beings* (New York: Cambridge University Press, 2023), 5. This approach aligns with a "context-oriented" approach of folklore studies that privileges "the ecological conditions and socioeconomic structures that give meaning to folkloric acts." Lauri Honko, "Methods in Folk Narrative Research," in *Nordic Folklore: Recent Studies*, Reimund Kvideland and Henning K. Sehmsdorf, eds. (Bloomington: Indiana University Press, 1989), 23. See, generally, Peter Burke, "History and Folklore: A Historiographical Survey," *Folklore* 115, no. 2 (2004): 133–39; Dan Ben-Amos, *Folklore Concepts: Histories and Critiques*, Henry Glassie and Elliott Oring, eds. (Bloomington: Indiana University Press, 2020), 99–109; J.D.A. Widdowson, "New Beginnings: Towards a National Folklore Survey," *Folklore* 127, no. 3 (2016): 257–69.

As with religion, so with demons, fairies, goblins, and their ilk: we have no data for the thing itself. What we have are words: definitions, contestations, refusals to define. And it is these words (and the stakes involved in using them, the theoretical or cultural assumptions they reveal, their polemical purport), which become our object of study. Our own insistence that neither we nor anyone else is quite sure what they are talking about when they talk about goblins and fairies and pucks and elves should redirect the study of such beings to the study of word choices and of rhetorical strategies. Lacking any readily available intersubjective basis for definitional consensus, goblins (etc.) are pure objects of definition. They are thus especially helpful markers for, or sites of contestation about, other definitional schema: superstition, religion, diabolism, magic.[12]

This lexical approach to the history of goblins also has the practical advantage of facilitating quantitative analysis that shows changes in word usage over time. Here, I humbly follow in the footsteps of Simon Young, who made great use of digital databases in his 2022 monograph, *The Boggart: Folklore, History, Place-names and Dialect*.[13] Online repositories with searchable texts like Early English Books Online, Archive.org, Google Books, Eighteenth Century Collections Online, and Newspapers.com contain millions of sources with the word "goblin" that broadly indicate interest and usage over time.[14] This lexeme has the advantage of not having other widespread connotations that can skew data, like how "ghost"

---

[12] In this article, Ostling and Forest use collocation (the study of the proximity of words to each other) to show how the words "goblin" and "fairy" were used interchangeably as an index of the "domain of the spooky, the eerie, the unknown" in early modern English texts. They argue that we ought to treat preternatural creatures, "as much as possible, as words: as moments of discourse with no reference beyond the associations into which texts put them." Ostling and Forest, "'Goblins, Owles and Sprites': Discerning Early-Modern English Preternatural Beings through Collocational Analysis," 547, 551, 564.

[13] Simon Young, *The Boggart: Folklore, History, Place-Names and Dialect* (Exeter: Exeter University Press, 2022).

[14] Sheena Gardner and Emma Moreton, "Written Corpora," in *The Routledge Handbook of English Language and Digital Humanities*, Svenja Adolphs and Dawn Knight, eds. (New York: Routledge, 2020), 26–48. The sources accessible in these databases change over time, too, in ways that are not transparent to users. When I typed "goblin" into Newspapers.com in January 2024, I received some 1,352,272 matches. That number rose to 1,384,001 by March 2024 and 1,664,124 by December 2024. This instability in source materials unfortunately makes it impossible for the exact parameters of my searches to be replicated. I have ensured, however, that the underlying trends (which are more important) remain consistent as these databases were updated.

and "spirit" are transformed with the word "holy" in front of them. Nor does it overlap with other English words that can complicate search functionality (like elf/elves with self/selves). By analyzing quantitative trends based on deployment of the word "goblin," I show (for example) the decline of goblins as Christian demons in the early modern period, the ascendency of goblins as creatures associated with Halloween instead of Christmas in the late nineteenth century, and surging interest in goblins within works of children's literature during the twenty-first century.[15] Occasionally, this need to prove tendencies over time requires, to borrow a phrase from Latham's foundational work on Elizabethan fairies, a "certain amount of repetition."[16] I hope that my combination of quantitative and qualitative analysis, however, proves effective for balancing this need to demonstrate trends across decades and (sometimes) centuries with the concision required of an academic monograph.

I have also made a handful of other editorial decisions about the goblins to include in this book. The first relates to anthroponyms. Some medieval and early modern texts mention individuals named *Gobelinus*. This appears to be a variant spelling of *Ghibbelin* or *Gibelin*. Albert of Aachen, a participant in the First Crusade, mentions the deposition of a cleric named Evremar, who was succeeded by Gibelin [*Gobelino*] of Arles.[17] A

---

[15] Franco Moretti, *Distant Reading* (New York: Verso, 2013). Digital repositories and the OCR technologies within them, though invaluable, are not without their flaws. Algorithms designed to identify letters often make mistakes that disrupt searches, especially for texts written before the nineteenth century, such as the rendering of a lower-case "l" as an upper-case "I" or confusing the medial "s" [ſ] with a modern "f." Duplicates of documents (especially in the case of Google Books) can risk skewing data, too. These technologies are also constrained by imperfections in the scans of documents: blurred or faded letters, misspellings by typesetters, and the omission of pages. I have tried to mitigate some of these issues by using the asterisk as a "wildcard" symbol in searches, which allows a search of *gob* to return hits with varied spellings like "hobgoblin," "gobelyn," or "gob-lin." When conducting searches like this, I have verified that the results of my searches are actual goblins and not (among others) the Gobelins Manufactory of Paris or a "goblet." Luciana Duranti and Patricia C. Franks, eds., "Digitization," in *Encyclopedia of Archival Science* (Lanham: Rowman & Littlefield, 2015). See also Timothy R. Tangherlini, "The Folklore Macroscope: Challenges for a Computational Folkloristics," *Western Folklore* 72, no. 1 (Winter 2013): 7–27; Jeffrey A. Tolbert and Eric D.M. Johnson, "Digital Folkloristics: Text, Ethnography, and Interdisciplinarity," *Western Folklore* 78, no. 4 (Fall 2019): 327–56.

[16] M.W. Latham, *Elizabethan Fairies: The Fairies of Folklore and the Fairies of Shakespeare* (New York: Columbia University Press, 1972), 13.

[17] Albert of Aachen, *Historia Hierosolymitanae Expeditionis*, vol. 166, Patrologia Latina (Paris: Garnier Fratres, 1894), 677.

medieval German author, Gobelinus Person [*Gobelinus Persona*], wrote a handful of texts in the late fourteenth and early fifteenth centuries as well.[18] In the early modern period, too, the Gobelin family of Paris established a thriving business making tapestries. Despite my best efforts, I could not find a connection between these names and the supernatural creatures of northern France and England. This does not mean that it does not exist, but it is more likely that these names were associated with family names like Ghibelline derived from the geography of southern Germany. I have likewise not analyzed placenames that have a phonetic similarity to the word goblin but are unrelated to the folkloric traditions at the heart of this narrative, as is the case with Beth Gibelin (modern Israel) or Gebelein (modern Egypt).[19] Words that sound similar to "goblin" but are not etymologically related (like the verb "to gobble") are only considered when invoked together.

The tradition of the French *gobelin* has a peculiar role in this history, too. As I discuss in Chap. 2, our earliest attestations of goblins come from two twelfth-century texts written in Normandy (northern France), one each in Latin (*gobelinus*) and Old French (*gobelin*). In subsequent decades, though, this lexeme fell out of favor in France for unclear reasons—especially compared to designators like *fée* and *lutin*. The first edition of the *Dictionnaire de l'Académie française* (*Dictionary of the French Academy*, 1694) does not include an entry for *gobelin*, nor are related preternatural creatures associated with it.[20] *Gobelin* makes its first appearance in the series in its 8th edition from 1932 as an archaic term defined as an *esprit follet*.[21] Indeed, translators of English texts into French since the early modern period have tended to translate "goblin" as anything other than *gobelin*.[22] Conversely, translators of French texts into English have been

---

[18] Thietmarus Merseburgensis, *Notitia in Thietmarum*, vol. 139, Patrologia Latina (Paris: Garnier Fratres, 1880), 1177.

[19] Mathias Piana, "Crusader Fortifications: Between Tradition and Innovation," in *The Crusader World*, ed. Adrian Boas (New York: Taylor & Francis, 2019), 437–59.

[20] *Dictionnaire de l'Académie françoise*, 1st ed., vol. I (Paris: Jean Baptiste Coignard, 1694), 525–26. The term *gobelin* (or any variations) does not appear in the Anglo-Norman Dictionary either: https://anglo-norman.net/.

[21] *Dictionnaire de l'Académie française*, 8th ed., vol. I (Paris: Librairie Hachette, 1932), 602. The word "Gobelins," however, appears as early as the 4th edition of the dictionary (1762) in reference to the tapestry manufacturers.

[22] See, for example, Samuel Butler, *Hudibras. Poëme.*, vol. II (London, 1757), 14–15, 297–98; John Milton, *L'Allegro et le Pensieroso de Milton*, trans. J. Ribouville (London, 1792), 13.

comfortable homogenizing a number of French lexemes into "goblin" or "hobgoblin," including terms with more literal translations like *loup garou* ("werewolf").[23]

Despite a lack of written attestations, the tradition of the *gobelin* certainly persisted in Normandy into the nineteenth century via oral tradition. Thomas Keightley, for example, recorded in *The Fairy Mythology* (1828) how the "house-spirit Follet" is also called "Gobelin" in Normandy. It is used to threaten little children as a fict, like "the Gobelin will eat you; the Gobelin will take you." Songs like "Les Goublins" by Norman songwriter Alfred Rossel further testify to its persistence in folklore.[24] That said, it appears that the *gobelin* tradition of Normandy had little bearing on the Anglophone goblin based on its general absence in written sources since the early modern period. Even in works of comparative folklore, like that of Keightley, the term is used sparingly. Instead, *lutin* and *esprit follet* provide more common points of Francophone comparison. While the Norman *gobelin* thus provides one of our first medieval attestations of the word and was part of a hazy interplay of oral traditions so poorly documented in the textual record, the word had a more demonstrably robust history across the English Channel.[25] Further research into the oral

---

[23] Loup-garou has a fairly straightforward translation of "werewolf," though it was rendered on a handful of occasions as "hobgoblin," which indicates the breadth of perceptions of the latter. An English translation of a French occult satire, *A History of the Ridiculous Extravagancies of Monsieur Oufle*, details how its titular character becomes so obsessed with the occult that he begins to think he is a werewolf. This word is rendered in French as "loup-garou" but translated into English as "hobgoblin." Laurent Bordelon, *L'histoire des imaginations extravagantes de Monsieur Oufle* (Amsterdam: Estienne Roger, Pierre Humbert, Pierre de Coup, & les Frers Chatelain, 1710), 32; Laurent Bordelon, *A History of the Ridiculous Extravagancies of Monsieur Oufle* (London: J. Morphew, 1711), 23. See also Molière, *The Works of Moliere, French and English*, vol. IX (London: D. Browne, 1755), 218–21.

[24] Par Pierre Ropert, "Des contes normands à Tolkien, d'où viennent les gobelins?," RadioFrance, February 9, 2023, https://www.radiofrance.fr/franceculture/des-contes-normands-a-tolkien-d-ou-viennent-les-gobelins-8677528.

[25] Thomas Keightley, *The Fairy Mythology*, vol. II (London: William Harrison Ainsworth, 1828), 297. In *Les Misérables* (1862), the term is used a few times as well—as in a garden "haunted by goblins." Hugo might have even chosen this term because of its antiquated reputation. Victor Hugo, *Les Misérables*, vol. IV (Paris: Pagnerre, 1862), 118. Dévigne's 1942 collection of French folklore classifies *lutins* as "French goblins" ("*gobelins français*"). Roger Dévigne, *Le légendaire de France* (Paris, 1942), 13. Belgian folklorist Albert Doppagne, too, notes that *gobelin* is a "kind of *lutin*, a familiar spirit" used to scare children. Albert Doppagne, *Esprits et génies du terroir* (Gembloux_ J. Duculot, 1977), 40.

traditions and archival records of Normandy could yield additional evidence on this topic.

Fairyland Across Disciplines

The contents of this book comprise over one thousand years of history, traverse countless political and geographical boundaries, and rely on an incredibly diverse pool of sources. Its arguments therefore utilize methodologies from a number of academic disciplines. Synthesizing this material has not been an easy task. Modern universities have long facilitated the siloing of academic disciplines and incentivized scholars to write on narrow topics that fall within their exclusive areas of expertise. While this trend has produced remarkable scholarship, it has simultaneously discouraged research that traces topics across broad stretches of time and space. The sheer amount of scholarship written in any given discipline, paired with the quantity of primary source materials accessible on the Internet, has likewise made it difficult to write on conceptually interdisciplinary topics like this one.[26]

This book draws on scholarship across a variety of academic fields, most prominently folklore studies (folkloristics), history, English literature, monster studies, religious studies, anthropology, game studies (ludology), media studies, disability studies, and cultural studies. However, it would be a mistake to see these disciplines as having neat boundaries when it comes to the world of Fairyland.[27] Monographs on fairy "belief" (a loaded term itself) often include a disclaimer about the interdisciplinarity required of this kind of research and/or the limitations of a given author. Richard Firth Green, for example, prefaces his history of medieval fairies by noting that "I have not been professionally trained as a folklorist, nor can I lay

[26] Louis Menand, *The Marketplace of Ideas: Reform and Resistance in the American University* (New York: W.W. Norton & Company, 2010); Robert Frodeman, *Sustainable Knowledge: A Theory of Interdisciplinarity* (New York: Palgrave Macmillan, 2013).

[27] It would also be a mistake to see these disciplines as working in sustained conversation with one another. Musharbash, for example, notes that "anthropology has not substantially joined in with the burgeoning interdisciplinary field of monster studies." Yasmine Musharbash, "Introduction: Monsters, Anthropology, and Monster Studies," in *Monster Anthropology in Australasia and Beyond*, Yasmine Musharbash and Geir Henning Presterudstuen, eds. (New York: Palgrave Macmillan, 2014), 1.

claim to any special proficiency in this area."[28] Dianne Purkiss, too, calls her foundational study on Fairyland "an imperfect and limping creature."[29] Ronald Hutton's examination of witchcraft mentions that the topic "badly needs and deserves serious treatment by more scholars in a number of different disciplines."[30] Piotr Spyra likewise notes that fairies are "a curious subject of scholarship and invite different interdisciplinary methodologies."[31]

Bearing in mind these messy disciplinary intersections, I have approached scholarship relevant to this book with curiosity and humility, knowing that every field provides insights into the history of goblins but equally aware that I cannot navigate all their contours. Some of the individual texts that I consider, like *The Canterbury Tales* of Chaucer, have been the subject of countless scholarly analyses but are only given a sentence or two of contextualization. This lack of analysis does not mean that such texts are not important enough to warrant meaningful consideration, but that they have a relatively small role to play in this history. Across this book, I have carved out room for brief discussions of relevant scholarship, though I will be the first to recognize that there is not enough space in it to provide adequate commentaries for every text considered therein.[32] This is particularly true of non-Anglophone fairy traditions, which have thematic overlap with many of my arguments but are less applicable to the "goblin" lexeme.

Of central importance to this book is the dialectic between folklore and literature, theater, digital media, and other forms of popular culture that evoke folkloric themes.[33] These iterations of the "folkloresque" (per Foster

---

[28] Richard Firth Green, *Elf Queens and Holy Friars: Fairy Beliefs and the Medieval Church* (Philadelphia: University of Pennsylvania Press, 2016), 7.

[29] Diane Purkiss, *At the Bottom of the Garden: A Dark History of Fairies, Hobgoblins, Nymphs, and Other Troublesome Things* (New York: NYU Press, 2003), xi.

[30] Ronald Hutton, *The Triumph of the Moon: A History of Modern Pagan Witchcraft* (New York: Oxford University Press, 1999), vii.

[31] Piotr Spyra, *The Liminality of Fairies: Readings in Late Medieval English and Scottish Romance* (New York: Routledge, 2020), 1–2.

[32] Auerbach is forthcoming about such limitations in her study of vampires. She notes that she has had to collapse genre distinctions "into episodes in a single story, leaving others to explore the borders between genres and to explain vampires' special affinity for long novels and films." Nina Auerbach, *Our Vampires, Ourselves* (Chicago: University of Chicago Press, 1995), 8.

[33] Although folklore studies has "never gained more than a marginal position in English academia," it has been prominent in Finland (especially) since the 1800s. Alaric Hall, *Elves*

and Tolbert) exist in a relationship to folklore "like a Möbius strip… magically, paradoxically, two different sides of the same surface, never intersecting because they are always already intersecting."[34] Folklore and the folkloresque are always influencing each other, though these exchanges often occur outside of written histories and are (at best) poorly glimpsed in surviving primary sources. For this history, the entanglement of folkloric goblins with those in English literature and theater is particularly pronounced, though academic coverage of the latter is extremely uneven. While there is no shortage of analysis of Shakespearean fairies, much of the subsequent media in which goblins have been featured (children's literature, fantasy, and science fiction in modern nomenclature) has long been considered unworthy of academic analysis. It is only with the cultural turn of the 1960s and movement away from a singular canon of Western literature that scholars have examined these genres as cultural products worthy of study. Such sea changes in higher education facilitated, too, the formation of newer fields like game studies and monster studies, which exist on the peripheries of academic departments and (if lucky) have homes in interdisciplinary centers.[35]

in Anglo-Saxon England: Matters of Belief, Health, Gender and Identity (Rochester: Boydell & Brewer, 2017), 167. See also Diarmuid Ó Giolláin, *Locating Irish Folklore: Tradition, Modernity, Identity* (Cork: Cork University Press, 2000), 76–93.

[34] Michael Dylan Foster, "Introduction: The Challenge of the Folkloresque," in *The Folkloresque: Reframing Folklore in a Popular Culture World*, Michael Dylan Foster and Jeffrey A. Tolbert, eds. (Logan: Utah State University Press, 2016), 25–26. "Folkloresque" provides a less judgmental space to consider works with folkloric themes than Dorson's "fakelore" (1950), which condemned (among others) the tradition of Paul Bunyan. Richard M. Dorson, *Folklore and Fakelore: Essays toward a Discipline of Folk Studies* (Cambridge: Harvard University Press, 1976); Alan Dundes, *Folklore Matters* (Knoxville: University of Tennessee Press, 1989), 40–56.

[35] Drawing on the work of Morin and Derrida (among others), Moser urges those in monster studies to think outside "the confines of a tiny epistemological box" tied to disciplinarity. Keith Moser, "Introduction," in *The Metaphor of the Monster: Interdisciplinary Approaches to Understanding the Monstrous Other in Literature*, Keith Moser and Karina Zelaya, eds. (New York: Bloomsbury Academic, 2020), 1–2. Koenig-Woodyard, Nanayakkara, and Khatri similarly argue that monster studies "transcends the very corporeality of English literary studies as manifested and practised institutionally in undergraduate and graduate English departments and programs." Chris Koenig-Woodyard, Shalini Nanayakkara, and Yashvi Khatri, "Introduction: Monster Studies," *University of Toronto Quarterly* 87, no. 1 (2018): 3. See also Marina Levina and Diem-My T. Bui, eds., *Monster Culture in the 21st Century: A Reader* (New York: Bloomsbury, 2013).

Writing this history of goblins, therefore, has often felt like an exercise in trying to bring together the methodologies of small, marginalized disciplines and the unfrequented corners of more established ones. I have been aided in this task by scholars from a variety of academic backgrounds whose work has tackled various aspects of the fairies and folkloric creatures: Hutton's *The Triumph of the Moon: A History of Modern Pagan Witchcraft*; Silver's *Strange and Secret Peoples: Fairies and Victorian Consciousness*; Magliocco's *Witching Culture: Folklore and Neo-Paganism in America*; Buccola's *Fairies, Fractious Women, and the Old Faith: Fairy Lore in Early Modern British Drama and Culture*; Hall's *Elves in Anglo-Saxon England: Matters of Belief, Health, Gender and Identity*; Talairach-Vielmas' *Fairy Tales, Natural History and Victorian Culture*; Foster's *The Book of Yokai: Mysterious Creatures of Japanese Folklore*; and Henderson's *Witchcraft and Folk Belief in the Age of Enlightenment: Scotland, 1670–1740* are a few of them.[36]

These studies of fairies provide crucial context and methodologies for this history, which is geographically and temporally broader but has a more specific lexical focus. This approach enables the analysis of continuities and ruptures in the evocation of goblins across contexts. It allows us to chart, for example, how the goblin morphed from a creature of folklore, often interchangeable with elves and dwarves, to a lowly antagonist of high fantasy literature that was defined in part by conflict with nobler creatures like elves and dwarves. It shows the vanishing of the demonic goblin from its heyday in the Middle Ages to its near-total erasure such that the suburban parents behind the Satanic Panic of the 1980s showed no interest in goblins despite their presence in the pages of the much-maligned *Dungeons & Dragons*. It highlights how the goblin evolved from a creature of masculine and monstrous deformity to an avatar for online

---

[36] Hutton, *The Triumph of the Moon: A History of Modern Pagan Witchcraft*; Carole G. Silver, *Strange and Secret Peoples: Fairies and Victorian Consciousness* (New York: Oxford University Press, 2000); Sabina Magliocco, *Witching Culture: Folklore and Neo-Paganism in America* (Pennsylvania: University of Pennsylvania Press, 2004); Regina Buccola, *Fairies, Fractious Women, and the Old Faith: Fairy Lore in Early Modern British Drama and Culture* (Selinsgrove: Susquehanna University Press, 2006); Hall, *Elves in Anglo-Saxon England: Matters of Belief, Health, Gender and Identity*; Laurence Talairach-Vielmas, *Fairy Tales, Natural History and Victorian Culture* (New York: Palgrave Macmillan, 2014); Michael Dylan Foster, *The Book of Yokai: Mysterious Creatures of Japanese Folklore* (Berkeley: University of California Press, 2015); Lizanne Henderson, *Witchcraft and Folk Belief in the Age of Enlightenment: Scotland, 1670–1740* (New York: Palgrave Macmillan, 2016).

communities particularly fitting for the LGBTQ+ community, especially non-binary people.

Scholars who have undertaken examinations of preternatural creatures (including those less associated with Fairyland) across contexts have shown the utility of this approach. Auerbach argues in *Our Vampires, Ourselves* that English vampires destabilized intimacies in class and familial relationships of the nineteenth century, while their later American counterparts embodied "seditious urbanity."[37] Purkiss' *At the Bottom of the Garden: A Dark History of Fairies, Hobgoblins, Nymphs, and Other Troublesome Things* catalogues fairy stories from ancient to modern to show their tendency to mediate major points of transition in human life: birth, sex, marriage, and death.[38] Hutton's *Queens of the Wild: Pagan Goddesses in Christian Europe: An Investigation* shows the persistence and variance of feminine "beings" that do not "fit very well into the categories of pagan or Christian."[39] Francis Young's *Twilight of the Godlings: The Shadowy Beginnings of Britain's Supernatural Beings* argues that fairy belief in Britain was not the result of literary constructs, but of "sustained interaction between learned and popular culture" between the Roman and Norman conquests.[40] A number of edited volumes, too, have provided explicitly comparative approaches to the fairies to great effect, including Narváez's *The Good People: New Fairylore Essays*, Ostling's *Fairies, Demons, and Nature Spirits:*

---

[37] Auerbach, *Our Vampires, Ourselves*, 7. Even broader in scope is Stephen T. Asma, *On Monsters: An Unnatural History of Our Worst Fears* (New York: Oxford University Press, 2009). In the case of these studies, authors inevitably have to make difficult classificatory decisions about what to include and omit. Hutton, in his study of witches, defines them as "an alleged worker" of "destructive magic," which knowingly omits certain, more positive definitions that have become more common in recent decades. Ronald Hutton, *The Witch: A History of Fear, from Ancient Times to the Present* (New Haven: Yale University Press, 2017), x.

[38] Fairies preside "over the borders of our lives, the seams between one phase of life and another." Purkiss, *At the Bottom of the Garden: A Dark History of Fairies, Hobgoblins, Nymphs, and Other Troublesome Things*, 4.

[39] Ronald Hutton, *Queens of the Wild: Pagan Goddesses in Christian Europe: An Investigation* (New Haven: Yale University Press, 2022), 40.

[40] Young, *Twilight of the Godlings: The Shadowy Beginnings of Britain's Supernatural Beings*, 20. Lindow's *Trolls: An Unnatural History*, Sugg's *Fairies: A Dangerous History*, and Scribner's *Merpeople: A Human History* also consider specific folkloric creatures, highlighting their intersections with American capitalism and modern film (among others). John Lindow, *Trolls: An Unnatural History* (London: Reaktion Books, 2014); Richard Sugg, *Fairies: A Dangerous History* (London: Reaktion Books, 2018); Vaughn Scribner, *Merpeople: A Human History* (London: Reaktion Books, 2020).

'Small Gods' at the Margins of Christendom, Teverson's *The Fairy Tale World*, and Young and Ermacora's *The Exeter Companion to Fairies, Nereids, Trolls and Other Social Supernatural Beings.*[41]

Broadly taken, these studies on the preternatural, in the realms of both folklore and the folkloresque, approach their subject matter with the goal of understanding the worlds of those who believed in and/or wrote about them. They do not seek to give definitive answers about the existence or ontology of fairies.[42] Nor do they attempt to connect them to observable natural phenomena or historical people (euhemerism).[43] Nor do they seek to use folklore to make claims about the fundamental nature of peoples and nations.[44] Fairies were not the product of a static rural environment, unchanged across the centuries, but rather the result of changing contexts that necessarily gave rise to diverse beliefs—a push and pull between past

[41] Peter Narváez, ed., *The Good People: New Fairylore Essays* (Lexington: University Press of Kentucky, 1991); Michael Ostling, ed., *Fairies, Demons, and Nature Spirits: "Small Gods" at the Margins of Christendom* (New York: Palgrave Macmillan, 2017); Andrew Teverson, ed., *The Fairy Tale World* (New York: Routledge, 2019); Simon Young and Davide Ermacora, eds., *The Exeter Companion to Fairies, Nereids, Trolls and Other Social Supernatural Beings: European Traditions* (Exeter: University of Exeter Press, 2024). Worth mentioning, too, are the primary source compilations by Penguin Press that focus on preternatural phenomena, including Cristina Bacchilega and Marie Alohalani Brown, eds., *The Penguin Book of Mermaids* (New York: Penguin, 2019); Scott G. Bruce, ed., *The Penguin Book of Dragons* (New York: Penguin, 2021).

[42] This trend in folklore studies overlaps with the ontological turn of anthropology, which emphasizes alterity and different ways of being as opposed to "a stable and universal 'nature'" that can be viewed through various cultural perspectives. Rather than attempting to pigeonhole different belief systems into a shared reality, anthropologists have emphasized the fundamentally different worlds (and not worldviews) that communities inhabit. Paolo Heywood, "Anthropology and What There Is: Reflections on 'Ontology,'" *The Cambridge Journal of Anthropology* 30, no. 1 (2012): 143. This is not to say that scholarship on the actual existence of folkloric creatures has entirely disappeared. See, for example, Benjamin Radford, *Tracking the Chupacabra: The Vampire Beast in Fact, Fiction, and Folklore* (Albuquerque: University of New Mexico Press, 2011).

[43] Writing in 1967, Katharine Briggs argues that "this is not an attempt to prove that fairies are real. My intention has been to report objectively what people believed themselves to have seen…. As far as my personal belief goes the most I can say is that I am agnostic on the subject." Katharine Briggs, *The Fairies in Tradition and Literature* (New York: Routledge, 1967), ix–x. Henderson and Cowan similarly write that they "are not concerned with proving the reality, or otherwise, of fairies; such an endeavor would be as futile as it is irrelevant." Lizanne Henderson and Edward J. Cowan, *Scottish Fairy Belief: A History* (Edinburgh: Tuckwell Press, Ltd, 2001), 2.

[44] Timothy Baycroft and David Hopkin, eds., *Folklore and Nationalism in Europe during the Long Nineteenth Century* (Leiden: Brill, 2012).

traditions and the "pull of present (and future) needs."[45] These traditions were historically contingent, grounded in genres and discourses informed by concerns that enveloped not only folkloric tradition, but literature and other forms of popular media gravitating around it, each of which influenced the other.[46] This evolving conversation between folklore and the folkloresque, so crucial but also frustratingly difficult to tease out with precision, is central to this history.[47]

CHAPTER SUMMARIES

This book explores many of the goblins that historical communities have imagined and crafted since the Middle Ages. Chapter 2 considers the origins of the lexeme "goblin" and its uses in Latin, Old French, and Middle English texts from the medieval period. Likely deriving from the ancient Greek *kobalos*, the term migrated into Latin as *gobelinus* and then Middle English as *gobelyn*. Medieval clerics writing in northern France and England wrote about both a particular demon named Goblin and groups of demonic goblins that were threats to non-Christians. These goblins

---

[45] Foster's introduction to his study of *yōkai* provides a useful synthesis of this tension. Foster, *The Book of Yokai: Mysterious Creatures of Japanese Folklore*, 27–31.

[46] In the late nineteenth century, folklorist Edwin Sidney Hartland defines folklore as "anthropology dealing with psychological phenomena of uncivilized man." This and other early definitions are discussed in Otis T. Mason, "Anthropology in 1886," in *Annual Report of the Board of Regents of the Smithsonian Institution* (Washington, D.C.: Government Printing Office, 1889), 540–42. William Henderson similarly romanticizes the countryside as a place where antiquity breathes: "It is difficult, while living on the surface of society, so smooth, so rational, so commonplace, to realise what relics of a widely different past linger in its depths.... Yet so it is: in almost every part of our island we occasionally come across such bits of stubborn antiquity, but in the North of England they abound." William Henderson, *Notes on the Folk-Lore of the Northern Counties of England and the Borders* (London: W. Satchell, Peyton and Co., 1879), 1. See also Hutton, *The Triumph of the Moon: A History of Modern Pagan Witchcraft*, 112–31.

[47] Tolbert argues that "the folkloresque embraces the diversity and creativity of folkloric adaptations and new folklore-like creations in various contexts; it is a critical but nonjudgmental term. Far from a recapitulation of concepts like fakelore and folklorism, the folkloresque enables us to begin to understand how folklore and its related concepts—for example, tradition, heritage, legend, myth—are invoked in non-scholarly contexts and the various ways new cultural products perform their connections to existing folklore." Jeffrey A. Tolbert, "Introduction: The Value of Recursion," in *Möbius Media: Popular Culture, Folklore, and the Folkloresque*, Jeffrey A. Tolbert and Michael Dylan Foster, eds. (Logan: Utah State University Press, 2024), 5.

tended to be associated with darkness, ugliness, and sin—often juxtaposed with the light, beauty, and salvation of God. Beneath these vitriolic condemnations of demonic goblins, though, we can glimpse widespread traditions of fairy belief among non-clerics, of which goblins, elves, and fairies were a vibrant part. These preternatural creatures tended to be associated not with satanic threats, but with the otherwise unexplainable (and often unfortunate) occurrences of daily life. They were part of a world that was alive with spirits, which are difficult to categorize as Christian or pagan or something else because such distinctions were of little relevance to those who encountered them. So ubiquitous and powerful were the fairies that, by the middle of the fifteenth century, rebels against the English monarchy affiliated themselves with the Fairy King and Fairy Queen, whose realm was outside the jurisdiction of any human government.

We are fortunate to have many more surviving texts from the early modern period (c. 1500–1800) that testify to the prevalence of goblins in England and its colonies. Chapter 3 shows how goblins were caught up in Reformation-era debates about the existence of demonic entities on Earth. Protestant authors largely dismissed preternatural creatures as conjurations of Catholic fearmongers or superstitions of the ignorant. With Protestant ascendency in Britain came the minimization of goblins as a threat to the Christian faithful. Underneath this demonological discourse, however, were goblins of folk traditions that operated alongside Christian practices. Some beliefs held that goblins could assist in household chores if provided with the appropriate provisions—reminiscent of another folkloric creature, the "hob," and linked to the creation of the hybrid "hobgoblin." Others considered goblins to be more dangerous creatures that could inflict harm on humans by kidnapping children, harassing travelers in the woods, and pinching people when they were not looking. The ballads of Robin Goodfellow and plays of Shakespeare depicted goblins that were comical, mischievous, or helpful depending on the circumstance. Lurking beneath these interpretations, however, was a clear association of the goblin with notions of harm, trickery, and abnormality. The literary deployment of the goblin not as a creature, but as an abstraction or descriptor, trended toward this malevolence more than merriment.

Chapter 4 examines the fate of the goblin as the imperial and colonial interests of the British Empire crossed the globe in the nineteenth century. Scholars studying the British Isles and Europe used folklore (the veracity of which they often questioned) to make overarching claims about ethnic genealogies, national identities, and the inherent characteristics of groups of people. Goblins or hobgoblins were sometimes seen as distinctly English phenomena that corresponded to other European creatures like the German *kobold*. More common, however, was the use of the goblin as a broad category of creature within the realm of Fairyland, perhaps best expressed in the category of "Goblindom" deployed by folklorists near the end of the nineteenth century. Such classificatory distinctions, however, were of little concern to colonial administrators, anthropologists, and missionaries operating in the Global South. They used goblins in their translations and analyses of belief systems to represent a range of entities. More important than parsing the differences between these creatures (ultimately fictional in their minds) was the civilizing mission undergirding these texts and the drive of their authors to eliminate the goblins of paganism. Simultaneously, some Victorian writers began to classify groups of people as goblins. They saw the "pygmies" of Central Africa as reminiscent of goblins or dwarves: the descendants of the original fairies that once lived in Europe. People with physical disabilities, especially dwarfism, were also infantilized using the language of Fairyland. The connotations of goblins as grotesque creatures, both monstrous and comical, thus seeped into the racist and ableist discourse of Victorian society. Peculiar natural landscapes, especially forests, were also given the goblin label outside of Britain in locations where such fairy traditions had never existed—an act of folkloric colonization that brought the familiar goblin to unfamiliar locations.

The emergence of new literary and theatrical forms in the nineteenth century led to additional iterations of goblins, as we explore in Chap. 5 through the analysis of four influential authors. The Gothic-inspired fiction of Walter Scott depicts goblins as monstrosities, somewhere between human and something else, whose unnatural appearance reflected the eerie atmosphere central to the genre. Charles Dickens puts a moralizing spin on the goblin within his Christmas stories. Equal parts startling and comical, goblins work to terrify miserly old protagonists into seeing the error of their ways. Such charitable framings of goblins are not reflected in Dickens' other writings, however, which disparagingly present humans with recognizable disabilities and erratic behaviors as goblins. The traditionally masculine presentation of goblins takes center stage in Christina Rossetti's *Goblin Market*, meanwhile, which frames them as the tempters of young women—as frenzied animals that seek to corrupt a pair of sisters with their forbidden fruit. Christian undertones also permeate George MacDonald's *The Princess and the Goblin*, which sees a crude kingdom of troglodytic goblins attempt to kidnap a human princess. They are physically devolved creatures, corrupted by years of living underground, and their eventual destruction set a precedent in fictional literature for the massacring of goblins being an act of heroism.

By the end of the nineteenth century, goblins existed in numerous forms across genres and contexts. From this milieu, though, emerged a particularly influential iteration of them within the realm of high fantasy universes. Chapter 6 shows how J.R.R. Tolkien, drawing on the work of George MacDonald in particular, formulated an enduring vision of goblins (also called "orcs") as evil, crafty, corrupted, dark-skinned troglodytes that threatened the well-being of the nobler races in Middle-earth. They are agents of evil in a binary conflict of lightness against darkness. As such, they are slaughtered without guilt across the pages of *The Hobbit* and *The Lord of the Rings*. These goblins retain their historical associations with darkness and malevolent conduct, but Tolkien infused them with racialized language that was common in contemporary English discourse and broadly associated them with a non-European other. Connotations of humor and merriment are gone in these goblins. Instead, they are antagonists whose destruction ought to be celebrated. Tolkien's American contemporaries did not craft the same kind of detailed worlds as Middle-earth, though they nonetheless drew on an amalgamation of folklore and literature in their works. Therein, goblins range from grim markers of the sinister supernatural to lowly, dark-skinned thralls in the service of more powerful creatures. However presented, they are a far cry from the valorous heroes in these fantasy stories, which tend to feature protagonists that reflect the audience of (primarily) young, white men that read these texts.

Chapter 7 considers how designers of tabletop games adapted (and later, rejected) the motifs of Tolkien. In the rulebooks for early editions of *Dungeons & Dragons* in the 1970s, Gary Gygax outlined distinct appearances and statblocks for the kind of monsters that parties of heroic adventures could expect to encounter in their games: goblins, orcs, kobolds, hobgoblins, and bugbears included. These goblins are dark-skinned, cruel, tricky, but ultimately weak creatures—the exact opposite of the virtuous, light-skinned heroes of this game whose appearance reflected its target audience. Designers of countless other tabletop games have expanded upon these ideas by making goblins low-level antagonists and vessels for malevolent conduct that righteous heroes can avenge. The staleness of this fantasy trope, though, has led an increasing number of game designers to sympathize with the goblin and transform it into an underdog hero of sorts that can use its predisposition for trickery for good rather than evil.

Players of the latest editions of *D&D* and *Pathfinder* can therefore embody heroic goblins whose species does not confine them to a life of predestined evil.

This rehabilitation of goblins in tabletop games has been paralleled in other forms of media since the mid-twentieth century, as explored in Chap. 8. Televised adaptations of *The Princess and the Goblin* sanitized MacDonald's novel by elevating its antagonists' comical attributes and potential for moral redemption. Original works of fantasy literature, too, have rejected the racialist framings of Tolkien and Gygax in favor of more complicated environments. Goblins, long depicted as antagonists destined for slaughter, thus become victims of systemic oppression within the volumes of Terry Pratchett and J.K. Rowling (among others). Authors of children's literature have similarly used the ugliness of the goblin to teach moralizing lessons about the dangers of stereotyping others. This is not to say that Tolkienian motifs have entirely disappeared. Goblins remain vile antagonists in many works of high fantasy. Alongside them, however, are more complicated creatures whose reappraisal mirrors other media that finds humanity in monstrosity. The phenomena of Goblincore and Goblin Mode, which encourage people to relate to the ugliness and weirdness of goblins as part of themselves, are extensions of this trend.

The variability in people's encounters with, depictions of, and attitudes toward goblins across this history is considerable. Trying to find a single unifying thread to connect all of them is inevitably a fool's errand. In searching for the most applicable through line, however, the characterization of the goblin as an object of atypical appearance and behavior is perhaps the most fitting (even if it is admittedly broad). This abnormality could be terrifying, eerie, ugly, confusing, humorous, prejudiced, racist, anti-Semitic, misunderstood, villainous, and/or heroic (among others). Goblins often manifested some combination of the following characteristics: short, humanoid, dark-skinned, long-limbed entities that lived in darkness on the peripheries of human settlement and were capable of supernatural acts ranging from merry pranks to evil deeds. The goblin's reputation for unnatural appearance and behaviors has resulted in the term being used to broadly characterize the irregular, and the difficulty that stems from slotting such irregularities into one's understanding of the world means that goblins have thrived on the margins: somewhere between human and inhuman, existing in dark spaces on the peripheries of the known world, and eerily resembling natural phenomena. To be a goblin is to be outside the realm of normal. This underlying alterity has given goblins remarkable longevity and diversity. At the same time, it has meant that goblins have often embodied the anxieties and prejudices at the heart of the people who have crafted them. It is only in the twenty-first century that these abnormalities have been widely reframed as positive attributes. Goblins remain atypical and ugly—but so is everyone.

A Note on Terminologies

In an interdisciplinary work like this, I have tried to make my writing as accessible as possible for an academic audience by limiting jargon and relegating the details of scholarly disagreements to footnotes. Nonetheless, a few words and ideas loom large enough to warrant introductory consideration. The first is "folklore," which has definitions "as many and varied as the versions of a well-known tale."[48] When I write of folklore, I do not mean to convey an irrational type of archaic belief. Instead, folklore should be seen as a historically contingent form of expression from a group of people "whose joint sense of what is right and appropriate shapes [a] story, performance, or custom" regardless of its alignment with powerful institutions.[49] These beliefs are part of a "definite realistic, artistic, and communicative process" that forms an ongoing dialectic with larger societal forces.[50] I use "folklore" in this broad sense alongside terminologies like "folk belief" and "folk tradition."

Two words that often crop up in discussions of folklore are "preternatural" and "supernatural." Although some scholars have unpacked the philosophical and theological differences between these words, I will be treating them synonymously.[51] As the roots of "preter" and "super" indicate, both words gravitate around something outside of the ordinary.

---

[48] Dan Ben-Amos, "Toward a Definition of Folklore in Context," *The Journal of American Folklore* 84, no. 331 (1971): 3.

[49] Jacqueline Simpson and Steve Roud, "Introduction," in *A Dictionary of English Folklore* (New York: Oxford University Press, 2003), v.

[50] Ben-Amos, "Toward a Definition of Folklore in Context," 4.

[51] Edward Feser, "Natural and Supernatural," in *Neo-Aristotelian Metaphysics and the Theology of Nature*, William M.R. Simpson, Robert C. Koons, and James Orr, eds. (New York: Routledge, 2021), 343–63. Handley makes a distinction between these two ideas, too, with preternatural meaning "something irregular, or out of step with the natural order of things" and supernatural being "something above the power of nature." Sasha Handley, *Visions of an Unseen World: Ghost Beliefs and Ghost Stories in Eighteenth Century England* (New York: Taylor & Francis, 2015). In a review of this book in *Fabula*, though, David Elton Gay argues that this distinction "simply does not work as an analytic device."

Preternatural and supernatural creatures exist in this world (or so many think) and have some features that are recognizable to humans. However, they also have unnatural powers and/or appearances that defy logical or scientific explanations. These creatures are often associated with the occult, though divine beings like angels are sometimes also classified using these terminologies.[52] Even the label of "creature" here is potentially fraught since it disassociates humans from the lifeforms around them. Given disciplinary trends, however, I have restricted my consideration of the more recent anthropological designator of "more-than-human" to Chap. 8.[53]

Goblins, elves, and dwarves are a few of the preternatural creatures that loom large in this history. Beginning in the late medieval period, it became increasingly common for English-language authors to refer to preternatural creatures like these as "fairies" (from the French *fée*). The term "fairy" has since been ascribed to an incredibly broad swath of creatures, peoples, and ideas such that the vagueness of the word has become one of its features.[54] Per Noel Williams, "…defining a name that refers to nothing is a complex problem… [and this] inherent vagueness and confusion is crucial to an understanding of the word, hence to the phenomena it is used to name."[55] Throughout this book, I try to emulate the terminologies used by historical authors when referring to preternatural creatures, though in cases of cross-cultural comparison and summation, I default to "fairies" and their home in "Fairyland."[56]

Ambiguities about fairies extend to the genres of literature in which they feature. Even a genre as commonplace as the "fairy tale," for

[52] Coree Newman, "The Good, the Bad and the Unholy: Ambivalent Angels in the Middle Ages," in *Fairies, Demons, and Nature Spirits: "Small Gods" at the Margins of Christendom*, ed. Michael Ostling (New York: Palgrave Macmillan, 2017), 103–22.

[53] David Abram, *The Spell of the Sensuous: Perception and Language in a More-Than-Human World* (New York: Vintage Books, 1996). Levy, Mageo, and Howard reject "supernatural" and other neologisms, pejoratively loaded as they can be, with the term "numinous" (per Rudolph Otto). Robert I. Levy, Jeannette Marie Mageo, and Alan Howard, "Gods, Spirits, and History: A Theoretical Perspective," in *Spirits in Culture, History, and Mind*, ed. Jeannette Marie Mageo and Alan Howard (New York: Routledge, 1996), 12–14.

[54] Regina Buccola, *Fairies, Fractious Women, and the Old Faith: Fairy Lore in Early Modern British Drama and Culture*, 38–41.

[55] Noel Williams, "The Semantics of the Word Fairy: Making Meaning Out of Thin Air," 457–58.

[56] Katharine Briggs, *An Encyclopedia of Fairies: Hobgoblins, Brownies, Bogies, and Other Supernatural Creatures*, 398–400, 422–24.

example, evades easy definition.[57] The *Oxford Companion to Fairy Tales* conveys some of this complexity by helpfully clarifying that "there is no such thing as the fairy tale; however, there are hundreds of thousands of fairy tales. And these fairy tales have been defined in so many different ways that it boggles the mind to think that they can be categorized as a genre."[58] Their messiness and complexity is such that scholars (per Aronstein) "quickly find themselves in a maze of caveats and contradictions, quibbling about the distinction between oral and literary texts, sorting through themes and motifs, and reducing plots and narratives to the simplest common denominators."[59] While acknowledging this messy history, I follow the lead of *The Oxford Dictionary of Literary Terms* in this book by restricting the usage of the fairy tale to oral traditions "adapted and written down for the entertainment of children" and usually featuring preternatural elements.[60] I consider the disputed boundaries of other genres as they are relevant to this book, usually in footnotes.

Much of this book considers the history of Britain, which comprises the modern countries of England, Scotland, and Wales. Although English is the dominant language in most of Britain today, this was not always the case, especially in the medieval and early modern periods. Acknowledged in my simple label of "Britain" during these time periods are the many languages spoken on the island and the many peoples living there, even though the English language was dominant in print.[61] This kind of geographic flattening is an unfortunate necessity in a history of this breadth,

---

[57] Ruth B. Bottigheimer, *Fairy Tales: A New History* (Albany: State University of New York Press, 2009), 3–10; Jennifer Schacker, *Staging Fairyland: Folklore, Children's Entertainment, and Nineteenth-Century Pantomime* (Detroit: Wayne State University Press, 2018).

[58] Jack Zipes, "Introduction: Towards a Definition of the Literary Fairy Tale," in *The Oxford Companion to Fairy Tales*, ed. Jack Zipes, 2nd ed. (New York: Oxford University Press, 2015), xv. See also Cristina Bacchilega, *Postmodern Fairy Tales: Gender and Narrative Strategies* (Philadelphia: University of Pennsylvania Press, 1997), 5–19.

[59] Susan Aronstein, "Introduction: Once Upon a Time in the Middle Ages," in *A Cultural History of Fairy Tales in the Middle Ages*, ed. Susan Aronstein (New York: Bloomsbury Academic, 2021), 2.

[60] Chris Baldick, ed., "Fairy Tale," in *The Oxford Dictionary of Literary Terms* (New York: Oxford University Press, 2015). As always, this definition is not without its problems. Namely, as Jack Zipes argues, Victorian authors of fairy tales "always had two implied ideal readers in mind: the middle-class parent *and* child." Jack Zipes, *Victorian Fairy Tales: The Revolt of the Fairies and Elves* (New York: Routledge, 1987), xix.

[61] See, for example, Ronald M. James, *The Folklore of Cornwall: The Oral Tradition of a Celtic Nation* (Exeter: University of Exeter Press, 2018), 1–5.

though I have tried to show regional distinctions in cases of substantial variation. Homogenization is sometimes necessary in terms of chronology, too. The first two body chapters of this book cover close to 700 years of history, and while I show broad changes over time within them, I have had to relegate minor variations to footnotes for the sake of narrative cohesion. I provide short historical introductions for the first three body chapters in this book (up to c. 1900) on events and trends of particular relevance. In Chaps. 2 and 3, I also modernize the English of medieval and early modern texts in cases where (in my judgment) the original work is too archaic to easily parse for modern readers.

References

Abram, David. 1996. *The Spell of the Sensuous: Perception and Language in a More-Than-Human World*. New York: Vintage Books.

Albert of Aachen. 1894. *Historia Hierosolymitanae Expeditionis*, Patrologia Latina. Vol. 166. Paris: Garnier Fratres.

Aronstein, Susan. 2021. Introduction: Once Upon a Time in the Middle Ages. In *A Cultural History of Fairy Tales in the Middle Ages*, ed. Susan Aronstein, 1–22. New York: Bloomsbury Academic.

Asma, Stephen T. 2009. *On Monsters: An Unnatural History of Our Worst Fears*. New York: Oxford University Press.

Auerbach, Nina. 1995. *Our Vampires, Ourselves*. Chicago: University of Chicago Press.

Bacchilega, Cristina. 1997. *Postmodern Fairy Tales: Gender and Narrative Strategies*. Philadelphia: University of Pennsylvania Press.

Bacchilega, Cristina, and Marie Alohalani Brown, eds. 2019. *The Penguin Book of Mermaids*. New York: Penguin.

Baldick, Chris. 2015. Fairy Tale. In *The Oxford Dictionary of Literary Terms*, 134–135. New York: Oxford University Press.

Baycroft, Timothy, and David Hopkin, eds. 2012. *Folklore and Nationalism in Europe during the Long Nineteenth Century*. Leiden: Brill.

Ben-Amos, Dan. 1971. Toward a Definition of Folklore in Context. *The Journal of American Folklore* 84 (331): 3–15.

Ben-Amos, Dan. 2020. *Folklore Concepts: Histories and Critiques*. Edited by Henry Glassie and Elliott Oring. Bloomington: Indiana University Press.

Bordelon, Laurent. 1710. *L'histoire des imaginations extravagantes de Monsieur Oufle*. Amsterdam: Estienne Roger, Pierre Humbert, Pierre de Coup, & les Frers Chatelain.

Bordelon, Laurent. 1711. *A History of the Ridiculous Extravagancies of Monsieur Oufle*. London: J. Morphew.

Bottigheimer, Ruth B. 2009. *Fairy Tales: A New History*. Albany: State University of New York Press.

Briggs, Katharine. 1967. *The Fairies in Tradition and Literature*. New York: Routledge.

Briggs, Katharine. 1976. *An Encyclopedia of Fairies: Hobgoblins, Brownies, Bogies, and Other Supernatural Creatures*. New York: Pantheon Books.

Bruce, Scott G., ed. 2021. *The Penguin Book of Dragons*. New York: Penguin.

Buccola, Regina. 2006. *Fairies, Fractious Women, and the Old Faith: Fairy Lore in Early Modern British Drama and Culture*. Selinsgrove: Susquehanna University Press.

Burke, Peter. 2004. History and Folklore: A Historiographical Survey. *Folklore* 115 (2): 133–139.

Butler, Samuel. 1757. *Hudibras. Poëme*. II Vols. London.

Carroll, Lewis, and Roger Lancelyn Green. 1989. *The Selected Letters of Lewis Carroll*. London: Palgrave Macmillan.

Cheeseman, Matthew, Matthew Cheeseman, and Carina Hart. 2022. Introduction. In *Folklore and Nation in Britain and Ireland*, 1–21. New York: Routledge.

Dévigne, Roger. 1942. *Le légendaire de France*. Paris.

Dictionnaire de l'Académie française. 1932. 8th ed. II vols. Paris: Librairie Hachette.

Dictionnaire de l'Académie françoise. 1694. 1st ed. II vols. Paris: Jean Baptiste Coignard.

Doppagne, Albert. 1977. *Esprits et génies du terroir*. Gembloux: J. Duculot.

Dorson, Richard M. 1976. *Folklore and Fakelore: Essays toward a Discipline of Folk Studies*. Cambridge: Harvard University Press.

Dundes, Alan. 1989. *Folklore Matters*. Knoxville: University of Tennessee Press.

Duranti, Luciana, and Patricia C. Franks. 2015. Digitization. In *Encyclopedia of Archival Science*, 173–176. Lanham: Rowman & Littlefield.

Feser, Edward. 2021. Natural and Supernatural. In *Neo-Aristotelian Metaphysics and the Theology of Nature*, ed. William M. R. Simpson, Robert C. Koons, and James Orr, 343–363. New York: Routledge.

Foster, Michael Dylan. 2016. Introduction: The Challenge of the Folkloresque. In *The Folkloresque: Reframing Folklore in a Popular Culture World*, ed. Michael Dylan Foster and Jeffrey A. Tolbert, 3–34. Logan: Utah State University Press.

Frodeman, Robert. 2013. *Sustainable Knowledge: A Theory of Interdisciplinarity*. New York: Palgrave Macmillan.

Gardner, Sheena, and Emma Moreton. 2020. Written Corpora. In *The Routledge Handbook of English Language and Digital Humanities*, ed. Svenja Adolphs and Dawn Knight, 26–48. New York: Routledge.

Gencarella, Stephen Olbrys. 2010. Gramsci, Good Sense, and Critical Folklore Studies. *Journal of Folklore Research* 47 (3): 221–252.

Goblin, n.1. 2022. In *Oxford English Dictionary*. New York: Oxford University Press, March. https://www.oed.com/view/Entry/79613. Accessed December 1, 2024.

Green, Richard Firth. 2016. *Elf Queens and Holy Friars: Fairy Beliefs and the Medieval Church*. Philadelphia: University of Pennsylvania Press.

Hall, Alaric. 2017. *Elves in Anglo-Saxon England: Matters of Belief, Health, Gender and Identity*. Rochester: Boydell & Brewer.

Handley, Sasha. 2015. *Visions of an Unseen World: Ghost Beliefs and Ghost Stories in Eighteenth Century England*. New York: Taylor & Francis.

Henderson, William. 1879. *Notes on the Folk-Lore of the Northern Counties of England and the Borders*. London: W. Satchell, Peyton and Co.

Henderson, Lizanne. 2016. *Witchcraft and Folk Belief in the Age of Enlightenment: Scotland, 1670–1740*. New York: Palgrave Macmillan.

Henderson, Lizanne, and Edward J. Cowan. 2001. *Scottish Fairy Belief: A History*. Edinburgh: Tuckwell Press, Ltd.

Heywood, Paolo. 2012. Anthropology and What There Is: Reflections on 'Ontology.'. *The Cambridge Journal of Anthropology* 30 (1): 143–151.

Honko, Lauri. 1989. Methods in Folk Narrative Research. In *Nordic Folklore: Recent Studies*, ed. Reimund Kvideland and Henning K. Sehmsdorf, 23–39. Bloomington: Indiana University Press.

Hugo, Victor. 1862. *Les Misérables*. V Vols. Paris: Pagnerre.

Hunt, Robert. 1865. *Popular Romances of the West of England, Or, The Drolls, Traditions and Superstitions of Old Cornwall*. 2 Vols. London: John Camden Hotten.

Hutton, Ronald. 1999. *The Triumph of the Moon: A History of Modern Pagan Witchcraft*. New York: Oxford University Press.

Hutton, Ronald. 2017. *The Witch: A History of Fear, from Ancient Times to the Present*. New Haven: Yale University Press.

Hutton, Ronald. 2022. *Queens of the Wild: Pagan Goddesses in Christian Europe: An Investigation*. New Haven: Yale University Press.

Jakobsson, Ármann. 2017. *The Troll Inside You: Paranormal Activity in the Medieval North*. Santa Barbara: Punctum Books.

James, Ronald M. 2018. *The Folklore of Cornwall: The Oral Tradition of a Celtic Nation*. Exeter: University of Exeter Press.

Keightley, Thomas. 1828. *The Fairy Mythology*. II Vols. London: William Harrison Ainsworth.

Koenig-Woodyard, Chris, Shalini Nanayakkara, and Yashvi Khatri. 2018. Introduction: Monster Studies. *University of Toronto Quarterly* 87 (1): 1–24.

Latham, M. W. 1972. *Elizabethan Fairies: The Fairies of Folklore and the Fairies of Shakespeare*. New York: Columbia University Press.

Leach, Maria, and Jerome Fried, eds. 1949. *Standard Dictionary of Folklore, Mythology, and Legend*. II Vols. New York: Funk & Wagnalls.

Levina, Marina, and Diem-My T. Bui, eds. 2013. *Monster Culture in the 21st Century: A Reader*. New York: Bloomsbury.

Levy, Robert I., Jeannette Marie Mageo, and Alan Howard. 1996. Gods, Spirits, and History: A Theoretical Perspective. In *Spirits in Culture, History, and Mind*, ed. Jeannette Marie Mageo and Alan Howard, 11–27. New York: Routledge.

Lindow, John. 2014. *Trolls: An Unnatural History*. London: Reaktion Books.

Lysaght, Patricia. 1986. *The Banshee: The Irish Death Messenger*. Boulder: Robert Rinehart Publishers.

Magliocco, Sabina. 2004. *Witching Culture: Folklore and Neo-Paganism in America*. Pennsylvania: University of Pennsylvania Press.

Mason, Otis T. 1889. Anthropology in 1886. In *Annual Report of the Board of Regents of the Smithsonian Institution*, 523–544. Washington, D.C.: Government Printing Office.

Menand, Louis. 2010. *The Marketplace of Ideas: Reform and Resistance in the American University*. New York: W.W. Norton & Company.

Milton, John. 1792. *L'Allegro et le Pensieroso de Milton*. Translated by J. Ribouville. London.

Molière. 1755. *The Works of Moliere, French and English*. X Vols. London: D. Browne.

Moretti, Franco. 2013. *Distant Reading*. New York: Verso.

Moser, Keith. 2020. Introduction. In *The Metaphor of the Monster: Interdisciplinary Approaches to Understanding the Monstrous Other in Literature*, ed. Keith Moser and Karina Zelaya, 1–16. New York: Bloomsbury Academic.

Musharbash, Yasmine. 2014. Introduction: Monsters, Anthropology, and Monster Studies. In *Monster Anthropology in Australasia and Beyond*, ed. Yasmine Musharbash and Geir Henning Presterudstuen, 1–24. New York: Palgrave Macmillan.

Narváez, Peter, ed. 1991. *The Good People: New Fairylore Essays*. University Press of Kentucky: Lexington.

Newman, Coree. 2017. The Good, the Bad and the Unholy: Ambivalent Angels in the Middle Ages. In *Fairies, Demons, and Nature Spirits: "Small Gods" at the Margins of Christendom*, ed. Michael Ostling, 103–122. New York: Palgrave Macmillan.

Ó Giolláin, Diarmuid. 2000. *Locating Irish Folklore: Tradition, Modernity, Identity*. Cork: Cork University Press.

Ostling, Michael. 2017a. Introduction: Where've All the Good People Gone? In *Fairies, Demons, and Nature Spirits: "Small Gods" at the Margins of Christendom*, ed. Michael Ostling, 1–53. New York: Palgrave Macmillan.

Ostling, Michael, ed. 2017b. *Fairies, Demons, and Nature Spirits: "Small Gods" at the Margins of Christendom*. New York: Palgrave Macmillan.

Ostling, Michael, and Richard Forest. 2014. 'Goblins, Owles and Sprites': Discerning Early-Modern English Preternatural Beings through Collocational Analysis. *Religion* 44 (4): 547–572.

Piana, Mathias. 2019. Crusader Fortifications: Between Tradition and Innovation. In *The Crusader World*, ed. Adrian Boas, 437–459. New York: Taylor & Francis.

Purkiss, Diane. 2003. *At the Bottom of the Garden: A Dark History of Fairies, Hobgoblins, Nymphs, and Other Troublesome Things.* New York: NYU Press.

Ropert, Par Pierre. 2023. Des contes normands à Tolkien, d'où viennent les gobelins? *RadioFrance*, February 9. https://www.radiofrance.fr/franceculture/des-contes-normands-a-tolkien-d-ou-viennent-les-gobelins-8677528. Accessed December 1, 2024.

Schacker, Jennifer. 2018. *Staging Fairyland: Folklore, Children's Entertainment, and Nineteenth-Century Pantomime.* Detroit: Wayne State University Press.

Scribner, Vaughn. 2020. *Merpeople: A Human History.* London: Reaktion Books.

Senior, W. A. 2002. Goblins. *Journal of the Fantastic in the Arts* 13 (2): 110–113.

Silver, Carole G. 2000. *Strange and Secret Peoples: Fairies and Victorian Consciousness.* New York: Oxford University Press.

Simpson, Jacqueline, and Steve Roud. 2003. Introduction. In *A Dictionary of English Folklore*, v–vii. New York: Oxford University Press.

Spence, Lewis. 1946. *British Fairy Origins.* London: Watts & Co.

Spyra, Piotr. 2020. *The Liminality of Fairies: Readings in Late Medieval English and Scottish Romance.* New York: Routledge.

Sugg, Richard. 2018. *Fairies: A Dangerous History.* London: Reaktion Books.

Talairach-Vielmas, Laurence. 2014. *Fairy Tales, Natural History and Victorian Culture.* New York: Palgrave Macmillan.

Tangherlini, Timothy R. Winter 2013. The Folklore Macroscope: Challenges for a Computational Folkloristics. *Western Folklore* 72 (1): 7–27.

Teverson, Andrew, ed. 2019. *The Fairy Tale World.* New York: Routledge.

Thietmarus Merseburgensis. 1880. *Notitia in Thietmarum*, Patrologia Latina. Vol. 139. Paris: Garnier Fratres.

Tolbert, Jeffrey A. 2024. Introduction: The Value of Recursion. In *Möbius Media: Popular Culture, Folklore, and the Folkloresque*, ed. Jeffrey A. Tolbert and Michael Dylan Foster, 3–37. Logan: Utah State University Press.

Tolbert, Jeffrey A., and Eric D. M. Johnson. Fall 2019. Digital Folkloristics: Text, Ethnography, and Interdisciplinarity. *Western Folklore* 78, no. 4:327–356.

Widdowson, J. D. A. 2016. New Beginnings: Towards A National Folklore Survey. *Folklore* 127 (3): 257–269.

Williams, Noel. 1991. The Semantics of the Word Fairy: Making Meaning Out of Thin Air. In *The Good People: New Fairylore Essays*, ed. Peter Narváez, 457–478. Lexington: University Press of Kentucky.

Young, Simon. 2013. Against Taxonomy: The Fairy Families of Cornwall. *Cornish Studies* 21 (1): 223–237.

Young, Simon. 2022. *The Boggart: Folklore, History, Place-Names and Dialect.* Exeter: Exeter University Press.

Young, Francis. 2023. *Twilight of the Godlings: The Shadowy Beginnings of Britain's Supernatural Beings.* New York: Cambridge University Press.

Young, Simon, and Davide Ermacora. 2024a. Introducing the Social Supernatural. In *The Exeter Companion to Fairies, Nereids, Trolls and Other Social Supernatural Beings: European Traditions*, ed. Simon Young and Davide Ermacora, 1–17. Exeter: University of Exeter Press.

Young, Simon, and Davide Ermacora, eds. 2024b. *The Exeter Companion to Fairies, Nereids, Trolls and Other Social Supernatural Beings: European Traditions.* Exeter: University of Exeter Press.

Zipes, Jack. 1987. *Victorian Fairy Tales: The Revolt of the Fairies and Elves.* New York: Routledge.

Zipes, Jack. 2015. Introduction: Towards a Definition of the Literary Fairy Tale. In *The Oxford Companion to Fairy Tales*, ed. Jack Zipes, 2nd ed., xv–xxxv. ed. New York: Oxford University Press.

CHAPTER 2

Medieval Origins

Finding a singular point of origin for any folkloric creature is almost always bound to be a fool's errand. The variability and ephemerality of oral tradition, a general lack of written evidence, and the inescapable biases of textual sources make it impossible to deduce with any degree of confidence when or where someone first used the word "goblin" (or a term like it). The origins of this lexeme might lie in ancient Greek or Germanic linguistic traditions, but our first medieval attestations of the word come from Normandy in the twelfth century. There, the monk Orderic Vitalis penned an account in Latin of the demon Zabulon, called *gobelinus* by commoners, who haunted the city of Évreux after being defeated by Saint Taurinus. Later that century, the chronicler Ambroise, writing in Old French, compared a traitorous noble to a *gobelin*. Whether perceived as a demon or something else entirely, this lexeme migrated to Britain, where it was rendered in Middle English as *gobelyn* or *gobelyne*.

Medieval clerics provide the most detailed descriptions of goblins. Although they were divided on whether this creature was a specific demon named Goblin or a broader category of sinister agent, they wrote of them as a threat to the Christian faithful. Lurking beneath the moralizing narratives of these Christian authors, though, we can glimpse a rich world of medieval fairy belief that was less concerned with the depths of Hell and more with explaining the otherwise unexplainable occurrences of daily life. Goblins were one of many creatures within this world of Fairyland

M. King, *A History of Goblins*, https://doi.org/10.1007/978-3-032-01063-6_2

that evolved along with the people migrating to and living in Britain. These oral traditions were widespread but poorly documented in written sources from largely skeptical or hostile authors, who give us a passing glimpse into these belief systems that operated alongside Christian practice.

ETYMOLOGICAL AMBIGUITIES

The linguistic origin of the term "goblin" is unknown, but the most commonly accepted etymology comes from the Greek κόβαλος, which transliterates to *kobalos* (plural *kobaloi* or *kobalous*).[1] The term was associated with mischief, trickery, and lying in ancient Greek texts, though it did not refer to a particular kind of creature with those attributes. Aristophanes, a comedic playwright who lived and wrote in ancient Athens, uses this term in his satire *Knights* when a sausage seller jokingly invokes tricksy Gods:

> When I saw that they were swallowing his story and being fooled by his flimflam, I said, 'Come on, you demons of Puffery, Quackery, Foolery, Chicanery [*kobaloi*], and Debauchery, and you Marketplace where I was reared as a boy, now give me boldness, a ready tongue, and a shameless voice!' As I was pondering this prayer, some bugger validated it by farting on my lucky side.[2]

Later in *Knights*, the same sausage seller is disparagingly called a *kobalos* (translated in one edition as "scamp") for his misdeeds.[3] This connotation is similarly seen in a passage from another of Aristophanes' plays, *Frogs*, in which a group of men are described as "not the civic shirkers, vulgarians, imps [*kobalous*], and criminals they are now."[4] In these entries, the *kobalos* is a term of mocking, meant (depending on the circumstance) to lampoon religious practices or disparage people who do not act as upstanding citizens. Aristophanes is not the only author to invoke this term. Cassius Dio,

---

[1] The etymology of "goblin" is considered in *OED*, "Goblin, n.1."

[2] Translation is from Aristophanes, *Aristophanes: Acharnians. Knights*, trans. Jeffrey Henderson, vol. 178, Loeb Classical Library (Cambridge: Harvard University Press, 2018), 306–7. The translation of Halliwell appears to render *kobaloi* as an adjective to describe the "deceitful" demons mentioned by the sausage vender (the demons of this translation are Flapdoodle, Bamboozle, and Fakery). Aristophanes, *Aristophanes: Acharnians, Knights, Wasps, Peace*, trans. Stephen Halliwell (Oxford: Oxford University Press, 2022), 115.

[3] Aristophanes, *Aristophanes: Acharnians. Knights*, 178:286–87.

[4] Aristophanes, *Aristophanes: Frogs. Assemblywomen. Wealth.*, trans. Jeffrey Henderson (Cambridge: Harvard University Press, 2002), 162–63.

a Roman scholar, also uses it within his *Roman History*. Herein, he documents a speech that Augustus made before the Roman senate as he was consolidating power in 27 BCE:

> I am sure that I shall seem to some of you, Conscript Fathers, to have made an incredible choice. For what each one of my hearers would not wish to do himself, he does not like to believe, either, when another claims to have done it, especially as everyone is jealous of anybody who is superior to him and so is more prone to disbelieve any utterance that is above his own standard. Besides, I know this, that those who say what appears to be incredible not only fail to persuade others but also appear to be impostors [*kobaloi*].[5]

This interpretation of *kobalos* bears some similarity to that found in Aristophanes' *Knights*, though they are not identical meanings. Aristophanes uses the term to denote criminal mischief and improper conduct; Cassius Dio deploys it through the mouth of Augustus to refer to imposters in the Roman senate. This lack of congruity is not particularly surprising. Aristophanes and Cassius Dio, though writing in the same language, lived some 500 years apart and were undertaking very different kinds of literary works. Still, the word persisted across these centuries indicating some kind of duplicity—or, as one modern scholar wrote, "tricksy impishness."[6]

---

[5] Translation is from Cassius Dio, *Roman History, Volume VI*, trans. Earnest Cary and Herbert Baldwin Foster, vol. 83, Loeb Classical Library (Cambridge: Harvard University Press, 1917), 198–99.

[6] Aristophanes and Benjamin Bickley Rogers, *The Comedies of Aristophanes* (London: George Bell & Sons, 1907), 32. The note of Rogers on this page further mentions that *kobalos* "is supposed to survive in the *Cobolds* of the Continent, and our own *goblins.*" A few Internet articles (and a handful of non-peer-reviewed books) mention the *kobaloi* as a specific kind of mischievous creature akin to a modern goblin, but I have not been able to find evidence for this in ancient Greek texts. It appears the ultimate source of this perception is Robert Brown, *The Great Dionysiak Myth*, vol. 2 (London: Longmans, Green, and Co., 1878), 230. This work, though, was perhaps informed by the lexicon of Lidell and Scott, who provide one definition of *kobaloi* as "a set of *mischievous goblins*, invoked by rogues" based on the speech of the sausage seller in Aristophanes' *Knights*. Henry George Liddell and Robert Scott, *A Greek-English Lexicon*, 4th ed. (Oxford: Oxford University Press, 1845), 750. See also E.W. Hopkins, "Sanskrit Kabāiras or Kubāiras and Greek Kabeiros," *Journal of the American Oriental Society* 22 (1913): 55–56. A linkage between the Greek *kerkopes* and the goblin, though widely circulated on the Internet, likewise does not have a foundation in ancient texts. William Smith, "Cerco'pes," in *Dictionary of Greek and Roman Biography and Mythology*, vol. I, III vols. (London: Taylor and Walton, 1844), 672; M.C. Howatson, ed.,

The process through which the term *kobalos* might have drifted from Greek into other languages and ultimately into "goblin" is an obscure one. Languages are not static monoliths that perpetually exist in a dictionary; they mutate in keeping with the evolving contexts in which people utilize them. The *Oxford English Dictionary* speculates that "goblin" entered into the English language from *kobalos*, which then evolved "probably via an unattested post-classical Latin form" like *cobalus* or *covalus* that found its way into Old French and then Middle English.[7] The details of this process are unknown, and the lack of written texts from the early medieval period (c. 500–1000) should give us little hope that additional evidence will surface.

Indeed, it is possible that ancient Greek does not provide the etymological root for the goblin at all. William Sayers speculates that an unattested form of the German *kobold* in Old English (*cofweald*) or Old Low Franconian (*kubawald*) could have morphed into something akin to "goblin" via phonological adaptations common in Gallo-Romance languages.[8] Like the etymological reconstruction of the *OED*, however, this one is speculative and hindered by a lack of written sources. Both of these proposed etymologies have centuries-long lacunae bridging ancient sources (or speculative ancient sources) to later medieval ones, the latter of which did not even have access to the former. Instead of searching for any ancient origin for the goblin, then, we must turn to the Central Middle Ages (c. 1000–1300) to consider the first usages of the word.

FAIRIES, *GOBELINUS*, AND A *GOBELIN*

The earliest written accounts of the goblin come from the twelfth century, when two authors in Normandy document it in Latin and Old French as *gobelinus* and *gobelin* (respectively). Around this time, too, the term moved across the Channel as people migrated within the domains of the King of England, who also controlled the Duchy of Normandy from 1066 until 1204. The lexeme "goblin" apparently found more traction in

---

"Cercō'pes," in *The Oxford Companion to Classical Literature*, 3rd ed. (Oxford: Oxford University Press, 2011), 138.

[7] *OED*, "Goblin, n.1."

[8] This origin is based on the *kobold* being "Protector of the Bedchamber" based on its two elements in Old High German: *kuba* ("room") and *walt* ("lord"). William Sayers, "The Dispossessed House Spirit: The Etymology of Goblin and Some Thoughts on Its Early History," *Tradition Today* 10 (December 2021): 34.

England than the continent. Substantially more sources from England use the term "goblin" than in France, where there is a gap in written usage from the late twelfth century to the mid-fifteenth century. Given this linguistic evidence and the Anglophone-centric definition of the goblin being used in this history, a cursory overview of the religious and folkloric landscape in (primarily) England will provide a foundation for examining these attestations.

Medieval writers typically provide precious few details about the lives of commoners, though we can still make reasonable generalizations about their living conditions. The vast majority of people in England and France lived in small, rural villages—upwards of 80% to 90% of the population.[9] People living in these areas were typically under the jurisdiction of a local elite, whose loyalty (in theory) ultimately led to a monarch. Local elites exploited their peasants, who in turn exploited their land. Peasants, whether they were technically "free" or "unfree" in the eyes of the law, labored year-round to cultivate lands that they were allowed to work. It was a difficult existence. Peasant laborers were one bad harvest away from possible starvation, and they had limited fallbacks if their crops failed. Their education was almost entirely practical. They did not learn to read or write, but instead were raised from birth to contribute to the agricultural and household tasks (based on gender) required to sustain their families.[10] Infant mortality was high, and medical treatments incorporated an uneven combination of herbal remedies, prayers, incantations, charms, and vestiges of classical theories like the four humors (depending on the location and local expert).[11]

Peasants lived in humble accommodations: hovels of a few small rooms where both humans and animals slept. Outside of these homes was a natural environment that was untamed and often dangerous. The wolf, which

---

[9] Any concrete statistics about medieval commoners should be approached with an abundance of caution. Dyer considers it "probable that in the fourteenth century at least 15 per cent of the population of England, and more likely 20 per cent, were located in towns." Before the fourteenth century, this number was likely lower. Christopher Dyer. *Everyday Life in Medieval England* (New York: Hambledon and London, 2000), 302.

[10] An accessible introduction to peasant life can be found in Judith M. Bennett, *A Medieval Life: Cecilia Penifader of Brigstock, c. 1295–1344* (New York: McGraw-Hill Education, 1998). On these issues generally, see Barbara A. Hanawalt, *The Ties That Bound: Peasant Families in Medieval England* (Oxford: Oxford University Press, 1986); Miriam Müller, ed., *The Routledge Handbook of Medieval Rural Life* (New York: Taylor & Francis, 2021).

[11] Anne Van Arsdall, *Medieval Herbal Remedies: The Old English Herbarium and Early-Medieval Medicine*, 2nd ed. (New York: Routledge, 2023), 53–58.

was a symbol of vice in medieval literature, was eventually hunted to extinction in England because of the dangers it posed to people and livestock. Accordingly, the boundless forest was a ubiquitous location in many romances and folk traditions because it was close enough to human settlements to be a known commodity, but wild enough that mysterious happenings could occur within it.[12]

Latin Christianity (i.e., Catholicism) was the dominant religion in Normandy and Britain by the Central Middle Ages. France/Gaul underwent waves of Christianization as part of the Roman Empire, and the conversion of the first Merovingian King at the end of the fifth century ensured Christian dominance. When pagan Vikings were ceded the Duchy of Normandy at the beginning of the tenth century, their leader and many of his entourage converted too. Across the Channel, conversion was slower. Ecclesiastical authors detail the conversion of English leaders beginning in the late sixth century, whose vassals and subjects gradually followed suit. Such was the gravitational pull of Christianity (politically and spiritually) that pagan lords from Scandinavia who migrated to Britain in the ninth and tenth centuries converted to it. By the Central Middle Ages, the Latin Church was an institution of immense power in both England and France. The Church influenced when people worked, who they could marry, what they should believe, how their bodily afflictions should be treated, and what behaviors were acceptable. People were born and raised with the idea that they would eventually be judged by God on the basis of their behaviors during their life, which could earn them a spot in Heaven, Hell, or (later) Purgatory. Peasants in the countryside received regular reminders about proper Christian conduct through their parish priests, who were tasked with transmitting religious orthodoxy upon those untrained in the specifics of Christian theology.

Modern understandings of how medieval commoners perceived the world around them are based largely on texts penned by ecclesiastical officials who sought to impose religious orthodoxy upon the uneducated masses. Their often-disparaging words give a sense of the religious syncretism that accompanied Christian practice. For many commoners

---

[12] Corinne J. Saunders, *The Forest of Medieval Romance: Avernus, Broceliande, Arden* (Cambridge: D.S. Brewer, 1993); Aleksander Pluskowski, *Wolves and the Wilderness in the Middle Ages* (Rochester: Boydell & Brewer, 2006). The idea that the genre of "fairy tale" existed in the Middle Ages is contested, though Zilkowski makes a compelling argument that it did. Jan M. Ziolkowski, *Fairy Tales from Before Fairy Tales: The Medieval Latin Past of Wonderful Lies* (Ann Arbor: University of Michigan Press, 2007).

in England, for example, the elves that inhabited the forests and water-ways near their homes (as experienced by their ancestors) were just as real and present as Jesus Christ.[13] Indeed, it is difficult to imagine the ubiquity of spiritual/religious/supernatural phenomena (however we try to define them) in the Middle Ages. This was a world "where every-thing was alive with spiritual presences" that transcend modern cat-egorizations like "folklore," "belief," and "religion."[14] Instead, these experiences were part of larger "cultural systems" shared within and across communities.[15] As Christianity spread across Britain, people assimilated Christian ideas with traditional pagan beliefs in ways that (while unproblematic to them) horrified high-ranking members of the Church.[16] Old English leechbooks and poems, for example, men-tion elves as a kind of sinister force that could bring harm to humans from their homes in the wilderness.[17] *Bald's Leechbook*, a tenth-century

[13] Young argues that these folkloric ideas developed between the Roman and Norman conquests of Britain "against a backdrop of Roman, Brittonic and Anglo-Saxon paganisms," and that (per Ostling) thinking with "small gods" rather than demons or saints helps to understand long-term cultural and religious histories. Young, *Twilight of the Godlings: The Shadowy Beginnings of Britain's Supernatural Beings*, 3–5, 29–30.

[14] Karen Louise Jolly, *Popular Religion in Late Saxon England: Elf Charms in Context* (Chapel Hill: University of North Carolina Press, 2015), 2. See also Young, *Twilight of the Godlings: The Shadowy Beginnings of Britain's Supernatural Beings*.

[15] Carl Watkins, "'Folklore' and 'Popular Religion' in Britain during the Middle Ages," *Folklore* 115, no. 2 (2004): 147.

[16] This kind of religious syncretism is attested across cultural contexts. Although pantheons of pagan gods tend to retreat in the face of Christian conversion, "…minor deities and nature spirits tend to stick around in ways that haunt Christian consciences for decades or centu-ries." Ostling, "Introduction: Where've All the Good People Gone?," 16. See also Ronald Hutton, "The Making of the Early Modern British Fairy Tradition," *The Historical Journal* 57, no. 4 (2014): 1135–56.

[17] Malcolm Laurence Cameron, *Anglo-Saxon Medicine* (Cambridge: Cambridge University Press, 1993), 141–42; Emily Kesling, *Medical Texts in Anglo-Saxon Literary Culture* (Cambridge: Cambridge University Press, 2020), 57–94. The fantastical elements of medi-eval texts were commonly disregarded by scholars of the nineteenth and twentieth centuries, and it is only since the cultural turn of the 1960s that their contents have been the subject of more serious analysis. In the case of Icelandic sagas, for example, these texts "have been reestablished as legitimate and valuable sources for mentalities and attitudes propagated in medieval Iceland, rendering debates of truth versus fiction as obsolete." Ármann Jakobsson and Miriam Mayburd, "Introduction: The Paranormal Encounter," in *Paranormal Encounters in Iceland 1150–1400*, ed. Ármann Jakobsson and Miriam Mayburd (Berlin: De Gruyter, 2020), 2.

Anglo-Saxon medical text, describes the remedy for one who has contracted the disease of the water-elf:

> When somebody gets the water-elf-disease, their nails will turn dark, their eyes will tear up, and they'll want to look down. Give them this remedy: carline thistle, hassock, the lower part of iris, ewe berry, lupine, elecampane, marsh-mallow sprout, water-mint, dill, lily, cockspur grass, pennyroyal, horehound, dock, elder-wood, earth-gall, wormwood, strawberry leaf, comfrey. Soak in ale, add holy water, and sing this [charm] three times.[18]

The general association of elves with evil doings is likewise seen in *Beowulf*, in which the creature Grendel is accompanied by "*eotenas ond ylfe ond orcneas*." Scholars typically translate *eotenas* as monstrous enemies like giants or ogres, while *orcneas* are seen as evil phantoms, spirits, or demons.[19] The *ylfe* ("elf") carries the same malevolent association. Like many folkloric creatures, these elves provided an explanation for the occasional injury, disappearance, disease, change in behavior, unfavorable weather, or otherwise unexplainable phenomena that were a regular part of daily life.[20]

Not all Anglo-Saxon elves had these expressly negative connotations. An Old English translation of the Bible mentions Sarah, the wife of Abraham, as being *ælfscýno* ("elf-bright"), which Hall sees as a "paradigmatic example of beauty."[21] Other texts mention elves forging high-quality weapons and conducting healing rituals for mortals. Anthroponyms like Ælfríc and toponyms like Elveden show the reach of elf belief in England during the early medieval period and hint at the complexities associated

[18] Translation is from Jacob Riyeff, "An Old English Galdor," *Exchanges*, Spring 2021, https://exchanges.uiowa.edu/ancient/issues/passage/against-the-water-elf-disease/.

[19] See, for example, Seamus Heaney, *Beowulf: A New Verse Translation* (New York: W.W. Norton & Company, Inc., 2000), 8–9.

[20] The phenomenon of "elf-shot," in which diminutive elves shot darts or other projectiles at unsuspecting humans or livestock, is contested. Hall, for example, argues that the "historiographical construct of *elf-shot* is ill-founded" even though elves were responsible for a variety of ailments in Anglo-Saxon texts. An image from the *Eadwine Psalter* that some had argued was a depiction of elf-shot is likely a more general depiction of demons attacking humans. Hall, *Elves in Anglo-Saxon England: Matters of Belief, Health, Gender and Identity*, 115.

[21] Hall, *Elves in Anglo-Saxon England: Matters of Belief, Health, Gender and Identity*, 92–93. See also Jean N. Goodrich, "Fairy, Elves and the Enchanted Otherworld," in *Handbook of Medieval Culture: Fundamental Aspects and Conditions of the European Middle Ages*, ed. Albrecht Classen, vol. 1 (Berlin: De Gruyter, 2015), 436.

with their regional variations.[22] These evolving traditions were intimately connected to the migration of people into Britain. As cross-Channel activity increased during the eleventh and twelfth centuries, French, Scandinavian, Irish, and German immigrants brought their belief systems from the continent to the island. For example, the "*fae*" or "*fée*" of Old French likely came to Britain sometime in the eleventh century, morphed into a variation of "fairy," and eventually became the preferred term for both the home of fantastical creatures like elves as well as a category of name for these creatures themselves.[23]

Accompanying this movement of people across the English Channel was the growing importance of written documentation, which legitimized and provided administrative consistency for the expanding power of secular and ecclesiastical elites.[24] These texts provide a hitherto unprecedented portrait of medieval cultures and societies, even if they were documented by elite male writers. One of them was Orderic Vitalis, who was born in England in 1075 CE and raised in Normandy.[25] While living in the Abbey of Saint-Evroul, he wrote the *Historia Ecclesiastica* (*Ecclesiastical History*), which catalogues the history of Saint-Evroul alongside developing states in modern-day England, France, Germany, and Italy. It contains the first written mention of an entity called Goblin, rendered in Latin as *gobelinus*. This creature appears in a section on the miracles of Saint Taurinus, who

---

[22] Young, *Twilight of the Godlings: The Shadowy Beginnings of Britain's Supernatural Beings*, 250–52. These interpretations were reproduced across generations and "became in turn part of the material from which tradition participants constructed and transmitted their own conceptions of the beliefs involved." Hall, *Elves in Anglo-Saxon England: Matters of Belief, Health, Gender and Identity*, 17. This same process, poorly glimpsed in contemporary sources but operating widely among the Anglo-Saxons, is true of other folkloric creatures like the dwarf (*dweorg*). Bill Griffiths, *Aspects of Anglo-Saxon Magic* (Norfolk: Anglo-Saxon Books, 2003), 187–88; Claude Lecouteux, *The Hidden History of Elves and Dwarfs: Avatars of Invisible Dreams*, trans. Jon E. Graham (Rochester: Inner Traditions, 2018), 76–126.

[23] Goodrich, "Fairy, Elves and the Enchanted Otherworld," 431; Green, *Elf Queens and Holy Friars: Fairy Beliefs and the Medieval Church*, 208.

[24] See, for example, Marco Mostert and Paul S. Barnwell, eds., *Medieval Legal Process: Physical, Spoken and Written Performance in the Middle Ages* (Turnhout: Brepols, 2011); Charity L. Urbanski, *Writing History for the King: Henry II and the Politics of Vernacular Historiography* (Ithaca: Cornell University Press, 2013).

[25] On the life and works of Orderic Vitalis, see Marjorie Chibnall, *The World of Orderic Vitalis: Norman Monks and Norman Knights* (Rochester: Boydell Press, 2001); Charles C. Rozier et al., eds., *Orderic Vitalis: Life, Works and Interpretations* (Rochester: Boydell & Brewer, 2017).

was the first bishop of the city of Évreux (Normandy) and died there in the early fifth century CE:

> Taurinus entered the temple of Diana, and compelled Zabulon, by the power of God, to stand visible before all the people, at which spectacle the heathen multitude was greatly terrified. For he appeared to them in the shape of an Ethiopian, black as soot, having a long beard, and breathing out flames of fire from his mouth. Then there came an angel of the Lord, shining like the sun, and in the sight of all bound the demon's hands and carried him off.... Then Taurinus entered the defiled temple of Diana, and, purifying it by exorcisms and prayers, consecrated it as a Christian church in honor of St. Mary, mother of God....
>
> [After the death of Taurinus], some miracles are also daily wrought by him at Évreux. For the demon which he expelled from the temple of Diana still haunts the city, appearing in various shapes, but hurting no one. The common people call it Goblin [*gobelinum*] and assert that it is restrained to this day from injuring mankind by the merits of St. Taurinus; and that because it obeyed his commands by breaking its own idols, it was not forthwith cast into the pit, but undergoes its punishment in the very place where it had reigned supreme, by witnessing the salvation of those whom it had before insulted and tormented.
>
> It is also said by the inhabitants, and it is true, that no venomous animal can exist in Évreux. At one time the rich soil, flooded by the waters of the river Iton, gave birth to such numbers of vipers and snakes that the city of Évreux was full of reptiles of that kind. The citizens complained of this pest, and Saint Taurinus prayed to the Lord to deliver them from the annoyance so that no venomous reptile should in future be suffered to live within the walls. His prayers were heard. If by any accident an adder or a toad is introduced in a bundle of grass, the moment it comes within the walls it dies.[26]

Orderic Vitalis presents Goblin/Zabulon as a demon vanquished by the righteous hand of Saint Taurinus and one of God's angels. The perspective of commoners, though thankfully acknowledged, is presented in this inescapably Christian perspective. Orderic even hints that he doubts his contemporaries' belief that Goblin still haunts their village, as he prefaces the next passage by saying "and it is true," which implies that he was less sold

---

[26] Translation is slightly modified from Orderic Vitalis, *The Ecclesiastical History of England and Normandy*, trans. Thomas Forester, vol. II (London: Henry G. Bohn, 1854), 132–37; Orderic Vitalis, *The Ecclesiastical History of Orderic Vitalis*, trans. Marjorie Chibnall, vol. 3 (Oxford: Clarendon Press, 1972), 44–45.

on the veracity of their Goblin story. Nonetheless, this reference indicates a belief among commoners that this particular creature (whether demonic or not) was little threat to humans. However vile it had once been in centuries past, it was a shell of a threat—haunting but not harming those in Évreux.

The Latin of Orderic Vitalis creates additional interpretative ambiguities. Latin does not have indefinite or definite articles like English, which means that *gobelinus* could refer to a single creature ("the goblin" or "Goblin") or a broader type of creature ("a goblin"). The earliest copy of *The Ecclesiastical History*, which was likely written and revised by Orderic himself, spells the word with the miniscule "g." However, Orderic generally uses this style with proper nouns that are not at the beginning of sentences, as seen a few pages earlier with the mention of King William as "*guilellmi regis*" (Fig. 2.1).

Modern editions of the *Ecclesiastical History* only add to this confusion, as scholars have rendered *gobelinus* with both a miniscule "g" and a

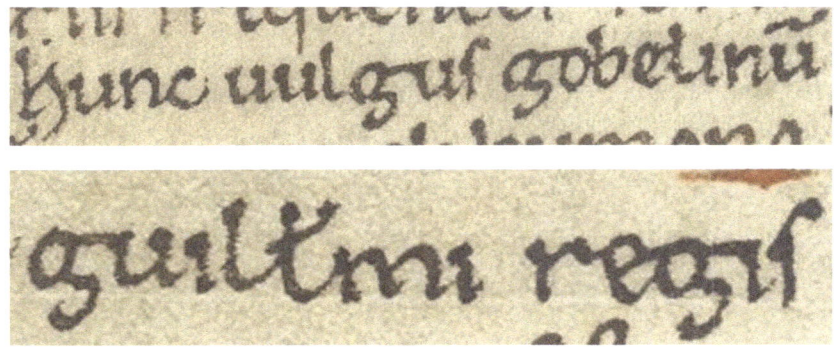

Fig. 2.1 The handwriting of Orderic Vitalis from the *Ecclesiastical History*. (Top) *hunc vulgus gobelinum [appellat]* ("The common people call it Goblin"). Image courtesy of the Bibliothèque nationale de France. (Bottom) *guilellmi regis* ("King William"). This excerpt shows the use of the miniscule "g" even when referring to the name of the king. Image courtesy of the Bibliothèque nationale de France (Orderic Vitalis, *Historia Ecclesiastica*, Bibliothèque nationale de France, Département des Manuscrits, Latin 5506 v. 2, 107r and 111r. Accessible here: https://archivesetmanuscrits.bnf.fr/ark:/12148/cc64462q/ca59764991046630)

majuscule "G" in their editions.[27] I have opted for "Goblin" in my translation because of the equation of Goblin with the demon Zabulon, though I recognize that one could make an argument for other renderings. For our first example of a goblin, then, we are already confronted with a handful of linguistic and contextual complexities. Less ambiguous, though, is the spiritual message undergirding the encounter between Saint Taurinus and Zabulon/Goblin. Orderic considers the confrontation as one of lightness pitted against darkness. When Taurinus compels this demon to appear, it materializes "in the shape of an Ethiopian, black as soot, having a long beard, and breathing out flames of fire from his mouth." Orderic juxtaposes this darkness and fire with the shining of the sun that accompanied an angel of the Lord descending to banish it. For readers, Saint Taurinus is one of countless examples of the triumph of God and his agents over the forces of darkness.

Although we do not have any surviving depictions of Goblin, its characteristics align with contemporary understandings of demons. Broadly speaking, demons in the Latin Christian tradition are monsters of ugliness, deformed and dark-skinned, whose wretched appearance matches their sinful nature and whose deeds correspond to cultural and religious anxieties.[28] Although demons were once angels, their failed rebellion against God and alignment with Satan perverted their ethereal bodies in horrifying ways.[29] This dichotomy, in which beauty corresponded to virtue and ugliness to sin, also extended to people who transgressed the boundaries of appropriate Christian conduct, especially "Ethiopians, Jews, Muslims, and Mongols."[30] These groups were commonly depicted as agents of

---

[27] The majuscule "G" can be found in Vitalis, *The Ecclesiastical History of England and Normandy*, II:136; Orderic Vitalis, *Historia Ecclesiastica*, ed. J.P. Migne, vol. 188, Patrologia Latina (Paris, 1855), 389. The miniscule "g" can be found in Chibnall's translation: Vitalis, *The Ecclesiastical History of Orderic Vitalis*, 3:44.

[28] Cohen calls the monster's body a "cultural body" and one "of pure culture." Ostling, though, argues that this interpretation overreaches, for "elves and their ilk are often metaphors, allegories, indices for credulity or exoticism or evil or the wild; but they are also, sometimes for people, real beings with whom real people understand themselves to interact." Jeffrey Jerome Cohen, ed., "Monster Culture (Seven Theses)," in *Monster Theory: Reading Culture* (Minneapolis: University of Minnesota Press, 1996), 4; Ostling, "Introduction: Where've All the Good People Gone?," 5.

[29] Juanita Feros Ruys, *Demons in the Middle Ages* (Kalamazoo: ArcHumanities Press, 2017), 2.

[30] Such terms were incredibly homogenizing. "Ethiopians," for example, was applied to Black people living across sub-Saharan and sub-Egyptian Africa. Debra Higgs Strickland,

Satan and, in some contexts, demons themselves. As authors in England documented the characteristics of these non-Christian "races" (a term deployed today with some controversy), they struggled with their heterogeneity and hybridity, which complicated authors' attempts at writing cohesive, unified histories.[31] Similar anxieties existed around those with physical disabilities. Theologians debated how God could allow such imperfect beings to exist—for nothing could defy His natural law, as argued by Saint Augustine and Isidore of Seville—and some even thought that these people were reminders of the "perfection that humanity may attain after the resurrection" (Fig. 2.2).[32]

Shapeshifting demons could take many forms, from the roughly humanoid to the more bestial: bears with menacing claws, hordes of pigs, flying horses, and monsters with huge mouths marking the entrance to Hell (the Hellmouth).[33] They were ethereal beings that could nonetheless pose corporeal threats to Christians and required constant vigilance and prayer to guard against. They could shift between masculine and feminine form at will. They were (per Leah DeVun) "duplicitous, diabolical, nonbinary figures."[34] Thus, Orderic Vitalis did not see Goblin as a metaphor for sin or some theological abstraction warning against heterodoxy. This

Saracens, Demons, & Jews: Making Monsters in Medieval Art (Princeton: Princeton University Press, 2003), 1–3, 61–93.

[31] Jews were one of many groups "monsterized" in post-conquest England, where they were imagined "to imperil the lives of Christians in the English cities where they cohabited. Narratives of separation in the guise of ethnography, history, and hagiography helped to bring exclusive political and cultural solidities into being." Jeffrey Jerome Cohen, *Hybridity, Identity, and Monstrosity in Medieval Britain: On Difficult Middles* (New York: Palgrave, 2006), 3. Such ideas had their origins in the Old Testament and the fate of Noah's sons: Shem, Japhet, and Ham. Geraldine Heng, "Jews, Saracens, 'Black Men,' Tartars: England in a World of Racial Difference," in *A Companion to Medieval English Literature and Culture c. 1350–1500*, ed. Peter Brown (New York: Wiley, 2007), 247–69; Debra Higgs Strickland, "Monstrosity and Race in the Late Middle Ages," in *The Ashgate Research Companion to Monsters and the Monstrous*, Asa Simon Mittman and Peter J. Dendle, eds. (New York: Routledge, 2012), 365–86.

[32] Christine M. Neufeld, "Monsters and the Monstrous: Tracking Medieval Monsters into Fairy-Tale Worlds," in *A Cultural History of Fairy Tales in the Middle Ages*, ed. Susan Aronstein (New York: Bloomsbury Academic, 2021), 115–16.

[33] These examples come from Peter the Venerable. Ruys, *Demons in the Middle Ages*, 35–37. See also the illustrations in Alixe Bovey, *Monsters & Grotesques in Medieval Manuscripts* (Toronto: University of Toronto Press, 2002).

[34] Leah DeVun, *The Shape of Sex_ Nonbinary Gender from Genesis to the Renaissance* (New York: Columbia University Press, 2021), 88.

Fig. 2.2 Demons from the early–mid-1200s. (Left) Demons seize souls and stuff them in a cauldron in this illustration from a *Bible Moralisée* ("Moralized Bible") produced in the second quarter of the 1200s in Paris. Image (cropped) courtesy of the British Library Collection (*Bible Moralisée*, British Library Collection, Harley MS 1526, f. 21r. Accessible here: https://blogs.bl.uk/digitisedmanuscripts/2015/04/the-devil-is-in-the-detail-a-thirteenth-century-bible-moralis%C3%A9e.html). (Right) A man wearing a fool's cap holds parchment that reads *non e[st] Deu[s]* ("there is no God"—taken from Psalm 52) as two demons encourage this thought. This image is from the Ingeborg Psalter, which was produced around Noyon in northeastern France c. 1205. Image (cropped) courtesy of the J. Paul Getty Museum (Ingeborg Psalter, J. Paul Getty Museum, Ms. 66 (99.MK.48), f. 56. Accessible here: https://www.getty.edu/art/collection/object/108FQQ)

demon had once physically stalked this world before being banished by the valor of Saint Taurinus and light of God. Even if Orderic was skeptical about commoners' belief that Goblin still haunted Évreux, he still saw fit to document this tradition within his chronicle.[35] In the absence of testimony from commoners about Goblin, we are left with this unavoidable tension between the Christian demonology of Orderic and the folk traditions operating alongside it.

[35] The life and veneration of Saint Taurinus is considered in Samantha Kahn Herrick, *Imagining the Sacred Past: Hagiography and Power in Early Normandy* (Cambridge: Harvard University Press, 2007), 33–37, 130.

In all likelihood, Goblin was an object of folk belief in Normandy that had existed for some time before Orderic shoehorned it into Christian demonology. Monastic writers served as mediators in cases like these, synthesizing the many folk beliefs around them into the "eclectic world" of literate theologians.[36] Indeed, a passing reference to a *gobelin* in the Old French chronicle of Ambroise of Normandy from the end of the twelfth century (the first vernacular attestation of the word) indicates its wider usage. When discussing political intrigue during the Third Crusade, Ambroise criticizes some nobles' support for German leaders instead of Richard the Lionheart.[37] To Ambroise, one of these characters, Balian of Ibelin, is "more false [*faus*] than a goblin [*gobelin*]" and (along with Reynald of Sidon) deserves to be "hunted with dogs."[38] This passage invokes, without any clarifying context, a goblin as being a deceitful creature whose reputation provides a point of comparison for the treacherous Balian. It provides a crucial piece of evidence that, even as Orderic wrote of Goblin the demon lurking around Évreux, there was a broader idea in the vernacular of goblins being creatures associated with falsehood.

We know unfortunately little about Ambroise's life to help inform our understanding of his goblins. He was likely from Normandy. He was likely a cleric, as there are "biblical echoes" across his chronicle, though he never achieved the exalted status of Orderic Vitalis.[39] Without getting weighed down in the sparse details of Ambroise's life, we can use this short passage to show that the people of Évreux were not alone in encountering a malevolent entity with the name "goblin" (or something of a similar morphology). The creature was well known enough that Ambroise used it as an accessible point of comparison to emphasize the machinations of a scheming noble. That said, demonological specifications take a clear back

[36] This process was not unique to medieval Europe. David Frankfurter, *Christianizing Egypt: Syncretism and Local Worlds in Late Antiquity* (Princeton: Princeton University Press, 2018), 30.

[37] Peter Edbury, "Setting the Record Straight? Ernoul's Account of the Fall of Jerusalem," *Crusades* 23, no. 1 (2024): 21–22.

[38] Translation is from Ambroise, *The History of the Holy War: Ambroise's Estoire de La Guerre Sainte*, trans. Malcolm Barber and Ailes Marianne, vol. I (Rochester: Boydell Press, 2003), 149. The Old French reads, "Ço fud Belians d'Ibelin / Qui iert plus faus de gobelin." Ambroise, *L'Estoire de la Guerre Sainte*, ed. Gaston Paris (Paris: Imprimerie Nationale, 1897), 233. As the word *faus* found its way into Middle English, it had connotations of deception, deceit, faithlessness, and treachery. This passage thus does not imply that Balian does not exist (as in a false apparition), but rather that he is deceitful.

[39] Ambroise, *The History of the Holy War: Ambroise's Estoire de La Guerre Sainte*, I:1.

seat in Ambroise's text. Instead, the goblin is used to emphasize the severity of Balian of Ibelin's malicious intent against the Angevin crown.

These two passages from Orderic and Ambroise provide a fleeting glimpse of goblins in twelfth-century Normandy. Goblin haunted Évreux as a malicious spirit that Orderic Vitalis classified as a demon: the shell of Zabulon neutered but not vanquished by Saint Taurinus. Though Orderic was skeptical of Goblin's continued presence in the village, local beliefs surrounding this creature were important enough for him to record them. Ambroise, conversely, compares the deceit of a scheming noble to that of a goblin. This passage, which invokes the goblin without any explanatory introduction, testifies to knowledge of this duplicitous creature outside of Évreux and, likely, across much of Normandy.

Demonic Goblins Across the Channel

The next group of texts to mention goblins are Latin and Middle English works produced in England during the Late Middle Ages (c. 1300–1500).[40] As elites and commoners alike migrated from Normandy to England during the eleventh and twelfth centuries, the *gobelin* or *gobelinus* assimilated with the rich tradition of Anglo-Saxon, Irish, Germanic, and Scandinavian fairy beliefs already present there. Over time, these traditions made their way into a number of texts that prioritized designators of French origin like "goblin" or "fairy."[41] Although clerics were divided on whether Goblin was a specific named agent of Satan or a more general type of creature (an ambiguity shared with other "small gods" in lay belief systems), they agreed that it was a malevolent entity that could harm Christians.[42] It is unclear why *gobelin* and its variants fall out of the written record in French lands around this time, but it has far fewer attestations in the late medieval period compared to designators like *fée* and *lutin*.[43]

---

[40] French texts are silent until the middle of the 1400s, when *gobelin* appears "clearly as a demonic spirit." Sayers, "The Dispossessed House Spirit: The Etymology of Goblin and Some Thoughts on Its Early History," 35.

[41] Williams, "The Semantics of the Word Fairy: Making Meaning Out of Thin Air," 469–71.

[42] Young, *Twilight of the Godlings: The Shadowy Beginnings of Britain's Supernatural Beings*, 70–72; Krešimir Vuković, *Wolves of Rome: The Lupercalia from Roman and Comparative Perspectives* (Berlin: De Gruyter, 2023), 173–201.

[43] Brüch is unequivocal that there is no relationship between the Gobelin family (of tapestry fame) and the folkloric creature. Josef Brüch, "Zu Gamillschegs etymologischem

The earliest attestation of the goblin in England comes from the *Fasciculus Morum* [*The Little Bundle of Morals*], a Latin handbook for Christian preachers from the early 1300s structured around the seven deadly sins and their seven counterposing virtues.[44] Goblins are mentioned in a section on lechery. Like the passage from Orderic, this text presents goblins in a Christian context but hints at the folk beliefs of non-clerical audiences:

> To lure a person to this sin [of lechery], the devil acts like a blacksmith. Since the latter cannot shape iron at will, he puts it in the fire and blows on it hard. In the same way, when the devil cannot lead a person after his will, he first lights the fire of lust around him.... And when the devil has thus set them on fire, he can bend them at his will....
>
> Therefore, it seems to me that when the devil seduces a person he acts literally as the goblin [*gobelino*] did in former times. For in the past, I have often heard that the following frequently happened to men who used to go at night to see their lovers and gratify other desires. When they set out on their way to some assigned place, they wandered all night long in a circle around a grove or a manor house as if suddenly led astray by some illusion, thinking all the time they were proceeding on a straight path.... But when at last dawn came, they realized that they had made no progress on the way they originally planned to go. And as in their astonishment and wonder they reflected that they were being deceived, they would hear a noise close by

Wörterbuch," *Zeitschrift fuer Romanische Philologie* 52 (1932): 340–41. Sayers argues that *gobelin* does not appear in any Anglo-French records and is "not the subject of tales of little people or of vernacular discussions of demonology." This does not necessarily indicate an abandonment of the term entirely, as the attestation of *gobelin* (in various spellings) in Middle English might indicate "wider use in Anglo-French than suggested by the lack of attested usage." Sayers, "The Dispossessed House Spirit: The Etymology of Goblin and Some Thoughts on Its Early History," 35. A satirical Middle French poem from Burgundy in the late fifteenth century includes a battle summons of soldiers near and far to wage battle against "that *gobellin*" called the king of pawns. Marie Bouhaïk-Gironès and Katell Lavéant, "Le Mandement de froidure de Jean Molinet: la culture joyeuse, un pont entre la cour de Bourgogne et les milieux urbains," in *Jean Molinet et son temps: Actes des rencontres internationales de Dunkerque, Lille et Gand (8–10 novembre 2007)*, Jean Devaux, Estelle Doudet, and Élodie Lecuppre-Desjardin, eds. (Turnhout: Brepols, 2013), 67–82.

[44] A Latin/English edition of this text can be found in Siegfried Wenzel, ed., *Fasciculus Morum: A Fourteenth-Century Preacher's Handbook* (University Park: Pennsylvania State University Press, 1989). See also Siegfried Wenzel, *Verses in Sermons: Fasciculus Morum and Its Middle English Poems* (Cambridge: The Mediaeval Academy of America, 1978).

that sounded like the laughter of some invisible being. According to some, this is a demon popularly called Goblin [*Gobelyn*].[45]

The anonymous author of the *Fasciculus Morum* compares the work of the devil, who manipulates Christians to sin like a blacksmith molds metal, to that of a goblin impeding men from reaching their (illicit) lovers at night. This comparison is an awkward one that speaks to some level of incongruity between the ecclesiastical and lay goblin. To the author of the *Fasciculus Morum*, Satan inflames humans with lust to bend them to his sinful will. A goblin, though, takes advantage of an existing lust within people and, far from leading them to sin, actually prevents them from carrying out their illicit affairs. The motivation of this folkloric goblin is one of mischief and humor, as indicated by the invisible laughter that comes when dawn arrives and the folly of the foolish lover becomes apparent. This disconnect between clerical and lay beliefs is reinforced by linguistic differences. We are given two different spellings of Goblin within this short passage: one from the Latin, rendered as *gobelino*, and another from the Middle English: *Gobelyn*.

A different kind of sinful association accompanies the vernacular Goblin of the "Harley Lyrics" manuscript (c. 1340). This work contains poems in a handful of languages that range in topic from political commentary to religious devotion. For our purposes, this manuscript is important for a satirical poem titled "Satire on the Retinues of the Great," which is "a riotous jumble of alliterative invective and coarse insult" framed through an unpaid bill and reflecting contemporary concerns about purveyance.[46]

---

[45] I was unfortunately unable to consult the manuscripts for this text, which could shine additional light on conventions relating to capitalization. Wenzel, *Fasciculus Morum: A Fourteenth-Century Preacher's Handbook*, 696–99. Young calls this kind of encounter "fairy disorientation." Simon Young, "Pixy-Led in Devon and the South-West," *Devonshire Association for the Advancement of Science, Literature and the Arts Report and Transactions* 148 (June 2016): 311–36.

[46] Susanna Fein, David Raybin, and Jan Ziolkowski, trans., *The Complete Harley 2253 Manuscript*, vol. 3 (Kalamazoo: Medieval Institute Publications, 2015), 218. This poem makes ample usage of French loan words, including "*rybauds, rolle,* and *harlotes*" from the first three lines. Rory G. Critten, "The Exploitation of French–English Lexical Transfer in Early Middle English Poetry," *Early Middle English* 4, no. 1 (2022): 41. See also Wendy Scase, "'Satire in the Retinues of the Great' (MS Harley 2253): Unpaid Bills and the Politics of Purveyance," in *Studies in Late Medieval and Early Renaissance Texts in Honour of John Scattergood*, Anne Marie D'Arcy and Alan J. Fletcher, eds. (Portland: Four Courts Press, 2005), 305–20.

This poem mentions an agent of Satan named Goblin and appears below in a modern translation of Middle English:

> Of rascals I rhyme and recount in my roll,
> Of low rogues, grooms, of Colin and of Colle,
> Scoundrels, horse-knaves, by pate and by head —
> I deliver them to the Devil, and offer tribute!…
>
> The scoundrels are lechers and chase after pleasure,
> The bastards are gluttons and drink till it dawns,
> Satan, their sire, said in his proverb:
> "Goblin [*Gobelyn*] set his storehouse in a groom's belly."
>
> The knave crams his paunch before the cock crows;
> He mumbles and munches and ruins his guts;
> When he's fully drunk and fallen over low,
> Dogs by the dozen couldn't drag him away!

"Satire on the Retinues of the Great" associates Goblin with gluttony, residing metaphorically in one's belly and driving people to sinful excess. This agent of Satan needs no introduction, presumably, because an audience reading or hearing the poem knows of this demon and his reputation. Goblin is at home in the stomachs of gluttons, knaves, and this broad ensemble of malefactors whose selfish dishonesty is central to this satire. The goblin is associated with improper, sinful conduct, though the dishonest company of those around it bears more resemblance to the duplicitous Balian of Ibelin (as described by Ambroise) than the illicit lover of the *Fasciculus Morum*.

The monumental *Piers Plowman* (c. 1370s) provides another gloss on the demonic Goblin and places it in Hell alongside a host of Satan's agents. Written by William Langland, this work is among the most important in the history of Middle English literature, serving not only as a foundational work of satire and allegory, but also an influence for Chaucer's *Canterbury Tales*.[47] In one scene, Christ tries to force Lucifer and his devils to legally defend their wrongful imprisonment of human souls.[48] This dialogue features the following interjection:

---

[47] A useful introduction to this text can be found in Emily Steiner, *Reading Piers Plowman* (Cambridge: Cambridge University Press, 2013), 1–20.

[48] Helen Barr, "Major Episodes and Moments in Piers Plowman B," in *The Cambridge Companion to Piers Plowman*, Andrew Cole and Andrew Galloway, eds. (Cambridge: Cambridge University Press, 2014), 28.

"But God can't be deceived!" cried the demon Goblin [*gobelyne*]. "There's no tripping him up! We have no genuine claim on [the souls] since their condemnation was brought about by means of a treacherous piece of deception."[49]

Sidestepping the tricky issue of who has the legal rights to a condemned soul, this passage places Goblin as a demon in Hell acting on behalf of Satan.[50] It appears as an individual demon rather than a class of creatures, and its role here is not the corruption of souls on Earth but the retention of them in Hell.

Not all of Longland's contemporaries, however, adhered to this interpretation. Other authors of the late fourteenth century use the term as a more generic catchall for entities that could bring harm to Christians. This is evident in the work of John Wycliffe, who was part of a team of scholars that translated the Latin Vulgate into Middle English in the late fourteenth century.[51] Within the so-called Wycliffe Bible, the term "goblin" appears in Psalm 91:

(91.4) With His shoulders He shall cover you; and you shall have hope in His refuge. His truth shall encircle you with a shield; (5) you shall not dread of the terrors of night, nor an arrow flying in the day, (6) nor a goblin [*gobelyn*] going into darkness, nor the destruction of a mid-day fiend.[52]

[49] This passage is from the B manuscript of *Piers Plowman* and rendered from the following translation: William Langland, *Piers Plowman: A New Translation of the B-Text*, trans. A.V.C. Schmidt (Oxford: Oxford University Press, 2000), 219. See also Siegfried Wenzel, "Medieval Sermons," in *A Companion to Piers Plowman*, ed. John A. Alford (Berkeley: University of California Press, 1988), 163.

[50] Barney suggests that the demonic names in this passage (goblin, the devil, and the fiend) are "by-names for Satan" and represent this singular character generally. In any case, the association of *gobelyne* with Satan and Hell is clear. Stephen A. Barney, *The Penn Commentary on Piers Plowman*, vol. 5, 5 (Pennsylvania: University of Pennsylvania Press, 2006), 61–62. See also Karl Shoemaker, "The Devil at Law in the Middle Ages," *Revue de l'histoire Des Religions* 4 (2011): 567–86.

[51] Mary Dove, *The First English Bible: The Text and Context of the Wycliffite Versions* (Cambridge: Cambridge University Press, 2007).

[52] Translated from Middle English. Josiah Forshall and Frederic Madden, eds., *The Holy Bible, Containing the Old and New Testaments, with the Apocryphal Books, in the Earliest English Versions Made from the Latin Vulgate by John Wycliffe and His Followers*, vol. 2 (Oxford: Oxford University Press, 1850), 831–32. Medieval editions of the Wycliffe Bible place this psalm as number 90, though today it is identified as number 91. I would like to thank Nicole Discenza for her assistance with this translation and for providing helpful resources on Middle English.

Although these translators do not present the goblin as a named agent of Satan, they still associate this creature with fear and darkness that can be overcome by faith in God. The inclusion of the goblin within this translation provides a powerful indicator of how widespread knowledge of this creature was by the end of the 1300s. The earliest versions of the Wycliffe Bible, which provide an incredibly literal translation of the Vulgate, do not mention this goblin—and, indeed, there is no clear-cut word in the Latin that could have inspired such a translation.[53] When associates of Wycliffe revised these early translations in the late fourteenth century to make them more accessible for those speaking and reading Middle English, however, they liberally rendered the Vulgate's *negotio* (commonly rendered in modern translations as "pestilence") as *gobelyn*. These translators thought that an apt and resonant designator for a malevolent force of darkness, and implicitly sin, was a goblin.

A contemporary sermon from a Wycliffite preacher generally echoes this idea of goblins being demons that could bring harm to humans. It also, helpfully, juxtaposes this sentiment with folkloric traditions believed by the laity:

And some dream of these fiends that some are elves and some goblins [*gobelynes*], and have but a little power to tempt men in harming the soul. But since we cannot prove this nor disprove this speedily, let us stay in the bounds that God tells us in His law. However, it is likely that these fiends have the power to create both wind and rain, thunder and lightning, and other weather.[54]

This preacher puts goblins and elves into the general category of "fiend." They are not particularly threatening demons, however, and the author is skeptical of their existence. Some of his congregation clearly think that these fiends can bring harm to Christians—why else would he acknowledge this issue in the first place? Rather than try to puzzle through the specifics of these beliefs, which cannot be easily proven or disproven, the preacher encourages his congregation to consider more easily interpretable aspects of God's law. This statement is immediately undercut, though, by the preacher's speculation that goblins and elves can probably

---

[53] Henry Hargreaves, "The Latin Text of Purvey's Psalter," *Medium Ævum* 24, no. 2 (1955): 78.

[54] Translated from Middle English. Anne Hudson, ed., *English Wycliffite Sermons*, vol. 1 (Oxford: Clarendon Press, 1983), 686. See also Richard Firth Green, "Changing Chaucer," *Studies in the Age of Chaucer* 25 (2003): 35–36.

control the weather. In trying to present a convincing argument to his flock about the totality of God's power, this preacher more successfully shows the awkwardness that comes from trying to wedge folkloric beliefs into Christian doctrine.

Demonic goblins were even brought into the Arthurian tradition. The *Polychronicon* of Ranulf Higden was a widely circulated history written in the fourteenth century that was the subject of later continuations and translations.[55] Part of this text considers the life of Merlin at the court of King Arthur. This was a common subject for medieval English writers, for whom Arthur was a potent and legitimizing symbol. They struggled, though, with how to interpret the character of Merlin, who had extraordinary powers and was born without a father, a narrative with uncomfortable parallels to Christianity.[56] The original Latin version of the *Polychronicon* questions the idea that Merlin was born "from an incubus" ("*ex incubo*"). When this text was translated into Middle English, *incubus* was rendered as goblin:

> But death slew Merlin,
> Merlin was ergo no goblin [*gobelyn*].[57]

This passage implies that goblins, as a demon reminiscent of the Latin *incubus*, could not die. Although some thought that Merlin was begotten

---

[55] Galbraith calls this text "the best seller of its age," with some one hundred manuscript copies surviving today. V.H. Galbraith, "An Autograph MS of Ranulph Higden's Polychronicon," *Huntington Library Quarterly* 23, no. 1 (1959): 1. See also Trevor Russell Smith, "Ranulf Higden's Polychronicon and Continuations: Texts and Manuscripts," *Traditio* 79 (2024): 257–348.

[56] Peter H. Goodrich and Raymond H. Thompson, eds., *Merlin: A Casebook* (New York: Taylor & Francis, 2004), 8–9. Medieval monarchs, too, feared sorcery—even though some of them were accused of using it. Some magic advisers, including Roger Bacon, even "took on the legendary mantle of Merlin" as they hoped to use alchemy to provide wealth to the monarchy and to use magical arts to better defend the kingdom. Francis Young, *Magic in Merlin's Realm: A History of Occult Politics in Britain* (New York: Cambridge University Press, 2022), 27. A romance about Alexander the Great from the 1400s provides a passing mention, too, of the armies that opposed him, which included the infamous Gog and Magog as well as lesser-known villains like "Gamarody the goblin." Walter W. Skeat, ed., *The Wars of Alexander: An Alliterative Romance* (London: N. Trübner & Co., 1886), 270.

[57] Translated from Middle English. Ranulf Higden, *Polychronicon Ranulphi Higden, Monachi Cestrensis*, ed. Churchill Babington, vol. 1 (Cambridge: Cambridge University Press, 2013), 418–21.

by a goblin, the fact that Merlin died proved otherwise.[58] The rendering of *gobelyn* from the Latin *incubus* reinforces the categorization of goblins as a demon. This particular demon was well known for assaulting victims as they slept. This assault on the faithful is explicitly considered by Thomas of Monmouth, who writes of a virgin in the village of Dunwich (Suffolk) being attacked by "one of those beings whom they call fairies and incubi [*faunos dicunt et incubos*], who are prone to lust and are often the seducers of women, changing himself into the form of a very beautiful young man." Though the woman was of the "weaker sex," she managed to resist the incubus' advances and restrain it thanks to a miracle facilitated by Saint William of Norwich.[59] We also see the incubus considered in an account from Gervase of Tilbury:

> [They are called] incubi, from their oppression [*incubation*] of the mind; for they afflict people's minds in their sleep, making them believe they are falling from a height or suffocating.... We have actually observed that some demons love women with such passion that they break out into unheard-of acts of lewdness, and when they come to bed with them they bear down upon them with extraordinary pressure, and yet are seen by no one else. There are also some demons which are only seen by virgins; for untainted flesh possesses great spiritual vision.[60]

According to Christian clerics, incubi could take the form of humans (often young men) and try to infiltrate the minds of women, whether through seductive flattery or dreamlike infiltration. These demons were visceral indicators of Christian anxieties about sex, especially the chastity of young women. They went by many names (fairies and goblins included), though their classificatory details were less relevant than the existential threats they posed. Demons were ethereal shapeshifters, incredibly variable in form, and able to mutate between male and female forms as the

[58] Medieval scholars were divided about the mortality of fairies. Matthew Paris, for example, mentions an *incuba* that died during childbirth. Green, *Elf Queens and Holy Friars: Fairy Beliefs and the Medieval Church*, 59–60.

[59] Latin and English accounts of this story are accessible in Thomas of Monmouth, *The Life and Miracles of St. William of Norwich*, Augustus Jessopp and Montague Rhodes James, eds. (Cambridge: Cambridge University Press, 1896), 79–85.

[60] Gervase of Tilbury, *Otia Imperialia: Recreation for an Emperor*, trans. S.E. Banks and J.W. Binns (Oxford: Clarendon Press, 2002), 96–97. A useful, though dated, overview of folklore in the *Otia Imperialia* can be found in C.C. Oman, "The English Folklore of Gervase of Tilbury," *Folklore* 55, no. 1 (1944): 2–15.

situation demanded. Indeed, many depictions of demons show them as having both male and female anatomy. Even pronouns that identify goblins as male (including some in the sources above) were not meant to be definitive statements about the gender of demons, which "transcended binary sex" altogether.[61] When medieval scholars tried to differentiate between the different kinds of demons with any degree of precision, the results were inevitably forced—as in Thomas of Cantimpré's classification of fairies as a kind of hornet demon.[62] These gendered and categorical ambiguities reflect, too, those of folkloric elves, which sometimes connoted a form of feminine beauty that was nonetheless transferrable to masculine creatures.[63]

The sources considered in this section show that theologians wrote about both a demon named Goblin and demons called goblins in late medieval England. The ephemerality of these malevolent agents meant that Goblin or goblins could appear in many forms and many places. Writers associated them with a handful of sins, including lechery and gluttony. Their relative threat to Christians varied—if taken as an incubus, they threatened the chastity and purity of women, but if construed as a lesser fiend alongside elves, they had little ability to harm the faithful (though they might bring about an inconvenient thunderstorm). It is unclear what exactly differentiated goblins from the hordes of other fiends operating on behalf of Satan. Indeed, trying to manufacture distinctions between them would undermine the larger goal of clerics writing about them: to steer the faithful closer to God by documenting the many ways in which Satan could seek to corrupt them. Lurking beneath these salvation-centric texts, however, was a cornucopia of folk traditions involving the creatures of Fairyland that were less concerned with these demonological issues. It is to these beliefs that we now turn.

[61] Some medieval theologians even argued that the combination of male and female sexes was the "original condition of humanity" before God separated Adam and Eve into their respective genders. DeVun, *The Shape of Sex_ Nonbinary Gender from Genesis to the Renaissance*, 11, 89. See also Peggy McCracken, "Chaste Subjects: Gender, Heroism, and Desire in the Grail Quest," in *Queering the Middle Ages*, ed. Glenn Burger and Steven F. Kruger (Minneapolis: University of Minnesota Press, 1999), 133–34.

[62] The *Third Cleopatra Glossary* from the tenth century also equated a Castilian nymph with a mountain-elf. Green, *Elf Queens and Holy Friars: Fairy Beliefs and the Medieval Church*, 3–4.

[63] Hall reads the elf as "part of a systematic gender inversion in early Anglo-Saxon mythologies." Hall, *Elves in Anglo-Saxon England: Matters of Belief, Health, Gender and Identity*, 157.

MEDIEVAL FAIRYLAND

Modern understandings of medieval Fairyland come from both monastic and lay authors who were generally (though not uniformly) skeptical of belief systems surrounding it. Their portraits of fairies and fairy interactions with humans provide a narrow window into the countless variations of disparate oral traditions long lost to time. Nonetheless, they reveal how Fairyland was (per Green) a "contested site in the struggle between the official and unofficial cultures of the Middle Ages."[64] Circulating around the demonic goblins of *Piers Plowman* and the *Polychronicon* was a sea of fairies at the intersections of Anglo-Saxon, French, Irish, Scandinavian, and Germanic traditions. Though goblins were less ubiquitous in this tradition than elves and fairies, they were nonetheless part of this preternatural milieu.

Attempting to categorize or classify the inhabitants of medieval Fairyland is an exercise in futility. It is impossible "to impose a logical order on spontaneous local traditions" in a satisfactory way.[65] As we consider the world of Fairyland, we should bear in mind this "fundamental uncertainty" that accompanies any sweeping claims about its inhabitants.[66] A handful of brief examples illustrate this complexity. Some monastic authors from England, though typically disapproving of fairy beliefs, nonetheless record these stories as moralizing tales and "curiosities" that could entertain elite readers.[67] Gerald of Wales, for example, details the life of a priest named Elidorus, who, as a young boy, was approached by "two little men of pygmy [*pygmææ*] stature" and taken to an otherworldly location that they promised would be "full of delights and sports." Elidorus obliged and was taken to a mysterious new land:

> Assenting and rising up, he followed his guides through a path, at first subterraneous and dark, into a most beautiful country, adorned with rivers and meadows, woods and plains, but obscure, and not illuminated with the full light of sun. All the days were cloudy, and the nights extremely dark, on

---

[64] Green, *Elf Queens and Holy Friars: Fairy Beliefs and the Medieval Church*, 2.

[65] Green, *Elf Queens and Holy Friars: Fairy Beliefs and the Medieval Church*, 4; Goodrich, "Fairy, Elves and the Enchanted Otherworld," 435.

[66] Sarah L. Higley, "Humans and Non-Humans: Writing the Fairy, Reading Melusine," in *A Cultural History of Fairy Tales in the Middle Ages*, ed. Susan Aronstein (New York: Bloomsbury Academic, 2021), 91.

[67] Goodrich, "Fairy, Elves and the Enchanted Otherworld," 450.

account of the absence of the moon and stars. The boy was brought before the king, and introduced to him in the presence of the court.... These men were of the smallest stature, but very well proportioned in their make; they were all of a fair complexion, with luxuriant hair falling over their shoulders like that of women. They had horses and greyhounds adapted to their size. They neither ate flesh nor fish, but lived on milk diet, made up into messes with saffron. They never took an oath, for they detested nothing so much as lies. As often as they returned from our upper hemisphere, they reprobated our ambition, infidelities, and inconstancies; they had no form of public worship, being strict lovers and reverers, as it seemed, of truth.[68]

According to Gerald, the boy Elidorus frequently traveled between our "upper hemisphere" and the lower hemisphere of these pygmy people (i.e., Fairyland).[69] When caught stealing a gold ball from the fairy king, though, he was unable to find his way back. Gerald frames this banishment as ultimately a good thing, as Elidorus was able to restore "his right way of thinking" and become a priest. A handful of other roughly contemporary writers, including Gervase of Tilbury and Walter Map, feature stories with similar motifs.[70] Some, however, were less receptive to the world of Fairyland. The *Fasciculus Morum*, which I considered in the previous section, denounces those who believe in "elvenland" and shows the many places where these demons could seduce the vulnerable, from jousts to dances to other games:

What shall we say of those superstitious wretches who claim that at night they see the most beautiful queens and other girls dancing in the ring with Lady Diana, the goddess of the heathens, who in our native tongue are

---

[68] Gerald of Wales, *Giraldi Cambrensis Opera*, ed. James F. Dimock, Rerum Britannicarum Medii Aevi Scriptores (London: Longmans, Green, Reader, and Dyer, 1868), 75–77. Translation is from Gerald of Wales, *The Historical Works of Giraldus Cambrensis*, trans. Thomas Wright (London: H.G. Bohn, 1863), 390–91.

[69] Celtic mythology's "Other Side" or "Otherworld" bears some similarity to this kind of Fairyland, as seen in an exchange in the eighth century between Saint Boniface (the "Apostle of Germany") and Vergil of Salzburg, who had previously been an abbot in Ireland. Vergil apparently "shocked" Boniface because of his belief in the Other Side, a "fairy counter-kingdom which flanked the human race." Peter Brown, *The Rise of Western Christendom: Triumph and Diversity, A.D. 200–1000* (New Jersey: Wiley-Blackwell, 2013), 421.

[70] Gervase of Tilbury, for example, mentions two children with green skin who emerged from the forest near Bury St Edmunds. After eventually eating beans offered by villagers, they returned to normal complexion and were baptized. Oman, "The English Folklore of Gervase of Tilbury," 10.

called *elves*? And they believe that these can change both men and women into other beings and carry them with them to *elvenland*.... All this is nothing but phantoms shown them by a mischievous spirit. For when the devil has subdued someone's soul into believing these things, he transforms himself, now into an angel, now into a man or a woman, not into other creatures, now [on] horses, now [on] foot, sometimes even at tournaments and jousts, sometimes, as I have said, at dances and other games. By all of these he deludes in many ways the soul of a wretch whom he has captivated through his credulity, so that he will believe and recount all this.[71]

The *Fasciculus Morum* depicts Fairyland as an illusion imparted by Satan, as deceitful as ever in his many forms, onto women and girls. This was a common trope among Latin Christian thinkers, who (drawing on Aristotle and Augustine) considered women to be inherently weak and requiring additional protection from strong, pious men.[72] The popularity of the *Fasciculus Morum* was such that later authors built upon ideas within it. In the early 1400s, a preacher in England provides a similar but more inflammatory description of elves and those who believe in them, culminating in the proclamation that "they should know that they have forsaken the faith of Christ, betrayed their baptism, and incurred the anger and enmity of God."[73] Although these authors condemn fairy belief and urge their readers to forge a more righteous path, the repetition of these arguments tells us that these folk beliefs persisted among the laity.

This tension is likewise seen in *Dives et Pauper*, which was written in the early fifteenth century by (likely) a Franciscan monk.[74] Framed as a dialogue between the titular Dives (Rich) and Pauper (Poor), this text outlines interpretations and controversies surrounding the Ten Commandments. One section considers superstitious practices, including a condemnation of witches and those who engage in superstitious rituals. Pauper singles out people who set out food or drink at night on a bench to feed the spirit or the goblin [*gobelyn*] at the new moon or new year;

---

[71] Translation is from Wenzel, *Fasciculus Morum: A Fourteenth-Century Preacher's Handbook*, 579–81. My use of italics reflects that of the translation. See also Green, *Elf Queens and Holy Friars: Fairy Beliefs and the Medieval Church*, 158–59.

[72] Jacqueline Murray, "Femininity and Masculinity," in *Women and Gender in Medieval Europe: An Encyclopedia*, ed. Margaret Schaus (New York: Routledge, 2006), 284–87.

[73] Translation is from Green, *Elf Queens and Holy Friars: Fairy Beliefs and the Medieval Church*, 1.

[74] Priscilla Heath Barnum, *Dives et Pauper*, vol. 2 (New York: Oxford University Press, 1976), xx–xxii.

move a plow around the fire for good luck; pay attention to astrology; perform divination based on the movement of birds; gather herbs; and write anything other than the Lord's Prayer.[75] Those who engage in such actions have forsaken the Church such that bishops must destroy these "witchcrafts" and chase those who practice them out of their dioceses.

This brief passage from *Dives et Pauper* broadly clusters folk beliefs about "the goblin" with other types of sinful conduct. It links together the "sins of superstition, idolatry, magic, and witchcraft" but, nonetheless, distinguishes between these harmful practices and the mindset of those who practiced them.[76] Pauper, for example, hints that intent is crucial in determining whether the use of charms is a malevolent act. Inscribing them with figures or characters forsakes Christian faith but adorning them with gospel texts or the *Pater noster* is permissible. Such arguments build on those of Augustine, who thought pious or scientific intent could redeem an otherwise impermissible activity.[77] Without delving too deeply into these theological specificities, this passage shows that the author of *Dives et Pauper* grappled with what kinds of folk rituals were permissible in Christian worship. The act of leaving food out to feed the spirit or goblin at certain times of year falls generally into the category of superstition and outside the boundaries of proper Christian conduct—though this designation did not mean all rituals should share this fate.

This tension between elite Christian theology and folk beliefs manifested in legal proceedings as well. Joan of Arc admitted during her fifteenth-century trial, for example, that one of her godmothers claimed to have seen fairies at a tree called the *arbre des dames* ("tree of women") in the village of Domrémy, but Joan adamantly denied having gone to any suspicious gatherings there.[78] Over thirty witnesses were questioned about

---

[75] *Diues [et] Pauper* (Westmonstre: Wynkyn de worde, 1496), xxxiiij.

[76] Kathleen Kamerick, "Shaping Superstition in Late Medieval England," *Magic, Ritual & Witchcraft* 3, no. 1 (Summer 2008): 38.

[77] Valerie Flint calls this entry from Augustine's *De Doctrina Christiana* an "enormous loophole" that allowed for decidedly non-Christian activities to be permissible. Valerie Flint, *The Rise of Magic in Early Medieval Europe* (Princeton: Princeton University Press, 1991), 301. See also Kamerick, "Shaping Superstition in Late Medieval England," 40.

[78] Joan apparently said that this godmother who had seen the fairies was nonetheless "not a fortune-teller or sorceress." When asked if she knew about people who consorted with fairies, Joan replied that "said she never did such a thing, nor does she know anything about it; but she did hear rumors of them, and that they went on Thursdays. But she does not believe in it and thinks it is just sorcery." Daniel Hobbins, trans., *The Trial of Joan of Arc* (Cambridge: Harvard University Press, 2005), 110, 114.

this tree, of which nine admitted to having heard stories about fairies around there. One worker, Jean Morel, mentioned that he had heard about women and fairies dancing beneath the tree, but that after the Gospel of Saint John was read aloud there, these dances ceased.[79] These exchanges, regardless of their veracity, served to smear Joan as affiliated with those who believed in fairies and did not properly practice Christianity.

In texts written outside of ecclesiastical circles, interactions between humans and fairies do not always bear this kind of prejudice. Breton lays (short romances), *Chansons de Gest* ("Songs of Heroic Deeds"), poetic retellings of classical stories, and vernacular romances adapted folkloric themes to literary forms for the entertainment of (primarily) lay elites. For this history, the extent to which elites believed these folkloresque stories to be true (in totality or partially) is less important than the adaptation of oral traditions surrounding Fairyland within them. In England, elites with connections to the continental nobility imported Old French romances, which sometimes spoke of the magical gifts that fairies imparted upon gallant heroes, the journeys to the Otherworld that these heroes endured, and sexual encounters between fairies and mortals.[80] These texts constituted a "coherent literary tradition of a fairy kingdom" by the Late Middle Ages that intersected with oral traditions in Britain to form an evolving body of literary and folkloric ideas crucial to the interpretation of fairies (and goblins) in the early modern period.[81] This is not to say, however, that fairies

[79] Green, *Elf Queens and Holy Friars: Fairy Beliefs and the Medieval Church*, 54.

[80] These literary traditions have dominated French scholarship on medieval fairies. As Young summarizes, French scholars have focused "not so much on the historical origins of fairies as on their functions, universality, archetypal character and roles in literature." Young, *Twilight of the Godlings: The Shadowy Beginnings of Britain's Supernatural Beings*, 23. The *Romance of the Rose* provides a similarly compelling story about the historicity of these beliefs in the context of the Norman invasion of England in 1066. "Huntsmen were accustomed to go to Barenton [in Normandy].... People were accustomed to seeing fairies and many other wonders there, if the Bretons are telling us the truth.... I went there to see wonders, I saw the forest and I saw the region; I searched for wonders but I didn't find any; I came back a fool— I went there a fool; I went there a fool— I came back a fool." Translation is from Green, *Elf Queens and Holy Friars: Fairy Beliefs and the Medieval Church*, 35.

[81] Hutton, "The Making of the Early Modern British Fairy Tradition," 1153. Young critiques Hutton's thesis that English fairy belief is "an essentially literary construct of the late Middle Ages" and sees fairy belief as the result of "sustained interaction between learned and popular culture over an extended period." Young, *Twilight of the Godlings: The Shadowy Beginnings of Britain's Supernatural Beings*, 19–20.

are uniform in these texts; each has their own "internal folklore" unique to the authors who wrote them and the oral traditions surrounding them.[82]

A few examples of vernacular fairy stories give a sense of their many forms. *Sir Orfeo*, a Middle English poem that retells the story of Orpheus and Eurydice, begins with the fairy king abducting queen Heurodis while she is picking the fruit of an "ympe-tre." This is a grafted tree designed to produce multiple kinds of fruits and a fitting place where the worlds of humans and fairies overlap.[83] In *Huon de Bordeaux*, the eponymous hero traverses the forests of the Fairy King, Oberon. This monarch is described as "that dwarf king of the fairies" whose appearance was "so fair" that our hero had never encountered such a sight.[84] Among the most popular vernacular romances of late medieval Europe was the Middle French *Melusine*, written by Jean d'Arras in the late fifteenth century.[85] It tells of the titular Melusine, a spirit cursed by her mother to take on a half-serpent, half-human form every Saturday. Melusine eventually marries Raymond of Poitou and bears him ten children before he finds out about her monstrous visage. She promptly turns into a dragon, gives Raymond a pair of magical rings, and flies away.[86] An English translation of this text invokes goblins (from the French *lutin*) in its opening lines:

> We have then heard say and tell of our ancestors, that in many parts of said land of Poitou have been shown to many one right familiarly many manners of things;
> Which some called Goblins [*Gobelyns*];
> Others fairies, and others "bonne dames" or good ladies;
> And they go by nighttime and enter into houses without opening or breaking any door;
> And take and bear sometimes with them the children out of their cradles.
> And sometimes they turn them out of their wit;

[82] James Wade, *Fairies in Medieval Romance* (New York: Palgrave Macmillan, 2011), 3.

[83] Spyra, *The Liminality of Fairies: Readings in Late Medieval English and Scottish Romance*, 61.

[84] These quotations are rendered in modern English based on a sixteenth-century translation. Huon of Bordeaux, *The Ancient, Honorable, Famous, and Delighfull Historie of Huon of Bourdeaux*, trans. John Bourchier Berners, 3rd ed. (London: Thomas Purfoot, 1601), chapters XX, XXIII.

[85] More than thirty manuscripts of *Melusine* survive. A full translation can be found in Jean d'Arras, *Melusine; or the Noble History of Lusignan*, trans. Donald Maddox and Sara Sturm-Maddox (University Park: Penn State University Press, 2015).

[86] Green, *Elf Queens and Holy Friars: Fairy Beliefs and the Medieval Church*, 29–30.

And sometimes they burn and roast them before the fire;
And when they depart from them, they leave them as whole as they
were before;
And some give great happiness and fortune in this world.[87]

The "Gobelyns" of Jean d'Arras were called different things by different people, and they could be benevolent or malevolent. They are presented as a rosy remnant of a past time, and they function as "ambiguous
supernatural" creatures that could "do things that are unexpected, unprecedented, and otherwise impossible."[88] This framing situates the fairies as
more prominent in the distant past than the present day, but still shows
continued sympathy for fairy belief and the traditions associated with
them. Indeed, the fairies were so ubiquitous and symbolically powerful
that they were invoked in the context of disputes between elite nobles and
their subjects. In early 1450, a rebellion formed in Kent against the government of King Henry VI. Motivated by the financial incompetence of
the English government, which extracted additional taxes to fund the
Hundred Years' War yet was still losing it, these rebels organized a small
army and demanded certain nobles be beheaded for their misdeeds. To
protect their identities, the leaders of the revolt adopted pseudonyms like
King of the Fairies and Queen of the Fairies. Another revolt organized
later that year also featured soldiers that called themselves "servants of the
Queen of the Fairies."[89]

These titles, beyond providing anonymity, were accessible to those dis-
satisfied with the power of English elites.[90] These rebels, by presenting
themselves as fairies or agents of the fairies, invoked a preternatural

---

[87] Jean d'Arras, *Melusine. Compiled (1382–1394 A.D.) by Jean d'Arras Englisht about 1500*,
ed. A.K. Donald (London: Kegan Paul, Trench, Trübner & Co., 1895), 4. See also Jean
d'Arras, *Melusine; or the Noble History of Lusignan*, 20. The circulation of Melusine in
English is considered in Lydia Zeldenrust, *The Mélusine Romance in Medieval Europe:
Translation, Circulation, and Material Contexts* (New York: Cambridge University Press,
2020), 183–220.

[88] Wade, *Fairies in Medieval Romance*, 1.

[89] I.M.W. Harvey, *Jack Cade's Rebellion of 1450* (Oxford: Oxford University Press, 1993),
65, 138.

[90] An uprising in 1489 also featured a leader who called himself "*Robyn God-felaws brodyr*"
("Robin Goodfellow's brother"). Green, *Elf Queens and Holy Friars: Fairy Beliefs and the
Medieval Church*, 22.

hierarchy that transcended the power of any human monarch.[91] The utilization of fairy lore in these contexts shows the extent to which they were known among non-elites and their widespread appeal as agents of antiestablishment thought. Such fairies had no demonic association; instead, they were avatars for popular discontent. Vernacular texts written outside of ecclesiastical circles showed a similar lack of concern with Christian demonology. Instead, the inhabitants of Fairyland were vessels for extraordinary journeys that could be deployed to various thematic ends.

Perpetually Receding Goblins

This overview of medieval goblins and the world of Fairyland has emphasized both the diversity of beliefs present in contemporary sources and the unescapably Christian context that informed them. Our first depiction of Goblin from Orderic Vitalis presents this creature as a dark-skinned demon that was defeated by Saint Taurinus and (according to some) still haunts the streets of Évreux. As the word "goblin" migrated from France to England, clerics presented Goblin or goblins as a demon that (like so many others) was associated with sin, darkness, and damnation. The powers of these goblins varied, from the ability to drag the faithful into the depths of Hell to control of the weather. This lack of consensus among clerics reflects the plurality of folk beliefs present in the minds of laypeople about goblins and their kin. These creatures (whether considered elves, dwarves, fairies, spirits, or something else) operated on the peripheries of human society. They were responsible for any number of deeds that were otherwise difficult to explain or stomach: a pregnancy out of wedlock, the disappearance of a child, or an unexpected sickness (to name a few). Though incongruous with the beliefs of Christian theologians, these traditions existed without issue for commoners, who had room in their worlds for both the vagaries of the elves and the miracles of Christ. These traditions became fodder for emergent literary forms of the Late Middle Ages,

---

[91] Toponyms for goblins are less attested in medieval Britain than elves, which had a longer presence on the island. There is a "Gobelynshole" at Portesham attested in 1461, but it is an apparent outlier. I admit that I unfortunately did not have the resources to undertake a systematic examination of goblin-related toponyms for this project, though I do consider some of them in Chap. 4. Jeremy Harte, "Fairy Barrows and Cunning Folk," in *Magical Folk: British and Irish Fairies: 500 AD to the Present*, Simon Young and Ceri Houlbrook, eds. (London: Gibson Square, 2018), 67.

which saw folkloric traditions appropriated and adapted primarily for the entertainment of elites.

Descriptions of fairy traditions from the Middle Ages occur in texts that simultaneously attest to their supposed disappearance. This is a recurrent theme in this history, and in fairy lore generally, that Barbara Rieti has dubbed the "perpetual recession of the fairies."[92] Writers from the Middle Ages through the modern era have documented the disappearance of goblins and their kin from the world around them even as these creatures clearly persisted in the popular imagination. Thus, even as medieval writers sought to differentiate themselves from the antiquated beliefs of their uneducated and rural contemporaries, they inadvertently documented the enduring popularity of such ideas.

We have encountered a few examples of this phenomenon already. The romance *Melusine* begins with an evocation of what the "ancestors" believed in the land of Poitou, including the presence of goblins and fairies. The author of the *Fasciculus Morum* likewise muses that "it seems to me that when the devil seduces a person he acts literally as the goblin [*gobelino*] did in former times." During Joan of Arc's trial, too, some of the inhabitants of Domrémy deflected questions about fairy belief by acknowledging that they had heard stories about it—but that these tales took place long ago.[93] The most famous iteration of this perpetual recession, though, comes from Chaucer's *The Canterbury Tales*. Therein, "The Wife of Bath's Tale" begins with a nostalgic description of the days of King Arthur and the elves, the latter of which could no longer be seen because of the spread of Christianity:

> In the old days, the days of King Arthur,
> He whom the Britons hold in great honour,
> All of this land was full of magic then.
> And with her joyous company the elf-queen
> Danced many a time on many a green mead.
> That was the old belief, as I have read:

[92] Barbara Rieti, *Strange Terrain: The Fairy World in Newfoundland* (Newfoundland: Memorial University of Newfoundland, 1991), 51. Briggs, too, saw the fairies as "always vanishing" but then "popping back up again." Katharine Briggs, *The Vanishing People: Fairy Lore and Legends* (New York: Pantheon Books, 1978), 8. See also Spyra, *The Liminality of Fairies: Readings in Late Medieval English and Scottish Romance*, 4–9.

[93] Karen Sullivan, *The Interrogation of Joan of Arc* (Minneapolis: University of Minnesota Press, 1999), 15–16.

I speak of many hundred years ago.
But now elves can be seen by men no more,
For now the Christian charity and prayers
Of limiters and other saintly friars
Who haunt each nook and corner, field and stream,
Thick as the motes of dust in a sunbeam,
Blessing the bedrooms, kitchens, halls, and bowers,
Cities and towns, castles and high towers,
Villages, barns, cattle-sheds and dairies,
Have seen to it that there are now no fairies.
Those places where you once would see an elf
Are places where the limiter himself
Walks in the afternoons and early mornings,
Singing his holy offices and matins,
While going on the rounds of his district.
Women may now go safely where they like:
In every bush, and under every tree,
They'll find no other satyr there but he:
And he'll do nothing worse than take their honour.[94]

Although this passage ends with a parting jab at the impropriety of friars, its emphasis is how Christian belief had long ago wiped out the elves. In other parts of *The Canterbury Tales*, too, Chaucer expresses skepticism about fairy belief such that they are portrayed as "an absurd delusion."[95] These descriptions stand in opposition to other texts from the fourteenth century that we have encountered in this chapter. Around the same time as the *Fasciculum Morum* and its imitators viciously condemned those who earnestly believed in the creatures of Fairyland, Chaucer dismissed their existence entirely. This incongruity is yet another testament to the many ideas circulating about Fairyland during the Late Middle Ages and the degrees to which educated and uneducated people, whether clerical or lay, believed in its existence. Such variability reaches us through a slim corpus of textual sources that scarcely scratch the surface of oral folklore operating around them. As we move into the early modern period, we are fortunate to have far more surviving sources to document fairy traditions.

[94] Geoffrey Chaucer, *The Canterbury Tales*, ed. Christopher Cannon, trans. David Wright (Oxford: Oxford University Press, 1986), 171–72.
[95] Green, *Elf Queens and Holy Friars: Fairy Beliefs and the Medieval Church*, 198.

References

Albu, Emily. 2017. *Orderic Vitalis: Life, Works and Interpretations*. Edited by Charles C. Rozier, Daniel Roach, Giles E.M. Gasper, and Elisabeth van Houts. Rochester: Boydell & Brewer.

Ambroise. 1897. *L'Estoire de la Guerre Sainte*. Edited by Gaston Paris. Paris: Imprimerie Nationale.

Ambroise. 2003. *The History of the Holy War: Ambroise's Estoire de La Guerre Sainte*. Translated by Malcolm Barber and Ailes Marianne. 2 Vols. Rochester: Boydell Press.

Aristophanes, and Benjamin Bickley Rogers. 1907. *The Comedies of Aristophanes*. London: George Bell & Sons.

Aristophanes. 2002. *Aristophanes: Frogs. Assemblywomen. Wealth*. Translated by Jeffrey Henderson. Cambridge: Harvard University Press.

Aristophanes. 2018. *Aristophanes: Archarnians. Knights*. Translated by Jeffrey Henderson. Vol. 178. Loeb Classical Library. Cambridge: Harvard University Press.

Aristophanes. 2022. *Aristophanes: Acharnians, Knights, Wasps, Peace*. Translated by Stephen Halliwell. Oxford: Oxford University Press.

Barney, Stephen A. 2006. *The Penn Commentary on Piers Plowman*. 5 Vols. Pennsylvania: University of Pennsylvania Press.

Barnum, Priscilla Heath. 1976. *Dives et Pauper*. 2 Vols. New York: Oxford University Press.

Barr, Helen. 2014. Major Episodes and Moments in Piers Plowman B. In *The Cambridge Companion to Piers Plowman*, ed. Andrew Cole and Andrew Galloway, 15–32. Cambridge: Cambridge University Press.

Bennett, Judith M. 1998. *A Medieval Life: Cecilia Penifader of Brigstock, c. 1295–1344*. New York: McGraw-Hill Education.

Bouhaïk-Gironès, Marie, and Katell Lavéant. 2013. Le Mandement de froidure de Jean Molinet: la culture joyeuse, un pont entre la cour de Bourgogne et les milieux urbains. In *Jean Molinet et son temps: Actes des rencontres internationales de Dunkerque, Lille et Gand (8–10 novembre 2007)*, ed. Jean Devaux, Estelle Doudet, and Élodie Lecuppre-Desjardin, 67–82. Turnhout: Brepols.

Bovey, Alixe. 2002. *Monsters & Grotesques in Medieval Manuscripts*. Toronto: University of Toronto Press.

Briggs, Katharine. 1978. *The Vanishing People: Fairy Lore and Legends*. New York: Pantheon Books.

Brown, Robert. 1878. *The Great Dionysiak Myth*. 2 Vols. London: Longmans, Green, and Co.

Brown, Peter. 2013. *The Rise of Western Christendom: Triumph and Diversity, A.D. 200–1000*. New Jersey: Wiley-Blackwell.

Brüch, Josef. 1932. Zu Gamillschegs etymologischem Wörterbuch. *Zeitschrift fuer Romanische Philologie* 52:321–350.

Cameron, Malcolm Laurence. 1993. *Anglo-Saxon Medicine.* Cambridge: Cambridge University Press.

Cassius Dio. 1917. *Roman History, Volume VI.* Translated by Earnest Cary and Herbert Baldwin Foster. Vol. 83. Loeb Classical Library. Cambridge: Harvard University Press.

Chaucer, Geoffrey. 1986. *The Canterbury Tales.* Edited by Christopher Cannon. Translated by David Wright. Oxford: Oxford University Press.

Chibnall, Marjorie. 2001. *The World of Orderic Vitalis: Norman Monks and Norman Knights.* Rochester: Boydell Press.

Cohen, Jeffrey Jerome. 1996. Monster Culture (Seven Theses). In *Monster Theory: Reading Culture*, 3–25. Minneapolis: University of Minnesota Press.

Cohen, Jeffrey Jerome. 2006. *Hybridity, Identity, and Monstrosity in Medieval Britain: On Difficult Middles.* New York: Palgrave.

Critten, Rory G. 2022. The Exploitation of French–English Lexical Transfer in Early Middle English Poetry. *Early Middle English* 4 (1): 31–50.

DeVun, Leah. 2021. *The Shape of Sex: Nonbinary Gender from Genesis to the Renaissance.* New York: Columbia University Press.

Diues [et] Pauper. 1496. Westmonstre: Wynkyn de worde.

Dove, Mary. 2007. *The First English Bible: The Text and Context of the Wycliffite Versions.* Cambridge: Cambridge University Press.

Dyer, Christopher. 2000. *Everyday Life in Medieval England.* New York: Hambledon and London.

Edbury, Peter. 2024. Setting the Record Straight? Ernoul's Account of the Fall of Jerusalem. *Crusades* 23 (1): 17–24.

Fein, Susanna, David Raybin, and Jan Ziolkowski, trans. 2015. *The Complete Harley 2253 Manuscript.* 3 Vols. Kalamazoo: Medieval Institute Publications.

Flint, Valerie. 1991. *The Rise of Magic in Early Medieval Europe.* Princeton: Princeton University Press.

Forshall, Josiah, and Frederic Madden, eds. 1850. *The Holy Bible, Containing the Old and New Testaments, with the Apocryphal Books, in the Earliest English Versions Made from the Latin Vulgate by John Wycliffe and His Followers.* 4 Vols. Oxford: Oxford University Press.

Frankfurter, David. 2018. *Christianizing Egypt: Syncretism and Local Worlds in Late Antiquity.* Princeton: Princeton University Press.

Galbraith, V. H. 1959. An Autograph MS of Ranulph Higden's Polychronicon. *Huntington Library Quarterly* 23 (1): 1–18.

Gerald of Wales. 1863. *The Historical Works of Giraldus Cambrensis.* Translated by Thomas Wright. London: H.G. Bohn.

Gerald of Wales. 1868. *Giraldi Cambrensis Opera*. Edited by James F. Dimock. Rerum Britannicarum Medii Aevi Scriptores. London: Longmans, Green, Reader, and Dyer.

Gervase of Tilbury. 2002. *Otia Imperialia: Recreation for an Emperor*. Translated by S.E. Banks and J.W. Binns. Oxford: Clarendon Press.

Goblin, n.1. 2022. In *Oxford English Dictionary*. New York: Oxford University Press, March. https://www.oed.com/view/Entry/79613. Accessed December 1, 2024.

Goodrich, Jean N. 2015. Fairy, Elves and the Enchanted Otherworld. In *Handbook of Medieval Culture: Fundamental Aspects and Conditions of the European Middle Ages*, ed. Albrecht Classen, vol. 1, 431–464. Berlin: De Gruyter.

Goodrich, Peter H., and Raymond H. Thompson, eds. 2004. *Merlin: A Casebook*. New York: Taylor & Francis.

Green, Richard Firth. 2003. Changing Chaucer. *Studies in the Age of Chaucer* 25:27–52.

Green, Richard Firth. 2016. *Elf Queens and Holy Friars: Fairy Beliefs and the Medieval Church*. Philadelphia: University of Pennsylvania Press.

Griffiths, Bill. 2003. *Aspects of Anglo-Saxon Magic*. Norfolk: Anglo-Saxon Books.

Hall, Alaric. 2017. *Elves in Anglo-Saxon England: Matters of Belief, Health, Gender and Identity*. Rochester: Boydell & Brewer.

Hanawalt, Barbara A. 1986. *The Ties That Bound: Peasant Families in Medieval England*. Oxford: Oxford University Press.

Hargreaves, Henry. 1955. The Latin Text of Purvey's Psalter. *Medium Ævum* 24 (2): 73–90.

Harte, Jeremy. 2018. Fairy Barrows and Cunning Folk. In *Magical Folk: British and Irish Fairies: 500 AD to the Present*, ed. Simon Young and Ceri Houlbrook, 65–78. London: Gibson Square.

Harvey, I. M. W. 1993. *Jack Cade's Rebellion of 1450*. Oxford: Oxford University Press.

Heaney, Seamus. 2000. *Beowulf: A New Verse Translation*. New York: W.W. Norton & Company, Inc.

Heng, Geraldine. 2007. Jews, Saracens, 'Black Men,' Tartars: England in a World of Racial Difference. In *A Companion to Medieval English Literature and Culture c. 1350–1500*, ed. Peter Brown, 247–269. New York: Wiley.

Herrick, Samantha Kahn. 2007. *Imagining the Sacred Past: Hagiography and Power in Early Normandy*. Cambridge: Harvard University Press.

Higden, Ranulf. 2013. *Polychronicon Ranulphi Higden, Monachi Cestrensis*. Edited by Churchill Babington. 9 vols. Cambridge: Cambridge University Press.

Higley, Sarah L. 2021. Humans and Non-Humans: Writing the Fairy, Reading Melusine. In *A Cultural History of Fairy Tales in the Middle Ages*, ed. Susan Aronstein, 89–1100. New York: Bloomsbury Academic.

Hobbins, Daniel, trans. 2005. *The Trial of Joan of Arc*. Cambridge: Harvard University Press.

Hopkins, E. W. 1913. Sanskrit Kabǎiras or Kubǎiras and Greek Kabeiros. *Journal of the American Oriental Society* 22:55–70.

Howatson, M. C. 2011. Cercõ'pes. In *The Oxford Companion to Classical Literature*, 3rd ed., 138. Oxford: Oxford University Press.

Hudson, Anne, ed. 1983. *English Wycliffite Sermons*. 5 Vols. Oxford: Clarendon Press.

Huon of Bordeaux. 1601. *The Ancient, Honorable, Famous, and Delightfull Historie of Huon of Bourdeaux*. Translated by John Bourchier Berners. 3rd ed. London: Thomas Purfoot.

Hutton, Ronald. 2014. The Making of the Early Modern British Fairy Tradition. *The Historical Journal* 57 (4): 1135–1156.

Jakobsson, Ármann, and Miriam Mayburd. 2020. Introduction: The Paranormal Encounter. In *Paranormal Encounters in Iceland 1150–1400*, ed. Ármann Jakobsson and Miriam Mayburd, 1–6. Berlin: De Gruyter.

Jean d'Arras. 1895. *Melusine. Compiled (1382–1394 A.D.) by Jean d'Arras Englisht about 1500*. Edited by A.K. Donald. London: Kegan Paul, Trench, Trübner & Co.

Jean d'Arras. 2015. *Melusine; or the Noble History of Lusignan*. Translated by Donald Maddox and Sara Sturm-Maddox. University Park: Penn State University Press.

Jolly, Karen Louise. 2015. *Popular Religion in Late Saxon England: Elf Charms in Context*. Chapel Hill: University of North Carolina Press.

Kamerick, Kathleen. Summer 2008. Shaping Superstition in Late Medieval England. *Magic, Ritual & Witchcraft* 3, no. 1:29–53.

Kesling, Emily. 2020. *Medical Texts in Anglo-Saxon Literary Culture*. Cambridge: Cambridge University Press.

Langland, William. 2000. *Piers Plowman: A New Translation of the B-Text*. Translated by A.V.C. Schmidt. Oxford: Oxford University Press.

Lecouteux, Claude. 2018. *The Hidden History of Elves and Dwarfs: Avatars of Invisible Dreams*. Translated by Jon E. Graham. Rochester: Inner Traditions.

Liddell, Henry George, and Robert Scott. 1845. *A Greek-English Lexicon*. 4th ed. Oxford: Oxford University Press.

McCracken, Peggy. 1999. Chaste Subjects: Gender, Heroism, and Desire in the Grail Quest. In *Queering the Middle Ages*, ed. Glenn Burger and Steven F. Kruger, 123–142. Minneapolis: University of Minnesota Press.

Mostert, Marco, and Paul S. Barnwell, eds. 2011. *Medieval Legal Process: Physical, Spoken and Written Performance in the Middle Ages*. Turnhout: Brepols.

Müller, Miriam, ed. 2021. *The Routledge Handbook of Medieval Rural Life*. New York: Taylor & Francis.

Murray, Jacqueline. 2006. Femininity and Masculinity. In *Women and Gender in Medieval Europe: An Encyclopedia*, ed. Margaret Schaus, 284–287. New York: Routledge.

Neufeld, Christine M. 2021. Monsters and the Monstrous: Tracking Medieval Monsters into Fairy-Tale Worlds. In *A Cultural History of Fairy Tales in the Middle Ages*, ed. Susan Aronstein, 111–134. New York: Bloomsbury Academic.

Oman, C. C. 1944. The English Folklore of Gervase of Tilbury. *Folklore* 55 (1): 2–15.

Ostling, Michael. 2017. Introduction: Where've All the Good People Gone? In *Fairies, Demons, and Nature Spirits: "Small Gods" at the Margins of Christendom*, ed. Michael Ostling, 1–53. New York: Palgrave Macmillan.

Pluskowski, Aleksander. 2006. *Wolves and the Wilderness in the Middle Ages*. Rochester: Boydell & Brewer.

Purkiss, Diane. 2003. *At the Bottom of the Garden: A Dark History of Fairies, Hobgoblins, Nymphs, and Other Troublesome Things*. New York: NYU Press.

Rieti, Barbara. 1991. *Strange Terrain: The Fairy World in Newfoundland*. Newfoundland: Memorial University of Newfoundland.

Riyeff, Jacob. 2021. An Old English Galdor. *Exchanges*, Spring. https://exchanges.uiowa.edu/ancient/issues/passage/against-the-water-elf-disease/. Accessed December 1, 2024.

Ruys, Juanita Feros. 2017. *Demons in the Middle Ages*. Kalamazoo: ArcHumanities Press.

Saunders, Corinne J. 1993. *The Forest of Medieval Romance: Avernus, Broceliande, Arden*. Cambridge: D.S. Brewer.

Sayers, William. December 2021. The Dispossessed House Spirit: The Etymology of Goblin and Some Thoughts on Its Early History. *Tradition Today* 10:33–39.

Scase, Wendy. 2005. 'Satire in the Retinues of the Great' (MS Harley 2253): Unpaid Bills and the Politics of Purveyance. In *Studies in Late Medieval and Early Renaissance Texts in Honour of John Scattergood*, ed. Anne Marie D'Arcy and Alan J. Fletcher, 305–320. Portland: Four Courts Press.

Shoemaker, Karl. 2011. The Devil at Law in the Middle Ages. *Revue de l'histoire Des Religions* 4:567–586.

Skeat, Walter W., ed. 1886. *The Wars of Alexander: An Alliterative Romance*. London: N. Trübner & Co.

Smith, William. 1844. Cerco'pes. In *Dictionary of Greek and Roman Biography and Mythology*, vol. 1, 672. London: Taylor and Walton.

Smith, Trevor Russell. 2024. Ranulf Higden's Polychronicon and Continuations: Texts and Manuscripts. *Traditio* 79:257–348.

Spyra, Piotr. 2020. *The Liminality of Fairies: Readings in Late Medieval English and Scottish Romance*. New York: Routledge.

Steiner, Emily. 2013. *Reading Piers Plowman*. Cambridge: Cambridge University Press.

Strickland, Debra Higgs. 2003. *Saracens, Demons, & Jews: Making Monsters in Medieval Art*. Princeton: Princeton University Press.

Strickland, Debra Higgs. 2012. Monstrosity and Race in the Late Middle Ages. In *The Ashgate Research Companion to Monsters and the Monstrous*, ed. Asa Simon Mittman and Peter J. Dendle, 365–386. New York: Routledge.

Sullivan, Karen. 1999. *The Interrogation of Joan of Arc*. Minneapolis: University of Minnesota Press.

Thomas of Monmouth. 1896. *The Life and Miracles of St. William of Norwich*. Edited by Augustus Jessopp and Montague Rhodes James. Cambridge: Cambridge University Press.

Urbanski, Charity L. 2013. *Writing History for the King: Henry II and the Politics of Vernacular Historiography*. Ithaca: Cornell University Press.

Van Arsdall, Anne. 2023. *Medieval Herbal Remedies: The Old English Herbarium and Early-Medieval Medicine*. 2nd ed. New York: Routledge.

Vitalis, Orderic. 1854. *The Ecclesiastical History of England and Normandy*. Translated by Thomas Forester. IV vols. London: Henry G. Bohn.

Vitalis, Orderic. 1855. *Historia Ecclesiastica*. Edited by J.P. Migne. Vol. 188. Patrologia Latina. Paris.

Vitalis, Orderic. 1972. *The Ecclesiastical History of Orderic Vitalis*. Translated by Marjorie Chibnall. 6 vols. Oxford: Clarendon Press.

Vuković, Krešimir. 2023. *Wolves of Rome: The Lupercalia from Roman and Comparative Perspectives*. Berlin: De Gruyter.

Wade, J. 2011. *Fairies in Medieval Romance*. New York: Palgrave Macmillan.

Watkins, Carl. 2004. 'Folklore' and 'Popular Religion' in Britain during the Middle Ages. *Folklore* 115 (2): 140–150.

Wenzel, Siegfried. 1978. *Verses in Sermons: Fasciculus Morum and Its Middle English Poems*. Cambridge: The Mediaeval Academy of America.

Wenzel, Siegfried. 1988. Medieval Sermons. In *A Companion to Piers Plowman*, ed. John A. Alford, 155–172. Berkeley: University of California Press.

Wenzel, Siegfried, ed. 1989. *Fasciculus Morum: A Fourteenth-Century Preacher's Handbook*. Pennsylvania State University Press: University Park.

Williams, Noel. 1991. The Semantics of the Word Fairy: Making Meaning Out of Thin Air. In *The Good People: New Fairylore Essays*, ed. Peter Narváez, 457–478. Lexington: University Press of Kentucky.

Young, Simon. June 2016. Pixy-Led in Devon and the South-West. *Devonshire Association for the Advancement of Science, Literature and the Arts Report and Transactions* 148:311–336.

Young, Francis. 2022. *Magic in Merlin's Realm: A History of Occult Politics in Britain*. New York: Cambridge University Press.

Young, Francis. 2023. *Twilight of the Godlings: The Shadowy Beginnings of Britain's Supernatural Beings*. New York: Cambridge University Press.

Zeldenrust, Lydia. 2020. *The Mélusine Romance in Medieval Europe: Translation, Circulation, and Material Contexts.* New York: Cambridge University Press.

Ziolkowski, Jan M. 2007. *Fairy Tales from Before Fairy Tales: The Medieval Latin Past of Wonderful Lies.* Ann Arbor: University of Michigan Press.

CHAPTER 3

Early Modern Variations

Early modern texts on demonology, politics, literature, theatre, music, medicine, and history detail perceptions of goblins in much greater depth than the medieval period. As might be expected from such a vast corpus, goblins take on many forms therein. In (skeptical) recordings of folk traditions, goblins could be temperamental household spirits that perform chores on behalf of a family if appropriately honored with nighttime offerings. In literature and plays, they could be part of an extravagant yet diminutive royal court with exquisite clothing to match developing capitalist consumption of English elites. In ballads, they could be malevolent agents vanquished by the merry Robin Goodfellow. In theological treatises, especially those written before the Reformation, they could be terrestrial demons or visions implanted by Satan to tempt the minds of weak Christians. More frequently, though, Protestant authors saw goblins as baseless superstitions perpetuated by women, children, the uneducated, and Catholics. Operating beneath these written sources, too, was a sea of oral traditions that both influenced these texts and were influenced by them.

Elites of the early modern period often saw goblins as a broad category of preternatural creature that was interchangeable with (among others) spirits and fairies. Some had more concrete ideas about what differentiated goblins from their kin, though there was no consensus about such classifications. Added to this milieu in the sixteenth century, too, was the

M. King, *A History of Goblins*,
https://doi.org/10.1007/978-3-032-01063-6_3

hobgoblin: a tautological combination of the folkloric "hob" (a diminutive form of Robin) and "goblin" that is first attested in 1530 and was commonplace by the end of the century.[1] Though hobgoblins and goblins were frequently synonymous, some authors saw a distinction between them. The equation of Hobgoblin with Robin Goodfellow, for example, was particularly popular in dictionaries of the sixteenth and seventeenth centuries and indicates a strong connection to merry and mischievous spirits, which sometimes actively rooted out more malevolent goblins. So too do we see early (and misinformed) etymological studies that trace the oppositional origins of goblins and elves to Italian politics, each apparently derived from the feuding houses of Ghibelline and Guelf. Collocational analysis further shows that goblins, when compared to fairies, were more likely to be surrounded by words associated with fear and darkness.

Lurking behind these countless texts must have been an overwhelming association of goblins with notions of harm, trickery, and abnormality. Indeed, the early modern period is when we see the rise of the lexeme "goblin" not as a creature but an abstraction: the frenzy of a bloody melee, the appearance of someone with facial abnormalities, and the fear of increased taxation (among many others). Even as goblins exhibited remarkable diversity across the early modern period as a preternatural creature interchangeable with many others, their more abstract association was synonymous with malintent and unnatural appearance—often in conjunction with some kind of darkness. Goblins were so ubiquitous in early modern England that they came to represent ideas that reflected the characteristics of their preternatural originators.

There is no shortage of scholarship about witchcraft, folklore, literature, theater, and the world of Fairyland in early modern Britain. This chapter seeks to provide a responsible synthesis of how goblins fit into this sizeable corpus of academic literature and, then, to consider whether goblins can be distinguished in any way from the milieu of hazily differentiated creatures in Fairyland. These discussions, given their breadth, require some degree of chronological flattening, though I have tried to show

---

[1] Palsgrave renders this word in English as *Hobgoblyng*, and it is defined as a *gobelin* or *mausse* (the latter an apparent derivation of *maufë*, meaning a demon or evil spirit in Anglo-Norman). I would like to thank Anne Latowsky for her assistance with this French text. John Palsgrave, *Lesclarcissement de la langue francoyse compose* (London: Richard Pynson, 1530). It is possible, too, that the "hob" of hobgoblin has its origin in the hob of the kitchen, which was a shelf adjacent to a fireplace used to keep items warm. *OED*, "Hobgoblin" and "Hob, n.1."

(especially in the case of the Reformation and witch trials) more concrete changes over time. Developments related to fairy tales, the Christmas story, and the academic field of anthropology, though they have their origins during the early modern period, will be considered in Chaps. 3 and 4.

HISTORICAL BACKGROUND

This chapter charts iterations of goblins from roughly 1500 to 1800 in (primarily) Britain. A handful of developments in these years have particular relevance for this history and deserve introductory consideration.[2] The first is the English Reformation, which saw the monarchy break away from the Catholic Church during the sixteenth century. This movement was fueled by a combination of Catholic corruption and power, doctrinal differences, the spread of Lutheranism, and monarchical ambitions. King Henry VIII oversaw the official split of the Church of England from the Catholic Church and the destruction of Catholic institutions during the 1530s. Despite attempts from Queen Mary I to restore Catholic power in England, pro-Protestant forces ultimately emerged triumphant, and scholars frequently cite the reign of Queen Elizabeth I (r. 1558–1603) as the end of the English Reformation. Theologians in Britain wrote extensively about Christian doctrine during this period and, thanks to the popularity and distribution of printed books, engaged with ideas cropping up across Christian Europe.[3] Though many were sympathetic to reformist ideas, they disagreed on doctrinal specifics, which motivated some to spurn the Church of England and form their own colonies in North America in the early seventeenth century. This migration across the Atlantic was one theater of British colonial ambitions in the early modern period: the East India Company was chartered in 1600; the trafficking of enslaved peoples from Africa to Europe and the Americas surged during the second half of

---

[2] The following texts provide useful syntheses of the content considered in this section: James Sharpe, *Early Modern England: A Social History 1550–1760*, 2nd ed. (New York: Bloomsbury, 1997); Peter C. Herman, *A Short History of Early Modern England: British Literature in Context* (Hoboken: Wiley, 2011); Robert Bucholz and Newton Key, *Early Modern England, 1485–1714: A Narrative History*, 2nd ed. (Malden: Blackwell Publishing, 2009); Keith Wrightson, ed., *A Social History of England, 1500–1750* (New York: Cambridge University Press, 2018).

[3] Around 800 books were published in England in the 1520s; this number rose to 3000 in the 1590s. Bucholz and Key, *Early Modern England, 1485–1714: A Narrative History*, 209.

the seventeenth century; and British convicts began settling Australia in the 1770s.

Roughly coinciding with the English Reformation was an increase in prosecutions related to witchcraft.[4] English Protestants were less likely than their Catholic counterparts to believe in the existence of and prosecute witches, though some saw these sorcerers as an active threat to the faithful. Emboldened by the Reformation and changes to criminal law that made convictions of vulnerable people easier to obtain, they sought to root out those who convened with devils or practiced magic (however defined). Witch trials in England surged during the first half of the seventeenth century, and theologians engaged in continent-wide debates about the nature of witchcraft, how to differentiate between divine and demonic occurrences, and the kinds of behaviors expected of witches.[5] Eventually, those skeptical of the feasibility of humans communing with demons emerged triumphant. The Witchcraft Act of 1735 criminalized accusations of witchcraft and, in doing so, presumed that no one could be a witch. By the end of these witch hunts, some 500 people in England were executed for witchcraft—and twenty-five more in the Massachusetts Bay Colony.

Witch trials in Britain targeted vulnerable women, poor widows, and spinsters especially, who had less clearly defined roles in patriarchal familial systems. Since these women were less likely to live with men who could testify to their appropriate conduct, they could easily fall victim to accusations of witchcraft. This is not to say that their accusers were uniformly malicious actors. Some probably were, but many also feared the machinations of witches and sought to remove them from their Christian communities. Stereotypes about the threat of female witches were reinforced by cheaply printed ephemera that featured women flying across the night sky with demons in tow. Testimonies from witch trials survive today from court transcripts, which gives some sense of how commoners viewed the practice of witchcraft. That said, these transcripts were still written by

---

[4] Brian P. Levack, *The Witch-Hunt in Early Modern Europe*, 3rd ed. (New York: Routledge, 2013), 74–108. On magic and the supernatural, see Euan Cameron, *Enchanted Europe: Superstition, Reason, and Religion 1250–1750* (New York: Oxford University Press, 2010); Mark A. Waddell, *Magic, Science, and Religion in Early Modern Europe* (New York: Cambridge University Press, 2021).

[5] One of the foundational texts on witchcraft and techniques for its prosecution, for example, was the *Malleus Maleficarum* (*The Hammer of Witches*), which was originally published in Germany in 1486. Hans Broedel, *The 'Malleus Maleficarum' and the Construction of Witchcraft: Theology and Popular Belief* (New York: Manchester University Press, 2003).

literate elites who standardized testimony based on their legal training and understanding of Christian doctrine.

The early modern period witnessed seismic changes to the culture and society of Britain. The Tudor period (1485–1603) saw the expansion of educational institutions such that literacy became increasingly common among families that could afford to send their children to grammar schools. Education was heavily based on classical texts, especially works of Classical Latin, which were fonts of inspiration for Tudor writers.[6] The popularity of Gutenberg's printing press enabled the production and distribution of printed texts at an unprecedented rate. Literature, drama, poetry, music, and the fine arts blossomed during the so-called English Renaissance, especially in London and during the time of Queen Elizabeth I, who reigned during a period of relative peace following the worst unrest of the English Reformation and violence in the seventeenth century during the Thirty Years' War and English Civil War. Though some reformist groups tried to limit these perceived excesses (including a brief window in which they succeeded in closing theaters in London), they were ultimately unsuccessful in staunching the cultural appetite of urbanites, who fueled demand for new written and theatrical works. London's population nearly quintupled from 200,000 inhabitants in 1600 to 960,000 in 1800.[7] Literacy rates hovered around 50% in Britain by the end of the early modern period, skewing toward people living in cities.[8]

The cultural effects of the English Renaissance were most acutely felt in cities, where wealth and educational access was clustered. These city-dwellers were still a substantial minority, though, as more than 80% of people in early modern England lived in the countryside practicing subsistence agriculture. Technological advancements allowed for more land to be farmed and increased crop yields from that land, though population increases sustained by these technologies meant that life for agricultural laborers was still precarious. Most modern estimates of life expectancy in England prior to 1800 place it below forty years old (whether rural or

---

[6] Deanne Williams and Richard Preiss, eds., *Childhood, Education and the Stage in Early Modern England* (New York: Cambridge University Press, 2017).

[7] Bucholz and Key, *Early Modern England, 1485–1714: A Narrative History*, 195; E.A. Wrigley, "Urban Growth in Early Modern England: Food, Fuel and Transport," *Past & Present* 225 (2014): 79–112.

[8] Such statistics are contingent upon what it means for someone to be "literate" in the first place. W.B. Stephens, "Literacy in England, Scotland, and Wales, 1500–1900," *History of Education Quarterly* 30, no. 4 (Winter 1990): 545–71.

urban), and though infant mortality declined during the eighteenth century, it was still common.[9] Disease outbreaks were a fact of life in both rural and urban areas. The Bubonic Plague re-occurred at regular intervals, the most dramatic of which was the Great Plague of London in 1665–1666. Medical treatments (depending on the doctor) involved a combination of classical humoral theory, folk remedies, and prayer. While some of these interventions brought temporary palliative effects, people were poorly equipped to treat the underlying symptoms of most infectious diseases.

The remainder of this chapter cuts across these 300 years of history to show the various ways in which people encountered goblins therein. This expansive chronology has required me to flatten some regional variations in favor of larger trends expressed across geographical contexts. We should not assume that the experience of rural people was consistent across time and space; the "cosmopolitan culture" and folkloric traditions of Scottish peasants did not necessarily reflect those of other parts of Britain, and even then, the lived experiences and beliefs of individuals varied from village to village.[10] So too does this chronology require the use of simplistic terminologies that do not do justice to the complexities of British society. Divisions between rich and poor, elite and common, urban and rural, literate and illiterate were not always clear cut.[11] The "high" culture produced by those in cities both reflected and was reflected by the "low" culture of the countryside, though the specifics of these exchanges are often unclear. The belief systems of rural people, too, often reach us via disparaging writings of urban elites, which complicates our analysis of these exchanges.

[9] Around the end of the sixteenth century, one out of eight children died within their first year of life, and one of four did not live past ten years of age. Bucholz and Key, *Early Modern England, 1485–1714: A Narrative History*, 172.

[10] Julian Goodare, "Scottish Witchcraft in Its European Context," in *Witchcraft and Belief in Early Modern Scotland*, Julian Goodare, Lauren Martin, and Joyce Miller, eds. (New York: Palgrave Macmillan, 2008), 31.

[11] Peter Burke, *Popular Culture in Early Modern Europe*, 3rd ed. (New York: Routledge, 2009); Andrew Hadfield, ed., *Literature and Popular Culture in Early Modern England* (New York: Taylor & Francis, 2016). See also Joan Kent, "The Rural 'Middling Sort' in Early Modern England, circa 1640–1740: Some Economic, Political and Socio-Cultural Characteristics," *Rural History* 10, no. 1 (April 1999): 19–54; Mark Hailwood, "Rethinking Literacy in Rural England, 1550–1700," *Past & Present* 260, no. 1 (2022): 38–70.

Goblins as Demons

Early modern writers, like their medieval predecessors, debated the role of fairies in Christian theology. These authors acknowledged the omniscience and ultimate power of God, but they clashed about how humans could use their observational powers to better understand His creation.[12] Their arguments drew on contemporary discourse about science, religion, history, and local issues like witch trials.[13] The classification of goblins and other preternatural creatures as a kind of demon persisted in the early modern period among elite authors, especially during the Reformation and height of witchcraft trials in England, though it fell out of favor such that it became a rarity by the eighteenth century. In these texts, authors presented goblins both as physical demons that stalked the earth with Satan and as mental ones that Satan implanted into the minds of Christians.

Two passages from the *Lucydarye* (published in multiple editions during the late fifteenth/early sixteenth centuries) give a sense of the ways that demonic goblins could manifest on Earth and in the minds of Christians. Written as a dialogue between a teacher and student, one passage sees the former inform the latter about goblins and their satanic kin:

> But elves, goblins, and helquins that men see by night, such as soldiers trotting on horseback in large companies—they are devils that are among us that show themselves in such a form and in many others like a dog, a horse, a tree, or a stone, and in many other forms to tempt a man into some vice and to make him err in the faith. Sometimes, these devils come into the stables, find a horse, and turn all that was above below in mockery of the man and to tempt him. Sometimes, they unbind little children and cast them

---

[12] In 1673, the anonymous author of *A Pleasant Treatise of Witches*, claims that "nothing has had more Defendants on either side, than the possibility of man's having familiarity with Demons." *A Pleasant Treatise of Witches* (London: H.B. for C. Wilkinson, 1673).

[13] Robin Briggs, *Witches & Neighbors: The Social and Cultural Context of European Witchcraft* (New York: Penguin, 1996); James Sharpe, *Instruments of Darkness: Witchcraft in Early Modern England* (Pennsylvania: University of Pennsylvania Press, 1997); Stuart Clark, *Thinking with Demons: The Idea of Witchcraft in Early Modern Europe* (New York: Oxford University Press, 1999); Rita Voltmer and Liv Helene Willumsen, "Introduction: Demonology and Witch-Trials in Dialogue," in *Demonology and Witch-Hunting in Early Modern Europe*, Julian Goodare, Rita Voltmer, and Liv Helene Willumsen, eds. (New York: Routledge, 2020), 1–18.

from the cradle to make the father and mother angry. Often, they kill the children when God permits it because of the sin of the father or mother.[14]

These demonic goblins present a range of threats, from the killing of children to the trashing of stables. Alongside this physical threat, though, is a mental one: a hallucination brought on by the devil. In another section of the dialogue, the pupil asks his teacher, "how do you see these women who say that they see in the air these fairies and goblins, which they call elves and many other things?" The teacher's answer is grounded in the susceptibility of women to sinful influences. He says that women are more influenced than men (as Eve was tempted before Adam) and that the devil often reveals his evil works to women. Witches, therefore, are sinful idolaters without proper faith who are easily led astray by these satanic schemes. These visions of fairies and goblins implanted by Satan resemble "those of a man who is drunk and who thinks the house is turning under his feet, which makes him fall, even though the house and the earth do not actually move."[15]

Within the *Lucydarye*, we see two different interpretations of goblins: a corporeal devil that roams the earth and a hallucinatory vision implanted by Satan. These interpretations are not mutually exclusive; they show readers two of the ways that Satan could harm Christians. Goblins are grouped with a handful of other creatures as demonic entities, though the author does not dwell on distinctions between them because, at their core, they are devils—even if people have bestowed different names on them.[16] Indeed, as Darren Oldridge summarizes:

[It was] conceivable that fairies were sometimes figments of the imagination and sometimes demons in disguise. Moreover, the Devil could be involved in both phenomena. This was because Satan was believed to operate through

---

[14] The Old French version of this text is a "free adaptation" of the Latin *Elucidarium* from the late eleventh century. The Middle English translator renders "goblins" from "*gibelins*" and "*gebelins*." Stephen Morrison, ed., *The Late Middle English "Lucydarye"* (Turnhout: Brepols, 2013), xi, 54–55.

[15] Morrison, 48–51.

[16] This kind of interchangeability is visible in texts across this chapter. Take, for example, Hieronymus Magomastix, *The Strange Witch at Greenwich, (Ghost, Spirit, or Hobgoblin) Haunting a Wench* (London: Thomas Harper, 1650).

both indirect and direct methods, and was prone to deceive the mind at least as often as the eyes.[17]

Other early modern authors warn readers about the threat of demonic goblins alongside anti-Catholic rhetoric typical of the Reformation, especially in the mid- to late sixteenth century.[18] A sermon from 1578, for example, paints goblins as a recent illusion brought by Satan in a long line of deceptions that includes the miracles of saints and the pains of purgatory, which "bewitched all who drank from the cup of his abomination."[19] Another from 1580 warns people to fear the various delusions brought by the devil and his ministers (i.e., Catholics), including "spirits, ghosts, goblins, and many vain apparitions and feigned miracles."[20] A treatise claims that all of the popes from Sylvester to Gregory VII were enchanters that "stirred up walking spirits, bugs, goblins, fierce sights, and various terrible ghosts and shapes."[21] Protestant writers presented aspects of Catholic doctrine as demonic illusions. In doing so, they rejected Catholic notions of an ambiguous purgatory between Heaven and Hell, corporeal devils battling the saints, and the existence of earthly spirits as anything more than the machinations of Satan.[22]

---

[17] Darren Oldridge, "Fairies and the Devil in Early Modern England." *The Seventeenth Century* 31, no. 1 (2016): 2.

[18] Peter Marshall, "Protestants and Fairies in Early-Modern England," in *Living with Religious Diversity in Early-Modern Europe,* C. Scott Dixon, Dagmar Freist, and Mark Greengrass, eds. (Burlington: Ashgate, 2009), 139–59. These frequent invectives against Catholics show their perceived influence despite persecution. Alan Dures and Francis Young, *English Catholicism 1558–1642* (New York: Routledge, 2022).

[19] William James, *A Sermon Preached before the Queenes Maiestie at Hampton Courte* (London: Henry Bynneman, 1578).

[20] Thomas Cooper, *Certaine Sermons Wherin Is Contained the Defense of the Gospell Nowe Preached against Such Cauils and False Accusations* (London: Ralphe Newbery, 1580), 81.

[21] John Bale, *The Pageant of Popes Contayninge the Lyues of All the Bishops of Rome* (London: Thomas Marshel, 1574), 73.

[22] This kind of language is mirrored in English-language texts refuting Protestant ideas, too. One account of the heretical tendencies of reformers, for example, mentions how Martin Luther admitted to buying a devil as a familiar and John Calvin confessed to being guided by goblins more than his own disposition. Henry Fitzsimon, *A Catholike Confutation of M. Iohn Riders Clayme of Antiquitie and a Caulming Comfort against His Caueat* (Douai: P. Auroi and C. Boscard, 1608), 136. Catholic attitudes toward witchcraft and demonic possession are considered in Francis Young, *English Catholics and the Supernatural, 1553–1829* (Aldershot: Ashgate, 2013). When Anglophone Catholics wrote about goblins, they largely retained their medieval associations. One author, for example, when narrating the life of

The gradual domination of Protestantism in England saw the tapering of texts that sought to position goblins as a Catholic folly. In the seventeenth century, though, the rise of witch trials encouraged some authors to consider the kinds of spirits that these enchanters could summon. Such examinations were less common than those that dismissed witchcraft entirely (more on that shortly), but they nonetheless show a continued association of goblins with Satan—in this case purveyed by witches instead of Catholics. Among the most detailed is Heywood's *Hierarchie of the Blessed Angels*, which classifies hobgoblins, fairies, and satyrs (among others) as lesser devils deployed by Satan and his agents "with great illusions" on this earth. Such creatures prefer living in subterranean areas like "concaves, pits, vaults, dens, and caverns deep."[23] They are "*Lucifugi*" (literally "those who shun the light") and responsible for modest inconveniences to humans, from snuffing out the lanterns of miners to making frightening noises in barns to dancing around kitchens at night. Though relatively benign in the greater hierarchy of Satanic agents, they are nonetheless classifiable as demonic threats.[24]

A handful of other texts echo this kind of classification. One from 1665 catalogues the spirits that witches could conjure. Hobgoblins are mentioned as one of many terrestrial spirits, which are subordinate to air spirits, distinct from infernal spirits, and occupy "woods, mountains, caves, fens, mines, ruins, desolate places, and ancient buildings" of this earth.[25] Among these terrestrial spirits are hobgoblins, which are "jocund and

---

Saint Godric of Finchale, tells how he performed miracles that put a "hellish Goblin" to flight. Jerome Porter, *The Flowers of the Liues of the Most Renowned Saincts of the Three Kingdoms England Scotland, and Ireland* (Douai: s.n., 1632), 482. See also Francis Trigge, *A Touchstone, Whereby May Be Easilie Discerned, Which Is the True Catholike Faith* (London: Peter Short, 1599), 211–12.

[23] Thomas Heywood, *The Hierarchie of the Blessed Angells* (London: Adam Islip, 1635), 568. Heywood compares pugs and hobgoblins to the *Kottri* and *Kobaldi* of Eastern Europe. Ostling argues that, in some cases, the *latawiec* of Poland bears a strong resemblance to the domestic "hobgoblins and pucks of Europe as a whole, mischievous but benevolent if given milk to drink." Michael Ostling, *Between the Devil and the Host: Imagining Witchcraft in Early Modern Poland* (New York: Oxford University Press, 2011), 199.

[24] Briggs calls them "the homelier type of devil." Katharine Briggs, "Heywood's Hierarchie of the Blessed Angells," *Folklore* 80, no. 2 (Summer 1969): 106.

[25] This passage is from an anonymous treatise attached to Reginald Scot, *The Discovery of Witchcraft* (London: Andrew Clark, 1665), II.51. The author of this text was apparently unaware that Scot was skeptical of witchcraft, for it is a non-satirical overview of the creatures associated with witchcraft. Philip C. Almond, *England's First Demonologist: Reginald Scot and "The Discoverie of Witchcraft"* (New York: I.B. Tauris, 2011), 6–8.

facetious" and responsible for replacing children with changelings, pinching people, and causing general mischief if not properly fed.[26] *A Pleasant Treatise of Witches* from 1673 undertakes a similar cataloguing of "familiar spirits, goblins, and fairies" that are broadly associated with Satan across historical contexts.[27] In one story, goblins invade the home of a man who had invited his friends for a meal. The man, recognizing these guests as demons, prays to God in fear. The goblins promptly vanish, leaving behind a foul odor in the room such that "few guests ever came into it afterwards."[28] In this treatise, goblins are distinct from specters and phantasms, apparitions of humanoid figures (sometimes the deceased) that torment those with whom they come into contact, as well as imps, which act as day-to-day assistants for witches and their various deeds. Like those of Heywood, these goblins pose a modest threat to humans even as demonic entities.

As agents of Satan, demonic goblins are sometimes depicted in the depths of Hell. *Flowers of Epigrammes* (1577) mentions how Christ once descended among the "goblins black of hell" in a grim reminder to the audience about their own mortality. In Shakespeare's drama *Hamlet* (c. 1600), when the titular character is confronted by a ghost, he calls upon the angels to defend him whether this entity is "a spirit of health or goblin damned / Bring with thee airs from heaven, or blasts from hell."[29] The enduring popularity of Shakespeare and resonance of this idea of a "goblin

[26] These ideas drew on discourse from continental Europe. A translation of Agrippa's Latin *De Occulta Philosophia Libri III*, for example, sees fairies and hobgoblins as spirits "not so noxious" but rather closer to men in behaviors and prone to live in grasslands (as opposed to the naiads, which live in fountains, or the nymphs, which reside in marshes and ponds). Henry Cornelius Agrippa, *Three Books of Occult Philosophy*, trans. James Freake (London: Gregory Moule, 1651), 450. See also Pierre de Lancre, *On the Inconstancy of Witches: Pierre de Lancre's Tableau de l'inconstance Des Mauvais Anges et Demons (1612)*, ed. Gerhild Scholz Williams (Turnhout: Brepols, 2006).

[27] Thomas Bromhall's history also provides examples throughout History of goblins and hobgoblins (used interchangeably), which he considers to be delusions brought by Satan. Thomas Bromhall, *An History of Apparitions, Oracles, Prophecies, and Predictions with Dreams, Visions, and Revelations and the Cunning Delusions of the Devil* (London: John Streater, 1658). Richard Bovet, too, analyzes demons from the ancient world to the present, including how the naiads of ancient Greece residing on the island of Samos were "old fashioned Goblins." In one contemporary anecdote, he also relates how a pious falconer was assaulted by a "frightful Goblin" one night. Richard Bovet, *Pandaemonium, or, The Devil's Cloyster* (London: J. Walthoe, 1684), 107, 198.

[28] *A Pleasant Treatise of Witches*, 75–76.

[29] William Shakespeare, *Hamlet*, ed. G.R. Hibbard, The Oxford Shakespeare (New York: Oxford University Press, 2008), 1.4, lines 44–46.

damned" was such that it was a common exclamation over the next several centuries. A description of Hell from a 1608 sermon includes the presence of "hobgoblins and infernal spirits" therein.[30] Milton uses many names, "Goblin" among them, to describe the dark and apparently formless shape that guarded the gates of Hell in *Paradise Lost* (1667).[31] Classificatory details aside, the goblin was an apt designator to describe some of Satan's agents.

Illustrations from these texts show that demons could take many forms. Some are humanoids with exaggerated features and monstrous append-ages like tails and horns. Others are more alien in appearance. They are often depicted flying or dancing. Though woodcuts provide limited opportunities for distinguishing between colors, some demons are black to match the sin and dark deeds with which they are associated.[32] Indeed, they were as ugly as their character—and their monstrous visage broadly corresponded to other groups whose deviancy reflected their appearance. As the British Empire expanded its reach across the globe, new groups of people were stereotyped based on this paradigm. I consider this theme in greater detail in Chap. 4 (Fig. 3.1).

Although some Protestant authors saw goblins as agents of Satan, their role within witch trials themselves is unclear. Documents from these cases (trial transcripts and witchcraft pamphlets especially) help us glimpse how commoners thought about the ability of humans to convene with demons, though they are complicated genres of texts in their own right.[33] Scribes wrote with standardizing hands using established conventions that dis-torted the words of those providing testimony in the courtroom. Later

[30] James, *A Sermon Preached before the Queenes Maiestie at Hampton Courte*, 33.

[31] John Milton, *Paradise Lost a Poem Written in Ten Books* (London: Peter Parker, 1667). The wildly popular allegory, *The Pilgrim's Progress* (1678), likewise mentions the presence of hobgoblins (alongside satyrs and dragons) dwelling within the Valley of the Shadow of Death. John Bunyan, *The Pilgrim's Progress* (London: Nathaniel Ponder, 1678), 76. A hand-ful of biblical commentaries clarify the kind of creatures that will one day inhabit fallen Babylon and Rome, including "spirits and Goblins" from Hell. See, for example, William Fulke, *Prælections Vpon the Sacred and Holy Reuelation of S. Iohn* (London: Thomas Purfoote, 1573).

[32] See also Paul Juvenal, *Vulcan's Rebuke* (London: s.n., 1788), 14.

[33] On these complexities, see Marion Gibson, *Reading Witchcraft* (New York: Taylor & Francis, 2005); James Sharpe, "English Witchcraft Pamphlets and the Popular Demonic," in *Demonology and Witch-Hunting in Early Modern Europe*, Julian Goodare, Rita Voltmer, and Liv Helene Willumsen, eds. (New York: Routledge, 2020), 127–46.

Fig. 3.1 Early modern demons. (Left) The frontispiece of Nathaniel Crouch's 1688 *The Kingdom of Darknes* showing, in the bottom-left corner, demons circling a person performing an incantation. Image (cropped) courtesy of the Internet Archive (published under a pseudonym: Robert Burton, *The Kingdom of Darkness* (London: Nathaniel Crouch, 1688), frontispiece. Accessible here: https://archive. org/details/TheKingdomOfDarknessOrTheHistoryOfDaemonsSpecters WitchesEtc.1688). (Right-top) Demons hover in the air above a house in Joseph Glanvill's 1681 *Saducismus Triumphatus*. Image (cropped) courtesy of the National Library of Medicine (Joseph Glanvill, *Saducismus Triumphatus* (London: J. Collins and S. Lownds, 1681), 181. Accessible here: https://collections.nlm. nih.gov/catalog/nlm:nlmuid-2354009R-bk). (Right-bottom) A demon flies through the air alongside human witches in Thomas Norris' 1720 *The History of Witches and Wizards*. Image (cropped) courtesy of the Wellcome Collection (W.P., *The History of Witches and Wizards* (London: Thomas Norris, 1720), 6. Accessible here: https://wellcomecollection.org/works/abkab8tq/items)

accounts of trials, too, are inevitably warped by authorial agendas and genre conventions.[34]

The difficulty of using witch trial texts for this history of goblins is best illustrated in a case study from the Salem witch trials of 1692–1693. During the trial of Bridget Bishop, a man named John Louder testified that a shapeshifting entity attacked him in his home.[35] He referred to this creature in a number of ways: a black pig, a monkey with the claws of a chicken and face of a man, a "black thing," a creature, and a devil. Although Louder was able to rid himself of the monster by proclaiming "the whole armor of God be between me and you," the dust that hit him in the stomach when the creature forcefully leapt away rendered him "struck dumb" for a few days. The testimony of Louder and others was enough to see Bishop executed—the first of twenty-five to die during these trials.

According to this court transcript, Louder did not call the creature that accosted him a goblin. The same cannot be said of the account of Louder's testimony provided by Cotton Mather, who defended his aggressively anti-witch conduct in *The Wonders of the Invisible World* (1693). While summarizing Louder's testimony (despite not attending the trial), Mather calls the entity in question a "goblin."[36] Mather, a trained theologian, imposed his own ideas about demonology onto Louder, as in the same text, he writes that there are many kinds of demons with different degrees of severity, including those "baser goblins that choose to nest in the filthy and loathsome rags of a beastly sorceress."[37] Since Mather saw Bridget Bishop as a witch, he was comfortable categorizing the entity that Louder encountered as a goblin.

This brief case study perhaps indicates a larger phenomenon. In my searches of digital repositories of trial transcripts, I was unable to find mentions of goblins, even in trials that involve witches accused of

---

[34] Authors critical of Charles I, for example, tied providential occurrences like the appearance of fairies to corruption in the monarchy, making accused witches complicit in his administration's misdeeds. Peter Elmer, *Witchcraft, Witch-Hunting, and Politics in Early Modern England* (New York: Oxford University Press, 2016), 87–90.

[35] "Testimony of John Louder v. Bridget Bishop" (Salem Witch Trials Documentary Archive and Transcription Project, 1692), https://salem.lib.virginia.edu/n13.html#n13.11.

[36] Cotton Mather, *The Wonders of the Invisible World* (Boston: Benjamin Harris, 1693), 111–12.

[37] Mather, *The Wonders of the Invisible World*, 10.

convening with fairies.[38] In these cases, scribes show a preference for terms like devils, spirits, imps, and familiars.[39] This linguistic trend broadly indicates that goblins were less associated with witchcraft among the laity—and that their evocation in contemporary theological discourse was more reflective of elite perspectives. That said, the preoccupation of scribes at these witchcraft trials was not the classification of these demonic associates, so it is possible that they elided testimony regarding goblins into other, more commonly used categories. Even so, Carla Suhr informed me that she did not find any mentions of goblins within the corpus of materials for her project, "Corpus of Early Modern English Witchcraft Pamphlets." It seems that goblins, however classified in Christian demonology, were not commonly invoked in these trials. Since I was unable to undertake a thorough examination of trial transcripts, however, I hope that more systematic research will reveal further details.

The texts considered in this section show that some early modern writers saw goblins as a form of demon, associated them with various harms that could befall Christians, and used them interchangeably with a handful of other devils like elves and fairies. The distinction between these creatures was less important to these authors than the spiritual threat posed by them. Many of these ideas were continuations of those developed during the Middle Ages, though authors modified them as they engaged in debates related to the Protestant Reformation and witch trials. The idea that goblins and their demonic kin were verifiable threats to Christians, however, was not the dominant force to emerge in demonology during the early modern period.

---

[38] I would like to thank Carla Suhr and Mikki Brock for their help on this topic. I consulted the following online repositories: Salem Witch Trials: Documentary Archive and Transcription Project; The Survey of Scottish Witchcraft, The National Archives (United Kingdom).

[39] Henderson and Cowan, *Scottish Fairy Belief: A History*, 116–32; Henderson, *Witchcraft and Folk Belief in the Age of Enlightenment: Scotland, 1670–1740*, 83. The process of translating folkloric creatures into the Latin language during legal proceedings was fraught, as Ostling explores in the case of early modern Poland. He shows that each translation was an "act of comparative ethnography, an attempt to gloss not just a foreign *term* but a foreign *thing*: each translation is accomplished through reference to some locally imagined spirit or creature or demon." Here, the terms in question are the Latin *incubus* and the Polish *latawiec*. Ostling, *Between the Devil and the Host: Imagining Witchcraft in Early Modern Poland*, 227–37.

FAKE GOBLINS

The classification of goblins as a demon declined in popularity during the early modern period. In its place emerged the idea that goblins and their preternatural kin were nothing more than fantasies conjured by misinformed Catholics and the uneducated masses. These arguments were closely connected to contemporary preoccupations with witchcraft. As a gradual consensus emerged that humans could not convene with the devil, creatures summoned by witches were increasingly seen as figments of the imagination. Gendered and classist language was common in these arguments, as writers blamed uneducated women for spreading a pointless fear among children about the existence of these creatures and thus perpetuating a needless superstition.

Among the most influential anti-witchcraft writings was Reginald Scot's 1584 *The Discoverie of Witchcraft*, which catalogues the ways that people could be fooled into believing things that were not true. Rational people, Scot argues, do not believe in goblins, fairies, or spirits. He notes that Robin Goodfellow and Hobgoblin "were as terrible, and also as credible to the people, as hags and witches be now: and in time to come, a witch will be as much derided and contemned, and as plainly perceived, as the illusion and knavery of Robin Goodfellow."[40] Here, Scot positions Hobgoblin as a creature that was once believed to exist but now is rightly known as fictitious. In another passage, he lists the illusions that cause people to be afraid of their own shadows and forsake proper Christian practice (i.e., Calvinism), spirits, elves, fairies, Tom Thumb, Hobgoblin, and Robin Goodfellow among them.[41] Distinctions between these creatures (however named) are ultimately unimportant because they are all figments of the imagination.

Numerous authors in the second half of the seventeenth century express similar skepticism about the existence of demonic goblins as enthusiasm for witch trials was waning and Protestantism was firmly established as the dominant strand of Christianity in Britain. Authors saw such creatures as superstitious relics of flawed belief systems, the root cause of which varied. Some Protestant authors blame Catholics for using them to scare people into submission. A sermon from 1657, for example, mentions how spirits

---

[40] Reginald Scot, *The Discouerie of Witchcraft* (London: Henry Denham, 1584), 131. See also Almond, *England's First Demonologist: Reginald Scot and "The Discovery of Witchcraft."*
[41] Scot, *The Discouerie of Witchcraft*, 153.

and hobgoblins were believed to exist in the days of "Popery and blindness" but that the light of Protestantism had vanished those false beliefs from the world.[42] Another from 1660 disparages the Catholics who use "so many ghosts and goblins to scare and amuse the common people."[43] Thomas Ady, a skeptic of witchcraft, even accuses demonologists themselves of concocting ridiculous stories (including one about a goblin trapped in an underground cellar) to bolster their own flawed opinions and enrich themselves.[44]

The uneducated masses were another target of ridicule. A 1652 treatise demeans the "fantasy of the most stupid idiot" that allows the mind to paint whatever false image it likes as real: chimeras, sirens, harpies, and goblins included.[45] A sermon preached at the University of Cambridge in 1658 claims that "people talk of Goblins to fright children and fools."[46] John Locke, among the most important thinkers of the Enlightenment, dismisses the existence of goblins and sprites, blaming their perpetuation on the "foolish maid" that places them into the mind of the child, whereupon they become synonymous with darkness.[47] The anonymous author of 1676's *The Doctrine of Devils* broadly and contemptuously dismisses the notion of witchcraft, goblins, and devils as inventions of the gullible masses:

> You'll find old Wives Tales, and Profane Fables, seconded by *Romantic* Inventions, and Poetical Fictions, to be the Original of all. Some Old, Crazy-Brained, Doting, Melancholical, Hypochondriac Dreamers in the Paroxysm of their Distempers, seem to see strange Sights, Creatures,

[42] John Everard, *The Gospel Treasury Opened* (London: John Owsley, 1657), 161.

[43] John Gauden, *A Sermon Preached in St. Pauls Church London* (London: Andrew Crook, 1660), 66. One pamphlet of an unknown date disparagingly refers to the Catholic religious service as "hobgoblin mass" and another refutes the "goblin witchcraft" of Catholic writer John Dryden. "A Passionate / Satyr / Upon the Devillish Great / He-Whore / That Lives Yonder at / Rome" (n.d.), Crawford.EB.1005, National Library of Scotland; Thomas Rymer, "An Epistle to Mr. Dryden" (Exeter, 1688), H.P.1056, Chetham's Library - Halliwell-Phillipps.

[44] Thomas Ady, *The Doctrine of Devils, Proved to Be the Grand Apostacy of These Later Times* (London: Thomas Ady, 1676), 187–88.

[45] Walter Charleton, *The Darkness of Atheism Dispelled by the Light of Nature: A Physico-Theologicall Treatise* (London: William Lee, 1652), 6.

[46] Nathaniel Ingelo, *The Perfection, Authority, and Credibility of the Holy Scriptures* (London: Luke Fawn, 1658), 146.

[47] John Locke, *An Essay Concerning Humane Understanding* (London: Awnsham and John Churchill, 1700), 223.

> Goblins, Devils, as they think; this they report, with Confidence; the Rabble
> is credulous....[48]

This group of texts dismisses the notion that goblins exist anywhere but the minds of the naïve and uneducated. Goblins are not distinguished from other kinds of creatures because they are representative of a backward and ultimately ungrounded set of beliefs from which authors seek to separate themselves. Authors in England were hardly alone in reaching this conclusion, and indeed, many of them drew on scholars from mainland Europe (including Erasmus) to buttress their conclusions.[49] Such arguments made their way into non-theological texts, too. The playwright William Cartwright satirizes archaic belief systems in *The Ordinary* (c. 1635) via Moth, an "antiquarian dupe who speaks an elaborately muddled form of Chaucerian Middle English," including one absurd prayer to the fairies of old:

> Saint *Francis*, and Saint *Benedict*,
> Blesse this house from wicked wight,
> From the Night-mare and the Goblin,
> That is [called] *good fellow Robin*.
> Keep it from all evil Spirits,
> Fairies, Weasels, Rats and Ferrets,
> From Curfew time
> To the next prime.[50]

Moth's delivery of this lofty, ye olde prayer reinforces the idea that belief in goblins and fairies is archaic. A 1664 play for students at a private grammar school similarly shows the extent to which some educators sought to distance their students from these backward beliefs.[51] At the

---

[48] *The Doctrine of Devils Proved to Be the Grand Apostacy of These Later Times* (London, 1676), 127.

[49] Erasmus' disdain for superstitions, including the "old wives' tales of sprites, of devils, of hobgoblin and the fairies," is on full display within *In Praise of Folly*, which was translated from Latin in the sixteenth century. Desiderius Erasmus, *The Praise of Folie* (London: Thomas Berthelet, 1549).

[50] William Cartwright, *The Ordinary, a Comedy* (London: Humphrey Moseley, 1651), 36; Adrian Streete, "Moderation and Religious Criticism in William Cartwright's The Ordinary (1635)," *The Seventeenth Century* 31, no. 1 (2016): 17–36.

[51] *School-Play Prepared for, and Performed in a Private Grammar-School in Middlesex* (London: S. Cripps, 1664), 41–42.

play's conclusion, students declare that Ignoramus, hags, and hobgoblins are henceforth banished from their realm. This proclamation shows the audience (likely teachers and parents) that the young performers of this play are aware that hobgoblins and their kin are not real, thus performatively separating themselves from their less educated peers.

Gendered and classist language is prominent in condemnatory descriptions of preternatural creatures. Women were largely responsible for the rearing of children during the early modern period, and elite men placed the blame on them for the persistence of folk traditions among the uneducated masses.[52] Educational texts across the early modern period urge their readers to avoid perpetuating these superstitions. One from 1550 cautions teachers that hobgoblins, witches, nightmares, spirits, and giants are nothing more than "naughty lies" and "evil sayings" learned as children from "dads, grandmothers, nurses, and maidens while they were spinning."[53] The time spent on these fantastical stories ought to instead have been used learning scripture, grammar, and oration. A 1699 manual for midwives, nurses, and young married women similarly recommends that they avoid frightening children with old wives' tales of goblins and specters. Early exposure to these kinds of stories, the author warns, can make them fall into epileptic fits or suffer from falling sickness (i.e., seizures).[54] Olinthus Gregory's instructional text for British youth from 1796 also laments the "too numerous" stories of "ghosts and apparitions, hobgoblins and spectres" perpetuated by "the great weakness and folly of some parents and nurses." Such superstitions are difficult to eradicate, ingrained as they are within older generations and based, in some way, on misconceptions of the natural world.[55]

[52] Wendy Wall, "Why Does Puck Sweep?: Fairylore, Merry Wives, and Social Struggle," *Shakespeare Quarterly* 52, no. 1 (2001): 68–69; Michelle D. Brock and David R. Winter, "Theory and Practice in Early Modern Epistemologies of the Preternatural," in *Knowing Demons, Knowing Spirits in the Early Modern Period*, Michelle D. Brock, Richard Raiswell, and David R. Winter, eds. (New York: Springer, 2018), 3–8.

[53] Rychard Sherry, *A Treatise of Schemes [and] Tropes Very Profitable for the Better Vnderstanding of Good Authors* (London: Iohn Day, 1550). See also George Savile Halifax, *Advice to a Daughter as to Religion, Husband, House, Family and Children, Behaviour and Conversation, Friendship, Censure, Vanity and Affectation, Pride, Diversions* (London: M. Gillyflower and B. Tooke, 1699), 7.

[54] Aristotle, *Aristotle's Manual of Choice Secrets*, trans. J.P. (London: John Back, 1699), 112.

[55] Olinthus Gregory, *Lessons Astronomical and Philosophical for the Amusement and Instruction of British Youth* (Cambridge: Benjamin Flower, 1796), 120.

Some medical doctors even present goblins and fairies as symptoms of diseases that could afflict the human body, especially melancholy. According to classical humoral theory, melancholy was associated with an overabundance of black bile in the body as well as the general conditions of coldness and dryness. This condition brought about false visions, or as one text calls them, "counterfeit goblins" through which "the brain (deprived of good judgment), deceives the heart."[56] Another treatise similarly associates melancholy with dreams of goblins and a host of other dismal topics: darkness, funerals, tombs, and other "sad and doleful matters."[57] Astrological calculations reinforce this medical diagnosis. One author writes that Saturn brings about diseases related to melancholy, which includes dropsy, gout, and fearful and "formidable fancies" of a hobgoblin.[58] These illusory goblins are symptoms of diseases brought by "inward Causes" and markers themselves of something that is not real.[59]

The texts considered in this section reject the notion that goblins exist in this world. Instead, authors saw them as a fantastical idea that could reach vulnerable minds via fearmongering Catholics, naïve women, the uneducated masses, or certain physical ailments. Authors invoked goblins in different contexts within this corpus, though they roundly dismissed the idea that these creatures were anything but a fantasy.

Across the texts considered within this chapter thus far, it is important to note that the word "goblin" itself was never the focal point of authors. Usually, the term is mentioned once or twice as part of larger lists of creatures (demonic, hallucinatory, or otherwise), but goblins themselves are never central to these narratives. Instead, they take a backseat to more common theological designators like devils, demons, familiars, spirits, and apparitions. The interchangeability of goblins with these creatures admittedly complicates any generalization we make about them—as a reader might have had a goblin in the back of their mind when an author discussed a "spirit" summoned by a witch, for example. As such, this

---

[56] Timothie Bright, *A Treatise of Melancholie* (London: Thomas Vautrollier, 1586), 103–4.

[57] Leonardus Lessius, *Hygiasticon* (Cambridge: Roger Daniel, 1634), 154.

[58] Nicholas Culpeper, *Semeiotica Uranica* (London: Nathaniell Brookes, 1651), 84.

[59] Thomas Tryon, *A Treatise of Dreams & Visions* (London: s.n., 1689), 24. These symptoms could be treated by certain roots, seeds, and gemstones (either emeralds or diamonds, depending on the author). William Langham, *The Garden of Health Conteyning the Sundry Rare and Hidden Vertues and Properties of All Kindes of Simples and Plants* (London: Christopher Barker, 1597), 483; *A Physicall Directory* (London: Peter Cole, 1649), 74; Simeon Partlicius, *A New Method of Physick* (London: Peter Cole, 1654), 158.

discussion of goblins could be applied with few changes to the numerous other preternatural creatures with which authors commonly grouped them.

GOBLINS IN BETWEEN

Situated between the poles of demonic and illusory goblins is a spectrum of beliefs related to the world of Fairyland that defy easy categorization. Some of the most influential depictions of goblins from early modern Britain come from the pens of authors and playwrights who were unconcerned with the nature of these creatures' existence and instead used folkloresque imagery to convey larger themes in their works. Fairies and goblins could be accessibly injected into narratives across genres, whether as central players or passing references. Depending on the work, they could reinforce monarchical structures, destabilize gender roles, embody hedonism, critique class hierarchies, blur the boundaries between real and fiction, scare people into proper behavior, or indicate a realm of the vaguely supernatural. These depictions simultaneously influenced folklore and were influenced by it. This section unpacks the many faces of goblins in early modern literature and theater, which in turn allows for a richer analysis of the oral traditions that operated alongside it in the next section of this chapter.

Fairy lore was a common subject for authors and "probably more prominent in British culture between 1560 and 1640 than at any time before or since."[60] An amorphous milieu of folk traditions coalesced in the fifteenth and sixteenth centuries around the fairy court—a class of supernatural creatures with a royal hierarchy mirroring earthly ones—that elite authors infused with their own perspectives and criticisms.[61] The court of Fairyland, for example, was expanded within literary and theatrical works intended for elite audiences such that it legitimized the English monarchy.[62] Edmund Spenser tied Queen Elizabeth I to fairy monarchies in his acclaimed *The Faerie Queen* (1590), and Prince Henry himself played Oberon in a 1611 production of *Oberon, the Faery Prince*.[63] The increased

[60] Hutton, "The Making of the Early Modern British Fairy Tradition," 1147.

[61] Young and Ermacora, "Introducing the Social Supernatural," 2–7.

[62] Marjorie Swann, "The Politics of Fairylore in Early Modern English Literature," *Renaissance Quarterly* 53, no. 2 (Summer 2000): 450–51.

[63] Joshua Poole provides a hierarchy of the fairy court in *The English Parnassus*. At the wedding of King Oberon and Queen Mab are the courtiers "Periwiggin, Periwinckle, Puck, Hobgoblin Tomalin, Tom Thumb" and the maids of honor "Hop, Mop, Drop, Pip, Trip,

wealth of England during the Stuart period (1603–1714) saw authors emphasize material possessions among the tiny inhabitants of Fairyland as a critique of elite excess. Although authors innovated on previous fairy traditions to suit their own circumstances, by 1640 "the standard characters and associations of fairyland were established in the British literary imagination" and "would not alter greatly for the rest of the early modern period."[64]

This is not to say that authors did not find new ways to use fairies in their works—but rather that the structure of the fairy court and its associations were well established in the 1600s. Fairies were often transgressive and challenged prevailing assumptions about class and gender hierarchies. The ruler of Fairyland was often a queen, whose presence in theatrical productions would be embodied by a male actor, though King Oberon was an important figure as well.[65] Fairies on stage, whether provided with an explicit gender or not, would "indiscriminately engage in activities socially ascribed to men or women specifically" and blur the lines between gender roles.[66] Robin Goodfellow, often described as a male fairy, thus performed household chores at night—an activity traditionally expected of women.[67] Fairies might encourage extramarital sex without consequence (for themselves, at least) and goad humans to engage in unacceptable behaviors for their own amusement. Human women, too, were more likely to transgress gender norms when working in tandem with fairies than if they were to challenge patriarchal hierarchies on their own. These

---

Skip, Fib, Tib, Tick, Pinke, Pin, Quick, Gill, Jin, Tit, Wap, Win, Nit." Revealingly, in this same compilation, Poole invokes a more sinister landscape of "raging fiends and goblins" when describing ancient Rome. Joshua Poole, *The English Parnassus* (London: Thomas Johnson, 1657), 295, 433.

[64] Hutton, "The Making of the Early Modern British Fairy Tradition," 1148. Such broad generalizations are echoed in other works on Fairyland, too. Simon Young argues that the idea of the boggart remained essentially unchanged from 1500 to 1800. Young, *The Boggart: Folklore, History, Place-Names and Dialect*, 48–49.

[65] Hutton, *Queens of the Wild: Pagan Goddesses in Christian Europe: An Investigation*, 75–109.

[66] Buccola, *Fairies, Fractious Women, and the Old Faith: Fairy Lore in Early Modern British Drama and Culture*, 41.

[67] Wall, "Why Does Puck Sweep?: Fairylore, Merry Wives, and Social Struggle," 67–68. Lamb argues, too, that Robin Goodfellow could serve as a "weapon of the weak" or a facilitator for "evading social control" depending on the context. Mary Ellen Lamb, "Taken by the Fairies: Fairy Practices and the Production of Popular Culture in A Midsummer Night's Dream," *Shakespeare Quarterly* 51, no. 3 (Autumn 2000): 279–80. See also Ezra Horbury, "Early Modern Transgender Fairies," *Transgender Studies Quarterly* 8, no. 1 (2021): 75–95.

fairies were generally tamer than their medieval antecedents, though their petite frames and comical antics should not entirely distract from their "formidable" tempers, which could still bring harm to humans.[68]

Goblins were sometimes part of this fairy tradition, though they could also retain their more malevolent, demonic connotation. This variability is exhibited within the plays of Shakespeare, wherein goblins range from Fairyland pranksters to denizens of Hell to general markers of the supernatural. In *The Comedy of Errors* (c. 1594), for example, Dromio of Syracuse proclaims the following as he tries to make sense of a situation in which (unbeknownst to him) he has been mistaken for his brother:

> O, for my beads! I cross me for a sinner.
> This is the fairy land. O spite of spites!
> We talk with goblins, owls, and sprites.
> If we obey them not, this will ensue:
> They'll suck our breath, or pinch us black and blue.

Dromio invokes goblins alongside owls and sprites as the kind of creatures that will harass humans if not obeyed—an adaptation of contemporary oral tradition for the stage. Rhetorically, this passage serves to reinforce the peculiarity of the situation in which the characters find themselves: servants mistaken as masters, strangers mistaken for husbands. Dromio of Syracuse expresses the oddity of this situation by positioning himself in the bizarre world of Fairyland with its goblins, owls, and sprites.

Fairies take center stage in another of Shakespeare's early plays, *A Midsummer Night's Dream* (c. 1595–1596), which features Robin Goodfellow as an agent of Oberon. His introduction gives a sense of the kind of deeds that he is known to commit:

> Either I mistake your shape and making quite,
> Or else you are that shrewd and knavish sprite
> Called Robin Goodfellow. Are not you he
> That frights the maidens of the villagery,
> Skim milk, and sometimes labor in the quern
> And bootless make the breathless huswife churn,
> And sometime make the drink to bear no barm,

---

[68] Katharine Briggs, *The Anatomy of Puck: An Examination of Fairy Beliefs among Shakespeare's Contemporaries and Successors* (London: Routledge and Kegan Paul, 1959), 42–45.

> Mislead night wanderers, laughing at their harm?
> Those that "Hobgoblin" call you and "sweet Puck,"
> You do their work, and they shall have good luck....[69]

Here we see the conflation of Robin Goodfellow, Hobgoblin, and Puck as three names for the same creature.[70] He is a trickster, sometimes pulling pranks upon people going about their business as a "merry wanderer of the night." Elsewhere in the play, Puck acts on behalf of Oberon and interferes in the lives of humans, including transforming one's head into a donkey and mimicking voices to lead two of them astray (though he only ever speaks directly to other fairies). The overall framing of *A Midsummer Night's Dream* reinforces the difficulty of pinpointing where and when one might encounter the fairies. The story is set in a magical forest in ancient Athens, though the play ends with Robin Goodfellow suggesting that this whole story might have been a dream. Shakespeare is not particularly sympathetic to those who are dismissive of this magical world, however. The chief skeptic of Fairyland is the pompous Duke Theseus, whose dismissiveness of such "antique fables" and "fairy toys" is undermined by other characters, especially his wife Hippolyta.[71]

The earliest surviving depiction of Robin Goodfellow from *A Midsummer Night's Dream* comes from Theobald's 1740 edition. Shown squeezing juice into the eyes of Lysander, he wears "a broad-collared Elizabethan shirt and... a jester's cap," which positions him as a fool in the court of Oberon.[72] Two paintings of Puck from the late eighteenth century present him as a cherubic figure, which was a common practice for fairy illustrations of the time, though they embrace very different parts of his personality. The painting by Joshua Reynolds is smiling and playful; the

---

[69] William Shakespeare, *A Midsummer Night's Dream*, ed. Sukanta Chaudhuri, The Arden Shakespeare Third Series (New York: Bloomsbury, 2017), 2.1, lines 33–42.

[70] This malleability is further reinforced in two manuscripts of *The Merry Wives of Windsor*: the folio provides stage directions for a "hobgoblin" and the quarto for a "puck." William Shakespeare, *A Midsummer Night's Dream*, ed. Peter Holland, The Oxford Shakespeare (New York: Oxford University Press, 2008), 41. In Drayton's *Nymphidia* (1627), we see a similar introduction of Puck, whom "most men call Hobgoblin." Michael Drayton, *Nymphidia or The Court of Faery* (London: George Routledge & Sons, Limited, 1906).

[71] Kristen Poole, *Supernatural Environments in Shakespeare's England: Spaces of Demonism, Divinity, and Drama* (New York: Cambridge University Press, 2011), 30–31. See also Ronald F. Miller, "A Midsummer Night's Dream: The Fairies, Bottom, and the Mystery of Things," *Shakespeare Quarterly* 26, no. 3 (Summer 1975): 254–68.

[72] Shakespeare, *A Midsummer Night's Dream*, 43.

one by Fuseli is vindictive and malevolent as he throws a traveler off his horse. Across these depictions, too, Puck has light skin, which opposes the demonological equation of devils with darkness and, instead, connects to the intertwining of nationality, folklore, and race in England near the end of the early modern period.[73] Like the character himself, the variation we see in these early works of art of Robin Goodfellow/Hobgoblin/Puck is substantial (Fig. 3.2).

Theatrical interpretations of fairies in other works of Shakespeare range from the playfully mischievous to the more sinister. In *The Merry Wives of Windsor* (1602), a group of children dress as fairies (including "Crier Hobgoblin") to pinch and punish Falstaff.[74] As mentioned earlier in this chapter, Hamlet questions whether a ghost is "a spirit of health or goblin damned." Later in the play, Shakespeare presents goblins as more of a generic marker of misfortune when Hamlet laments the many "bugs and goblins" in his life.[75] We see a similarly sinister evocation in *Troilus and Cressida* (c. 1602), in which Troilus threatens to "haunt thee like a wicked conscience still / That moldeth goblins swift as frenzy's thoughts."[76] In *The Winter's Tale* (1611), too, Mamillius proclaims that "A sad tale's best for winter. I have one / Of sprites and goblins." These goblins are representative of an entire kind of story, the kind that can frighten with tales of darkness and the supernatural.[77] The merry mischief of Hobgoblin and the capricious world of Fairyland ought to be juxtaposed with these more sinister goblins.

Some of Shakespeare's plays that feature fairies take place in the ancient world—and this is no coincidence. Ancient Roman texts were crucial parts of the curriculum at grammar schools, and the mythological monsters of these texts were inspirational to early modern authors. Translations of classical texts and Latin-English dictionaries' entries across the early modern

---

[73] Mary Floyd-Wilson, *English Ethnicity and Race in Early Modern Drama* (New York: Cambridge University Press, 2003); Patricia Akhimie, ed., *The Oxford Handbook of Shakespeare and Race* (New York: Oxford University Press, 2024).

[74] William Shakespeare, *The Merry Wives of Windsor*, Callan Davies, Sarah Neville, and Emma Smith, eds. The New Oxford Shakespeare (New York: Oxford University Press, 2024), 5.5, lines 40–52.

[75] Shakespeare, *Hamlet*, 5.2, line 25.

[76] William Shakespeare, *Troilus and Cressida*, ed. Kenneth Muir (New York: Oxford University Press, 2008), 5.11, lines 30–31.

[77] William Shakespeare, *The Winter's Tale*, ed. Stephen Orgel, The Oxford Shakespeare (New York: Oxford University Press, 2008), 2.1, lines 34–37.

Fig. 3.2 Depictions of Puck from *A Midsummer Night's Dream*. (Top) Puck administering flower juice to a sleeping Lysander (whom he believed to be Demetrius) in a 1740 edition of *A Midsummer Night's Dream*. Image (cropped) courtesy of Wikimedia (William Shakespeare, *The Works of Shakespeare*, ed. Lewis Theobold, vol. 1 (London: H. Lintott, 1740), 71. Accessible here: https://commons.m.wikimedia.org/wiki/File:The_Works_of_Shakespeare_(1740)_-_Vol._1.pdf). (Bottom-left) A cherubic Puck smiles and waves in a 1789 painting by Joshua Reynolds for the Boydell Gallery. Image courtesy of Wikimedia

period reinforce a connection between ancient and contemporary goblins in particular. A 1566 English translation of Seneca the Younger's *Medea* sees the eponymous princess entreat "ugly bugs and goblins grim" as she seeks revenge on her ex-husband Jason.[78] A 1658 dictionary clarifies how the Latin "lemures" is "vulgarly called hobgoblin," and a 1746 translation of Horace's epistles wonders if readers can laugh "at the Schemes / of magic Terrours, visionary Dreams, / Portentous Wonders, witching Imps of Hell, / The nightly Goblin, and enchanting Spell?"[79] Latin texts and their English translations provided a well of inspiration for early modern authors, Shakespeare included, that shaped their interpretations of Fairyland.[80]

Shakespeare was hardly alone among his contemporaries in depicting (or referencing) goblins on stage. A 1584 translation of an Italian play lists "Robin Goodfellow, Hobgoblin, the devil and his dam" within a long list

---

[78] Seneca the Younger, *The Seuenth Tragedie of Seneca, Entituled Medea*, trans. Iohn Studley (London: Thomas Colwell, 1566), 34. See also Horace, *The Epistles and Art of Poetry of Horace*, trans. Philip Francis (London: A. Millar, 1746), 245.

[79] The same is true in translations of non-English texts. See, for example, the frequent usage of "goblin" in Miguel de Cervantes, *The History of the Most Renowned Don Quixote of Mancha* (London: Thomas Hodgkin, 1687).

[80] Some scholars explicitly compare ancient and contemporary preternatural creatures. Thomas Nash sees similarities in the *lares* of Rome; the fawnes, satyres, dryads, and hamadryas of Greece; and the Robin Goodfellows, elves, fairies, and hobgoblins "of our latter age." Thomas Nash, *The Terrors of the Night* (London: Iohn Danter, 1594). Henry Stubbe, conversely, argues in his analysis of the *Oneirocrticia* that the creature Empusa was not a hobgoblin, for Stubbe had not encountered descriptions of the latter describing it hopping on one leg or having the foot of a donkey. Henry Stubbe, *Clamor, Rixa, Joci, Mendacia, Furta, Cachini* (London: s.n., 1657), 28–38.

Fig 3.2 (continued) (Joshua Reynolds, *Puck*, 1789, oil on canvas, 1789. Accessible here: https://en.m.wikipedia.org/wiki/File:Reynolds-Puck.JPG. Early reviews of this painting were quite negative, with Horace Walpole calling this version of Puck "an ugly little imp, but with some character." Kevin Pask, *The Fairy Way of Writing: Shakespeare to Tolkien* (Baltimore: The Johns Hopkins University Press, 2013), 91. (Bottom-right) Puck flies through the air as a horse and its human rider fall while attempting to cross a stream in a 1790 painting by Henry Fuseli for the Boydell Gallery. Image courtesy of Wikimedia (Henry Fuseli, *Puck*, 1790, oil on canvas, 1790. Accessible here: https://commons.wikimedia.org/wiki/File:F%C3%BCssli_Robin_Goodfellow-Puck_1787-1790.jpg)

of "baser sprites" that could be conjured.[81] A comedy from 1600 notes that a bandit was running "like hobgoblin up and down" the fields.[82] An Elizabethan burlesque jokingly attributed to Robin Goodfellow, *Tarlton's Jests, and News Out of Purgatory*, provides similarly comedic situations.[83] In 1638, John Suckling's play titled *The Goblins* premiered, featuring a band of bandits that roamed across the land, pulling pranks and performing acts of vigilante justice—likely in a nod to the occasional conflation of Robin Goodfellow with Robin Hood.[84] In other plays (both comedies and dramas), we encounter "villainous goblins" haunting churchyards and inhabiting the depths of Hell.[85] Across these theatrical works, goblins and hobgoblins are referenced as singular and plural entities, sometimes capitalized and sometimes not, with no consistency. Authors rarely dwell on their gender, too, though they typically refer to them with masculine pronouns, which matches depictions of Puck and those in broadside ballads (more on that shortly). The mention of a "she-goblin" within one play indicates that some saw the potential for these creatures to take female form, though the simpler "goblin" was presumably meant to indicate a masculine creature.[86]

Goblins within early modern plays were thus varied yet so ubiquitous that playwrights could use them across contexts without issue. People viewing these plays, too, could both delight in the antics of fairies on stage and condemn them from the pews. Take, for example, King James VI (of

---

[81] Luigi Pasqualigo, *Fedele and Fortunio: The Deceites in Loue*, trans. A.M. (London: John Charlewood, 1585), act 2, scene 2.

[82] *A Pleasant Commodie, Called Looke about You* (London: Edward Allde, 1600). See also Dabridgcourt Belchier, *Hans Beer-Pot His Inuisible Comedie* (London: Bernard Alsop, 1618).

[83] Jane Belfield, "Tarlton's News Out of Purgatory (1590): A Modern-Spelling Edition, with Introduction and Commentary" (Birmingham, University of Birmingham, 1978).

[84] John Suckling, *The Goblins: A Comedy* (London: Humphrey Moseley, 1646). This conflation persisted into the nineteenth century. Guiney, for example, notes that "Hobgoblin is the same as Rob or Bob-Goblin, a goblin whose full name seemed to be Robert. Robin Hood, the famous outlaw, dear to all of us, was thought to have been christened after Robin Hood the fairy, because he, too, was tricksy and sportive, wore a hood, and lived deep in the forest." Louise Imogen Guiney, *Brownies and Bogles* (Boston: D. Lothrop Company, 1888), 86–87.

[85] John Day, *Humour out of Breath* (London: Richard Bradock, 1608); *The Merry Deuill of Edmonton* (London: Henry Ballard, 1608); John Dryden, *Tyrannick Love, or, The Royal Martyr a Tragedy* (London: H. Herringman, 1670), 67; William Hemings, *The Jewes Tragedy, or, Their Fatal and Final Overthrow by Vespatian and Titus* (London: Matthew Inman, 1662), 27.

[86] John Mason, *The Turke A Worthie Tragedie* (London: Edward Allde, 1610).

Scotland) and I (of England). In response to Scottish witch trials and Scot's *The Discoverie of Witchcraft*, James wrote *Daemonologie*, which endorses the existence of witches, their familiars, and efforts to root them from society. This text also condemns fairies as tricks of the devil and associates them with the follies of Catholic doctrine.[87] Later in his life, though, James watched "with apparent equanimity" as his son (the aforementioned Prince Henry) played the title role in *Oberon, The Faery Prince* in a 1611 English production.[88] Attempts at divining any kind of singular nature for goblins and their kin are impossible when they could evidently vary within the mind of one individual.

Similar variations are seen in poetry as well. Poets depict goblins convening with witches to help "give the Devil his due," ravaging the lands that would eventually be tamed by a leader of the First Crusade, and being compared to a disheveled knight.[89] Some poets even looked wistfully at them as representatives of a bygone time and place. Inspired by the idylls of Roman authors and the unpleasant realities of early modern cities, these authors nostalgically cast an eye to a rural past full of simpler people and ideas. Churchyarde's *A Handeful of Gladsome Verses* (1592) invokes a time when the world was full of merriment and stories were passed around with glee:

> Of old Hobgoblin's guise
> That walked like a ghost in sheets
> With maids that would not early rise
> For fear of bugs and sprites.
>
> Some say the fairies fair
> Did dance on Bednall Green
> And fine familiars of the air
> Did talk with men unseen....[90]

---

[87] James VI and I, *Daemonologie* (Edinburgh: Robert Walde-Graue, 1597), 74–75. See also Henderson and Cowan, *Scottish Fairy Belief: A History*, 121–27.

[88] Hutton, "The Making of the Early Modern British Fairy Tradition," 1152. See also Marisa R. Cull, *Shakespeare's Prince of Wales: English Identity and the Welsh Connection* (New York: Oxford University Press, 2014), 120–49.

[89] Robert Dixon, *Canidia, or, The Witches a Rhapsody* (London: S. Roycroft, 1683), 5; Torquato Tasso, *Godfrey of Bulloigne, or The Recouerie of Ierusalem* (London: Ar. Hatfield, 1600), 58; Samuel Butler, *Hudibras in Three Parts* (London: W. Rogers, 1684).

[90] Thomas Churchyard, *A Handeful of Gladsome Verses* (Oxford: Ioseph Barnes, 1592).

Though Churchyarde recounts these stories with fondness, he is skeptical of these "fables feigned" and sees them as a pastime to keep people entertained.[91] Samuel Rowlands, too, recounts in the 1613 poem *Of Ghosts and Goblins* how the kindly Robin Goodfellow of times long past has given way to a more sinister Robin Badfellow, who pilfers and steals at night.[92] John Milton, too, remembers the merry traditions of English rural folk in L'Allegro (1645):

> With stories told of many a feat,
> How Faery Mab the junkets eat,
> She was pinched and pulled she said,
> And he by friar's lantern led,
> Tells how the drudging goblin sweat,
> To earn his cream-bowl duly set,
> When in one night, ere glimpse of morn,
> His shadowy flail hath threshed the corn....[93]

Milton's rosy remembrance of this bucolic lifestyle, which is replete with references to classical poetry, does not dwell on the actual existence of goblins and their kin. Instead, he uses them to set a pleasant scene that celebrates rural life (in a marked departure from the Hell-dwelling Goblin of his later poem *Paradise Lost*). Similarly framed is a 1700 translation of Chaucer from John Dryden. Near the beginning of the "The Wife of Bath's Tale," Dryden mentions the "merry goblins" driven away by Christianity, despite that specific label not being used in *The Canterbury Tales*.[94] Chaucer had written of fairies and elves in his own reminiscence about the days of King Arthur, but when Dryden updated this language to better resonate with his contemporaries, he inserted the ubiquitous goblin into this milieu too. Goblins were thus part of a rosy, fairy-filled reminiscence among poets about the beauty and quaint simplicity of the rural past—another iteration of the perpetual recession of the fairies.

Debating the precise nature of goblins and fairies was not a priority for these authors and playwrights, who instead used them for various rhetorical ends: evoking a general feel of the dismal, critiquing elite consumption,

---

[91] Edmund Spenser, *Amoretti and Epithalamion* (London: William Ponsonby, 1595).

[92] Samuel Rowlands, *More Knaves Yet? The Knaves of Spades and Diamonds* (London, 1613), F2.

[93] John Milton, *Poems* (London: Ruth Raworth, 1645), 34.

[94] John Dryden, trans., *Fables, Ancient and Modern* (London: Jacob Tonson, 1700), 480.

facilitating transgressive behavior among humans, yearning for an idyllic rural past, and encouraging audiences to question the realities of their world. The ubiquity of goblins and the world of Fairyland was such that they required no introduction and could serve in these many roles without confusion. These writers fused folklore with these folkloresque traditions to forge new, intertwining interpretations of goblins.

FOLKLORIC GOBLINS

Details about folklore in the early modern period reach us in texts that document it with varying degrees of incredulity, curiosity, and hostility. They show us that many in early modern Britain believed that fairies existed and played an active role in their lives. The world was "alive with spirit activity" that was grounded in a combination of community traditions, lived experience, and scripture.[95] Fairies were "small gods" for "small people, and small things."[96] Commoners tended not to dwell on the exact intersection of fairies with Christian theology but instead saw them as part of a universe of unexplainable occurrences that were realities of daily life.[97]

Within these folkloric traditions, the idea of how to best approach the nature of "belief" in fairies is a tricky one.[98] Many of the sources

[95] Brock and Winter, "Theory and Practice in Early Modern Epistemologies of the Preternatural," 5. Floyd-Wilson similarly argues that elites and commoners alike in early modern England "conducted their lives with the conviction that their emotions, behavior, and practices were affected by, and dependent on, secret sympathies and antipathies that coursed through the natural world." Mary Floyd-Wilson, *Occult Knowledge, Science, and Gender on the Shakespearean Stage* (New York: Cambridge University Press, 2013), 1.

[96] Ronald Hutton, "Afterword," in *Fairies, Demons, and Nature Spirits: "Small Gods" at the Margins of Christendom*, ed. Michael Ostling (New York: Palgrave Macmillan, 2017), 349–56. See also Joyce Underwood Munro, "The Invisible Made Visible: The Fairy Changeling as a Folk Articulation of Failure to Thrive in Infants and Children," in *The Good People: New Fairylore Essays*, ed. Peter Narváez (Lexington: University Press of Kentucky, 1991), 251–83.

[97] Goodare calls these fairies "probably the most important group of non-humans beings." Julian Goodare, *The European Witch-Hunt* (New York: Routledge, 2016), 130.

[98] Linda Dégh, *Legend and Belief: Dialectics of a Folklore Genre* (Bloomington: Indiana University Press, 2001); Carlo Ginzburg, *The Cheese and the Worms*, trans. Anne C. Tedeschi and John Tedeschi (Baltimore: Johns Hopkins University Press, 2013); Ostling and Forest, "'Goblins, Owles and Sprites': Discerning Early-Modern English Preternatural Beings through Collocational Analysis," 564–65; Henderson, *Witchcraft and Folk Belief in the Age of Enlightenment: Scotland, 1670–1740*, 29–37.

encountered in this chapter were written by fairy skeptics who associated these creatures with the superstitious, uneducated masses.[99] This attitude, though, belies a wide spectrum of beliefs: people actively trying to interface with fairies using the spells of a grimoire, skeptics putting out a small serving of milk overnight at certain times of year as part of a longstanding familial ritual, and parents telling ficts to their children.[100] When elite authors talk about the seemingly absurd beliefs of commoners, we should bear in mind the various ways in which belief itself could manifest.

Many of the demonological sources already mentioned in this chapter provide crucial evidence for folk beliefs of the early modern period. Reginald Scot, for example, dismisses the idea that fairies exist in *The Discoverie of Witchcraft* (1584), but he nonetheless narrates some of the traditions associated with them:

> An incubus is a spirit; and I trust you know that a spirit has no flesh or bones, etc. and that he neither eats nor drinks. Indeed, your grandma's maids were wont to set a bowl of milk before him and his cousin Robin Goodfellow for the grinding of malt or mustard and sweeping the house at midnight. You have also heard that he would be exceedingly angry of the maid or housewife of the house, having compassion for his nakedness, laid any clothes for him besides his offering of white bread and milk, which was his standing fee. For in that case, he said, 'What have we here? Hemton hamten, here will I nevermore tread nor stomp.'[101]

[99] Ostling and Forest, "'Goblins, Owles and Sprites': Discerning Early-Modern English Preternatural Beings through Collocational Analysis," 563–65; Jean Pouillon, "Remarks on the Verb 'to Believe,'" Michel Izard and Pierre Smith, eds. trans. John Leavitt, *HAU: Journal of Ethnographic Theory* 6, no. 3 (2016): 485–92.

[100] Some magicians, for example, likely saw fairies as easier to summon than creatures in Heaven or Hell. Daniel M. Harms, "Hell and Fairy: The Differentiation of Fairies and Demons Within British Ritual Magic of the Early Modern Period," in *Knowing Demons, Knowing Spirits in the Early Modern Period*, Michelle D. Brock, Richard Raiswell, and David R. Winter, eds. (New York: Springer, 2018), 55–78. The evocative (and controversial) case of Isabel Gowdie provides one example of how an accused witch claimed to commune with fairies. Emma Wilby, *The Visions of Isobel Gowdie: Magic, Witchcraft and Dark Shamanism in Seventeenth-Century Scotland* (Liverpool: Liverpool University Press, 2010). A spell from the year 1600 about how to "summon, supplicate, control, and copulate" with fairies is also illustrative. Frederika Bain, "The Binding of the Fairies: Four Spells," *Preternature: Critical and Historical Studies on the Preternatural* 1, no. 2 (2012): 323–54.

[101] Scot, *The Discouerie of Witchcraft*, 85–86.

Although writing with an eye toward disproving these folk practices, Scot gives us a sense of those that circulated around his time. Other early modern texts help us glimpse additional fairy-related rituals. Many of them revolve around household labor.[102] Properly sweeping the floors and watching over children could result in a spirit providing a reward like a coin in the shoe or a chore performed during the night. Not tending to these affairs, though, could see this spirit turn malevolent and perform more destructive acts like dirtying the house or bathing a child in beer. Sometimes spirits might force a woman to do chores on their behalf and then claim credit for that work. This kind of household spirit went by many names as immigrants to Britain from Ireland and the European continent fused their folkloric traditions with local ones: brownies, pucks, elves, fairies, and hobgoblins (often capitalized and presented as a singular entity) are among the most common. Variations of these stories were likewise as plentiful as names for the spirits featured in them.

When humans physically encountered fairies, it was rarely a positive experience. Take, for example, a 1510 translation of *The Distaff Gospels*. One tale narrates how a woman's husband was riding on horseback at night when he saw a goblin on the side of the road. He did not have time to draw his sword because of the speed with which he had to flee from the creature.[103] Other encounters between fairies and humans typically turned out poorly for the latter: children who saw them at night were frightened by their appearance and unable to sleep; babies were kidnapped by them and replaced with changelings; extramarital affairs might be punished with pinches and bruises from fairies; women were whisked away to Fairyland and forced to nurse fairy babies; those who entered fairy circles could be bewitched and unable to function. These encounters, in a continuation of medieval tradition, were frequently associated with the darkness of night and dangers of untamed nature.

Although folkloric fairies existed on this earth, they typically existed in spaces just outside of human reach. Fairies occupied households when people were asleep. They could be heard in a nearby tunnel by miners

---

[102] Many of these stories are summarized in Briggs, *The Anatomy of Puck: An Examination of Fairy Beliefs among Shakespeare's Contemporaries and Successors*, 71–81; Briggs, *The Fairies in Tradition and Literature*, 66–73.

[103] Henry Watson, trans., *The Gospelles of Dystaues* (London: Wynkyn de worde, 1510) (Wednesday) chapter xx. Stories like this frequently had a moral dimension, too. Madeleine Jeay and Kathleen Garay, trans., *The Distaff Gospels: A First Modern English Edition of Les Évangiles Des Quenouilles* (Peterborough: Broadview Press, 2006), 44–45.

working underground. They inhabited treacherous bodies of water and expansive forests. They lived in an ill-defined Fairyland that could be reached by humans under the right conditions—but a person's safe return was never guaranteed. Fairies could operate alone or cluster together in troupes, including those that danced in fairy circles and created peculiar formations of plants as a result. Some of them, too, were connected to a larger fairy kingdom that mirrored (either crudely or sublimely) monarchies on earth, though this tradition was more coherently expressed in literature and theater.

These folk traditions were more than stories to amuse and frighten; they also explained the otherwise unexplainable. Parents could blame the fairies for the disappearance of a child, and travelers could blame them for getting lost at night. The displacement of tableware or other household goods could be the result of fairies frolicking and dancing in the house at night.[104] Concerns like these sometimes intersected with issues of development, disability, and disease. When a baby showed signs of mental disability, parents could claim that their real child had been switched out for a deformed changeling instead. Medical issues that incapacitated people or saw them experiencing visions could likewise be blamed on malevolent spirits.

Fairies also served to reinforce appropriate behavior. They incentivized women to regularly perform their household chores. They encouraged children to sleep at night and not wander outside of the home. They motivated parents to monitor and tend to their babies. They encouraged people not to risk traveling at night. Fairy beliefs helped to "reinforce some of the standards upon which the effective working of society depended," especially in rural areas where state surveillance was less present.[105] Thus, although these fairies shared their names with those invoked in literature and theater, their functions in folk traditions were often quite different.

The ubiquity of Fairyland in early modern Britain is glimpsed in court cases involving scammers who convinced people to give them money so that they could have favorable relationships with fairies. In 1613, John and

---

[104] A humorous description from the early eighteenth century of women overly obsessed with looking at (but not buying) tea dishes compares their frantic rearrangement of this tableware to the work of "Night Goblins." This quotation comes from issue 337 of *The Spectator* but was reprinted in John Ashton, *Social Life in the Reign of Queen Anne*, vol. I (London: Chatto & Windus, 1882), 96–97.

[105] Keith Thomas, *Religion and the Decline of Magic* (New York: Charles Scribner's Sons, 1971), 612.

Alice West were convicted of impersonating fairies to fleece a man named Thomas Moore. They staged a meeting between Moore and fairies, where they brought him into a room and showed him "two attired like the king and queen of fairies, and by them little elves and goblins" and many bags apparently filled with money, one of which had written on it "This is for Thomas Moore."[106] Despite receiving no return on his investments, Moore continued to pay money to the Wests for various services from the fairies, including a healing ritual. Stories like this illustrate that fairy belief was common enough for people to claim to be able to commune with the fairies on behalf of others for a fee. This kind of scam (or well-intentioned fairy intervention, if we want to be generous to the Wests) was also believable enough to attract people like Thomas Moore, whose seemingly unshakeable belief in the power of fairies led to his own financial downfall.

It is difficult to estimate how many people believed in fairies and to what extent they did at various points in the early modern period. Elite authors reported that these traditions were "barely surviving or tenaciously thriving" depending on the context, and quantitative demographic data from these centuries does not yield workable evidence.[107] Placenames from the early modern period sometimes indicate local beliefs in the presence of goblins or fairies, though they have not been systematically recorded such that a larger quantitative analysis can be conducted.[108] Instead, the many arguments across the early modern period about the decline of fairy belief, whether caused by the light of Protestant theology or the rational advances of the Scientific Revolution, ironically attest to its persistence among non-elites.

Although the precise beliefs of those sympathetic to the fairies are largely lost to time, some of the less judgmental (or even sympathetic) texts written by elites give a sense of how these creatures could exist in

---

[106] Joseph Ritson, ed., *Fairy Tales: Legends and Romances* (London: Frank & William Kerslake, 1875), 223–38; David Hawkes, *Money and Magic in Early Modern Drama* (London: Bloomsbury, 2022), 66–67.

[107] Marshall, "Protestants and Fairies in Early-Modern England."

[108] A 1787 legal document from the Bedfordshire Archives, for example, reports the sale of a parcel of land "commonly called Goblin's Hole." In any case, the presence of a toponym does not indicate contemporary belief in its preternatural origin. "Release Forming a Conveyance between Edward Baber of Park Street" (1787), Acc.No.8112, Bedfordshire Archives.

hierarchies alongside angels and humans.[109] Robert Kirk's *The Secret Commonwealth*, which was compiled in the late seventeenth century, catalogues folkloric traditions in the Scottish Highlands in an attempt to promote Christianity and disprove atheism. Therein, Kirk notes the presence of numerous spirits (none of which he calls goblins) that exist as a "middle nature" between humans and angels.[110] These fairies could shapeshift, were best observed at twilight (though only by those with "second sight"), and were responsible for the kind of behaviors already considered in this section. Other authors associate fairies with fallen angels or the souls of the dead—as is the case with two Scottish women accused of communing with fairies "through men who were once ordinary living, breathing mortals."[111] Daniel Higgs, in his 1699 report of a young girl who was bewitched in Ireland, is forthcoming about his own uncertainties about the nature of fairies. When discussing the circumstances of this bewitching, he writes that "it is unsearchable to us, how far God leaves invisible, intellectual powers to free will about inferior things… and whether those called fairies and goblins are not such."[112] Higgs argues that spirits cannot do anything except by God's will, even if those details are "unknown to us." Goblins, fairies, and other spirits thus occupy an uncertain position in the natural order of the world as permitted by the will of God. Such arguments about the presence of fairies somewhere between angels and humans were buttressed by traditions outside of the British Isles, where scholars mobilized the arguments of the Enlightenment and Scientific Revolution to support, rather than condemn, the presence of preternatural creatures.[113]

---

[109] Goodare considers this tradition in Scotland particularly, where some argued that "there existed a distinct class of spirit beings that were intermediate between humans and angels" based on Renaissance-era scientific theories. Julian Goodare, "Between Humans and Angels: Scientific Uses for Fairies in Early Modern Scotland," in *Fairies, Demons, and Nature Spirits: "Small Gods" at the Margins of Christendom*, ed. Michael Ostling (New York: Palgrave Macmillan, 2017), 169–90.

[110] Robert Kirk, *The Secret Commonwealth of Elves, Fauns, & Fairies*, ed. Andrew Lang (London: David Nutt, 1893), 5.

[111] Henderson and Cowan, *Scottish Fairy Belief: A History*, 19.

[112] Daniel Higgs, *The Wonderfull and True Relation of the Bewitching a Young Girle in Ireland* (s.n., 1699), 3–5.

[113] For the case of Iceland, see Terry Gunnell, "The Álfar, the Clerics and the Enlightenment: Conceptions of the Supernatural in the Age of Reason in Iceland," in *Fairies, Demons, and Nature Spirits: "Small Gods" at the Margins of Christendom*, ed. Michael Ostling (New York: Palgrave Macmillan, 2017), 191–212.

Some folkloric traditions survive in a new medium of text that emerged during the early modern era: the broadside ballad. These pamphlets, which were printed on cheap paper for distribution in both urban and rural areas, include printings of folk songs that are less hostile to fairy beliefs and show little interest in their intersection with Christian theology. Similar to the broadside ballad is the chapbook, which could stretch to twenty-four pages in length. The stories and songs within these texts were admittedly printed in cities and penned by literate elites, though they give at least some sense of the stories that circulated among commoners.[114] In some instances, we see the equation of Hobgoblin with Robin Goodfellow, which reflected the language of Shakespeare and, in turn, reinforced these identifiers in folk traditions. A ballad from around 1628, for example, narrates how long ago, when fairies used to walk the earth, Robin Goodfellow was born as the offspring of the fairy king Oberon and a human woman. This entity was mischievous to the core, took on many appearances, and went by many names:

> Sometimes a cripple he would seeme,
>   sometimes a soldier brave:
> Sometimes a fox, sometimes a hare;
>   brave pastimes would he have.
>
> Sometimes an owl he'd seem to be,
>   sometimes a skipping frog;
> Sometimes a kirne, in Irish shape,
>   to leap over mire or bog:
> Sometime he'd counterfeit a voice,
>   and travelers call astray,
> Sometimes a walking fire he'd be,
>   and lead them from their way.
>
> Some call him Robin Good-fellow,
>   Hob goblin, or mad Crisp,
> And some again do term him oft
>   by name of Will the Wisp;
> But call him by what name you list,
>   I have studied on my pillow,

---

[114] The utility of these ballads for analyzing folk beliefs is contested. I follow the argumentation of Henderson and Cohen, who show that (despite their limitations) ballads "do preserve valuable material and that they do indeed provide an important articulation of folk belief." Henderson and Cowan, *Scottish Fairy Belief: A History*, 5.

I think the best name he deserves
    is Robin the Good Fellow.[115]

This ballad was not the originator of folk traditions relating to Robin Goodfellow. References to this creature stretch back in printed form to the late fifteenth century and were frequently adapted into other genres over the next two centuries.[116] It is likely that the name itself originated in English folklore but widened to include other traditions too, including brownies (Scotland), pucks (Scandinavia), goblins (France), and hobs (northern Britain). Indeed, many of these creatures were given colloquial Christian names, too, as in Tom Thumb, Will-o'-the-Wisp, or Robin Goodfellow.[117] The combination and elision of these identifiers resulted in numerous variations, including Robgoblin and Hobgoblin.[118] I compare the relative usages of goblins and hobgoblins in greater detail at the end of this chapter.

Robin Goodfellow, also known as Hobgoblin, sometimes serves as a benevolent force to scare off more malicious creatures.[119] In a 1625 ballad, Robin Goodfellow soars through the air, driving off hags, ghosts, and goblins:

More swift than lightning can I fly
And round about this air [cloud] soon,
And in a minute's space discern
Each thing that's done beneath the moon.
There's not a Hag,
Nor Ghost shall wag,
Nor cry Goblin where I do go,

---

[115] J. Payne Collier, ed., *The Mad Pranks and Merry Jests of Robin Goodfellow: Reprinted from the Edition of 1628* (London: The Percy Society, 1841), xviii.

[116] There is a "massive body of reference to Robin throughout the sixteenth and seventeenth centuries." Shakespeare, *A Midsummer Night's Dream: The Oxford Shakespeare*, 38.

[117] The name "Goodfellow" itself brings to mind other colloquial names for fairies that appeal to their better nature despite their propensity for malice, like the Aos Sí as "good people" in Ireland or the Furies as "kindly ones" in Greece.

[118] Jonathan Gil Harris, "Puck/Robin Goodfellow," in *Fools and Jesters in Literature, Art, and History: A Bio-Bibliographical Sourcebook*, ed. Vicki K. Janik (Westport: London, 1998), 351–52.

[119] A two-part ballad from 1628 clarifies in the second part's title that Robin Goodfellow is "commonly called Hob-Goblin." *Robin Good-Fellow, His Mad Prankes, and Merry Jests Full of Honest Mirth, and Is a Fit Medicine for Melancholy* (London: Miles Flesher, 1628).

But *Robin* I,
Their feats will spy,
And feat them home with, "ho ho ho."[120]

The ballad concludes with a list of creatures that know of Robin Goodfellow and his deeds (fiends, ghosts, sprites, hags, and goblins), which reinforces the distinction between him and these more sinister creatures. Goblins had this malevolent nature; Hobgoblin did not. In other ballads from the early seventeenth century, we see Robin Goodfellow counted as a fairy but also as distinct from them. One song, for example, is prefaced by a short story in which fairies ask him to dance with them, seemingly marking him as a creature outside of their kind.[121] This ambiguity mirrors Robin Goodfellow's roles in literary contexts, as he can appear both as a member of the fairy court and as a preternatural being roughly adjacent to it—in either case, though, a clearly social creature. Robin Goodfellow's appearance likewise varies because of his shapeshifting abilities, though the images that accompany these ballads are revealing (Fig. 3.3).

These illustrations of Robin Goodfellow show a handful of the forms that he can assume, ranging from a hairy humanoid to a rabbit to a priapic satyr. Other stories mention him being able to fit through key-holes, but at other times he is large enough to be easily seen by people and perform household chores. When taking humanoid form, he presents as a smiling man, though his attire and hairiness vary. Indeed, a common theme in these ballads is the association of Robin Goodfellow with joy and merriment. One ballad considers his exploits a "medicine for melancholy," which suggests that his deeds serve as a fond reminiscence or fantasy for the downtrodden.[122] A pamphlet from 1643 similarly introduces Robin Goodfellow as "the harmless spirit and the merry."[123] This characterization runs counter to those described in aforementioned medical texts, which depict goblins as a symptom of melancholy, and demonological ones that (in one case) classify hobgoblins and Robin Goodfellows as a

---

[120] Ben Jonson, "The Mad-Merry Prankes of Robbin Good-Fellow" (H.G., 1610–1640).

[121] *Robin Good-Fellow, His Mad Prankes, and Merry Jests Full of Honest Mirth, and Is a Fit Medicine for Melancholy*, part 2.

[122] *Robin Good-Fellow, His Mad Prankes, and Merry Jests Full of Honest Mirth, and Is a Fit Medicine for Melancholy*.

[123] *The Mid-Nights Watch, or, Robin Good-Fellow His Serious Observation* (London: George Lindsey, 1643), 2.

Fig. 3.3 Depictions of Robin Goodfellow from broadside ballads. (Top-left) Robin Goodfellow as a rabbit in a ballad by Ben Jonson set to the tune of "Dulcina" from (likely) the first half of the seventeenth century. Image (cropped) courtesy of the British Library Collection (Jonson, "The Mad-Merry Prankes of Robbin Good-Fellow." Located in the British Library Roxburghe Ballad Collection (C.20.f.7.230–231) and accessible through the English Broadside Ballad Archive (EBBA 30163): https://ebba.english.ucsb.edu/ballad/30163/). (Top-right) Robin Goodfellow as a dancing satyr on the title page of *Robin Good-Fellow, His*

"bigger kind" of terrestrial devil that could bring the "most harm" to people.[124]

The evolution of Robin Goodfellow between folkloric and literary contexts gives some sense of a messy dialectic that is poorly documented in surviving sources. Reginald Scot provides a skeptical retelling of stories associated with Robin Goodfellow in his *Discoverie of Witchcraft*. Other writers like Thomas Churchyarde fondly remember (but are nonetheless skeptical of) similar tales in poetry from the late sixteenth century. Shakespeare encountered some of these texts and infused their folkloric ideas with other oral traditions as well as themes from classical literature.[125] In *A Midsummer Night's Dream*, then, we have Puck/Hobgoblin/Robin Goodfellow making mischief for humans in a mystical forest outside of ancient Athens. The popularity of Shakespeare meant that his works spawned offshoots and copycats, ensuring that his rendering of Robin Goodfellow reached an audience beyond those who saw productions of his plays. Hence, some of the illustrations in broadside ballads show this creature as a satyr. We can thus see a hazy interplay between elite discourse and folk beliefs in an ongoing dialectic in which one influenced the other.[126]

[124] Richard Burton, *The Anatomy of Melancholy* (Oxford: John Lichfield and James Short, 1621), 65.

[125] Harris, "Puck/Robin Goodfellow," 353–54; Lamb, "Taken by the Fairies: Fairy Practices and the Production of Popular Culture in A Midsummer Night's Dream," 294–308.

[126] Walsham calls this a "mutually enriching equilibrium" and refutes the idea that Protestantism helped to destroy oral traditions. Alexandra Walsham, "Reformed Folklore?

Fig 3.3 (continued) *Mad Prankes and Merry Jests* (1639). Image (cropped) courtesy of the Folger Shakespeare Library (this image was featured on a number of broadside ballads as well. *Robin Good-Fellow, His Mad Prankes, and Merry Jests Full of Honest Mirth* (London: Thomas Cotes, 1639). Accessible here: https://digitalcollections.folger.edu/img59020). (Bottom) Two humanoid Robin Goodfellows stand holding a tree branch (left) or spear (right) from *The Mad Merry Pranks of Robin Good-fellow*, which is set to the tune of "Dulcina." Image (cropped) courtesy of University of Glasgow Archives & Special Collections, Euing Collection, Euing Ballads 203 (Ben Jonson, "The Mad-Merry Prankes of Robin Good-Fellow" (F. Coles, T. Vere, and J. Wright, 1663–1674). Located in the University of Glasgow Library (Euing Ballads 203) and accessible through the English Broadside Ballad Archive (EBBA 31962): https://ebba.english.ucsb.edu/ballad/31962/)

DEFINITIONS AND ASSOCIATIONS

Most of this chapter has been a goblin-centric synthesis of Christian demonology, witchcraft, theater, literature, and folklore in early modern Britain. This overview has shown that goblins, elves, pucks, Robin Goodfellows, and fairies (among others) were frequently synonymous and could be invoked in many situations for many purposes. They were ubiquitous and deployed in different contexts to different ends without contradiction. The remainder of this chapter asks if it is possible to find any meaningful differences between goblins and these other creatures. Were goblins distinct in some way from the other inhabitants of Fairyland or Hell? Can we pull something uniquely "goblin" from this preternatural morass?[127]

I approach these questions through both quantitative and qualitative means. We begin with the former by using data from dictionary entries to assess how goblins were perceived in relation to other lexemes over time. Dozens of monolingual and bilingual dictionaries from the early modern period provide snapshots of how individual authors thought of words in relation to one another. In the case of preternatural creatures, which were amorphous and taxonomically evasive, the relational nature of these definitions speaks to overarching trends not explicitly considered in other texts.

Dictionaries published during the early modern period were products of their changing environments.[128] Those from the 1500s were short and primarily used as memory or teaching aids, including Coote's 1596 *The English Schoole-Maister*, which provides definitions for nearly 1400 words with difficult spellings. Academics of this century, though, were conscious of how their texts lagged behind those in mainland Europe (especially France) and sought to create more substantive texts to standardize the

Cautionary Tales and Oral Tradition in Early Modern England," in *The Spoken Word: Oral Culture in Britain, 1500–1850* (New York: Manchester University Press, 2002), 173. See also Henderson, *Witchcraft and Folk Belief in the Age of Enlightenment: Scotland, 1670–1740*, 13.

[127] Ostling and Forest found genre-based association with imps, incubi, and familiars, but they saw goblins and fairies as more definitional and synonymous, indicating "a twilight domain of the spooky, the eerie, the unknown." Ostling and Forest, "'Goblins, Owles and Sprites': Discerning Early-Modern English Preternatural Beings through Collocational Analysis," 547.

[128] John Considine, *Dictionaries in Early Modern Europe: Lexicography and the Making of Heritage* (New York: Cambridge University Press, 2008); John Considine, *Academy Dictionaries 1600–1800* (New York: Cambridge University Press, 2014); Sarah Ogilvie, ed., *The Cambridge Companion to English Dictionaries* (New York: Cambridge University Press, 2020).

English language. These dictionaries were published with increasing frequency and detail in the 1600s, both in monolingual and bilingual editions like *The New World of English Words* and *A Dictionary of Barbarous French*. The 1700s saw the publication of even more expansive dictionaries, including Samuel Johnson's *A Dictionary of the English Language* (1755), which has been widely taught (and debated) as the "first English dictionary."[129] Although some criticized Johnson's inclusion of particularly obscure words, *A Dictionary of the English Language* was widely praised and became a standard point of reference for later dictionaries published in the eighteenth century (and beyond).

Over these 300 years of dictionary production, one important circumstance shaped their publication: the lack of a centralized, governmental body that sought to regulate authors. This absence of a singular authority for the English language—as opposed to the *Académie Française* across the Channel—meant that authors were able to publish words and their definitions as they saw fit. Dictionary entries, whether original or based on earlier texts, speak to the ideas of their authors at a given point in time and help us glimpse how they perceived goblins in relation to other creatures and ideas. This data admittedly skews toward the perspectives of well-educated men, though its quantity and temporal breadth nonetheless reveal changes over time within this population (Fig. 3.4).

This graph uses data from 173 entries in thirty-five dictionaries and grammatical schoolbooks stored in Lexicons of Early Modern English, Early English Books Online (EEBO), and Google Books to show words that were associated with the lexemes "goblin" and "hobgoblin" (inclusive of spelling variations) either as the dictionary headword or part of an accompanying definition.[130] This data is distributed by century to give a sense of broad changes in word usage across the early modern period. It

---

[129] Jack Lynch, "Samuel Johnson and the 'First English Dictionary,'" in *The Cambridge Companion to English Dictionaries*, ed. Sarah Ogilvie (New York: Cambridge University Press, 2020), 142–54.

[130] I have included here only English-language words in these entries, which means that words like "*larva*" and "*lemures*" (Latin) are not included. I have standardized spellings, too, and removed adjectival variations. Thus, in this data, a "spirit appearing by night" and a "ghost of such as die before their time" are rendered simply as "spirit" and "ghost" (respectively). When dictionary entries have multiple definitions within them that are separated by a period or semi-colon, I have only included the definition with "goblin." For example, in the following entry for "*larve*" from Cotgrave's 1611 *A Dictionarie of the French and English Tongues*, only the words hag, spirit, goblin, and night-ghost (simplified to "ghost") appear in this data: "A Hag, Spirit, **Goblin**, Night-ghost; also, a leane, pale, meagar, withered scrag; one that looks like death, or like a ghost." When "goblin" or "hobgoblin" is the headword

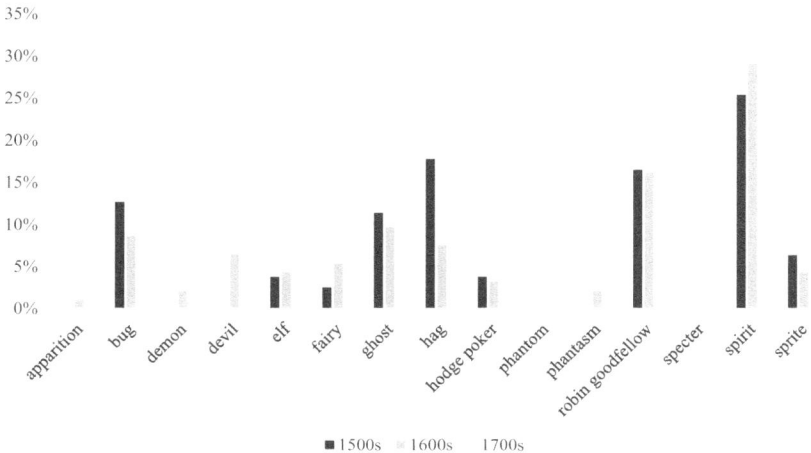

35%
30%
25%
20%
15%
10%
5%
0%

apparition bug demon devil elf fairy ghost hag hodge poker phantom phantasm robin goodfellow specter spirit sprite

■ 1500s   1600s   1700s

Fig. 3.4 English-language lexemes shared with "goblin" or "hobgoblin" in early modern dictionaries. (Dictionaries from the early modern period show a strong correlation of goblins and hobgoblins with "spirit" across all three centuries, but with more varied associations in other cases (including falling associations with "Robin Goodfellow" in the 1700s and rising association with "fairy" in the 1700s))

helps to quantify a handful of trends that have loomed large in this chapter.[131] The first is that goblins were defined in relation to many other preternatural creatures, the most common of which was the "spirit" (perhaps the broadest categorization of all within this list) across all three centuries. Other creatures had strong associations, too, but in more limited timeframes. Goblins were sometimes equated with devils and demons in dictionaries from the seventeenth century, when witch trials were at their peak, but less so in flanking centuries. Goblins were also associated in the sixteenth and seventeenth centuries with Robin Goodfellow, but this association plummeted in frequency by the eighteenth century. So too were goblins less associated with bugs, ghosts, and hags over time; they instead were replaced by apparitions, elves, phantoms, and (especially) fairies. This

of an entry, I have included all definitions. Randle Cotgrave, *A Dictionarie of the French and English Tongues* (London: Adam Islip, 1611).

[131] Since I standardized spellings within this dataset, it does not show the gradual dominance of the spellings of "hobgoblin" and "goblin" over earlier variations. We can see this trend in play within two editions of Reginald Scot's *The Discovery of Witchcraft*, which uses "hobbgoblin" in the original 1584 edition but "hobgoblin" in a revised 1665 edition.

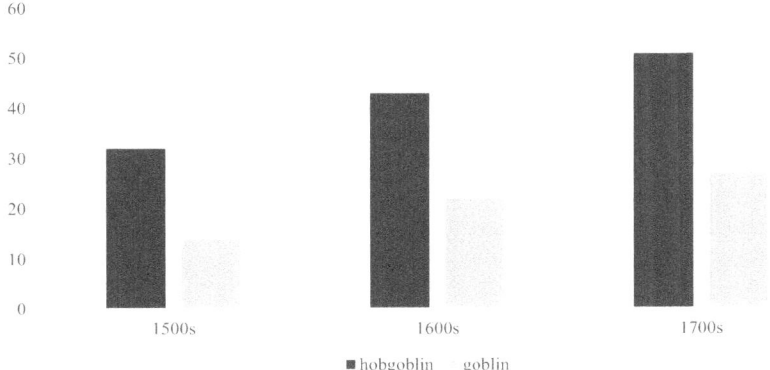

60
50
40
30
20
10
0

1500s   1600s   1700s

■ hobgoblin   goblin

Fig. 3.5 Relative uses of "goblin" and "hobgoblin" in early modern dictionaries. (Dictionaries from the early modern period show a preference for the term "hobgoblin" over "goblin" with a ratio of around 2:1 across all three centuries)

data shows that words associated with goblins changed over time—and indeed, these associated words had shifting meanings too—but it does not suggest a transcendent uniqueness to goblins (Fig. 3.5).

These dictionaries also show the relative popularity of the term "hobgoblin" over the simpler "goblin" across all three centuries. Though "hobgoblin" was used more frequently than "goblin," it is unclear if authors perceived a meaningful difference between the two lexemes. Most entries use synonymous words when defining them—and, indeed, one is often defined as the other. At times, though, authors give the sense that hobgoblins were a more benevolent form of creature. Defoe's 1735 *A New English Dictionary*, for example, defines hobgoblins as "imaginary apparitions, spirits, fairies" but goblins as "evil spirits, bugbears, or hobgoblins."[132] Even though Defoe was skeptical of the existence of these creatures, he nonetheless indicates a more sinister association for goblins. This idea is further supported by the disproportionate association of the lexemes "hobgoblin" and "Robin Goodfellow," which were mentioned twenty-four times in association with each other (as opposed to only five

---

[132] Benjamin Defoe, *A New English Dictionary* (Westminster: John Brindley, 1735). Samuel Johnson's dictionary provides a similar distinction. Goblins are "an evil spirit; a walking spirit; a frightful phantom" and "a fairy; an elf." Hobgoblins are "a frightful fairy" in the 1773 edition of the dictionary, and the 1755 edition curiously omits a definition entirely (providing instead only an etymology).

for "goblin"). Data for "hobgoblin" and "goblin" from Early English Books Online, too, shows that the most unique collocate for each word in comparison to the other is "Robin" and "ghost" (respectively).[133] The equation of Robin Goodfellow and Hobgoblin (especially in Shakespeare) as a creature that traffics in mischief more than evil is a likely reason for this divergence. So too is the ubiquity of Shakespeare likely the reason for the relative popularity of hobgoblin over goblin in dictionaries from the 1600s and 1700s, as larger databases of early modern texts show more overall hits for goblins than hobgoblins.[134]

Behind this quantitative data are more detailed definitions that do not lend themselves well to graphs like the ones above. Some express skepticism about the existence of goblins, calling them an "illusion," an "imaginary apparition," a "vain apparition," a "thing to affright children with," a "false terror," and a "devil (like) fiction."[135] These associations are seen across the early modern period, though with greater frequency in texts from the seventeenth and eighteenth centuries, which aligns with the ascendancy of antiwitchcraft ideas. So too does this data hide the frequent equation of goblins or hobgoblins as a "night spirit" or "nightwalking spirit"—associations that stem from the common motif of goblins and their kin being most active under the cover of darkness.[136] Such associations are more explicit in collocation data, which have been scraped from Early English Books Online for lexemes with more than fifteen total hits (Table 3.1).

This data reflects the consistent association of goblin and its derivations (including "hobgoblin") with other preternatural entities like spirits,

---

[133] These comparisons (with stop words removed) were made via https://www.english-corpora.org.

[134] Early English Books Online, for example, indicates that some 690 sources use the term "goblin" compared to 593 that use "hobgoblin." Eighteenth Century Collections Online, meanwhile, indicates that "goblin" was used in 2.61% of texts while "hobgoblin" was used in 0.44% of them.

[135] John Florio, *A Worlde of Wordes* (London: Arnold Hatfield, 1598); John Florio, *Queen Anna's New World of Words* (London: Melch. Bradwood, 1611); John Wilkins, *An Essay towards a Real Character and a Philosophical Language* (London: Sa. Gellibrand, 1668); Defoe, *A New English Dictionary*; Joseph Scott, *A New Universal Etymological English Dictionary* (London: T. Osborne and J. Shipton, 1755); John Ebers, *The New and Complete Dictionary of the German and English Languages* (Leipzig: Breitkopf and Haertel, 1796).

[136] John Colet, *A Short Introduction of Grammar* (London: Reyner Wolfe, 1567); Thomas Cooper, *Thesaurus Linguae Romanae et Brittanicae* (London: H. Denham, 1578); Cotgrave, *A Dictionarie of the French and English Tongues*; Thomas Jones, *The British Language in Its Lustre* (London: Lawrence Baskervile, 1688).

Table 3.1   "Goblin" collocates from Early English Books Online

Rank	Lexeme	Hits		Rank	Lexeme	Hits
1	Spirit(s)	89		10	Called	20
2	Like	57		11	Fright	19
3	Ghost(s)	74		12	Children	18
4	Fairy/Fairies	66		13	Devils	17
5	Night	25		14	Robin	17
6	Make	24		15	Shall	16
7	Men	24		16	Witches	16
8	Haunted	23		17	Fiends	15
9	Away	21				

Collocates for the word "goblin" show strong associations with spirits, ghosts, fairies, and night

Table 3.2   "Fairy" collocates from Early English Books Online

Rank	Lexeme	Hits		Rank	Lexeme	Hits
1	Queen(s)	376		8	Elf/Eves	47
2	Land(s)	175		9	Man/Men	47
3	Like	140		10	Lady/Ladies	44
4	King(s)	91		11	Hobgoblin(s)	37
5	Dance(s)	61		12	Court(s)	32
6	Knight(s)	57		13	Nymph(s)	29
7	Oberon	49		14	Goblin(s)	27

Collocates for the word "fairy" (which has more attestations than "goblin" in early modern texts) show strong associations with queen, land, king, dance, knight, and Oberon

ghosts, and fairies.[137] It also shows the prominence of words associated with fear and darkness—far more than the tradition of merriment seen in ballads. Glimpsed in this data, too, is the gendered identification of goblins as male creatures, as masculine pronouns have far more collocates (122 total) than their feminine counterparts (seventeen total). Comparing this data, too, with collocates for the word "fairy" and its many spelling variations (minimum twenty-five hits) shows that the two terms were developing unique associations (Table 3.2).

---

[137] This data was processed by https://www.english-corpora.org and tested for collocates within five words of *goblin* in this corpus. I have removed stop words based on the list from Voyant Tools: https://voyant-tools.org/.

Although numerous editions of *The Faerie Queen* of Spenser are likely skewing this data, other collocates of the word show a meaningful divergence from lexemes deployed around "goblin."[138] We are more likely to encounter words associated with the royal court around "fairy" than those that evoke dread and darkness. The sheer number of collocates for "fairy" also shows that this lexeme was deployed much more frequently than "goblin." Even though goblins were often juxtaposed with fairies, the inverse was not quite as true (though both "hobgoblin" and "goblin" make appearances near the end of this list). Fairies had much wider purchase as an identifier of preternatural creatures, the land in which they resided, and the genre of story in which they were featured.

Etymological studies also hint at a perceived difference between goblins and elves. Beginning in the late sixteenth century, some authors postulated that the origin of these words was tied to Italian political strife. Edmund Spenser's *The Shepheardes Calendar* (1579) argues that fairies are the invention of Catholic friars, and that their name does not have its origins in folk tradition. Instead, during conflict between the Guelph and Ghibellines, parents told misbehaving children that the Guelfs or the Ghibellines were coming. These words morphed over time into elf and goblin (respectively) alongside a number of other unspecified words.[139] Edmund Spenser took this division one step further in *The Faerie Queen*, which narrates the noble deeds of the descendants of Elfe, including the defeat of the "wicked Gobbelines" in battle.[140] This perspective gained traction over the next century such that one historian felt the need to specify that he did not "quarrel with the tradition that elves and goblins in

---

[138] I used the same search parameters via English Corpora and stop words as my data for *goblin*. Because of the many spelling variations of "fairy," I synthesized data from the following searches: faerie*, faery*, faieri*, fairie*, fairy*, farey*, farie*, fary*, fayri*, fayry*, feiri*, feyrye*, and pharie*. These findings provide a different result than the corpus used by Ostling and Forest, which (to their surprise) did not return "any strong descriptive correlations for *puck, elf, fairy, goblin/hobgoblin,* or *sprite.*" Ostling and Forest, "'Goblins, Owles and Sprites': Discerning Early-Modern English Preternatural Beings through Collocational Analysis," 556.

[139] Edmund Spenser, *The Shepheardes Calender* (London: Hugh Singleton, 1579). This perspective is echoed in William Lightfoot, *The Complaint of England* (London: Iohn Wolfe, 1587). See also James F. Royster, "E. K.'S Elf < Guelph, Goblin < Ghibelline," *Modern Language Notes* 43, no. 4 (April 1928): 249–52.

[140] Edmund Spenser, *The Faerie Queene* (London: William Ponsonbie, 1590), 345. Samuel Johnson recognized the implausibility of the Guelph/elf and Ghibbeline/goblin derivation in his dictionary (tracing "elf" to Welsh and "goblin" to German).

our English tongue" had their origins in "the names of Guelfs and Ghibellines."[141] To be clear, this perspective was never a central preoccupation in literary discourse—but this etymological divergence was part of a small group that differentiated goblins from elves and, in the case of Spenser, made them enemies of each other.

The texts considered in this section provide a glimpse into what a small group of well-educated men thought about goblins as they attempted to standardize the English language and clarify its relationship to other tongues. They should not be used to make totalizing statements about perceptions and ideas surrounding these creatures. Instead, they hint at a handful of trends and ideas that are clarified in other contemporary texts. Goblins were broadly equated with many different kinds of preternatural creatures. These associations changed over time as goblins were caught up in debates about witchcraft, used in popular theater productions, and mentioned metaphorically in various kinds of discourse. There was never a singular and immutable definition of these creatures; they instead evolved along with the people who invoked them.

The ubiquity of the goblin in the early modern period facilitated the use of this lexeme in more abstract contexts.[142] Beginning in the late sixteenth century, authors began to use "goblin" to label ideas, institutions, and objects that they considered atypical or harmful. Protestant authors refer to the "vain hobgoblins" of Catholic doctrine, the hobgoblin budget of the papacy, and the threat of "that great[est] hobgoblin of all, transubstantiation."[143] These abstract goblins were applied to other groups and institutions with increasing frequency in the seventeenth century. One political commentator wrote a treatise against the "terrible Goblin called

---

[141] Thomas Fuller, *The Historie of the Holy Warre* (Cambridge: Thomas Buck, 1639), 167. See also Peter Heylyn, *Cosmographie in Four Bookes* (London: Henry Seile, 1652), 109.

[142] The *OED* notes attributive, appositive, and instrumental deployments of "goblin." In a letter from 1799, we even see hobgoblin rendered as a verb. One belief among German peasants, as described by Samuel Taylor Coleridge, involves the fate of one who vows to go on a pilgrimage but is unable to complete it, which results in them hovering "between heaven and earth, and at times hobgoblins his relations till they perform it for him." Samuel Taylor Coleridge, *Letters of Samuel Taylor Coleridge*, ed. Ernest Hartley Coleridge, vol. I (London: William Heinemann, 1895), 291.

[143] Jean Calvin, *A Little Booke of Iohn Caluines* (London: H. Wykes, 1567), 104; Henry Foulis, *The History of Romish Treasons & Usurpations* (London: J.C., 1671), 267; Thomas Jekyll, *Popery, a Great Mystery of Iniquity Proved in a Sermon Preached in the Parish Church of Newland* (London: Jonathan Robinson, 1681), 22.

Slavery" that was sweeping through Britain and its colonies.[144] Another refers to an argument about the fortifying of naval garrisons as a "terrible Goblin," and a writer from the Massachusetts Bay Colony describes the threat of the "Hobgoblin Monster" of the Salem witch trials.[145] These ideas persisted into the eighteenth century and were deployed with some degree of regularity in speeches and treatises. One zealous politician denounced the possible passage of a "Hobgoblin Excise Bill" in a short pamphlet that satirized stockbrokers' obsession with tax increases; another bid farewell to that "Goblin thing" called a subpoena.[146]

The sixteenth century also provides the first evidence of authors referring to disagreeable people as goblins. *A Treatise of Treasons against Q. Elizabeth* calls one author a "Hobgoblin" because he hides "his name and person still in darkness... framing his speech so obscurely as shall abide no light of answer or trial, and by telling us lies still and nothing else, as such fowl spirits are wont to do."[147] This anonymous hobgoblin author lurks in the darkness, telling lies alongside so many other repulsive spirits. Similar language is seen in other texts. One author from the American colonies attacks "that Goblin Tom Case," a Quaker leader.[148] Cotton Mather goes wider with his critiques when he laments the unsavory conduct of the masses as they swore, broke the Sabbath, committed adultery, and drank heavily—all of which is more befitting a monster or "goblin."[149] A comedic play describes a frantic scene wherein a man had to wade into a bloody brawl of men and women, whom the author calls goblins; a novel featuring a Robin Hood-esque protagonist regards police sergeants as "devils" and compares their seemingly infinite legions of enforcers to "the

[144] *Remarks upon a Scurrilous Libel* (London: s.n., 1697), 1, 7.

[145] *Remarks on the Present Condition of the Navy* (London: s.n., 1700), 11; Increase Mather, *A Further Account of the Tryals of the New-England Witches* (London: J. Dunton, 1693), 10.

[146] *Change-Alley Excised: Or, The Bulls and Bears in an Uproar* (London: W. Webb, 1733). See also John Humfrey, *After-Consideration for Some Members of the Parliament, upon the Occasional Bill Dismiss'd* (London: B. Bragg, 1704), 22, 26. See also *The / Salamanca Doctor's Farewel* (London: G.C., 1685); "The Downfall of the Chancery" (n.d.), C.20.f.4.(66.), British Library Collection - Luttrell Ballads.

[147] *A Treatise of Treasons against Q. Elizabeth* (Leuven: J. Fowler, 1572), 5.

[148] *Some Few Remarks, upon a Scandalous Book, against the Government and Ministry of New-England* (Boston: T. Green, 1701), 56.

[149] Mather, *The Wonders of the Invisible World*, Enchantments Encountred I.

Hobgoblins underground."[150] Royals were not immune from these attacks, either. One member of a political club in the mid-eighteenth century argues that Don Carlos, son of King Philip V of Spain (and future king of Spain himself), was "made into the hobgoblin" for his fearmongering regarding a treaty.[151]

In these texts, the goblin becomes an insult and indicates that someone or something has transgressed the bounds of appropriate conduct. Hence, a goblin could be a misguided Spanish royal, the institution of slavery, a drunk American colonist, or the practice of transubstantiation. This kind of categorization stretched to the realm of physical appearance, too. As early as the sixteenth century, a dictionary equates hobgoblins with "deformed and misshapen images."[152] Such associations became more pronounced in the seventeenth century as "taste for monsters became a disease" in England, spurred by curiosities imported from the New World.[153] One work on human musculature calls the look of those suffering from strabismus (crossed eyes) as "Goblin-like" and prone to scaring others.[154] An anti-Catholic treatise took a swipe at medieval artisans, whose depictions of sacred figures were similar to those of monsters and hobgoblins rather than men.[155] Another Protestant author described a

---

[150] Monsieur Scarron, *The Comical Romance* (London: John Playfere, 1665), 77. This novel is a translation of the picaresque Spanish novel *Guzmán de Alfarache*. Carlos Garcia, *Lavernæ, or, The Spanish Gipsy*, trans. W. M. (London, 1650), 24–25; Jane Smith, "The Commonwealth Cavalier," *Studies in Philology* 114, no. 3 (Summer 2017): 609–40.

[151] Decius Magius, "Proceedings and Debates in the Political Club," *The London Magazine*, September 1748, 400.

[152] Another dictionary traces the origins of "ugly" to "ouph" (i.e., a "goblin"). Cooper, *Thesaurus Linguae Romanae et Brittanicae*; Scott, *A New Universal Etymological English Dictionary*.

[153] Henry Morley, *Memoirs of Bartholomew Fair* (London: Frederick Warne, 1874), 246. These spectacles declined in popularity during the mid-eighteenth century (Semonin sees *Gulliver's Travels* of 1726 as a marker of this trend), though popular interest surged again in the nineteenth century. Paul Semonin, "Monsters in the Marketplace: The Exhibition of Human Oddities in Early Modern England," in *Freakery: Cultural Spectacles of the Extraordinary Body*, ed. Rosemarie Garland-Thomson (New York: New York University Press, 1996), 69.

[154] The author calls the "squinting muscle" responsible for this phenomenon the "tragic or hobgoblin muscle." John Bulwer, *Pathomyotamia, or, A Dissection of the Significative Muscles of the Affections of the Minde* (London: Humphrey Moseley, 1649), 170.

[155] Alexander Cooke, *Pope Ioane: A Dialogue Betweene a Protestant and a Papist* (London: R. Field, 1610), 5. The Jesuits were the targets of one invective from the late seventeenth century, in which the author asks whether they were "Giant or Monster, or some Goblin

Catholic assembly resembling one "not of Bishops, but of Hobgoblins" because of their sycophantic enabling and corruption.[156] A pamphlet chastising bad writing calls these authors goblins with "bladder cheeks puffed out like a Swiss' britches" and thin heads that "live upon the scraps of invention."[157] Plays use similar language when characters indicate that they did not look their normal selves. In one comedy, a man asks a woman "am I such a hobgoblin that you start at the sight of me?" In another, a woman declares that she is "a strange hobgoblin, sure!"[158]

When humans are described as goblins, their unusual appearance or harmful behaviors take center stage. Such characterizations place them adjacent to evolving language of teratology, but in the growing body of literature and advertisements produced for cultural spectacles of monstrous humans, I was unable to locate humans described as goblins. This is not to say that such associates did not exist, but rather that other terms (especially "dwarf") were preferred ways of designating humans with physical disabilities or atypical characteristics.[159] Broadsides advertising monster shows and treatises from elite authors condemning these spectacles do not label the people or creatures therein as goblins—even as some compared monstrous humans to satyrs, troglodytes, and pygmies (among others).[160] Thus, although goblins were occasionally deployed to pejoratively describe humans, this association was not widespread enough to

---

dress't / In Angels Colours fair above the rest...." Thomas Rogers, *The Conspiracy of Guts and Brains: Or An Answer to the Twinn-Shams* (London, 1694), 2.

[156] Daniel Featley, *The Grand Sacrilege of the Church of Rome* (London: Felix Kyngston, 1630), 224.

[157] Thomas Dekker, *The Wonderfull Yeare. 1603 Wherein Is Shewed the Picture of London, Lying Sicke of the Plague* (London: Thomas Creede, 1603).

[158] Colly Cibber, "Flora; or, Hob in the Well," in *A Collection of the Most Esteemed Farces and Entertainments Performed on the British Stage*, vol. 4 (Edinburgh: C. Elliot, 1786), 309; "The Spirit of Contradiction," in *A Collection of the Most Esteemed Farces and Entertainments Performed on the British Stage*, vol. 4 (Edinburgh: C. Elliot, 1786), 350.

[159] James Paris du Plessis' manuscript "A Short History of Human Prodigies, and Monstrous Births: of Dwarfs, Sleepers, Giants, Strong Men, Hermaphrodites, Numerous Births, and Extreme Old Age" (early 1730s) gives a sense of this preferred nomenclature.

[160] Semonin, "Monsters in the Marketplace: The Exhibition of Human Oddities in Early Modern England," 74–75; Whitney Dirks, *Monstrosity, Bodies, and Knowledge in Early Modern England: Curiosity to See and Behold* (Amsterdam: Amsterdam University Press, 2024), 83–120. See also Asma, *On Monsters: An Unnatural History of Our Worst Fears*, 141–62.

widely permeate contemporary discourse about monstrous bodies.[161] Instead, goblins were more suitable as insulting descriptions and comparisons for those who looked or behaved contrary to what a given author considered appropriate. Whatever benevolence we might have encountered in other interpretations of goblins and hobgoblins washes away in these descriptions, which instead emphasize harm and irregularity.

CONCLUSION

Goblins were as ubiquitous as they were variable in the early modern period. Depending on the context, they could reinforce hierarchies in rural households or satirize traditional gender roles on theater stages. They could provide merriness for those suffering from melancholy or drag the gullible into the depths of Hell. They could help people perform household chores or disrupt their daily lives. Goblins were often grouped together with elves, hobs, brownies, and Robin Goodfellows—but in some ballads, they were oppositional to them. Goblins and hobgoblins were frequently interchanged with each other, and they fluctuated between being a singular named entity and a category of preternatural creature. Goblins needed no introduction or definition because they were so commonplace, and the variability in their deployment did not result in confusion for those who encountered them.

Existing alongside these iterations of demonic, folkloric, literary, and theatrical goblins were more abstract ideas that trended toward the malevolent. Writers uprooted the goblin from its preternatural origins and distilled it into a malignant and irregular essence. The merriness of Robin Goodfellow had little place in this abstraction, which instead elevated evil characteristics that, if anything, were more reminiscent of demons or medieval fairies. As authors of the early modern era sanitized the fairies of the Middle Ages, then, the goblin retained a more sinister association when abstractly deployed. As we turn our gaze toward the nineteenth century, we will see how these many interpretations of goblins evolved alongside new literary forms produced against a backdrop of the colonial expansion of the British Empire.

[161] These kinds of "non-normative bodies" at the intersection of monster studies and disability studies are considered in Richard H. Godden and Asa Simon Mittman, "Embodied Difference: Monstrosity, Disability, and the Posthuman," in *Monstrosity, Disability, and the Posthuman in the Medieval and Early Modern World*, Richard H. Godden and Asa Simon Mittman, eds. (New York: Palgrave Macmillan, 2019), 4.

REFERENCES

A Passionate / Satyr / Upon the Devillish Great / He-Whore / That Lives Yonder at / Rome. n.d. Crawford.EB.1005. National Library of Scotland.

A Physicall Directory. 1649. London: Peter Cole.

A Pleasant Commodie, Called Looke about You. 1600. London: Edward Allde.

A Pleasant Treatise of Witches. 1673. London: H.B. for C. Wilkinson.

A Treatise of Treasons against Q. Elizabeth. 1572. Leuven: J. Fowler.

Ady, Thomas. 1676. *The Doctrine of Devils, Proved to Be the Grand Apostacy of These Later Times.* London: Thomas Ady.

Agrippa, Henry Cornelius. 1651. *Three Books of Occult Philosophy.* Translated by James Freake. London: Gregory Moule.

Akhimie, Patricia, ed. 2024. *The Oxford Handbook of Shakespeare and Race.* New York: Oxford University Press.

Almond, Philip C. 2011. *England's First Demonologist: Reginald Scot and "The Discoverie of Witchcraft".* New York: I.B. Tauris.

Aristotle. 1699. *Aristotle's Manual of Choice Secrets.* Translated by J.P. London: John Back.

Ashton, John. 1882. *Social Life in the Reign of Queen Anne.* II Vols. London: Chatto & Windus.

Asma, Stephen T. 2009. *An Unnatural History of Our Worst Fears.* New York: Oxford University Press.

Bain, Frederika. 2012. The Binding of the Fairies: Four Spells. *Preternature: Critical and Historical Studies on the Preternatural* 1 (2): 323–354.

Bale, John. 1574. *The Pageant of Popes Contayninge the Lyues of All the Bishops of Rome.* London: Thomas Marshel.

Belchier, Dabridgcourt. 1618. *Hans Beer-Pot His Inuisible Comedie.* London: Bernard Alsop.

Belfield, Jane. 1978. Tarlton's News Out of Purgatory (1590): A Modern-Spelling Edition, with Introduction and Commentary. University of Birmingham.

Bovet, Richard. 1684. *Pandaemonium, or, The Devil's Cloyster.* London: J. Walthoe.

Briggs, Katharine. 1959. *The Anatomy of Puck: An Examination of Fairy Beliefs among Shakespeare's Contemporaries and Successors.* London: Routledge and Kegan Paul.

Briggs, Katharine. 1967. *The Fairies in Tradition and Literature.* New York: Routledge.

Briggs, Katharine. Summer 1969. Heywood's Hierarchie of the Blessed Angells. *Folklore* 80 (2): 89–106.

Briggs, Robin. 1996. *Witches & Neighbors: The Social and Cultural Context of European Witchcraft.* New York: Penguin.

Bright, Timothie. 1586. *A Treatise of Melancholie.* London: Thomas Vautrollier.

Brock, Michelle D., and David R. Winter. 2018. Theory and Practice in Early Modern Epistemologies of the Preternatural. In *Knowing Demons, Knowing*

Spirits in the Early Modern Period, ed. Michelle D. Brock, Richard Raiswell, and David R. Winter, 3–19. New York: Springer.

Broedel, Hans. 2003. *The 'Malleus Maleficarum' and the Construction of Witchcraft: Theology and Popular Belief*. New York: Manchester University Press.

Bromhall, Thomas. 1658. *An History of Apparitions, Oracles, Prophecies, and Predictions with Dreams, Visions, and Revelations and the Cunning Delusions of the Devil*. London: John Streater.

Buccola, Regina. 2006. *Fairies, Fractious Women, and the Old Faith: Fairy Lore in Early Modern British Drama and Culture*. Selinsgrove: Susquehanna University Press.

Bucholz, Robert, and Newton Key. 2009. *Early Modern England, 1485–1714: A Narrative History*. 2nd ed. Malden: Blackwell Publishing.

Bulwer, John. 1649. *Pathomyotamia, or, A Dissection of the Significative Muscles of the Affections of the Minde*. London: Humphrey Moseley.

Bunyan, John. 1678. *The Pilgrim's Progress*. London: Nathaniel Ponder.

Burke, Peter. 2009. *Popular Culture in Early Modern Europe*. 3rd ed. New York: Routledge.

Burton, Richard. 1621. *The Anatomy of Melancholy*. Oxford: John Lichfield and James Short.

Burton, Robert. 1688. *The Kingdom of Darkness*. London: Nathaniel Crouch.

Butler, Samuel. 1684. *Hudibras in Three Parts*. London: W. Rogers.

Calvin, Jean. 1567. *A Little Booke of Iohn Caluines*. London: H. Wykes.

Cameron, Euan. 2010. *Enchanted Europe: Superstition, Reason, and Religion 1250–1750*. New York: Oxford University Press.

Cartwright, William. 1651. *The Ordinary, a Comedy*. London: Humphrey Moseley.

Cervantes, Miguel de. 1687. *The History of the Most Renowned Don Quixote of Mancha*. London: Thomas Hodgkin.

Change-Alley Excised: Or, The Bulls and Bears in an Uproar. 1733. London: W. Webb

Charleton, Walter. 1652. *The Darkness of Atheism Dispelled by the Light of Nature: A Physico-Theologicall Treatise*. London: William Lee.

Churchyard, Thomas. 1592. *A Handeful of Gladsome Verses*. Oxford: Ioseph Barnes.

Cibber, Colly. 1786. Flora; or, Hob in the Well. In *A Collection of the Most Esteemed Farces and Entertainments Performed on the British Stage*, vol. 4, 301–328. Edinburgh: C. Elliot.

Clark, Stuart. 1999. *Thinking with Demons: The Idea of Witchcraft in Early Modern Europe*. New York: Oxford University Press.

Coleridge, Samuel Taylor. 1895. *Letters of Samuel Taylor Coleridge*. Edited by Ernest Hartley Coleridge. II vols. London: William Heinemann.

Colet, John. 1567. *A Short Introduction of Grammar*. London: Reyner Wolfe.

Collier, J. Payne, ed. 1841. *The Mad Pranks and Merry Jests of Robin Goodfellow: Reprinted from the Edition of 1628*. London: The Percy Society.

Considine, John. 2008. *Dictionaries in Early Modern Europe: Lexicography and the Making of Heritage*. New York: Cambridge University Press.

Considine, John. 2014. *Academy Dictionaries 1600–1800.* New York: Cambridge University Press.

Cooke, Alexander. 1610. *Pope Ioane: A Dialogue Betweene a Protestant and a Papist.* London: R. Field.

Cooper, Thomas. 1578. *Thesaurus Linguae Romanae et Brittanicae.* London: H. Denham.

Cooper, Thomas. 1580. *Certaine Sermons Wherin Is Contained the Defense of the Gospell Nowe Preached against Such Cauils and False Accusations.* London: Ralphe Newbery.

Cotgrave, Randle. 1611. *A Dictionarie of the French and English Tongues.* London: Adam Islip.

Cull, Marisa R. 2014. *Shakespeare's Prince of Wales: English Identity and the Welsh Connection.* New York: Oxford University Press.

Culpeper, Nicholas. 1651. *Semeiotica Uranica.* London: Nathaniell Brookes.

Day, John. 1608. *Humour out of Breath.* London: Richard Bradock.

Defoe, Benjamin. 1735. *A New English Dictionary.* Westminster: John Brindley.

Dégh, Linda. 2001. *Legend and Belief: Dialectics of a Folklore Genre.* Bloomington: Indiana University Press.

Dekker, Thomas. 1603. *The Wonderfull Yeare. 1603 Wherein Is Shewed the Picture of London, Lying Sicke of the Plague.* London: Thomas Creede.

Dirks, Whitney. 2024. *Monstrosity, Bodies, and Knowledge in Early Modern England: Curiosity to See and Behold.* Amsterdam: Amsterdam University Press.

Dixon, Robert. 1683. *Canidia, or, The Witches a Rhapsody.* London: S. Roycroft.

Drayton, Michael. 1906. *Nymphidia or The Court of Faery.* London: George Routledge & Sons, Limited.

Dryden, John. 1670. *Tyrannick Love, or, The Royal Martyr a Tragedy.* London: H. Herringman.

Dryden, John, trans. 1700. *Fables, Ancient and Modern.* London: Jacob Tonson.

Dures, Alan, and Francis Young. 2022. *English Catholicism 1558–1642.* New York: Routledge.

Ebers, John. 1796. *The New and Complete Dictionary of the German and English Languages.* Leipzig: Breitkopf and Haertel.

Elmer, Peter. 2016. *Witchcraft, Witch-Hunting, and Politics in Early Modern England.* New York: Oxford University Press.

Erasmus, Desiderius. 1549. *The Praise of Folie.* London: Thomas Berthelet.

Everard, John. 1657. *The Gospel Treasury Opened.* London: John Owsley.

Featley, Daniel. 1630. *The Grand Sacrilege of the Church of Rome.* London: Felix Kyngston.

Fitzsimon, Henry. 1608. *A Catholike Confutation of M. Iohn Riders Clayme of Antiquitie and a Caulming Comfort against His Caueat.* Douai: P. Auroi and C. Boscard.

Florio, John. 1598. *A Worlde of Wordes.* London: Arnold Hatfield.

Florio, John. 1611. *Queen Anna's New World of Words*. London: Melch. Bradwood.

Floyd-Wilson, Mary. 2003. *English Ethnicity and Race in Early Modern Drama*. New York: Cambridge University Press.

Floyd-Wilson, Mary. 2013. *Occult Knowledge, Science, and Gender on the Shakespearean Stage*. New York: Cambridge University Press.

Foulis, Henry. 1671. *The History of Romish Treasons & Usurpations*. London: J.C.

Fulke, William. 1573. *Prælections Vpon the Sacred and Holy Reuelation of S. Iohn*. London: Thomas Purfoote.

Fuller, Thomas. 1639. *The Historie of the Holy Warre*. Cambridge: Thomas Buck.

Fuseli, Henry. 1790. *Puck*. Oil on canvas.

Garcia, Carlos. 1650. *Lavernæ, or, The Spanish Gipsy*. Translated by W. M. London.

Gauden, John. 1660. *A Sermon Preached in St. Pauls Church London*. London: Andrew Crook.

Gibson, Marion. 2005. *Reading Witchcraft*. New York: Taylor & Francis.

Ginzburg, Carlo. 2013. *The Cheese and the Worms*. Translated by Anne C. Tedeschi and John Tedeschi. Baltimore: Johns Hopkins University Press.

Glanvill, Joseph. 1681. *Saducismus Triumphatus*. London: J. Collins and S. Lownds.

Godden, Richard H., and Asa Simon Mittman. 2019. Embodied Difference: Monstrosity, Disability, and the Posthuman. In *Monstrosity, Disability, and the Posthuman in the Medieval and Early Modern World*, ed. Richard H. Godden and Asa Simon Mittman, 3–31. New York: Palgrave Macmillan.

Goodare, Julian. 2008. Scottish Witchcraft in Its European Context. In *Witchcraft and Belief in Early Modern Scotland*, ed. Julian Goodare, Lauren Martin, and Joyce Miller, 26–50. New York: Palgrave Macmillan.

Goodare, Julian. 2016. *The European Witch-Hunt*. New York: Routledge.

Goodare, Julian. 2017. Between Humans and Angels: Scientific Uses for Fairies in Early Modern Scotland. In *Fairies, Demons, and Nature Spirits: "Small Gods" at the Margins of Christendom*, ed. Michael Ostling, 169–190. New York: Palgrave Macmillan.

Gregory, Olinthus. 1796. *Lessons Astronomical and Philosophical for the Amusement and Instruction of British Youth*. Cambridge: Benjamin Flower.

Guiney, Louise Imogen. 1888. *Brownies and Bogles*. Boston: D. Lothrop Company.

Gunnell, Terry. 2017. The Álfar, the Clerics and the Enlightenment: Conceptions of the Supernatural in the Age of Reason in Iceland. In *Fairies, Demons, and Nature Spirits: "Small Gods" at the Margins of Christendom*, ed. Michael Ostling, 191–212. New York: Palgrave Macmillan.

Hadfield, Andrew, ed. 2016. *Literature and Popular Culture in Early Modern England*. New York: Taylor & Francis.

Hailwood, Mark. 2022. Rethinking Literacy in Rural England, 1550–1700. *Past & Present* 260 (1): 38–70.

Halifax, George Savile. 1699. *Advice to a Daughter as to Religion, Husband, House, Family and Children, Behaviour and Conversation, Friendship, Censure, Vanity and Affectation, Pride, Diversions.* London: M. Gillyflower and B. Tooke.

Harms, Daniel M. 2018. Hell and Fairy: The Differentiation of Fairies and Demons Within British Ritual Magic of the Early Modern Period. In *Knowing Demons, Knowing Spirits in the Early Modern Period*, ed. Michelle D. Brock, Richard Raiswell, and David R. Winter, 55–78. New York: Springer.

Harris, Jonathan Gil. 1998. Puck/Robin Goodfellow. In *Fools and Jesters in Literature, Art, and History: A Bio-Bibliographical Sourcebook*, ed. Vicki K. Janik, 351–362. London: Westport.

Hawkes, David. 2022. *Money and Magic in Early Modern Drama.* London: Bloomsbury.

Hemings, William. 1662. *The Jewes Tragedy, or, Their Fatal and Final Overthrow by Vespatian and Titus.* London: Matthew Inman.

Henderson, Lizanne. 2016. *Witchcraft and Folk Belief in the Age of Enlightenment: Scotland, 1670–1740.* New York: Palgrave Macmillan.

Henderson, Lizanne, and Edward J. Cowan. 2001. *Scottish Fairy Belief: A History.* Edinburgh: Tuckwell Press, Ltd.

Herman, Peter C. 2011. *A Short History of Early Modern England: British Literature in Context.* Hoboken: Wiley.

Heylyn, Peter. 1652. *Cosmographie in Four Bookes.* London: Henry Seile.

Heywood, Thomas. 1635. *The Hierarchie of the Blessed Angells.* London: Adam Islip.

Higgs, Daniel. 1699. *The Wonderfull and True Relation of the Bewitching a Young Girle in Ireland.* s.n.

Horace. 1746. *The Epistles and Art of Poetry of Horace.* Translated by Philip Francis. London: A. Millar.

Horbury, Ezra. 2021. Early Modern Transgender Fairies. *Transgender Studies Quarterly* 8 (1): 75–95.

Humfrey, John. 1704. *After-Consideration for Some Members of the Parliament, upon the Occasional Bill Dismiss'd.* London: B. Bragg.

Hutton, Ronald. 2014. The Making of the Early Modern British Fairy Tradition. *The Historical Journal* 57 (4): 1135–1156.

Hutton, Ronald. 2017. Afterword. In *Fairies, Demons, and Nature Spirits: "Small Gods" at the Margins of Christendom*, ed. Michael Ostling, 349–356. New York: Palgrave Macmillan.

Hutton, Ronald. 2022. *Queens of the Wild: Pagan Goddesses in Christian Europe: An Investigation.* New Haven: Yale University Press.

Ingelo, Nathaniel. 1658. *The Perfection, Authority, and Credibility of the Holy Scriptures.* London: Luke Fawn.

James, William. 1578. *A Sermon Preached before the Queenes Maiestie at Hampton Courte.* London: Henry Bynneman.

James VI and I. 1597. *Daemonologie.* Edinburgh: Robert Walde-Graue,.

Jeay, Madeleine, and Kathleen Garay, trans. 2006. *The Distaff Gospels: A First Modern English Edition of Les Évangiles Des Quenouilles*. Peterborough: Broadview Press.

Jekyll, Thomas. 1681. *Popery, a Great Mystery of Iniquity Proved in a Sermon Preached in the Parish Church of Newland*. London: Jonathan Robinson.

Jones, Thomas. 1688. *The British Language in Its Lustre*. London: Lawrence Baskervile.

Jonson, Ben. 1601–1640. The Mad-Merry Prankes of Robbin Good-Fellow. H.G.

Jonson, Ben. 1663–1674. The Mad-Merry Prankes of Robin Good-Fellow. F. Coles, T. Vere, and J. Wright.

Juvenal, Paul. 1788. *Vulcan's Rebuke*. London: s.n.

Kent, Joan. April 1999. The Rural 'Middling Sort' in Early Modern England, circa 1640–1740: Some Economic, Political and Socio-Cultural Characteristics. *Rural History* 10 (1): 19–54.

Kirk, Robert. 1893. *The Secret Commonwealth of Elves, Fauns, & Fairies*. Edited by Andrew Lang. London: David Nutt.

Lamb, Mary Ellen. Autumn 2000. Taken by the Fairies: Fairy Practices and the Production of Popular Culture in A Midsummer Night's Dream. *Shakespeare Quarterly* 51 (3): 277–312.

Langham, William. 1597. *The Garden of Health Conteyning the Sundry Rare and Hidden Vertues and Properties of All Kindes of Simples and Plants*. London: Christopher Barker.

Lessius, Leonardus. 1634. *Hygiasticon*. Cambridge: Roger Daniel.

Levack, Brian P. 2013. *The Witch-Hunt in Early Modern Europe*. 3rd ed. New York: Routledge.

Lightfoot, William. 1587. *The Complaint of England*. London: Iohn Wolfe.

Locke, John. 1700. *An Essay Concerning Humane Understanding*. London: Awnsham and John Churchill.

Lynch, Jack. 2020. Samuel Johnson and the 'First English Dictionary'. In *The Cambridge Companion to English Dictionaries*, ed. Sarah Ogilvie, 142–154. New York: Cambridge University Press.

Magius, Decius. 1748. Proceedings and Debates in the Political Club. *The London Magazine*, September, 398–404.

Magomastix, Hieronymus. 1650. *The Strange Witch at Greenwich, (Ghost, Spirit, or Hobgoblin) Haunting a Wench*. London: Thomas Harper.

Marshall, Peter. 2009. Protestants and Fairies in Early-Modern England. In *Living with Religious Diversity in Early-Modern Europe*, ed. C. Scott Dixon, Dagmar Freist, and Mark Greengrass, 139–159. Burlington: Ashgate.

Mason, John. 1610. *The Turke A Worthie Tragedie*. London: Edward Allde.

Mather, Cotton. 1693. *The Wonders of the Invisible World*. Boston: Benjamin Harris.

Mather, Increase. 1693s. *A Further Account of the Tryals of the New-England Witches*. London: J. Dunton.

Miller, Ronald F. Summer 1975. A Midsummer Night's Dream: The Fairies, Bottom, and the Mystery of Things. *Shakespeare Quarterly* 26 (3): 254–268.

Milton, John. 1645. *Poems*. London: Ruth Raworth.

Milton, John. 1667. *Paradise Lost a Poem Written in Ten Books*. London: Peter Parker.

Morley, Henry. 1874. *Memoirs of Bartholomew Fair*. London: Frederick Warne.

Morrison, Stephen, ed. 2013. *The Late Middle English "Lucydarye."*. Turnhout: Brepols.

Munro, Joyce Underwood. 1991. The Invisible Made Visible: The Fairy Changeling as a Folk Articulation of Failure to Thrive in Infants and Children. In *The Good People: New Fairylore Essays*, ed. Peter Narváez, 251–283. Lexington: University Press of Kentucky.

Nash, Thomas. 1594. *The Terrors of the Night*. London: Iohn Danter.

Ogilvie, Sarah, ed. 2020. *The Cambridge Companion to English Dictionaries*. New York: Cambridge University Press.

Oldridge, Darren. 2016. Fairies and the Devil in Early Modern England. *The Seventeenth Century* 31 (1): 1–15.

Ostling, Michael. 2011. *Between the Devil and the Host: Imagining Witchcraft in Early Modern Poland*. New York: Oxford University Press.

Ostling, Michael, and Richard Forest. 2014. 'Goblins, Owles and Sprites': Discerning Early-Modern English Preternatural Beings through Collocational Analysis. *Religion* 44 (4): 547–572.

Palsgrave, John. 1530. *Lesclarcissement de la langue francoyse compose*. London: Richard Pynson.

Partlicius, Simeon. 1654. *A New Method of Physick*. London: Peter Cole.

Pask, Kevin. 2013. *The Fairy Way of Writing: Shakespeare to Tolkien*. Baltimore: The Johns Hopkins University Press.

Pasqualigo, Luigi. 1585. *Fedele and Fortunio: The Deceites in Loue*. Translated by A.M. London: John Charlewood.

Pierre de Lancre. 2006. *On the Inconstancy of Witches: Pierre de Lancre's Tableau de l'inconstance Des Mauvais Anges et Demons (1612)*. Edited by Gerhild Scholz Williams. Turnhout: Brepols.

Poole, Joshua. 1657. *The English Parnassus*. London: Thomas Johnson.

Poole, Kristen. 2011. *Supernatural Environments in Shakespeare's England: Spaces of Demonism, Divinity, and Drama*. New York: Cambridge University Press.

Porter, Jerome. 1632. *The Flowers of the Liues of the Most Renowned Saincts of the Three Kingdoms England Scotland, and Ireland*. Douai: s.n.

Pouillon, Jean. 2016. Remarks on the Verb 'to Believe.' Edited by Michel Izard and Pierre Smith. Translated by John Leavitt. *HAU: Journal of Ethnographic Theory* 6 (3): 485–92.

Release Forming a Conveyance between Edward Baber of Park Street. 1787. Acc. No.8j112. Bedfordshire Archives.

Remarks on the Present Condition of the Navy. 1700. London: s.n.

Remarks upon a Scurrilous Libel. 1697. London: s.n.

Reynolds, Joshua. 1789. *Puck*. Oil on canvas.

Ritson, Joseph, ed. 1875. *Fairy Tales: Legends and Romances.* London: Frank & William Kerslake.

Robin Good-Fellow, His Mad Prankes, and Merry Jests Full of Honest Mirth, and Is a Fit Medicine for Melancholy. 1628. London: Miles Flesher.

Robin Good-Fellow, His Mad Prankes, and Merry Jests Full of Honest Mirth. 1639. London: Thomas Cotes.

Rogers, Thomas. 1694. *The Conspiracy of Guts and Brains: Or An Answer to the Twinn-Shams.* London.

Rowlands, Samuel. 1613. *More Knaves Yet? The Knaves of Spades and Diamonds.* London.

Royster, James F. April 1928. E. K.'S Elf < Guelph, Goblin < Ghibelline. *Modern Language Notes* 43 (4): 249–252.

Rymer, Thomas. 1688. An Epistle to Mr. Dryden. Exeter. H.P.1056. Chetham's Library - Halliwell-Phillipps.

Scarron, Monsieur. 1665. *The Comical Romance.* London: John Playfere.

School-Play Prepared for, and Performed in a Private Grammar-School in Middlesex. 1664. London: S. Cripps.

Scot, Reginald. 1584. *The Discouerie of Witchcraft.* London: Henry Denham.

Scot, Reginald. 1665. *The Discovery of Witchcraft.* London: Andrew Clark.

Scott, Joseph. 1755. *A New Universal Etymological English Dictionary.* London: T. Osborne and J. Shipton.

Semonin, Paul. 1996. Monsters in the Marketplace: The Exhibition of Human Oddities in Early Modern England. In *Freakery: Cultural Spectacles of the Extraordinary Body,* ed. Rosemarie Garland-Thomson, 69–81. New York: New York University Press.

Seneca the Younger. 1566. *The Seuenth Tragedie of Seneca, Entituled Medea.* Translated by Iohn Studley. London: Thomas Colwell.

Shakespeare, William. 1740. *The Works of Shakespeare.* Edited by Lewis Theobold. 8 vols. London: H. Lintott.

Shakespeare, William. 2008a. *Hamlet.* Edited by G.R. Hibbard. The Oxford Shakespeare. New York: Oxford University Press.

Shakespeare, William. 2008b. *A Midsummer Night's Dream.* Edited by Peter Holland. The Oxford Shakespeare. New York: Oxford University Press.

Shakespeare, William. 2008c. *Troilus and Cressida.* Edited by Kenneth Muir. New York: Oxford University Press.

Shakespeare, William. 2008d. *The Winter's Tale.* Edited by Stephen Orgel. The Oxford Shakespeare. New York: Oxford University Press.

Shakespeare, William. 2017. *A Midsummer Night's Dream.* Edited by Sukanta Chaudhuri. The Arden Shakespeare Third Series. New York: Bloomsbury.

Shakespeare, William. 2024. *The Merry Wives of Windsor*. Edited by Callan Davies, Sarah Neville, and Emma Smith. The New Oxford Shakespeare. New York: Oxford University Press.

Sharpe, James. 1997a. *Early Modern England: A Social History 1550–1760*. 2nd ed. New York: Bloomsbury.

Sharpe, James. 1997b. *Instruments of Darkness: Witchcraft in Early Modern England*. Pennsylvania: University of Pennsylvania Press.

Sharpe, James. 2020. English Witchcraft Pamphlets and the Popular Demonic. In *Demonology and Witch-Hunting in Early Modern Europe*, ed. Julian Goodare, Rita Voltmer, and Liv Helene Willumsen, 127–146. New York: Routledge.

Sherry, Rychard. 1550. *A Treatise of Schemes [and] Tropes Very Profytable for the Better Vnderstanding of Good Authors*. London: Iohn Day.

Smith, Jane. Summer 2017. The Commonwealth Cavalier. *Studies in Philology* 114 (3): 609–640.

Some Few Remarks, upon a Scandalous Book, against the Government and Ministry of New-England. 1701. Boston: T. Green.

Spenser, Edmund. 1579. *The Shepheardes Calender*. London: Hugh Singleton.

Spenser, Edmund. 1590. *The Faerie Queene*. London: William Ponsonbie.

Spenser, Edmund. 1595. *Amoretti and Epithalamion*. London: William Ponsonby.

Stephens, W. B. Winter 1990. Literacy in England, Scotland, and Wales, 1500–1900. *History of Education Quarterly* 30 (4): 545–571.

Streete, Adrian. 2016. Moderation and Religious Criticism in William Cartwright's The Ordinary (1635). *The Seventeenth Century* 31 (1): 17–36.

Stubbe, Henry. 1657. *Clamor, Rixa, Joci, Mendacia, Furta, Cachini*. London: s.n.

Suckling, John. 1646. *The Goblins: A Comedy*. London: Humphrey Moseley.

Swann, Marjorie. Summer 2000. The Politics of Fairylore in Early Modern English Literature. *Renaissance Quarterly* 53 (2): 449–473.

Tasso, Torquato. 1600. *Godfrey of Bulloigne, or The Recouerie of Ierusalem*. London: Ar. Hatfield.

Testimony of John Louder v. Bridget Bishop. 1692. Salem Witch Trials Documentary Archive and Transcription Project. https://salem.lib.virginia.edu/n13.html#n13.11. Accessed December 1, 2024.

The / Salamanca Doctor's Farewel. 1685. London: G.C.

The Doctrine of Devils Proved to Be the Grand Apostacy of These Later Times. 1676. London.

The Downfall of the Chancery. n.d. C.20.f.4.(66.). British Library Collection - Luttrell Ballads.

The Merry Deuill of Edmonton. 1608. London: Henry Ballard.

The Mid-Nights Watch, or, Robin Good-Fellow His Serious Observation. 1643. London: George Lindsey.

The Spirit of Contradiction. 1786. In *A Collection of the Most Esteemed Farces and Entertainments Performed on the British Stage*, 4:329–57. Edinburgh: C. Elliot.

Thomas, Keith. 1971. *Religion and the Decline of Magic*. New York: Charles Scribner's Sons.

Trigge, Francis. 1599. *A Touchstone, Whereby May Be Easilie Discerned, Which Is the True Catholike Faith*. London: Peter Short.

Tryon, Thomas. 1689. *A Treatise of Dreams & Visions*. London: s.n.

Voltmer, Rita, and Liv Helene Willumsen. 2020. Introduction: Demonology and Witch-Trials in Dialogue. In *Demonology and Witch-Hunting in Early Modern Europe*, ed. Julian Goodare, Rita Voltmer, and Liv Helene Willumsen, 1–18. New York: Routledge.

W.P. 1720. *The History of Witches and Wizards*. London: Thomas Norris.

Waddell, Mark A. 2021. *Magic, Science, and Religion in Early Modern Europe*. New York: Cambridge University Press.

Wall, Wendy. 2001. Why Does Puck Sweep?: Fairylore, Merry Wives, and Social Struggle. *Shakespeare Quarterly* 52 (1): 67–106.

Walsham, Alexandra. 2002. Reformed Folklore? Cautionary Tales and Oral Tradition in Early Modern England. In *The Spoken Word: Oral Culture in Britain, 1500–1850*, 173–195. New York: Manchester University Press.

Watson, Henry, Trans. 1510. *The Gospelles of Dystaues*. London: Wynkyn de worde.

Wilby, Emma. 2010. *The Visions of Isobel Gowdie: Magic, Witchcraft and Dark Shamanism in Seventeenth-Century Scotland*. Liverpool: Liverpool University Press.

Wilkins, John. 1668. *An Essay towards a Real Character and a Philosophical Language*. London: Sa. Gellibrand.

Williams, Deanne, and Richard Preiss, eds. 2017. *Childhood, Education and the Stage in Early Modern England*. New York: Cambridge University Press.

Wrightson, Keith, ed. 2018. *A Social History of England, 1500–1750*. New York: Cambridge University Press.

Wrigley, E. A. 2014. Urban Growth in Early Modern England: Food, Fuel and Transport. *Past & Present* 225:79–112.

Young, Francis. 2013. *English Catholics and the Supernatural, 1553–1829*. Aldershot: Ashgate.

Young, Simon. 2022. *The Boggart: Folklore, History, Place-Names and Dialect*. Exeter: Exeter University Press.

Young, Simon, and Davide Ermacora. 2024. Introducing the Social Supernatural. In *The Exeter Companion to Fairies, Nereids, Trolls and Other Social Supernatural Beings: European Traditions*, ed. Simon Young and Davide Ermacora, 1–17. Exeter: University of Exeter Press.

CHAPTER 4

Goblins of Nations and Empires

The nineteenth century brought new faces to the creatures, peoples, objects, and ideas called goblins. Scholars researching the folklore of Europe produced detailed studies about the world of Fairyland that found new ways to taxonomize their inhabitants based on linguistic and national origin. Some argued that goblins or hobgoblins were distinctly English creatures that, though similar to other creatures of European folklore like the *kobold* (Germany) or *nisse* (Scandinavia), had characteristics reflective of the peoples that produced them. Others saw the English goblin as an impoverished corruption of earlier folk traditions embellished by the imaginative pen of Shakespeare and other early modern writers. Operating alongside these discussions was the continued use of "goblin" as a broad category of creature comprising many (if not all) of the creatures of Fairyland. These academic discussions are not reflective of texts produced by Anglophone authors writing about the belief systems of the Global South.[1] These writers, from missionaries to colonial administrators to

---

[1] I use the term "Global South" to demarcate those lands outside of Europe and North America that were subject to colonial exploitation. It is an admittedly imperfect and anachronistic term, though it broadly conveys a geographic region of incredible diversity that is otherwise difficult to succinctly express. Stewart Patrick and Alexandra Huggins, "The Term 'Global South' Is Surging. It Should Be Retired," Carnegie Endowment for International Peace, August 15, 2023, https://carnegieendowment.org/posts/2023/08/the-term-global-south-is-surging-it-should-be-retired?lang=en.

© The Author(s), under exclusive license to Springer Nature Switzerland AG 2026
M. King, *A History of Goblins*,
https://doi.org/10.1007/978-3-032-01063-6_4

academics, used the ubiquitous goblin to represent a wide range of entities in their translations and analyses of world belief systems. Parsing the differences between goblins and their kin was of less importance to these authors than the colonial project at the heart of their works, especially conversion to Christianity. Goblins served their purpose as an accessible label for preternatural entities across religions.

The longstanding association of goblins with ideas of darkness, sin, and grotesque appearance led to new groups being assigned this dubious title. Victorian ideologies about what constituted proper appearance spread widely in the Anglophone world such that those who transgressed them were subject to persecution and dehumanization. The so-called pygmies of Central Africa were one target. Colonial authors compared their dark skin, short stature, and peculiar conduct to European fairies—and some concluded that they were the original inspiration for the creatures of Fairyland. People with physical disabilities, especially forms of dwarfism, were also dehumanized in circuses and freak shows as fairies. Both of these groups were rarely called goblins themselves, though they were given labels of creatures that existed in the world of Fairyland (especially "dwarfs") and were sometimes conflated with goblins. Natural phenomena that appeared atypical, too, were associated with goblins. This was particularly true of mossy and knotted trees, which dotted the landscape as goblin forests even in places that did not have folkloric traditions connected to these creatures.

HISTORICAL BACKGROUND

The nineteenth century witnessed colossal changes to Great Britain and its empire.[2] The economic incentives provided by industrialization facilitated the influx of people into cities, turning a predominantly rural society into an urban one. By 1900, around 80% of the population of Great Britain lived in cities, most of them working in factories as part of a capitalist economy responsible (by 1880) for around 41% of manufacturing

---

[2] As with any broad historical overview, some of these trends elide complex historical events and historiographical debates. I echo Hewitt's introduction to the Victorians, which "underestimates complexity, smooths over unevenness, and excludes difference" in ways that would "dissolve on closer scrutiny." Martin Hewitt, *The Victorians: A Very Short Introduction* (Oxford University Press, 2023), 1.

entering world trade.[3] Immigration and increasing birth rates led to population increases. In England and Wales, a population of 7.5 million in 1750 ballooned to thirty-six million in 1911.[4] The wealth of workers increased when compared to the meager pay of subsistence agriculturalists, but urban life brought new challenges. Cities, inundated with new arrivals and without adequate housing infrastructure, became breeding grounds for disease. Infant mortality remained high, though the sanitary movement and ascendency of germ theory in the late nineteenth century led to gradual improvements in public health.[5] Despite its drawbacks, urban life offered employment, amenities, and some degree of security for millions of migrants to cities. London remained the cosmopolitan heart of the empire, home to its government and around 6.5 million people, though its seedy underbelly was globally renowned for prostitution and vice. Travel across urban centers in Britain was made easier and more affordable by steam-powered trains and boats.

Urbanization and industrialization transformed family dynamics. The industrial workplace was commonly seen as the domain of men, and the household was the sphere of women. Men were paid for their work and exercised authority across public venues; women were unpaid for their domestic labor, which included the bulk of childrearing, and were largely confined to this more private sphere.[6] Access to education became widespread over the course of the nineteenth century through church- and government-funded programs, including free instruction to children into their early teens. Nonetheless, child labor was a recurrent concern, and reformers lobbied for bills that limited the hours children could work and made schooling compulsory. By the end of the century, around 90% of people in England and Wales were literate. Christianity continued to permeate all aspects of society and inspired numerous moralistic movements dedicated to proper conduct: abolition; children's rights; sexual morality;

[3] Martin Daunton, "Society and Economic Life," in *The Nineteenth Century: The British Isles, 1815–1901*, ed. Colin Matthew (New York: Oxford University Press, 2000), 41.

[4] This population growth was uneven and geographically contingent across the nineteenth century (especially in the case of Ireland). W.D. Rubinstein, *Britain's Century: A Political and Social History* (New York: Arnold, 1998), 261.

[5] Robert Woods, *The Demography of Victorian England and Wales* (New York: Cambridge University Press, 2000), 203–309.

[6] These changes were not universal, though, and gendered continuities from the early modern period persisted as well. Robert B. Shoemaker, *Gender in English Society, 1650–1850: The Emergence of Separate Spheres?* (New York: Taylor & Francis, 2014), 10–11.

charity; and the avoidance of vices like alcohol, gambling, prostitution, homosexuality, and cruelty to people and animals.

Accompanying urbanization and an increased emphasis on education was the rise of modern universities in the mid- to late nineteenth century that more closely resemble those of the present day.[7] Although Christianity remained culturally dominant, academic modes of inquiry focused less on the omniscience of God and more on observable phenomena explainable without appealing to the divine.[8] Universities also emphasized original research to a degree not seen prior, and more specialized disciplines cohered into departments with their own evolving and contested methodologies (though they were still a far cry from the disciplinary silos seen today).[9] In this environment, scholars developed new ways to understand and categorize the world around them. Biologists taxonomized wildlife; historians divided the past into recognizable eras; linguists crafted phylogenetic trees to show shared language families; anthropologists found new ways to classify societies of people. The establishment of periodicals and academic journals, including *The Folk-Lore Record* (1878), allowed for the wider dissemination of research.[10] Though some disparaged the study of folklore as the realm of the uneducated and barbarous, the field found defendants in the form of intellectuals like Andrew Lang, whose publications included collections of fairy tales and more academic explorations of folk beliefs. As the discipline evolved, authors frequently framed their folkloric studies using language of nationalism that sought to impose modern

[7] William C. Kirby, *Empires of Ideas: Creating the Modern University from Germany to America to China* (Cambridge: Harvard University Press, 2022). In the United States, the number of universities exploded from eighteen in the year 1800 to more than 450 a century later. Roger L. Geiger, "Introduction: New Themes in the History of Nineteenth-Century Colleges," in *The American College in the Nineteenth Century*, ed. Roger L. Geiger (Nashville: Vanderbilt University Press, 2000), 1–36.

[8] Robert Anderson, *British Universities Past and Present* (New York: Bloomsbury Academic, 2006); John C. Moore, *A Brief History of Universities* (New York: Palgrave Macmillan, 2018).

[9] Bernard Lightman and Bennett Zon, eds., *Victorian Culture and the Origin of Disciplines* (New York: Taylor & Francis, 2019).

[10] Burke argues that, prior to World War I, historians and folklorists existed in an "age of harmony" before methodological differences related to the nation-state and "scientific" methods drove them apart. Peter Burke, "History and Folklore: A Historiographical Survey," 113. More generally, periodicals "proliferated to an astonishing degree" in the Victorian period. Jane Garnett, "Religious and Intellectual Life," in *The Nineteenth Century: The British Isles, 1815–1901*, ed. Colin Matthew (New York: Oxford University Press, 2000), 200.

identities onto historical communities.[11] Embedded in much of this scholarship, too, was an ideology of scientific racism linked to the expansion of European empires and subjugation of indigenous people in the Global South.[12]

The solidification of European states and expansion of their empires during the nineteenth century spurred ongoing discussions about national identities. White Europeans looked to history for ways to differentiate between groups of people and carved out unique characteristics for each that related to a broader sense of the state. They also frequently disparaged the perceived lack of civilization among non-white groups in the Global South, on whom they sought to impose capitalism and Christianity as part of a larger "civilizing mission." To be sure, English expansion across the Atlantic and Indian Oceans stretched back to the 1500s, but increased material demands from an emerging middle class during the mid- to late nineteenth century fueled further colonial ambitions. The so-called Scramble for Africa led the majority of the continent to be ruled by European colonial administrations; the British Crown took direct control of India in 1858 and established governments in Australia and New Zealand during the mid-nineteenth century; European victories over China initiated the "century of humiliation" for the latter in 1839; American conquests, motivated by the ideology of Manifest Destiny, dramatically expanded the borders of the United States. Governmental reforms in these empires granted increasing powers to the administrative state, which looked for new ways to surveil and categorize those under their control—and to dehumanize the monstrous "freaks" that transgressed normative boundaries.[13]

This chapter is the first of two to consider the many faces of goblins during the nineteenth century. Non-fiction works are the primary object

[11] Folklore and nationalism were connected by "the search for 'the people' and its authentic voice." Timothy Baycroft, "Introduction," in *Folklore and Nationalism in Europe during the Long Nineteenth Century*, Timothy Baycroft and David Hopkin, eds. (Leiden: Brill, 2012), 1. See also Matthew Cheeseman and Carina Hart, eds., *Folklore and Nation in Britain and Ireland* (New York: Routledge, 2022).

[12] Eram Alam, Dorothy Roberts, and Natalie Shibley, eds., *Ordering the Human: The Global Spread of Racial Science* (New York: Columbia University Press, 2024).

[13] The freak "challenges the conventional boundaries between male and female, sex and sexless, animal and human, large and small, self and other, and consequently between reality and illusion, experience and fantasy, fact and myth." Leslie Fiedler, *Freaks: Myths and Images of the Secret Self* (New York: Simon & Schuster, 1978), 24.

of analysis for this chapter: academic texts from the fields of history, English literature, anthropology, sociology, biology, botany, medicine, and folklore studies; accounts of traders, government officials, academics, and missionaries to the Global South; travel guides; government reports; and newspaper articles. Chapter 5 focuses on the role of goblins in works of literary fiction and theater. It would be a mistake, though, to see these genres functioning independently of one another or to neatly divide them as such, especially in the case of fairy tale collections, which sometimes feature expositions about the nature of these stories (this chapter) along-side the tales themselves (next chapter). I occasionally mention interplay between works of non-fiction and fiction within this chapter, though the majority of this analysis comes in the next one. Fans of Dickens, Rossetti, and MacDonald hold tight—their time in the spotlight will come shortly.

Categorizing Goblins and Their Kin

The nineteenth century saw goblins feature prominently in studies of folk beliefs in the British Isles and Europe. Scholars approached these traditions with a variety of goals and methodologies that multiplied over the course of the century as folklore studies developed as a discipline alongside overlapping fields like anthropology (ethnology) and history.[14] The search for the defining characteristics of peoples and their nations was a central project of this scholarship. By comparing folklore (as well as language, dress, food, etc.) across communities, academics thought they could pin-point larger ethnogenetic truths about the Teutons, Celts, Scots, and others.[15] The work of the Brothers Grimm, who were deeply committed to the cause of German nationalism, was translated into English beginning in the 1820s and further legitimized the use of folklore and fairy tales to

[14] The early history of the Folklore Society of London speaks to some of these disciplinary (and imperialist) tensions. Chris Wingfield and Chris Gosden, "An Imperialist Folklore? Establishing the Folk-Lore Society in London," in *Folklore and Nationalism in Europe during the Long Nineteenth Century*, Timothy Baycroft and David Hopkin, eds. (Leiden: Brill, 2012), 255–74. See also Francesca Bihet, "Fairies and Folklore: The History of Fairies in the Folklore Society, 1878–1845" (Doctoral Dissertation, University of Chichester, 2020).

[15] In a study dedicated to Walter Scott, MacCulloch writes that the study of superstitions "is a contribution, not only towards that of the human mind, but to that of the descent of nations; for the superstitions and the tales of a people will be found to possess very wide, and often, very unexpected connexions." John MacCulloch, *The Highlands and Western Isles of Scotland*, vol. 4 (London: Longman, Hurst, Rees, Orme, Brown, and Green, 1824), 321.

parse modern identities.[16] Implicit in these ideas was the existence of static traditions and rural populations whose beliefs provided a window into a previous era.

The process of classifying oral traditions in the British Isles involved a handful of interrelated projects: analyzing the islands' folklore using historical texts (both literary and scholarly), cataloguing and editing contemporary stories, comparing these accounts to continental traditions, and using this information to make larger claims about the people that crafted them. Folklorists did not operate under any unifying set of methodologies, and even the classification of their works as "academic" might give undue credibility to some research that took extreme liberties with source materials.[17] It was commonplace, for example, for authors to synthesize multiple accounts of oral traditions to fit what they saw as an idealized narrative. Accusations of embellishment and falsification were not uncommon.[18] More critical methods in folklore studies emerged as the century progressed, including attempts by folklorists to catalogue "original" versions of stories and to categorize them across cultures by shared "tale

---

[16] Jakob Norberg, *The Brothers Grimm and the Making of German Nationalism* (New York: Cambridge University Press, 2022). Linke sees a combination of "romantic nationalism and administrative particularism" as crucial to the emergence of folklore scholarship in Germany. The "romantic folklorists" sought to cultivate "a politically unified nation based on a common cultural and historical heritage," while the "administrative folklorists" looked to "enhance the governing power of single German states by introducing novel procedures" (like folklore surveys) to better understand their people. Uli Linke, "Colonizing the National Imaginary: Folklore, Anthropology, and the Making of the Modern State," in *Cultures of Scholarship*, ed. S.C. Humphreys (Ann Arbor: University of Michigan Press, 1997), 99. The fairy tale compilations of the Brothers Grimm, though monumental, took a backseat in their own lifetimes to their two-volume *Deutsche Sagen* ("*German Legends*") and their scholarship on medieval poetry. Terry Gunnell, "Introduction," in *Grimm Ripples: The Legacy of the Grimms' Deutsche Sagen in Northern Europe*, ed. Terry Gunnell (Leiden: Brill, 2022), 1–25.

[17] Henderson refers to the "sleight of hand" performed by Walter Scott to "cut corners or to make assertions that others would have considered questionable at best." Henderson and Cowan, *Scottish Fairy Belief: A History*, 196. See also Terry Gunnell, "Daisies Rise to Become Oaks. The Politics of Early Folktale Collection in Northern Europe," *Folklore* 121, no. 1 (April 2010): 12–37.

[18] Keightley, for example, accused Croker of falsifying some of his folk tales. Nonetheless, Croker has retained an "honorable, if not frequent, mention in the historiography of folklore study" as the first field collection in Great Britain. Richard M. Dorson, "The First Group of British Folklorists," *The Journal of American Folklore* 68, no. 267 (1955): 2–3; Jennifer Schacker, *National Dreams: The Remaking of Fairy Tales in Nineteenth-Century England* (Pennsylvania: University of Pennsylvania Press, 2003), 46–77.

types."[19] In Scotland, the designation of "seelie" and "unseelie" became one way to delineate between benevolent and malevolent fairies.[20] Anna Eliza Bray, a novelist and folklorist, facilitated the adoption of the "pixie" as a category of folkloric creature and as a folkloresque figure in contemporary literature and visual culture.[21]

Tied up in these studies of folklore was an evolution in language that reflected debates about biological and societal progress. Carl Linnaeus' ideas on taxonomy, which were published in a series of texts beginning in 1735, gradually led scholars to use more standardized terms to refer to life forms, including "genus" and "species." The theories of Charles Darwin in the middle of the nineteenth century built on this scholarship, and his theory of evolution encouraged scientists to look for shared ancestries among species and to critically examine those that deviated from their usual characteristics.[22] Accompanying this taxonomizing impulse was racist ideology used to justify the surveillance and subjugation of groups based on the needs of those in the seats of power.[23] Even those who opposed the work of Linnaeus and his successors found ways to justify slavery and colonial oppression. Samuel Stanhope Smith, for example, argued that those with bad moral character had darker complexion (i.e.,

[19] A common designation is the "tale type," which was coined in 1946 but applies to the systems of Hahn and Aarne from decades prior. Hans-Jörg Uther, "Tale Type," in *Folktales and Fairy Tales: Traditions and Texts from Around the World*, Anne E. Duggan, Donald Haase, and Helen J. Callow, eds. vol. III, IV vols. (New York: Bloomsbury, 2016). The current standard in folklore studies is Hans-Jörg Uther, *The Types of International Folktales: A Classification and Bibliography, Based on the System of Antti Aarne and Stith Thompson*, III vols. (Helsinki: Finnish Academy of Science and Letters, 2011).

[20] One text notes that the seelie court was "kind, courteous, and charitable" while the unseelie court was malicious to those who offended its members, stealing their wares or killing livestock with elf-shot. Patrick Buchan, *The Guidman O' Inglismill, and the Fairy Bride* (Edinburgh: Edmonston and Douglas, 1873), xvii.

[21] Paul Manning, "Pixies' Progress: How the Pixie Became Part of the Nineteenth-Century Fairy Mythology," in *The Folkloresque: Reframing Folklore in a Popular Culture World*, Michael Dylan Foster and Jeffrey A. Tolbert, eds. (Logan: Utah State University Press, 2016), 81–103.

[22] Asma, *On Monsters: An Unnatural History of Our Worst Fears*, 163–79.

[23] Émile Durkheim and Marcel Mauss, *Primitive Classification*, ed. Rodney Needham (Chicago: University of Chicago Press, 1967); George M. Fredrickson, *Racism: A Short History* (Princeton: Princeton University Press, 2002), 49–96.

Black Africans), but the proximity that some slaves had to white culture improved them and made their skin lighter.[24]

These taxonomic ideas seeped into academic folklore such that goblins and their kin were frequently divided into "various orders and degrees" of preternatural creatures—even if the characteristics undergirding these divisions were unclear.[25] We thus encounter attestations of a creature of the "half human semi-goblin race, uncanny hybrids, of pigmy character but great strength" and another that "must belong to some genus in the spirit world," whether it be "the hobgoblin species, or... of the brownie or fairy extraction, or of the elf, witch, or wizard kind."[26] Because most authors writing of folkloric goblins did not see them as anything more than a superstition, they were grouped into categories based on defining characteristics like national origin, appearance, or behavior. Applying rigid classifications to preternatural creatures forced authors to distill them into a simplifying essence that adhered to a particular tradition of beliefs—but also flattened their many variations.

Although scholars never reached a consensus about the nature of goblins and/or hobgoblins, a handful of ideas became commonplace. One thread situated them as the uniquely English archetype of a particular household spirit with clear parallels in other linguistic and national traditions like the *kobold*, *nisse*, and brownie. The characteristics of this goblin varied depending on the author, ranging from haunting a particular location to delighting in mischief to harassing the non-industrious. Simultaneously, though, scholars used goblins as broad designators of often-malevolent spirits that could cut across cultural boundaries without issue.

The works of Walter Scott loom large in this discourse. His three-volume *Minstrelsy of the Scottish Border* (initially published in 1802),

---

[24] Samuel Stanhope Smith, *An Essay on the Causes of the Variety of Complexion and Figure in the Human Species* (New Brunswick: J. Simpson, 1810).

[25] Frederick Cobley, *On Foot Through Wharfedale* (Otley: William Walker and Sons, 1882), 235.

[26] "Cathedral Legends," *The Glasgow Herald*, December 14, 1857; "A Goondiwindi Ghost," *The Week*, March 17, 1877. Similar language can be found in some fairy tale compilations, too. In the story of "The Cauld Lad of Hilton" from 1890's *English Fairy Tales*, for example, a brownie is introduced as follows: "'What's a Brownie?' you say. 'Oh, it's a kind of a sort of a Bogle, but it isn't so cruel as a Redcap! What! you don't know what's a Bogle or a Redcap! Ah, me! what's the world a-coming to? Of course a Brownie is a funny little thing, half man, half goblin, with pointed ears and hairy hide.'" Joseph Jacobs, *English Fairy Tales* (London: David Nutt, 1890), 203–4.

written in collaboration with John Leyden and a handful of other scholars, is a foundational examination of ballads collected in the Scottish border-land.[27] Therein, Scott catalogues the "sundry classes of subordinate spirits" described by commoners: fairies, brownies, elves, and bogles/goblins. He differentiates the brownies, a "class of beings… meagre, shaggy, and wild" in appearance, from the "freakish and mischievous elves." Fairies are important enough to warrant an entire volume in this anthology, and bogles/goblins are another kind of creature entirely:

> A being, totally distinct from those hitherto mentioned, is the Bogle, or Goblin; a freakish spirit, who delights rather to perplex and frighten mankind, than either to serve, or seriously hurt, them. This is the *Esprit Follet* of the French; and *Puck*, or *Robin Goodfellow*, though enlisted by Shakespeare among the fairy band of *Oberon*, properly belongs to this class of phantoms. *Shellycoat*, a spirit, who resides in the waters, and has given his name to many a rock and stone upon the Scottish coast, belongs also to the class of bogles….
>
> Of all these classes of spirits it may be, in general observed, that their attachment was supposed to be local, and not personal. They haunted the rock, the stream, the ruined castle, without regard to the persons or families to whom the property belonged. Hence, they differed entirely from that species of spirits, to whom, in the Highlands, is ascribed the guardianship, or superintendence of a particular clan, or family of distinction; and who, perhaps yet more than the Brownie, resemble the classic household gods.[28]

To Scott, goblins are tied to a particular landscape, whether natural or manmade, and perplex or frighten (but do not seriously injure) humans that pass through it. They are distinct from brownies, which haunt houses during the daytime, perform household chores at night, and can have more personal relationships with families.[29] This categorization makes

---

[27] Published in several editions during the early nineteenth century, this text "was the single most influential publication on the subject of fairies, frequently reprinted and perennially plundered by would-be authorities." Henderson and Cowan, *Scottish Fairy Belief: A History*, 196.

[28] The first edition of this text was published in 1802 but, due to its popularity, was expanded into a three-volume edition the following year. Walter Scott, *Minstrelsy of the Scottish Border*, vol. 1 (Edinburgh: James Ballantyne, 1803), lxxxi–lxxxvi.

[29] Scott's belief in the existence of fairies evolved over the course of his life, from the view that they "were essentially fictional creatures" fused from a handful of folkloric traditions to the idea that dwarfs or pygmies were "the prototypes of the fairies." Silver, *Strange and Secret Peoples: Fairies and Victorian Consciousness*, 10–11.

Scott comfortable with reclassifying the "drudging goblin" of Milton's *L'Allegro* as a brownie. It also elevates Scottish folklore over its English counterpart. Scott argues that Shakespeare's interpretation of the merry Puck (i.e., Hobgoblin) was an improvement upon "the vulgar belief" of the people in his time and shifted fairies in the English consciousness to a new kind of playfully mischievous creature removed from the harsher characteristics of dwarves and elves. These alterations made the fairies of England distinct from their Scottish counterparts, which Scott characterizes as more "ancient" and thus of a more "appropriate character."[30] (Fig. 4.1)

Scott was not alone in seeing early modern writers as distorting English folklore. Scholars of the nineteenth century frequently saw England as a folkloric vacuum that was populated first by continental traditions and then embellished by the imaginative pens of figures like Shakespeare and Milton. W.B. Yeats, for example, depicts English fairies as (per Levy and Mendlesohn) "extensions of French fancy" and unlike Irish fairies, which have real "authenticity behind them."[31] This disparagement of English folklore compared to that of Scandinavian, Germanic, and Celtic origin was such that it became something of a tradition for Victorian authors to complain "about the lack of attention paid to English vernacular culture and folklore."[32] Travel writer Johann Georg Kohl, who visited Britain in the 1840s, is explicit about this lack of tradition among English miners compared to their German counterparts:

[They have] invented none of these pretty traditions about under-earth goblins [*kobolden*], mountain spirits, and divining rods with which our German miners are so abundantly provided. These mines untenanted by demon or spirit, are illustrative of the sound, intelligent, but unimaginative character of the English people.[33]

[30] Walter Scott, *Minstrelsy of the Scottish Border*, vol. 2 (Edinburgh: James Ballantyne, 1802), 212–13.

[31] Michael Levy and Farah Mendlesohn, *Children's Fantasy Literature: An Introduction* (New York: Cambridge University Press, 2016), 30.

[32] Jonathan Roper, "England—The Land without Folklore?," in *Folklore and Nationalism in Europe during the Long Nineteenth Century*, Timothy Baycroft and David Hopkin, eds. (Leiden: Brill, 2012), 227.

[33] J.G. Kohl, *England and Wales* (London: Frank Cass & Co. Ltd., 1968), 81. The original German can be found in J.G. Kohl, *Reisen in England und Wales*, vol. II (Leipzig: Arnold, 1844), 36. See also Diarmuid Ó Giolláin, "The Leipreachán and Fairies, Dwarfs and the Household Familiar: A Comparative Study," *Béaloideas* 52 (1984): 75–150. Lecouteux defines the kobold as "the name of a local land spirit that is attached to various places and has

Fig. 4.1   *The Goblin* by William Blake (1816–1820). Blake's painting of a goblin evaporating into the night sky was inspired by Milton's *L'Allegro*. Image courtesy of Wikimedia (accessible here: https://commons.wikimedia.org/wiki/File:Penseroso_%26_L%27Allegro_William_Blake5.jpg. This is one of twelve watercolors that Blake designed from Milton's *L'Allegro* and *Il Penseroso* for a commission for Thomas Butts. William Blake, *The Goblin*, watercolor, 1816–1820, The Morgan Library & Museum)

This perspective, however, was not universal. William Thoms, for example, argues that the fairies of Shakespeare were representative of contemporary beliefs and not literary appropriations. He views Robin Goodfellow/Hobgoblin as the English equivalent of a handful of other creatures, including the German *Narrenkolbe* and the Danish *Nissen God dreng*.[34] Thoms advocates for the existence of a respectable English folk tradition, and his career reflects this perspective, as he was the coiner of the term "folklore" and the journal (partially) dedicated to it, *Notes and Queries* (1849). Thoms' efforts paid off, and English folklore eventually became an object of serious study alongside other Celtic beliefs—a term invigorated (and contested) during the Celtic Revival of the nineteenth century.[35] Joseph Jacobs, an editor of *Folklore*, opens his 1890 *English Fairy Tales* with the question "Who says that English folk have no fairy-tales of their own?"[36] When the American folklorist Walter Evans-Wentz published his expansive study of folk beliefs in 1911, he did not dismiss English folklore, but rather looked for commonalities across the "Celtic" world. The *lutins* of French tradition thus "show affinity with Pucks and such shape-shifting hobgoblins as are found in Wales." So too do the *lutin* and Breton *Corrigan* belong to the Celtic elfish peoples that include "pixies in Cornwall, Robin Good-fellows in England, goblins [*bwganod*] in Wales, or brownies in Scotland." They might haunt a house or protect it; they might lead a traveler astray or dance merrily when the moon is bright.

---

a multitude of names depending on the country and region. He corresponds to the goblin and the gnome." Claude Lecouteux, *Encyclopedia of Norse and Germanic Folklore, Mythology, and Magic*, ed. Michael Moynihan, trans. Jon E. Graham (Rochester: Inner Traditions, 2016), 165. In Cornwall, spirits associated with mines were commonly called Tommyknockers or Knockers, and such creatures even made their way across the Atlantic with Cornish immigrants to the American southwest in the nineteenth century. Ronald M. James, "Knockers, Knackers, and Ghosts: Immigrant Folklore in the Western Mines," *Western Folklore* 51, no. 2 (April 1992): 153–77.

[34] Articles published on the folklore of Shakespeare in 1847 in the journal *Athenaeum* were later compiled in William Thoms, "The Folk-Lore of Shakespeare," in *Three Notelets on Shakespeare* (London: John Russell Smith, 1865), 87–88.

[35] This revival was particularly pronounced in literature. See, for example, Gerard Carruthers and Alan Rawes, eds., *English Romanticism and the Celtic World* (New York: Cambridge University Press, 2003); Thomas M. Curley, *Samuel Johnson, the Ossian Fraud and the Celtic Revival in Great Britain and Ireland* (New York: Cambridge University Press, 2009).

[36] Jacobs, *English Fairy Tales*, vii.

Though their dispositions varied, they were part of a folkloric corpus encompassing a perceived "ancient empire of the Celts."[37]

When Evans-Wentz wrote of Celtic fairies, he was operating in a long tradition of folklorists attempting to classify the many inhabitants of Fairyland. In the previous chapter, we saw some authors classify goblins as "terrestrial devils" and the like. The specificity of Walter Scott's classifications in the early nineteenth century, though, and the gradual absorption of methods employed by continental folklorists like the Brothers Grimm, meant that scholars found new, more detailed ways to taxonomize the creatures of Fairyland.[38] In *Fairy Legends and Traditions of the South of Ireland* (1825–1828), for example, Thomas Croften Croker sees a strong resemblance between the *kobold, brownie, cluricaune, tomte gubbe, nisse-god-dreng, duende, trasgo, lutin*, goblin, and hobgoblin.[39] This class of spirits is defined by attachment to a family or household, which lasts as long as the family does. Although this "domestic spirit" can be active, good-natured, and skillful, if its relationship with a family sours, it can also turn "very revengeful." Croker shows the forms this creature can take across cultural traditions, and he categorizes it primarily as a benevolent spirit that delights in "mischief and mockery."[40]

Mischievous antics (ranging from the playfully benevolent to more malicious) were a common trait that scholars assigned to goblins. John Roby considers the Greek *kobalos* as the ultimate point of origin for the puck, bogle, *esprit follet*, goblin, and *kobold*, all of which are defined by

[37] Evans-Wentz speculates that "there seems to have been a time in the evolution of animism when the ancient Celts of Britain, of Ireland, and of Continental Europe too, held, in common with the ancient Greeks, Romans, and Teutons, an original Aryan doctrine." Walter Evans-Wentz, *The Fairy-Faith in Celtic Countries* (London: Henry Frowde, 1911), xvii, 207, 220, 243–44.

[38] Éilís Ní Dhuibhne Almqvist, "Pioneers: Thomas Crofton Croker and the Brothers Grimm," in *Grimm Ripples: The Legacy of the Grimms' Deutsche Sagen in Northern Europe* (Leiden: Brill, 2022), 259–87.

[39] Thomas Crofton Croker, *Fairy Legends and Traditions of the South of Ireland*, vol. 3 (London: John Murray, 1828), 111–12. The importance of Croker's work is such that Almqvist used him as the boundary for the first two phases of his four-part chronology: pre-Croker, Croker to Hyde, Delargy, and post-Delargy. Bo Almqvist, "Irish Migratory Legends on the Supernatural: Sources, Studies and Problems," *Béaloideas* 59 (1991): 1–43.

[40] In general, Croker draws a distinction between the Shakespearian Robin Goodfellow and the Hobgoblin of Milton, the latter of which is apparently the appropriate English "hobgoblin." The simpler "goblin" meanwhile serves as a broader category that comprises a handful of Irish lexemes including *far darrig, dullahan*, and the many variations of *sia*.

their "sole delight" in perplexing humans.[41] Joseph Jekyll, a Whig politician, sees mischief as one of several markers of the British hobgoblin, as described in an 1825 letter:

> I don't believe they possess in France our true species of British hobgoblin. Ours is neither *mauvais fée*, nor *loup garou*, nor, as old Boyer stupidly has it, *esprit spectre fantôme*.[42] Our true hobgoblin is ugly, tragic, mischievous; but I should not know how to dress the character for a fancy ball at a county member's. It would be Dalmation difficult.[43]

The connection between a goblin and human family often involved the former performing household labor (if treated well) on behalf of the latter. In *The Fairy Mythology* (1828), Thomas Keightley argues that the German *kobold* is "exactly the same being as the Danish Nis, Scottish Brownie, and English Hobgoblin. He performs the very same services for the family to whom he attaches himself."[44] These creatures are all subsumed under the umbrella of elf or fairy, which itself has two classes: domestic spirits and the spirits inhabiting the wilderness. These shared folkloric taxonomies, when taken in their entirety, promote to Keightley the idea of a "common origin of the Caucasian race."[45]

Keightley was not alone in associating goblins with chores and labor performed on behalf of a family. One study of the Walloons (roughly located in the Low Countries) argues that the performance of "household duties" is the defining characteristic of the "goblin race," which comprises *kobolds*, brownies, and the lubber fiend of Milton.[46] Egerton Brydges, who edited a number of early modern texts, places his own spin on the creature of Milton's *L'Allegro*. He notes that this household helper was the "true British goblin," for it only worked its mischief on "sluttish housemaids

---

[41] John Roby, *Traditions of Lancashire*, 2nd ed., vol. I (London: Longman, Rees, Orme, Brown, and Green, 1831), xviii.

[42] These French terms are (roughly) "bad fairy," "werewolf," and "spirit ghost phantom." The latter of these categorizations is from a pre-1825 version of Boyer's *Royal Dictionary Abridged*, though in this letter from Jekyll they are rendered without commas.

[43] Joseph Jekyll, *Correspondence of Mr. Joseph Jekyll*, ed. Algernon Bourke (London: John Murray, 1894), 153.

[44] Keightley, *The Fairy Mythology*, 1828, II:41.

[45] Thomas Keightley, *The Fairy Mythology*, vol. I (London: William Harrison Ainsworth, 1828), ix.

[46] "Walloon Traditions," *Chambers's Journal* 65 (1888): 40–41.

and lazy hinds" but not virgins, the good, or the industrious.[47] This version of goblin, in other words, was harmless to upstanding British people and only punished those who transgressed the kind of values that Brydges saw as central to their identity. Gone are the mischievous pranks of Robin Goodfellow that could befall practically anyone—instead, this British goblin works in service of a higher moral character.[48]

The above classification systems show considerable variability, and some scholars were forthcoming about the difficulties that arose from attempting to classify the fairies.[49] The authors of *The Occult Sciences* (1855) note in the chapter "Goblins and Bogles" that the distinctions they draw between various kinds of entities are "more artificial than real."[50] Still, they spend much of this chapter trying to determine which creatures bear "the genuine goblin stamp" and to subdivide those entities using terminologies like a "goblin of the bogle-boe species." They conclude confusingly that the hobgoblin is a hopping goblin, the goblin is a *kobalos*, the *kobalos* is a harsh kind of spirit from ancient Greek tradition, and that goblins cannot be classified as spirits or demons. Internal contradictions and ambiguities like these abound within classification schemes as authors sought to impose from the top down a rigid structure upon disparate folk traditions. Such complexities only multiply when authors attempted translations of non-Anglophone traditions or cross-cultural comparisons.[51]

---

[47] John Milton, *The Poetical Works of John Milton*, ed. Egerton Brydges, vol. V (London: John Macrone, 1835), 262–63.

[48] This more benevolent goblin was uncommon, though not unprecedented. Charles Scott, an American philologist, defines a goblin as "a demon, often of a friendly disposition." Charles P.G. Scott, "The Devil and His Imps: An Etymological Inquisition," *Transactions of the American Philological Association* XXVI (1895): 79–146.

[49] Indeed, the many classifications and definitions found within these works led to confusion among some readers. One author within *Notes and Queries* inquired about when the word "bug" ceased to mean goblin and became used only for the insect. Jaydee, "A Note on Bugs," *Notes and Queries* 9, no. 235 (1860): 500. An early translation of the Brothers Grimm also notes that "we have no nomenclature sufficiently accurate for the classification of the goblin tribes of the North." Jacob Grimm and Wilhelm Grimm, *German Popular Stories Translated from the Kinder Und Kinder Und Haus-Märchen, Collected by M. M. Grimm, from Oral Tradition*, trans. Edgar Taylor (London: C. Baldwyn, 1823), 231.

[50] Edward Smedley et al., *The Occult Sciences* (London: Richard Griffin, 1855), 26, 72–78.

[51] Leland, for example, renders the Italian *folletto* as "goblin" in his 1896 compilation of Florentine folk traditions. He acknowledges, though, that *folletto* was "originally an airy tricksy sprite" but "is now applied not only to fairies and goblins in general, but also to every kind of supernatural apparition. I have a book in which even comets are described as *folletti*."

Wirt Sikes, an American diplomat, details these difficulties in the introduction to 1880's *British Goblins*:

> Fairies being creatures of the imagination, it is not possible to classify them by fixed and immutable rules. In the exact sciences, there are laws which never vary, or if they vary, their very eccentricity is governed by precise rules. Even in the largest sense, comparative mythology must demean itself modestly in order to be tolerated in the severe company of the sciences. In presenting his subjects, therefore, the writer in this field can only govern himself by the purpose of orderly arrangement.[52]

Feeling compelled to adopt contemporary scientific methodologies to the world of Fairyland, Sikes uses the goblin as a base unit of analysis. As its title implies, *British Goblins* uses "lowly goblins" as an overarching category that encompasses fairies, ghosts, spirits, and any number of other preternatural creatures encountered in Britain. This text abounds with goblins of every shape, size, and disposition. Sikes, though, is more careful with his classification of the hobgoblin. He sees this creature as the English iteration of the household spirit, erroneously derived from the Welsh *hob* (meaning "to hop") and *coblynau* (defined as "mine fairies" and equivalent to gnomes).[53] Sikes further equates the hobgoblin with the *nisse*, brownie, *bwbach* (Wales), and *kobold*, all of which have a "double character" as both helpful performers of household chores and malevolent tricksters. The breadth of the goblin, then, does not extend to the uniquely English hobgoblin.

Charles Godfrey Leland, *Legends of Florence: Collected from the People* (London: David Nutt, 1895), 21.

[52] Sikes notes that the divisions proposed by Keightley are "entirely arbitrary" but also "perhaps as satisfactory as another." Wirt Sikes, *British Goblins: Welsh Folk-Lore, Fairy Mythology, Legends and Traditions* (London: Sampson Low, Marston, Searle, & Rivington, 1880), 11–12, 32.

[53] *A Dictionary of Celtic Mythology* defines *coblynau* as "Welsh mine goblins, not unlike the knockers of Cornwall. Although usually seen as quite ugly and standing only 18 inches high, they are perceived as being friendly and helpful. They know where rich lodes of ore may be found." The lexeme *coblynau* (singular, *coblyn*) undoubtedly derives from the French *gobelin*, likely via the English "goblin." James MacKillop, "Coblynau, Coblynnod," in *A Dictionary of Celtic Mythology* (New York: Oxford University Press, 2004), 10.1093/acref/9780198609674.001.0001.

The Handbook of Folklore (1890), written by the director of the Folklore Society, George Gomme, conveys a similarly broad sentiment about the goblin in a chapter titled "Goblindom:"

> The belief in spirits which assume a form and possess characteristics more or less like mankind is prevalent nearly everywhere. These spirits appear either as very diminutive or as gigantic; as nimble, merry, and clever; or as heavy, plodding, and stupid. The name generally given to them is that of fairy or goblin.[54]

Following this description is a "perhaps tolerably perfect" list of special names given to these spirits, which includes many considered in the last few chapters like Hobgoblin, Robin Goodfellow, and Puck. Dozens of questions at the end of this chapter give a sense of the many types of creature subsumed under this banner, ranging from physical appearance ("Beautiful? Hideous? Small in stature? Different at different times?") to mortality ("Can he be killed? Or changed into stone?").[55] The expansive framing of Gomme's goblins allows for the existence of, say, a "Spanish goblin" or "German goblin" without issue.[56] Indeed, the provenance of this text, written by the director of the Folklore Society, indicates that this framing had some degree of popularity near the end of the nineteenth century.[57] Arguments about a distinguishing feature of a British or English goblin have no place here because the goblin is a category of creature that crosses cultural boundaries.

[54] The creatures of Goblindom are further divided into eight categories: elves, household familiars, ancestral spirits, individual demons haunting single places, ghosts, the wild hunt, enchanted heroes, and beings that represent ancient goddesses. George Laurence Gomme, *The Handbook of Folklore* (London: David Nutt, 1890), 30–38.

[55] A similarly expansive list can be found in the mid-century work of Denham, who lists out (with some repetition, including use of the word "hobgoblin" twice) the spirits observed in the time of Shakespeare, likely deriving from the list provided in Scot's *Daemonologie*. Michael Aislabie Denham, *The Denham Tracts: A Collection of Folklore*, ed. James Hardy (London: The Folklore Society, 1895), 77–80.

[56] Indeed, such terms pre-dated Gomme's work. See, for example, MacCulloch, *The Highlands and Western Isles of Scotland*, 4:329, 332.

[57] The seventh annual report from the Folklore Society, for example, contains a number of definitions of folklore from leading scholars, including Charlotte Sophia Burne (first woman president of the society and editor of its journal). She divides folklore into four major components, including "Superstitious Belief and Practice," which itself is divided into Goblindom, Witchcraft, Astrology, and "Superstitions connected with material things." "Seventh Annual Report of the Council," *The Folk-Lore Journal* 3, no. 4 (1885): 389.

Alongside broad classifications like these was the rhetorical use of the goblin to indicate that a writer was going to discuss the supernatural. Some authors write of the irrational beliefs of people in the "days of ghosts and goblins" or the childhood fear of the "ghost or goblin."[58] New derivations of the word cropped up to convey these notions, often with a degree of derision. We can thus read of the "nursery goblinism" of Dante's *Divine Comedy*, the exploitative goblinism of the French, or the alternating "tenderness, hobgoblinism and imaginative conceits of the old storyteller."[59] One writer of the mid-nineteenth century even references the array of academic disciplines that have cropped up "from the buried teeth of the old dragons of mythology and goblinology."[60] Another notes how a genre of play is "particularly well suited to goblinries and weirdnesses of all kinds."[61] Goblins were so ubiquitously associated with a certain kind of folklore that authors morphed the word into a representation of superstition writ large.

Persistent across the nineteenth century, too, is the familiar contempt that elite authors had for the traditions of the countryside and (in another iteration of the perpetual recession of the fairies) their documentation of a decline in fairy belief accompanying advances in science. Keightley, for example, notes that belief in fairies is confined to certain areas of Wales but that "the sounds of the cotton-mill, the steam-engine, and, more than all, the whistle of the railway train, more powerful than any exorcists, have banished, or soon will banish, the fairy tribes from all their accustomed haunts" in England proper.[62] Writers commonly reference this kind of sentiment, in which the spread of technology and scientific rationality has driven away the ignorance and metaphorical darkness of superstition—an

[58] W. Howells, *Cambrian Superstitions* (Tipton: Thomas Danks, 1831), 17; "Notes on Ghosts and Goblins," *The Cornhill Magazine* XXVII (1873): 451–66.

[59] William Beckford, *Memoirs of William Beckford*, vol. II (London: Charles J. Skeet, 1859), 41; Peter Bayne, "Milton," *The Contemporary Review* XXII (1873): 453; "Review of 'The Fairy Tales of Hans Christian Andersen,'" *The Artist* XXV (1899): lxxi–lxxii.

[60] Mary Irving, "The 'Spirits' of the Age," *The Literary American* IV, no. 25 (June 22, 1850): 462–63. The oldest reference I could locate for "goblinology" comes from a work of an 1825 work of fiction, though it conveys a similar sentiment. One character claims to "know something of these witcheries, and have been instructed in all the goblinology of the North of Ireland, which, I assure you, is very profound." *The Adventurers*, vol. I (London: Longman, Hurst, Rees, Orme, Brown, and Green, 1825), 118.

[61] Lafcadio Hearn, *Glimpses of Unfamiliar Japan*, vol. 2 (New York: Houghton Mifflin and Company, 1894), 646.

[62] Keightley, *The Fairy Mythology*, 1828, II:117–18.

idea in keeping with the supposed "disenchantment of the world."[63] According to this line of reasoning, places with more rural, uneducated populations (like Wales) had less exposure to these advancements and were thus more prone to maintaining vestiges of these backward traditions.[64]

Goblins could thus range in specificity from a mischievous spirit tied to a particular environment to an overarching category of preternatural creatures. The number of stories related within these volumes involving goblins is resultingly massive, ranging from the "Goblin Builders" that tear down construction projects to the wandering goblins that lead travelers astray to the gluttonous goblins that devour food at certain times of year. They inhabit just about any place on the peripheries of human settlement: mines, forests, ancient ruins, the dark corners of homes, etc. They sometimes invoked fear, sometimes merriment, sometimes both. Images accompanying these stories show some of the ways that people envisioned these creatures—typically humanoid and diminutive, though their shape-shifting powers make their appearance hard to define. Nonetheless, these images influenced subsequent depictions of fairies just as they themselves were influenced by earlier written and visual representations. I consider depictions of goblins in greater detail in the next chapter, as the corpus of illustrations in works of literature and theater is more extensive (Fig. 4.2).

For this history, what is more important than relating these manifold stories and showing every accompanying illustration of goblins is to see how the categorizing impulses of authors during the nineteenth century pushed them to consider what exactly made a goblin a goblin as opposed

[63] Barker, for example, argues that humans suffer from "the darkness of ignorance and error" but can be liberated by the "the day-light of science [which] shows us that the ghosts and goblins, that startled us in the dark, are in truth our benefactors and our friends." J.F. Berg and Joseph Barker, *Great Discussion of the Origin, Authority, and Tendency of the Bible* (Boston: J.B. Yerrinton & Son, 1854), 9. The idea of the "disenchantment of the world" brought by advances in science, secular thought, and government (popularized by Weber) is contested. Gauchet argues, for example, that "the disappearance of enchanters and powerful supernatural beings is only the superficial sign of a much deeper revolution in relations between heaven and earth." Marcel Gauchet, *The Disenchantment of the World: A Political History of Religion* (Princeton: Princeton University Press, 1997), 3.

[64] Sikes goes a step further and even notes that "among the vulgar in Wales, the belief in fairies is less nearly extinct than casual observers would be likely to suppose. Even educated people who dwell in Wales, and have dwelt there all their lives, cannot always be classed as other than casual observers in this field." Sikes, *British Goblins: Welsh Folk-Lore, Fairy Mythology, Legends and Traditions*, 2–3.

Fig. 4.2 Goblins in folklore scholarship from the nineteenth century. (Left) Rowli and the Ellyll conversing from a story in Sikes' *British Goblins* (1880). Image courtesy of Project Gutenberg (Sikes, *British Goblins: Welsh Folk-Lore, Fairy Mythology, Legends and Traditions*, 16. Accessible here: https://www.gutenberg. org/ebooks/34704). (Top-right) The *Far Darrig* (Red Man) of Ireland, which bears a great resemblance to "that merry goblin" Puck or Robin Goodfellow, from Croker's *Fairy Legends and Traditions* (1828). Image courtesy of Project Gutenberg (Thomas Crofton Croker, *Fairy Legends and Traditions of the South of Ireland*, vol. 2 (London: John Murray, 1828), 153, 162. Accessible here: https:// www.gutenberg.org/cache/epub/39752/pg39752-images.html. The influence of the illustrations in Croker's works extended outside of Britain, too, and proved important for depictions of Norwegian folk legends. Terry Gunnell, "Thomas Crofton Croker, The Fairy Legends, and the Arrival of the Illustrated Folk Legend in Northern Europe," *Irish University Review* 54, no. 1 (2024): 101–11.). (Bottom-right) The half-human, half-goblin brownie from "The Cauld Lad of Hilton" as told in Jacobs' *English Fairy Tales* (1890). Image courtesy of Wikimedia (Jacobs, *English Fairy Tales*, 203. Accessible here: https://commons.wikimedia. org/wiki/File:Goblin_illustration_from_19th_century.jpg)

to a fairy, elf, dwarf, or other creature. National identity, malevolent trick-ery, and household attachment were some of the ways that authors dis-tilled the goblin into a particular folkloric entity—and inevitably flattened other interpretations of it in the process. The hobgoblin, too, was com-monly (though not universally) tied to the English literary tradition of Shakespeare and Milton, which differentiated it from the broader label of "goblin."

OLD IDEAS, NEW CONTEXTS

Debates about the nature of goblins and their kin were prominent in stud-ies of British and European folklore, though they were less central in works centered on different geographical contexts. When Anglophone authors wrote about the non-Christian belief systems of people in the Global South, especially during the wave of colonial expansion in the late nine-teenth century, they used goblins to indicate countless entities ranging from the quirky to the downright evil. Translations of religious texts use goblins to refer to entire classes of beings, like one of the six realms of Buddhism, as well as more specific creatures, like a Japanese goblin badger (*tanuki*) that might lead travelers astray. Authors applied this term with-out contradiction to belief systems of indigenous peoples in Africa, India, China, and the Americas. The distinction between the hobgoblin and goblin, too, is nonexistent. As such, the umbrella of what could be called a goblin expanded to fit the societies encountered by Anglophone empires.

The variety of texts that mention goblins in the Global South is sub-stantial. Politicians, academics, missionaries, tourists, and traders (many of whom fall under multiple of these designators) produced texts that con-sidered the indigenous people of the Global South and North America with differing degrees of curiosity, benevolence, and contempt.[65] Some were abolitionists who abhorred the practice of slavery; others believed that African peoples were inferior to Europeans and that the institution of slavery was ultimately a benevolent one. Regardless of their position on any other slew of contemporary issues, Anglophone writers served as

---

[65] H.H. Risley, for example, was both senior official in the colonial government of British India and one of its foremost anthropologists. C.J. Fuller, *Anthropologist and Imperialist: H.H. Risley and British India, 1873–1911* (New York: Routledge, 2023). See also Russell McDougall and Iain Davidson, eds., *The Roth Family, Anthropology, and Colonial Administration* (New York: Taylor & Francis, 2008).

agents of colonial power, and their attempts to chart out the belief systems of indigenous peoples created and reinforced categories that were not necessarily present therein.[66] For this history, though, our concern lies with analyzing how these authors invoked goblins and other creatures, rather than attempting to use such texts to make larger claims about the beliefs of those subject or adjacent to colonialism.

Publications dedicated to the discussion of organized religion, especially Christianity, were far and away the most common produced in Britain during the nineteenth century. Indeed, churches were the "central social force" of the time—and missionaries traveling to non-Christianized parts of the world sought to spread this religion and its accompanying social customs.[67] Texts written by and for Christian missionaries catalogued the belief systems of people in the Global South so that readers could better proselytize to them.[68] Goblins were often used therein as a designator of superstition and aversion to Christian doctrine. An 1878 report on missionary work in China mentions how its people are "full of fearful hobgoblin stories" because of Buddhist writings that exhort people to avoid certain practices.[69] Another article disparages Taoist beliefs "in goblins and genii" that are "largely responsible for the deep and strong superstitions of the people."[70] One missionary broadly defined the beliefs

[66] Hence the moniker commonly bestowed on the discipline of anthropology: the "Handmaiden of Colonialism." In the case of British India, Channa argues that "conquest, administration, and control were central to all forms of scholarship and pedagogical efforts." Subhadra Mitra Channa, "Introduction: Establishing an Empire," in *Colonial Anthropology: Technologies and Discourses of Dominance, 1886–1936*, Subhadra Mitra Channa and Lancy Lobo, eds. (New York: Routledge, 2024), 5. See also Peter Pels and Oscar Salemink, eds., *Colonial Subjects: Essays on the Practical History of Anthropology* (Ann Arbor: University of Michigan Press, 1999); Marvin Harris, *The Rise of Anthropological Theory: A History of Theories of Culture* (New York: AltaMira Press, 2001).

[67] Rubinstein, *Britain's Century: A Political and Social History*, 298.

[68] Christian evangelists of the nineteenth century were primarily indigenous people who "selectively rejected, utilized, or retranslated Christianity for their own ends and needs." The relationship between missionary activity and abolitionism, capitalism, and imperialism is likewise contested. A useful overview can be found in Michael Gladwin, "Mission and Colonialism," in *The Oxford Handbook of Nineteenth-Century Christian Thought*, Joel D.S. Rasmussen, Judith Wolfe, and Johannes Zachhuber, eds. (New York: Oxford University Press, 2017), 282–304.

[69] Charles Reed, ed., *The Seventy-Ninth Annual Report of the Religious Tract Society* (London: Pardon and Son, 1878), 170–71.

[70] J.C. Garritt, "Popular Account of the Canonization of the Gods, Illustrated," *The Chinese Recorder and Missionary Journal* XXX (1899): 162.

of rural people around Singrauli, India, as consisting of "ghost or hobgoblin worship, extensively associated with witchcraft and sorcery."[71] Lamentations abound in a description of the difficulties missionaries may have in converting the "superstitious people" of southern Africa, who believe in a "host of goblins and sprites" and a number of other strange ideas.[72] The beliefs of people in Central Africa receive similar treatment in a reference guide for missionaries:

> And as beneath the dull, leaden skies of the distant north there are believed to be structures haunted by ghosts and goblins, so here the forest, with its tenantry of owls and bats, is the abode of malignant spirits, and the rustling of the foliage at eventide is their mysterious dialogue. Shadowy vagueness and superstitious terror are cardinal elements of Central African religion.[73]

Because missionaries were predominately concerned with conversion and salvation, they broadly grouped the entities of non-Christian belief systems into simple, recognizable categories like ghosts, goblins, and spirits. Quibbles about distinctions between goblins and other preternatural creatures have no place in this discourse.[74] Instead, the goblin is a suitably generic term applicable to non-Christian (and ultimately fictitious) entities that fulfills a basic didactic purpose for missionaries: to indicate that the people living in a given location believe in baseless superstitions. The association of indigenous belief systems with creatures routinely featured in

---

[71] W. Jones, "The Singrowli Mission," in *The Chronicle of the London Missionary Society for the Year 1870*, ed. Joseph Mullens (London: Directors of the London Missionary Society, 1870), 116. One author generalizes that non-Christians of India formed beliefs based on "a goblin of their own imagination" because they had never been exposed to Christianity. H. Carre Tucker, "Christianity in India," *The Foreign Missionary* XVIII (June 1859): 18. Another operating in India notes that Hindus have superstitions associated with the ashes of the dead, which they believe exist as ghosts that "often hover in goblin forms about them, not always kindly disposed to the passer-by." T.J. Scott, *Missionary Life among the Villages in India* (Cincinnati: Hitchcock and Walden, 1876), 248.

[72] James Mackinnon, *South African Traits* (Edinburgh: James Gemmell, 1887), 294. Another text on the Zulus catalogues the duties expected of young women, who by age thirteen or fourteen have been "duly instructed by the old women in all the folk-lore and goblin stories with which to frighten the younger children committed to her care." C.L. Boyd, "The Medical Missionary and Africa," *The Medical Missionary* 1, no. 1 (1891): 50.

[73] Edward Davies, *An Illustrated Handbook on Africa* (Reading: Holiness Book Concern, 1886), 12.

[74] See, generally, Kirsteen Kim and Alison Fitchett-Climenhaga, eds., *The Oxford Handbook of Mission Studies* (New York: Oxford University Press, 2022).

children's fairy tales further served to infantilize and barbarize non-Christians. An 1837 essay on Zulu beliefs even explicitly notes that these people were "of a kindred nature with some of the hobgoblin stories I used to hear in childhood."[75] Positioning indigenous belief systems as akin to superstitious folklore and fairy tales reinforced the paternalistic, civilizing ideas that were at the heart of missionary activities.

Translations of religious texts exhibit similar patterns. The act of translation is inherently one of linguistic domestication and cultural transference that bastardizes an original text. In this colonial context, translators reconfigured non-Christian beliefs using language and ideas that were familiar to them.[76] The creatures of Fairyland provided an accessible group of entities for this task. Within texts on Buddhism, for example, "goblin" is a common rendering for a handful of terminologies. One of the six realms of existence is home to the *preta*, which modern scholars broadly characterize as a hungry ghost housed in one of the "unfortunate realms" of the cosmos.[77] Colonial scholars sometimes render *preta* as goblin, placing them on this karmic tier.[78] In another translation, though, we see the *preta* rendered as a sprite and the goblin as a *pishacha*, which is a more malevolent, flesh-eating kind of demon in Hindu and Buddhist

---

[75] George Champion, "Southern Africa: Journal of Mr. Champion at Ginani," *The Missionary Herald* XXXIV, no. 1 (January 1838): 212.

[76] Bassnett and Trivedi forcefully argue that "translation does not happen in a vacuum, bit in a continuum; it is not an isolated act, it is part of an ongoing process of intercultural transfer. Moreover, translation is a highly manipulative activity that involves all kinds of stages in that process of transfer across linguistic and cultural boundaries. Translation is not an innocent, transparent activity but is highly charged with significance at every stage." Susan Bassnett and Harish Trivedi, "Introduction: Of Colonies, Cannibals and Vernaculars," in *Post-Colonial Translation: Theory and Practice*, Susan Bassnett and Harish Trivedi, eds. (New York: Routledge, 2012), 1–18. See also Abdelmajid Hannoum, "Translation and the Colonial Imaginary: Ibn Khaldūn Orientalist," *History and Theory* 42, no. 1 (February 2003): 61–81.

[77] They are "pitiful figures, possessing mouths as narrow as the eye of a needle, distended stomachs, and naked skeletal bodies" defined by their never-sated hunger. Depictions of these creatures vary considerably. Adeana McNicholl, *Of Ancestors and Ghosts: How Preta Narratives Constructed Buddhist Cosmology and Shaped Buddhist Ethics* (New York: Oxford University Press, 2024), 2–8.

[78] M.J. Walhouse, "On the Belief in Bhutas—Devil and Ghost Worship in Western India," *Journal of the Royal Anthropological Institute* V (1876): 408; Monier Williams, "Notes on Indian Folk-Lore," *The Indian Antiquary, a Journal of Oriental Research* VIII (1879): 209–11.

traditions.[79] Another translator goes in the opposite direction and characterizes the *preta* as ghosts or specters, while the goblin is equated with the *kumbhāṇḍa*: animal–human hybrids that were lesser deities.[80] Within these translations, then, authors advocated for different types of goblins and (thus) different types of Buddhism—yet the frequency of goblins being used in these translations shows their perceived accessibility for English readers.

Goblins appear in descriptions of belief systems across the globe outside of missionary contexts, too. An 1826 account of an American Indian tradition features a "spirit or goblin" named Siwanticot that smoked a pipe with such intensity that the island of Nantucket emerged from its ashes.[81] Articles published in the early years of the journal *American Anthropologist* record goblins in the belief systems of Mayans, Inuit, French Canadians, and Powhatan Indians.[82] Compilations of Japanese folk tales mention spider goblins, river goblins, goblin foxes, goblin badgers, and the goblin mountain (among others).[83] An 1840 survey of Hindu literature includes a translation and analysis of a "wild goblin scene" featuring a host of skeleton-like creatures.[84] A history of the Venḍa people of Southern Africa notes how they are haunted by gods, ghosts, and "all sorts of hobgoblins."[85] An author from the Royal Niger Company writes of the fear that locals have "of these were-wolves, and the dread of malicious goblins" such that they rarely dare "to leave the shelter of his house or compound or the

[79] Pramadá-Dása Mitra, *The Mirror of Composition* (Calcutta: C.B. Lewis, 1875), 250.

[80] H. Kern, *Manual of Indian Buddhism* (Strassburg: Karl J. Trübner, 1896), 59–60.

[81] This story circulated in a handful of newspapers, including "The Creation of the Island of Nantucket," *Alexandria Gazette*, August 24, 1826.

[82] One claims that "elves, goblins, and fairies are native on American soil." Ruth Edna Kelley, *The Book of Hallowe'en* (Boston: Lothrop, Lee & Shepard Co., 1919). See also Cyrus Thomas, "Are The Maya Hieroglyphs Phonetic?," *American Anthropologist* 6, no. 3 (1893): 241–70; Signe Rink, "The Girl and the Dogs - Further Comments," *American Anthropologist* 11, no. 7 (1898): 209–15; William Wallace Tooker, "Some Powhatan Names," *American Anthropologist* 6, no. 5 (December 1904): 670–94.

[83] Lafcadio Hearn, *Glimpses of Unfamiliar Japan*, 2 vols. (New York: Houghton Mifflin and Company, 1894); Fanny Bradley Greene, Hisa Tateishi, and Mari Kosugi, trans., "The Goblin Mountain," in *Iwaya's Fairy Tales of Old Japan* (Tokyo: Bun Yo Do To Mita, 1914).

[84] Hugh Murray et al., *Historical and Descriptive Account of British India*, vol. 2 (Edinburgh: Oliver & Boyd, 1840), 313–14.

[85] E. Gottschling, "The Bawenda: A Sketch of Their History and Customs," *The Journal of the Anthropological Institute of Great Britain and Ireland* 35 (December 1905): 371.

cheerful circle of his 'club' fire after nightfall."[86] The ethnographer and British officer A.B. Ellis writes of one Yoruba tale about a goblin (*iwin*) that punishes a dishonest girl by siccing a horde of wild beasts onto her.[87] A history of the Māori discusses how people construct a particular kind of house to catch a *taniwha*, which is rendered as "goblin."[88]

As Anglophone writers in the nineteenth century translated and synthesized religious texts from unfamiliar belief systems, they mobilized familiar English vocabulary from the world of folklore. Goblins were ubiquitous and had such widespread associations with mischief, malevolence, and playful trickery that authors could slot them into traditions featuring entities with roughly similar characteristics. Within these translations, the larger significance of goblins was contingent upon a given belief system and could be applied to creatures of different dispositions without issue: wandering ghosts of the dead, deities inhabiting the body of an earthly animal, haunters of places where terrible events once transpired, or manifestations of evil itself. These many translations and syntheses broadened the generic category of goblins to include entities within non-European belief systems, though they flattened the complexities of these religions to make them accessible to Anglophone audiences. They also implicitly aligned non-Christian belief systems with the kind of folklore and superstition associated with children and the uneducated, which contributed to the civilizing mission at the heart of colonialism.

DEMONIC GOBLINS DIMINISHED

This chapter has shown the breadth of creatures subsumed under the goblin banner during the nineteenth century. Running contrary to this trend is the goblin of Christian demonology, which had fallen out of favor in the

[86] Harry Johnston, "Report by Vice-Consul Johnson on the British Protectorate of the Oil River (Niger Delta)," 1888, 301, FO 403/76, United Kingdom Foreign Office.

[87] A.B. Ellis, *The Yoruba-Speaking Peoples of the Slave Coast of West Africa* (London: Chapman & Hall, 1894). See also J.D.Y. Peel, *Religious Encounter and the Making of the Yoruba* (Bloomington: Indiana University Press, 2000).

[88] John White, *Ancient History of the Maori, His Mythology and Traditions, Tai-Nui*, vol. V (Wellington: George Didsbury, 1888), 79. Another English-language account of a Māori tradition of first contact with English colonists notes that "the people of Mercury Bay" knew that the English "were goblins, because a boat's crew pulled ashore rowing with their backs to the land. Only goblins have eyes in the backs of their heads." William Pember Reeves, *The Long White Cloud: Ao Tea Roa*, 2nd ed. (London: Horace Marshall & Son, 1899), 83–86.

early modern period and remained a rarity in the nineteenth century. Very few texts indicate that people believed in goblins as terrestrial devils or illusions of Satan that could interfere in their lives. A few folklorists note that this association persisted, as the author of 1831's *Cambrian Superstitions* records that "it is the opinion of many" that goblins are tools of the devil.[89] Religious texts do not bear out this claim, though. When goblins appear in nineteenth-century sermons (a rarity in itself), they are typically presented as part of fantastical tales told to children or as figments of the imagination.[90] We see occasional references to the goblin of Bunyan's *The Pilgrim's Progress* or the "goblins damned" of *Hamlet*—but no accounts interrogating the dangers of goblins like those seen in centuries prior.[91] A revealing footnote from an 1896 edition of Milton's *Paradise Lost* notes that goblins are presently associated with "the idea of smallness and quaintness, but evidently no such meaning was in Milton's mind" based on the demonic goblin that guarded the gates of Hell.[92]

An updated edition of "The Pilgrim's Song" shows that the resonance of goblins as a kind of demon had fallen out of favor among the Christian faithful. Originally appearing in the second part of *The Pilgrim's Progress* (1684), the song was revised in the early twentieth century by Percy Dearmer:

> Original 1684 Lyrics
> Hobgoblin, nor foul fiend,
> Can daunt his spirit;
> He knows at the end
> Shall life inherit.

---

[89] Howells, *Cambrian Superstitions*, 12.

[90] Reginald Heber, *Sermons on the Lessons, the Gospel, or the Epistle*, vol. II (London: John Murray, 1837), 56. One of the most prolific publishers of religious texts during the nineteenth century was the Religious Tract Society. Their publications have not been fully digitized and OCR'd, but a partial collection housed on the Internet Archive gives a sense of their contents: 337 texts in total (including duplicates). Of those texts, goblins and hobgoblins appear in only four of them. Therein, their role is restricted to descriptions of folklore, other belief systems, and moralizing stories for children. Authors (at least in this sample) do not view them as a real threat to Christians.

[91] Harvey Goodwin, *The Doctrines and Difficulties of the Christian Faith*, The Hulsean Lectures (Cambridge: Deighton, Bell and Co., 1856), 209; Charles Haddon Spurgeon, *Sermons of the Rev. C.H. Spurgeon* (New York: Sheldon, Blakeman & Company, 1857), 183.

[92] John Milton, *Milton's Paradise Lost*, ed. Edward Everett Hale (New York: Longmans, Green, and Co., 1896), 65.

Revised 1906 Lyrics
Since, Lord, thou dost defend
Us with thy Spirit,
We know we at the end
Shall life inherit.

The threat of the hobgoblin and foul fiend, which had resonance for an audience of the late seventeenth century, was sufficiently diminished by the beginning of the twentieth century that Dearmer removed them from this hymn. This minimization of demonic goblins within Protestant Christianity elevated the other uses detailed in this chapter and the next one. Instead of residing in the realm of Christian demonology, goblins were embedded in folklore and folkloresque media on a global scale.

DARK AND GROTESQUE GOBLINS

Goblins had been associated with darkness and atypical appearance since the Middle Ages. These themes took on new forms in the nineteenth century, especially in discourse surrounding race and physical disability. Some argued that groups of short, dark-skinned people in Central Africa were the ultimate inspiration for creatures of European folklore that shared similar physical characteristics. Commonly called "pygmies" (from the ancient Greek), these people were depicted as descendants of the original dwarves, goblins, and/or fairies. People with physical disabilities or peculiarities could be goblins, too, in keeping with developing Victorian notions of the "freak"—though this characterization was less common than that of "dwarf" or "fairy." The connection of goblins to the grotesque (here carrying connotations of unnatural, heterogeneous distortion as well as astonishment and laughter) even extended to wildlife, especially forests.[93] Although geographic toponyms had long been associated with folkloric traditions, this arboreal goblin was situated in recently colonized geographies without stories relating to European folklore. Atypical appearance, rather than local tradition, defined them.

---

[93] On the idea of the grotesque in the nineteenth century, see Isabelle Hervouet-Farrar, "Introduction: The Grotesque in the Nineteenth Century," in *The Grotesque in the Fiction of Charles Dickens and Other 19th-Century European Novelists* (Newcastle upon Tyne: Cambridge Scholars Publishing, 2015), 1–11.

The drive to taxonomize every conceivable thing and idea in the nineteenth century was not restricted to the ivory tower.[94] Across Great Britain and the United States, elites sought to protect their interpretation of what they saw as a regular body and to favorably juxtapose it with those that were transgressive or exceptional. They wanted to see more white, able-bodied people within their empire—and those not within these parameters were subjected to persecution and dehumanization, especially those with disabilities who could not work in factories and contribute to the capitalist economy. Discrimination seeped into all levels of society and forms of media during the nineteenth century, from the novel (to be considered in the next chapter) to the freak show. These manifestations of intolerance intersected with state regulation of the body, the rising importance of image as a marker of social standing, and the normative values of the heterosexual nuclear family. Those who fell outside of these acceptable markers were called many things. Goblin was one of them.

British colonists saw opposites when comparing themselves to the people of sub-Saharan Africa: white or Black skin, civilization or barbarism, Christianity or paganism. Renowned missionary David Livingstone makes this comparison when he notes that "most writers believe the blacks to be savages, nearly all blacks believe the whites to be cannibals. The nursery hobgoblin of the one is black, of the other white."[95] Livingstone's sweeping statement about racial attitudes envelops the hobgoblin, which had lurked for so long in the shadows that, in the eyes of Livingstone, it itself had become universally black and the opposite of the white hobgoblin of Black Africans.[96] This is a clear oversimplification (as the images within this chapter and the next make clear), but it was a powerful way for Livingstone to highlight the diametric opposites between Africans and the British. This

[94] People classified as freaks "imperiled categories and dichotomies common in Western thought" like man–woman, animal–human, and those that transcended those categories were fascinating but sickening. John Woolf, "Freaks and the Victorian Imagination," in *The Palgrave Handbook of Steam Age Gothic*, ed. Clive Bloom (New York: Palgrave Macmillan, 2021), 674. See also Elizabeth Grosz, "Freaks," *Social Semiotics* 1, no. 2 (1991): 22–38.

[95] David Livingstone and Charles Livingstone, *Narrative of an Expedition to the Zambesi and Its Tributaries* (London, 1865), 67. In a similar account, Livingstone chastises women in Southern Africa for "making a hobgoblin of the white man and telling their children that they would send for him to bite them." David Livingstone, *Missionary Travels and Researches in South Africa* (London: John Murray, 1857), 465.

[96] Boyd similarly remarks in a study of people along the Zambezi River how strangers with blue eyes and red whiskers are "regarded as a hob-goblin" and cause terror among girls and children. James P. Boyd, *Stanley in Africa* (Stanley Publishing Co., 1889), 339.

anecdote was re-interpreted in a handful of texts about Livingstone, too. One author uses it to disparage the "unsophisticated" peoples of Africa; another applies the hobgoblin label to those who are "far removed from their standard of beauty."[97] The latter of these interpretations is explicit about how people conceive hobgoblins as being oppositional to beauty, which in this case inherently disparages people with Black skin.[98]

Some authors went a step further in their association of Africans with goblins and argued that they were the ultimate source of inspiration for folkloric fairies. British authors typically called these people "pygmies," though they comprised many groups spread across Central Africa around the Congo Basin. Dark-skinned and relatively short in stature, they became fodder for the imagination of colonial writers. Harry Johnston, an administrator who spent much of his life in Africa, summarizes this perspective in a 1902 article:

> The demeanour and actions of the little Congo Dwarfs at the present day remind one over and over again of the traits attributed to the brownies and goblins of our fairy stories. Their remarkable power of becoming invisible by adroit hiding in herbage and behind rocks, their probable habits in sterile or open countries of making their homes in holes and caverns, their mischievousness and their prankish good-nature, all seem to suggest that it was some race like this which inspired most of the stories of Teuton and Celt regarding the dwarfish people of quasi-supernatural attributes.[99]

Johnston provides a handful of other associations within this article that suggest a linkage between ancient European folklore and pygmies. Embedded within these notions is scientific racism that positioned Black people as inferior to their white counterparts, diminished in both physical and mental abilities.[100] Johnston's article circulated in contemporary newspapers and was not unique in its comparison of African people to the world of Fairyland. Robert Haliburton, for example, wrote a handful of

[97] W.G. Blaikie, "An Evening with Dr. Livingstone," ed. Thomas Guthrie, *The Sunday Magazine*, September 1, 1866, 292.

[98] An 1893 philological text groups the following words as cognates: demon, devil, goblin, bad, black, night, death, and bogie. R.P. Greg, *Comparative Philology of the Old and New Worlds in Relation to Archaic Speech* (London: Kegan Paul, Trench, Trübner & Co., 1893), 7.

[99] Harry Johnston, "The Pygmies and Ape Like Men of the Uganda Borderland," *The Pall Mall Magazine* 26 (1902): 178.

[100] Silver calls this "a new amalgam" and "further degradation in status." Silver, *Strange and Secret Peoples: Fairies and Victorian Consciousness*, 128–29.

works that looked for the survival of primordial "dwarf races" across the globe: the Atlas Mountains, the New World, the Pyrenees, and Central Africa. In *Dwarf Survivals, and Traditions as to Pygmy Races* (1895) he compares the Taata of the Atlas Mountains to the brownies of Scotland, the latter of which he calls "little dark-complexioned smiths."[101] Other authors use a combination of folkloric traditions and classical texts like the *Iliad* to trace the history of this diminutive "race," which are typically called dwarfs or pygmies.[102] Comparison to folkloric goblins and brownies exist within these texts, though they typically take a backseat to these other identifiers.[103] Goblins thus hovered around these descriptions but were not central to them.

The label of goblin was not restricted to people with dark skin; it could be applied to people with recognizable disabilities too. The evidence for this comes primarily from works of literary fiction, which will be considered in the next chapter, though texts from outside this genre are illuminating as well. As early as Scott's *Minstrelsy*, goblins and their kin were associated with "freakish" behavior.[104] In the early nineteenth century, this label did not have an expressly negative connotation, but instead denoted something playful, capricious, fanciful, or eccentric. The word developed more sinister connotations mid-century and was applied to people with physical, behavioral, and/or mental disabilities. The persecution and dehumanization of people with atypical bodies had existed for centuries, but it took on new forms as the scientific language of teratology recast freaks from the "prodigious monster" without clear explanation to

---

[101] He argues that this "dwarf race" existed in the "early ages of the New World" and were "objects of veneration" in the Old World. R.G. Haliburton, "Dwarf Survivals, and Traditions as to Pygmy Races," *Proceedings of the American Association for the Advancement of Science* 44 (1895): 337–44.

[102] Silver, *Strange and Secret Peoples: Fairies and Victorian Consciousness*, 117–47.

[103] C.W. Leadbeater, a pioneering theosophist, saw nature spirits as aboriginal peoples. He thinks fairies can evolve into angels within discrete hierarchies. Fairies are evolutionarily distinct from humans and have been called many things by many peoples, but "fairies" are the type "best known to man." C.W. Leadbeater, *The Hidden Side of Things* (Madras: The Theosophical Publishing House, 1913), 216; Silver, *Strange and Secret Peoples: Fairies and Victorian Consciousness*, 52. See also Morgan Daimler, "The Victorians, the Theosophists and the Cottingley Fairies: The Reshaping of Modern Fairy Belief," in *The Cottingley Fairy Photographs: New Approaches to Fairies, Fakes and Folklore*, ed. Simon Young (Pwca Books and Pamphlets, 2024), 182–95.

[104] Scott, *Minstrelsy of the Scottish Border*, 1802, 1:cvi.

abnormal and intolerable evolutionary oddities.[105] Circuses and freak shows provided venues for the exploitative display of people with these differences, and the owners of these exhibits sometimes invoked the denizens of Fairyland to sell tickets.

Two common preternatural designators within these shows were "dwarf" and "fairy," though other labels were applied to people as it suited the spectacle of a given act. Handbills use any combination of atypical traits to entice visitors, including "Adonis, the Marvellous African Dwarf" and "Little Queen Mab: The Smallest and Prettiest Dwarf ever exhibited."[106] In America, P.T. Barnum advertised the wedding of Charles Stratton (i.e., General Tom Thumb) and Lavinia Warren, two Americans with dwarfism called the "Loving Lilliputians," as a Fairy Wedding. According to a *New York Times* article, some 20,000 women lined up to view the procession, one of whom shouted, "It's like a fairy scene!"[107] The language surrounding this scene (alternatingly maternal, feminizing, cutesy, and infantilizing) brought the world of Fairyland into this real-life legal ceremony and shows the mass cultural appeal of an event that combined folkloric mythos with the spectacle of the freak show.[108] The tendency to associate women with fairies, as opposed to the more masculine goblin, is explored in the next chapter.

People with recognizable disabilities were equated with the creatures of Fairyland and dehumanized through these preternatural labels—especially those with short stature. Within circus playbills and advertisements for freak shows, though, the association of people with goblins was

---

[105] Thomson argues that the tensions of modernity shifted pre-modern practices involving the interpretation of "extraordinary bodies" toward "the secular and the rational, [and] it flourished as never before within the expanding marketplace, institutionalized under the banner of the freak show." Rosemarie Garland-Thomson, "Introduction: From Wonder to Error - A Genealogy of Freak Discourse in Modernity," in *Freakery: Cultural Spectacles of the Extraordinary Body*, ed. Rosemarie Garland Thomson (New York: New York University Press, 1996), 4. See, generally, Cohen, "Monster Culture (Seven Theses)"; Jeffrey Andrew Weinstock, "Introduction: A Genealogy of Monster Theory," in *The Monster Theory Reader*, ed. Jeffrey Andrew Weinstock (Minneapolis: University of Minnesota Press, 2020), 1–36.

[106] "Unparalleled Programme of Holiday Entertainments," nineteenth century, https://wellcomecollection.org/works/kq66hx8j/items; "P.T. Barnum's Own and Only Greatest Show on Earth," 1879, ht4210529_1, The Ringling Museum.

[107] "The Loving Lilliputians," *The New York Times*, February 11, 1863.

[108] Lori Merish, "Cuteness and Commodity Aesthetics: Tom Thumb and Shirley Temple," in *Freakery: Cultural Spectacles of the Extraordinary Body*, ed. Rosemarie Garland-Thomson (New York: New York University Press, 1996), 192–95.

uncommon. I was unable to find any person within these exhibits advertised as "goblins" during the nineteenth century, a paucity that was frankly
surprising. A man named Vernon L. Sweet was apparently billed as the
"Goblin Man" in the 1920s for the Ringling Bros. and Barnum & Bailey
Side Show, though I was unable to locate further documentation about
him.[109] Robert Heller, an Australian musician and magician, deployed a
"Goblin Drum Corps" in the 1870s, though the emphasis here was not
on the disfigured appearance of any person, but the seeming invisibility of
a musician playing on a suspended drum.[110] I suspect a more systematic
examination of ephemera from circuses and freak shows will yield further
materials, but the scope of this book is such that I am unable to undertake
this deep dive myself. This is not to say that the goblin label was never
applied to people in freak shows and circuses, but that it was rare in this
context when compared to other Fairyland identifiers. The owners of
these exhibits, and presumably the audiences they sought to attract, differentiated between goblins and the dwarfs, giants, and fairies advertised
in their acts.

The association of non-normative bodies with goblins existed in other
contexts, though. An 1887 travelogue documenting a trip to Asia Minor,
for example, recounts the steadfast devotion and work ethic of a passen-
ger's servant, who was nicknamed Goblin because of his short stature.[111]
Editions of *Webster's Dictionary* from the mid-nineteenth century define a
goblin as a gnome (among others) and a gnome as "a dwarf; a goblin; a
person of small stature or misshapen features, or of a strange appearance."[112]
Newspaper articles associate goblins with various forms of freakery, as in
descriptions of "ghosts, goblins, freaks and fairies" or "freaks, fairies and
goblins." Even if goblins were not explicitly named in playbills or advertisements for freak shows, they were nonetheless hovering around the bor-

[109] "The Final Curtain," *The Billboard*, July 10, 1943.

[110] "Heller's Wonders," *The Argus*, February 5, 1870; Ryan Howard, *Punch and Judy in 19th Century America: A History and Biographical Dictionary* (Jefferson: McFarland & Company, Inc., 2014), 39; Jessie Fillerup, "Robert Heller's Magic Mystery Tours," *19th Century Music* 47, no. 1 (Summer 2023): 3–32. On Australian fairy tales, see Rebecca-Anne Do Rozario, "Fairies in a Strange Land: Colonization, Migration, and the Invention of the Australian Fairy Tale," in *The Fairy Tale World*, ed. Andrew Teverson (New York: Routledge, 2019), 368–77.

[111] William Cochran, *Pen and Pencil in Asia Minor* (London: Sampson Low, Marston, Searle, & Rivington, 1887), 407–9.

[112] Noah Webster, Chauncey A. Goodrich, and Noah Porter, *Dr. Webster's Complete Dictionary of the English Language* (London: Bell and Daldy, 1864), 576.

ders of this ill-defined grouping of atypical people that provided a spectacle for those without (or with less recognizable) disabilities. These ideas, though admittedly limited in this chapter, are reinforced by literature considered in the next.

More evidence attests to the use of "goblin" as a descriptor of natural environments. Folkloric traditions had long inspired geographic place-names, and the stories behind these sites were documented with increasing frequency in the nineteenth century, especially within the pages of travel guidebooks. These texts show that goblin-related toponyms existed for both natural and manmade locations in the Anglophone world. When authors consider places recently colonized or being colonized, though, the evocation of goblins shifts. Because these sites did not have Anglophone traditions of fairy lore, authors use the goblin to mark a particularly grotesque or abnormal aesthetic (especially forests) that defies their expectation for a given natural phenomenon. Through this goblin label, authors colonized natural landscapes with the creatures of Fairyland.

Placenames related to folk creatures and beliefs stretch back as far as recorded history.[113] As the tourism industry bloomed in the 1830s, spurred by the rise of a middle class with disposable income, guidebooks recorded these names and their purported origins. In one forested area in Clevedon (southwest England), for example, tradition held that a girl had once been taken to Fairyland when she wandered into a small valley, but that she was freed because she had been holding a primrose: hence the name "Goblin Combe." *Chilcott's Clevedon New Guide* describes this site (when compared to nearby Brockley Combe) as a "wilder and more sequestered scene, but presenting the same features of sylvan beauty."[114] Similar descriptions are seen in guidebooks for Scotland, where visitors to the Trossachs can find Goblin's Cave (*Coir-nan-Uriskin*), which derives its name from the belief that it is the abode of the *Urisks*, a "race of sprites"

---

[113] Jeremy Harte, "Names and Tales: On Folklore and Place Names," *Folklore* 130, no. 4 (2019).

[114] *Chilcott's Clevedon New Guide*, 2nd ed. (Bristol: J. Chilcott, 1840), 46. Later editions of this guide replace "sequestered" with "romantic," though they retain the remainder of the description. Such narratives are tied up in nationalist discourse, too, which simultaneously present the English as lovers of nature and valorize the English defeat of the villainous wolves lurking within their forests. Jeremy Harte, "Forest Murmurs: Wood and Wild in the Making of England," in *Folklore and Nation in Britain and Ireland*, Matthew Cheeseman and Carina Hart, eds. (New York: Routledge, 2022), 48–62.

akin to brownies.[115] So too can visitors to Chester encounter the "Goblin's Tower," the name of which is unexplained beyond "some *ghostly* reason."[116] Descriptions like these reinforced the appeal of folklore for tourists and, more broadly, its relevance to national identity.[117]

Goblins were also used to describe locations that authors perceived as atypical and reminiscent of the eeriness associated with supernatural hauntings. These descriptions were most common in the late nineteenth century and not restricted to the genre of the guidebook. Peculiar trees were the most likely to receive this designation. A scientific journal article from 1883 asks the reader "who has not seen a mean, shabby, little oak tree—a vegetable hobgoblin, and living libel on its species—yet literally covered, season by season, with acorns?"[118] Another author reminisces

---

[115] *The Scottish Tourist, and Itinerary*, 4th ed. (Edinburgh: Stirling and Kenney, 1832), 84–85; *The Trosachs and Loch Lomond* (Edinburgh: Oliver & Boyd, 1860), 44–45. Denham records the presence of "Goblin Field" near Mold, Flintshire, as well. Denham, *The Denham Tracts: A Collection of Folklore*, 78.

[116] Thomas Hughes, *The Stranger's Handbook to Chester and Its Environs* (Chester: Thomas Catherall, 1851), 24. In Wales, too, Denbigh Castle has its own Goblin Tower. "Garden Fete," *North Wales Chronicle*, July 5, 1873, 1. See also James De Mille, "The Goblin Tower: A Tale of Tuscany," *Gleason's Pictorial* VII, no. 15 (October 14, 1854): 230.

[117] Murray's guidebooks in particular were founded "on the illusion of a collective national identity" for English people visiting continental Europe. As a genre, though, there was variation in how national identity factored into descriptions of tourist destinations. Rebecca Butler, "'Can Any One Fancy Travellers without Murray's Universal Red Books'? Mariana Starke, John Murray and 1830s' Guidebook Culture," *The Yearbook of English Studies* 48 (2018): 157. See also Rudy Koshar, "'What Ought to Be Seen': Tourists' Guidebooks and National Identities in Modern Germany and Europe," *Journal of Contemporary History* 33, no. 3 (July 1998): 323–40. One could also encounter a "Goblin Hill" in northern Massachusetts with a "reputation for horrid sights," especially for the travelers crossing it at night. "Goblin Hill," *The United States Gazette*, February 5, 1830. The process of mapping placenames associated with goblins is a compelling one, but it is unfortunately too onerous to be included in the scope of this project. A brief examination of goblin-based placenames in the United States recorded by the United States Geological Survey shows a few locations in the east coast (Appalachia broadly) but a greater clustering in the west coast beginning with the Rocky Mountains—and a clear paucity of them in the Great Plains. Given the association of goblins with forests and mountains, this result is perhaps expected, though a more detailed survey that considers other sources is needed before firmer conclusions can be made. The methods of Houlbrook and Young provide a useful template for larger mapping projects like these. Ceri Houlbrook, *The Magic of Coin-Trees from Religion to Recreation* (New York: Palgrave Macmillan, 2018); Young, *The Boggart: Folklore, History, Place-Names and Dialect*, 51–76. Collaborative projects like ISEBEL (http://search.isebel.eu/), which focuses on the Netherlands, Denmark, and northeastern Germany, show the utility of mapping out oral traditions alongside GIS data.

[118] "Waste," *The Journal of Science* V (July 1883): 380.

about a "hobgoblin tree" that grew on a particular patch of dirt near the playground of his school.[119] A late nineteenth-century travelogue describes a goblin's baobab tree that looked "like a small grey tower, with a black cavity gouged in one side" in pale light.[120] The "Goblin Tree" of Wistow (Leicestershire) was a "huge and lightning-blasted oak, standing with gaunt arms extending like some bleached skeleton" that only the stout of heart could pass without fear.[121] These trees deviated from what authors perceived as being a normal tree and thus labeled as a goblin variant.

Entire species and locations sometimes fell under this designator. A study of Japanese folk traditions broadly claims that Japan, "like the tropical world, has its goblin trees," including varieties within the hemp and willow families that are associated with haunting spirits.[122] The "twisted trunks" of olive trees in Italy could take "grotesque goblin shapes" in the moonlight.[123] The marshy, forested home of a flock of blue herons deep within the New Hampshire wilderness is also a "goblin town. . sixty feet high in gnarled beeches among rock maples and scattered firs."[124] An American war correspondent traveling through the Central Asian Steppe describes a goblin forest and its ominous appearance:

> While riding back to the path we were following, I remarked that the sax-aul here, although so large, owing probably to the greater richness and humidity of the soil or sand, still maintained its peculiar characteristics—hard, dry,

[119] Josiah Thomas Slugg, *Woodhouse Grove School: Memorials and Reminiscences* (London: T. Woolmer, 1885), 32.

[120] Walter Montagu Kerr, *The Far Interior: A Narrative of Travel and Adventure*, vol. II (London: Sampson Low, 1886), 93.

[121] Edmund Bogg, *The Old Kingdom of Elmet: York and the Ainsty District* (London: John Heywood, 1902), 233. This tree was felled in the early twenty-first century, and according to one local historian, "...they say it was because the tree had become too dangerous, but I can't help but think it might have had something to do with the farmer and his staff, having to work the fields on late autumn evenings, sensing the prickle of their hair standing up on the back of their neck, with a feeling almost as if someone was watching them from the branches of the Goblin Tree." "History of Wistow Village," Wistow Parish Council, 2022, https://wistowparishcouncil.gov.uk/wp-content/uploads/2022/09/History-of-Wistow-Village2-1.pdf.

[122] Hearn, *Glimpses of Unfamiliar Japan*, 1894, 2:358–59.

[123] Elizabeth Robins Pennell, "Italy, From a Tricycle," *The Century* XXXI (1886): 855.

[124] This author admits that such associations are "fancy," but "the noise [of the herons] was there, and it seems as reasonable to ascribe it to goblins as to any wild creatures one meets in an ordinary tramp in the woods. And indeed the birds that made it are no ordinary wild creatures of the woods." Winthrop Packard, "The Blue Herons of New Hampshire; Their Shy Character and Their Far Retreats," *Boston Evening Transcript*, July 28, 1915, 19.

knotty, scrubby, gnarly and twisted as a ram's horn.[125] Half of it seemed to be dead or dying, and as the spring leaves had not yet come out, the whole presented a bleak forbidding aspect, like a goblin forest that had been scorched and withered by some terrible curse.[126]

Goblin trees transcended species and geography. An 1886 article in the children's magazine *St. Nicholas*, which circulated widely in newspapers (often in columns intended for children), details the peculiarities and uses of the Yucca plant of the American southwest, which is "a curious, mis-shapen, grotesque and twisted plant that seems more like a goblin tree than a real one."[127] Thousands of miles from the American southwest, goblin trees could likewise be found in the rainy climate of the North Island of New Zealand. A travel handbook from the late nineteenth century notes the forest around Mount Taranaki as having a "weird and peculiar" appearance that justified its name of the "Goblin Bush."[128] A newspaper article from 1912 references its "gnarled and moss-covered" trees that bring to mind Longfellow's "Evangeline," and one photographer referred to this site as an "ancient forest" that transports visitors "back to the youth of the world—a million years ago."[129] The peculiar appearance of these moss-covered trees created a primordial forest reflecting those once home to goblins.[130]

The above accounts of goblin forests represent very different ecologies, from the steppe of Central Asia to the deserts of the southwestern United States to the forests of New Zealand. Underlying taxonomies and ecosystems mattered less to these authors than the aesthetic of these trees, the twisted and gnarled appearance of which brought to mind the deformities associated with goblins. These environments were sometimes called

---

[125] This is *Haloxylon ammodendron*, which has a handful of naming conventions similar to "saxaul" or "saksaul."

[126] Januarius Aloysius MacGahan, *Campaigning on the Oxus* (London: Sampson Low, Marston, Low, and Searle, 1874), 46.

[127] "The Newspaper Plant," *St. Nicholas* XIII (May 1886): 553.

[128] F.W. Pennefather, *A Handbook for Travellers in New Zealand*, Murray's Foreign Handbooks (London: John Murray, 1893), 65.

[129] "The Mt. Egmont Line," *Taranaki Daily News*, February 6, 1912.

[130] Later in the twentieth and twenty-first centuries, New Zealand scientists argued about whether the "Goblin Forest" comprised a specific combination of species and environmental characteristics. The term is widely used today in promotional materials for the area around Mount Taranaki. J. Bastow Wilson, "Cockayne & the Mt. Egmont 'Goblin Forest' - Reply," *Botanical Society of Otago Newsletter* 27 (2001): 5–6.

goblin forests and sometimes compared to the kinds of locations reminiscent of goblins. The underlying peculiarity of these places varied, too, though they share a certain atypical characteristic that brought to mind the goblin more so than, say, a fairy or elf.

Although the designation of goblin landscapes was most common for forests, other natural phenomena could fulfill this criterion too.[131] *Schistostega pennata*, a luminous moss, was colloquially called "goblin gold" because of its curious-yet-beautiful glow within dark caves.[132] *Mitsukurina owstoni*, a shark catalogued by an American scientist at the University of Tokyo in the late nineteenth century, was later named a "goblin shark" based on its peculiar appearance and one of its Japanese names: *tenguzame* (derived from the *tengu*).[133] One area of Yellowstone National Park was referred to as "Goblin Land" or "Goblin Labyrinths" because of its many hoodoos.[134] The superintendent of Yellowstone sketched these "many weird wonders of erosion" in an 1881 report and wrote that "nearly every form, animate or inanimate, real or chimerical ever actually seen or conjured by the imagination may here be observed."[135] Other guidebooks for Yellowstone from the late nineteenth century

---

[131] It is rare for human settlements to bear the goblin label, although it was used to name ancient or haunted structures within towns (like the house in Sutton Bonington called "Hobgoblins"). The sole exception I could locate from the nineteenth century is the settlement of Goblintown and its accompanying creek in modern Virginia. Today, it is best known for its grist mill, but I was unable to locate the ultimate point of (presumed) folkloric origin for this site, which is documented in newspapers as early as the mid-eighteenth century. The proximity of Goblintown to Fairy Stone State Park speaks to some degree of folkloric inspiration in the area; I hope that a deeper dive into the archives of the Clarke County Historical Association will yield additional results. "New York," *The Pennsylvania Journal*, September 6, 1764, 2; "Round the Villages. Sutton Bonington," *Loughborough Echo*, September 5, 1913, 6.

[132] Abel Joel Grout, *Mosses with Hand-Lens and Microscope: A Non-Technical Hand-Book of the More Common Mosses of the Northeastern United States*, vol. 4 (New York City: Mount Pleasant Press, 1903), 187.

[133] An article from 1910 claims that the shark "is certainly grotesque, well deserving of his sobriquet 'goblin.'" Edward J. Wheeler, ed., "The Newly Discovered Goblin Shark" XLVIII (June 1910): 402–3. The now-extinct genus *Scapanorhynchus* was identified as a "goblin shark" (likely because of its atypically flattened snout) as well. Frederick Chapman, *Descriptions and Revisions of the Cretaceous and Tertiary Fish-Remains of New Zealand* (Marcus F. Marks, 1918), 9, 29.

[134] P.W. Norris, "Fifth Annual Report of the Superintendent of the Yellowstone National Park" (Washington: Department of the Interior, 1881), 47.

[135] P.W. Norris, "The Yellowstone National Park," *Science* 2, no. 43 (1881): 186–87.

referred to the area as a "weirdly wild region," a "strangle locality," and a "ghostly region" because of these rock formations.[136] Unlike, say, Icelandic traditions that saw elves living within peculiarly shaped rocks, these goblin rocks reflected the peculiar appearance and eeriness of their preternatural inspiration (Fig. 4.3).[137]

Although these landscapes did not have longstanding English-language traditions of goblins or other creatures from Fairyland, their visitors and colonizers brought the goblin to them. In the case of the western United States and Oceania especially, colonial settlers saw certain corners of an expansive wilderness as natural embodiments of the goblin's grotesqueness or eeriness. Such characterizations allowed for the transplantation of Fairyland from the Old World across the high seas, where traditions associated with fairies were less common.[138] Make no mistake, many of these landscapes had incredible significance to the belief systems of indigenous peoples.[139] For colonial newcomers, though, these environments did not have the picturesque stone ruins or decades-old fairy traditions of the Old World—so they invoked the goblin as a familiar creature that was reminiscent of their abnormal appearance.[140]

The association of goblins with a certain aesthetic, ranging from the spooky to the unnatural to the downright ugly, extended to manmade works as well. Wyke Bayliss, a renowned painter of churches during the Victorian era, condemned any aesthetic he disliked as a hobgoblin. After spending a few chapters on the "Hobgoblins by the Great Masters," he rejoiced in leaving them behind and never revisiting them again:

[136] Henry J. Winser, *The Yellowstone National Park* (New York: G.P. Putnam's Sons, 1883), 84; Hezekiah Butterworth, *Zigzag Journeys in the Western States of America* (London: Dean & Son Publishers, 1884), 248–51; A.B. Guptill, *Yellowstone Park Guide* (St. Paul: F. Jay Haynes, 1894), 78.

[137] Matthias Egeler, Dagrún Ósk Jónsdóttir, and Jón Jónsson, "Patterns in Icelandic Elf Hills," *Folklore* 135, no. 3 (September 2024): 388–414.

[138] In Australia, attempts at cultivating a "distinctive fairy-tale tradition" in the late nineteenth and early twentieth centuries "largely failed." Danielle Wood, "Renegotiating 'Once Upon a Time:' Fairy Tales in Contemporary Australian Writing," in *The Fairy Tale World*, ed. Andrew Teverson (New York: Routledge, 2019), 378.

[139] See, for example, G.N. Devy and Geoffrey V. Davis, *Environment and Belief Systems* (London: Routledge, 2020). Like any archaeological artifact, a landscape is a "cultural product." It is dynamic, and has been "colonised, developed, declined, and endured decay, damage and reuse." Martin Brown and Pat Bowen, "The Last Refuge of the Faeries: Archaeology and Folklore in East Sussex," in *Archaeology and Folklore*, Amy Gazin-Schwartz and Cornelius Holtorf, eds. (New York: Routledge, 1999), 251.

[140] Paul Manning, "No Ruins. No Ghosts," *Preternature: Critical and Historical Studies on the Preternatural* 6, no. 1 (2017): 63–92.

Fig. 4.3 Goblin landscapes of Yellowstone National Park and New Zealand. (Left) The rocky hoodoos of the "Goblin Labyrinths" are depicted in an annual report of the Superintendent of Yellowstone. Image courtesy of the Open Parks Network and Clemson University (P.W. Norris, "Annual Report of the Superintendent of the Yellowstone National Park to the Secretary of the Interior for the Year 1880" (Washington: Department of the Interior, 1881), 8. Accessible here: http://purl.clemson.edu/E8A812FFBFC9F127695ED1FE79DF5C38). (Right) The goblin forest of Mount Taranaki on the North Island of New Zealand. Image courtesy of the Museum of New Zealand | Te Papa Tongarewa (James Walter Chapman-Taylor, "The Goblin Bush," 1920s, O.002450, Museum of New Zealand | Te Papa Tongarewa. Accessible here: https://collections.tepapa.govt. nz/object/224484)

Let us have done with these Hobgoblins. We will shut up our library, or at least will lock the offending bookcase. We will go to no more exhibitions to see the apotheosis of ugliness—landscapes of mud painted with mud; bundles of rags held cleverly together upon lay-figures; or curious affectations of eccentricity which give pleasure only in proportion as they astonish. Above all things we will not visit Florence; or if we do we will spend our mornings there without guide-books and try to forget the name of [Simone] Memmi.[141]

As in centuries prior, authors continued to associate goblins with the harmful, peculiar, and supernatural across contexts and genres. Goblins were often metaphors for harmful ideas, as in the "goblin of folly and prejudice" or the widely cited Emerson quotation, "...a foolish consistency is the hobgoblin of little minds, adored by little statesmen and philosophers and divines."[142] Goblins could also indicate a supernatural or superhuman quality (even a positive one), like the work ethic of politician Amos Kendall, who conducted business "of goblin extent and with goblin speed, which makes men look about... with superstitious wonder."[143] This could apply to animals, too, as is the case with the unnerving gaze of owls that "suggests goblins and graveyards and witchcraft."[144] Doctors disparaged belief in goblins, astrology, and palmistry (among others) as being contrary to the tenets of evidence-based practices.[145] One even said that physicians ought not to speak of "hobgoblin-pathy" and other forms of pseudo-medicine like Indian-pathy and homeopathy.[146] Disagreeable politicians and their arguments remained goblins, like an uppity "anti-English hobgoblin," the "hobgoblin argument" of communism, or the "hobgoblin of re-distribution of seats" in British parliament.[147] One political car-

[141] Wyke Bayliss, *The Higher Life in Art, With a Chapter on Hobgoblins by the Great Masters* (London: David Bogue, 1879), 139.

[142] Ralph Waldo Emerson, "Self-Reliance," in *Essays* (Boston: James Munroe and Company, 1841), 47; J.R. Kendrick, "The Spectre of Negro Rule," *The Andover Review* XII (December 1889): 606.

[143] This quotation comes from an 1834 letter transcribed partially in "Review of Stickney's Autobiography of Amos Kendall," *The North American Review* 116, no. 238 (1873): 166.

[144] "A Talk About Owls," *Hull Evening News*, May 24, 1894.

[145] "Popular Lecture on Animal Magnetism," *The New England Journal of Medicine* 15, no. 22 (January 1837): 349–52.

[146] "Medical Miscellany," *The New England Journal of Medicine* 88, no. 4 (January 1873): 95.

[147] Henry Wikoff, *The Adventures of a Roving Diplomatist* (New York: W.P. Fetridge & Co., 1857). Speeches from the House of Commons dated to February 14, 1879 and August 4, 1880 are the source of these latter two quotations. They are available online at https://hansard.parliament.uk/Commons. Eminent historian Charles A. Beard, in a 1938 speech to the House Naval Affairs Committee, argues that the current administration sought to foment war by falsely arguing that "the Fascist goblins of Europe" pose a credible threat to nations in the Americas. "Life on the American Newsfront: Historian and Admiral Join the War Debate," *Life*, February 21, 1938, 16.

toon from 1913 even shows a goblinified William Redfield, the United States Secretary of Commerce, menacingly showing workers how his tariffs will not affect their wages beneath the Annie-inspired tagline, "The goblin will get you if you don't watch out!" (Fig. 4.4)

Fig. 4.4 "The Goblin Will Get You If You Don't Watch Out!" Cover image from a 1913 issue of *Puck Magazine*. It bears the caption, "The goblin will get you if you don't watch out!" Image (cropped) courtesy of the Library of Congress (L.M. Glackens, "The Goblin Will Get You If You Don't Watch Out!" *Puck Magazine* 73, no. 1892 (1913): cover. Accessible here: https://www.loc.gov/item/2011649597/)

Even as folklorists argued about the precise nature of goblins and hob-goblins, authors outside of this relatively narrow academic world showed little concern for these distinctions. Instead, the goblin existed as a designator for people, natural phenomena, objects, and ideas that transgressed what they perceived as normal or right. Those with dark skin and physical disabilities were sometimes subsumed under this goblin banner by authors (most of whom were able-bodied white men) who saw these differences as harmful or subhuman abnormalities. This same label could be applied to the natural world, especially to gnarled or misshapen trees. Goblin forests could thus exist in spaces without longstanding folkloric traditions associated with these creatures; their peculiar appearance was enough to justify this label. Ideas, arguments, works of art, and the people behind them could similarly be grouped under the ever-expanding goblin banner.

Conclusion

When the authors of the first edition of the *Oxford English Dictionary* (then called *A New English Dictionary on Historical Principles*) confronted the lexemes "goblin" and "hobgoblin" in the fourth and fifth volumes of their trailblazing collection (published in 1901), they synthesized a handful of traditions that had developed over the last few hundred years. They define the former as the following:

1. A mischievous and ugly demon.
2. *attrib.* and *Comb.* a. attributive, passing into an adj. (of, pertaining to, or suitable for goblins), as *goblin appearance, cave, cheek, sport, story, word*; b. appositive, as *goblin man*, c. instrumental, as *goblin-haunted, -peopled* adjs.[148]

The definitions of hobgoblin are more numerous:

1. A mischievous, tricksy imp or sprite; another name for Puck or Robin Goodfellow; hence, a terrifying apparition, a bogy.
2. *fig.* An object which inspires superstitious dread or apprehension; a bogy, bugbear.

---

[148] Derived from goblin are rarer forms like goblinish, goblinism, goblinize, and goblinry. These definitions are accompanied by historical examples dating back to Orderic Vitalus. *Oxford English Dictionary*, 1st edition, IV:266.

3. *humorous*. An animal that causes terror.
4. *attrib.* and *adj.* Or, pertaining to, or connected with hobgoblins; like a hobgoblin.[149]

These definitions apply to many of the ideas encountered in this chapter. Goblins and hobgoblins served as overarching categories for spirits, often mischievous or malevolent, that were applicable across cultures. Some folklorists sought to locate goblins as a more specific category of creatures associated with household labor, geographical location, or national origin—though there was no agreement about how to taxonomize these inhabitants of Fairyland. The works of Shakespeare loomed large in discourse about hobgoblins in particular, as some saw it as a distinctly English creature. This process of classification was part of a larger nationalist discourse in which authors (intentionally or not) sought to define the quintessential nature of people and their nations in a sea of disparate folkloric traditions. Such distinctions were of little relevance to those writing in areas far removed from European folk traditions. Instead, these authors used the goblin as an accessible category of creatures across belief systems that they saw as reminiscent in some way of its folkloric namesake.

The ubiquity of goblins and hobgoblins—however defined—led to additional uses that revolved around fear, malintent, grotesque appearance, and the supernatural. These associations had long existed, though they took on new forms in keeping with evolving ideas about appropriate conduct and appearance. Authors, drawing on theories of scientific racism, occasionally presented Black Africans as reminiscent of goblins and theorized that they could have been descendants of the fairies described in European folklore. They also applied the label of goblin to those of short stature or physical deformity, though in the case of circuses and freak shows the term "dwarf" "or fairy" was preferred. Plants and animals could likewise be subsumed under a goblin aesthetic that defied expectations for how that lifeform ought to look.

The characteristics that authors of the nineteenth century associated with goblins in this chapter both reflected and influenced developments in the world of literature and theater. It is to this rich corpus of works that we now turn.

---

[149] Hobgoblin also has variants like hobgoblinet, hobgoblinism, and hobgoblinry. *Oxford English Dictionary*, 1ˢᵗ edition, V:317.

REFERENCES

Alam, Eram, Dorothy Roberts, and Natalie Shibley, eds. 2024. *Ordering the Human: The Global Spread of Racial Science*. New York: Columbia University Press.

Alexandria Gazette. 1826. The Creation of the Island of Nantucket. August 24.

Almqvist, Bo. 1991. Irish Migratory Legends on the Supernatural: Sources, Studies and Problems. *Béaloideas* 59:1–43.

Almqvist, Éilís Ní Dhuibhne. 2022. Pioneers: Thomas Crofton Croker and the Brothers Grimm. In *Grimm Ripples: The Legacy of the Grimms' Deutsche Sagen in Northern Europe*, 259–287. Leiden: Brill.

Anderson, Robert. 2006. *British Universities Past and Present*. New York: Bloomsbury Academic.

Asma, Stephen T. 2009. *On Monsters: An Unnatural History of Our Worst Fears*. New York: Oxford University Press.

Bassnett, Susan, and Harish Trivedi. 2012. Introduction: Of Colonies, Cannibals and Vernaculars. In *Post-Colonial Translation: Theory and Practice*, ed. Susan Bassnett and Harish Trivedi, 1–18. New York: Routledge.

Baycroft, Timothy. 2012. Introduction. In *Folklore and Nationalism in Europe during the Long Nineteenth Century*, ed. Timothy Baycroft and David Hopkin, 1–10. Leiden: Brill.

Bayliss, Wyke. 1879. *The Higher Life in Art, With a Chapter on Hobgoblins by the Great Masters*. London: David Bogue.

Bayne, Peter. 1873. Milton. *The Contemporary Review* XXII:427–460.

Beckford, William. 1859. *Memoirs of William Beckford*. II Vols. London: Charles J. Skeet.

Berg, J. F., and Joseph Barker. 1854. *Great Discussion of the Origin, Authority, and Tendency of the Bible*. Boston: J.B. Yerrinton & Son.

Bihet, Francesca. 2020. Fairies and Folklore: The History of Fairies in the Folklore Society, 1878–1845. Doctoral Dissertation, University of Chichester.

Blaikie, W. G. 1866. An Evening with Dr. Livingstone. Edited by Thomas Guthrie. *The Sunday Magazine*, September 1, 291–96.

Blake, William. 1816–1820. *The Goblin*. Watercolor. The Morgan Library & Museum.

Bogg, Edmund. 1902. *The Old Kingdom of Elmet: York and the Ainsty District*. London: John Heywood.

Boyd, James P. 1889. *Stanley in Africa*. Stanley Publishing Co.

Boyd, C. L. 1891. The Medical Missionary and Africa. *The Medical Missionary* 1 (1): 48–50.

Brown, Martin, and Pat Bowen. 1999. The Last Refuge of the Faeries: Archaeology and Folklore in East Sussex. In *Archaeology and Folklore*, ed. Amy Gazin-Schwartz and Cornelius Holtorf, 246–263. New York: Routledge.

Buchan, Patrick. 1873. *The Guidman O' Inglismill, and the Fairy Bride*. Edinburgh: Edmonston and Douglas.

Burke, Peter. 2004. History and Folklore: A Historiographical Survey. *Folklore* 115 (2): 113–139.

Butler, Rebecca. 2018. 'Can Any One Fancy Travellers without Murray's Universal Red Books'? Mariana Starke, John Murray and 1830s' Guidebook Culture. *The Yearbook of English Studies* 48:148–170.

Butterworth, Hezekiah. 1884. *Zigzag Journeys in the Western States of America*. London: Dean & Son Publishers.

Carruthers, Gerard, and Alan Rawes, eds. 2003. *English Romanticism and the Celtic World*. New York: Cambridge University Press.

Champion, George. January 1838. Southern Africa: Journal of Mr. Champion at Ginani. *The Missionary Herald* XXXIV (1): 208–220.

Channa, Subhadra Mitra. 2024. Introduction: Establishing an Empire. In *Colonial Anthropology: Technologies and Discourses of Dominance, 1886–1936*, ed. Subhadra Mitra Channa and Lancy Lobo, 1–23. New York: Routledge.

Chapman, Frederick. 1918. *Descriptions and Revisions of the Cretaceous and Tertiary Fish-Remains of New Zealand*. Marks: Marcus F.

Chapman-Taylor, James Walter. The Goblin Bush, 1920s. O.002450. Museum of New Zealand | Te Papa Tongarewa.

Cheeseman, Matthew, and Carina Hart, eds. 2022. *Folklore and Nation in Britain and Ireland*. New York: Routledge.

Chilcott's Clevedon New Guide. 1840. 2nd ed. Bristol: J. Chilcott.

Cobley, Frederick. 1882. *On Foot Through Wharfedale*. Otley: William Walker and Sons.

Cochran, William. 1887. *Pen and Pencil in Asia Minor*. London: Sampson Low, Marston, Searle, & Rivington.

Cohen, Jeffrey Jerome. 1996. Monster Culture (Seven Theses). In *Monster Theory: Reading Culture*, 3–25. Minneapolis: University of Minnesota Press.

Croker, Thomas Crofton. 1825–1828. *Fairy Legends and Traditions of the South of Ireland*. 3 Vols. London: John Murray.

Curley, Thomas M. 2009. *Samuel Johnson, the Ossian Fraud and the Celtic Revival in Great Britain and Ireland*. New York: Cambridge University Press.

Daimler, Morgan. 2024. The Victorians, the Theosophists and the Cottingley Fairies: The Reshaping of Modern Fairy Belief. In *The Cottingley Fairy Photographs: New Approaches to Fairies, Fakes and Folklore*, ed. Simon Young, 182–195. Pwca Books and Pamphlets.

Daunton, Martin. 2000. Society and Economic Life. In *The Nineteenth Century: The British Isles, 1815–1901*, ed. Colin Matthew, 41–84. New York: Oxford University Press.

Davies, Edward. 1886. *An Illustrated Handbook on Africa*. Reading: Holiness Book Concern.

De Mille, James. October 14, 1854. The Goblin Tower: A Tale of Tuscany. *Gleason's Pictorial* VII (15): 230.

Dearmer, Percy. 1906. *The English Hymnal.* London: Henry Frowde.

Denham, Michael Aislabie. 1895. *The Denham Tracts: A Collection of Folklore.* Edited by James Hardy. London: The Folklore Society.

Devy, G. N., and Geoffrey V. Davis. 2020. *Environment and Belief Systems.* London: Routledge.

Do Rozario, Rebecca-Anne. 2019. Fairies in a Strange Land: Colonization, Migration, and the Invention of the Australian Fairy Tale. In *The Fairy Tale World*, ed. Andrew Teverson, 368–377. New York: Routledge.

Dorson, Richard M. 1955. The First Group of British Folklorists. *The Journal of American Folklore* 68 (267): 1–8.

Durkheim, Émile, and Marcel Mauss. 1967. *Primitive Classification.* Edited by Rodney Needham. Chicago: University of Chicago Press.

Egeler, Matthias, Dagrún Ósk Jónsdóttir, and Jón Jónsson. September 2024. Patterns in Icelandic Elf Hills. *Folklore* 135 (3): 388–414.

Ellis, A. B. 1894. *The Yoruba-Speaking Peoples of the Slave Coast of West Africa.* London: Chapman & Hall.

Emerson, Ralph Waldo. 1841. Self-Reliance. In *Essays*, 35–74. Boston: James Munroe and Company.

Evans-Wentz, Walter. 1911. *The Fairy-Faith in Celtic Countries.* London: Henry Frowde.

Fiedler, Leslie. 1978. *Freaks: Myths and Images of the Secret Self.* New York: Simon & Schuster.

Fillerup, Jessie. Summer 2023. Robert Heller's Magic Mystery Tours. *19th Century Music* 47 (1): 3–32.

Fredrickson, George M. 2002. *Racism: A Short History.* Princeton: Princeton University Press.

Fuller, C. J. 2023. *Anthropologist and Imperialist: H.H. Risley and British India, 1873–1911.* New York: Routledge.

Garland-Thomson, Rosemarie. 1996. Introduction: From Wonder to Error - A Genealogy of Freak Discourse in Modernity. In *Freakery: Cultural Spectacles of the Extraordinary Body*, ed. Rosemarie Garland-Thomson, 1–19. New York: New York University Press.

Garnett, Jane. 2000. Religious and Intellectual Life. In *The Nineteenth Century: The British Isles, 1815–1901*, ed. Colin Matthew, 195–228. New York: Oxford University Press.

Garritt, J. C. 1899. Popular Account of the Canonization of the Gods, Illustrated. *The Chinese Recorder and Missionary Journal* XXX:162–174.

Gauchet, Marcel. 1997. *The Disenchantment of the World: A Political History of Religion.* Princeton: Princeton University Press.

Geiger, Roger L. 2000. Introduction: New Themes in the History of Nineteenth-Century Colleges. In *The American College in the Nineteenth Century*, ed. Roger L. Geiger, 1–36. Nashville: Vanderbilt University Press.

Glackens, L. M. 1913. The Goblin Will Get You If You Don't Watch Out! *Puck Magazine* 73 (1892): cover.

Gladwin, Michael. 2017. Mission and Colonialism. In *The Oxford Handbook of Nineteenth-Century Christian Thought*, ed. Joel D. S. Rasmussen, Judith Wolfe, and Johannes Zachhuber, 282–304. New York: Oxford University Press.

Gomme, George Laurence. 1890. *The Handbook of Folklore*. London: David Nutt.

Goodwin, Harvey. 1856. *The Doctrines and Difficulties of the Christian Faith*, The Hulsean Lectures. Cambridge: Deighton, Bell and Co.

Gottschling, E. December 1905. The Bawenda: A Sketch of Their History and Customs. *The Journal of the Anthropological Institute of Great Britain and Ireland* 35:365–386.

Greene, Fanny Bradley, Hisa Tateishi, Mari Kosugi, and trans. 1914. The Goblin Mountain. In *Iwaya's Fairy Tales of Old Japan*. Tokyo: Bun Yo Do To Mita.

Greg, R. P. 1893. *Comparative Philology of the Old and New Worlds in Relation to Archaic Speech*. London: Kegan Paul, Trench, Trübner & Co.

Grimm, Jacob, and Wilhelm Grimm. 1823. *German Popular Stories Translated from the Kinder Und Kinder Und Haus-Märchen, Collected by M. M. Grimm, from Oral Tradition*. Translated by Edgar Taylor. London: C. Baldwyn.

Grosz, Elizabeth. 1991. Freaks. *Social Semiotics* 1 (2): 22–38.

Grout, Abel Joel. 1903. *Mosses with Hand-Lens and Microscope: A Non-Technical Hand-Book of the More Common Mosses of the Northeastern United States*. 5 Vols. New York City: Mount Pleasant Press.

Gunnell, Terry. 2010. Daisies Rise to Become Oaks. The Politics of Early Folktale Collection in Northern Europe. *Folklore* 121 (1): 12–37.

Gunnell, Terry. 2022. Introduction. In *Grimm Ripples: The Legacy of the Grimms' Deutsche Sagen in Northern Europe*, ed. Terry Gunnell, 1–25. Leiden: Brill.

Gunnell, Terry. 2024. Thomas Crofton Croker, The Fairy Legends, and the Arrival of the Illustrated Folk Legend in Northern Europe. *Irish University Review* 54 (1): 101–111.

Guptill, A. B. 1894. *Yellowstone Park Guide*. St. Paul: F. Jay Haynes.

Haliburton, R. G. 1895. Dwarf Survivals, and Traditions as to Pygmy Races. *Proceedings of the American Association for the Advancement of Science* 44:337–344.

Hannoum, Abdelmajid. 2003. Translation and the Colonial Imaginary: Ibn Khaldūn Orientalist. *History and Theory* 42 (1): 61–81.

Harris, Marvin. 2001. *The Rise of Anthropological Theory: A History of Theories of Culture*. New York: AltaMira Press.

Harte, Jeremy. 2019. Names and Tales: On Folklore and Place Names. *Folklore* 130 (4): 373–394.

Harte, Jeremy. 2022. Forest Murmurs: Wood and Wild in the Making of England. In *Folklore and Nation in Britain and Ireland*, ed. Matthew Cheeseman and Carina Hart, 48–62. New York: Routledge.

Hearn, Lafcadio. 1894. *Glimpses of Unfamiliar Japan*. 2 Vols. New York: Houghton Mifflin and Company.

Heber, Reginald. 1837. *Sermons on the Lessons, the Gospel, or the Epistle*. II Vols. London: John Murray.

Henderson, Lizanne, and Edward J. Cowan. 2001. *Scottish Fairy Belief: A History*. Edinburgh: Tuckwell Press, Ltd.

Hervouet-Farrar, Isabelle. 2015. Introduction: The Grotesque in the Nineteenth Century. In *The Grotesque in the Fiction of Charles Dickens and Other 19th-Century European Novelists*, 1–11. Newcastle upon Tyne: Cambridge Scholars Publishing.

Hewitt, Martin. 2023. *The Victorians: A Very Short Introduction*. Oxford University Press.

Houlbrook, Ceri. 2018. *The Magic of Coin-Trees from Religion to Recreation*. New York: Palgrave Macmillan.

Howard, Ryan. 2014. *Punch and Judy in 19th Century America: A History and Biographical Dictionary*. Jefferson: McFarland & Company, Inc.

Howells, W. 1831. *Cambrian Superstitions*. Tipton: Thomas Danks.

Hughes, Thomas. 1851. *The Stranger's Handbook to Chester and Its Environs*. Chester: Thomas Catherall.

Hull Evening News. 1894. A Talk About Owls. May 24.

Irving, Mary. June 22, 1850. The 'Spirits' of the Age. *The Literary American* IV (25): 462–463.

Jacobs, Joseph. 1890. *English Fairy Tales*. London: David Nutt.

James, Ronald M. April 1992. Knockers, Knackers, and Ghosts: Immigrant Folklore in the Western Mines. *Western Folklore* 51 (2): 153–177.

Jaydee. 1860. A Note on Bugs. *Notes and Queries* 9 (235): 500.

Jekyll, Joseph. 1894. *Correspondence of Mr. Joseph Jekyll*. Edited by Algernon Bourke. London: John Murray.

Johnston, Harry. 1888. Report by Vice-Consul Johnson on the British Protectorate of the Oil River (Niger Delta), FO 403/76. UK Foreign Office.

Johnston, Harry. 1902. The Pygmies and Ape Like Men of the Uganda Borderland. *The Pall Mall Magazine* 26:173–184.

Jones, W. 1870. The Singrowli Mission. In *The Chronicle of the London Missionary Society for the Year 1870*, ed. Joseph Mullens, 113–118. London: Directors of the London Missionary Society.

Keightley, Thomas. 1828. *The Fairy Mythology*. II Vols. London: William Harrison Ainsworth.

Kelley, Ruth Edna. 1919. *The Book of Hallowe'en*. Boston: Lothrop, Lee & Shepard Co.

Kendrick, J. R. December 1889. The Spectre of Negro Rule. *The Andover Review* XII:596–606.

Kern, H. 1896. *Manual of Indian Buddhism*. Strassburg: Karl J. Trübner.

Kerr, Walter Montagu. 1886. *The Far Interior: A Narrative of Travel and Adventure*. II Vols. London: Sampson Low.

Kim, Kirsteen, and Alison Fitchett-Climenhaga, eds. 2022. *The Oxford Handbook of Mission Studies*. New York: Oxford University Press.

Kirby, William C. 2022. *Empires of Ideas: Creating the Modern University from Germany to America to China*. Cambridge: Harvard University Press.

Kohl, J. G. 1844. *Reisen in England und Wales*. III Vols. Leipzig: Arnold.

Kohl, J. G. 1968. *England and Wales*. London: Frank Cass & Co. Ltd.

Koshar, Rudy. 1998. 'What Ought to Be Seen': Tourists' Guidebooks and National Identities in Modern Germany and Europe. *Journal of Contemporary History* 33 (3): 323–340.

Leadbeater, C. W. 1913. *The Hidden Side of Things*. Madras: The Theosophical Publishing House.

Lecouteux, Claude. 2016. *Encyclopedia of Norse and Germanic Folklore, Mythology, and Magic*. Edited by Michael Moynihan. Translated by Jon E. Graham. Rochester: Inner Traditions.

Leland, Charles Godfrey. 1895. *Legends of Florence: Collected from the People*. London: David Nutt.

Levy, Michael, and Farah Mendlesohn. 2016. *Children's Fantasy Literature: An Introduction*. New York: Cambridge University Press.

Life. 1938. Life on the American Newsfront: Historian and Admiral Join the War Debate. February 21.

Lightman, Bernard, and Bennett Zon, eds. 2019. *Victorian Culture and the Origin of Disciplines*. New York: Taylor & Francis.

Linke, Uli. 1997. Colonizing the National Imaginary: Folklore, Anthropology, and the Making of the Modern State. In *Cultures of Scholarship*, ed. S. C. Humphreys, 97–138. Ann Arbor: University of Michigan Press.

Livingstone, David. 1857. *Missionary Travels and Researches in South Africa*. London: John Murray.

Livingstone, David, and Charles Livingstone. 1865. *Narrative of an Expedition to the Zambesi and Its Tributaries*. London.

Loughborough Echo. 1913. Round the Villages. Sutton Bonington. September 5.

MacCulloch, John. 1824. *The Highlands and Western Isles of Scotland*. 4 Vols. London: Longman, Hurst, Rees, Orme, Brown, and Green.

MacGahan, Januarius Aloysius. 1874. *Campaigning on the Oxus*. London: Sampson Low, Marston, Low, and Searle.

MacKillop, James. 2004. Coblynau, Coblynnod. In *A Dictionary of Celtic Mythology*. New York: Oxford University Press. https://doi.org/10.1093/acref/9780198609674.001.0001.

Mackinnon, James. 1887. *South African Traits*. Edinburgh: James Gemmell.

Manning, Paul. 2016. Pixies' Progress: How the Pixie Became Part of the Nineteenth-Century Fairy Mythology. In *The Folkloresque: Reframing Folklore in a Popular Culture World*, ed. Michael Dylan Foster and Jeffrey A. Tolbert, 81–103. Logan: Utah State University Press.

Manning, Paul. "No Ruins. No Ghosts." *Preternature: Critical and Historical Studies on the Preternatural* 6, 1 (2017): 63–92.

McDougall, Russell, and Iain Davidson, eds. 2008. *The Roth Family, Anthropology, and Colonial Administration*. New York: Taylor & Francis.

McNicholl, Adeana. 2024. *Of Ancestors and Ghosts: How Preta Narratives Constructed Buddhist Cosmology and Shaped Buddhist Ethics*. New York: Oxford University Press.

Medical Miscellany. January 1873. *The New England Journal of Medicine* 88 (4): 95.

Merish, Lori. 1996. Cuteness and Commodity Aesthetics: Tom Thumb and Shirley Temple. In *Freakery: Cultural Spectacles of the Extraordinary Body*, ed. Rosemarie Garland-Thomson, 185–203. New York: New York University Press.

Milton, John. 1835. *The Poetical Works of John Milton*. Edited by Egerton Brydges. VI Vols. London: John Macrone.

Milton, John. 1896. *Milton's Paradise Lost*. Edited by Edward Everett Hale. New York: Longmans, Green, and Co.

Mitra, Pramadá-Dása. 1875. *The Mirror of Composition*. Calcutta: C.B. Lewis.

Moore, John C. 2018. *A Brief History of Universities*. New York: Palgrave Macmillan.

Murray, Hugh, R. K. James Wilson, Professor Jameson Greville, Whitelaw Ainslie, and Clarence Dalrymple. 1840. *Historical and Descriptive Account of British India*. 3 Vols. Edinburgh: Oliver & Boyd.

Norberg, Jakob. 2022. *The Brothers Grimm and the Making of German Nationalism*. New York: Cambridge University Press.

Norris, P. W. 1881a. *Annual Report of the Superintendent of the Yellowstone National Park to the Secretary of the Interior for the Year 1880*. Washington: Department of the Interior.

Norris, P. W. 1881b. *Fifth Annual Report of the Superintendent of the Yellowstone National Park*, 1881. Washington: Department of the Interior.

Norris, P. W. 1881c. The Yellowstone National Park. *Science* 2 (43): 186–187.

North Wales Chronicle. 1873. Garden Fete. July 5.

Notes on Ghosts and Goblins. 1873. *The Cornhill Magazine* XXVII: 451–66.

Ó Giolláin, Diarmuid. 1984. The Leipreachán and Fairies, Dwarfs and the Household Familiar: A Comparative Study. *Béaloideas* 52:75–150.

P.T. Barnum's Own and Only Greatest Show on Earth. 1879. Ht4210529_1. The Ringling Museum.

Packard, Winthrop. July 28, 1915. The Blue Herons of New Hampshire; Their Shy Character and Their Far Retreats. *Boston Evening Transcript*.

Patrick, Stewart, and Alexandra Huggins. 2023. The Term 'Global South' Is Surging. It Should Be Retired. Carnegie Endowment for International Peace, August 15. https://carnegieendowment.org/posts/2023/08/the-term-global-south-is-surging-it-should-be-retired?lang=en. Accessed December 1, 2024.

Peel, J. D. Y. 2000. *Religious Encounter and the Making of the Yoruba*. Bloomington: Indiana University Press.

Pels, Peter, and Oscar Salemink, eds. 1999. *Colonial Subjects: Essays on the Practical History of Anthropology*. Ann Arbor: University of Michigan Press.

Pennefather, F. W. 1893. *A Handbook for Travellers in New Zealand*, Murray's Foreign Handbooks. London: John Murray.

Pennell, Elizabeth Robins. 1886. Italy, From a Tricycle. *The Century* XXXI:839–859.

Popular Lecture on Animal Magnetism. January 1837. *The New England Journal of Medicine* 15 (22): 349–52.

Reed, Charles, ed. 1878. *The Seventy-Ninth Annual Report of the Religious Tract Society*. London: Pardon and Son.

Reeves, William Pember. 1899. *The Long White Cloud: Ao Tea Roa*. 2nd ed. London: Horace Marshall & Son.

Review of 'The Fairy Tales of Hans Christian Andersen.' 1899. *The Artist* XXV: lxxi–lxxii.

Review of Stickney's Autobiography of Amos Kendall. 1873. *The North American Review* 116 (238): 166–76.

Rink, Signe. 1898. The Girl and the Dogs - Further Comments. *American Anthropologist* 11 (7): 209–215.

Roby, John. 1831. *Traditions of Lancashire*. II Vols. 2nd ed. London: Longman, Rees, Orme, Brown, and Green.

Roper, Jonathan. 2012. England—The Land without Folklore? In *Folklore and Nationalism in Europe during the Long Nineteenth Century*, ed. Timothy Baycroft and David Hopkin, 227–253. Leiden: Brill.

Rubinstein, W. D. 1998. *Britain's Century: A Political and Social History*. New York: Arnold.

Schacker, Jennifer. 2003. *National Dreams: The Remaking of Fairy Tales in Nineteenth-Century England*. Pennsylvania: University of Pennsylvania Press.

Scott, Walter. 1803. *Minstrelsy of the Scottish Border*. 3 Vols. Edinburgh: James Ballantyne.

Scott, T. J. 1876. *Missionary Life among the Villages in India*. Cincinnati: Hitchcock and Walden.

Scott, Charles P. G. 1895. The Devil and His Imps: An Etymological Inquisition. *Transactions of the American Philological Association* XXVI:79–146.

Seventh Annual Report of the Council. 1885. *The Folk-Lore Journal* 3 (4): 385–96.

Shoemaker, Robert B. 2014. *Gender in English Society, 1650–1850: The Emergence of Separate Spheres?* New York: Taylor & Francis.

Sikes, Wirt. 1880. *British Goblins: Welsh Folk-Lore, Fairy Mythology, Legends and Traditions.* London: Sampson Low, Marston, Searle, & Rivington.

Silver, Carole G. 2000. *Strange and Secret Peoples: Fairies and Victorian Consciousness.* New York: Oxford University Press.

Slugg, Josiah Thomas. 1885. *Woodhouse Grove School: Memorials and Reminiscences.* London: T. Woolmer.

Smedley, Edward, W. Cooke Taylor, Henry Thompson, and Elihu Rich. 1855. *The Occult Sciences.* London: Richard Griffin.

Smith, Samuel Stanhope. 1810. *An Essay on the Causes of the Variety of Complexion and Figure in the Human Species.* New Brunswick: J. Simpson.

Spurgeon, Charles Haddon. 1857. *Sermons of the Rev. C.H. Spurgeon.* New York: Sheldon, Blakeman & Company.

Taranaki Daily News. 1912. The Mt. Egmont Line. February 6.

The Adventurers. 1825. III Vols. London: Longman, Hurst, Rees, Orme, Brown, and Green.

The Argus. 1870. Heller's Wonders. February 5.

The Billboard. 1943. The Final Curtain. July 10.

The Glasgow Herald. 1857. Cathedral Legends. December 14.

The New York Times. 1863. The Loving Lilliputians. February 11.

The Newspaper Plant. 1886. *St. Nicholas* XIII (May): 553.

The Pennsylvania Journal. 1764. New York. September 6.

The Scottish Tourist, and Itinerary. 1832. 4th ed. Edinburgh: Stirling and Kenney.

The Trosachs and Loch Lomond. 1860. Edinburgh: Oliver & Boyd.

The United States Gazette. 1830. Goblin Hill. February 5.

The Week. 1877. A Goondiwindi Ghost. March 17.

Thomas, Cyrus. 1893. Are The Maya Hieroglyphs Phonetic? *American Anthropologist* 6 (3): 241–270.

Thoms, William. 1865. The Folk-Lore of Shakespeare. In *Three Notelets on Shakespeare*, 25–112. London: John Russell Smith.

Tooker, William Wallace. December 1904. Some Powhatan Names. *American Anthropologist* 6 (5): 670–694.

Tucker, H. Carre. June 1859. Christianity in India. *The Foreign Missionary* XVIII:17–19.

Unparalleled Programme of Holiday Entertainments, 19th century. https://wellcomecollection.org/works/kq66hx8j/items. Accessed December 1, 2024.

Uther, Hans-Jörg. 2011. *The Types of International Folktales: A Classification and Bibliography, Based on the System of Antti Aarne and Stith Thompson.* III Vols. Helsinki: Finnish Academy of Science and Letters.

Uther, Hans-Jörg. 2016. Tale Type. In *Folktales and Fairy Tales: Traditions and Texts from Around the World*, ed. Anne E. Duggan, Donald Haase, and Helen J. Callow, vol. III. New York: Bloomsbury.

Walhouse, M. J. 1876. On the Belief in Bhutas—Devil and Ghost Worship in Western India. *Journal of the Royal Anthropological Institute* V:408–422.

Walloon Traditions. 1888. *Chambers's Journal* 65: 40–41.

Waste. 1883. *The Journal of Science* V (July): 377–84.

Webster, Noah, Chauncey A. Goodrich, and Noah Porter. 1864. *Dr. Webster's Complete Dictionary of the English Language*. London: Bell and Daldy.

Weinstock, Jeffrey Andrew. 2020. Introduction: A Genealogy of Monster Theory. In *The Monster Theory Reader*, ed. Jeffrey Andrew Weinstock, 1–36. Minneapolis: University of Minnesota Press.

Wheeler, Edward J., ed. 1910. The Newly Discovered Goblin Shark. XLVIII (June): 402–3.

White, John. 1888. *Ancient History of the Maori, His Mythology and Traditions, Tai-Nui*. XIII Vols. Wellington: George Didsbury.

Wikoff, Henry. 1857. *The Adventures of a Roving Diplomatist*. New York: W.P. Fetridge & Co.

Williams, Monier. 1879. Notes on Indian Folk-Lore. *The Indian Antiquary, a Journal of Oriental Research* VIII:209–211.

Wilson, J. Bastow. 2001. Cockayne & the Mt. Egmont 'Goblin Forest' - Reply. *Botanical Society of Otago Newsletter* 27:5–6.

Wingfield, Chris, and Chris Gosden. 2012. An Imperialist Folklore? Establishing the Folk-Lore Society in London. In *Folklore and Nationalism in Europe during the Long Nineteenth Century*, ed. Timothy Baycroft and David Hopkin, 255–274. Leiden: Brill.

Winser, Henry J. 1883. *The Yellowstone National Park*. New York: G.P. Putnam's Sons.

Wistow Parish Council. 2022. History of Wistow Village. https://wistowparish-council.gov.uk/wp-content/uploads/2022/09/History-of-Wistow-Village2-1.pdf. Accessed December 1, 2024.

Wood, Danielle. 2019. Renegotiating 'Once Upon a Time:' Fairy Tales in Contemporary Australian Writing. In *The Fairy Tale World*, ed. Andrew Teverson, 378–388. New York: Routledge.

Woods, Robert. 2000. *The Demography of Victorian England and Wales*. New York: Cambridge University Press.

Woolf, John. 2021. Freaks and the Victorian Imagination. In *The Palgrave Handbook of Steam Age Gothic*, ed. Clive Bloom, 671–690. New York: Palgrave Macmillan.

Young, Simon. 2022. *The Boggart: Folklore, History, Place-Names and Dialect*. Exeter: Exeter University Press.

CHAPTER 5

Goblins in Literature and Theater of the Nineteenth Century

As new forms of literature emerged in the nineteenth century, so too did the goblins invoked therein. The folkloresque goblins of Gothic fiction embodied the eeriness and darkness that was central to the genre's aesthetic, while those in Dickensian Christmas stories used their grotesque appearance, simultaneously comical and scary, to motivate people to live better lives. When Christmas goblins were adapted into theatrical productions, directors amplified the comical elements of these curiosities with the dances, songs, and slapstick expected of pantomime shows. The popularity of children's literature (fairy tales included) in the mid- to late nineteenth century brought new variations on goblins, too, especially those that had to be destroyed or outsmarted for a happy ending to be achieved. Depending on the genre, authors could present goblins as supernatural peculiarities without explanation in our world, humans with atypical looks or behaviors, or very real creatures within fantasy worlds.

A handful of recurring themes emerged in these new interpretations of literature and theater. Goblins continued to serve as an overarching category of creature that marked the presence of the supernatural, especially in dark and eerie environments. The intent of these goblins varied from the terrifying-yet-benevolent to the maliciously evil, but across this spectrum readers could expect goblins to befuddle or terrify the humans with whom they interacted. Goblins could take many physical forms but were most often deformed humanoids, short but with long limbs, through which

M. King, *A History of Goblins*, https://doi.org/10.1007/978-3-032-01063-6_5

writers emphasized irregular movements (especially jumping and flying). Illustrations accompanying these works, which were produced in higher quantity and quality than academic texts on folklore, provide a sense of this range. In some cases, too, the language surrounding the appearance of goblins (dark skinned, grotesque, ugly, unnatural, freakish) reinforced contemporary understandings of racial hierarchies and teratology.

When goblins were important enough in a story to be named or speak with other characters, they were typically masculine creatures. Atop their crude hierarchies was a goblin king that often provided a villainous counterpart to the character of the fairy queen or godmother. In children's literature especially, authors presented fairies and goblins as countervailing forces of good and evil, light and dark, beautiful and grotesque. Goblins fittingly lived deep underground or within dark forests in societies that crudely mirrored those of humans, whereas fairies inhabited more pleasant places. Although folkloric goblins and fairies had long been conflated, many authors of nineteenth-century fiction saw these creatures as diametrically opposed entities. Thus, although the goblin remained a label for the supernatural and unnatural throughout the 1800s, some strands of fiction cohered around these more specific characteristics.

The bulk of this chapter considers these themes across four sections. Each provides a case study for an author of enduring popularity from the nineteenth century—Walter Scott, Charles Dickens, Christina Rossetti, and George MacDonald—and uses their writing as a foundation on which to consider larger trends. I conclude with a handful of quantitative observations about goblins across print media, including the ascendency of the term "goblin" over "hobgoblin" and the gradual association of goblins with the festivities of Halloween instead of Christmas.

THE UNNATURAL GOBLINS OF WALTER SCOTT

Walter Scott's synthesis of ballads in *Minstrelsy of the Scottish Border* (1802) was written early in his literary career. Over the next few decades, Scott produced a corpus of history-inspired poems and novels that attracted a wide readership. These texts drew heavily on themes from Gothic fiction, which emphasized an atmosphere of darkness, gloom, eeriness, and fear— often in combination with elements of the folkloresque supernatural that confronted the limitations of scientific or religious knowledge.[1] Though folkloric themes were central to many of these works, Scott abandoned the classification system for goblins and their kin established in *Minstrelsy*.[2] Instead, goblins are categorically ambiguous, somewhere between monster and man, and defined by their grotesque appearance and supernatural powers. In 1805's *The Lay of the Last Minstrel*, for example, Scott introduces the character of the "goblin page" in the service of Lord Cranstoun:

> … And, like a tennis-ball by raquet tossed,
>   A leap, of thirty feet and three,
> Made from the gorse this elfin shape,
> Distorted like some dwarfish ape,
>   And lighted at Lord Cranstoun's knee …
> But where he rode one mile, the dwarf ran four,
> And the dwarf was first at the castle door.
>
> Use lessens marvel, it is said.
> This elvish dwarf with the Baron staid;
> Little he eat, and less he spoke,
> Nor mingled with the menial flock …
>   He was waspish, arch, and litherlie,
>   But well Lord Cranstoun served he …
> All, between Home and Hermitage,
> Talked of Lord Cranstoun's goblin page.[3]

[1] Gothic fiction thus oscillates "between the earthly laws of conventional reality and the possibilities of the supernatural." Jerrold E. Hogle, "Introduction: The Gothic in Western Culture," in *The Cambridge Companion to Gothic Fiction*, ed. Jerrold E. Hogle (New York: Cambridge University Press, 2002), 2. The stock features of these stories led to ridicule among some authors and literary critics. Robert D. Hume, "Gothic versus Romantic: A Revaluation of the Gothic Novel," *PMLA* 84, no. 2 (March 1969): 282–90; Michael Gamer, *Romanticism and the Gothic: Genre, Reception, and Canon Formation* (Pennsylvania: University of Pennsylvania Press, 2000).

[2] Scott is often regarded as the "uncontested progenitor" of the historical novel, which drew heavily on Gothic themes. Christina Morin, *The Gothic Novel in Ireland: C. 1760–1829* (Manchester: Manchester University Press, 2018), 29. Perhaps unsurprisingly, Scott's vision of history reflects his own preoccupations with contemporary Scottish identity. More broadly, Scottish Gothic literature uses history to undo the ascendency of the British state. David Punter, "Scottish and Irish Gothic," in *The Cambridge Companion to Gothic Fiction*, ed. Jerrold E. Hogle (New York: Cambridge University Press, 2002), 107–13; Ian Duncan, "Walter Scott, James Hogg, and Scottish Gothic," in *A New Companion to the Gothic*, ed. David Punter (Malden: Wiley-Blackwell, 2012), 123–34.

[3] Walter Scott, *The Lay of the Last Minstrel* (London: Longman, Hurst, Rees, and Orme, 1805), 57–58.

This goblin page is distorted like an ape, comparable to a prickly shrub, capable of great feats of athleticism, but unable to socialize with those around him. He is peculiar, in other words, in appearance and manner—somewhere between a human, elf, dwarf, and something else. This ambiguity is central to Scott's goblins. Elshie from *The Black Dwarf* (1816), for example, is "deformed to the eye" and "grotesque" in appearance.[4] He has a large head disproportionate to his dwarfish frame, thick and muscly limbs, weathered skin, and a mane of tangled hair.[5] Based on an actual Scottish man (David Ritchie) who had shunned society and retreated into the wilderness, Scott infuses this character with local border tales of an "angry goblin."[6] He elevates Ritchie's superstitions into preternatural powers within this story, including second sight, though Scott ultimately reveals this hideous gnome to be benevolent in nature and instrumental in facilitating the marriage of two protagonists (Fig. 5.1).

Even in cases of unambiguously human characters, Scott uses goblins to emphasize their unnatural appearance and behaviors. The titular character of *Rob Roy* (1817), for example, has "something wild, irregular, and, as it were, unearthly, to his appearance" reminiscent of the barbarous old Picts, who were "a sort of half goblin half human beings, distinguished, like this man, for courage, cunning, ferocity, the length of their arms, and the squareness of their shoulders." These grotesque features corrupt an otherwise "very handsome man" and mark him as otherworldly.[7] *Kenilworth* (1821) also features an "ugly urchin" nicknamed "Hobgoblin." As this boy takes Tressilian on a taxing journey through the wilderness, he performs a peculiar ritual, as he "began to clap his long, thin hands, point with his skinny fingers, and twist his wild and ugly features into such an extravagant expression of laughter and derision" that he looked like "an

[4] Walter Scott, *The Black Dwarf*, Tales of My Landlord (Edinburgh: William Blackwood, 1816), 81, 321.

[5] This kind of "grotesque realism" is common in Gothic literature, especially when applied to villainous characters. Mark M. Hennelly, "Framing the Gothic: From Pillar to Post-Structuralism," *College Literature* 28, no. 3 (Fall 2001): 73.

[6] This description comes from a later edition of this novel with an extended footnote about the origins of the story. Walter Scott, *The Black Dwarf. A Legend of Montrose.* (Leipzig: Bernhard Tauchnitz, 1858), 13. Silver calls Scott's portrait of Elshie a "strange waver between the natural and supernatural." The eventual revelation of the Elshie's benevolence reveals "a fairy godfather in goblin's clothing." Silver, *Strange and Secret Peoples: Fairies and Victorian Consciousness*, 13.

[7] Walter Scott, *Rob Roy*, vol. II (Edinburgh: James Ballantyne and Co., 1818), 213–14.

Fig. 5.1   Elshie from *The Black Dwarf* (1832). A depiction of Elshie from an 1832 edition of Walter Scott's *The Black Dwarf*, drawn by Henry James Richter and engraved by Timothy Stansfeld Engleheart. Image (cropped) courtesy of the Walter Scott Image Collection at the University of Edinburgh. (Accessible here: https://images.is.ed.ac.uk/luna/servlet/UoEwal%7E1%7E1)

actual hobgoblin."[8] For Scott, then, the label of goblin indicates grotesque appearance and behaviors that make a character (whether expressly human or not) seem unnatural. These goblins are exclusively male, and their physical oddities center around long limbs disproportionate to their short stature.[9]

When not associated with specific characters in Scott's works, goblins serve as indicators of a malevolent supernatural presence. We can thus read of a "goblin grim" within an ancient castle or nightmares "of spectres, and of goblins" or stories of "Highland goblins and fairy folk."[10] Goblins could also be attached to a certain location, as in the site of a "Goblin Cave" near Loch Katrine or "Goblin Hall" beneath Castle Gifford.[11] These goblins transcend historical context, and they feature in stories of different eras and locations—from medieval Catholic monks to a Highlander of the eighteenth century. These goblins need no additional identifiers because their actual presence in the story is less important than the haunted aesthetic that they indicate to readers.

Scott was not alone in using goblins as avatars for the haunted supernatural in the early nineteenth century. Authors in the United States, where fiction related to Fairyland was considerably less popular than in Britain, use them to similar ends.[12] Take, for example, a scene from

[8] Walter Scott, *Kenilworth; A Romance*, vol. I (Edinburgh: Archibald Constable and Co., 1821), 245–50.

[9] Shortness is a common but not universal trait of goblins in literary fiction of the early nineteenth century. An embedded story in *The Antiquary* features "the woodland goblin" of the Harz forest in Germany, which is "in the shape of a wild man, of huge stature, his head wreathed with oak leaves." Walter Scott, *The Antiquary*, vol. II (Edinburgh: James Ballantyne and Co., 1816), 191.

[10] Walter Scott, *The Bridal of Triermain* (Edinburgh: James Ballantyne and Co., 1813), 36; Walter Scott, *The Monastery. A Romance.*, vol. II (Edinburgh: Longman, Hurst, Rees, Orme, and Brown, 1820), 212; Walter Scott, *Chronicles of the Canongate*, vol. I (Philadelphia: Carey, Lea & Carey, 1827), 230.

[11] Walter Scott, *The Lady of the Lake*, 2nd ed. (Edinburgh: John Ballantine and Co., 1810), 111, 131; Walter Scott, *Marmion; A Tale of Flodden Field* (Edinburgh: J. Ballantyne and Co., 1808), lvi–lvii, 151.

[12] Colonial and early American authors tend to "play down the fantastic, either rationalizing the tales, that is finding non-fantastic explanations for what in the original story was a clearly supernatural event" or situating them in a far-off (often European) context. Levy and Mendlesohn, *Children's Fantasy Literature: An Introduction*, 50. See also Brian Attebery, *The Fantasy Tradition in American Literature: From Irving to Le Guin* (Bloomington: Indiana University Press, 1980). The same tradition exists in the English tradition, too. *The Fakenham Ghost: A True Tale* by Bloomfield tells of a woman struck with terror as she is

Washington Irving's 1820 influential short story, "The Legend of Sleepy Hollow," which sets up Ichabod Crane's eventual encounter with the Headless Horseman:

> All the stories of ghosts and goblins that Ichabod had heard in the after-noon, now came crowding upon his recollection. The night grew darker and darker; the stars seemed to sink deeper in the sky, and driving clouds occasionally hid them from his sight. He had never felt so lonely and dismal.[13]

Elsewhere, Irving calls the headless entity that chases Ichabod Crane a goblin, though whether it is the ghost of a decapitated Hessian soldier or a disguised human is left unresolved. The precise nature of this creature is less important than the fear it instills in the story's protagonist. Another American author, James Kirke Paulding, foregrounds the narrative of *The Backwoodsman* (1818) as a story that will not feature goblins or the tropes of Fairyland:

> My humble theme is of a hardy swain,
> The lowliest of the lowly rural train,
> Who left his native fields afar to roam,
> In western wilds, in search of happier home.
> Simple the tale I venture to rehearse,
> For humble is the Muse, and weak her verse;
> She hazards not, to sing in lofty lays,
> Of steel-clad knights, renown'd in other days …
> Or tell of stately dames of royal birth,
> That scorn'd communion with dull things of earth,
> With fairies leagu'd, and dwarfs of goblin race,
> Of uncouth limbs, and most unseemly face,
> Tremendous wights! That erse in nursery-keep
> Were used to scare the forward babe to sleep.[14]

---

chased by a monster (called both a ghost and goblin) through the night. She faints upon reaching her home, and her family only then realizes that the monster is "no goblin he; no imp of sin" but a playful donkey. Charmette Kendrick, "The Goblins Will Get You! Horror in Children's Literature from the Nineteenth Century," *Children and Libraries* 7, no. 1 (Spring 2009): 19–23.

[13] Washington Irving, *The Sketch Book of Geoffrey Crayon*, vol. I (New York: C.S. Van Winkle, 1819), 107.

[14] James Kirke Paulding, *The Backwoodsman. A Poem* (Philadelphia: M. Thomas, 1818), 7.

Paulding, writing in the midst of westward American expansion, tells his readers that his rural heroes are not the kind that interact with fairies or "dwarfs of goblin race." This story will not be a fict with supernatural themes. It will be one about real, hardworking people and their struggles. Indeed, the backlash to fairy-inspired fiction of the early nineteenth century was such that some critics used the ubiquitous goblin to broadly critique it. One chastised the entire group of "novelist goblin-mongers" for putting such horrifying visions within the minds of readers.[15] Another writer favorably juxtaposes the work of Lord Byron with the "muddied imagination" of the German "goblin-mongers," whose work ought to be exorcised.[16]

Although Walter Scott and his contemporaries commonly associated goblins with darkness, the labeling of entire groups of people as goblins or goblin-like was uncommon in the early nineteenth century. We see a glimpse of it, though, in the American novel *Symzonia: A Voyage of Discovery* (1820) during an encounter between Captain Seaborn and a group of mysterious beings with startlingly white skin. Seaborn, aware of his "dark and hideous appearance" from his long journey, sees one of these beings considering whether "a mortal or a goblin" stood before him. As they circle each other, Seaborn muses that "the sootiest African does not differ more from us in darkness of skin and grossness of features, than this man did from me in fairness of complexion and delicacy of form."[17] Though Seaborn himself is white, his appearance relative to these mysterious people is such that he compares himself to the grotesqueness of dark-skinned goblins and Africans. This kind of racial comparison was rare in the early nineteenth century but became more commonplace as the century progressed.

---

[15] "Invective against Novelist Goblin-Mongers," *Flowers of Literature* I (1803): 393.

[16] J.M. Milligen and George Byron, *The Life, Writings, Opinions, and Times of the Right Hon. George Gordon Noel Byron*, vol. I (London: Matthew Iley, 1825), 362.

[17] *Symzonia* was published under a pseudonym, though the real author might have been Nathaniel Ames. Adam Seaborn, *Symzonia; A Voyage of Discovery* (New York: J. Seymour, 1820), 107–8. This encounter is an inversion of tropes associated with contemporary adventure novels, in which civilized white explorers meet barbarous dark-skinned peoples. The appearance of the Belzubians (a hybrid of Beelzebub and Nubian) is further explained by moral deterioration, in which their beautiful white appearance was physically darkened by improper behaviors. Charles D. Martin, *The White African American Body: A Cultural and Literary Exploration* (New Brunswick: Rutgers University Press, 2002), 97–99.

These eerie and deformed goblins were not the only variation of these creatures circulating in the early nineteenth century. More comedic interpretations, inspired by the merry tales of Robin Goodfellow and cheerful readings of Shakespeare, persisted in some circles. An athletic-yet-diminutive goblin serves as the titular character in 1809's *The Goblin Groom: A Tale of Dunse*, a parody of the early fiction of Walter Scott:

> He was of little form, and tight;
> His weight, if man, had been full light:
> In short, he was a sportsman-sprite …
> The goblin sprite enjoys each joke,
> Though never once the while he spoke,
> But lent a civil listening ear,
> Resolved minutely all to hear;
> And every toast with ready will
> His elfin hand consents to fill.[18]

Trending more toward the comedic than the dramatic, this goblin is an adept jockey that wears green clothing and is afraid of water. Indeed, the peculiar behaviors and movements of goblins—framed as eerie and spooky in Gothic fiction—were ripe for visual comedy. Pantomime of the late 1700s and early 1800s frequently adapted fairy tales for the stage, providing an accessible and influential interpretation of fairies for audiences across social classes. Therein, the character of the "good fairy" or fairy godmother was responsible for a crucial act of transformation near the end of an opening scene that initiated the comedic "harlequinade" portion of the entertainment featuring (among others) the stock characters of Harlequin and Columbine.[19] Music and dancing were staples of pantomime, though the introduction of the spoken word allowed for more complex stories from English, French, and German traditions to be told as

---

[18] A note within the text explains the appearance of this goblin: "The dress of this little stranger, and his manner of introducing himself to the festival, must satisfy the reader that the Goblin Groom is one of those supernatural sportsmen usually termed Fairies. In the sequel, however, it will appear evident, that he owes his origin to the hardy race of northern Elves, rather than to the more delicate family of eastern Peris." R.O. Fenwick, *The Goblin Groom; A Tale of Dunse* (Edinburgh: Alex. Lawrie & Co., 1809), 29, 96.

[19] Schacker, *Staging Fairyland: Folklore, Children's Entertainment, and Nineteenth-Century Pantomime*, 10.

the century progressed.[20] The popularity of these performances led to increasingly ornate set designs in fairy tale "extravaganzas" that were especially popular during the Christmas holidays.[21]

These pantomimes feature goblins simultaneously frightening and jovial, often moving erratically in frantic dances. A 1770 folkloresque pantomime about Mother Shipton describes creatures swarming from the sky and underground in a frenzied dance:

> With Hoppings and Hobblings,
> With Fricks and Vagaries,
> Come Fairies and Goblins,
>   Come Goblins and Fairies![22]

In subsequent decades, viewers could see goblins in numerous pantomimes: the fire goblin Glow Glimmer in *Harlequin and the Swans* (1813), the titular character in *The Yellow Dwarf; or Harlequin King of the Golden Mines* (1820), a goblin sprite in *Harlequin and Friar Bacon* (1821), the queen of the Goblin Wood in *Harlequin and Golden Eyes* (1825), or Flickerflame the goblin in *Harlequin and the Princess of the Hidden Island* (1829).[23] These goblins were interchangeable with other small creatures (especially dwarves and gnomes) that operated underground and/or in darkness. They could be played by men or women, though the former was more common. Folkloresque tropes about goblins living underground made them natural fits for pantomimes situated in these spaces, which ranged in scope from satires about industrialization to more romantic

---

[20] Pantomimes of the early eighteenth century alternated between dramatic and comedic sections, the former drawing on mythology and the latter on stock characters. The popularity of comic scenes relegated more serious ones to the beginnings and endings of shows. Jonathan Buckmaster, *Dickens's Clowns: Charles Dickens, Joseph Grimaldi and the Pantomime of Life* (Edinburgh: Edinburgh University Press, 2019), 17–22. The interpretations of folklore and fairy tales from continental Europe in English pantomime are considered in Schacker, *Staging Fairyland: Folklore, Children's Entertainment, and Nineteenth-Century Pantomime*, 105–73.

[21] Jeffrey Richards, *The Golden Age of Pantomime: Slapstick, Spectacle and Subversion in Victorian England* (New York: Bloomsbury, 2014), 56–64, 82–123.

[22] George Colman, *The Recitatives, Airs, &c. In the New Pantomime Entertainment of Mother Shipton* (London, 1770).

[23] The British Library has a large (and searchable) archive of pantomime playbills: https://blplaybills.org/.

dramas about mysteries within ancient mines.[24] *The Fire Goblin and the Three Charcoal Burners* (1818), for example, juxtaposes the fantastical realm of Hazrock, "Fire Goblin, King of the Wastes and Mines," with that of real-world charcoal burners, who are eventually turned into stock characters during the harlequinade. The show's culminating scene is the triumph of the "good genie" Glendoveer over Hazrock and a celebration in the palace of the Queen of the Air—a typical ending of good/light defeating evil/dark. Though these goblins live in darkness and perform acts of mischief, the genre of pantomime elevated their comedic tendencies with genre-appropriate comedy, music, and dancing.

The formulaic structure of pantomimes relegated certain creatures of Fairyland to repetitive roles based on stock characteristics. Fairies were relatively benevolent entities associated with light, femininity, and the power of transformation that initiated the harlequinade. Goblins, meanwhile, were antagonists living in the darkness of mines or forests.[25] This juxtaposition was by no means uniform in the early nineteenth century, though it became more commonplace during the Victorian era (1837–1901).

MORALIZING AND GROTESQUE DICKENSIAN GOBLINS

The Victorians were "utterly fascinated by the fairies" and filled books, theater halls, and art galleries with their many forms.[26] The genre of the literary fairy tale was particularly popular across social classes and, though ostensibly written for children, had broad appeal to parents and caregivers

---

[24] Frederick Burwick, *British Drama of the Industrial Revolution* (New York: Cambridge University Press, 2015), 145–47. The first edition of the *OED* even defines the "fairy of the mine" as "a goblin supposed to inhabit mines."

[25] This division between fairies and goblins can be glimpsed in contemporary art, too. A 1786 watercolor by William Blake shows pale-skinned fairies from "A Midsummer Night's Dream" dancing in the forest in flowing robes. They harmoniously exist within nature, some with butterfly wings or leaves in their hair. Blake's depiction of Milton's drudging goblin, meanwhile, draws on folkloric traditions associated with household labor. Fairies were commonly depicted in Romantic-era art, though the evocation of goblins specifically therein is rare. Silver, *Strange and Secret Peoples: Fairies and Victorian Consciousness*, 25–28. See also Nicola Brown, *Fairies in Nineteenth-Century Art and Literature* (New York: Cambridge University Press, 2006).

[26] Silver, *Strange and Secret Peoples: Fairies and Victorian Consciousness*, 3.

as well.[27] These texts had their origins on the European continent. The first collection of literary fairy tales was (arguably) Madame d'Aulnoy's 1697 *Les Contes des Fées* ("*Tales of the Fairies*"), which was followed by numerous other Francophone works that catalogued stories circulating in French salons. The Brothers Grimm collected folk tales for their 1812 publication, *Kinder- und Hausmärchen* ("*Children's and Household Tales*"), the contents of which were sanitized in later editions for the children that were likely to encounter them. These stories were translated into English in the 1820s, saw surging sales mid-century in Britain, and were reprinted over the course of the century.[28] Additional translations of continental fairy tales followed, including those from Hans Christian Andersen, and the cultivation of written fairy lore from within the British Isles likewise prospered (often lumping together Irish, English, Scottish, and Welsh traditions). Newspapers and other periodicals provided additional venues for an increasingly literate population to encounter these stories.[29]

Though detractors in Great Britain lamented the deleterious effects of the fairy tale, which they saw as damaging the moral education of young people, this perspective fell out of favor by the mid-nineteenth century. Fairy tales, according to a new crop of authors, could use whimsy to cultivate the imaginations of innocent children and provide valuable commentary on appropriate conduct in a changing industrial society. This is not to say that authors were united in the mobilization of Fairyland for these didactic means. Some thought that fairies were well suited to protect Victorian norms and to guide readers into acceptable behaviors, especially

[27] See, generally, Zipes, *Victorian Fairy Tales: The Revolt of the Fairies and Elves*, xiii–xix; Silver, *Strange and Secret Peoples: Fairies and Victorian Consciousness*; Jack Zipes, *Fairy Tales and the Art of Subversion: The Classical Genre for Children and the Process of Civilization*, 2nd ed. (Routledge: New York, 2006); Caroline Sumpter, *The Victorian Press and the Fairy Tale* (New York: Palgrave Macmillan, 2008); Talairach-Vielmas, *Fairy Tales, Natural History and Victorian Culture*; Melanie Keene, *Science in Wonderland: The Scientific Fairy Tales of Victorian Britain* (New York: Oxford University Press, 2015).

[28] The Brothers Grimm were not the first to record fairy tales, though they were crucial in popularizing the genre and establishing early methodologies for collecting them. Jack Zipes, *Grimm Legacies: The Magic Spell of the Grimms' Folk and Fairy Tales* (Princeton: Princeton University Press, 2014).

[29] The press "did more than keep Queen Mab in the news. By continually bringing the genre into the contemporary moment, the press also helped to reinvent the fairy tale, and secured its cherished place at the heart of Victorian culture." Sumpter, *The Victorian Press and the Fairy Tale*, 2.

marriage and (for women) the maintenance of a certain feminine aesthetic. Others saw fairies as vessels to show the absurdities of these mores.[30] Dickens himself penned a critique of the re-writing of fairy tales to serve moral purposes in "Frauds on the Fairies" (1853), which satirized George Cruikshank's emphasis on the contemporary evils of alcoholism.[31] Near the end of his career, Andrew Lang also complained about the number of published fairy tales written for children that were far removed from the original fairies of folklore.[32]

Goblins were mainstays of Anglophone fairy tale compilations of the nineteenth century. A popular set of translations of the Brothers Grimm was marketed in several editions as *Grimm's Goblins*, which catalogued "Goblin Legends" with their "marvellous whimsicalities and exquisite subtleties of fancy."[33] Like so many texts considered in the last two chapters, the goblin was a broad indicator of a supernatural creature.[34] Other authors were more selective in what they were willing to call goblins—like J.R. Planché in his 1855 translation of Madame d'Aulnoy's foundational *Tales of the Fairies*.[35] Within an appendix, he explains the possible English translations of the character Prince Lutin, including "Hobgoblin Prince" and "Prince Elfin." Planché argues, though, that this prince "certainly is not" an elf, because an elf is a kind of fairy that influences humans without the use of magical powers. The powers of fairies, meanwhile, are limited to

---

[30] Zipes calls these two schools of thought "conventionalism" and "utopianism." Zipes, *Victorian Fairy Tales: The Revolt of the Fairies and Elves*, xxiii. Fairy tales foreground "the idea that femininity is closely linked to aestheticization, and that beauty is a feminine virtue which needs to be cultivated." Laurence Talairach-Vielmas, *Moulding the Female Body in Victorian Fairy Tales and Sensation Novels* (Burlington: Aldershot, 2007), 5.

[31] Harry Stone, "Dickens, Cruikshank, and Fairy Tales," *The Princeton University Library Chronicle* 35, no. 1/2 (1973): 213–47.

[32] More broadly, Lang dreamt of "the destruction of his own texts, as well as the end of science and civilization" to bring back a "true" fairy tale. Sumpter, *The Victorian Press and the Fairy Tale*, 177.

[33] Jacob Grimm and Wilhelm Grimm, *Grimm's Goblins*, trans. E. Taylor (London: R. Meek, 1877).

[34] Lang's fairy tale compilations include (from the French tradition) "The Goblin Pony" and a translation of Andersen's "The Goblin and the Grocer." Andrew Lang, *The Grey Fairy Book* (London: Longmans, Green, and Co., 1900), 16–18; Andrew Lang, *The Pink Fairy Book* (London: Longmans, Green, and Co., 1897), 12–17.

[35] Many of Madame d'Aulnoy's works were translated into English as early as the seventeenth century, though reception of them was uneven. She became best known for her fairy tale collections due to the work of Planché. Melvin D. Palmer, "Madame d'Aulnoy in England," *Comparative Literature* 27, no. 3 (Summer 1975): 237–53.

invisibility, teleportation, and being ethereal. Goblin could be a translation of Lutin, too, but this creature has a more abstract connotation that "conveys the idea of something frightful, or at least grotesque, in appearance, and generally mischievous in character." Having eliminated these options, Planché settles on "Prince Sprite" as an apt translation for this character (though he also likes "Invisible Prince").[36] Compilers of written fairy tales thus transposed their own ideas about underlying characteristics of folkloresque goblins, elves, and fairies onto a rich and growing tapestry of their stories.

Fairies were particularly important around Christmas time. This association stretched back into the early modern period, as the "goblin story" (as it was sometimes called) provided entertainment during these dark-yet-celebratory days.[37] Newspapers, published in increasing quantities mid-century, provided accessible venues for new interpretations of these supernatural tales. Therein, preternatural entities were often used as plot devices through which larger moral truths could be told. Within two such stories, Charles Dickens paints vivid descriptions of goblins with grotesque visages and supernatural abilities that scared miserly old protagonists into living better lives. These stories bring the goblin, so long associated with the rural poor, into urban households and larger critiques of improper behavior and economic inequality in Victorian society. In other genres, though, when Dickens portrays certain individuals as goblins or goblin-like, the connotation is overwhelmingly negative. The antagonistic dwarf Quilp in *The Old Curiosity Shop* and an old woman giving a tour at the medieval palace of Avignon show that human goblins were monstrosities with fittingly peculiar appearance and characteristics—but without the preternatural powers that could help the miserly.

Although Dickens was skeptical of the existence of ghosts and other preternatural entities, he was nonetheless fond of their stories.[38] He wrote

---

[36] Countess d'Aulnoy and J.R. Planché, *Fairy Tales* (London: G. Routledge, 1855), 612.

[37] One verse from 1738 reads, "Mean-time the Village rouzes up the Fire; / While well attested, and as well believ'd, / Heard solemn, goes the Goblin-Story round; / Till superstitious Horror creeps o'er all." James Thomson, *The Works of Mr. Thomson*, vol. I, II vols. (London: A. Millar, 1738). Another promises tales of "Fairies, Ghosts, Hobgoblins, Witches, Bull-beggars, Rawheads and Bloody-Bones" for entertainment on cold winter evenings. *Round about Our Coal-Fire: Or, Christmas Entertainments* (London: J. Roberts, 1732).

[38] Dickens' reputation as an enthusiast for the supernatural and occult has been amplified through his presentation in modern media (as in his dubious membership in the so-called Ghost Club in *Assassin's Creed: Syndicate*). Shari Hodges Holt, "Dickens 'Was Dead: To

more than twenty of them, often embedded in novels, and infused those set around Christmas with social commentary.[39] One of his early serialized novels, *The Posthumous Papers of the Pickwick Club* (1836–1837), includes the Christmas story called "The Story of the Goblins Who Stole a Sexton," which is introduced by a group gathered around the fire on a snowy night. Some dispute the veracity of the tale, though the most forceful believer in it is an old lady, whose conviction leads her son Wardle to narrate it. Therein, a crotchety sexton named Gabriel Grub encounters a goblin king while drinking and preparing to dig a grave on Christmas Eve. Dickens describes this encounter and the visage of the goblin in some detail:

> Seated on an upright tombstone, close to him, was a strange unearthly fig-ure, whom Gabriel felt at once, was no being of this world. His long fantas-tic legs which might have reached the ground, were cocked up, and crossed after a quaint, fantastic fashion; his sinewy arms were bare, and his hands rested on his knees. On his short round body he wore a close covering, ornamented with small slashes; and a short cloak dangled at his back; the collar was cut into curious peaks, which served the goblin in lieu of ruff or neckerchief; and his shoes curled up at the toes into long points. On his head he wore a broad-brimmed sugar loaf hat, garnished with a single feather. The hat was covered with the white frost, and the goblin looked as if he had sat on the same tombstone very comfortably, for two or three hundred years ....[40]

This goblin king—somewhere between comical, peculiar, and scary in appearance—berates Grub for his misdeeds before a horde of goblins emerges from the church and encircles the terrified sexton. They leap between tombstones with "marvellous dexterity" in a contorted sort of game as the church organ plays with increasing tempo. The goblin king

Begin with': Charles Dickens's Ghostly Afterlife in Neo-Victorian Narratives," *Dickens Studies Annual: Essays on Victorian Fiction* 51, no. 2 (2020): 375–410. Dickens also admired the work of Walter Scott; he served on a committee to help raise funds for a Scott monument in Edinburgh (though he was displeased with the eventual result). Ian Duncan, *Modern Romance and Transformations of the Novel: The Gothic, Scott, Dickens* (New York: Cambridge University Press, 1992), 177–78.

[39] The economic critiques of *A Christmas Carol*, for example, are less apparent in the tale of Gabriel Grub, which focuses on the importance of interpersonal relationships. Andrew Smith, "Dickens' Ghosts: Invisible Economies and Christmas," *Victorian Review* 31, no. 2 (2005): 36–55.

[40] Charles Dickens, *The Posthumous Papers of the Pickwick Club* (London: Chapman & Hall, 1837), 301.

then whisks Grub away to his court, wherein Grub is forced to drink "liquid fire" and watch a handful of visions that teach him to live a better life. When Grub awakes the next day in the churchyard, he finds no traces of the goblins (which he rationalizes because spirits would "leave no visible impression behind") and leaves town. Ten years later, he returns to the city as a "ragged, contented, rheumatic old man" to the confusion of the town's inhabitants, who eventually imbue his saga with moral messaging about the need to be good and social at Christmas.

In the saga of Gabriel Grub, Dickens uses a horde of goblins, terrifying to an inebriated Grub but more comical for readers, to serve a moralizing message to his audience.[41] Two illustrations for this story, one from English artist Hablot Knight Browne (Phiz) and the other from American cartoonist Thomas Nast, provide different renderings of the goblin king (Fig. 5.2).

Phiz's 1837 work shows a vaguely masculine, humanoid creature perched atop a tombstone, short and squat in height but with long limbs, wearing the strange ensemble described by Dickens. He smiles mischievously as he looks down at a petrified Grub. The tree in the foreground is eerie, its knots resembling human faces and its many leafless branches snaking upward. A cathedral in the background rounds out this Gothic environment. Nast's 1873 interpretation, conversely, leans more heavily into the comedic exchange between the intoxicated Grub and the goblin king. The latter has a head like a pumpkin with a mocking tongue stuck out, and the graveyard around him is stripped of its Gothic motifs. These depictions of the goblin king give some sense of how their peculiar, weird,

---

[41] David J. Greenman, "Alcohol, Comedy, and Ghosts in Dickens's Early Short Fiction," *Dickens Quarterly* 17, no. 1 (March 2000): 3–13.

Fig. 5.2   (continued) Depictions of the first encounter between Gabriel Grub and the goblin king. (Top) The goblin king and Gabriel Grub as drawn by Phiz in 1837. This image (cropped) was scanned by Philip V. Allingham for *The Victorian Web*. (Accessible here: https://victorianweb.org/art/illustration/phiz/pickwick/24.html). (Bottom) The goblin king and Gabriel Grub as drawn by Thomas Nast in 1873. This image (cropped) was scanned by Philip V. Allingham for *The Victorian Web*. (Accessible here: https://victorianweb.org/art/illustration/nast/33.html. Phiz made another illustration for the 1874 Household Edition of *The Pickwick Papers*, which was modeled on the original 1837 version)

Fig. 5.2

unnatural characteristics could fluctuate between terrifying and comical based on how individuals interpreted the underlying story. Wherever goblins land on this spectrum, though, their decidedly strange appearance functions in service of the greater good by reforming the miserly Grub. Audiences understood these goblins to be fictional, but they still helped convey a real-world, moral truth.

Grub's tale is not the only Christmas story by Dickens to include goblins. Though the entities that haunt Ebenezer Scrooge in *A Christmas Carol* (1843) are usually called ghosts or spirits, at one point he laments that he might be "persecuted by a legion of goblins" for the rest of his life.[42] Goblins are more central to 1844's *The Chimes: A Goblin Story of Some Bells that Rang an Old Year Out and a New Year In*, which echoes the structure of "The Story of the Goblins Who Stole a Sexton." Therein, the ticket-porter Toby "Trotty" Veck has a few awful experiences that make him wonder if the poor are naturally wicked. When drawn to a clanging bell tower on New Year's Eve, he encounters the Spirits of the Bells, which Dickens describes as a Goblin Sight:

> [Trotty] saw the tower, whither his charmed footsteps had brought him, swarming with dwarf phantoms, spirits, elfin creatures of the Bells. He saw them leaping, flying, dropping, pouring from the Bells without a pause. He saw them, round him on the ground; above him, in the air; clambering from him, by the ropes below; looking down upon him, from the massive iron-girded beams; peeping in upon him, through the chinks and loopholes in the walls; spreading away and away from him in enlarging circles, as the water ripples give way to a huge stone that suddenly comes plashing in among them. He saw them, of all aspects and all shapes. He saw them ugly, handsome, crippled, exquisitely formed. He saw them young, he saw them old, he saw them kind, he saw them cruel, he saw them merry, he saw them grim; he saw them dance, and heard them sing; he saw them tear their hair, and heard them howl ....[43]

Trotty then speaks to the Goblin of the Great Bell, who informs him that he had died climbing this tower. The goblin forces Trotty to watch scenes of his loved ones being miserable without him and chastises him for not seeing how people can improve themselves. Then, Trotty wakes up in his bed. Forever grateful at being given a second chance, he witnesses the happy marriage of his daughter. The story ends with Dickens inviting readers to reflect on "the stern realities from which these shadows come"

---

[42] Charles Dickens, *A Christmas Carol* (London: Chapman & Hall, 1843), 29.
[43] Charles Dickens, *The Chimes: A Goblin Story* (London: Chapman & Hall, 1845), 93–94.

Fig. 5.3 Depictions of Goblins from *The Chimes*. (Left) The frontispiece for the 1844 edition of *The Chimes* produced by Maclise and Becker. This image was scanned by Philip V. Allingham for *The Victorian Web*. (Accessible here: https:// www.victorianweb.org/art/illustration/chimes/1.html).   (Right)   An   interior image from the same printing of *The Chimes* (page 92) produced by Doyle and Linton. This image was scanned by Philip V. Allingham for *The Victorian Web*. (Accessible here: https://www.victorianweb.org/art/illustration/chimes/9.html)

and to "endeavor to correct, improve, and soften them" in the New Year. The Goblin of the Great Bell and his minions fulfill a similar purpose to the goblin king by scaring an old man into seeing the error of his ways.[44] Illustrations that accompany this story depict the chaotic "Goblin Sight" of a multitude of spirits swarming out of ringing bells. Their appearance and behaviors, though, are contingent upon the artist (Fig. 5.3).

[44] Reviews of this story were more lukewarm than the overwhelming praise for *A Christmas Carol*; literary scholars have likewise shown less enthusiasm for Trotty's tale. Marilyn J. Kurata, "Fantasy and Realism: A Defense of 'The Chimes,'" *Dickens Studies Annual* 13 (1984): 19–34.

The image from Maclise and Becker shows creatures that are broadly angelic or cherubic in appearance. They are half-naked, pale-skinned, and proportional humanoids. Many of them are kissing or caressing one another, though some are averting their gaze from this sight. In the center of the image is the Goblin of the Great Bell: a masculine figure that leers at the reader. The image from Doyle and Linton shows the same swarming scene but with substantial variations. These goblins are all diminutive and disfigured creatures that overwhelm Trotty. Some have bulging heads and antennae; others appear more animal than human; others are seemingly shaded to depict darker skin tones. They swarm across the scene, surrounding Trotty and tormenting him with visions of his loved ones suffering, as they ring a trio of calamitous bells.

Like the goblin king of Gabriel Grub, the image of these goblins was contingent on the perspective of artists. They could grotesquely torment Trotty in one depiction and be lithely kissing in the next—though the sexual tone of this latter frontispiece could have been a marketing gambit by the book's publishers. Despite these variations, Dickens presents some continuities across these two Christmas stories. The first is that these goblins had a hierarchy with a masculine goblin at its top, whether the goblin king or the Goblin of the Great Bell. Beneath this leader was a swarming host of minions with unnatural appearances and movements that used their preternatural powers to scare a person into living a better life. These monstrosities, though, were only visible to a single person in each of these stories, and the nature of their existence is unexamined. More important is the underlying message of these stories about the very real problems of urban Victorian society.

G.K. Chesteron, an English author, Christian apologist (sometimes veering into anti-Semitism), and admirer of Dickens, saw the grotesque appearance of goblins and ghosts as one of three central pillars to his Christmas works, alongside "dramatic quality" and a wintry setting. He argues that the grotesque is "the natural expression of joy" and that Dickens understood how happiness could be "best expressed by ugly figures" in these festive tales:

> When real human beings have real delights they tend to express them entirely in grotesques—I might almost say entirely in goblins. On Christmas Eve one may talk about ghosts so long as they are turnip ghosts. But one would not be allowed (I hope, in any decent family) to talk on Christmas Eve about astral bodies. The boar's head of old Yule-time was as grotesque

as the donkey's head of Bottom the Weaver. But there is only one set of goblins quite wild enough to express the wild goodwill of Christmas. Those goblins are the characters of Dickens.[45]

Indeed, the joyous attributes of Dickens' grotesque figures were elevated in theater.[46] When directors adapted his Christmas stories for the stage, they imbued these literary stories with the conventions of pantomime, a genre of which Dickens was a lifelong supporter.[47] Therein, goblins are still unnatural and weird, but they have additional comical scenes, dancing numbers, and colorful costumes. Two hand-painted "magic lantern slides" used for an 1875 production of *Gabriel Grub and the Grim Goblin* at the Royal Polytechnic Institution in London give a sense of these depictions.[48] The goblin king has a costume that combines the peculiar outfit described in Dickens' text with the bright colors characteristic of pantomime. Accompanying goblins come in many different shapes, sizes, and colors—though they are recognizably shorter than Grub, and many of them have green skin. Though Dickens' story provides the framework for this production, it adopts a more "humorous tone" and contains frequent interruptions of the narrative to allow for expected songs and dances.[49] Trumping the narrative structure of Dickens' original work, then, are the conventions of pantomime and the moral core of the story that sees Grub become a better man.

[45] G.K. Chesterton, *Appreciations and Criticisms of the Works of Charles Dickens* (London: J.M. Dent, 1911), 110–11.

[46] The "grotesques" of Dickens are "objects of humor, pathos, disgust, and horror in his fiction… they reference a world of gothic, exotic, and theatrical excess, yet they do not belong to any distant, marginal, or outside spaces." Andrew Mangham, *We Are All Monsters: How Deviant Organisms Came to Define Us* (The MIT Press, 2023), 9.

[47] Edwin M. Eigner, *The Dickens Pantomime* (Berkeley: University of California Press, 1989). In an 1883 column, George Lancaster writes that "a Drury Lane pantomime is an English institution. We can no more do without it than roast beef, plum-pudding, and mince-pies. A Boxing Day without pantomime would be as empty as a Christmas Day without dinner." George Lancaster, "Notes on the Pantomimes," *The Theater* I (June 1883): 12–13. See also Schacker, *Staging Fairyland: Folklore, Children's Entertainment, and Nineteenth-Century Pantomime*, 12.

[48] Accessible here: https://collection.sciencemuseumgroup.org.uk/objects/co8210972/collection-of-royal-polytechnic-institution-magic-lantern-slides.

[49] Phillip Roberts, "Optical Pantomimes at the Royal Polytechnic Institution: George Buckland's 1875 Production of Gabriel Grub and the Grim Goblin," *Film History: An International Journal* 28, no. 1 (2016): 26.

Dickens was one of many Victorian authors to write about goblins and other preternatural creatures within Christmas stories. These tales circulated widely via newspapers, which devoted sections to them near the end of the calendar year and provided suitable reading for the whole family. Goblins take on familiar roles therein. They are identifiers of the supernatural, as in the haunting residents of the "goblin domain" or the spooky shadows cast by furniture looking like a "weird, goblin aspect."[50] When goblins take on more important roles, they are curiosities with supernatural powers whose actions confuse and harm humans in the ultimate service of a moral message. The 1863 short story "Shadow-Land," for example, features a hoard of swarming goblins with all kinds of visual oddities:

> They were of all sorts and of all sizes, were these goblin comicalities—some long and slender, some short and squat, others with overwhelmingly large heads, others with infinitely small ones, some with wings of finest gauze, and others with leathern wings or no wings at all.[51]

Reminiscent of Dickens, these swarming goblins come in all shapes and sizes. Serving as "messengers of Christmas," they deliver a valuable lesson about the importance of this holiday to the malevolent Madame Querg. They cause warts to appear all over her face and threaten to blemish her further if she does not let her workers go home. By weaponizing ugliness, these goblins strong-arm Querg into embracing the generous behaviors that represent the Christmas spirit. A similar structure is found in "Jabez Jones," which was published in the United States in 1859.[52] The wealthy Mr Jones encounters a goblin, a "diminutive little hunchback man" with peculiar clothing and an inhuman laugh, that shows him through a series of fiery visions how he is rich in wealth but poor in happiness. Jones decides to be more generous with his wealth, and the story concludes with an invitation for readers to shame any loved ones for whom "a goblin visit might prove a blessing." These stories, like those of Dickens, insert

---

[50] "Bits of Books for Christmas Reading," *The Birmingham Journal*, December 25, 1847; "Gabriella: A Child's Story," *The Birmingham Daily Post*, December 25, 1872. The former entry is an excerpt from *Fireside Horrors for Christmas*.

[51] "Shadow-Land," *The Birmingham Post*, December 25, 1863.

[52] "Jabez Jones. A Goblin Story," *The Brookville Jeffersonian*, October 13, 1859. This story was originally printed in the New York *Sunday Mercury*. Though published in October, the story is set on a "cold December evening."

goblins into Christmas stories, using folkloresque tropes to convey larger messages about contemporary societal ills.[53]

The preternatural goblins of Dickens' Christmas stories, which are strange but ultimately benevolent in intent, are not matched by humans given this label. Instead, Dickens equates the grotesque appearance of these people with their behaviors.[54] The character of Daniel Quilp from *The Old Curiosity Shop* (1841) exemplifies this. A dwarf with "monstrous head and little body," Quilp is presented as a peculiarity of nature—an "evil spirit" with fittingly amoral behaviors that antagonize the novel's protagonist, the girl Nell. In one scene, Dickens describes Quilp's gait as he advanced "with a sort of skip, which, what with the crookedness of his legs, the ugliness of his face, and the mockery of his manner, was perfectly goblin-like." The spiritual bankruptcy of Quilp is seen throughout the text, including when the clerk Sampson sees Quilp looking at a "great, goggle-eyed, blunt-nosed figure-head of some old ship" that resembles "a goblin or hideous idol whom the dwarf worshipped." Sampson, confused as to whether Quilp saw this as a sort of "family portrait" for himself or as the likeness of some enemy, watches as Quilp destroys the statue (Fig. 5.4).[55]

Scholars have written at length about the monstrous particularities of Quilp, but for this history, his association with goblins is paramount.[56] Dickens had a broad interest in "the aberrant, the anomalous, and the grotesque" as defined by contemporary understandings of teratology and the Victorians' pathologizing impulses.[57] Quilp was one such curiosity: a dwarf, freak, monster, animal, and (thus) goblin-like. His physical

---

[53] Marie Corelli's *The Strange Visitation* operates in Dickensian tradition, too. The preternatural creature at its heart is "Professor Goblin," a spirit of a greedy soul condemned to Hell, who appears as "a kind of nondescript semi-human thing such as drunkards might possibly see in delirious dreams." It is like "an unpleasantly huge spider" with a human head and features described sometimes as hairy and others as skeletal. Marie Corelli, *The Strange Visitation* (New York: Hodder and Stoughton, 1910), 50–52.

[54] Chesterton describes, for example, the "uproarious villainy" of Quilp. Chesterton, *Appreciations and Criticisms of the Works of Charles Dickens*, 214.

[55] Charles Dickens, *The Old Curiosity Shop* (London: Chapman & Hall, 1841), 87, 96, 146–47.

[56] Michael Hollington, *Dickens and the Grotesque*, Routledge Revivals (New York: Routledge, 2016).

[57] Mangham, *We Are All Monsters: How Deviant Organisms Came to Define Us*, 130.

Fig. 5.4   Quilp from *The Old Curiosity Shop*. A simian Quilp destroys a statue, which is rendered by Phiz in an 1840 edition of *The Old Curiosity Shop* to resemble Admiral Horatio Nelson. This image was scanned by Philip V. Allingham for *The Victorian Web*. (Accessible here: https://victorianweb.org/art/illustration/phiz/305.html)

deformities match this character.[58] He appears and disappears in an unnatural manner, drinks copious amounts of alcohol, wildly swings his limbs in rage, contorts his wrinkly face in peculiar ways, is consumed with sexual energy, and devours food with the appetite of a household fairy—and the label of goblin is thus an apt one to describe him.[59] Though he does not

[58] Quilp is "monstrous in appearance and personality, he embodies the demonic disabled, a relative of such literary characters as Shakespeare's Richard III or Captain Ahab in Moby Dick." This is one of two archetypes for disabled people in Victorian literature (especially), the other being the "blessed" disabled person. Helen Williams, "'Blank Epochs': Narratives of Disability in Charles Dickens's The Old Curiosity Shop and Dinah Mulock Craik's John Halifax, Gentleman," *Victorians: A Journal of Culture and Literature* 122 (2012): 122.

[59] Dickens' representation of people with disabilities overall was nonetheless complex. Rodas argues that "his relationship with disabled identity and his representations of disabled

possess the preternatural powers of Christmas goblins, Quilp is still a monstrous vessel through which Dickens transports the timeless rural goblin
into a more immediate urban context. To be clear, Quilp is not a goblin,
but he is like one, and his peculiar appearance and behaviors match this
folkloresque archetype.

The tragic Nell, conversely, is associated with fairies. As she sleeps in the
curiosity shop, Master Humphries describes her as "so very young, so
spiritual, so slight and fairy-like a creature" in opposition to the material
oddities surrounding her.[60] She is very much the opposite of the goblin-
like Quilp. The opposition of the goblin to the fairy thus migrated into the
immensely popular work of Dickens. This duality speaks (per Hillard) to a
"rapid cultural consensus" about these two entities, which fixed "the supposed essence of each creature in nearly indelible opposition."[61] Dickens
reinforced the idea that goblins were a force of malevolence and darkness
(embodied by a deformed and evil human) while fairies were a counterposing force of benevolence and lightness (embodied by an innocent
young girl).

The labeling of humans as goblins is seen in one of Dickens' non-fiction
works, too: his 1846 travelogue *Pictures from Italy*. While passing through
Avignon, he describes a "she-goblin" working in the medieval Palace of
the Popes:

> A little, old, swarthy woman, with a pair of flashing black eyes,—despite
> proof that the world hadn't conjured down the devil within her, though it
> had had between sixty and seventy years to do it in,—came out of the
> Barrack Cabaret …. But such a fierce, little, rapid, sparkling, energetic she-
> devil I never beheld. She was alight and flaming, all the time. Her action was
> violent in the extreme. She never spoke, without stopping expressly for the
> purpose. She stamped her feet, clutched us by the arms, flung herself into
> attitudes, hammered against walls with her keys, for mere emphasis: now

bodies (and minds) appear to be more complex than some would believe." Dickens invites
"the audience to read past the idea of this figure as a familiar icon of pathos and sentimental-
ity toward an understanding of disability as a site of a complex and powerful identity, one not
to be easily appropriated, manipulated, or exploited." Admittedly, this article does not consider Quilp. Julia Miele Rodas, "Tiny Tim, Blind Bertha, and the Resistance of Miss
Mowcher: Charles Dickens and the Uses of Disability," *Dickens Studies Annual* 34
(2004): 51–97.

[60] Dickens, *The Old Curiosity Shop*, 47.

[61] Molly Clark Hillard, "Dangerous Exchange: Fairy Footsteps, Goblin Economies, and
'The Old Curiosity Shop,'" *Dickens Studies Annual* 35 (2005): 75.

whispered as if the Inquisition were there still: now shrieked as if she were on the rack herself; and had a mysterious, hag-like way with her forefinger, when approaching the remains of some new horror—looking back and walking stealthily, and making horrible grimaces ....[62]

She-Goblin (after first mention simply called Goblin) leads Dickens on a tour of the palace with "goblin energy," including a trip to a torture chamber where she re-enacts the heinous techniques used in the room with accompanying shouts and screeches. Though not a fictional scene, this encounter emphasizes some of the strands of thought seen in the other Dickensian goblins. This woman is erratic. She moves with strange speed, her arms flail about as she gesticulates, and she shouts "like a fiend" as she reveals the secrets of the palace. The designation of this woman as "She-Goblin" dehumanizes her; we never even learn her real name. So too does this entry reinforce that Dickens perceived of these creatures as generally masculine—so much so that he needed to clarify to readers that Goblin is a woman. The moralizing function of preternatural goblins in Dickensian Christmas stories is thus absent in these human goblins, fictional or otherwise. Instead, Dickens highlights their oddities, which range from the malicious to the comical.

CHRISTINA ROSSETTI'S GOBLIN SEDUCERS

Although goblins were rarely invoked as a demonic force in the nineteenth century, the titular antagonists of Christina Rossetti's *Goblin Market* (1862) are infused with Christian imagery and morality.[63] This poem tells the story of two sisters, Laura and Lizzie, the former of whom is seduced into eating fruit sold by goblin merchants living down by the river. Craving more fruit, Laura is horrified to find that she can no longer hear the calls of the goblin men, and she rapidly wastes away. Lizzie manages to save her sister by acquiring fruit from the goblins but not eating it, and then feeding Laura the pulp that had accrued on her clothing. The poem concludes with a warning about the "quaint fruit-merchant men" whose wares (though tempting to taste) poison the blood, and a statement about the power of the bond between sisters.

---

[62] Charles Dickens, *Pictures from Italy* (London: Bradbury & Evans, 1846), 24–25.

[63] Published in Christina Rossetti, *Goblin Market and Other Poems* (Cambridge: Macmillan and Co., 1862), 1–30.

The religious overtones of *Goblin Market* belie thematic undercurrents that scholars have debated for decades. Indeed, when Rossetti wrote this poem, she was able to draw on a rich corpus of literature that she had encountered as a child in London: fairy tales, Romantic-era poetry, novels, works of classical literature, and (most prominently) Anglican religious texts. A devout Christian, Rossetti's works frequently address issues of salvation and presume a Christian belief system guided by the will of God. She was particularly drawn to *The Pilgrim's Progress* of Bunyan and even adapted one of its scenes for *Goblin Market* in which a boy nearly dies from eating fruit from the orchard of Beelzebub. Rossetti was also drawn to folklore; she was family friends with Thomas Keightley, author of *The Fairy Mythology*, whom she personally visited in the late 1850s.[64]

These religious and folkloric inspirations are central to *Goblin Market*, even if some of Rossetti's underlying motivations in writing it remain unclear. She provided mixed messages about whether the poem was intended for children or adults (or both).[65] Modern scholars have likewise read a variety of messages into it: an exploration of forbidden sexuality, a critique of capitalism, anti-Semitism encoded into the goblin men, a reinterpretation of the expulsion from Eden, a view on the exclusion of women from various aspects of Victorian society, and the redemption of a fallen woman (among many others).[66] My analysis of this poem centers specifically on her goblin antagonists, whose apparent sole purpose in this fantasy world is to tempt young women. They use their animalistic features to seduce Laura into buying fruit for a lock of hair:

> When they reach'd where Laura was
> They stood stock still upon the moss,

---

[64] Jan Marsh, *Christina Rossetti: A Literary Biography* (London: Jonathan Cape, 1994), 3–123; Christina Rossetti, *Christina Rossetti: Poems and Prose*, ed. Simon Humphries (New York: Oxford University Press, 2008), xviii–xxxiii.

[65] Indeed, it could have been a "cross-audienced" poem with messaging for both children and adults. Lorraine Janzen Kooistra, "Goblin Market as a Cross-Audienced Poem: Children's Fairy Tale, Adult Erotic Fantasy," *Children's Literature* 25 (1997): 181–204.

[66] See, for example, Elizabeth Campbell, "Of Mothers and Merchants: Female Economics in Christina Rossetti's 'Goblin Market,'" *Victorian Studies* 33, no. 3 (Spring 1990): 393–410; Cynthia Scheinberg, *Women's Poetry and Religion in Victorian England: Jewish Identity and Christian Culture* (New York: Cambridge University Press, 2002), 126–33; Rebecca F. Stern, "'Adulterations Detected': Food and Fraud in Christina Rossetti's 'Goblin Market,'" *Nineteenth-Century Literature* 57, no. 4 (2003): 477–511; Simon Humphries, "The Uncertainty of 'Goblin Market,'" *Victorian Poetry* 45, no. 4 (Winter 2007): 391–413.

Leering at each other,
Brother with queer brother;
Signalling each other,
Brother with sly brother ...
The cat-faced purr'd,
The rat-faced spoke a word
Of welcome, and the snail-paced even was heard;
One parrot-voiced and jolly
Cried "Pretty Goblin" still for "Pretty Polly;"—
One whistled like a bird.[67]

These "goblin men" prod and tempt Laura with their repeated pleas to "come buy" before she succumbs to their entreaties. They have a seductive quality about them, using their synchronized coos "like the voice of doves" to encourage her to taste their fruit. As Laura succumbs to her mysterious illness, Lizzie seeks out the goblins at twilight—and they hurtle toward her in frenzied and animalistic movements: leaping, flying, hobbling, running, mowing, clucking, puffing, and gobbling their way to the young woman.[68] When Lizzie refuses to eat their fruit, their behaviors become more sinister:

No longer wagging, purring,
But visibly demurring,
Grunting and snarling.
One call'd her proud,
Cross-grain'd, uncivil;
Their tones wax'd loud,
Their looks were evil.
Lashing their tails
They trod and hustled her,
Elbow'd and jostled her,
Claw'd with their nails,
Barking, mewing, hissing, mocking,
Tore her gown and soil'd her stocking,

---

[67] Rossetti, *Goblin Market and Other Poems*, 6–7.

[68] Mayer reads this animalistic language to shine light on the plight of both animals and women as objects of exchange in the nineteenth century. Jed Mayer, "'Come Buy, Come Buy!': Christina Rossetti and the Victorian Animal Market," in *Animals in Victorian Literature and Culture*, Laurence W. Mazzeno and Ronald D. Morrison, eds. (New York: Palgrave, 2017), 213–31.

> Twitch'd her hair out by the roots,
> Stamp'd upon her tender feet,
> Held her hands and squeez'd their fruits
> Against her mouth to make her eat.[69]

The animalistic nature of these goblins—cute and inviting at one moment, scary and threatening in the next—shows both their seductive power and the danger that awaits any woman that ventures into "the haunts of goblin men." The frontispiece for the 1862 edition of *Goblin Market*, made by Rossetti's brother, Dante, visualizes Laura's fateful purchase (Fig. 5.5).

A founding member of the Pre-Raphaelite Brotherhood, Dante applied the Renaissance-inspired principles of this movement, which emphasized attention to detail and moral sincerity, to this piece.[70] It shows a flock of anthropomorphized goblins leering at the fateful Laura as she cuts a lock of her hair in exchange for their fruit. A mouse goblin gestures at a departing Lizzie, trying to beckon her back to them.

When Christina Rossetti drafted this poem, she was aware of a panoply of creatures from Fairyland and Christian theology that could embody its villainous seducers, and from this extensive group, she chose the goblin. More so than any other entity, goblins had the requisite associations to embody these unnatural variations of familiar creatures that had both human and animal qualities.[71] Rossetti's goblin men act as tempters, seeking to poison chaste women through their seductive appeal and hearkening back to Christian traditions associated with demons like the incubus. In this way, Rossetti inverts the goblin formula seen in Dickensian Christmas stories, in which goblins initially terrify a human but ultimately serve to help him lead a better life. In *Goblin Market*, the goblin men appear warm and inviting, a ploy that masks the harmful effects of their

---

[69] Rossetti, *Goblin Market and Other Poems*, 21–22.

[70] Dante was an important collaborator in Christina's work and provided crucial revisions for *Goblin Market* (including the title for the poem, which Christina had initially drafted as *A Peep at the Goblins*). Alison Chapman, "Defining the Feminine Subject: D. G. Rossetti's Manuscript Revisions to Christina Rossetti's Poetry," *Victorian Poetry* 35, no. 2 (Summer 1997): 139–56. Christina was also influenced by the Pre-Raphaelite movement, which encouraged her to see a world "at once Christological and ecological." Emma Mason, *Christina Rossetti: Poetry, Ecology, Faith* (New York: Oxford University Press, 2018), 70.

[71] Kristen Layne Figgins, "'What Is It?' 'It Is a Lewd Goblin': Taking Critical Cues from Illustrative Adaptations of Christina Rossetti's Goblin Market," *Adaptation* 16, no. 3 (2023): 314–29.

Fig. 5.5 "Buy from Us with a Golden Curl." Laura exchanges a lock of hair for the goblin's fruit in the frontispiece for Christina Rossetti's 1862 *Goblin Market and Other Poems* (drawn by Dante Gabriel Rossetti). Image (cropped) courtesy of Wikimedia and the Metropolitan Museum of Art. (Accessible here: https://www.metmuseum.org/art/collection/search/642949)

lethal fruit, and (eventually) when Lizzie refuses to eat the fruit, they become horrifying. Even then, their appearance and behaviors are not enmeshed in language of teratology so common in the work of Scott and Dickens (among others). These "goblin men" are not described as ugly or grotesque. They are not freaks, dwarves, or curiosities. Their appearance and behaviors are admittedly somewhere between the human and the animal—though this hybridity is subservient to the seductive role these goblins play in the poem.

The world in which Rossetti situates *Goblin Market* permits this pivot away from non-normative human bodies.[72] The stories of Scott and Dickens are set in mysterious versions of our world, and the extraordinary happenings that occur within them are ultimately beyond explanation. Gabriel Grub has a fleeting encounter with goblins, for example, that only readers can perceive, and no one else in Grub's world is aware of his experience. Within *Goblin Market*, though, Rossetti crafts a world for us, both fantastical and allegorical, with established rules that follow an unquestioned internal logic: goblins exist, they tempt young women with poisonous fruit, and its consumption can be lethal.[73] Laura and Lizzie do not question the existence of these animalistic creatures or the biology behind their fruit.[74] They are taken as part of this reality, which then serves as a real-world commentary about (depending on your reading) Christian redemption, sisterhood, the role of women in Victorian society, the industrial economy, etc.[75] By placing "goblin men" within this fantasy realm,

[72] The genre of fantasy developed in the nineteenth century despite protestations about its regressive themes in a developing world of science; Wordsworth framed these discussions around "the distinction between fancy and imagination." Gary K. Wolfe, "Fantasy from Dryden to Dunsany," in *The Cambridge Companion to Fantasy Literature* (New York: Cambridge University Press, 2012), 9.

[73] Roberts calls *Goblin Market* a form of "children's-Gothic" literature, though admittedly he thinks that "almost any mainstream Victorian writer" has Gothic characteristics in their works. Adam Roberts, "Gothic and Horror Fiction," in *The Cambridge Companion to Fantasy Literature*, Edward James and Farah Mendlesohn, eds. (New York: Cambridge University Press, 2012), 31–32.

[74] Levy and Mendlesohn see *Goblin Market* as an "interesting exception" to a general rule of nineteenth-century fantasy, which did not have "full fantasy" worlds akin to what later authors like Tolkien would develop. Levy and Mendlesohn, *Children's Fantasy Literature: An Introduction*, 47.

[75] Norcia sees *Goblin Market* and a handful of other fairy-inspired works of the 1860s as being united by this "trope of unstable ground," through which fantastical or imaginary worlds could "reveal uncertainties of sciences… the inadequacies of education, and the legacy of empire." Megan A. Norcia, "Impossible Monsters, Rabbit Holes, and New Worlds:

Rossetti removes the need to justify the existence of these monsters as creatures of folklore, deformed humans, demons, or something in between. They can simply exist.

Rossetti's interpretation of goblins—the first detailed description of these creatures in a work of English literature authored by a woman—also emphasizes their role as masculine seducers. Their singular role in this universe is to tempt young women, and their encounters with Laura and Lizzie are replete with sexual imagery.[76] They are thus monsters of a fantasy world, but Rossetti still uses humanizing language on occasion ("goblin men" and "evil people") to emphasize the threat they pose to women. This is not the first time we have encountered goblins in this vein. Medieval and early modern authors wrote of demons that could sexually assault people in their sleep. Dickens and his contemporaries equated physical disfigurement (i.e., Quilp) with perverse sexual appetite. *Goblin Market* draws on both as Rossetti, echoing the structure of Bunyan's *The Pilgrim's Progress*, frames goblins around a seemingly insatiable sexual desire that threatens the health and purity of women.

Rossetti was hardly the first writer to depict goblins as masculine creatures, though she makes their gender and sexuality a more central component of her narrative than most. Ballads featuring Robin Goodfellow from the early seventeenth century depict him in human form as a man; artistic depictions of Shakespeare's Puck follow suit (whether drawn as an adult or baby). Walter Scott's named goblins are all masculine, even though he blurs their categorization as human or monster. Dickens, too, felt the need to specify that the woman who took him on a tour of Avignon was a "She-Goblin" because of a presumed masculinity without this prefix. Though swarms of goblins might have more gender-inclusive descriptions, those creatures important enough to have speaking roles were overwhelmingly male. Rossetti operated within this larger tradition, but she made seductive masculinity a more central component to these goblins and a larger

The Unstable Ground of Science and Education in the Children's Fairy Tale and Fantasy Literature of the 1860s," in *Nineteenth-Century Literature in Transition: The 1860s*, ed. Pamela K. Gilbert (New York: Cambridge University Press, 2024), 94–110.

[76] The function of this sexual imagery is contested, especially when it comes to same-sex eroticism between Laura and Lizzie. Mary Wilson Carpenter, "'Eat Me, Drink Me, Love Me': The Consumable Female Body in Christina Rossetti's Goblin Market," *Victorian Poetry* 29, no. 4 (Winter 1991): 415–34; Victor Roman Mendoza, "'Come Buy': The Crossing of Sexual and Consumer Desire in Christina Rossetti's Goblin Market," *ELH* 73, no. 4 (Winter 2006): 913–47.

driver of the plot than (say) shapeshifting powers or vision-inducing liquid fire.

Goblin Market features a horde of goblin men without an apparent leader, a lack of hierarchy that departs from the developing motif of swarming goblins united under a goblin king. Indeed, around the time that Rossetti was writing *Goblin Market*, creators of pantomimes and fairy tales were expanding upon this trope. We have seen a few goblin kings in this chapter already, including Hazrock ("Fire Goblin, King of the Wastes and Mines") from the pantomime tradition, as well as the creature perched atop the tombstone that terrified Gabriel Grub. A number of other authors invoke goblin kings within their works of the early to mid-nineteenth century.[77] These creatures rule from halls of darkness, usually underground or within a forest, whence they crudely plan their acts of japery or destruction. It is uncommon for them to have a goblin queen. Instead, the goblin king and his male minions try to kidnap human women to force into marriage.[78]

As goblins and fairies were juxtaposed as forces of dark and light (respectively), the goblin king provided a villainous counterpart to a fairy queen or godmother. The precedent for this trope extended back to the late medieval and early modern periods, when the character of the fairy queen was at her height of popularity in England and lowland Scotland, though it found new life across genres in the mid- to late nineteenth century.[79] A Christmas story from 1853 juxtaposes the benevolent and

[77] See, for example, E.P. Wolferstan, *The Enchanted Flute, with Other Poems* (London: Longman, Hurst, Rees, Orme, and Brown, 1823), 424; D.L.J., "The Diamond Ring," *The Ladies' Museum* 1 (1830): 225; Julia Goddard, *More Stories* (London: Arthur Hall, Smart, and Allen, 1863), 96.

[78] Goblin queens were rare compared to their male counterparts (especially in the early to mid-nineteenth century). A character, for example, from one of Yeats' poems refers to an enchantress as a "goblin queen." An operetta features a "Goblin Queen" who is repelled by a prince loyal to the "Queen of the Fairies." William Butler Yeats, *The Wanderings of Oisin: Dramatic Sketches, Ballads & Lyrics* (London: T. Fisher Unwin, 1892), 143; "Scenes in Fairyland," *The San Francisco Examiner*, September 30, 1896.

[79] Hutton sees the revivals of the fairy queen in the nineteenth and twentieth centuries (the latter via Galadriel in *The Lord of the Rings*) as "mere echoes" of her glory in the medieval and early modern periods. Hutton, *Queens of the Wild: Pagan Goddesses in Christian Europe: An Investigation*, 108–9. Many French fairy tales of the early modern period "placed the power of metamorphosis in the hands of women.... Gifted women writers at the seventeenth century preferred to address themselves to a fairy and to have a fairy resolve the conflicts in their fairy tales than the Church with its male-dominated hierarchy." Jack Zipes, *When Dreams Came True: Classical Fairy Tales and Their Tradition* (New York: Routledge, 1999),

beautiful fairies of the forest with the mischievous cave-dwelling goblin, which was "an ugly little monster" of short stature and a "dark brown face."[80] Those from the 1870s, which were increasingly written for children, moved away from the Dickensian goblin to one that needed to be defeated by child protagonists—a broader reflection of fairy tales that saw the righteous defeat of an antagonistic creature. An 1872 story takes places in a version of Fairyland where goblins and fairies are "always at war." The former live in an appropriately dark "Goblin Land," which has gloomy weather, black water, weird trees with gnarled trunks, and no flowers except for the deadly nightshade.[81] The 1873 story "Jonquil and Azalea" similarly features a dark and hazardous "Goblin Land" filled with "Goblins of Darkness" that are oppositional to the "Fairies of Light."[82]

Theater and musical productions sometimes utilized this theme, too.[83] An 1854 pantomime juxtaposes a goblin's "den of doom" with the idyllic "fairy glade" lit by the moonlight.[84] A similar comparison was sometimes made between goblins and elves. An 1860 pantomime adaptation of *The Life and Adventures of Peter Wilkins* (1751) received a positive review from one critic, who notes the difference between the "grim and fantastic" dance of the goblins (which had "distorted physiognomies") compared to the "picturesque and graceful" ballet of the elves of Elfinland.[85] The concert program for an 1890 performance of Mendelssohn's overture for *A*

13. The role of Queen Victoria in this ascension is clear, as she was represented as a range of folkloric figures during her reign, from Titania to the Queen of Hearts. Eric C. Brown, "The Influence of Queen Victoria on England's Literary Fairy Tale," *Marvels & Tales* 13, no. 1 (1999): 31–51.

[80] Notable in this story, too, are internal differences between goblins. Our heroes allow one of the more helpful goblins to live as long as he "would in future amend his life and morals" while the other two are tied together and left to annoy themselves indefinitely. "The Three Sisters—The Three Goblins—And the Three Counts," *Illustrated News*, March 4, 1853.

[81] "The Goblin of the Eagle's Cliff," *The Birmingham Post*, December 25, 1872.

[82] "Jonquil and Azalea: A Fairy Tale," *The Birmingham Post*, December 25, 1873.

[83] The juxtaposition of fairies and goblins as vessels of lightness and darkness was not universal. In an 1848 pantomime, *The Land of Light*, for example, all of the fairies (including Oberon, Puck, and Queen Mab) are driven underground to the Goblin Coal Mine to "escape the advance of science." In this case, the internal divisions among the creatures of Fairyland were less important than their vulnerability to technological advances. Richards, *The Golden Age of Pantomime: Slapstick, Spectacle and Subversion in Victorian England*, 189.

[84] "Robin Hood; Or, Harlequin, Friar Tuck, and the Merrie Men of the Merrie Greenwood," *Aris's Birmingham Gazette*, December 25, 1854.

[85] This performance is considered in Richards, *The Golden Age of Pantomime: Slapstick, Spectacle and Subversion in Victorian England*, 237–38.

Midsummer Night's Dream describes "goblin horns now sounding a deep base" and counterbalancing higher, more aerial notes.[86] A 1914 children's guide to playing the piano even juxtaposes the "black houses" (i.e., keys) of the goblins with the "white houses" of the fairies.[87]

Across genres, goblins and fairies could serve as opposites of each other—forces of black and white with all of their accompanying connotations. They were not constantly in opposition to one another in these stories, nor was there always a goblin king antagonistic to a fairy queen (the latter was far more common). Nonetheless, by the middle of the nineteenth century, we can see clearly diverging paths for these folkloresque creatures that were once (and for some, still) synonymous entities. The same is true for other preternatural creatures, too, though we do not have space in this book to consider them in detail. To provide one brief example, elves became increasingly associated with construction in the mid-nineteenth century, both in Fairyland and the North Pole workshop of Santa Claus.[88] Sometimes these skills even led to cooperation with goblins. In 1891's *Lancelot and Guenevere: A Poem in Dramas*, for example, goblins provide the raw materials for elves to construct into a bridge.[89] Like the associations of goblins and fairies, this trend was not universal—though it indicates a larger process of essentializing the creatures of Fairyland into defining characteristics that stripped away folkloric ambiguities.

GEORGE MACDONALD AND HIS DEVOLVED GOBLINS

In 1872, George MacDonald published *The Princess and the Goblin*, a fantasy novel for children based on serialized short stories written over the previous two years, to warm reviews and strong sales. Central to its plot is an underground kingdom of antagonistic goblins whose appearance and

[86] G.H. Wilson, *Boston Symphony Orchestra Concert Programs Season 10* (Boston: C.A. Ellis, 1890), 308.

[87] In this case, though, the goblins and fairies work together in acoustic harmony. Samuel Fallows and Henry Ruoff, eds., "The Wonderful Land of Sound," in *The Human Interest Library*, vol. I, IV vols. (Chicago: The Midland Press, 1914), 280–81.

[88] Louisa May Alcott completed (but did not publish) an 1856 book: *Christmas Elves*. An 1873 work in *Godey's Lady's Book* also features Santa, toys, and elves. These depictions (especially in the United States) are tied to factory labor, for these elves "were not unlike immigrants… the best of them worked hard, long, and unselfishly." Penne Lee Restad, *Christmas in America: A History* (New York: Oxford University Press, 1997), 148–49.

[89] Richard Hovey, *Lancelot and Guenevere: A Poem in Dramas* (New York: United States Book Company, 1891), 54–56.

behaviors proved influential in subsequent works of fantasy, especially to the orcs of Tolkien. MacDonald presents goblins as devolutions of humans whose presence is enough to corrupt animals around them. They live within the dark depths of a mountain in a society that crudely reflects the aboveground human kingdom, complete with a goblin monarchy and royal court. Using their mining prowess, the goblins hatch a plan to tunnel into the nearby castle and kidnap the young princess, Irene. This plan is eventually thwarted by the actions of Curdie, a young miner, and the goblins are destroyed in a massive flood.

The Princess and the Goblin was part of a burgeoning corpus of children's literature produced in the mid- to late nineteenth century.[90] Authors drew on themes, settings, and characters from the world of folklore in stories designed for an audience of (increasingly literate) children. Instead of discouraging belief in goblins and fairies, as had been commonplace, these writers looked to the imagination of the innocent child as a font of inspiration. They crafted narratives with relatable, flawed protagonists that stood in marked contrast to the impossibly perfect children of earlier literature.[91] The presence of fantastical elements in these stories could both stimulate a child's imagination and provide guidance on how to conduct oneself in the real world. Authors disagreed, though, about the most fitting way to amend fairy lore for this new market, which reflected larger discussions in Victorian society about the nature of childhood itself.[92] Most authors instilled some kind of moralizing message within their children's literature, but this message was as varied as the writers who produced them—from George MacDonald's pro-Christian spirituality to

---

[90] See, generally, Maria Nikolajeva, "The Development of Children's Fantasy," in *The Cambridge Companion to Fantasy Literature*, Edward James and Farah Mendlesohn, eds. (New York: Cambridge University Press, 2012), 50–61; Levy and Mendlesohn, *Children's Fantasy Literature: An Introduction*, 27–48.

[91] Jackie C. Horne, *History and the Construction of the Child in Early British Children's Literature* (New York: Routledge, 2011). An 1836 article from *Youth's Companion* opens by asking whether its readers believe in hobgoblins and then telling a story about a supposed hobgoblin that turns out to be a few "roguish boys." "Hobgoblins," *Youth's Companion. And Sabbath School Recorder* IX, no. 51 (May 6, 1836): 203.

[92] As the nineteenth century progressed authors drifted away from using an omniscient narrator and instead told stories through the eyes of child protagonists. It also became more common for stories to reject children as blank slates onto which stories could happen and instead to show how a story intersected with the needs and understandings of a child. Levy and Mendlesohn, *Children's Fantasy Literature: An Introduction*, 34–47.

Lewis Carroll's critique of modern mores.[93] As authors of children's literature embraced the fantastic, those writing for adults trended toward
domestic realism, as (in a self-fulfilling prophecy) they saw fantasy and the
folkloresque as the realm of children.[94]

The fantasy worlds of George MacDonald drew on his anti-Calvinist
interpretation of Christianity, regional folklore, and fairy tales that he
encountered as a child in Scotland. One of MacDonald's maternal uncles
was editor of the *Gaelic Highland Dictionary*, his paternal grandfather
supported the publication of an edition of (the forged) *Ossian*, and his
step-uncle was a Shakespeare scholar.[95] Though he was raised Calvinist,
MacDonald pivoted away from the more repressive ideas of his church as
he trained to be a preacher. He did not find a congregation receptive to
these ideas of redemption and benevolence, so he turned to teaching and
writing for income. His first novel, *Phantastes* (1858), which depicts a
student's adventure when his room gradually turns into a magical forest,
is arguably one of the "earliest modern fantasy novels."[96] Spurred by the
success of *Phantastes*, MacDonald published a steady stream of novels and
short stories over the next thirty-seven years that, though imbued with
varying degrees of fantastical influences and whimsy, were undergirded by
a theological weight reflecting his belief in the potential for Christians to
achieve moral growth and atonement.[97] The widespread acclaim of these
books brought MacDonald fame and notoriety; he even mentored and

[93] Daniel Gabelman, "Organised Innocence: MacDonald, Lewis, and Literature 'For the
Childlike,'" in *Informing the Inklings: George MacDonald and the Victorian Roots of Modern
Fantasy*, ed. Michael Partridge and Kirstin Jeffrey Johnson (Hamden: Winged Lion Press,
2018), 69–94.

[94] Wolfe, "Fantasy from Dryden to Dunsany," 14.

[95] Kirstin Jeffrey Johnson, "Rooted Deep: Discovering the Literary Identity of Mythopoeic
Fantasist George MacDonald," *Linguaculture* 2 (2014): 28–29. In reflections on his childhood, MacDonald speaks of reading *The Arabian Nights* obsessively; of loving, if not understanding, his father's copy of "The Rime of The Ancient Mariner"; and of finding a passion
for Shakespeare. Barbara Amell, *The Art of God: Lectures on the Great Poets by George
MacDonald*. (Portland: Wingfold Books, 2004), 103.

[96] Wolfe, "Fantasy from Dryden to Dunsany," 13. Contemporaries of MacDonald referred
to *Phantastes* as a fairy tale, as the established genre and terminology of "fantasy" did not
yet exist.

[97] Daniel Gabelman, *George MacDonald: Divine Carelessness and Fairytale Levity* (Waco:
Baylor University Press, 2023).

urged Lewis Carroll to submit for publication his manuscript of *Alice's Adventures in Wonderland.*[98]

Contemporary discussions about folklore seeped into MacDonald's works and were crucial to the titular antagonists of *The Princess and the Goblin.*[99] He frames this story as a fairy tale of sorts. The opening sentence of the story, "There was once a little princess whose father was king over a great country full of mountains and valleys," provides a familiar landscape into which fantastical elements are soon layered. MacDonald introduces his antagonists with an acknowledgment of their ambiguities, as they are a "strange race of beings, called by some gnomes, by some kobolds, by some goblins."[100] However they are named, they used to live like humans but were driven underground by royal persecution—at the bottom of the hierarchy of lifeforms present in this world.[101] MacDonald considers the grotesque transformation that accompanied this process:

> They were now, not ordinarily ugly, but either absolutely hideous, or ludicrously grotesque both in face and form. There was no invention, they said, of the most lawless imagination expressed by pen or pencil, that could surpass the extravagance of their appearance. And as they grew mis-shapen in body, they had grown in knowledge and cleverness, and now were able to do things no mortal could see the possibility of. But as they grew in cunning, they grew in mischief, and their great delight was in every way they could think of to annoy the people who lived in the open-air-story above them.[102]

Goblins are a heinous race beyond description, though MacDonald's subsequent attempt utilizes language of ugliness and the grotesque that was a common marker for these creatures. They have disproportionately

---

[98] He also published a collection of his own fairy tales. George MacDonald, *Dealing with the Fairies* (London: Alexander Strahan, 1867).

[99] John Patrick Pazdziora, *Haunted Childhoods in George MacDonald* (Leiden: Brill, 2020), 137, 165.

[100] George MacDonald, *The Princess and the Goblin* (Philadelphia: J.B. Lippincott & Co., 1872), 7.

[101] Aline Sidny Faben, "Folklore in the Fantasies and Romances of George MacDonald" (Doctoral Dissertation, Buffalo, SUNY Buffalo, 1978), 111. In the book's sequel, *The Princess and Curdie*, MacDonald notes that "a mountain is a strange an awful thing… to me they are beautiful terrors." George MacDonald, *The Princess and Curdie* (London: Blackie & Son, 1888), 1.

[102] MacDonald, *The Princess and the Goblin*, 8–9.

large (and vulnerable) feet and a crippling aversion to song, both of which contribute to their eventual defeat.[103] Matching the goblins' hideous appearance is their hatred of humans. Using their keen intellect and cunning—an apparent product of their hideous devolution—the goblins hatch a handful of evil schemes, most prominently the plot to kidnap Princess Irene. The corrupting aura of these creatures is such that they even devolve animals around them:

> They were of course household animals belonging to the goblins, whose ancestors had taken their ancestors many centuries before from the upper regions of light into the lower regions of darkness. The original stocks of these horrible creatures were very much the same as the animals now seen about farms and homes in the country…. But in the course of time all had undergone even greater changes than had passed upon their owners. They had altered—that is, their descendants had altered—into such creatures as I have not attempted to describe except in the vaguest manner—the various parts of their bodies assuming, in an apparently arbitrary and self-willed manner, the most abnormal developments.[104]

The fantastical goblins of MacDonald have a detailed origin story that sets them apart from their predecessors. Depending on the context, other iterations of goblins encountered for this book were malevolent demons stalking the earth on behalf of Satan, some sort of intermediate entity between Christian angels and demons, figments of the imagination, one of countless creatures of folklore believed by some and rejected by others, or unexplainable fantastical creatures embedded in works of fiction. Across these interpretations, little attention is paid to their origins. MacDonald's goblins are decidedly creatures of fantasy, though they draw on contemporary understandings of natural science—a reinterpretation that brought narrative consequences. As devolved humans, the antagonists of *The Princess and the Goblin* retain many of the characteristics of human society. They speak English, have (crude) names, are grouped into families living in cave-houses, are excellent miners, and are organized into a monarchy with a king, queen, and prince. They are also mortal, as this story ends

---

[103] Some of these traits (and a few of the story elements of *The Princess and the Goblin*) likely derive from a story within *Granny's Wonderful Chair*. Colin Manlove, "George MacDonald and the Fairy Tales of Francis Paget and Frances Browne," *North Wind: A Journal of George MacDonald Studies* 18 (1999): 17–32.

[104] MacDonald, *The Princess and the Goblin*, 89.

with much of the goblin colony drowning beneath the mountain while the survivors flee.

The influence of evolutionary theory within this interpretation of goblins is clear.[105] MacDonald was familiar with the work of Darwin, as he directly referred to it in his novels *Malcolm* (1875) and *Lilith* (1895).[106] In *The Princess and the Goblin*, the antagonists are driven underground and evolve in keeping with their new environment—and MacDonald even toys with controversies surrounding evolutionary theory when Curdie discovers that goblins have no toes.[107] As Curdie discusses this with other miners, one of them "who had had more schooling than the rest" argues that "such must have been the primordial condition of humanity, and that education and handicraft had developed both toes and fingers."[108] Thus, this miner applies Darwinian thought to challenge the idea that goblins devolved from humans (instead, it was humans that evolved from goblins), inviting readers to challenge the discourse of evolutionary degeneracy and teratology of these creatures. Some of these goblins even try to use their perceived inferiorities to their advantage. When one goblin inspires his comrades to attack the humans and their castle, he proclaims that humans look upon them "as a degraded race" even though the goblins "excel them as far in mental ability."[109]

The eventual defeat of the goblins provides them, perhaps counterintuitively, with an opportunity for improvement. Although many perished in this great flood beneath the mountain, the survivors became "milder in

[105] Darwin published *On the Origin of Species* in 1859, and though its central theory remained the subject of debate across the nineteenth century, "evolutionism was triumphant" by the 1870s in Britain. Peter J. Bowler, *Evolution: The History of an Idea*, 3rd ed. (Berkeley: University of California Press, 2003), 179.

[106] One of the characters in *Malcolm*, "long before the younger Darwin arose, had suspected a close relationship—remote identity, indeed, in nature and history, between the animal and human worlds." In *Lilith*, Darwin and James Clerk Maxwell are compared to "Ptolemy, Dante, the two Bacons, and Boyle." George MacDonald, *Malcolm*, 2nd ed., vol. I (London: Henry S. King & Co., 1875), 76–77; George MacDonald, *Lilith*, 2nd ed. (London: Chatto & Windus, 1896), 2.

[107] MacDonald did not always write as if goblins were a distinct species. In his 1858 *Phantastes*, for example, he writes of "the gnomes or goblin-fairies, who inhabit the ground and earthy creeping plantings" and of a "desert region of dry sand and glittering rocks, peopled principally by goblin-fairies." George MacDonald, *Phantastes: A Faerie Romance for Men and Women* (London: Smith, Elder and Co., 1858), 35, 110.

[108] MacDonald, *The Princess and the Goblin*, 55; Sarah Ellis, "Darwin's Goblins," *Humanist in Canada* 36, no. 147 (2004).

[109] MacDonald, *The Princess and the Goblin*, 62.

character, and indeed became very much like the Scotch Brownies."[110] Additional changes accompanied this evolution: their skulls and hearts became softer, their feet harder, and they became friendlier with the other inhabitants of the mountain (miners included).[111] Though goblins devolved from humans, MacDonald makes explicit their ability to rise from this state of corruption and transform into something less evil. Circling around this depiction of goblins is language that reflects contemporary discourse about the lineage of fairies among the pygmies. As explored in the previous chapter, scholars sometimes considered groups in Central Africa to be the modern descendants of the European fairies and to accordingly behave "goblin-like." Racist evolutionary ideas dictated that pygmies were less evolved than their counterparts (hence frequent comparisons to primates) and that the color of their dark skin reflected their sin and grotesquery. MacDonald's goblins reflect this tradition to some degree —his goblins bear the same descriptions of darkness and evolutionary degeneracy—though he does not make the explicit connection between these antagonistic goblins and any group on this earth. Variations in depictions of these goblins, per Holdsworth, might even indicate that MacDonald wanted to throw into question these theories (Fig. 5.6).[112]

Indeed, the visual appearance of these goblins (as drawn by Arthur Hughes) is irregular. At times, they appear darker than the night around them, but at other times they are fairer in complexion. Most have long beards, though the scene in the king's wine cellar shows them clean-shaven. That said, MacDonald's written descriptions are more consistent in counterposing the blackness of goblins with the whiteness of Irene's great-great-grandmother, who functions more or less as a fairy godmother (despite never being called as such). When Irene emerges from an encounter with the goblins beneath the mountain, for example, she is thrilled to escape "from the darkness and fear through which she had come" and to

---

[110] MacDonald, *The Princess and the Goblin*, 202.

[111] The use of evolutionary ideas in fairy tales was "not uncommon" in the second half of the nineteenth century. Keene, *Science in Wonderland: The Scientific Fairy Tales of Victorian Britain*, 111.

[112] Holdsworth argues that the "unreliable narration, juxtaposition, and contradiction between text and image" of *The Princess and the Goblin* "suggests, through the goblins, that the ideas that underpin eugenics discourses, physiognomy, phrenology, and degeneration theory are flawed." Dylan Holdsworth, *The Government of Disability in Dystopian Children's Texts* (New York: Palgrave Macmillan, 2024), 21.

Fig. 5.6   The antagonists of *The Princess and the Goblin*. Depictions of goblins and their beasts from the 1872 edition of *The Princess and the Goblin* (illustrated by Arthur Hughes). Images (cropped) courtesy of HathiTrust. (MacDonald, *The Princess and the Goblin*, 8, 59, 88, 119, 142, 181. Accessible here: https://babel. hathitrust.org/cgi/pt?id=hvd.hwrfdk&seq=1)

the light of her grandmother's room, which was as if she was "going into the heart of the milkiest pearl." The goblins live a grotesque existence in "universal and constant darkness" under the mountain, while the great-great-grandmother is beautiful, with skin "smooth and white" accompanied by silver hair.[113]

---

[113] MacDonald, *The Princess and the Goblin*, 15–16, 97. See also Dimitra Fimi, *Tolkien, Race and Cultural History: From Fairies to Hobbits* (Basingstoke: Palgrave Macmillan, 2008), 31–32.

Although MacDonald's goblins drew heavily on folkloresque motifs, he broke with them in making goblins unambiguously mortal. By situating goblins as a kind of devolved human, MacDonald gave these creatures a human life cycle complete with birth, marriage, birth, and death. He avoids the more risqué components of this subject matter, though explicit in the kidnapping plot of the goblins is the forced marriage of the Goblin Prince to Irene so that they can have a hybrid human/goblin family. The climactic scene of *The Princess and the Goblin* is the foiling of this plan and the resultant mass destruction of these goblins in a flash flood. Never before had goblins been so thoroughly slaughtered in any piece of folklore or literature (to my knowledge), even if earlier fairy tales had provided a permission structure for heroic children righteously defeating their foes. Though MacDonald's goblins exist in the pages of an expressly fictional work, they are framed using evolutionary theory that justifies their wretched appearance and behaviors—and this same framework permits some of them to crawl out of these depraved depths and to behave in a more humane way.

MORE GOBLINS OF THE LATE NINETEENTH CENTURY

The enduring popularity of MacDonald's goblins in fantasy literature did not preclude continued diversity in representations of these creatures across genres and audiences in the late nineteenth century. Though some Victorian-era authors used Fairyland to challenge prevailing cultural mores, others used it to scare children into appropriate behavior. The poem "The Goblin Cat" (1876) recounts the fate of a young boy who drowned a cat and her brood in exchange for money with which to buy candy. The sweet in his pocket, however, eventually transforms into a "goblin grim," an ethereal manifestation of the drowned cat with "six spectral kittens" dangling from her mouth, which causes the boy to run endlessly away from the terror and its "shrieks of feline laughter."[114] James Whitcomb Riley's 1885 poem "The Elf-Child," which changed to the more enduring "Little Orphant Annie" in a later printing, was widely cir-culated in the United States and the subject of a handful of adaptations in the early twentieth century. This fict tells of goblins snatching away

---

[114] Peter Bell, "The Goblin Cat," in *Little Folks' Speeches and Dialogues*, Beadle's Dime Dialogues 17 (New York: Beadle and Adams, 1876), 77–78.

impudent children who do not obey their elders or help those in need. Each of its stanzas ends with an emphatic warning:

> An' the Gobble-uns 'at gits you
> > Ef you
> > > Don't
> > > > Watch
> > > > > Out![115]

Goblins also continued to serve as markers of the supernatural. In penny dreadfuls, which were cheaply produced and marketed toward young working-class men, we see characters looking to unearth "the hob-goblin devils" of the night or encountering a "ghost-haunted hole" with oddly shaped rocks that might be hobgoblins."[116] These broad evocations could also be used to denote a time now past, one in which people believed in the presence of the fairies—another iteration of their perpetual recession. In one of the stories from Rudyard Kipling's fantasy anthology, *Puck of Pook's Hill* (1906), for example, Puck laments how the people of the hills, "giants, trolls, kelpies brownies, goblins, imps" (and many more), have departed this land.[117] The equation of goblins and other supernatural beings, especially dwarves, was commonplace. The short story "The Revenge of the Dwarfs" (1904) speaks interchangeably of the "Dwarf King" and the "King of the Hob-goblins." Flipping the script of MacDonald and hearkening back to the fairy tales of the Brothers Grimm, though, this goblin kills an evil villager who delighted in terrorizing his neighbors.[118]

When goblins feature more prominently in stories, they are monstrous and irregular. In *Nailed to the Mast* (1885), a "deformed" and "ugly dwarf" that emerges from the sea is initially described as "some hideous, distorted goblin."[119] *The Golden Goblin* (1906), too, includes goblins with

---

[115] Early editions of this poem were published in American newspapers. James Whitcomb Riley, "The Elf-Child," *The Indiana State Sentinel*, November 25, 1885.

[116] *The Skeleton Crew* (London: Newsagents' Publishing Company, 1867), 32; Edwin Harcourt Burrage, *The Brigands of Palestra* (London, 1893), 90. See also John Springhall, "'Disseminating Impure Literature': The 'Penny Dreadful' Publishing Business Since 1860," *The Economic History Review* 47, no. 3 (August 1994): 567–84.

[117] Rudyard Kipling, *Puck of Pook's Hill* (New York: Charles Scribner's Sons, 1906), 13.

[118] "The Revenge of the Dwarfs," *The Lichfield Mercury*, October 14, 1904.

[119] In a later scene, when the protagonists sail into a goblin cave, they are greeted with a supernatural cavern without a clear exit or entrance: "The walls were irregular, and the pro-

"features of human beings being rendered grotesque by long green mustaches and greet green, bushy eyebrows" and large, webbed hands and feet. The titular creature, his "Cantankerous Majesty," meanwhile, is "so grotesque" that one of the characters is "tempted to laugh aloud."[120] The short story "Mordreda, The White Wolf" (1880) tells of a seemingly ageless sorceress with a penchant for eating children. When she gives birth to a son and prepares to eat him, Odin turns the child into a fiendish changeling in a "series of goblin evolutions."[121] Eventually named Oolf, this hideous creature is described alternatingly as a pygmy, dwarf, and goblin—echoing the racialized language of contemporary anthropology and evolutionary theory. Although the text of this story describes Oolf as having a yellow and dried-up complexion like a mummy, the art accompanying this text (limited by black-and-white printing) emphasizes his darkness (Fig. 5.7).

Oolf is a supernatural evil cut from the same heinous cloth as his mother and has dark skin to match. This association is no coincidence. Surging interest in serialized adventure stories for young men roughly coincided with waves of European colonial expansion into the Global South during the late nineteenth century. The connection between goblins, dark skin, grotesque appearance, and evil deeds reinforced racist attitudes of the time. Goblins—like some people—were freaks in appearance and behavior.[122] We can see these intersections explicitly in an 1885 serialized story about the legendary Caratacus, a chieftain who resisted Roman rule. One of the villains he encounters is the slaver Zaba, a "goblin-like dwarf" from Ethiopia. With skin "black as night," Zaba delights in making Christians

---

jections and deep indentures took hideous goblin forms under the blue light. Crystals were imbedded in some places, and sparkled like diamonds, whilst from the ceiling long stalactites of various hues hung, giving the place a beautiful but goblin appearance." *Nailed to the Mast* (London: Boys of England Office, 1885), 38, 79–80.

[120] Curtis Dunham, *The Golden Goblin* (Indianapolis: The Bobbs-Merrill Company, 1906), 115–16, 128.

[121] "Mordreda, the White Wolf," *Barons of Old* II (1880): 4.

[122] We encounter poetry, for example, that describes "music of some goblin freak" and the "freak the moody goblin plays." In prose, too, we hear of the "freak of some goblin" and the equation of a freak with a "suggestion of the Goblin Whim." Geoffrey Oldcastle, "Visits from the Other World," *The Canterbury Magazine* I, no. 4 (October 1834): 159; Henry Austen Driver, *Harold de Burun: A Semi-Dramatic Poem* (London: Longman, Rees, Orme, Brown, Green, and Longman, 1835), 5; Amelia B. Edwards, *Barbara's History*, vol. I (Leipzig: Bernhard Tauchnitz, 1864), 307; Rose Haig Thomas, *Pan: A Collection of Lyrical Poems* (London: Bliss, Sands and Co., 1897), 29.

Fig. 5.7 Cover image of "Mordreda, The White Wolf." "Do not despise me, mother," cried the goblin sprite. Image (cropped) courtesy of the British Library Collection (located on page 1 of Shelfmark C.140.a.12)

suffer even more than Nero himself.[123] Another story from 1889 implies that evil and darkness can corrupt a person's physical appearance in a juxtaposition of two brothers, the fair-haired and blue-eyed Cecil (a "picture of his good, open-hearted mother") and the malicious, dark-skinned Michael:

> Michael, in contradiction to his brother's personal appearance, was dark, small-eyed, and so evil of aspect that the country folk shunned him, and even some of the superstitious went so far as to whisper that he was a goblin changeling.[124]

The darkness and evil of Michael are such that the superstitious associate him with the kind of creature that embodies these qualities: a goblin changeling. This is not to say that all goblins had dark skin. One of the central characters of 1890's *The Boys of Hawkhouse School* is a white boy

---

[123] *Caractacus: Champion of the Arena* (London: Hogarth House, 1885), 19.
[124] *Cheeky Charlie* (London: C. Fox, 1889), 10.

nicknamed "Goblin Jim," who was "always gobbling up something eatable or drinkable."[125] These dietary habits are perhaps Goblin Jim's most redeemable quality, though, as he performs many acts of evil across this story. Before meeting his ultimate demise (tarred and set aflame before jumping into the sea), Goblin Jim is described in no uncertain terms as "by nature a coward, and extremely cruel, delighting in witnessing another's pain." Goblin Jim had such strange behaviors and performed such wicked deeds that "goblin" was an apt nickname.

The specter of race loomed over goblins in other media, too. The lyrics to "The Ragtime Goblin Man" (1911) describe how a goblin man follows people around with a hook in his hand, hoping to kidnap them and make them part of his "raggedy band"—either that or "he'll beat you, then he'll eat you." The undertones of these lyrics, however, change radically depending on the cover art of the song's sheet music (Fig. 5.8). The racist connotations of the right image are unmistakable, as a devilish Black goblin zaps two petrified white people. The creature's exaggerated facial features are characteristic of racist minstrel shows and blackface. Indeed, the song itself provides an example of white musicians (Sterling and Von Tilzer) co-opting a Black art form and then using racist tropes to sell copies of it. The white goblin on the left, though, does not pose the same kind of threat. It is small, goofy, and pale—standing on a piano and toothily grinning around a sea of musical notes, equipped with bass and treble clefs. These two printings of "The Ragtime Goblin Man," beyond highlighting racist tropes gravitating around goblins, reinforce that the appearance of these creatures could change to suit a given agenda and target audience.[126]

---

[125] *The Boys of Hawkhouse School* (London: Alfred Bradley, 1890), 5. The equation of the goblin and the act of gobbling up food, though the words were not etymologically related, is echoed in some works of fiction (both intended for children and adults) from the mid- to late nineteenth century—often for comedic effect. Henry W. Wynn, *Ravencourt* (London: Simpkin, Marshall and Company, 1843), 50; Francis Davis, *Earlier and Later Leaves* (Belfast: W.H. Greer, 1878), 12; Alice Corkran, *Down the Snow Stairs* (London: Blackie & Son, 1887), 196.

[126] It is possible that the left cover was intended for display and use on a parlor piano, while the right was part of a small booklet intended for personal use—though this is admittedly speculation. I would like to thank Eric Lott for his advice on this matter. The threat of a hungry goblin man with a "great big mouth and eyes," preying on naughty boys and those who stay out late, is also central to the 1904 piece "The Goblin Man" from the comic opera *The Girl and the Bandit*. Ed Rose and Ted Snyder, *The Girl and the Bandit* (New York: F.A. Mills, 1904).

Fig. 5.8 Two covers for "The Ragtime Goblin Man." (Images courtesy of the University of Maine's Vocal Popular Sheet Music Collection (left) and the Lester S. Levy Sheet Music Collection, The Sheridan Libraries, Johns Hopkins University (right). Andrew B. Sterling and Harry Von Tilzer, *The Ragtime Goblin Man* (New York: Harry Von Tilzer Music Publishing Co., 1911). The left image is score 5569 in the Vocal Popular Sheet Music Collection at the University of Maine and is accessible here: https://digitalcommons.library.umaine.edu/mmb-vp/5569/. The right image is box 154, item 082 in the Lester S. Levy Sheet Music Collection: https://levysheetmusic.mse.jhu.edu/collection/154/082)

Although goblins were often rendered as malicious characters, more comical interpretations of them persisted. Pantomime and burlesque theater provided slapstick and merry adaptations of fairy tales with increasing complexity and budgets by the end of the nineteenth century. The production of *The Grim Goblin* (1876–1880), for example, features a giant mechanical octopus and mechanical trickery that allowed "giants to shrink to dwarfs" and actors to perform seemingly impossible jumps.[127] An 1874 performance of *Jack and the Beanstalk* includes goblin trees that confuse,

---

[127] "Versatile George Conquest: Something About the English Pantomimist and the 'Grim Goblin,'" *The New York Times*, July 24, 1880.

attack, and dance around two of the characters during a lightning storm.[128] Satires like *The Goblin Snob* use the inhabitants of Fairyland to poke fun at more serious interpretations of fairy tales, and one of the first humor magazines in the United States was titled *Puck* (founded in 1876) after Shakespeare's fairy.[129] An 1869 poem fondly recalls this merry interpretation of Puck several years before the magazine itself was launched:

> Puck is the maddest merriest of them all;
> Puck, that old goblin, ugly, quaint, and small,
> Who, though he knoweth no delight unless
> He work some mischief, or what men so call,
> Yet only hateth to behold distress,–
> He, the chief source and spring of their lightheartedness.[130]

Some of the goblins within children's literature reflected these comical traditions, too. Canadian author Palmer Cox wrote comical fairy stories in his collection *Queer People Such as Goblins, Giants, Merry-men and Monarchs, and their Kweer Kapers*.[131] Lewis Carroll ultimately rejected the title *Alice Among the Goblins* in favor of *Alice's Adventures in Wonderland*. One of his imitators, however, evidently preferred the sentiment of the latter. In 1884–1885, American author Charles E. Carryl published *Davy and the Goblin*, featuring a goblin that leads Davy on a number of adventures through a Wonderland-like world, a comical reflection of our earth, replete with comical mischief and pranks.[132] In *Johnnykin and the Goblins* (1876), a similar story unfolds when Johnnykin protects an odd stone

---

[128] J.F. McArdle, *Grand Comic Christmas Pantomime, Jack and the Beanstalk* (Liverpool: Daily Post Steam Printing Works, 1874), 38–39.

[129] Henry L. Stephens, *The Goblin Snob* (New York: De Witt & Davenport, 1850); Tom Culbertson, "Illustrated Essay: The Golden Age of American Political Cartoons," *The Journal of the Gilded Age and Progressive Era* 7, no. 3 (July 2008): 276–95. This magazine is separate from *Goblin*, a Canadian humor magazine founded by students at the University of Toronto in the 1920s. Issues have been digitized here: https://archive.org/details/uoftarchives?tab=collection&query=%22the+goblin%22.

[130] Arthur Compton Auchmuty, *Verses: Original and Translated* (Exeter: William Roberts, 1869), 9.

[131] Here, the term "goblin" ought to be taken as a generic category, as no named goblins appear specifically in these tales. Palmer Cox, *Queer People Such as Goblins, Giants, Merry-Men and Monarchs, and Their Kweer Kapers* (Philadelphia: Hubbard Brothers, 1888).

[132] This goblin has a familiarly grotesque-yet-comical appearance: "He was only about a foot high, but his head was as big as a coconut, and he had great, bulging eyes, like a frog, and a ridiculous turned-up nose…. His mouth was so wide that when he smiled it seemed to

statue from a group of boys.[133] The statue then comes to life as "the Goblin" and shepherds Johnnykin through a series of magical adventures. These goblins, though their initial appearance startles the stories' antagonists, are ultimately benevolent forces through which children are transported into a world of magic.

SOME QUANTITATIVE CONCLUSIONS

By the beginning of the twentieth century, goblins were mainstays of folklore as both a particular kind of impish creature and a broad category of analysis for scholars. Their reputation for supernatural mischief and freakish appearance led to broad applications of the term to refer to humans, wildlife, objects, and ideas. Anglophone writers—the vast majority of whom were elite, white men—saw human goblins in particular as grotesque perversions. They used teratology, scientific racism, and pro-colonial rhetoric to justify this classification, which dehumanized those that transgressed acceptable conduct and appearance, especially Black groups in Central Africa and people with disabilities (namely dwarfism). In works of literary fiction, many goblins retained their longstanding association with darkness, malevolence, and the supernatural—though the tradition of the merry and comical goblin persisted in some circles. The rise of fantastical elements in children's literature in particular led to more detailed descriptions of goblins, and these depictions were accompanied in some cases by illustrations that visualized their grotesque appearance.

The last two chapters have articulated these ideas across the nineteenth century. In this analysis, I have considered both authors of lasting influence and those whose work has left less of a mark on the historical record. This breadth, I hope, has provided a sense of the many ways in which goblins were invoked—though this emphasis on qualitative synthesis admittedly runs the risk of overlooking broader trends across a voluminous corpus of print media. By looking quantitatively at nineteenth-century sources through digitized databases containing thousands of texts, however, we can glimpse such trends. This analysis shows how the popularity of Halloween in the United States pulled goblins from

go quite behind his ears, and there was no way of knowing where the smile ended." Charles E. Carryl, *Davy and the Goblin* (Boston: Ticknor and Company, 1885), 13.

[133]When these boys retreat, they "look like goblins themselves... like little black imps." Charles Godfrey Leland, *Johnnykin and the Goblins* (London: MacMillan, 1876), 12.

Christmas to this spookier holiday, how goblins came to eclipse hobgoblins in usage, and how authors were slotting the creatures of Fairyland into specific cultural niches that differentiated these once-synonymous entities.

Most of this book has grouped together literary trends in Britain and the United States. The circulation of literature across the Atlantic was indeed commonplace, especially for popular authors.[134] American authors, though, developed their own traditions relating to Fairyland. The folkloric traditions of England, as well as folkloresque media that invoked its themes, did not translate directly to its colonies, where opposition to these pagan ideas on religious grounds was commonplace.[135] Scottish and Irish immigration in the nineteenth century, however, brought new traditions to All Hallow's Eve (eventually elided into Halloween) that gradually expanded past these communities and into the broader cultural fabric of the United States.[136]

The movement of goblins from creatures of Christmas to those of Halloween can be glimpsed through newspaper data. Figures 5.9 and 5.10 show the frequency of the words "goblin" and "hobgoblin" within newspaper articles published in New York and England during the late nineteenth and early twentieth centuries. The first shows the relative percentage of occurrences of these terms in the week surrounding Christmas (December 22 to 28) and Halloween (October 28 to November 3) in New York. It indicates that the 1890s was an inflexion point for when these creatures were more associated with Halloween than Christmas. Even a cursory glance at newspaper articles from this decade (both within and outside of New York) shows the ubiquity of creatures of Fairyland—ghosts, goblins, and fairies especially—with all of their accompanying frights and merriment intended primarily for the entertainment of

---

[134] One story (which "probably has some mythic if not material truth to it") relates that American readers flocked to the docks to find out the fate of Nell. Patten, Robert L., "Publishing in Parts," in *Palgrave Advances in Charles Dickens Studies*, John Bowen and Robert L. Patten, eds. (New York: Palgrave Macmillan, 2005), 34.

[135] Variation existed in the United States, too. Southern author William Gilmore Simms disparages Santa Claus as a "dapper little Manhattan goblin" when compared to the "much more respectable" Father Christmas in an 1852 short story. William Gilmore Simms, *The Golden Christmas* (Charleston: Walker, Richards and Co., 1852), 150. This is not to say that American colonists did not develop their own folklore, but rather that fairy traditions of the Old World were less widespread there. See, for example, Ronald M. James. *Monumental Lies: Early Nevada Folklore of the Wild West* (Reno: University of Nevada Press. 2023).

[136] Nicholas Rogers, *Halloween: From Pagan Ritual to Party Night* (Oxford University Press, 2002), 67–101.

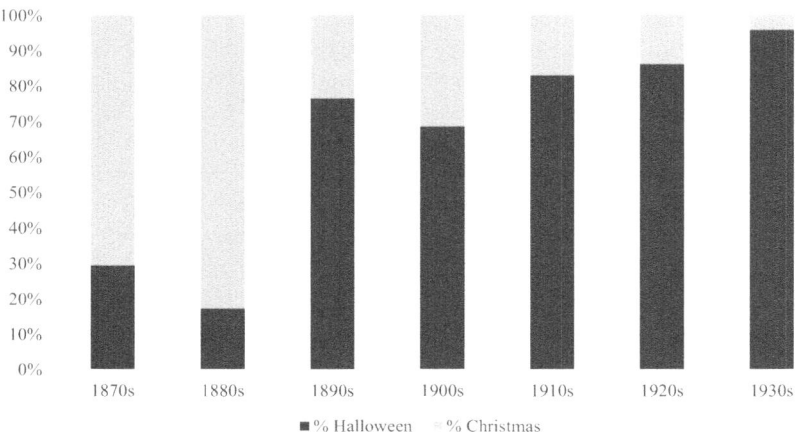

Fig. 5.9 Relative instances of "Goblin" and "Hobgoblin" in newspapers from New York. (Newspapers from New York show more instances of "goblin" and "hobgoblin" in the week surrounding Christmas in the 1870s and 1880s, but a clear association with Halloween in subsequent decades through the 1930s)

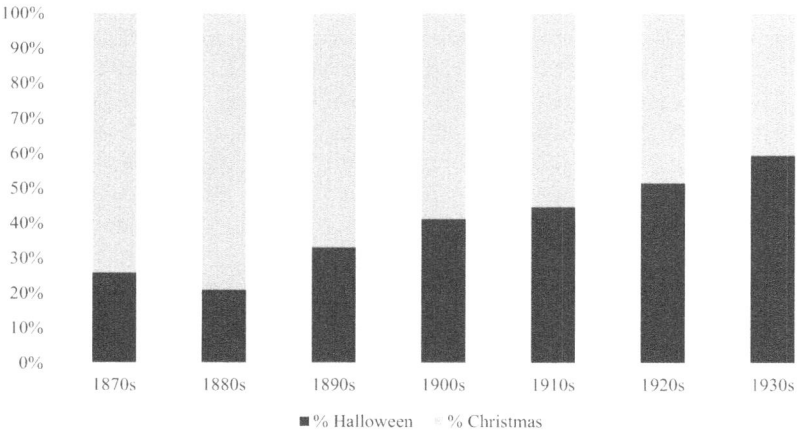

Fig. 5.10 Relative instances of "Goblin" and "Hobgoblin" in newspapers from England. (Newspapers from England show more instances of "goblin" and "hobgoblin" in the week surrounding Christmas instead of Halloween during the late nineteenth century, but begin to slightly favor Halloween by the 1920s and 1930s)

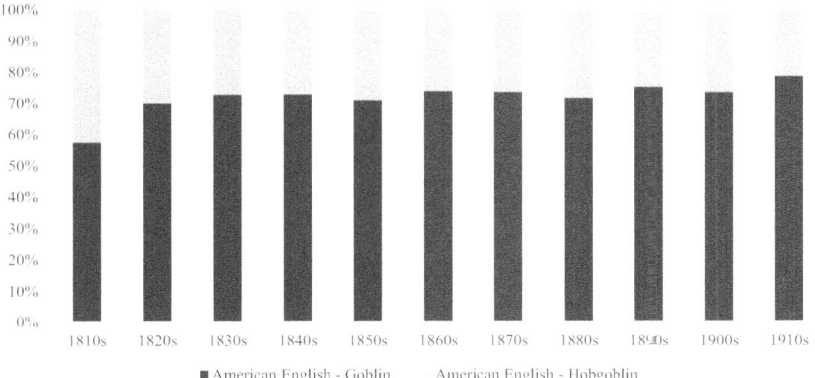

Fig. 5.11 Relative uses of "Goblin" and "Hobgoblin" in American English. (Texts in American English show a preference for the use of the word "goblin" instead of "hobgoblin" from 1810 to 1919)

children.[137] The second graph shows a less abrupt transition in England as the tradition of goblins in Christmas stories and pantomimes persisted well into the twentieth century but in diminishing numbers.

The nineteenth century also saw the ascendency of the lexeme "goblin" over "hobgoblin" in usage. It appears that the labeling of the hobgoblin as a particular kind of English spirit, often with ties to Puck and Robin Goodfellow of *A Midsummer Night's Dream*, meant that fewer authors invoked in outside of these contexts. This was not universal—the metaphorical invocation from Emerson of the "hobgoblin of little minds" is a notable exception—but the breadth of historic uses for the word "goblin" led to its appearance in more texts than its preternatural derivation. Figures 5.11 and 5.12 show relative uses of goblin, hobgoblin, and their derivations across the century in data extracted from Google Books via English Corpora.[138]

---

[137] See, for example, "Hallowe'en Aftermath. Goblins, Ghosts and Bogies Stalk Abroad. Everybody Makes Merry," *The Wayne Republican*, November 2, 1895; "It's Halloween: Goblins and Fairies Will Be Roaming Abroad To-Night," *The Philadelphia Inquirer*, 1898.

[138] See, generally, Douglas Biber and Randi Reppen, eds., *The Cambridge Handbook of English Corpus Linguistics* (New York: Cambridge University Press, 2015). This dataset is much larger than that of the dictionary data used in Chap. 3, which helps to explain the relative difference in usage of "goblin" and "hobgoblin" between the eighteenth and nineteenth centuries. It seems that compilers of early dictionaries, eager to relate the English language

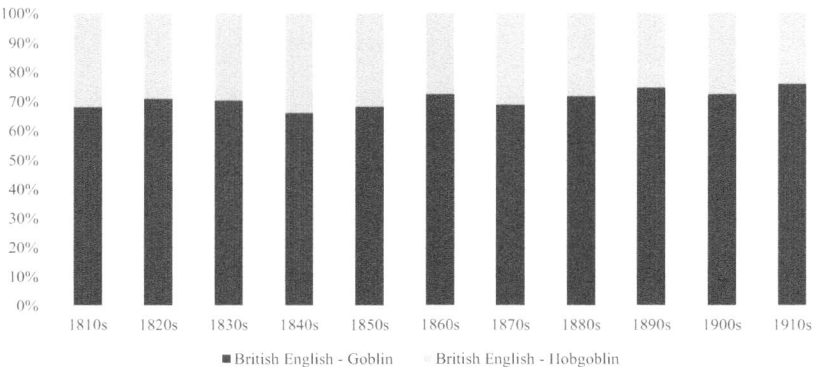

Fig. 5.12 Relative uses of "Goblin" and "Hobgoblin" in British English. (Texts in British English also show a preference for the use of the word "goblin" instead of "hobgoblin" from 1810 to 1919)

By the end of the nineteenth century, goblins and fairies were frequently opposing forces of dark and light (with all of their accompanying associations) in works of literature. The deployment of these terms to describe humans highlights this divergence. People with dark skin and men with physical disabilities were most likely to be associated with goblins. Fairies, conversely, had overarching associations of beauty and femininity. Women, children, and (pejoratively) men who behaved like women could be labeled as such.[139] Other creatures of Fairyland were also beginning to carve out niches for themselves, and though there are not enough pages in this book to relate these details, quantitative data can give a sense of one such divergent path. Ghosts, for example, became associated with ethereal spirits of the departed and were used as labels for stories with supernatural elements. Figure 5.13 shows the relative frequency of the terms "Fairy Story," "Ghost Story," and "Goblin Story" during the nineteenth century from Google Ngrams (both American and British

to its greatest playwright, elevated the hobgoblin to levels not reflected in other written media.

[139] The *OED* cites an 1896 article from the *American Journal of Psychology* as the earliest use of "fairy" as a pejorative for a gay man or a "man who behaves in a way stereotypically associated with women or gay men." *OED*, "Fairy."

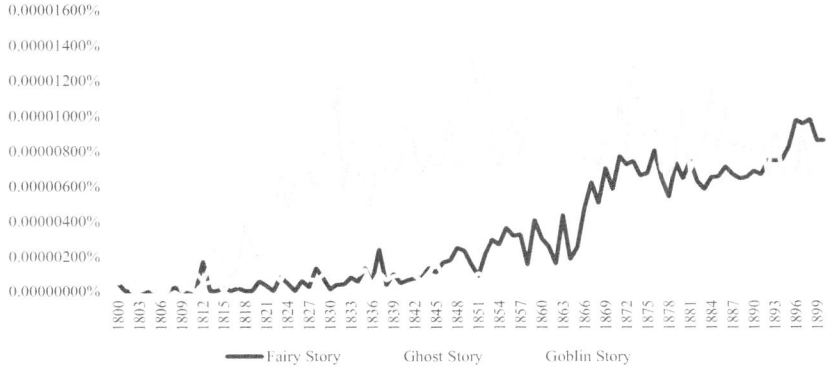

Fig. 5.13 Frequency of "Fairy Story," "Ghost Story," and "Goblin Story." (Data from Google Books shows the terms "Fairy Story" and "Ghost Story" overtake "Goblin Story" as the preferred designators for a preternatural tale during the mid- to late nineteenth century)

English).[140] Though the Goblin Story was used as a label for supernatural tales through the middle of the nineteenth century, it declined in use during the 1850s. Ghosts and fairies, rather than goblins, became the titular creatures of these stories, and published compilations of them might not even include the word "goblin." The world of "Goblindom" as described by folklorists, then, never had the traction of these other designators in popular literature.[141]

Turning our gaze to the beginning of the twentieth century, we see that centuries of folkloric and folkloresque traditions surrounding goblins were coalescing into a handful of dominant literary themes. The centuries-old use of goblins as markers of the supernatural (often used to disparage superstitious beliefs) remained, though their presence was not so ubiquitous as to be the appropriate umbrella name for this kind of story. When these creatures played more prominent roles in stories, they ranged in demeanor from comical to mischievous to malevolent (and sometimes all of the above). They were virtually guaranteed to inspire fear in humans

[140] I have not included a related chart of "Ghost Tale," "Goblin Tale," and "Fairy Tale," because the latter so thoroughly outnumbers the other two.

[141] In the preface to *English Fairy Tales*, Joseph Jacobs notes that "one cannot imagine a child saying, 'Tell us a folk-tale, nurse,' or 'Another nursery tale, please, grandma'" because of the ubiquity of the "fairy tale." Jacobs, *English Fairy Tales*, viii.

that encountered them (at least initially), and their monstrous appearance was sometimes couched in language of teratology and scientific racism aimed at populations that transgressed the boundaries of acceptable appearance. Goblins made their home in dark spaces outside of human settlements, usually deep within forests or beneath mountains, whence they launched campaigns to kill or abduct humans. Organized in crude societies under a goblin king, they were coded as masculine creatures—and increasingly ones that had to be fought or killed by righteous protagonists supported by a benevolent fairy queen or godmother. Even as folklorists remained comfortable with incredibly wide-ranging definitions of goblins, then, authors of fiction were gravitating toward these themes. They were by no means universal, but they were commonplace—and foundational to the works of Tolkien and other authors of fantasy literature in the twentieth century.

References

Amell, Barbara. 2004. *The Art of God: Lectures on the Great Poets by George MacDonald*. Portland: Wingfold Books.

Aris's Birmingham Gazette. 1854. Robin Hood; Or, Harlequin, Friar Tuck, and the Merrie Men of the Merrie Greenwood., December 25.

Attebery, Brian. 1980. *The Fantasy Tradition in American Literature: From Irving to Le Guin*. Bloomington: Indiana University Press.

Auchmuty, Arthur Compton. 1869. *Verses: Original and Translated*. Exeter: William Roberts.

Bell, Peter. 1876. The Goblin Cat. In *Little Folks' Speeches and Dialogues*, 77–78. Beadle's Dime Dialogues 17. New York: Beadle and Adams.

Biber, Douglas, and Randi Reppen, eds. 2015. *The Cambridge Handbook of English Corpus Linguistics*. New York: Cambridge University Press.

Bowler, Peter J. 2003. *Evolution: The History of an Idea*. 3rd ed. Berkeley: University of California Press.

Brown, Eric C. 1999. The Influence of Queen Victoria on England's Literary Fairy Tale. *Marvels & Tales* 13 (1): 31–51.

Brown, Nicola. 2006. *Fairies in Nineteenth-Century Art and Literature*. New York: Cambridge University Press.

Buckmaster, Jonathan. 2019. *Dickens's Clowns: Charles Dickens, Joseph Grimaldi and the Pantomime of Life*. Edinburgh: Edinburgh University Press.

Burrage, Edwin Harcourt. 1893. *The Brigands of Palestra*. London.

Burwick, Frederick. 2015. *British Drama of the Industrial Revolution*. New York: Cambridge University Press.

Campbell, Elizabeth. 1990. Of Mothers and Merchants: Female Economics in Christina Rossetti's 'Goblin Market'. *Victorian Studies* 33 (3, Spring): 393–410.

Caractacus: Champion of the Arena. 1885. London: Hogarth House.

Carpenter, Mary Wilson. 1991. 'Eat Me, Drink Me, Love Me': The Consumable Female Body in Christina Rossetti's Goblin Market. *Victorian Poetry* 29 (4, Winter): 415–434.

Carryl, Charles E. 1885. *Davy and the Goblin.* Boston: Ticknor and Company.

Chapman, Alison. 1997. Defining the Feminine Subject: D. G. Rossetti's Manuscript Revisions to Christina Rossetti's Poetry. *Victorian Poetry* 35 (2, Summer): 139–156.

Cheeky Charlie. 1889. London: C. Fox.

Chesterton, G. K. 1911. *Appreciations and Criticisms of the Works of Charles Dickens.* London: J.M. Dent.

Colman, George. 1770. *The Recitatives, Airs, &c.* In the New Pantomime Entertainment of Mother Shipton. London.

Corelli, Marie. 1910. *The Strange Visitation.* New York: Hodder and Stoughton.

Corkran, Alice. 1887. *Down the Snow Stairs.* London: Blackie & Son.

Countess d'Aulnoy, and J.R. Planché. 1855. Fairy Tales. London: G. Routledge.

Cox, Palmer. 1888. *Queer People Such as Goblins, Giants, Merry-Men and Monarchs, and Their Kweer Kapers.* Philadelphia: Hubbard Brothers.

Culbertson, Tom. 2008. Illustrated Essay: The Golden Age of American Political Cartoons. *The Journal of the Gilded Age and Progressive Era* 7 (3): 276–295.

D.L.J. 1830. The Diamond Ring. *The Ladies' Museum* 1:225–228.

Davis, Francis. 1878. *Earlier and Later Leaves.* Belfast: W.H. Greer.

Dickens, Charles. 1837. *The Posthumous Papers of the Pickwick Club.* London: Chapman & Hall.

Dickens, Charles. 1841. *The Old Curiosity Shop.* London: Chapman & Hall.

Dickens, Charles. 1843. *A Christmas Carol.* London: Chapman & Hall.

Dickens, Charles. 1845. *The Chimes: A Goblin Story.* London: Chapman & Hall.

Dickens, Charles. 1846. *Pictures from Italy.* London: Bradbury & Evans.

Driver, Henry Austen. 1835. *Harold de Burun: A Semi-Dramatic Poem.* London: Longman, Rees, Orme, Brown, Green, and Longman.

Duncan, Ian. 1992. *Modern Romance and Transformations of the Novel: The Gothic, Scott, Dickens.* New York: Cambridge University Press.

Duncan, Ian. 2012. Walter Scott, James Hogg, and Scottish Gothic. In *A New Companion to the Gothic*, ed. David Punter, 123–134. Malden: Wiley-Blackwell.

Dunham, Curtis. 1906. *The Golden Goblin.* Indianapolis: The Bobbs-Merrill Company.

Edwards, Amelia B. 1864. *Barbara's History.* II Vols. Leipzig: Bernhard Tauchnitz.

Eigner, Edwin M. 1989. *The Dickens Pantomime.* Berkeley: University of California Press.

Ellis, Sarah. 2004. Darwin's Goblins. *Humanist in Canada* 36 (147):

Faben, Aline Sidny. 1978. *Folklore in the Fantasies and Romances of George MacDonald.*" Doctoral Dissertation,. SUNY Buffalo.

Fallows, Samuel, and Henry Ruoff, eds. 1914. "The Wonderful Land of Sound" In *The Human Interest Library*, vol. I, 280–281. Chicago: The Midland Press.

Fenwick, R. O. 1809. *The Goblin Groom; A Tale of Dunse.* Edinburgh: Alex. Lawrie & Co.

Figgins, Kristen Layne. 2023. 'What Is It?' 'It Is a Lewd Goblin': Taking Critical Cues from Illustrative Adaptations of Christina Rossetti's Goblin Market. *Adaptation* 16 (3): 314–329.

Fimi, Dimitra. 2008. *Tolkien, Race and Cultural History: From Fairies to Hobbits.* Basingstoke: Palgrave Macmillan.

Gabelman, Daniel. 2018. Organised Innocence: MacDonald, Lewis, and Literature 'For the Childlike.'. In *Informing the Inklings: George MacDonald and the Victorian Roots of Modern Fantasy*, ed. Michael Partridge and Kirstin Jeffrey Johnson, 69–94. Hamden: Winged Lion Press.

Gabelman, Daniel. 2023. *George MacDonald: Divine Carelessness and Fairytale Levity.* Waco: Baylor University Press.

Gamer, Michael. 2000. *Romanticism and the Gothic: Genre, Reception, and Canon Formation.* Pennsylvania: University of Pennsylvania Press.

Goddard, Julia. 1863. *More Stories.* London: Arthur Hall, Smart, and Allen.

Greenman, David J. 2000. Alcohol, Comedy, and Ghosts in Dickens's Early Short Fiction. *Dickens Quarterly* 17 (1): 3–13.

Grimm, Jacob, and Wilhelm Grimm. 1877. Grimm's Goblins. Translated by E. Taylor. London: R. Meek.

Hennelly, Mark M. 2001. Framing the Gothic: From Pillar to Post-Structuralism. *College Literature* 28 (3, Fall): 68–87.

Hillard, Molly Clark. 2005. Dangerous Exchange: Fairy Footsteps, Goblin Economies, and 'The Old Curiosity Shop.'. *Dickens Studies Annual* 35:63–86.

"Hobgoblins". 1836. *Youth's Companion. And Sabbath School Recorder* IX (51): 203.

Hogle, Jerrold E. 2002. Introduction: The Gothic in Western Culture. In *The Cambridge Companion to Gothic Fiction*, ed. Jerrold E. Hogle, 1–20. New York: Cambridge University Press.

Holdsworth, Dylan. 2024. *The Government of Disability in Dystopian Children's Texts.* New York: Palgrave Macmillan.

Hollington, Michael. 2016. *Dickens and the Grotesque. Routledge Revivals.* New York: Routledge.

Holt, Shari Hodges. 2020. Dickens 'Was Dead: To Begin with': Charles Dickens's Ghostly Afterlife in Neo-Victorian Narratives. *Dickens Studies Annual: Essays on Victorian Fiction* 51 (2): 375–410.

Horne, Jackie C. 2011. *History and the Construction of the Child in Early British Children's Literature.* New York: Routledge.

Hovey, Richard. 1891. *Lancelot and Guenevere: A Poem in Dramas*. New York: United States Book Company.

Hume, Robert D. 1969. Gothic versus Romantic: A Revaluation of the Gothic Novel. *PMLA* 84 (2): 282–290.

Humphries, Simon. 2007. The Uncertainty of 'Goblin Market.'. *Victorian Poetry* 45 (4, Winter): 391–413.

Hutton, Ronald. 2022. *Queens of the Wild: Pagan Goddesses in Christian Europe: An Investigation*. New Haven: Yale University Press.

Illustrated News. 1853. The Three Sisters—The Three Goblins—And the Three Counts, March 4.

"Invective against Novellist Goblin-Mongers". 1803. *Flowers of Literature* I: 393.

Irving, Washington. 1819. *The Sketch Book of Geoffrey Crayon*. VII Vols. New York: C.S. Van Winkle.

Jacobs, Joseph. 1890. *English Fairy Tales*. London: David Nutt.

James, Ronald M. 2023. *Monumental Lies: Early Nevada Folklore of the Wild West*. Reno: University of Nevada Press.

Johnson, Kirstin Jeffrey. 2014. Rooted Deep: Discovering the Literary Identity of Mythopoeic Fantasist George MacDonald. *Linguaculture* 2:25–44.

Keene, Melanie. 2015. *Science in Wonderland: The Scientific Fairy Tales of Victorian Britain*. New York: Oxford University Press.

Kendrick, Charmette. 2009. The Goblins Will Get You! Horror in Children's Literature from the Nineteenth Century. *Children and Libraries* 7 (1, Spring): 19–23.

Kipling, Rudyard. 1906. *Puck of Pook's Hill*. New York: Charles Scribner's Sons.

Kooistra, Lorraine Janzen. 1997. Goblin Market as a Cross-Audienced Poem: Children's Fairy Tale, Adult Erotic Fantasy. *Children's Literature* 25:181–204.

Kurata, Marilyn J. 1984. Fantasy and Realism: A Defense of 'The Chimes.'. *Dickens Studies Annual* 13:19–34.

Lancaster, George. 1883. Notes on the Pantomimes. *The Theater* I:12–20.

Lang, Andrew. 1897. *The Pink Fairy Book*. London: Longmans, Green, and Co.

Lang, Andrew. 1900. *The Grey Fairy Book*. London: Longmans, Green, and Co.

Leland, Charles Godfrey. 1876. *Johnnykin and the Goblins*. London: MacMillan.

Levy, Michael, and Farah Mendlesohn. 2016. *Children's Fantasy Literature: An Introduction*. New York: Cambridge University Press.

MacDonald, George. 1858. *Phantastes: A Faerie Romance for Men and Women*. London: Smith, Elder and Co.

MacDonald, George. 1867. *Dealing with the Fairies*. London: Alexander Strahan.

MacDonald, George. 1872. *The Princess and the Goblin*. Philadelphia: J.B. Lippincott & Co.

MacDonald, George. 1875. *Malcolm*. III Vols. 2nd ed. London: Henry S. King & Co.

MacDonald, George. 1888. *The Princess and Curdie*. London: Blackie & Son.

MacDonald, George. 1896. *Lilith*. 2nd ed. London: Chatto & Windus.

Mangham, Andrew. 2023. *We Are All Monsters: How Deviant Organisms Came to Define Us*. The MIT Press.

Manlove, Colin. 1999. George MacDonald and the Fairy Tales of Francis Paget and Frances Browne. *North Wind: A Journal of George MacDonald Studies* 18:17–32.

Marsh, Jan. 1994. *Christina Rossetti: A Literary Biography*. London: Jonathan Cape.

Martin, Charles D. 2002. *The White African American Body: A Cultural and Literary Exploration*. New Brunswick: Rutgers University Press.

Mason, Emma. 2018. *Christina Rossetti: Poetry, Ecology, Faith*. New York: Oxford University Press.

Mayer, Jed. 2017. 'Come Buy, Come Buy!': Christina Rossetti and the Victorian Animal Market. In *Animals in Victorian Literature and Culture*, ed. Laurence W. Mazzeno and Ronald D. Morrison, 213–231. New York: Palgrave.

McArdle, J. F. 1874. *Grand Comic Christmas Pantomime, Jack and the Beanstalk*. Liverpool: Daily Post Steam Printing Works.

Mendoza, Victor Roman. 2006. 'Come Buy': The Crossing of Sexual and Consumer Desire in Christina Rossetti's Goblin Market. *ELH* 73 (4, Winter): 913–947.

Milligen, J. M., and George Byron. 1825. *The Life, Writings, Opinions, and Times of the Right Hon. George Gordon Noel Byron*. III Vols. London: Matthew Iley.

"Mordreda, the White Wolf". 1880. *Barons of Old* II: 1–16.

Morin, Christina. 2018. *The Gothic Novel in Ireland: C. 1760–1829*. Manchester: Manchester University Press.

Nailed to the Mast. 1885. London: Boys of England Office.

Nikolajeva, Maria. 2012. The Development of Children's Fantasy. In *The Cambridge Companion to Fantasy Literature*, ed. Edward James and Farah Mendlesohn, 50–61. New York: Cambridge University Press.

Norcia, Megan A. 2024. Impossible Monsters, Rabbit Holes, and New Worlds: The Unstable Ground of Science and Education in the Children's Fairy Tale and Fantasy Literature of the 1860s. In *Nineteenth-Century Literature in Transition: The 1860s*, ed. Pamela K. Gilbert, 94–110. New York: Cambridge University Press.

Oldcastle, Geoffrey. 1834. Visits from the Other World. *The Canterbury Magazine* I (4): 157–163.

Palmer, Melvin D. 1975. Madame d'Aulnoy in England. *Comparative Literature* 27 (3, Summer): 237–253.

Patten, Robert L. 2005. Publishing in Parts. In *Palgrave Advances in Charles Dickens Studies*, ed. John Bowen and Robert L. Patten, 11–47. New York: Palgrave Macmillan.

Paulding, James Kirke. 1818. *The Backwoodsman. A Poem*. Philadelphia: M. Thomas.

Pazdziora, John Patrick. 2020. *Haunted Childhoods in George MacDonald.* Leiden: Brill.

Punter, David. 2002. Scottish and Irish Gothic. In *The Cambridge Companion to Gothic Fiction*, ed. Jerrold E. Hogle, 105–124. New York: Cambridge University Press.

Restad, Penne Lee. 1997. *Christmas in America: A History.* New York: Oxford University Press.

Richards, Jeffrey. 2014. *The Golden Age of Pantomime: Slapstick, Spectacle and Subversion in Victorian England.* New York: Bloomsbury.

Riley, James Whitcomb. 1885. *The Elf-Child.* The Indiana State Sentinel, November 25.

Roberts, Adam. 2012. Gothic and Horror Fiction. In *The Cambridge Companion to Fantasy Literature*, ed. Edward James and Farah Mendlesohn, 21–35. New York: Cambridge University Press.

Roberts, Phillip. 2016. Optical Pantomimes at the Royal Polytechnic Institution: George Buckland's 1875 Production of Gabriel Grub and the Grim Goblin. *Film History: An International Journal* 28 (1): 1–42.

Rodas, Julia Miele. 2004. Tiny Tim, Blind Bertha, and the Resistance of Miss Mowcher: Charles Dickens and the Uses of Disability. *Dickens Studies Annual* 34:51–97.

Rogers, Nicholas. 2002. *Halloween: From Pagan Ritual to Party Night.* Oxford University Press.

Rossetti, Christina. 1862. *Goblin Market and Other Poems.* Cambridge: MacMillan and Co.

Rossetti, Christina. 2008. *Christina Rossetti: Poems and Prose.* Edited by Simon Humphries. New York: Oxford University Press.

Round About Our Coal-Fire: Or, Christmas Entertainments. 1732. London: J. Roberts.

Schacker, Jennifer. 2018. *Staging Fairyland: Folklore, Children's Entertainment, and Nineteenth-Century Pantomime.* Detroit: Wayne State University Press.

Scheinberg, Cynthia. 2002. *Women's Poetry and Religion in Victorian England: Jewish Identity and Christian Culture.* New York: Cambridge University Press.

Scott, Walter. 1805. *The Lay of the Last Minstrel.* London: Longman, Hurst, Rees, and Orme.

Scott, Walter. 1808. *Marmion; A Tale of Flodden Field.* Edinburgh: J. Ballantyne and Co.

Scott, Walter. 1810. *The Lady of the Lake.* 2nd ed. Edinburgh: John Ballantine and Co.

Scott, Walter. 1813. *The Bridal of Triermain.* Edinburgh: James Ballantyne and Co.

Scott, Walter. 1816a. *The Antiquary.* III Vols. Edinburgh: James Ballantyne and Co.

Scott, Walter. 1816b. *The Black Dwarf. Tales of My Landlord.* Edinburgh: William Blackwood.

Scott, Walter. 1818. *Rob Roy.* III Vols. Edinburgh: James Ballantyne and Co.

Scott, Walter. 1820. *The Monastery. A Romance.* III Vols. Edinburgh: Longman, Hurst, Rees, Orme, and Brown.

Scott, Walter. 1821. *Kenilworth; A Romance.* III Vols. Edinburgh: Archibald Constable and Co.

Scott, Walter. 1827. *Chronicles of the Canongate.* II Vols. Philadelphia: Carey, Lea & Carey.

Scott, Walter. 1858. *The Black Dwarf. A Legend of Montrose.* Leipzig: Bernhard Tauchnitz.

Seaborn, Adam. 1820. *Symzonia; A Voyage of Discovery.* New York: J. Seymour.

Silver, Carole G. 2000. *Strange and Secret Peoples: Fairies and Victorian Consciousness.* New York: Oxford University Press.

Simms, William Gilmore. 1852. *The Golden Christmas.* Charleston: Walker, Richards and Co.

Smith, Andrew. 2005. Dickens' Ghosts: Invisible Economies and Christmas. *Victorian Review* 31 (2): 36–55.

Springhall, John. 1994. 'Disseminating Impure Literature': The 'Penny Dreadful' Publishing Business Since 1860. *The Economic History Review* 47 (3): 567–584.

Stephens, Henry L. 1850. *The Goblin Snob.* New York: De Witt & Davenport.

Stern, Rebecca F. 2003. Adulterations Detected': Food and Fraud in Christina Rossetti's 'Goblin Market. *Nineteenth-Century Literature* 57 (4): 477–511.

Stone, Harry. 1973. Dickens, Cruikshank, and Fairy Tales. *The Princeton University Library Chronicle* 35 (1/2): 213–247.

Sumpter, Caroline. 2008. *The Victorian Press and the Fairy Tale.* New York: Palgrave Macmillan.

Talairach-Vielmas, Laurence. 2007. *Moulding the Female Body in Victorian Fairy Tales and Sensation Novels.* Burlington: Aldershot.

Talairach-Vielmas, Laurence. 2014. *Fairy Tales, Natural History and Victorian Culture.* New York: Palgrave Macmillan.

The Birmingham Daily Post. 1872. Gabriella: A Child's Story. December 25.

The Birmingham Journal. 1847. Bits of Books for Christmas Reading. December 25.

The Birmingham Post. 1863. Shadow-Land. December 25.

The Birmingham Post. 1872. The Goblin of the Eagle's Cliff. December 25.

The Birmingham Post. 1873. Jonquil and Azalea: A Fairy Tale. December 25.

The Boys of Hawkhouse School. 1890. London: Alfred Bradley.

The Brookville Jeffersonian. 1859. Jabez Jones. A Goblin Story. October 13.

The Lichfield Mercury. 1904. The Revenge of the Dwarfs. October 14.

The New York Times. 1880. Versatile George Conquest: Something About the English Pantomimist and the 'Grim Goblin.' July 24.

The Philadelphia Inquirer. 1898. It's Halloween: Goblins and Fairies Will Be Roaming Abroad To-Night.

The San Francisco Examiner. 1896. Scenes in Fairyland. September 30.

The Skeleton Crew. 1867. London: Newsagents' Publishing Company.

The Wayne Republican. 1895. Hallowe'en Aftermath. Goblins, Ghosts and Bogies Stalk Abroad. Everybody Makes Merry. November 2.

Thomas, Rose Haig. 1897. *Pan: A Collection of Lyrical Poems.* London: Bliss, Sands and Co.

Thomson, James. 1738. *The Works of Mr. Thomson.* II Vols. London: A. Millar.

Williams, Helen. 2012. 'Blank Epochs': Narratives of Disability in Charles Dickens's The Old Curiosity Shop and Dinah Mulock Craik's John Halifax, Gentleman. *Victorians: A Journal of Culture and Literature* 122:117–128.

Wilson, G. H. 1890. *Boston Symphony Orchestra Concert Programs Season 10.* Boston: C.A. Ellis.

Wolfe, Gary K. 2012. Fantasy from Dryden to Dunsany. In *The Cambridge Companion to Fantasy Literature*, 7–20. New York: Cambridge University Press.

Wolferstan, E. P. 1823. *The Enchanted Flute, with Other Poems.* London: Longman, Hurst, Rees, Orme, and Brown.

Wynn, Henry W. 1843. *Ravencourt.* London: Simpkin, Marshall and Company.

Yeats, William Butler. 1892. *The Wanderings of Oisin: Dramatic Sketches, Ballads & Lyrics.* London: T. Fisher Unwin.

Zipes, Jack. 1987. *Victorian Fairy Tales: The Revolt of the Fairies and Elves.* New York: Routledge.

Zipes, Jack. 1999. *When Dreams Came True: Classical Fairy Tales and Their Tradition.* New York: Routledge.

Zipes, Jack. 2006. *Fairy Tales and the Art of Subversion: The Classical Genre for Children and the Process of Civilization.* 2nd ed. New York: Routledge.

Zipes, Jack. 2014. *Grimm Legacies: The Magic Spell of the Grimms' Folk and Fairy Tales.* Princeton: Princeton University Press.

CHAPTER 6

Of Orcs and Goblins

This chapter considers goblins within works of fantasy literature in the early-mid twentieth century. Long perceived as a subject matter most suitable for children, the realm of fantasy gradually opened to adult readers, especially after World War I. In Britain, the Middle-earth works of J.R.R. Tolkien stand out for their genre-shaping depiction of goblins. Drawing particularly on the antagonists of George MacDonald's *The Princess and the Goblin*, Tolkien crafted goblins (more commonly called "orcs") as an unambiguously evil race, corrupted from a purer species, that inhabits the dark corners of Middle-earth. They commit acts of violence against the nobler races of this fantasy world—successful only when employing devious tricks or present in overwhelming numbers—and are slaughtered without remorse across *The Hobbit* and *The Lord of the Rings*. Racialized language in these texts paint goblins as dark-skinned, barbaric, monstrous, unredeemable Others that stand in stark contrast to the whiter, nobler, more civilized races of the world. Minimized in these descriptions are any vestige of goblins as comical or merry; instead, they are evil antagonists without hope for salvation.

Across the Atlantic, meanwhile, American authors embedded the creatures of Fairyland in pulp magazines like *Weird Tales* for audiences of teenagers and young men. When goblins are mentioned in these stories, they typically serve as indicators of malevolent supernatural forces. Although this idea was not particularly new, the more mature themes of these

© The Author(s), under exclusive license to Springer Nature Switzerland AG 2026
M. King, *A History of Goblins*,
https://doi.org/10.1007/978-3-032-01063-6_6

stories, many of which revolved around violence, cosmic horror, and sexual exploitation, transported goblins to these adult narratives. As book-length works of high fantasy became more widespread in the middle of the twentieth century, American authors inserted goblins into their detailed worlds. Poul Anderson's *The Broken Sword*, for example, positions goblins as a lowly race of dark-skinned creatures that exist as servants or slaves to more powerful races in a mythologized northern Europe. Within this emerging genre of sword-and-sorcery fantasy, the diminutive and dark-skinned goblin exists near the bottom of a racialized hierarchy that valorizes the exploits of (typically) white, male heroes.

THE WORLDS OF TOLKIEN

John Ronald Reuel Tolkien was born in 1892 in British South Africa, though he spent most of his childhood in England, where he was raised Roman Catholic. He was an avid reader and found particular pleasure in books about the preternatural, including Lang's *Red Fairy Book*, William Morris' translation of Viking sagas, and MacDonald's *The Princess and the Goblin*.[1] Reflecting on his upbringing, Tolkien claims that his "real taste" for fairy stories emerged as a young adult; it was "wakened by philology on the threshold of manhood, and quickened to full life by war."[2] In 1915, a year before shipping off to France to fight in World War I, he penned for his fiancée Edith the poem "Goblin Feet." Inspired by her love of "spring and flowers and trees, and little elfin people," it depicts a raucous procession of fairies:

> … I must follow in their train
> Down the crooked fairy lane
> Where the coney-rabbits long ago have gone.

---

[1] Humphrey Carpenter, *J.R.R. Tolkien: A Biography* (Boston: Houghton Mifflin Company, 2000), 22; John Garth, "A Brief Biography," in *A Companion to J.R.R. Tolkien*, 2nd ed. (New York: Wiley Blackwell, 2022), 3–18. See, generally, Tom Shippey, *The Road to Middle-earth: How J.R.R. Tolkien Created a New Mythology* (Boston: Houghton Mifflin Company, 2003); Elizabeth A. Whittingham, *The Evolution of Tolkien's Mythology: A Study of the History of Middle-earth* (Jefferson: McFarland & Company, Inc., 2007); Jane Chance, ed., *Tolkien and the Invention of Myth: A Reader* (Lexington: University of Kentucky Press, 2008); Fimi, *Tolkien, Race and Cultural History: From Fairies to Hobbits*; Robert Stuart, *Tolkien, Race, and Racism in Middle-earth* (Cham: Palgrave Macmillan, 2022).

[2] J.R.R. Tolkien, *Tolkien: On Fairy-Stories*, ed. Verlyn Flieger and Douglas A. Anderson (New York: HarperCollins, 2014), 56.

And where silvery they sing
In a moving moonlit ring
All a twinkle with the jewels they have on.
They are fading round the turn
Where the glow worms palely burn
And the echo of their padding feet is dying!
O! it's knocking at my heart-
Let me go! O! let me start!
For the little magic hours are all a-flying.

O! the warmth! O! the hum! O! the colours in the dark!
O! the gauzy wings of golden honey-flies!
O! the music of their feet - of their dancing goblin feet!
O! the magic! O! the sorrow when it dies.[3]

Tolkien presents leprechauns, gnomes, and fairies as part of this merry goblin procession: a cheerful interpretation of Fairyland reminiscent of Victorian whimsy. Later in life, however, Tolkien claimed that this poem represented all that he had come to "fervently dislike" about fairies, which were informed more by Victorian fancies than the more severe medieval and early modern folklore on which they were based.[4] As a professional philologist, Tolkien was well positioned to make this comparison. He worked for the Oxford English Dictionary, translated prominent medieval texts like *Sir Gawain and the Green Knight* and *Beowulf*, and landed a job as professor of Anglo-Saxon at Oxford University. Tolkien's changing attitude toward goblins as he was formulating the world of Middle-earth can be glimpsed in Christmas stories that he wrote to his children in 1932 and 1933. Framed as letters written by Father Christmas, they tell of violent

---

[3] J.R.R. Tolkien, "Goblin Feet," in *Oxford Poetry*, ed. G.D.H.C. and T.W.E. (Oxford: B.H. Blackwell, 1915), 64–65; Carpenter, *J.R.R. Tolkien: A Biography*, 80–87. The lack of "terminological consistency" in this poem was characteristic of Victorian and Edwardian precedent. Fimi, *Tolkien, Race and Cultural History: From Fairies to Hobbits*, 30. See also Dimitra Fimi, "'Come Sing Ye Light Fairy Things Tripping So Gay': Victorian Fairies and the Early Work of J.R.R. Tolkien," *Working with English: Medieval and Modern Language, Literature and Drama* 2 (2005–06): 10–26.

[4] John Garth, *Tolkien and the Great War: The Threshold of Middle-earth* (Boston: Houghton Mifflin Harcourt, 2013), 75. The 1920 edition of this poem includes an illustration by Warwick Goble, which shows a diverse and spooky ensemble of creatures marching through the forest at night: anthropomorphized animals, a man with a long beard and pointy hat, and green-skinned humanoids with peculiar facial features. Dora Owen, ed., *The Book of Fairy Poetry* (New York: Longmans, Green, and Co., 1920).

encounters between evil goblins and the inhabitants of the North Pole. The 1932 letter sees Father Christmas stumbling upon an expansive goblin cavern, whose inhabitants are "very much what rats are to you, only worse, because they are very clever." Ever the philologist, Tolkien provides within the letter a complete goblin script, the characters of which resemble pictograms reminiscent of cave paintings.[5] These goblins are not dangerous themselves, though Father Christmas worries about the dangers of their caves, which emanate with "queer noises & false echoes." Eventually, he discovers that the goblins have used their mining prowess to tunnel between their caves and his home, stealing all of the toys they could find. The story ends with a brief battle between the red gnomes and goblins, which sees the latter defeated (hundreds captured and more driven out into the snow) and peace temporarily restored.[6]

Drawing on the goblin tradition of George MacDonald, Tolkien presents goblins as lowly, troglodytic, scheming miners that more closely reflect those of *The Hobbit* (which Tolkien was simultaneously writing) than "Goblin Feet." Similar themes are present in the Christmas story that Tolkien wrote a year later, which narrates a goblin attack on the workshop of Father Christmas. He glimpses "bat-riding Goblins" (not seen since the goblin war of 1453) alongside a ground invasion of his home that saw the ground "black with goblins." The attack is eventually thwarted by the heroics of Polar Bear, who "was squeezing, squashing, trampling, boxing, and kicking Goblins sky-high, and roaring like a zoo, and the Goblins were yelling like engine whistles." Many goblins die, and Father Christmas delights in this sight: "SAY NO MORE: I ENJOYED IT IMMENSELY."[7] Such was the inherent mischief, evil, and inhumanity of these goblins that, even in a Christmas story meant to entertain children, Tolkien did not need to justify their slaughter. An illustration accompanying this story even shows Polar Bear obliterating a hoard of jet-black goblins.

---

[5] Paul Nolan Hyde, "A Philologist at the North Pole: J.R.R. Tolkien and The Father Christmas Letters," *Mythlore* 15, no. 1 (Autumn 1988): 23–27. The translation for this letter, which is a Christmas greeting that mentions how Tolkien's children are excelling in real-world languages, is provided in a 1936 letter.

[6] Father Christmas expects that the goblins will "crop up again in a century or so." J.R.R. Tolkien, *The Father Christmas Letters*, ed. Baillie Tolkien (Boston: Houghton Mifflin Company, 1976), 1932 Letter. Tolkien likely adapted elements from these stories for *The Hobbit*, which he was writing simultaneously. Kris Swank, "'The Hobbit' and 'the Father Christmas Letters,'" *Mythlore* 32, no. 1 (Fall/Winter 2013): 127–44.

[7] Tolkien, *The Father Christmas Letters*, 1933 Letter.

The Princess and the Goblin had established a fantasy precedent for the mass destruction of goblins in children's literature, and Tolkien embraced this motif. As the world of Middle-earth was forming in Tolkien's mind, the goblins populating it were thus moving away from the dancing procession of "Goblin Feet" and toward the more malevolent cave-dwellers associated with George MacDonald.[8]

This is not to say that Tolkien had fully formed Middle-earth when he published *The Hobbit* in 1937. Its construction was a lifelong process, beginning with recognizable excerpts in 1914 and extending through *The Lord of the Rings* trilogy (1954–55) and other stories published posthumously.[9] Middle-earth was an evolving amalgamation of folklore, European mythologies, medieval epics, Romantic-era art and theater, philology, anti-industrial sentiment, children's literature, and Christian morality.[10] Tolkien's early writings on this world, which borrowed heavily from Victorian and Edwardian fairy tales, gradually gave way to a more detailed enterprise inspired by the literature and folklore of medieval England and Scandinavia.[11] Tolkien took this process of world-building seriously. He

[8] Tolkien wrote large portions of *The Hobbit* during his holiday breaks in the early 1930s, simultaneous to his writing of these Christmas letters. Rateliff argues that the 1932 and 1933 letters in particular "represent a dramatic shift in tone" due to his progress on the latter parts of *The Hobbit* (including the potential inclusion of Gollum and Smaug in the illustration accompanying the 1932 letter). John D. Rateliff, *The History of The Hobbit*, vol. I (Boston: Houghton Mifflin Company, 2007), xvi. Goblins are less featured in later Christmas stories. The 1938 one, for example, mentions "The GOBLINS, you'll be glad to hear / have not been seen at all this year / not near the Pole. But I am told / they're moving *south* and getting bold / and coming back to many lands / and making with their wicked hands / new mines and caves. But do not fear! / They'll hide away when I appear." The 1939 letter also mentions goblins using the chaos of World War II as cover to attack the North Pole. They are eventually defeated thanks to the heroism of Polar Bear and his family. Tolkien, *The Father Christmas Letters*, 1938 and 1939 letters.

[9] Per Stuart, "we should never assume the absolute coherence of Tolkien's views–even at a particular moment during the interminable gestation of his legendarium, and certainly not from one period of creativity to another." Stuart, *Tolkien, Race, and Racism in Middle-earth*, 66.

[10] To borrow the nomenclature from Leppälahti, Tolkien had a broad "shared fantasy pool" on which to draw for his Middle-earth works, and these texts in turn became a fantasy product that was eventually (due to its popularity) introduced into this shared fantasy pool. Merja Leppälahti, "From Folklore to Fantasy," trans. Clive Tolley, *Journal of the Fantastic in the Arts* 29, no. 2 (2018): 179–200.

[11] In attempting to make Middle-earth seem "realistic," Tolkien even tried to publish manuscript facsimiles of texts encountered by the Fellowship. Fimi, *Tolkien, Race and Cultural History: From Fairies to Hobbits*, 192–93.

argued in an influential 1947 essay (based on an earlier lecture) that magic within fairy stories should not be "laughed at nor explained away."[12] He thought this fantastical creation, though grounded in a world removed from our own, could nonetheless (in the words of Edward James) "express real and important truths—truths that were regarded as worthy of an adult audience in the Middle Ages, and should be now."[13] Tolkien carefully populated his intricate fantasy world with languages, peoples, histories, cultures, and geographies that were unprecedented for its time.[14] Unlike those in "Goblin Feet," the goblins lurking in the darkness of Middle-earth were a villainous and vile race.

Given the scope of this book, I do not have the space to recount the details of *The Hobbit* and *The Lord of the Rings*. Below, though, is a brief (and goblin-centric) summary of their contents. Tolkien's first Middle-earth publication was 1937's *The Hobbit, or There and Back Again*. It tells the story of Bilbo Baggins, a hobbit who is dragged on a quest with thirteen dwarves at the behest of the wizard Gandalf to slay the dragon Smaug. When crossing beneath the Misty Mountains, the party is captured by goblins, taken to their cavernous home of Goblin-town, and confronted by the Great Goblin:

> [The goblins] seized Bilbo and the dwarves and hurried them along. It was deep, deep, dark, such as only goblins that have taken to living in the heart of the mountains can see through. The passages there were crossed and tangled in all directions, but the goblins knew their way, as well as you do to the nearest post-office; and the way went down and down, and it was most horribly stuffy. The goblins were very rough, and pinched unmercifully, and

---

[12] This essay was also a serious engagement with prevailing theories in folklore and philology, faulting both Müller and Lang for their mining of fairy stories for data rather than the enchantment they were meant to inspire. For Tolkien, "it matters less where fairy-stories came from, or what they might originally have referred to, than what they have to give the reader in that *now* which he so strongly emphasized." Verlyn Flieger, "'There Would Always Be a Fairy-Tale': J. R. R. Tolkien and the Folklore Controversy," in *Tolkien the Medievalist*, ed. Jane Chance (Routledge: New York, 2003), 35.

[13] Edward James, "Tolkien, Lewis and the Explosion of Genre Fantasy," in *The Cambridge Companion to Fantasy Literature*, ed. Edward James and Farah Mendlesohn (New York: Cambridge University Press, 2012), 67.

[14] Tolkien even criticized his friend and fellow "Inklings" member C.S. Lewis for his "bricolage approach to fantasy." Peter Hunt, "The Children's Novel," in *The Oxford History of the Novel in English: Volume 7: British and Irish Fiction Since 1940*, ed. Peter Boxall and Bryan Cheyette (New York: Oxford University Press, 2016), 317.

chuckled and laughed in their horrible stony voices ... For goblins eat horses and ponies and donkeys (and other much more dreadful things), and they are always hungry ...

There in the shadows on a large flat stone sat a tremendous goblin with a huge head, and armed goblins were standing round him carrying the axes and the bent swords that they use. Now goblins are cruel, wicked, and bad-hearted. They make no beautiful things, but they make many clever ones. They can tunnel and mine as well as any but the most skilled dwarves, when they take the trouble, though they are usually untidy and dirty. Hammers, axes, swords, daggers, pickaxes, tongs, and also instruments of torture, they make very well, or get other people to make to their design, prisoners and slaves that have to work till they die for want of air and light. It is not unlikely that they invented some of the machines that have since troubled the world, especially the ingenious devices for killing large numbers of people at once, for wheels and engines and explosions always delighted them, and also not working with their own hands more than they could help; but in those days and those wild parts they had not advanced (as it is called) so far ...[15]

The party of dwarves, aided by Gandalf's slaying of the Great Goblin, barely manages to flee from the goblins. Bilbo, isolated during the chaotic escape, chances upon a magical ring that turns the wearer invisible and uses it to evade the ring's previous owner, the creature Gollum. Bilbo and the dwarves eventually manage to defeat Smaug and his allies at the Battle of Five Armies, including goblins that banded together after the killing of the Great Goblin.

When Tolkien began *The Hobbit*, he was unaware it was going to be the first entry in an epic fantasy series. Tolkien had long been writing about Middle-earth and sketching out loosely related short stories about its inhabitants, but this mythology largely did not trickle into the first editions of this text—intended as it was for an audience of children (especially his own). The success of *The Hobbit*, though, gave Tolkien the latitude with publishers to develop his other stories intended for an older audience.[16] Some of them became *The Lord of the Rings* trilogy, which was

[15] J.R.R. Tolkien, *The Hobbit, or There and Back Again* (New York: Ballantine Books, 2001), 60–62.

[16] Tolkien did not tailor *The Lord of the Rings* "for anyone but himself, or for a select audience only: his son Christopher, and C.S. Lewis." Wayne G. Hammond, "Whose Lord of the Rings Is It, Anyway?," *Canadian C.S. Lewis Journal* 97 (Spring 2000): 64. Tolkien was aware of the dramatic tonal shift between *The Hobbit* and *The Lord of the Rings*; publishers

published in three parts in 1954 and 1955: *The Fellowship of the Ring*, *The Two Towers*, and *The Return of the King*. The central plot of these books is the epic journey of the eponymous Fellowship to destroy the Ring of Power of the Dark Lord Sauron by casting it into the fires of Mount Doom. Various tribes of goblins—some working on behalf of Sauron, some bred by the wizard Saruman, and others existing as independent agents of chaos—populate the dark corners of Middle-earth and pose a persistent threat to its inhabitants. The bearers of the One Ring, the hobbits Frodo and Samwise, manage to defeat and evade these goblins (among many other monsters) on their quest to rid Middle-earth of Sauron.

The reception to *The Lord of the Rings* in Great Britain was mixed upon its release. Supporters of the text compared it to the greatest epics in English literature, while its detractors criticized Tolkien's archaic prose and fairy-inspired subject matter. When the trilogy was released in paperback editions within the United States in the 1960s, though, it found widespread acceptance and acclaim (especially among young adults).[17] Revisions to *The Hobbit* in later editions reflected the narrative of *The Lord of the Rings*, and the popularity of Middle-earth as a "mythology for England" (a contested term) persisted into the twenty-first century.[18] Tolkien, though, did not publish any additional Middle-earth materials during his lifetime. Christopher Tolkien, the literary executor to his father's estate, collected and edited unpublished stories and fragments in *The Silmarillion* (1977) and twelve-part *The History of Middle-earth* (1983–96). I will consider reception to the works of Tolkien in greater detail in the next two chapters.

When Tolkien was formulating *The Lord of the Rings* in the early-mid twentieth century, he was part of a growing cohort of writers crafting fantastical worlds for adult readers. Authors of the Victorian Era had emphasized the importance of imagination and fairy tales among primarily

---

were also alarmed at this change, as many had been hoping that Tolkien would publish a sequel intended for children.

[17] Joseph Ripp, "Middle America Meets Middle-earth: American Discussion and Readership of J. R. R. Tolkien's The Lord of the Rings, 1965–1969," *Book History* 8, no. 1 (2005): 245–86.

[18] Carl F. Hostetter and Arden R. Smith, "A Mythology for England," *Mythlore* 21, no. 2 (1996): 281–90; Anders Stenström, "A Mythology? For England?," *Mythlore* 21, no. 2 (1996): 310–14.

children.[19] The late nineteenth and early twentieth centuries, especially after World War I, saw increased interest in fantastical literature written for adults (though the genre of "fantasy" itself did not emerge until the 1960s).[20] Drawing on Victorian fairy literature and the folklore on which it was based, these authors crafted worlds with themes befitting an older audience.

George Knight, for example, explores the theme of mortality in "The Showman of Goblintown" (1896), whose titular inhabitants (half-gnome, half-moon-people) live the "sweetest" life on earth as "perfect lovers" until their world is disrupted by a traveling showman.[21] One of Lord Dunsany's 1916 short stories takes place amid an ongoing war between elves and goblins, though these creatures have little relevance beyond this thematic backdrop.[22] Goblins do play a more prominent role in Dunsany's 1924 novel, *The King of Elfland's Daughter*, in which humans interact with the "gnomes, trolls, elves and goblins" of Elfland—a familiar interpretation of Fairyland that exists on the periphery of our world and does not adhere to our understandings of nature or science.[23] Goblins and trolls have a particular kinship in this land, as a group of humans encounters on

---

[19] Though some authors like MacDonald, Ruskin, and Morris embraced fantastical elements in their adult novels, they were outliers in the mid-late nineteenth century.

[20] The defining characteristics of "fantasy" as a genre remain contested; Mendlesohn and James call early-twentieth century fantastical literature "weird fancy." Farah Mendlesohn and Edward James, *A Short History of Fantasy* (London: Middlesex University Press, 2009), 25–42. See also Jamie Williamson, *The Evolution of Modern Fantasy: From Antiquarianism to the Ballantine Adult Fantasy Series* (New York: Palgrave Macmillan, 2009), 127–66.

[21] Knight relates how, "When one of the tiny people is a year and a day old, its wonderful eyes open (for the Goblins are born blind), and straightway it loves and is loved. A hundred years the two live and love, and then together they fade and disappear. Where they have been 143 lies a drop of bright dew. This the gnomes gather up and bury it deep, deep in the earth, for a hundred years more. As the years pass the drop grows hard and clear as crystal, and glorious with a thousand broken lights and shattered rainbow tints. And at the last, men dig for the opals, and prize them greatly. But always there is a fear that they are unlucky, and perhaps the fear is just, since to tear an opal from its bed is to violate a grave. Also the love of the Goblins is chaste and pure, whilst that of human lovers—who most of all fear to give the opal as a gift—is fierce and passionate... Such is the life and death of the people of Goblintown." George Knight, "The Showman of Goblintown," in *Dust in the Balance* (London, 1896), 141–43.

[22] Lord Dunsany, *Tales of Wonder* (London: Elkin Mathews, 1917), 53–54.

[23] Lord Dunsany, *The King of Elfland's Daughter* (New York: G.P. Putnam's Sons, 1924), 170. Schweitzer argues that Elfland "is both a place and a state of existence. It doesn't conform to mundane rules of geography or anything else... It is also a literalized, multiplex metaphor for the imagination, for the lost innocence of childhood, for everything which lies

an eerie night "goblin laughter and the unbridled mirth of the trolls … amongst all manner of mysteries, queer sounds, queer shapes, and queer shadows."[24] The association of goblins with the strange and sinister, a common trope in preceding decades, persists in the work of Dunsany. In Hope Mirrlees' 1926 *Lud-in-the-Mist*, too, we see goblins serve as markers of peculiar appearance, as in "a grotesque hobgoblin tabby cat" and a peculiar symbol that looked "as if it had been some hideous goblin."[25]

A more taxonomized variation of the fairies is found in E.R. Eddison's 1922 novel, *The Worm Ouroboros*. Written in pseudo-early-modern prose, this story tells of conflicting kingdoms vying for control of a fantastical Mercury: Witchland, Demonland, Goblinland, Pixyland, and Impland.[26] The goblins of *The Worm Ouroboros* are notable for their infighting, as the traitorous goblin, Lord Gro, collaborates with witches against their demon and goblin enemies. We also witness the "unruly rabble" of Goblinland's army, which crumbles during an ill-fated assault on the capital of the witches.[27] Goblins take on a secondary role in the larger conflict between witches and demons, but when they do take center stage, their subterfuge and tactical incompetence is highlighted. Indeed, Tolkien regarded Eddison as "the most convincing writer of 'invented worlds'" and an inspiration for Middle-earth (despite some misgivings about his writing process).[28] Although the worlds of Dunsany, Mirrlees, and Eddison did not yet exhibit the depth of a fully formed "secondary world" like Middle-earth, they were more detailed than their Victorian and Edwardian

beyond our grasp." Darrell Schweitzer, *Pathways to Elfland: The Writings of Lord Dunsany* (Philadelphia: Owlswick Press, 1989), 79.

[24] Dunsany, *The King of Elfland's Daughter*, 272.

[25] Hope Mirrlees, *Lud-in-the-Mist* (New York: Alfred A. Knopf, 1927), 110, 125.

[26] E.R. Eddison, *The Worm Ouroboros* (London: Jonathan Cape LTD, 1924). Eddison attended two of the meetings of the Inklings, and C.S. Lewis blurbed his unfinished *Mezentian Gate*. Richard C. West, "Where Fantasy Fits: The Importance of Being Tolkien," *Mythlore* 33, no. 1 (Fall/Winter 2014): 12.

[27] Eddison, *The Worm Ouroboros*, 70.

[28] Williamson, *The Evolution of Modern Fantasy: From Antiquarianism to the Ballantine Adult Fantasy Series*, 148–49.

predecessors.[29] The inhabitants of Fairyland, goblins included, thus found new yet familiar homes in fiction written for adults.[30]

Middle-earth, too, became more detailed and saturated with mature themes as Tolkien moved from writing *The Hobbit* to *The Lord of the Rings*. This process was particularly significant for the goblin, which was a central antagonist in the former but was linguistically replaced in the latter by the "orc" (borrowed from the Old English *orcneas* in *Beowulf*).[31] Tolkien provides this point of linguistic clarification in later editions of *The Hobbit*:

> *Orc* is not an English word. It occurs in one or two places but is usually translated *goblin* (or *hobgoblin* for the larger kinds). *Orc* is the hobbits' form of the name given at that time to these creatures, and it is not connected at all with our *orc*, *ork*, applied to sea-animals of dolphin-kind.[32]

[29] The term "secondary world" originated in Tolkien's essay, "On Fairies Stories," and has since been used to differentiate fantasy worlds removed from our own and those more reminiscent of Fairyland, which exist within or adjacent to our own. Maria Nikolajeva, "Fairy Tale and Fantasy: From Archaic to Postmodern," *Marvels & Tales* 17, no. 1 (2003): 142.

[30] The mythology of King Arthur was prominent in these works, too. In *The Sword in the Stone* (1938), T.H. White references nineteenth-century theories about fairies to frame his story of Arthur's childhood: "Some people say [the fairies] are the Oldest Ones of All, who lived in England before the Romans came here—before us Saxons, before the Old Ones themselves—and that they have been driven underground. Some say they look like humans, like dwarfs, and others that they look ordinary, and others that they don't look like anything at all, but put on various shapes as the fancy takes them. Whatever they look like, they have the knowledge of the ancient Gaels." T.H. White, *The Once and Future King* (New York: G.P. Putnam's Sons, 1958), 93.

[31] Tolkien completed a prose translation of *Beowulf* in 1926. Christopher Tolkien eventually edited and published this text in 2014. Therein, Tolkien translates *eotenas ond ylfe ond orcneas* (which I mentioned in chapter 2) as "ogres and goblins and haunting shapes of hell." J.R.R. Tolkien, *Beowulf: A Translation and Commentary Together with Sellic Spell*, ed. Christopher Tolkien (New York: Houghton Mifflin Harcourt, 2014), 16.

[32] J.R.R. Tolkien, *The Hobbit, or There and Back Again* (London: HarperCollins, 2012), 9. Some editions of *The Hobbit* do not include this note, including the Ballantine edition cited earlier in this chapter. Tolkien's language evolved as he wrote his works on Middle-earth. In early drafts of the stories that would become *The Book of Lost Tales*, for example, "elves" were called "fairies" in keeping with Victorian tradition. Fimi, *Tolkien, Race and Cultural History: From Fairies to Hobbits*, 11–23. In the first French translation of *The Hobbit*, Francis Ledoux renders "goblin" as "gobelin" (who live in Gobelinville) but does not provide this clarifying note about orcs and goblins. J.R.R. Tolkien, *Bilbo, le Hobbit*, trans. Francis Ledoux (Paris: Hachette, 1979).

Tolkien equates the terms "orcs" and "goblins" in *The Hobbit* such that we should see the two as the same within his texts—even as his treatment of these creatures changed along with the evolving mythos of Middle-earth.[33] This interpretation is supported within *The Lord of the Rings* as well, in which the two terms are occasionally conflated.[34] As Tolkien re-tooled Middle-earth for an adult audience, however, he preferred to iden-tify these creatures as orcs instead of goblins. He saw the latter, so long a staple of folklore and children's literature, as a poor fit for the increasingly mature themes of *The Lord of the Rings*, and used the former to designate the lowly soldiers in service of a faceless, sinister evil. The movement within Tolkien's legendarium from "goblin" to "orc" thus paralleled the evolution of Middle-earth, moving his "race of evil creatures from the folk matrix" to a developing tradition of epic fantasy.[35] For the remainder of this chapter, I will refer to the "goblins" of Tolkien rather than "orcs" when analyzing these creatures for the sake of consistency, though any quotations will retain Tolkien's original verbiage.

[33] Thomas Honegger, "From Old English Orcneas to George MacDonald's Goblins with Soft Feet: Sources of Inspiration and Models for Tolkien's Orcs from English Literature," in *Eine Kleine Geschichte Der Orks: Der Monströse Feind Im Wandel Der Zeit*, ed. Delila Jordan and Droß-Krüpe, 2024, 45–46.

[34] J.R.R. Tolkien, *The Fellowship of the Ring* (New York: Ballantine Books, 2001), 378; J.R.R. Tolkien, *The Two Towers* (New York: Ballantine Books, 2001), 6, 44. Rateliff has shown that the terms "goblin" and "orc" were used "more or less interchangeably in the early material" of Tolkien and that, if there was any distinction, it had to do with a preference for the word "orc" in stories that were linked to *The Silmarillion* tradition while "goblin" was used in more light-hearted content. Rateliff, *The History of The Hobbit*, I:137–38. As with so much of Tolkien's writings, internal contradictions complicate these conclusions. A 1938 letter to *The Observer*, for example, Tolkien claims that, in *The Hobbit*, "*elf, gnome, goblin, dwarf* are only approximate translations of the Old Elvish names for beings of not quite the same kinds and functions." Fimi, *Tolkien, Race and Cultural History: From Fairies to Hobbits*, 32. In a 1954 letter, too, Tolkien writes in a parenthetical aside that orcs "are not 'goblins,'" though it seems as though he means that the orcs of Middle Earth do not cor-respond to earlier interpretations of goblins in folklore and literary fantasy. J.R.R. Tolkien, *The Letters of J.R.R. Tolkien*, ed. Humphrey Carpenter and Christopher Tolkien (Boston: Houghton Mifflin Harcourt, 2013), letter 131.

[35] Honegger, "From Old English Orcneas to George MacDonald's Goblins with Soft Feet: Sources of Inspiration and Models for Tolkien's Orcs from English Literature," 57.

The Goblins of Middle-Earth

Middle-earth is teeming with goblins. They are an evil race, corrupted from elves or men yet distinct from them in appearance, language, and demeanor. Dark-skinned and monstrous, goblins stand in stark contrast to the valorous and light-skinned races of Middle-earth. Whether read as a racist transposition of the non-white Other or a Catholic allegory dissociated from our world, Tolkien presents goblins as one of many distinct groups of Middle-earth using racialist language that was common in the early twentieth century. The slaughter of goblins can be done without guilt or remorse, and when goblins are lucky enough to defeat their nobler foes, it is due to their trickery or overwhelming numbers. Tolkien's emphasis on the inherent evil of goblins and their many vile deeds diminishes some of their other historical associations, especially their comedic merriment.

Though Tolkien's Middle-earth was influenced by a host of literary, theological, folkloric, and historical sources, *The Princess and the Goblin* is paramount for this history. Tolkien admitted that his goblins owe "a good deal to the goblin tradition" of George MacDonald and that they "to some extent resemble" those in *The Princess and the Goblin*.[36] This is particularly true in the case of *The Hobbit*, wherein we encounter a goblin tribe, cunningly adept at mining and united under a male leader, wreaking havoc on their neighbors with malicious glee. The evolutionary lineage of Middle-earth goblins as explored in *The Lords of the Rings* and a handful of posthumous texts, too, are based on the corruption of purer species. In *The Return of the King*, Sam speculates that "The Shadow that bred [orcs] can only mock, it cannot make … I don't think it gave life to the orcs, it only ruined them and twisted them; and if they are to live at all, they have to live like other living creatures."[37] In *The Two Towers*, Treebeard notes that "Trolls are only counterfeits, made by the Enemy in the Great

---

[36] Tolkien, *The Letters of J.R.R. Tolkien*, letters 144 and 151. Tolkien wrote that *The Hobbit* was not informed by Victorian literature except for George MacDonald. Near the end of his life, Tolkien's feelings toward MacDonald cooled. In a 1966 interview, Tolkien said that "I now find that I can't stand George MacDonald books at any price at all. I find that now I can't take him." This quotation can be found in John D. Rateliff, "She and Tolkien, Revisited," in *Tolkien and the Study of His Sources: Critical Essays*, ed. Jason Fisher (Jefferson: McFarland & Company, Inc., 2008), 145.

[37] J.R.R. Tolkien, *The Return of the King* (New York: Ballantine Books, 2001), 201.

Darkness, in mockery of Ents, as Orcs were of Elves."[38] *The Silmarillion* has a similar passage in which Tolkien discusses how orcs were initially elves that were tortured and bred by the divinity Morgoth.[39] This picture is complicated from a passage in *Morgoth's Ring*, however, in which Tolkien writes that orcs could have been corrupted men.[40] These passages broadly agree that goblins are corrupted forms of other races, though the details are murky. Tolkien admits as much in a 1954 letter, acknowledging that they "are nowhere clearly stated to be of any particular origin," but he reasons that their existence as "servants of the Dark Power" indicates that they must be "corruptions" of some kind.[41]

Goblins, therefore, are perversions of purer species and associated with the forces of evil. Such an ignoble lineage is reflected in their language. In an appendix to *The Lord of the Rings*, Tolkien mentions that goblins "had no language of their own, but took what they could of other tongues and perverted it to their own liking," including many words from the Black Speech of Sauron. These creatures, "filled with malice," crafted "many barbarous dialects" to reflect their expanding numbers and tribes.[42] When goblins speak, they tend to do so in short, crude sentences to reflect (as Tolkien saw it) their appropriation of other dialects. Departing from the goblins of MacDonald, which speak similarly to humans, Tolkien imbues his goblins with primitive speech to reflect the extent of their corruption. The names of Tolkien's goblins are likewise reflective of the languages of Middle-earth (Uglúk and Azog) and not the more comical English-language names like Glump, Podge, and Harelip in *The Princess and the Goblin*.

Explicit in the goblins of Tolkien, too, is their classification as a specific "race" of creature.[43] This is a common feature throughout *The Lord of the Rings*. Tolkien delineates the various groups therein along racial lines, which inform their cultures, histories, and geographies.[44] Some races can

---

[38] Tolkien, *The Two Towers*, 91.

[39] J.R.R. Tolkien, *The Silmarillion*, ed. Christopher Tolkien (London: HarperCollins, 1999), 50.

[40] Rateliff, *The History of The Hobbit*, I:137–43; Stuart, *Tolkien, Race, and Racism in Middle-earth*, 32–38.

[41] Tolkien, *The Letters of J.R.R. Tolkien*, Letter 144.

[42] Tolkien, *The Return of the King*, 457–58.

[43] Stuart, *Tolkien, Race, and Racism in Middle-earth*, 28–29.

[44] He mentions, for example, the "race of Númenor," the "race of Gonder," the "race of those that are named the Black Númenóreans," the "race of the West," the "race of uruks,"

even miscegenate to terrifying effect, as seen in the "wickedest deed" of the wizard Saruman and his predecessor Morgoth: the breeding of goblins and men to create "Men-orcs large and cunning, and Orc-men treacherous and vile."[45] This trend of classification based on race was praised by C.S. Lewis, as it allows for "character delineation ... done simply by making the character an elf, a dwarf, or a hobbit. The imagined beings have their insides on the outside."[46] Although MacDonald briefly mentioned goblins being a "race" of creatures, the degree to which Tolkien crafted a fantasy universe based on racial identities was innovative, as "few if any novelists had previously grouped Elves and Dwarves (and trolls and goblins and fairies, for that matter) as 'races.'"[47]

Tolkien's racialist framing of Middle-earth reflected contemporary English understandings of the peoples and nations of the world. Race continued to be a crucial category of analysis for understanding a given group's (supposedly) inherent natures and abilities, often in ways that framed white Europeans as superior to non-whites. Books like *Origin of the Anglo-Saxon Race* (1906), *The Story of the British Race* (1907), and *Poems of the English Race* (1921) give some indication of the prominence of this kind of discourse.[48] Philologists, too, advocated for an intertwined English language and Anglo-Saxon race since the Middle Ages—a theory

the "race of the Twilight," the "races of the world," the "races of Orcs and Men," the "mortal race," a "strange" race of long-dead elves, and a time of friendship "between folk of different race, even between Dwarves and Elves." Tolkien, *The Fellowship of the Ring*, 50, 215, 318, 340; Tolkien, *The Two Towers*, 34, 76; Tolkien, *The Return of the King*, 94, 171, 270, 365, 458.

[45] J.R.R. Tolkien, *Morgoth's Ring*, ed. Christopher Tolkien, The History of Middle-earth (New York: HarperCollins, 1994), 418–19.

[46] C.S. Lewis, "The Dethronement of Power," in *Tolkien and the Critics: Essays on J.R.R. Tolkien's The Lord of the Rings*, ed. Neil D. Isaacs and Rose A. Zimbardo (Notre Dame: University of Notre Dame Press, 1968), 15.

[47] Daniel Smith-Rowsey, "Whose Middle-earth Is It? Reading The Lord of the Rings and New Zealand's New Identity Form a Globalized, Post-Colonial Perspective," in *How We Became Middle Earth: A Collection of Essays on the Lord of the Rings*, ed. Adam Lam and Nataliya Oryshchuk (Zollikofen: Walking Tree Press, 2007), 133.

[48] Thomas William Shore, *Origin of the Anglo-Saxon Race: A Study of the Settlement of England and the Tribal Origin of the Old English People*, ed. T.W. Shore and L.E. Shore (London: Elliot Stock, 1906); John Munro, *The Story of the British Race* (New York: D. Appleton and Company, 1907); Raymond MacDonald Alden, ed., *Poems of the English Race* (New York: Charles Scribner's Sons, 1921). See also Peter Mandler, *The English National Character: The History of an Idea from Edmund Burke to Tony Blair* (New Haven: Yale University Press, 2006).

that allowed for white people anywhere in the British Empire (or former parts of it like the United States) to claim a specific ethno-linguistic identity.[49] Scientific racism remained embedded in this discourse, and scientists of the early twentieth century thought it was "entirely legitimate and scientifically acceptable to divide humankind into races with fixed physical characteristics and mental abilities."[50] Eugenics, building on theories of the nineteenth century, emerged as a field of study that predictably elevated white Europeans as genetically superior to those with darker skin. This ideology fit all too comfortably with Christian associations of an eternal battle between light and dark, enmeshed as it was in the conquests and civilizing mission of colonialism.

Although some of the arguments surrounding eugenics lost popularity by the 1930s, they were still firmly rooted in British society as Tolkien was developing the world of Middle-earth.[51] This is not to say that Tolkien was enamored with this scientific field (as he unequivocally denounced the eugenic ideologies of the Nazi party), but rather that he was educated in a world in which it was acceptable to sort people into racial groups and to see these groups as naturally different than each other. These ideas seeped into Middle-earth, which is constructed based on racial divisions and mapped out accordingly in a fictional geography.[52] Of note, too, is the awkwardness with which this idea of "race" in Middle-earth maps onto biological classifications. It is unclear which races of Middle-earth can procreate with one another. Tolkien, reluctant as ever to write about women

---

[49] Helen Young, *Race and Popular Fantasy Literature: Habits of Whiteness* (New York: Routledge, 2016), 20–25. The discipline of philology revolved around an "amalgamation of concepts surrounding nationhood and language community" when Tolkien was studying it. Philippa Levine, "Anthropology, Colonialism, and Eugenics," in *The Oxford Handbook of the History of Eugenics*, ed. Alison Bashford and Philippa Levine (New York: Oxford University Press, 2010), 43–61.

[50] Fimi, *Tolkien, Race and Cultural History: From Fairies to Hobbits*, 132.

[51] Rich argues that the emergence of a more established class of professional scholars in the 1920s and 1930s helped to "shift mainstream and middle opinion from the older racial ideology, especially with the emergence of studies in genetics," even though scientific racism remained commonplace in some circles. Paul B. Rich, *Race and Empire in British Politics*, 2nd ed. (New York: Cambridge University Press, 1990), 8–9.

[52] Per Jerng, "elves are different than orcs because of their varying physical and cultural traits but also because they are plotted into different times and spaces." Mark C. Jerng, *Racial Worldmaking: The Power of Popular Fiction* (New York: Fordham University Press, 2017), 106. See also Robert T. Tally Jr., *J.R.R. Tolkien's The Hobbit: Realizing History through Fantasy: A Critical Companion* (New York: Palgrave Macmillan, 2022), 65–84.

and sex, sometimes implies that the mixing of different races was a corrupting act (i.e., Morgoth's breeding of goblins and men) and other times
that it could be an act of healing (i.e., the marriage of Aragorn and Arwen).
Given these ambiguities, Robert Stuart argues that men, elves, hobbits,
and goblins ought to be seen as "breeds of a single human species, each
breed a racial representative of an aspect of that species' multiple
characteristics."[53] In the absence of clarifications from Tolkien himself,
though, these biological details are less revealing than how Tolkien detailed
the appearance and actions of these races in Middle-earth.

Here, there is much less ambiguity. Tolkien's goblins are unequivocally
associated with darkness and evil. Tolkien often refers to those with malicious intent as being dark or black, as seen in the title of the "Dark Lord"
Sauron, the "Black Riders" that served as his agents, and the lowly goblins
in his armies.[54] Their skin tone varies from "sallow" to "dark skin of greenish scales" to "black-skinned" depending on the tribe—though all of them
bleed black.[55] Even the evil "Mannish" races of Middle-earth from the
unexplored East and South are darker than the more righteous men
against whom they wage war on behalf of Sauron.[56] Conversely, heroic
figures in *The Lord of the Rings* are often (though not uniformly) associated with lightness. Tolkien's elves, for example, are replete with references to their bright skin. The elven lords of Lothlórien are "clad wholly
in white; and the hair of the Lady was of deep gold, and the hair of the
Lord Celeborn was of silver long and bright."[57] As Charles Moseley summarizes, these valorous forces "are clean-limbed, white, dark-haired, grey-
eyed examples of Northern European physical excellence."[58] They embody
the qualities that Tolkien most admired, and the opposite is true of goblins and their allies.

[53] Stuart, *Tolkien, Race, and Racism in Middle-earth*, 35.

[54] Per Rearick, "It is undeniable that darkness and the color black are continually associated
throughout Tolkien's universe with unredeemable evil, specifically Orcs and the Dark Lord
Sauron." He sees this as a reflection of Judeo-Christian values rather than racial ones.
Anderson Rearick III, "Why Is the Only Good Orc a Dead Orc? The Dark Face of Racism
Examined in Tolkien's World," *MFS Modern Fiction Studies* 50, no. 4 (Winter 2004): 861–62.

[55] The "sallow" reference comes from a description of human allies of Sauron who have
"goblin-faces, sallow, leering, squint-eyed." Tolkien, *The Fellowship of the Ring*, 324; Tolkien,
The Two Towers, 187; Tolkien, *The Return of the King*, 214.

[56] Stuart, *Tolkien, Race, and Racism in Middle-earth*, 104.

[57] Tolkien, *The Fellowship of the Ring*, 397–98.

[58] Charles Moseley, *J.R.R. Tolkien* (Liverpool: Liverpool University Press, 1997), 63. See
also Stuart, *Tolkien, Race, and Racism in Middle-earth*, 105.

Tolkien was (at times) forthcoming about how these races of Middle-earth mapped onto those of our world. In a 1964 interview, Tolkien mentions that hobbits are "just rustic English people" and that the tongue of dwarves is based on Semitic languages.[59] Indeed, critics have long shown the tendency of Tolkien to caricature dwarves based on anti-Semitic tropes, including ideas of insatiable greed and a lost homeland, even as he was outspoken about the horrors perpetrated against Jews during his lifetime.[60] Goblins likewise draw on tropes about a vaguely defined anti-European Other. In a widely cited letter, Tolkien refers to them as "squat, broad, flat-nosed, sallow-skinned, with wide mouths and slant eyes; in fact degraded and repulsive versions of the (to Europeans) least lovely Mongol-type."[61] The appearance of goblins, then, had some relation to the "Mongol-type," though their dark skin (of multiple shades), tribal structure, primitive language, and barbarous acts broadly map onto a generic Other that seeks to destroy the nobler races of elves and men.[62] These goblins have clear parallels to those associated with non-white peoples in works of anthropology and literary fiction from preceding decades.[63]

Complicating this mapping of goblins onto real-world peoples, though, is the theological framing of Middle-earth. Tolkien wrote that *The Lord of the Rings* is a "fundamentally religious and Catholic work" in which this "religious element is absorbed into the story and the symbolism."[64] If the heroic journey of Frodo and Sam is an allegory for salvation (as many have argued), then goblins represent a "particular distillate" of Satanic forces of evil.[65] Modern scholars, weighing this theological backdrop against Tolkien's racialist language, are divided on how to most appropriately read

[59] "J.R.R. Tolkien Interview," Radio, *Reluctant Olympians* (BBC, November 26, 1964).

[60] Thus, "Tolkien can be found denouncing racism even while constructing racialized fantasies." Stuart, *Tolkien, Race, and Racism in Middle-earth*, 67. See also Renée Vink, "'Jewish' Dwarves: Tolkien and Anti-Semitic Stereotyping," *Tolkien Studies* 10 (2013): 123–45.

[61] Tolkien, *The Letters of J.R.R. Tolkien*, Letter 210.

[62] The disparaging category of "Mongoloid," too, could be applied to those with mental disabilities in the early-mid twentieth century. Its utility to describe the goblins of Tolkien is mixed—for they were barbarous and less civilized than their nobler counterparts, but they were crafty and tricky in a way that did not reflect contemporary uses of "Mongoloid." Fimi, *Tolkien, Race and Cultural History: From Fairies to Hobbits*, 154–57.

[63] Tolkien even wrote (with some regret later in life) that medieval Ethiopia "was hot and its people black. That Hell was similar in both respects would occur to many." Stuart, *Tolkien, Race, and Racism in Middle-earth*, 102.

[64] Tolkien, *The Letters of J.R.R. Tolkien*, Letter 142.

[65] Stuart, *Tolkien, Race, and Racism in Middle-earth*, 155.

goblins and other agents of evil in Middle-earth.[66] Some argue that it is "extremely difficult to rescue Tolkien from accusations of racism" based on the repeated massacres (even genocide) of dark-skinned, somewhat-human creatures; others reject this interpretation and see his work as a Christian allegory, which means that goblins "do *not* symbolize the racial animosities, ethnic cleansings, and bloody genocides of our tormented times."[67] Such debates delve into unresolved questions about the nature of these fictional creatures (do goblins have free will or souls?) in lengthy interrogations of Tolkien's contradictory corpus.[68] My goal here is not to make definitive claims about the nature of these Middle-earth goblins, but rather to show that—whatever Tolkien's intent—they are depicted using racialized language common of the early-mid twentieth century, which both differentiated them from nobler races and unequivocally associated them with darkness and evil.

Whether interpreted as racial transposition, Catholic allegory, or something else entirely, goblins are cannon fodder for the heroes of Middle-earth. They are rank-and-file soldiers in the armies of the Dark Lord and his allies, rarely named as individuals but instead a horrifying throng of evil.[69] Some goblins (like the Uruk-Hai) are stronger than their brethren, yet even these genetically engineered variants are usually weaker than the heroes they confront. Before Gandalf kills the Great Goblin in *The Hobbit*, for example, he immolates the other goblins around him, whose shrieks are worse than "several hundred wild cats and wolves being slowly roasted alive"—a story that makes our heroes laugh when it is recounted later in the book.[70] Boromir, the tragic hero who dies at the beginning of *The Two*

[66] Robin Anne Reid, "Race in Tolkien Studies: A Bibliographic Essay," in *Tolkien and Alterity*, ed. Christopher Vaccaro and Yvette Kisor (Cham: Palgrave Macmillan, 2017), 33–74.

[67] Gregory Hartley, "Civilized Goblins and Talking Animals: How The Hobbit Created Problems of Sentience for Tolkien," in *The Hobbit and Tolkien's Mythology: Essays on Revisions and Influences*, ed. Bradford Lee Eden (Jefferson: McFarland & Company, Inc., 2014), 113–35; Stuart, *Tolkien, Race, and Racism in Middle-earth*, 155. Tolkien's framing of Middle-earth has been influential to a handful of conservative leaders, including Italy's far-right Prime Minister, Giorgia Meloni. Jason Horowitz, "Inspiration for Leader of Italy's Hard Right: World of Hobbits," *The New York Times*, September 21, 2022, sec. A.

[68] Rateliff, *The History of The Hobbit*, I:138–39.

[69] Franz Klug, "'The Board Is Set, the Pieces Are Moving': Horrifying Armies of Darkness and Their Function as Embodiments of Evil and Catalysts of Change Within Subcreated Worlds,'" *Hither Shore* 14 (2017): 95–110.

[70] Tally notes the "abject cruelty" of Gandalf in this scene, as the "savage delight with which goblins are violently murdered is hard to ignore." Tally Jr., *J.R.R. Tolkien's The Hobbit: Realizing History through Fantasy: A Critical Companion*, 81.

Towers, only succumbs after slaying many goblins that were "piled all about him and his feet." During the epic confrontation at Helms Deep, so many goblins are slain that they "were piled in great heaps" without any survivors, as opposed to the villainous "hillmen" taken prisoner.[71]

The threat of goblins, then, comes not from their individual skill, but from their sheer numbers and inventive trickery. They die in hordes throughout *The Hobbit* and *The Lord of the Rings* yet somehow manage to always come crawling out of some otherwise unsettled dark corner of Middle-earth. Tolkien was not the first to invent a fictional world in which large numbers of goblins could be killed; Eddison and (more influentially) MacDonald had established this precedent. In the case of MacDonald, though, the explicit origin of goblins as devolved humans means that there is hope for their re-evolution, as some who survive the flooding of the mountain become "milder in character" and more reminiscent of the "Scotch Brownies."[72] Tolkien provides no such hope of salvation for his goblins, which are the subject of such a vile corruption that he sees no possibility for their improvement.[73]

Goblins also have long-standing antagonism against other races of Middle-earth. They clash with dwarves, with whom they vie for control over mines in the mountains, and elves, from whom they were likely descended, in wars across Tolkien's legendarium. When transposed into Middle-earth, the once-synonymous inhabitants of Fairyland are pitted against each other in conflicts often based on mutual racial animosity. To some degree, this trend reflected the dichotomy between the dark goblins and light fairies of the nineteenth century. Tolkien, however, is notable for pitting goblins and dwarves against each other, as these creatures had been more frequently synonymous in preceding works. In rare cases when the goblins of Middle-earth make alliances with these races, it is not because goblins have improved themselves, but because other races have fallen into evil—as is the case with a group of "wicked dwarves" mentioned in *The*

---

[71] Tolkien, *The Two Towers*, 4, 163.

[72] MacDonald, *The Princess and the Goblin*, 202.

[73] Robert T. Tally Jr., "Demonizing the Enemy, Literally: Tolkien, Orcs, and the Sense of the World Wars," *Humanities* 8, no. 1 (2019): 54, https://doi.org/10.3390/h8010054. This is not to say that Tolkien broadly advocated for the destruction of certain groups, as scholars have shown his value of individual life (noting especially the empathy of Sam)—just not with regard to orcs. These issues are summarized in Stuart, *Tolkien, Race, and Racism in Middle-earth*, 143–49.

Hobbit.[74] Other races are more naturally inclined to work with the evil goblins. Likely drawing on the corrupted animals of *The Princess and the Goblin*, Tolkien shows goblins cooperating with the wolf-like "warg" on a handful of occasions—an alliance widespread enough to warrant the mantra, "where the warg howls, there also the orc prowls."[75] Wargs have the same vaguely evil origin story as goblins (perhaps bred by Morgoth or possessed by evil spirits) and thus make natural allies.[76]

As will be explored in the next two chapters, Tolkien's interpretation of goblins—troglodytic, crafty, cruel, tribal, dark-skinned, masculine, evil, and eminently killable—has been foundational to fantasy media. Equally important are the folkloresque trends associated with goblins that he discarded (intentionally or not). Although Tolkien acknowledged the debt that his goblins had to those of George MacDonald, he did away with their soft feet and aversion to song. The diminutive stature of goblins is also minimized in Middle-earth, as goblins can range from the size of hobbits to human men based on the circumstances of their breeding. The familial structure of goblins is likewise unexplored. Tolkien was admittedly uncomfortable writing female characters (human or otherwise) and left it to the imagination of readers how exactly goblins procreated. Goblin women and children are omitted from these texts, and any talk of reproduction is done so using animalistic terms, as in "all the orcs ever spawned" or "the Shadow that bred them."[77] Tolkien writes of no goblin queens or women; goblins are coded as men and presumed as such across his corpus. We do not encounter any humanizing descriptions of their families or cultures, only the crude, fractious, and masculine tribes that terrorize the inhabitants of Middle-earth.

Predictably discarded in this villainous rendering of goblins is the tradition of merriment associated with Robin Goodfellow and the pantomime tradition. Goblins sing a crude and sinister tune as they descend beneath the Misty Mountains in *The Hobbit*, though Tolkien provides no additional examples of goblin song in the more mature environment of *The Lord of the Rings*.[78] The association of goblins with freakishness is similarly

[74] Tolkien, *The Hobbit, or There and Back Again*, 2001, 62.

[75] Tolkien, *The Fellowship of the Ring*, 334.

[76] Rateliff downplays this connection to MacDonald, and instead sees wargs as owing "less to literary tradition than [Tolkien's] own imagination, stimulated as always by philology," in this case the Old English "wearg." Rateliff, *The History of The Hobbit*, I:217.

[77] Tolkien, *The Return of the King*, 194, 201.

[78] Tolkien, *The Hobbit, or There and Back Again*, 2001, 60–61.

diminished. Whatever the ultimate origin of these creatures, they are so differentiated from other humanoids of short stature, especially dwarves, that rhetorical tropes about disfigured humans are thrust upon to other races in Middle-earth. Indeed, a 1938 letter to Tolkien asks whether hobbits (not goblins) were inspired by the "little furry men" apparently spotted in Africa.[79] Though Tolkien perceived of goblins as corrupted forms of humans or elves, their evil deeds and clear differentiation from other races were enough to limit comparisons to real-world humans with physical or mental disabilities.

In the previous two chapters, we saw how the lexeme "hobgoblin" had fallen out of favor compared to the simpler "goblin" in most contexts. This trend seeped into Middle-earth, too. Tolkien acknowledges that hobgoblins exist in *The Hobbit*, but they play virtually no role within the narrative—only mentioned in passing as inhabitants of the Grey Mountains.[80] Tolkien's linguistic note clarifies that hobgoblins are simply larger goblins, so we can perhaps presume that the Uruk-Hai and other larger orcs could be classified as such (even though hobgoblins are never mentioned in *The Lord of the Rings*). It is unclear where Tolkien derived the idea that hobgoblins are larger variants than goblins. A 1621 medical text classifies hobgoblins and Robin Goodfellows as a "bigger kind" of terrestrial devil than most—but this entry runs counter to the general trend of hobgoblins being merrier than their goblin counterparts.[81] Perhaps Tolkien made this pronouncement without the kind of linguistic consideration for which he was known, since ultimately it had little bearing on the world of Middle-earth? Whatever the case, this minor pronouncement had lasting consequences for differentiations between goblins and hobgoblins in the fantasy genre (to be explored in the next chapter).

Weird American Fiction

Middle-earth was pioneering. No other author had crafted such a detailed fantasy world, but it took time for Tolkien's work to become the standard bearer of adult fantasy literature, especially in the United States.[82] It was

[79] Tolkien responded in the negative to this question. Tolkien, *The Letters of J.R.R. Tolkien*, Letter 25.

[80] Tolkien, *The Hobbit, or There and Back Again*, 2012, 138.

[81] Burton, *The Anatomy of Melancholy*, 65.

[82] Although Tolkien hints that *The Lord of the Rings* takes place "in the prehistory of our own world, that is not sustained, and to all intents and purposes Middle-earth is a separate

not until the 1960s, when cheap paperbacks of *The Hobbit* and *The Lord of the Rings* became readily available, that the aesthetic and themes of Middle-earth permeated the fantasy sphere. American authors of the early-mid twentieth century, then, developed their own style of fantasy that drew on some of the same sources as Tolkien but manifested in different ways. Of particular importance are the short stories featured in low-cost pulp magazines that targeted the imaginations of young American men. Among these publications, *Weird Tales* stands out for its authors' evocation of goblins as generic markers of supernatural eeriness. Therein, goblins indicate to readers that something is out of the ordinary, whether in describing the appearance of a living thing (like a goblin bat) or a superstitious tale from long ago. Even though goblins had long had this association, the violent and sexual themes that ran through these stories re-framed them for the target demographic of this media.

Pulp magazines were designed for mass consumption and became popular among working-class American teens and young men in the late nineteenth and early twentieth centuries.[83] The first pulp, *Argosy*, began in 1896 and was dedicated to children's fiction. Its success spawned other magazines that focused on different audiences and tropes: wartime aviation, murder mysteries, westerns, science fiction, and fantasy (among others). The popularity and affordability of pulps were such that they survived the Great Depression, but they struggled to maintain readership when faced with paper shortages from World War II and (later) the rise of comic books, paperback novels, and television. Into the 1950s, though, pulps provided a source of cheap literature and proved influential to later generations of authors and fantasy enthusiasts. That said, these magazines

creation." James, "Tolkien, Lewis and the Explosion of Genre Fantasy," 65. This idea, though, is disputed, due in no small part to the "several different accounts" of the origins of Middle-earth that Tolkien provides. Catherine Butler, "Tolkien and Worldbuilding," in *J.R.R. Tolkien*, ed. Peter Hunt (New York: Palgrave Macmillan, 2013), 106–20.

[83] These books built off the success of penny dreadfuls in England and dime novels in the United States. Some of them made their way to the United Kingdom, too, and a handful of magazines like *The Pall Mall Magazine* (1893–1937) contained fantastical stories. See, generally, Mendlesohn and James, *A Short History of Fantasy*, 25–42; Roger Luckhurst, "American Weird," in *The Cambridge Companion to American Science Fiction*, ed. Gerry Canavan (New York: Cambridge University Press, 2015), 194–205; Jeffrey H. Shanks and Justin Everett, eds., *The Unique Legacy of Weird Tales: The Evolution of Modern Fantasy and Horror* (New York: Rowman & Littlefield, 2015); Betsy Huang, "SF and the Weird," in *The Cambridge Companion to American Horror*, ed. Stephen Shapiro and Mark Storey (New York: Cambridge University Press, 2022), 169–82.

did not receive widespread attention from contemporary critics or scholars; they were an "ephemeral literary ghetto" populated by authors who received measly stipends for their stories and certainly did not have the time to craft a world as involved as Middle-earth.[84]

Goblins abound in the pages of *Weird Tales*. Published from 1923 to 1954, *Weird Tales* printed short stories and poetry from primarily male writers, including the famed trio of H.P. Lovecraft, Robert E. Howard, and Clark Ashton Smith.[85] The editors of *Weird Tales*, each with their own literary preferences, published stories that (today) fall under the designation of science fiction, horror, and fantasy but were grouped into the genre of "weird" fiction at the time.[86] Such stories were, according to one editor, "taboo in the publishing world."[87] Young, white men were the primary consumers of *Weird Tales*, as its cover art makes apparent in scenes depicting strapping white men adventuring in exotic locales or semi-nude white women being held captive by heinous, dark-skinned monsters. Racist undertones permeated many of these stories, a reflection of American authors projecting their own attitudes about immigration from

[84]Williamson, *The Evolution of Modern Fantasy: From Antiquarianism to the Ballantine Adult Fantasy Series*, 167–68. Their inspirations were more likely Edgar Allen Poe than *Beowulf*, and they were more likely to use their stories to interrogate anxieties around modernity and mortality than proper Christian conduct. Jason Ray Carney, *Weird Tales of Modernity: The Ephemerality of the Ordinary in the Stories of Robert E. Howard, Clark Ashton Smith and H. P. Lovecraft* (Jefferson: McFarland, 2019).

[85]This is not to say that women did not read or contribute to these magazines, but rather that they were not the editors' primary demographic. Melanie Anderson, ed., *The Women of Weird Tales: Stories by Everil Worrell, Eli Colter, Mary Elizabeth Counselman and Greye La Spina* (Richmond: Valancourt Books, 2020).

[86]Williamson divides the stories of *Weird Tales* into three distinct groups: "(1) the proto-Dark Fantasy of Lovecraft and Smith; (2) the swashbuckling proto-Sword and Sorcery adventure fiction of Howard and Leiber; and (3) the more speculative fantasy of the Pratt/de Camp collaborations." Williamson, *The Evolution of Modern Fantasy: From Antiquarianism to the Ballantine Adult Fantasy Series*, 169. The stories in *Weird Tales* evolved with its editors and contributing authors. Its emphasis under Farnsworth Wright, for example, shifted from ghost stories to those "of torture and diabolical revenge" with less supernatural influences. Robert Weinberg, "Weird Tales," in *Science Fiction, Fantasy, and Weird Fiction Magazines*, ed. Marshall Tymn and Michael Ashley (Westport: Greenwood Press, 1985), 727–36.

[87]"Why Weird Tales," *Weird Tales* 4, no. 2 (July 1924): 1. Literary critics disparaged the writing found in pulp magazines. A 1933 *Vanity Fair* article calls the magazines "gaudy, blatant, banal" and their authors "hacks." Erin Smith, "Pulp Sensations," in *The Cambridge Companion to Popular Fiction*, ed. David Glover and Scott McCracken (New York: Cambridge University Press, 2012), 141.

East Asia (in particular).[88] Though the themes of these stories were not always as straightforward as this summary might imply, the editors of *Weird Tales* presumed this audience of young men—a relatively unedu-cated market disparagingly noted by one contemporary critic as "those who move their lips when they read."[89]

The stories of *Weird Tales* exhibit a tendency toward violence and hor-ror that distinguish them from contemporary interpretations of a folklor-esque Fairyland. The works of Dunsany, Eddison, and Mirrlees trend more toward antiquated language and the mystery of Fairyland than exis-tential dread. One of their American contemporaries, David MacGregor Cheney, similarly emphasizes the importance of whimsy and escapism for adults in his 1924 edition of *The Golden Goblin*:

> Some folks are wise enough never to grow old. For them, in defiance of maturity, care, and sorry, imagination still glows. For them half-shut eyes will bring again to field and forest the dancing fairies. It is the privilege of such fortunate grown-ups to forget the harsh realisms, for a time, in some such fantasy as this ....[90]

Compare this, then, to H.P. Lovecraft reflecting on the stories that were central to his writing and so many other authors in *Weird Tales*:

> The true weird tale has something more than secret murder, bloody bones, or a sheeted form clanking chains according to rule. A certain atmosphere of breathless and unexplainable dread of outer, unknown forces must be present; and there must be a hint, expressed with a seriousness and porten-tousness becoming its subject, of that most terrible conception of the human brain—a malign and particular suspension or defeat of those fixed laws of Nature which are our only safeguard against the assaults of chaos and the daemons of unplumbed space ... Atmosphere is the all-important thing, for the final criterion of authenticity is not the dovetailing of a plot but the creation of a given sensation.[91]

[88] Luckhurst, "American Weird," 197.

[89] Advertisements likewise indicate this audience. One of the more amusing ads (from volume IV, issue 2) promises to answer age-old questions for young men like, "Does a pet-ting party stop with a kiss or does it go further? Is spooning dangerous?"

[90] David MacGregor Cheney, *The Golden Goblin* (Arlington: The House of the Golden Goblin, 1924).

[91] H.P. Lovecraft, *Supernatural Horror in Literature* (New York: Ben Abramson, 1945), 15–16. Paul Manning sees the aesthetics of the weird tale as informed by a lack of ancient

In these weird stories, goblins were natural fits as atmospheric markers for malevolent supernatural forces. The initial run of *Weird Tales* comprised 279 issues, of which 109 include goblins or hobgoblins, most of which are rhetorically deployed to this eerie end. A 1925 story from Robert E. Howard, for example, mentions horrific creatures "transmitted through the ages in tales of ogres and goblins, of werewolves and beastmen."[92] Clark Ashton Smith narrates in a 1931 tale how the unconsecrated tombs of a pair of sorcerers were the subject of "grisly tales … stories of loup-garous and goblins, of fays and devils and vampires."[93] One of his poems similarly invokes ghouls and goblins to emphasize the perils of an abandoned forest:

> Through ghoul-watched wood unthridden,
> By goblin mere and midden,
> No ivory horn will blow,
> No gold lamp lighten gloom-ward,
> But we will carry doom-ward.
> The broken beauty caught from long ago ….[94]

Such evocations, in which goblins are peripheral to a story but used to denote a particularly dark supernatural atmosphere, are featured across *Weird Tales*.[95] A story from 1940 tells of the "devils and hobgoblins leaping in demoniac glee" as an evil family murders "helpless victims" with

---

ruins in the New World, which inspired authors to craft "new kinds of ruin and new forms of haunting, including imagined sublime ruins of vast age that predate European settlement." Manning, "No Ruins. No Ghosts.," 63.

[92] Robert E. Howard, "Spear and Fang," *Weird Tales* 6, no. 1 (July 1925): 112.

[93] Clark Ashton Smith, "A Rendezvous in Averoigne," *Weird Tales* 17, no. 3 (May 1931): 364. Another short story of Smith's from 1933 sees a group of adventurers paddling down a river through the heart of a dark forest, wherein the orchids leer with "goblin faces." Clark Ashton Smith, "The Seed of the Sepulcher," *Weird Tales* 22, no. 4 (October 1933): 499.

[94] Clark Ashton Smith, "O Golden-Tongued Romance," *Weird Tales* 44, no. 3 (March 1952): 33.

[95] Smith's career extended beyond the written word and into the realm of the visual arts. He produced artwork for several of his stories, including sculptures that he fired at home using cheap, local materials (a necessity because of the Great Depression). Two of these busts he identified as goblins, one each made of dark and light clay. They are broadly humanoid, one featuring what appears to be a triangular cap, though the admittedly poor quality of these images and lack of context behind them makes it hard to draw larger conclusions. Dennis Rickard, *The Fantastic Art of Clark Ashton Smith* (Baltimore: The Mirage Press, Ltd., 1973).

their blades.[96] Another from 1950 mentions fantastic stories replete with "ghosts and goblins and djinns and werewolves and other assorted horrors."[97] Goblins could be used to describe a creature or object that is abnormal, as in a "grotesque goblin-ship of snow and ice," a "hobgoblin realm full of terrible things," or an adventure "through goblin space."[98] The pervasiveness of the goblin as a representation of supernatural darkness and horror was such that Lovecraft and Howard (part of the same writing circle) created a fictional publishing company within their works called "Golden Goblin Press."[99]

Whether goblins are mentioned in the context of demons, superstitious folklore, or cosmic horrors, they set the scene for supernatural phenomena. As such, authors feel little need to differentiate them from other creatures. A 1946 story from Ray Bradbury laments how "ghosts, leprechauns, trolls, goblins, spirits" are nothing but "pitiful epithets, meaningless syllables to describe the waiting gloom."[100] Advertisements from back pages of the 1950s issues of *Weird Tales* also list goblins as one of the many creatures that readers could expect to encounter therein (even when they are not otherwise mentioned by name in that issue).

Regardless of the kind of world that authors were crafting, from a medieval-inspired kingdom in a sword-and-sorcery adventure to a grim future of cosmic horror, goblins could serve as markers of darkness and eeriness.[101] Another recurrent trend in *Weird Tales* is for authors to use goblins and their supernatural kin (initially) as markers of unfounded superstition. This is hardly a new motif, though authors sometimes subvert it within their stories by eventually revealing these superstitions to be true—thus rendering skeptical characters and readers as the ignorant ones. One story from 1928, for example, invokes goblins in the tales of a

[96] Clyde Irvine, "The Horror in the Glen," *Weird Tales* 35, no. 2 (March 1940): 9.

[97] Harold Lawlor, "Unknown Lady," *Weird Tales* 42, no. 6 (September 1950): 55.

[98] Volney G. Mathison, "The Death Bottle," *Weird Tales* 5, no. 3 (March 1925): 38; Walter G. Detrick, "Dead Hands," *Weird Tales* 5, no. 6 (June 1925): 458; Harry Houdini and H.P. Lovecraft, "Imprisoned with the Pharaohs," *Weird Tales* 4, no. 2 (July 1924): 9.

[99] Lovecraft writes, too, of a "primal blackness of the void" except for thin, austere peaks of granite that "stood out goblin-like." H.P. Lovecraft, "The Dream-Quest of Unknown Kadath," in *At the Mountains of Madness, and Other Novels* (Sauk City: Arkham House, 1964), 306–407. Today, Golden Goblin Press is a company dedicated to producing content for the *Call of Cthulhu* RPG.

[100] Ray Bradbury, "The Night," *Weird Tales* 39, no. 6 (July 1946): 26.

[101] The sword-and-sorcery genre traditionally begins with the *Conan* tales of Robert E. Howard, and the term itself was likely coined by Fritz Leiber.

European maid, for the skeptical narrator had "heard of devils in my child-hood, for my nurse was a Hungarian woman, a peasant of the old Magyar stock, and as full of stories of vampires, demons and hobgoblins as a chest-nut shell is of prickles."[102] Another from 1937 mentions how one charac-ter "had recounted olden whispers of goblin-folk, the dark dwarfs and gnomes that burrowed in the bogs and swamps."[103] A 1940 poem, "Inheritance," provides a fond reminiscence about the fanciful creatures invoked by previous generations, distinguishing the graceful fairies with the eeriness of ogres, hobgoblins, and gnomes:

> I'm grateful to people, a thousand years back,
> Who let their minds run on a fanciful track —.
> Saw silver-winged fairies dance lightly in rain;
> Heard witches conniving at trickery and pain;
> Felt shivers when ogres, hobgoblins and gnomes.
> Shrieked nightly in forests or haunted their homes.[104]

Although goblins serve as general indicators of supernatural evil, they rarely feature as primary antagonists. Instead, they set the thematic back-drop for the arrival of more nefarious creatures. At times, too, the goblin label is applied to humans or other creatures to indicate their peculiar, often sinister, appearance. An early story in the *Conan* series of Howard, for example, sees a human with the appearance of a "dark-faced, lank-haired goblin" leading our heroes through an ancient city.[105] In other stories, we encounter a bat emerging from the darkness "like a dragon-winged goblin," a woman so wretched in appearance that she becomes "a veritable goblin of perverseness," and a dark-skinned corpse floating "like an ebony goblin."[106] Though the use of goblins to show this kind of gro-tesque, distorted appearance had centuries of precedent, its continued use in "weird" fiction for adults testifies to its resonance for authors and their young adult audiences in the early-mid twentieth century.

---

[102] Seabury Quinn, "Mephistopheles and Company, Ltd.," *Weird Tales* 11, no. 2 (February 1928): 198.

[103] Robert Bloch, "The Brood of Bubastis," *Weird Tales* 29, no. 3 (March 1937): 274.

[104] Sudie Stuart Hager, "Inheritance," *Weird Tales* 35, no. 4 (July 1940): 111.

[105] Robert E. Howard, "Red Nails (Part 2)," *Weird Tales* 28, no. 2 (September 1936): 208.

[106] David Baxter, "Nomads of the Night," *Weird Tales* 6, no. 4 (October 1925): 553; Nictzin Dyalhis, "The Oath of Hul Jok," *Weird Tales* 12, no. 3 (September 1928): 339; Robert E. Howard, "The Grisly Horror," *Weird Tales* 25, no. 2 (February 1935): 182.

Authors writing in other pulp magazines adapted goblins for their respective genres and audiences. The stories of *Weird Tales* tended to feature supernatural themes that had long been the domain of goblins, ghosts, and ghouls. In pulps like *Adventure*, though, authors wrote swashbuckling tales that were less concerned with the realms of fantasy and science fiction. Nonetheless, goblins sometimes were mentioned in these stories to describe how a natural occurrence invoked a kind of supernatural weirdness: limestone rocks that looked like goblins, a giant squid with "huge goblin eyes," disoriented camels looking like "goblins in a panic," and a young Ethiopian boy called "the little goblin."[107] In these cases, goblins conveyed the weirdness of exotic places, creatures, and people in a continuation of themes seen in penny dreadfuls and adventure literature from the late nineteenth century.

It was less common for goblins to feature in science fiction pulps, though there was precedent for it. An alien species in "Beyond Pluto" (1932) adorns their halls with "garish murals of goblins" that clearly did not impress their human visitors.[108] Another tale from *Startling Stories* (1940) sees a character struggling to describe the creatures they encounter: "just big goblins, all black and shiny."[109] Clark Ashton Smith repeatedly uses goblins to describe the unearthly creatures in "The Visitors from Mlok," published in a 1933 issue of *Wonder Stories*.[110] Therein, we encounter four-foot-tall monstrosities with "numberless interbranching tendrils or feelers like a floral arabesque" and "unknown goblin features, some of which may have been eyes, of a peculiarly elongated and oblique sort." As the protagonist of this story is further tortured by these frightful visions, he encounters "a shrine of alien diabolism, hateful and menacing and he wanted to scream aloud with a nameless horror when the goblin creatures bore him toward it and urged him through its portals." The peculiar appearance of goblins was such that they could apply to alien life

[107]Talbot Mundy, "The Seventeen Thieves of El-Kalil," *Adventure* 33, no. 2 (February 1922): Chapter VII; F. St. Mars, "De Profundis," *Adventure* 34, no. 4 (May 1922): 130; Talbot Mundy, "The Invisible Guns of Kabul," *Adventure* 72, no. 6 (December 1929): 81; Gordon MacCreagh, "Slaves for Ethiopia," *Adventure* 124, no. 2 (January 1951): 87.

[108]John Scott Campbell, "Beyond Pluto," *Wonder Stories Quarterly* 3, no. 4 (Summer 1932): 467.

[109]Raymond Z. Gallun, "Nemesis from Lilliput," *Startling Stories* 3, no. 3 (May 1940): 126.

[110]Clark Ashton Smith, "The Visitors from Mlok," *Wonder Stories* 4, no. 12 (May 1933): 962–69.

encountered in works of science fiction, though such evocations were admittedly rare.[111] Authors more regularly provide a new name for an alien species that might otherwise be described as a goblin.

As pulp magazines lost ground to cheaply printed paperback novels in the 1950s, writers adapted the tropes of their short stories for longer works. One genre to emerge from the milieu of weird fiction was sword-and-sorcery fantasy, which built on the heroic tales of Howard's *Conan* stories in particular.[112] Like Tolkien's Middle-earth, these worlds were inspired by the Middle Ages, though American authors emphasized different aspects of its history and folklore.[113] Poul Anderson's 1954 novel *The Broken Sword* in particular shows how medieval source materials could produce different kinds of fantasy worlds.[114] Published in the same year as *The Fellowship of the Ring*, this novel takes place in a mythologized version of northern Europe that features elves, changelings, witches, and fairies.[115] The text draws heavily on medieval epics (and Romantic-era medievalism) in its presentation of a brutal and violent world of Faerie that minimizes the Christian themes so prevalent in the works of MacDonald and Tolkien. Set amid a war between elves and trolls, goblins feature on a handful of occasions. We learn that goblins had once been powerful, but that few remain due to the destruction caused by the elf Imric. Now, they are "furtive cave dwellers" with knowledge of "curious goblin lore." Many of them, too, are subservient to the more powerful races of elves and trolls,

---

[111] See also (originally published in 1939) William G. Bogart and Lester Dent, *World's Fair Goblin: A Doc Savage Adventure* (New York: Bantam Books, 1969).

[112] The boundaries of this genre were disputed (especially in relation to "high fantasy" and "epic fantasy"). Williamson divides this landscape of early fantasy into "literary" (Dunsany, Eddison, Tolkien) and "popular" (Smith, Howard, Lieber) based on the publication venues of the Ballantine Adult Fantasy Series (1969–74). Williamson, *The Evolution of Modern Fantasy: From Antiquarianism to the Ballantine Adult Fantasy Series*, 127, 132.

[113] The same is true in comparing Tolkien's elves to those of Pratchett and Rowling, all of whom drew on medieval and early modern evidence. Jacqueline Simpson, "On the Ambiguity of Elves," *Folklore* 122, no. 1 (2011): 76–83.

[114] Some of the brutality and violence of *The Broken Sword* was sanitized in a 1971 edition. The edition that I consulted uses the original 1954 prose, though its eBook formatting rendered page numbers variable. I have thus provided chapters instead. Poul Anderson, *The Broken Sword*, ed. Michael Dirda (New York: Open Road Media, 2014), Introduction.

[115] One critic referred to Anderson's work as "similar" to Tolkien "but not derivative." Margaret Parish, "Pick of the Paperbacks: Fantasy," *The English Journal* 66, no. 7 (October 1977): 93.

with whom they have long fought.[116] At the scene of a troll feast, Anderson describes the great hall:

> It was huge, hewn out of rock but furnished with magnificence raided from elves, dwarfs, goblins, and other folk, men among them. Great gems gleamed on the walls amid subtle tapestries, costly goblets and cloth bedecked tables of ebony and ivory, and the fires burning down the length of the hall lit rich garments on the troll lords and their ladies. Thralls of elf, dwarf, or goblin race moved about with trenchers of meat and cups of drink. This was a high feast, for which human and Faerie babies had been stolen as well as cattle, horses, pigs, and wines of the south.[117]

Anderson describes goblins in *The Broken Sword* as one of many races of creatures in this world. They are thralls (slaves) in the service of more powerful trolls, separated from their historical wealth like elves and dwarves. Anderson does not delve too deeply into the origins of goblins, but he associates them with interbreeding. One group of goblin thralls is a "race halfway between elf and troll, green-skinned and squat but of not unpleasant aspect." Another tribe of "wild chieftains" from Pictland have dark skin and short stature due to the mixing of "blood of troll and goblin and still older folk in them, as well as Pictish women stolen in long-gone days." Anderson thus sees goblins as dark-skinned hybrids, though their appearance and behaviors are not by definition devolved and crude. In one case, goblins are even compared favorably to "filthy troll savages."[118] Indeed, by the end of the novel, goblins have capitalized on the defeats of the trolls and initiated an uprising in the towns of Trollheim.

Even in lands where goblins are not enslaved or working in the service of another race, they have a reputation for being weak. One soldier recalls how "a few odd goblins and dwarfs ... scarcely count" in the greater scope of an elf army. In another conversation between two warriors, one sees "small danger from goblins and trash like that." The other chastises this idea, though: "Mock not the goblins. They are good warriors when they have the weapons they need." We get a glimpse of the kind of technology developed by goblins in a later battle, as one armada includes goblins equipped on "their own slim red snake-prowed ships." In the ensuing

---

[116] Anderson, *The Broken Sword*, chapter 4.

[117] Anderson, *The Broken Sword*, chapter 9.

[118] Quotations from this paragraph are from (in order) Anderson, *The Broken Sword*, chapters 11, 15, 19.

combat, though, the goblins fall quickly to the heroic Skafloc and his elf allies. Anderson even describes a graphic sequence in which goblins are cloven in two, cut open, decapitated, and impaled by a spear.[119]

Similar motifs related to goblins are found in Anderson's *Three Hearts and Three Lions* (1961), which was expanded from a 1953 novella. This story sees a World War II engineer transported abruptly into an alternate reality of our world, which is divided between forces of Chaos (Faerie) and those of Law (human kingdoms). Within Fairie, warriors and sorcerers exist at the top of a social hierarchy that relegates "goblins, kobolds, and other backward tribes" to slavery. In one scene, unnamed goblin slaves (short and green-skinned) attend to the hero Alfric, escorting him through an expansive estate and attending to his needs.[120] Goblins are only referenced in this context, and they are distinct from the more esteemed dwarves, who play a more significant role in the novel's plot.

Though Anderson was inspired by much of the same history and folklore as Tolkien, the fantastical goblins that emerge from his pen are quite different. Goblins are not barbaric or evil in the universes of *The Broken Sword* or *Three Hearts and Three Lions*, nor do they serve as allegorical representations of evil in an extended Christian allegory. They are pitiable dark-skinned creatures who usually exist as servants and slaves to more powerful races within chaotic worlds inspired by medieval Fairyland. Such depictions are part of a larger thematic consistency in works of mid-century sword-and-sorcery fantasy: a "default setting" of whiteness that relegates non-white humans and creatures to antagonistic or peripheral roles.[121] Like the country these American authors inhabited, where racial segregation was enshrined into law until 1954, it was perfectly accessible to segment groups in fantasy settings based on racial identities. This simplicity was a cherished feature of the genre. As L. Sprague de Camp remarks in a 1963 essay, stories of heroic fantasy hearken back to "prehistoric or medieval worlds, when (it's fun to imagine) all men were mighty, all women were beautiful, all problems were simple, and all life was adventurous."[122]

---

[119] Anderson, *The Broken Sword*, chapters 13, 15.

[120] Poul Anderson, *Three Hearts and Three Lions* (New York: Open Road Media, 2015), chapters 7, 8.

[121] Young, *Race and Popular Fantasy Literature: Habits of Whiteness*, 58. By the 1970s, non-white authors like Samuel R. Delany were upending these tropes to "explore issues of race, power, and desire" within the genre. Brian Attebery, *Fantasy: How It Works* (New York: Oxford University Press, 2012), 139.

[122] L. Sprague de Camp, ed., *Swords and Sorcery* (New York: Pyramid Books, 1963), 4.

Dark-skinned goblins, recognizable as part of a larger fairy milieu but not afforded the same kind of respect as some of their kin, were thus consigned to antagonistic and/or subservient archetypes within this genre.

CONCLUSION

Although goblins played a crucial role in the genre-defining legendarium of Middle-earth, it would be a mistake to see them as ubiquitous across all of the fantasy literature produced in the early-mid twentieth century. They are conspicuously absent in the medieval-inspired fantasies of T.H. White (*The Once and Future King*) and C.S. Lewis' *Chronicles of Narnia* series, for example.[123] In American pulp magazines, too, although goblins are most frequently mentioned in *Weird Tales*, they are still accounted for in less than half of the overall issues (109 issues out of 279). In pulps dedicated to other genres of stories, including adventure and science fiction, this number is even lower.

This is not to say that goblins were unimportant. Rather, this data shows that we should not take for granted that goblins' ubiquitous presence in Middle-earth was reflected in other contemporary literature. Tolkien's corpus, however, provided a lasting model for their appearance and behaviors in fantasy settings. The goblins of Middle-earth were an evil race that committed horrific acts against nobler peoples before retreating back into their dark lairs. Race was a defining characteristic of their world, and goblins were an unambiguously malevolent and corrupted one. They were dark in appearance and deed, so much so that the light-skinned heroes of Middle-earth could slaughter them en masse without a shred of guilt. Contemporary American high fantasy from Poul Anderson lacked the detailed world-building of Tolkien, but it nonetheless adhered to a similar racial paradigm. Anderson saw dark-skinned goblins as racial hybrids and depicted them as lowly creatures, subservient in various circumstances to the more powerful races around them. They lacked the malevolence of Tolkien's goblins but retained their status at the bottom of fantastical racial hierarchies.

---

[123] They only are mentioned once in the latter. During a scene from *The Last Battle*, Farsight orders his men "away from this accursed stable, and whatever goblin lives inside it." C.S. Lewis, *The Last Battle* (New York: HarperCollins, 2005), 153.

In other "weird" genres, particularly those written in the United States, goblins served as supernatural markers and indicators of atypical (often eerie) appearance. The short stories of *Weird Tales* testify to this enduring resonance across genres and authors, whose works ranged in setting from the barbaric Middle Ages to the distant future. Even though goblins rarely took on leading roles in these texts, they nonetheless persisted as mood-setting descriptions in tales marketed toward young men. With such an audience in mind, authors emphasized violence, horror, and heteronormative sex appeal that frequently saw young, white men as the protagonists within worlds of supernatural horror and adventure.

Among the consumers of fantasy literature were a group of wargamers in the American Midwest. Looking to innovate on the historical combat of their tabletop games, these young men infused the themes of Tolkien, Anderson, and their contemporaries into new systems that allowed players to actively take on the role of mythical heroes. The resulting game systems, most importantly *Dungeons & Dragons*, allowed players embody heroes on their epic quests—many of which involved the indiscriminate slaying of goblins.

References

"J.R.R. Tolkien Interview". 1964. Radio. Reluctant Olympians. *BBC*, November 26.

"Why Weird Tales". 1924. *Weird Tales* 4 (2): 1–2.

Alden, Raymond Mac Donald, ed. 1921. *Poems of the English Race*. New York: Charles Scribner's Sons.

Anderson, Poul. 2014. In *The Broken Sword*, ed. Michael Dirda. New York: Open Road Media.

Anderson, Poul. 2015. *Three Hearts and Three Lions*. New York: Open Road Media.

Anderson, Melanie, ed. 2020. *The Women of Weird Tales: Stories by Everil Worrell, Eli Colter, Mary Elizabeth Counselman and Greye La Spina*. Richmond: Valancourt Books.

Attebery, Brian. 2012. *Fantasy: How It Works*. New York: Oxford University Press.

Baxter, David. 1925. Nomads of the Night. *Weird Tales* 6 (4): 551–558.

Bloch, Robert. 1937. The Brood of Bubastis. *Weird Tales* 29 (3): 274–284.

Bogart, William G., and Lester Dent. 1969. *World's Fair Goblin: A Doc Savage Adventure*. New York: Bantam Books.

Bradbury, Ray. 1946. The Night. *Weird Tales* 39 (6): 23–27.

Burton, Richard. 1621. *The Anatomy of Melancholy*. Oxford: John Lichfield and James Short.

Butler, Catherine. 2013. Tolkien and Worldbuilding. In *J.R.R. Tolkien*, ed. Peter Hunt, 106–20. New York: Palgrave Macmillan.

de Camp, L. Sprague. 1963. *Swords and Sorcery*. New York: Pyramid Books.

Campbell, John Scott. 1932. Beyond Pluto. *Wonder Stories Quarterly* 3 (4, Summer): 438–483.

Carney, Jason Ray. 2019. *Weird Tales of Modernity: The Ephemerality of the Ordinary in the Stories of Robert E. Howard, Clark Ashton Smith and H. P. Lovecraft*. Jefferson: McFarland.

Carpenter, Humphrey. 2000. *J.R.R. Tolkien: A Biography*. Boston: Houghton Mifflin Company.

Chance, Jane, ed. 2008. *Tolkien and the Invention of Myth: A Reader*. Lexington: University of Kentucky Press.

Cheney, David Mac Gregor. 1924. *The Golden Goblin*. Arlington: The House of the Golden Goblin.

Detrick, Walter G. 1925. Dead Hands. *Weird Tales* 5 (6): 458–462.

Dunsany, Lord. 1917. *Tales of Wonder*. London: Elkin Mathews.

Dunsany, Lord. 1924. *The King of Elfland's Daughter*. New York: G.P. Putnam's Sons.

Dyalhis, Nictzin. 1928. The Oath of Hul Jok. *Weird Tales* 12 (3): 337–362.

Eddison, E. R. 1924. *The Worm Ouroboros*. London: Jonathan Cape LTD.

Fimi, Dimitra. 2005–2006. 'Come Sing Ye Light Fairy Things Tripping So Gay': Victorian Fairies and the Early Work of J.R.R. Tolkien. *Working with English: Medieval and Modern Language, Literature and Drama* 2: 10–26.

Fimi, Dimitra. 2008. *Tolkien, Race and Cultural History: From Fairies to Hobbits*. Basingstoke: Palgrave Macmillan.

Flieger, Verlyn. 2003. 'There Would Always Be a Fairy-Tale': J. R. R. Tolkien and the Folklore Controversy. In *Tolkien the Medievalist*, ed. Jane Chance, 26–35. New York: Routledge.

Gallun, Raymond Z. 1940. Nemesis from Lilliput. *Startling Stories* 3 (3): 113–128.

Garth, John. 2013. *Tolkien and the Great War: The Threshold of Middle-Earth*. Boston: Houghton Mifflin Harcourt.

Garth, John. 2022. A Brief Biography. In *A Companion to J.R.R. Tolkien*, 2nd ed., 3–18. New York: Wiley Blackwell.

Hager, Sudie Stuart. 1940. Inheritance. *Weird Tales* 35 (4): 111.

Hammond, Wayne G. 2000. Whose Lord of the Rings Is It, Anyway? *Canadian C.S. Lewis Journal* 97 (Spring): 59–65.

Hartley, Gregory. 2014. Civilized Goblins and Talking Animals: How The Hobbit Created Problems of Sentience for Tolkien. In *The Hobbit and Tolkien's Mythology: Essays on Revisions and Influences*, ed. Bradford Lee Eden, 113–135. Jefferson: McFarland & Company, Inc.

Honegger, Thomas. 2024. From Old English Orcneas to George MacDonald's Goblins with Soft Feet: Sources of Inspiration and Models for Tolkien's Orcs from English Literature. In *Eine Kleine Geschichte Der Orks: Der Monströse Feind Im Wandel Der Zeit*, ed. Delila Jordan and Droß-Krüpe, 41–60.

Horowitz, Jason. 2022. Inspiration for Leader of Italy's Hard Right: World of Hobbits. *The New York Times*, September 21, sec. A.

Hostetter, Carl F., and Arden R. Smith. 1996. A Mythology for England. *Mythlore* 21 (2): 281–290.

Houdini, Harry, and H. P. Lovecraft. 1924. Imprisoned with the Pharaohs. *Weird Tales* 4 (2): 3–12.

Howard, Robert E. 1925. Spear and Fang. *Weird Tales* 6 (1): 111–115.

Howard, Robert E. 1935. The Grisly Horror. *Weird Tales* 25 (2): 169–188.

Howard, Robert E. 1936. Red Nails (Part 2). *Weird Tales* 28 (2): 205–220.

Huang, Betsy. 2022. SF and the Weird. In *The Cambridge Companion to American Horror*, ed. Stephen Shapiro and Mark Storey, 169–182. New York: Cambridge University Press.

Hunt, Peter. 2016. The Children's Novel. In *The Oxford History of the Novel in English: Volume 7: British and Irish Fiction Since 1940*, ed. Peter Boxall and Bryan Cheyette, 310–327. New York: Oxford University Press.

Hyde, Paul Nolan. 1988. A Philologist at the North Pole: J.R.R. Tolkien and The Father Christmas Letters. *Mythlore* 15 (1, Autumn): 23–27.

Irvine, Clyde. 1940. The Horror in the Glen. *Weird Tales* 35 (2): 7–19.

James, Edward. 2012. Tolkien, Lewis and the Explosion of Genre Fantasy. In *The Cambridge Companion to Fantasy Literature*, ed. Edward James and Farah Mendlesohn, 62–78. New York: Cambridge University Press.

Jerng, Mark C. 2017. *Racial Worldmaking: The Power of Popular Fiction*. New York: Fordham University Press.

Klug, Franz. 2017. The Board Is Set, the Pieces Are Moving': Horrifying Armies of Darkness and Their Function as Embodiments of Evil and Catalysts of Change Within Subcreated Worlds. *Hither Shore* 14:95–110.

Knight, George. 1896. The Showman of Goblintown. In *Dust in the Balance*, 141–163. London.

Lawlor, Harold. 1950. Unknown Lady. *Weird Tales* 42 (6): 54–63.

Leppälahti, Merja. 2018. From Folklore to Fantasy. Translated by Clive Tolley. *Journal of the Fantastic in the Arts* 29 (2): 179–200.

Levine, Philippa. 2010. Anthropology, Colonialism, and Eugenics. In *The Oxford Handbook of the History of Eugenics*, ed. Alison Bashford and Philippa Levine, 43–61. New York: Oxford University Press.

Lewis, C. S. 1968. The Dethronement of Power. In *Tolkien and the Critics: Essays on J.R.R. Tolkien's The Lord of the Rings*, ed. Neil D. Isaacs and Rose A. Zimbardo, 12–17. Notre Dame: University of Notre Dame Press.

Lewis, C. S. 2005. *The Last Battle*. New York: HarperCollins.

Lovecraft, H. P. 1945. *Supernatural Horror in Literature*. New York: Ben Abramson.

Lovecraft, H. P. 1964. The Dream-Quest of Unknown Kadath. In *At the Mountains of Madness, and Other Novels*, 306–407. Sauk City: Arkham House.

Luckhurst, Roger. 2015. American Weird. In *The Cambridge Companion to American Science Fiction*, ed. Gerry Canavan, 194–205. New York: Cambridge University Press.

MacCreagh, Gordon. 1951. Slaves for Ethiopia. *Adventure* 124 (2): 74–103.

MacDonald, George. 1872. *The Princess and the Goblin*. Philadelphia: J.B. Lippincott & Co.

Mandler, Peter. 2006. *The English National Character: The History of an Idea from Edmund Burke to Tony Blair*. New Haven: Yale University Press.

Manning, Paul. 2017. No Ruins. No Ghosts. *Preternature: Critical and Historical Studies on the Preternatural* 6 (1): 63–92.

Mathison, Volney G. 1925. The Death Bottle. *Weird Tales* 5 (3): 33–38.

Mendlesohn, Farah, and Edward James. 2009. *A Short History of Fantasy*. London: Middlesex University Press.

Mirrlees, Hope. 1927. *Lud-in-the-Mist*. New York: Alfred A. Knopf.

Moseley, Charles. 1997. *J.R.R. Tolkien*. Liverpool: Liverpool University Press.

Mundy, Talbot. 1922. The Seventeen Thieves of El-Kalil. *Adventure* 33 (2): 3–56.

Mundy, Talbot. 1929. The Invisible Guns of Kabul. *Adventure* 72 (6): 56–83.

Munro, John. 1907. *The Story of the British Race*. New York: D. Appleton and Company.

Nikolajeva, Maria. 2003. Fairy Tale and Fantasy: From Archaic to Postmodern. *Marvels & Tales* 17 (1): 138–156.

Owen, Dora, ed. 1920. *The Book of Fairy Poetry*. New York: Longmans, Green, and Co.

Parish, Margaret. 1977. Pick of the Paperbacks: Fantasy. *The English Journal* 66 (7): 90–93.

Quinn, Seabury. 1928. Mephistopheles and Company, Ltd. *Weird Tales* 11 (2): 193–212.

Rateliff, John D. 2007. *The History of The Hobbit*. II Vols. Boston: Houghton Mifflin Company.

Rateliff, John D. 2008. She and Tolkien, Revisited. In *Tolkien and the Study of His Sources: Critical Essays*, ed. Jason Fisher, 145–161. Jefferson: McFarland & Company, Inc.

Rearick, Anderson, III. 2004. Why Is the Only Good Orc a Dead Orc? The Dark Face of Racism Examined in Tolkien's World. *MFS Modern Fiction Studies* 50 (4, Winter): 861–874.

Reid, Robin Anne. 2017. Race in Tolkien Studies: A Bibliographic Essay. In *Tolkien and Alterity*, ed. Christopher Vaccaro and Yvette Kisor, 33–74. Cham: Palgrave Macmillan.

Rich, Paul B. 1990. *Race and Empire in British Politics*. 2nd ed. New York: Cambridge University Press.

Rickard, Dennis. 1973. *The Fantastic Art of Clark Ashton Smith*. Baltimore: The Mirage Press, Ltd.

Ripp, Joseph. 2005. Middle America Meets Middle-Earth: American Discussion and Readership of J. R. R. Tolkien's The Lord of the Rings, 1965–1969. *Book History* 8 (1): 245–286.

Schweitzer, Darrell. 1989. *Pathways to Elfland: The Writings of Lord Dunsany*. Philadelphia: Owlswick Press.

Shanks, Jeffrey H., and Justin Everett. 2015. *The Unique Legacy of Weird Tales: The Evolution of Modern Fantasy and Horror*. New York: Rowman & Littlefield.

Shippey, Tom. 2003. *The Road to Middle-Earth: How J.R.R. Tolkien Created a New Mythology*. Boston: Houghton Mifflin Company.

Shore, Thomas William. 1906. In *Origin of the Anglo-Saxon Race: A Study of the Settlement of England and the Tribal Origin of the Old English People*, ed. T. W. Shore and L. E. Shore. London: Elliot Stock.

Simpson, Jacqueline. 2011. On the Ambiguity of Elves. *Folklore* 122 (1): 76–83.

Smith, Clark Ashton. 1931. A Rendezvous in Averoigne. *Weird Tales* 17 (3): 364–373.

Smith, Clark Ashton. 1933a. The Visitors from Mlok. *Wonder Stories* 4 (12): 962–969.

Smith, Clark Ashton. 1933b. The Seed of the Sepulcher. *Weird Tales* 22 (4): 497–505.

Smith, Clark Ashton. 1952. O Golden-Tongued Romance. *Weird Tales* 44 (3): 33.

Smith, Erin. 2012. Pulp Sensations. In *The Cambridge Companion to Popular Fiction*, ed. David Glover and Scott McCracken, 141–158. New York: Cambridge University Press.

Smith-Rowsey, Daniel. 2007. Whose Middle-Earth Is It? Reading The Lord of the Rings and New Zealand's New Identity Form a Globalized, Post-Colonial Perspective. In *How We Became Middle Earth: A Collection of Essays on the Lord of the Rings*, ed. Adam Lam and Nataliya Oryshchuk, 129–145. Zollikofen: Walking Tree Press.

St. Mars, F. 1922. De Profundis. *Adventure* 34 (4): 127–131.

Stenström, Anders. 1996. A Mythology? For England? *Mythlore* 21 (2): 310–314.

Stuart, Robert. 2022. *Tolkien, Race, and Racism in Middle-Earth*. Cham: Palgrave Macmillan.

Swank, Kris. 2013. The Hobbit' and 'the Father Christmas Letters. *Mythlore* 32 (1, Fall/Winter): 127–144.

Tally, Robert T. Jr. 2022. *J.R.R. Tolkien's The Hobbit: Realizing History Through Fantasy: A Critical Companion*. New York: Palgrave Macmillan.

Tally, Robert T., Jr. 2019. Demonizing the Enemy, Literally: Tolkien, Orcs, and the Sense of the World Wars. *Humanities* 8 (1): 54. https://doi.org/10.3390/h8010054.

Tolkien, J. R. R. 1976. In *The Father Christmas Letters*, ed. Baillie Tolkien. Boston: Houghton Mifflin Company.

Tolkien, J. R. R.. 1979. *Bilbo, le Hobbit*. Translated by Francis Ledoux. Paris: Hachette.

Tolkien, J. R. R. 1994. *Morgoth's Ring*. Edited by Christopher Tolkien. The History of Middle-Earth. New York: HarperCollins.

Tolkien, J. R. R. 1999. *The Silmarillion*. Edited by Christopher Tolkien. London: HarperCollins.

Tolkien, J. R. R. 2001a. *The Fellowship of the Ring*. New York: Ballantine Books.

Tolkien, J. R. R. 2001b. *The Hobbit, or There and Back Again*. New York: Ballantine Books.

Tolkien, J. R. R. 2001c. *The Return of the King*. New York: Ballantine Books.

Tolkien, J. R. R. 2001d. *The Two Towers*. New York: Ballantine Books.

Tolkien, J. R. R. 2012. *The Hobbit, or There and Back Again*. London: HarperCollins.

Tolkien, J. R. R. 2013. *The Letters of J.R.R. Tolkien*. Edited by Humphrey Carpenter and Christopher Tolkien. Boston: Houghton Mifflin Harcourt.

Tolkien, J. R. R.. 2014a. *Beowulf: A Translation and Commentary Together with Sellic Spell*. Edited by Christopher Tolkien. New York: Houghton Mifflin Harcourt.

Tolkien, J. R. R.. 2014b. Tolkien: On Fairy-Stories. Edited by Verlyn Flieger and Douglas A. Anderson. New York: HarperCollins.

Tolkien, J. R. R. 1915. Goblin Feet. In *Oxford Poetry*, ed. G.D.H.C. and T.W.E, 64–65. Oxford: B.H. Blackwell.

Vink, Renée. 2013. 'Jewish' Dwarves: Tolkien and Anti-Semitic Stereotyping. *Tolkien Studies* 10:123–145.

Weinberg, Robert. 1985. Weird Tales. In *Science Fiction, Fantasy, and Weird Fiction Magazines*, ed. Marshall Tymn and Michael Ashley, 727–736. Westport: Greenwood Press.

West, Richard C. 2014. Where Fantasy Fits: The Importance of Being Tolkien. *Mythlore* 33 (1, Fall/Winter): 5–36.

White, T. H. 1958. *The Once and Future King*. New York: G.P. Putnam's Sons.

Whittingham, Elizabeth A. 2007. *The Evolution of Tolkien's Mythology: A Study of the History of Middle-Earth*. Jefferson: McFarland & Company, Inc.

Williamson, Jamie. 2009. *The Evolution of Modern Fantasy: From Antiquarianism to the Ballantine Adult Fantasy Series*. New York: Palgrave Macmillan.

Young, Helen. 2016. *Race and Popular Fantasy Literature: Habits of Whiteness*. New York: Routledge.

CHAPTER 7

Tabletop Goblins

In the 1970s, Gary Gygax and Dave Arneson developed the rules for *Dungeons & Dragons*, a tabletop role-playing game (TTRPG) in which players embody (usually) heroic characters in fantastical worlds. The setting of *D&D* was a synthesis of historical, folkloric, folkloresque, literary, and religious themes that designers united under a single ruleset that could accommodate adventures as broad as players' imaginations. Inspired by the meticulous rules of historical wargames, those of *D&D* required some degree of rigidity. Gygax and his co-authors provided statistics and abilities for monstrous races that players could expect to encounter on their campaigns, including goblins, hobgoblins, kobolds, and orcs. In early editions of *D&D*, goblins are lowly humanoid monsters—short, dark-skinned, evil, and living in darkness—that relish violence and the enslavement of those that they conquer. They are natural antagonists for any group of low-level adventurers (typically coded as morally righteous, white, and masculine) hoping to obtain fortune and glory.

The interpretation of goblins in early editions of *D&D* has cast a wide shadow on other TTRPG systems, which tend to portray them along the same lines. Nonetheless, it would be a mistake to see *D&D* as having a wholly homogenizing impact on fantasy goblins in tabletop games. In the 1980s, other role-playing systems sought to distance themselves from Tolkien-centric themes, and *GURPS Fantasy* even embraced goblins as peaceful, enterprising traders that players could personify in their games.

© The Author(s), under exclusive license to Springer Nature Switzerland AG 2026
M. King, *A History of Goblins*,
https://doi.org/10.1007/978-3-032-01063-6_7

Over the last decade in particular, fantasy game designers have consciously crafted more diverse worlds that minimize racial determinism in their rule-sets. This process has resulted in a reimagining of goblins. Recent itera-tions of *D&D* and *Pathfinder* have seen designers reject goblins' inherent evil and instead portray them as crafty, resourceful humanoids with as much capacity for valor as mischief. Players of TTRPGs can thus use these rulesets to embody heroic goblins instead of relegating them to a fate of predestined malevolence.

The Creation and Influences of *Dungeons & Dragons*

Dungeons & Dragons emerged from wargaming communities of the mid-twentieth century, in which groups of (primarily) young, white men devised rules for simulated combat across historical time periods.[1] They created battle maps on large tables, often with complex terrain features, and moved clusters of soldier figurines around them with the goal of best-ing their opponent's forces.[2] Gygax was part of the wargaming community in Lake Geneva, Wisconsin, and devised (along with co-author Jeff Perren)

---

[1] Scholarship on *D&D* and TTRPGs cuts across the disciplines of history, game studies, English literature, anthropology, sociology, psychology, and cultural studies (especially). It is "admittedly an awkward one still in search of an appropriate academic home." Scott M. Bruner, "Constructing a Canon for 'Dungeons & Dragons': A Generative Analysis of Gary Gygax's Appendix N." (Master's Thesis, San Diego, San Diego State University, 2017), 3. The most detailed book-length accounts of the history of *D&D* are Shannon Appelcline, *Designers & Dragons: The '70s* (Silver Spring: Maryland, 2013); David M. Ewalt, *Of Dice and Men: The Story of Dungeons & Dragons and The People Who Play It* (New York: Scribner, 2013); Jon Peterson, *Playing at the World: A History of Simulating Wars, People and Fantastic Adventures, from Chess to Role-Playing Games*, 2nd ed. (San Diego: Unreason Press, 2012); Jon Peterson, *Game Wizards: The Epic Battle for Dungeons & Dragons* (Cambridge: Massachusetts Institute of Technology, 2021); Ben Riggs, *Slaying the Dragon: A Secret History of Dungeons and Dragons* (New York: JABberwocky Literary Agency, Inc., 2022); Aaron Trammell, *The Privilege of Play: A History of Hobby Games, Race, and Geek Culture* (New York: NYU Press, 2024).

[2] Most wargamers simulated combat of the nineteenth and early twentieth centuries. Gygax was notable for being one of the few members of this community (alongside Tony Bath) to explore ancient and medieval warfare. Gygax's 1970 newsletter for the Castle & Crusade Society, *Domesday Book*, circulated rules for simulations of medieval combat. Jon Peterson, "A Game Out of All Proportions: How a Hobby Miniaturized War," in *Zones of Control: Perspectives on Wargaming*, ed. Pat Harrigan and Matthew G. Kirschenbaum (Cambridge: The MIT Press, 2016), 20–21.

his own set of rules for a wargame called *Chainmail* in 1971.[3] Although the focus of this ruleset is combat between human armies, it also contains a "Fantasy Supplement" that provides guidelines for simulating conflict between battalions of wizards, elves, goblins, balrogs, and dragons (among others). The first ruleset for *Dungeons & Dragons* (*OD&D*), which Gygax published with Dave Arneson in 1974, is an outgrowth of this supplement and outlines a system of gameplay based on a process of collaborative storytelling.[4]

OD&D introduced the idea of players embodying individual characters and working together as a party within a shared fantasy world crafted by a Dungeon Master (DM).[5] These games do not have prescribed endings (unless the DM uses a pre-written adventure module), though they do see the gradual ascent of player characters via levels accumulated, treasure amassed, and reputation grown. This process of narrative creation, in which players negotiate with a DM to inform the actions they want their in-game characters to perform, has provided the basic gameplay formula across editions of *D&D* and become standard for TTRPGs across genres and settings.[6] As players defeat monsters and solve puzzles within the

[3] I was unable to locate a copy of the first edition of *Chainmail* and instead used the second edition, which was published in 1972. The scholarship mentioned in footnote 1 of this chapter does not indicate any substantial changes to the fantasy supplement between these two editions. Gary Gygax and Jeff Perren, *Chainmail: Rules for Medieval Miniatures*, 2nd ed. (Maine: Guidon Games, 1972).

[4] Gary Gygax and Dave Arneson, *Dungeons & Dragons: Rules for Fantastic Medieval Wargames Campaigns Playable with Paper and Pencil and Miniature Figures* (Lake Geneva: TSR, Inc., 1974).

[5] The terminology used in this initial edition was the "referee," a term borrowed from wargaming conventions. The factors that motivate players to inhabit certain kinds of characters (based on appearance, reputation, attitude, etc.) have been a subject of growing interest among psychologists over the last decade. Sören Henrich and Rachel Worthington, "Let Your Clients Fight Dragons: A Rapid Evidence Assessment Regarding the Therapeutic Utility of 'Dungeons & Dragons,'" *Journal of Creativity in Mental Health*, December 4, 2021, https://doi.org/10.1080/15401383.2021.1987367; Daniel Luccas Arenas, Anna Viduani, and Renata Brasil Araujo, "Therapeutic Use of Role-Playing Game (RPG) in Mental Health: A Scoping Review," *Simulation & Gaming* 53, no. 3 (2022): 285–311, https://doi.org/10.1177/10468781211073720

[6] That said, the parameters of what defines a "role-playing game" and even a "game" are contested. Zagal and Deterding argue that RPGs are "maybe the most contentious game phenomenon: the exception, the outlier, the not-quite-a-game game." José P. Zagal and Sebastian Deterding, "Definitions of 'Role-Playing Games,'" in *Role-Playing Game Studies: Transmedia Foundations*, ed. José P. Zagal and Sebastian Deterding (New York: Routledge, 2018), 19. Salen and Zimmerman use *D&D* as a case study for testing the limits of what can

game, their characters become more powerful. They can cast more lethal spells, become harder to kill in combat, and gain access to valuable equipment. These specifics are largely determined by a player's class. *OD&D* had only three classes in its original form (cleric, fighting man, and magic-user), but later editions expanded on both the classes and character races that players could embody.

Gygax and his collaborators drew on a handful of themes when crafting their rules for *Chainmail* and *OD&D* (both published by TSR, Inc.). Military history, especially that of medieval Europe, provided them with archetypes for different kinds of weapons, armor, factions, cultures, and societies within their worlds. Fantasy literature, fairy tales, horror films, science fiction, and world religions, meanwhile, informed the supernatural components of this ruleset. Gygax outlined these inspirations in a list of "Inspirational and Educational" reading in Appendix N of the *Dungeons Masters Guide* for the first edition of *Advanced Dungeons & Dragons* (*AD&D*):

Science fiction, fantasy, and horror movies were a big influence. In fact, all of us tend to get ample helpings of fantasy when we are very young, from fairy tales such as those written by the Brothers Grimm and Andrew Long. This often leads to reading books of mythology, paging through bestiaries, and consultation of compilations of the myths of various lands and peoples. Upon such a base I built my interest in fantasy, being an avid reader of all science fiction and fantasy literature since 1950 ....[7]

Following this preface is a list of media that was most influential to Gygax, including *The Hobbit* and *The Lord of the Rings*. Gygax was hardly alone in finding inspiration from Tolkien. The ascendancy of Middle-earth in fantasy literature during the 1960s and 1970s is hard to overstate. Elevated by the publication of cheap paperbacks of *The Lord of the Rings*, young Americans flocked to this trilogy such that it was a "cult classic" by

---

be considered a game, since it often does not have a fixed endpoint. Instead, *D&D* campaigns are "structured like serial narratives that grow and evolve from session to session." The authors overcome this quandary (since it is "ridiculous" to conclude that RPGs are not games) by seeing session-to-session goals and missions as representing quantifiable goals as required in their definition. Katie Salen and Eric Zimmerman, *Rules of Play: Game Design Fundamentals* (Cambridge: The MIT Press, 2003), 81–82.

[7] Gary Gygax, *AD&D Dungeon Masters Guide*, Lake Geneva (TSR, Inc., 1979), 224. See also Jeffro Johnson, *Appendix N* (Zug: Castalia House, 2017); Peter Bebergal, ed., *Appendix N: The Eldritch Roots of Dungeons and Dragons* (London: Strange Attractor Press, 2021).

the late 1960s.[8] Publishers, seeing the commercial potential of this kind of writing, rushed to define the fantasy genre. Ballantine Books reprinted classics of so-called Adult Fantasy, including Dunsany, Eddison, and MacDonald, which facilitated a "commercial boom" in the 1970s.[9] None of them reached the popularity of Tolkien, however, and his model for fantasy—a medieval-inspired secondary world separate from our own—inspired countless imitators.[10] Indeed, the prevalence of Tolkienian mythology within early editions of *D&D* was such that Tolkien Enterprises threatened legal action.[11] Lawyers demanded the removal of certain creatures (ents, goblins, hobbits, orcs, wargs, and balrogs) from the game, alleging that they were the intellectual property of Tolkien. The suit was settled out of court when Gygax and Arneson agreed to replace the balrog, hobbit, and warg with more generic alternatives.[12] Goblins, which had clear precedent outside Middle-earth, thus endured within the pages of *D&D*.

The works of Robert E. Howard, H.P. Lovecraft, and Poul Anderson, whose short stories were collected in paperback compilations during the 1960s and 1970s, are among those listed in Appendix N as well. So too are book-length fantasy novels, which became more common during these decades thanks to the success of Tolkien. Many works of high fantasy used a medieval-esque backdrop similar to that of Middle-earth, though American authors tended to emphasize brutal violence and horrifying

[8] James, "Tolkien, Lewis and the Explosion of Genre Fantasy," 72.

[9] Edward James and Farah Mendlesohn, "Unending Romance: Science Fiction and Fantasy in the Twentieth Century," in *The Cambridge History of the English Novel*, ed. Robert L. Caserio and Clement Hawes (New York: Cambridge University Press, 2012), 874–75. See also Williamson, *The Evolution of Modern Fantasy: From Antiquarianism to the Ballantine Adult Fantasy Series*, 192–98.

[10] One of Tolkien's lasting contributions to fantasy media was that "the default cultural model for the fantasy world was the Middle Ages." James, "Tolkien, Lewis and the Explosion of Genre Fantasy," 70. See also Peterson, *Playing at the World: A History of Simulating Wars, People and Fantastic Adventures, from Chess to Role-Playing Games*, 84.

[11] Peterson, *Game Wizards: The Epic Battle for Dungeons & Dragons*, 81–82.

[12] Tolkien Enterprises saw the commercial potential for TTRPGs and licensed their own system, *Middle-earth Role Playing* (*MERP*) in 1984. This system categorizes the groups of Middle-earth into more concrete categories than Tolkien. Within *MERP*, one of the groupings of "Non-Mannish Races" is the cluster of Common Orcs, Uruk-hai, and Half-orcs (goblins omitted entirely). These "hideous creatures" were descended from Elves but "twisted and perverted" by Morgoth. Though not "inherently evil, they are culturally and mentally predisposed toward Darkness." Coleman Charlton, *Middle-earth Role Playing* (Charlottesville: Iron Crown Enterprises, 1984), 11, 106.

monsters in their secondary worlds. In L. Sprague de Camp's *The Goblin Tower* (1968), for example, the titular spire is constructed from an army of goblins turned to stone by wizards—yet another example of lowly goblins destroyed at the hands of more powerful actors.[13]

When Gygax and his co-authors began writing the rules for *Chainmail* and *OD&D*, they had a growing corpus of fantasy literature to inform their many monsters. Their first description of goblins comes from the "Fantasy Supplement" of *Chainmail*. The entry for goblins (and kobolds, which are apparently different creatures but with the same statistical attributes) is brief but establishes the characteristics that inform later descriptions:

> Goblins and Kobolds see well in dimness or dark, but they do not like bright light. When fighting in full daylight or bright light they must subtract 1 from their Morale Rating, as well as 1 from any die rolled. Because of their reciprocal hatred, Goblins (Kobolds) will automatically attack any Dwarves (Gnomes) within charging distance.[14]

Built into the idea of goblins in *Chainmail* is that they are creatures of darkness. They see well in the dark but take penalties when in bright light. So too they are imbued, by virtue of their species, with a natural hatred of other subterranean groups: the dwarves and gnomes. This ruleset further clarifies the relationship between orcs and goblins, classifying the former as "nothing more than over-grown Goblins."[15] This distinction was likely informed by the association of goblins with *The Hobbit* and more imposing orcs with *The Lord of the Rings*. Goblins, kobolds, and orcs are likewise listed in sequence in a lineup of creatures that are agents of "Chaos," as opposed to those that fall under the "Law" (including hobbits, dwarves, gnomes) and "Neutral" (including sprites, pixies, elves, fairies) categories of this system.[16]

Even in this relatively brief supplement, Gygax and Perren established the precedent for rigidly dividing fantasy creatures into categories based on their immutable, quintessential nature. The characterization of goblins

---

[13] The story culminates in the destruction of the tower and the transformation of the goblins back into their original forms. L. Sprague de Camp, *The Goblin Tower* (New York: Del Rey, 1983).

[14] Gygax and Perren, *Chainmail: Rules for Medieval Miniatures*, 1972, 26.

[15] Gygax and Perren, *Chainmail: Rules for Medieval Miniatures*, 27.

[16] Gygax and Perren, *Chainmail: Rules for Medieval Miniatures*, 35.

as chaotic creatures that live in darkness and hate their cave-dwelling neighbors derived heavily from Tolkien, but the genre of tabletop gaming pushed Gygax and Perren to provide concrete statistics to clearly differentiate goblins from other supernatural monstrosities. Indeed, within tabletop rules, whether it is a wargame like *Chainmail* or an RPG like *D&D*, there is a need for specificity when it comes to the kind of creatures that players fight. Different species of enemies have different hit points, armor classes, attacks, and natural abilities that affect how they function within the game. Players and DMs need to know these details in order to effectively play. Gygax was aware of the need for this kind of consistency, as he explains in an early edition of the *Player's Handbook*:

> There is a need for a certain amount of uniformity from campaign to campaign in D&D … Uniformity means that classes are relatively the same in abilities and approach to solving problems with which the campaign confronts them. Uniformity means that treasure and experience are near a reasonable mean. Uniformity means that the campaign is neither a give-away show nor a killer—that rewards are just that, and great risk will produce commensurate rewards, that intelligent play will give characters a fighting chance of survival.[17]

This need for consistency led Gygax and Perren to note distinctions and unique characteristics among goblins and other monsters. This process began in *Chainmail* but became more refined in *OD&D*.[18] Therein, Gygax and Arneson give goblins, kobolds, orcs, and hobgoblins their own subheadings in the "Monster Descriptions" section.[19] Orcs have some physical similarities to goblins, namely, that they "do not like full daylight, reacting as do Goblins." Kobolds, too, should be treated "as if they were Goblins" (though with a small difference in hit points). Gygax further clarifies the relationship between goblins and hobgoblins, mentioning that the latter "are large and fearless Goblins"—a rendering likely deriving from Tolkien's introductory note in *The Hobbit*. Goblins themselves bear

[17] Gary Gygax, *AD&D Players Handbook*, Lake Geneva (TSR, Inc., 1978), 6.

[18] The third edition of *Chainmail* makes hobgoblins stronger than goblins, specifying that the former "fight as Armored Foot and defend as Heavy Foot." This edition also contains the typo of "Hoblins." Gary Gygax and Jeff Perren, *Chainmail: Rules for Medieval Miniatures*, 3rd ed. (Lake Geneva: TSR, Inc., 1975), 29.

[19] The rules for *OD&D* were initially distributed in three rulebooks. Gygax and Arneson, *Dungeons & Dragons: Rules for Fantastic Medieval Wargames Campaigns Playable with Paper and Pencil and Miniature Figures*, II.7–8.

the same characteristics as in *Chainmail*, though Gygax notes that they are organized under a goblin king. In the 1975 *Greyhawk* supplement to *OD&D*, Gygax expands the goblin family to include bugbears, which are "great hairy goblin-giants."[20]

The minor details that Gygax provides about goblin societies and their relationship to other monsters should not obfuscate the unambiguously antagonist role that goblins play in *Chainmail* and *OD&D*. Any semblance of the merry or quirky goblin is wiped away in favor of a singular vision of goblins as an evil monstrosity that players can kill for treasure and experience points. This phenomenon is admittedly not unique to goblins. To some degree, all of the monstrosities in *OD&D* are designed with combat against player characters in mind. They are stripped of their categorical ambiguities, encoded with specific appearances and behaviors, and made possible to defeat.[21] They become "objects of play," rather than objects of fear.[22] Within this system, too, goblins are near the bottom of the proverbial ladder. Gygax provides six "Monster Level Tables" for randomized encounters that give some sense of the relative power of various creatures, the first three of which are printed in Table 7.1.

Goblins occupy an unenviably position at the bottom of this monstrous hierarchy. They might be powerful enough to raid peaceful villages and ambush unwary travelers from their crude hideouts, but they are among the weakest enemies in *OD&D*. They are fodder for low-level characters to gain experience and middling amounts of treasure before these heroes become powerful enough to fight more dangerous foes.

There are few depictions of goblins and their kin in the rules of *Chainmail* and *OD&D*. The budget for both of these systems was minimal and left

---

[20] Gary Gygax and Rob Kuntz, *Supplement I: Greyhawk* (Lake Geneva: TSR, Inc., 1975), 34. The word "Bugbear" (per the *OED*) is attested as early as the sixteenth century and could refer to both an imaginary terror and a more specific creature that could eat misbehaving children. *OED*, "Bugbear."

[21] D&D allows players "to confront a hostile world in a way that was familiar to American, mostly white middle-class players—through turning challenges into capital based on calculable strategies." Jaroslav Švelch, "Encoding Monsters: 'Ontology of the Enemy' and Containment of the Unknown in Role-Playing Games," in *The Philosophy of Computer Games Conference* (Copenhagen, 2018).

[22] Švelch argues that literature can "keep its secrets thanks to *indeterminacy*" (per Iser) but that such secrets are inevitably revealed (and made less horrifying) in games. Jaroslav Švelch, "Monsters by the Numbers: Controlling Montrosity in Video Games," in *Monster Culture in the 21st Century: A Reader*, ed. Marina Levina and Diem-My T. Bui (New York: Bloomsbury, 2013), 195–97.

Table 7.1 Monster-level tables from *OD&D*

Level 1	Level 2	Level 3
Kobolds	Hobgoblins	Wights
Goblins	Zombies	Heroes
Skeletons	Lizards	Giant Hogs
Orcs	Warriors	Giant Ants
Giant Rats	Conjurers	Ochre Jelly
Centipedes	Gnolls	Thaumaturgists
Bandits	Thouls	Swashbucklers
Spiders	Ghouls	Magicians
–	Berserkers	Giant Snakes
–	Theurgists	Giant Weasels[a]

Difficulty levels of monsters from OD&D show that goblins (alongside creatures like kobolds, skeletons, orcs, and bandits) are among the weakest creatures in the game

[a] Gygax and Arneson, *Dungeons & Dragons: Rules for Fantastic Medieval Wargames Campaigns Playable with Paper and Pencil and Miniature Figures*, III.10–11

little room for game art. For *OD&D*, the art budget was around only $100, and the resulting illustrations appear "amateurish, even crude" because most contributors were not trained artists but "doodlers" working "as a favor to Gygax."[23] These illustrators provide one labeled illustration each of goblins and orcs: the former a bearded humanoid with a cape and axe, the latter a wrinkled, tunic-wearing humanoid with a sword. These sketches give a vague sense of how Gygax and his colleagues might have considered these creatures, though they provide few additional clarifying details. Given that the presumed audience for this game was wargamers already familiar with *Chainmail* and fantasy literature, Gygax perhaps thought that he did not need to overly explain their appearance.[24] Nonetheless, within the rules of *Chainmail* and *OD&D*, we can see how goblins evolved as Gygax and his co-authors adapted them for the medium of tabletop gaming. They were monsters with defined combat statistics alongside ambiguously related humanoids like orcs, kobolds, bugbears, and hobgoblins—all of which had malicious tendencies that made them natural foils for parties of low-level adventurers. In subsequent editions of *D&D*, Gygax built on these ideas to create more detailed and enduring interpretations of these creatures.

[23] Michael Witwer et al., *Dungeons & Dragons Art & Arcana: A Visual History* (New York: Clarkson Potter/Ten Speed, 2018), 26.

[24] Peterson, *Playing at the World: A History of Simulating Wars, People and Fantastic Adventures, from Chess to Role-Playing Games*, chapter 5.

Refining Goblins in *Advanced D&D*

Chainmail and *OD&D* were poorly funded endeavors meant to appeal to a niche market of wargamers in the United States. Their success, however, inspired additional supplements and editions of *D&D* that widened the market for the game.[25] The *Dungeons & Dragons Basic Set* (1977) was marketed as an introductory version for those without any prior experience to tabletop games, while *Advanced Dungeons & Dragons* (1977–1979, henceforth *AD&D*) substantially expanded the rules of the original edition with three full-length books: *Player's Handbook*, *Dungeon Master's Guide*, and *Monster Manual* (so-called core rulebooks), alongside a host of supplementary materials. Some of these materials detailed new heroes and monsters; others provided new campaign settings in which DMs could situate their campaigns. By 1979, around 400,000 people worldwide (most in the United States) were playing *AD&D*, and its books were grossing some $2 million annually for TSR, Inc.[26]

AD&D's description of goblins in the *Monster Manual* and *Dungeon Master's Guide* expands upon the foundations of *Chainmail* and *OD&D*.[27] Goblins live in "a tribal society, the strongest ruling the rest, allowing fealty to the goblin king." They inhabit dismal, dark surroundings (especially caves), which has made them skilled miners and natural foes to gnomes and dwarves such that goblins "will attack them in preference to any other creature." Cruel by default, goblins are "slave takers and fond of torture," and would rather "steal, rob, and kill for their income" than work for other creatures. They have average intelligence but are still relatively weak fighters. Though classified as "uncommon" creatures, when goblins do appear, they do so in large groups numbering between 40 and 400. Their skin color ranges from "yellow through dull orange to brick red" with matching red or yellow eyes.

The lowly status of goblins is reinforced in the 1983 edition of the *Dungeons & Dragons Players Manual*, which was designed as an accessible

---

[25] Appelcline characterizes the 1980s roleplaying industry as revolving around twenty-two companies that published a variety of "wargame holdovers, roleplaying originals, old guard resurrections, and small press publishers." Shannon Appelcline, *Designers & Dragons: The '80s* (Silver Spring: Maryland, 2014), 1.

[26] William J. White, *Tabletop RPG Design in Theory and Practice at the Forge, 2001–2012: Designs and Discussions* (New York: Palgrave Macmillan, 2020), 1–2.

[27] Gary Gygax, *AD&D Monster Manual*, Lake Geneva (TSR, Inc., 1977), 47; Gygax, *AD&D Dungeon Masters Guide*, 106.

introduction to *AD&D*. A sample encounter at the beginning of this book, "Your First Adventure," fittingly begins with a goblin:

> Suddenly, you see a goblin! He is smaller than you are, and looks like an ugly little man with gray skin. He sees you, gives a scream, waves his sword, and attacks. You dodge his blow, and raise your sword to swing … If you miss, the goblin tries again, but misses. You can swing again; roll again to see if you hit. If you hit the goblin, he screams and runs away, down the corridor and into the darkness ….[28]

New players are thus introduced to goblins through a combat scenario in which the goblin swings aimlessly at a low-level player character until it is hit and scampers away into the darkness. Later in the book, readers encounter a pitiable goblin enslaved by an evil wizard ("Please master! Don't hurt!" it whimpers) that nonetheless is slain and looted by a group of adventurers. In official adventure modules for *AD&D*, goblins consistently serve as antagonists to low-level characters—fodder for heroes to gain modest amounts of experience and treasure. One of these scenarios, "The Forest Oracle" (1984), outlines a scenario in which players need to defeat a band of goblins that live in the ruins of an uninhabited castle and had recently captured two female prisoners picking berries near the river (a possible reference to *Goblin Market*).[29]

The classification of goblins in relation to other monsters is briefly considered in *AD&D*; they are "smaller cousins" of bugbears and might be distantly related to kobolds.[30] We are also introduced to an aquatic variant of the hobgoblin called the koalinth, which is "similar to their land-dwelling cousins in most respects" and pillage shallow waters much as hobgoblins do on land.[31] Gygax evidently uses the familial term "cousin" to indicate a shared lineage between creatures like goblins/bugbears and hobgoblins/koalinths (as well as other species like gnomes/dwarves), though he does not provide additional details. Curiously, too, he does not mention any sort of taxonomic relationship between goblins and hobgoblins. He instead presents hobgoblins as a larger, more vicious, more

[28] This encounter comes in the Mentzer edition of the *Basic Set* from 1983. Gary Gygax and Dave Arneson, *Dungeons & Dragons Players Manual*, ed. Frank Mentzer (Lake Geneva: TSR, Inc., 1983), 3–8.

[29] Carl Smith, *The Forest Oracle* (Lake Geneva: TSR, Inc., 1984).

[30] Gygax, *AD&D Monster Manual*, 15, 47.

[31] Gygax, *AD&D Monster Manual*, 53.

omnipresent (they can live virtually anywhere), and more industrious goblins—and with darker skin tone from "dark reddish-brown to gray black" to match this brutality.[32]

The proximity of goblins to certain creatures is implied in their languages, too. Many of the monsters in the *AD&D Monster Manual* are able to speak their "racial" tongue (i.e., a dwarf speaking dwarfish) alongside a handful of languages based on creatures with whom they have frequent contact. Not all of this linguistic knowledge is reciprocal. The middling intelligence of goblins is such that they can mutually speak the respective languages of their monstrous kin: orcs, kobolds, and hobgoblins. They are unable, however, to speak the languages of more powerful monsters and heroic races like bugbears, halflings, gnomes, elves, dwarves—even though these groups can speak the tongue of goblins.

Depictions of goblins and their cousins in *AD&D* were produced in greater number and quality than in *OD&D*.[33] Artists worked in collaboration with Gygax on these illustrations, and the clear differences between them speak to how the game's developers sought to visually differentiate between them. All of these portraits depict bipedal humanoids armed with weapons, but each has distinguishing features—from the pig-like orc to the reptilian kobold to the hairy bugbear to the hyena-like gnoll.[34] Gygax mentions that interbreeding was a possibility between these monsters, especially in the case of orcs, who will "breed with anything" to create "unsavory mongrels with orcish blood, particularly orc-goblins,

---

[32] Gygax, *AD&D Monster Manual*, 52–53.

[33] Gnolls can speak hobgoblin and are "generally on friendly terms with orcs, hobgoblins, bugbears, ogres, and even trolls." An early illustration of a bugbear for a 1975 *OD&D* supplement featured a pumpkin head because of a miscommunication between Gygax and illustrator Greg Bell. Gary Gygax, "Q&A with Gary Gygax, Part VI," Dragonsfoot Forums, May 20, 2002, https://www.dragonsfoot.org/forums/viewtopic.php?p=328256

[34] In a 2002 forum post, Gygax summarizes his basic description of these creatures on terms that roughly correspond to the images in *AD&D*, though the pig-like appearance of orcs is replaced with a resemblance to apes:

"Kobolds: Greenish little humanoids with imp-like faces.Goblins: Orange-skinned little humanoids with bulbous heads and bodies.Orcs: Brutish, ape-man-like humanoids with small eyes and snout noses.Hobgoblins: Larger goblins, reddish of skin, also with skinny limbs.Gnolls: Hyena-men that smell and sound like hyenas when they cry out.Bugbears: Big, hairy hobgoblins with large, round heads."

Gary Gygax, "Q&A with Gary Gygax, Part VIII," Dragonsfoot Forums, May 20, 2002, https://www.dragonsfoot.org/forums/viewtopic.php?p=351833

orc-hobgoblins, and orc-humans."[35] Though these races are of different "stock," they are still able to miscegenate in grotesque ways. Gygax intentionally avoids the mechanical particularities of interbreeding, however. He elaborates on this rationale in a 1979 column:

> Should half-dwarves, half-gnomes, and half-halflings (and is a half-halfling a quartling, perchance?) be allowed? How about dwarf-elf, dwarf-gnome, dwarf-halfling, elf-gnome, elf-halfling, and gnome-halfling crossbreeds? Then there are tri-racial mixtures. Those involving humans and orcs add still more confounding factors. And now somebody decided that ogres could cross with humans! Could they cross with elves also? How about hill giants interbreeding with humans? with elves? with ogres? with ettins? Why leave out goblins? hobgoblins? gnolls? bugbears? Because of the potential for absolute madness in the game, I included only the half-elf, hoping that the rest would not arise to plague the placid waters of racial selection, but it is apparent that it was not meant to be.[36]

Gygax goes on to consider the difficulties of "designing a race" for game purposes and the impossibility of assigning balanced abilities and statistics for characters from different racial backgrounds.[37] Although Gygax adopts the racialized language of fantasy that was commonplace in the works of Tolkien and Anderson (among others), he restricts its biological implications for the purpose of game design. He is still comfortable, though, using race as a determining factor for numerous other mechanics in the game. Character classes are restricted to certain races, some races can obtain higher maximum levels than others, and races are predisposed toward being hostile or friendly to other races. They are also sorted into a system of morality based on axes of "lawful-neutral-chaotic" and "good-neutral-evil." Goblins fall into the "lawful evil" sector of this chart. They respect their particular version of tribal law and order, through which they seek to "impose their yoke upon the world," but they see no value in "life, beauty, truth, freedom and the like."[38] The creation of this alignment system allows DMs and players to broadly understand how monsters tend to act in given situations and how certain spells function (or do not function) against them.

[35] Gygax, *AD&D Monster Manual*, 76.
[36] Gary Gygax, "The Half-Ogre, Smiting Him Hip and Thigh," *Dragon* IV, no. 3 (September 1979): 12.
[37] In *OD&D*, Gygax preferred the term "creature" to "race," a change in both vocabulary and mechanics likely inspired by fantasy literature that divided imaginary worlds based on racial lines.
[38] Gygax, *AD&D Players Handbook*, 33.

The language of morality used in *AD&D* reflected broader ideas in the wargaming community about the nature of good and evil. These groups were small in size and tended to be more conservative than other youth movements of the 1960s and 1970s: mostly young, white men with an interest in military history (some of whom had served in the American military).[39] Writing during the Vietnam War and the Cold War, many of them had crystallized ideas about the nature of good and evil based on binaries of the time: capitalism vs. communism, America vs. the USSR, West vs. East, etc.[40] The fantasy novels that they read, too, were often situated in worlds with clearly defined and simplistic forces of good and evil. Hearkening back to de Camp's 1963 essay, these were worlds in which "all men were mighty, all women were beautiful, all problems were simple, and all life was adventurous."[41] These perspectives left little room for moral ambiguity, and we can see this expressed in the alignment system of *AD&D*, which has concrete ideas for what makes a particular creature good or evil, lawful or chaotic. As we will see shortly, not everyone in the wargaming community adhered to these binaries, but they were prevalent in the mind of Gygax and his co-authors.

This alignment system also intersected with contemporary strands of thought regarding gender and race. Fantasy game systems, though self-acknowledged as works of imagination, nonetheless have the perspectives and biases of their creators embedded within them. Studies of the presentation of women within early editions of *D&D* have shown how they were both less represented than men (in illustrations especially), received mechanical penalties to their strength score to reflect a presumed weakness, and were the subject of other sexist rules like the infamous "Random

---

[39] Fine even begins his pioneering 1983 monograph on fantasy gaming with a minimization of its size and importance: "By any standards the fantasy gaming world is a rather small, perhaps trivial, social world. It doesn't have a massive economic impact, it isn't a representative sample of American life and culture, and it does not exemplify any particular social problem. It certainly is not the most important subsegment of American society on which one might choose to do research." Gary Alan Fine, *Shared Fantasy: Role Playing Games as Social Worlds* (Chicago: University of Chicago Press, 1983), 1.

[40] When supplements to *AD&D* drew on geographic inspirations from outside Western Europe (especially the "Orient"), they reduced "the complexity of eastern culture to a set of problematically racist and sexist stereotypes." Aaron Trammell, "How Dungeons & Dragons Appropriated the Orient," *Analog Game Studies* III, no. I (January 11, 2016), https://analoggamestudies.org/2016/01/how-dungeons-dragons-appropriated-the-orient/

[41] De Camp, *Swords and Sorcery*, 4. An overview of this kind of "color coding" within fantasy can be found in Stuart, *Tolkien, Race, and Racism in Middle-earth*, 95–97.

Harlot Encounter Table" in the *AD&D Dungeon Masters Guide*.[42] Although Gygax and his peers are comfortable envisioning worlds filled with magic and supernatural monsters, those worlds require that men be naturally stronger than women.[43] The racialist framing of *AD&D* further positions light-skinned characters of human or demi-human lineage (elves, dwarves, gnomes, and halflings) as being appropriate for valorous player characters. The inhabitants of the *Monster Manual*, though, are frequently dark-skinned deviations from this heroic norm. This tendency is even codified within the rules, as some races (like dwarves and goblins) have such historic hatred for one another that they will prioritize attacking each other over other enemies.[44] Illustrations across the core rulebooks for *AD&D* and its many supplements reinforce this trope of light-skinned

[42] Aaron Trammell, "Misogyny and the Female Body in Dungeons & Dragons," *Analog Game Studies* I, no. III (2014), https://analoggamestudies.org/2014/10/constructing-the-female-body-in-role-playing-games/; Antero Garcia, "Privilege, Power, and Dungeons & Dragons: How Systems Shape Racial and Gender Identities in Tabletop Role-Playing Games," *Mind, Culture, and Activity* 24, no. 3 (2017): 232–46; Sarah Stang and Aaron Trammell, "The Ludic Bestiary: Misogynistic Tropes of Female Monstrosity in Dungeons & Dragons," *Games and Culture* 15, no. 6 (2020), https://doi.org/10.1177/1555412019850059. This should not obfuscate the role that women like Lee Gold played in the early years of *D&D* through communities like *Alarums & Excursions*. Aaron Trammell, *The Privilege of Play: A History of Hobby Games, Race, and Geek Culture*, 109–32.

[43] Gygax provides mix messages on how he interpreted gender and diversity within *D&D*. He is explicit in the *AD&D* player's handbook about wanting to embrace players with a "wide range of diversity" and is pleased that "even a fair number of women are counted among those who regularly play the game." This attempt at inclusivity, though is thoroughly undermined in his entry within a 1975 column about "Women in Wargaming" in which Gygax emphatically states, "I have been accused of being a nasty old sexist-male-Chauvinist-pig, for the wording in D&D isn't what it should be. Damn right I am a sexist. It doesn't matter to me if women get paid as much as men… They can jolly well stay away from wargaming in droves for all I care. I've seen many a good wargame and wargamer spoiled thanks to the fair sex." Gary Gygax, "Women and Wargaming," *Europa* 10/11 (1975): 86–94. A culture of masculinity, indeed, is traceable across editions of *D&D* and only in very recent publications been minimized. Aaron Trammell, "Militarism and Masculinity in Dungeons & Dragons," in *Masculinities in Play*, ed. Nicholas Taylor and Gerald Voorhees (New York: Palgrave Macmillan, 2018), 129–48.

[44] Outcry over an official history of the early years of *D&D*, in which its authors (rightfully) note the embedded biases of its creators, shows that this issue remains controversial. Ben Riggs, "D&D Co-Creator Gary Gygax Was Sexist. Talking About It Is Key to Preserving His Legacy.," Ben Rigg's Blog, July 7, 2024, https://www.writerbenriggs.com/blog/4h8ich5klfw83ehgcxamqko6u1yrg7; J.R. Zambrano, "D&D History Book Mentions Sexism and the Internet Has Big Feelings About It," Bell of the Souls, July 10, 2024, https://www.bello-

adventurers fighting dark-skinned, grotesque monsters en route to trea-sure and glory.[45]

Complementing the mechanical need for differentiated races of crea-tures in the fantasy worlds of *AD&D* was a practical one. Wargames and early TTRPGs were meant to be played on physical surfaces that allow players to simulate combat and movements. Player characters and mon-sters were frequently embodied in small plastic miniatures a few inches in height (for those who could afford them). These miniatures needed to be distinctive enough for players to differentiate between their own charac-ters and the monsters they were fighting. Regardless of the genetic rela-tionship between goblins, hobgoblins, kobolds, orcs, and other humanoid monsters, they needed to look different enough to be easily spotted on a tabletop. This material reality is apparent in advertisements for *AD&D* miniatures, which testify to the quality and variability of poses for mon-strous races.[46]

The clustering of goblins with other monsters like hobgoblins and orcs also had the inadvertent effect of insulating them from critiques of *AD&D* that emerged during the so-called Satanic Panic of the 1980s.[47] Spurious accusations of Satanic or occult rituals among *AD&D* players were part of a larger moral outcry against perceived anti-Christian media that ranged from horror movies like *The Exorcist* (1973) to heavy-metal music.[48] Although this hysteria had little basis in reality, it is true that demonic and cult imagery is present within the rulebooks of *AD&D*. Its *Monster*

---

flostsouls.net/2024/07/dd-history-book-mentions-sexism-and-the-internet-has-big-feel-ings-about-it.html

[45] Trammell argues that the "players and designers of *Dungeons & Dragons* were engaged in a white supremacist feedback loop which takes for granted and centers the human experi-ence as universal, powerful, attractive, and good, while simultaneously producing an inferior racialized other against which one's humanity can be judged." Aaron Trammell, "The Rules for Race: Dungeons & Dragons in the Suburbs," Gamers with Glasses, 2021, https://www.gamerswithglasses.com/features/the-rules-for-race-dungeons-amp-dragons-in-the-suburbs

[46] See, for example, "At Last, The Real Thing...," *Dragon* X, no. 9 (February 1986): 75.

[47] Frankfurter considers this incident as one of many "myth(s) of evil conspiracy" that, though distinct in historical contests, are framed through similar patterns. David Frankfurter, *Evil Incarnate: Rumors of Demonic Conspiracy and Satanic Abuse in History* (Princeton: Princeton University Press, 2006), 5–6.

[48] Joseph P. Laycock, *Dangerous Games: What the Moral Panic over Role-Playing Games Says about Play, Religion, and Imagined Worlds* (Oakland: University of California Press, 2015); Daniel Martin and Gary Alen Fine, "Satanic Cults, Satanic Play: Is 'Dungeons and Dragons' a Breeding Ground for the Devil?," in *The Satanism Scare*, ed. James T. Richardson, Joel Best, and David G. Bromley (New York: Routledge, 2017), 107–25.

Manual contains entries for six named demons (i.e., Juiblex, the Faceless Lord), six demon archetypes, eleven named devils, and associated creatures like imps.[49] Goblins are not mentioned at all in these entries, nor are they referenced as the kind of creature that could exist in their fiery domains. A 1984 article within a *D&D* magazine, "Nine Hells Revisited: More 'Facts' about Devildom" even differentiated between the "legions of the hells" as opposed to "the goblin races, men, and demons."[50] Although goblins had their origins as medieval demons, their association with Christian theology had so diminished that Gygax and his co-authors did not think to group them with actual demons. The second edition of *D&D*, whose authors wanted to distance themselves from this controversy, minimized references to devils, demons, and cults. Goblins and their kin, though, escaped this self-censorship because game designers and their critics saw them as unrelated to the depths of Hell.[51]

PLAYER PERSPECTIVES

While the goblins of *AD&D* reflect the imagination and game-design philosophy of Gary Gygax and his co-authors, they do not necessarily represent the perspective of the growing number of people who played the game in the 1970s and 1980s.[52] As the designers of *AD&D* acknowledged and embraced, their game could be modified and adapted.[53] Dedicated

---

[49] Gygax, *AD&D Monster Manual*, 16–23.

[50] Ed Greenwood, "Nine Hells Revisited: More 'Facts' about Devildom," *Dragon* IX, no. 6 (November 1984): 34.

[51] Fallout from the Satanic Panic is considered in Laycock, *Dangerous Games: What the Moral Panic over Role-Playing Games Says about Play, Religion, and Imagined Worlds*, chapter 5.

[52] This consideration of the perspective of both game designers and players is informed by the larger debate in game studies about the importance of "Ludology" as opposed to "Narratology," which centers on the "tension between rule-based systems and story-based systems" within games (especially videogames). Ian Bogost, *Unit Operations: An Approach to Videogame Criticism* (Cambridge: MIT Press, 2006), 68. In a keynote address, Bogost distills this debate into a simple question, "Is a game a system of rules, or is a game a kind of narrative?" Ian Bogost, "Videogames Are a Mess: My DiGRA 2009 Keynote, on Videogames and Ontology," *Writing* (blog), September 3, 2009. These theories need not be framed in opposition to one another. Amy McManus and Andrew Hale Feinstein, "Narratology and Ludology: Competing Paradigms or Complementary Theories in Simulation," *Developments in Business Simulation and Experiential Learning* 33 (2006): 363–72.

[53] Gygax wrote that, while there are "no optionals for the major systems" of *AD&D*, Dungeon Masters should exercise their discretion to "maintain excitement" and enjoyment of the game. Gygax, *AD&D Dungeon Masters Guide*, 9.

players discussed their own interpretations of it in official magazines, appropriately titled *Dungeon* and *Dragon*. The latter was longer-lived and included more diverse content than the former.[54] *Dragon* was published in print form for 359 issues from 1976 to 2007, the pages of which contain adventure modules, rule supplements, and discussions of materials related to TTRPGs. Its contents allow us to glimpse how the most dedicated players of *AD&D* interpreted, expanded upon, and changed the game's rules to fit their imaginative visions in the years when *AD&D* was at the height of its popularity.[55]

Goblins are commonplace within the pages of *Dragon*. Of the first 200 issues of the magazine from June 1976 to December 1993, 172 of them mention goblins or hobgoblins (for a total of 1610 instances).[56] Articles designed to inspire DMs frequently use goblins as troglodytic antagonists whose malevolent actions initiate a campaign and provide an introductory encounter or two for a party of adventurers.[57] One campaign setting introduces the "goblin-races" (kobolds, goblins, orcs, and hobgoblins) as the "most hated of all enemies," spurred by such an extended history of conflict with the dwarves that their "mutual hatred seems inborn."[58] Another

---

[54] *Dungeon* was published from 1986 to 2003. It focuses on adventure modules that players can adapt for their own campaigns. The first issue outlines its scope: "You, the readers, may share your own adventures and scenarios from *AD&D*® and *D&D*® gaming with the legions of other fantasy gamers. Each issue offers a number of fairly short (but often quite complicated and long-playing) modules, selected from the best we receive." Roger E. Moore, "Out of the Dungeon, Into the Fire," *Dungeon* 1 (October 1986): 1.

[55] Trammell has shown how the idea of "warrior masculinity" is prevalent in *Dragon* magazine and serves three main functions: "It erases women from discourses to affirm the TTRPG as a male preserve, they reinforce stereotypes of women as sources of protection or comedy, and they minimize the role of women in gaming to that of sidekicks and aberrations. Through these mechanisms, *Dragon* magazine served to marginalize women which lead to their erasure in the history of the game *Dungeons & Dragons*." Steven L. Dashiell, "Chasing the Dragon (Magazine): Gender Erasure Through Discourse in Dragon Magazine, 1978–2005," *Cultural Studies ↔ Critical Methodologies* 22, no. 6 (December 2022): 620–30.

[56] OCR copies of *Dragon* are accessible via the Internet Archive: https://archive.org/details/DragonMagazine260_201801/Dragon%20Magazine%2C%20The%20Art%20of/. I would love to be able to conduct a similar analysis of *Alarums & Excursions*, which was not affiliated with the publishers of *D&D*, but it has not been digitized and made available on the internet.

[57] See, for example, Charles Sagui, "A Short History of Adamanite," *Dragon* III, no. 3 (August 1978): 31–33.

[58] This idea is informed by Middle-earth. Roger E. Moore, "Hate Orcs? You'll Love This Campaign," *Dragon* V, no. 5 (November 1980): 56. The most detailed goblin mythology

references "relatively safe encounters" for a party of low-level characters involving only "a few Goblins or a Kobold or two."[59] One contributor even notes that their level-12 monk "rarely gets XP for kobolds, goblins, centipedes, etc." by their DM because they are "too easy" to defeat.[60] Despite their weakness in small groups, goblins could still be used to lethal effect when mobilized in large numbers. An article that catalogued some 600 player and hireling deaths over the course of a bloody campaign calculated that 10.1% of these deaths were at the hands of so-called "goblin races" or "goblin types" (the highest of any category):

> "Goblin types", while not being strong individually (although they may have the occasional troll or ogre with them), are usually found in large groups, eager to destroy, and can be encountered practically anywhere or anytime according to the monster encounter tables. Typically, you will come across up to 300 or 400 orcs or goblins, who will proceed to pepper your group with a huge cloud of arrows, wiping out all the low level players and hirelings. Very few higher level players ever get done in by these creatures, however.[61]

This DM mobilized goblins in huge numbers (often alongside more threatening monsters) to pose a real threat to players.[62] Some authors in the pages of *Dragon* even go a step further and encourage players to disregard certain rules in *AD&D* and to break free from its tropes.[63] Tom Armstrong, for example, encourages his peers to "look further than the

---

that I could locate during the first decade of *AD&D* is Glenn Rahman, "The History of Zorn and the Goblins," *Dragon* V, no. 12 (June 1981): 44–47.

[59] Charles Sagui, "Hirelings Have Feelings Too," *Dragon* III, no. 12 (June 1979): 26–27. Another writer calls goblins and kobolds "the worst" of the humanoid races. Arthur Collins, "Boulder-Throwers and Humanoid Hordes," *Dragon* XIII, no. 8 (January 1989): 34–36.

[60] Edgar W. Francis IV, "The Forum: Opinions and Observations," *Dragon* IX, no. 4 (September 1984): 6.

[61] Lyle Fitzgerald, "It's a Good Day to Die (Death Statistics of D & D Players)," *Dragon* III, no. 6 (November 1978): 26–27.

[62] *Dungeon* magazine, likewise, is filled with encounters that feature low-level goblins. David Howery, "Falcon's Peak," *Dungeon* 3 (February 1987): 4–10; Robert Kelk, "They Also Serve... Who Misappropriate," *Dungeon* 2, no. 4 (April 1988): 12–22.

[63] Some authors even inserted mechanics from *AD&D* into folkloric and historical people. A regular series within *Dragon* from TSR staff writers, "Giants in the Earth: Classic Heroes from Fiction & Literature," provides statblocks and descriptions for how to incorporate figures like John Henry (a level seven fighter) and Finn MacCumhall (a level fifteen ranger) into *AD&D*. The latter description mentions that Finn defeated a "goblin armed with a magical

book" when implementing monsters within the game. He writes of having his players stumble across "such things as kobolds with 18/00 strength, a rock troll (made of real rock), and lawful good goblins" in order to "shake up the average player's complacency."[64] Joseph Clay also provides guidelines for how players can create their own kobold and goblin characters, giving these "bad guys … a little glory for a change." For players wanting to create a goblin, they must give it physical abnormalities, which Clay sees as "a fact of life" and range from "unfortunate deformities to useful new abilities." Distinct from the traditional races of *AD&D*, Clay forces players to randomly assign abnormalities to their goblinoid characters, which includes colorblindness, insanity, infrared vision, stupidity, ugliness, and a thick skull.[65] These traits are more wide-ranging than previous kinds of disabilities associated with goblins, but for Clay, they are embedded in their essence.[66]

Other articles steered toward more theoretical issues. Like Tolkien, DMs took their world-building seriously and wanted to design universes that, while fantastical, were undergirded by taxonomies that reflected real-world science. They also needed to be consistent with the appearance of these creatures so that players could differentiate their plastic miniatures on a tabletop. This latter consideration inspired Lance Harrop to provide his own taxonomies in a 1979 article.[67] Harrop, noting the "wide variety" and ambiguity of representations of orcs and their kin, mimics Linnaeus' classification system to differentiate between them and visualizes them for readers in a gnarled and leafless phylogenetic tree: *Genus koboldus*, *Genus ogres*, *Genus goblus*, *Genus hoblus*, and *Genus orkus* (subdivided into lesser

harp," a reference to the story of the fire-breathing Áillen. Roger E. Moore, "Giants in the Earth: Classic Heroes from Fiction & Literature," *Dragon* VII, no. 2 (August 1982): 17.

[64] Tom Armstrong, "The Best DMs Will Look Further than the Book," *Dragon* VI, no. 2 (August 1981): 62.

[65] Joseph Clay, "Hey, Wanna Be a Kobold? Humanoids as Player Characters in AD&D® Games," *Dragon* XIII, no. 8 (January 1989): 38–43.

[66] Although Gygax advocates for some degree of conformity and consistency in *AD&D*, articles like these show that TSR, Inc. encouraged players to modify its rules and themes. The rules for the 1981 edition of the *Basic Set* even specify that "anything in this booklet… should be thought of as changeable" based on player and DM preference. Gary Gygax, Dave Arneson, and Tom Moldvay, *Dungeons & Dragons Fantasy Adventure Game Basic Rulebook* (Lake Geneva: TSR, Inc., 1981), B3.

[67] Lance Harrop, "Would the Real Orc Please Step Forward? Dealing with the Proliferation of Orcish Miniatures," *Dragon* III, no. 11 (May 1979): 18–19.

orcs, great orcs, and man orcs). Gnolls and trolls, meanwhile, are related to each other, but not these "goblin races".

Harrop was not alone in considering the genealogical varieties of humanoids in *AD&D*. A multi-part article series, "Fantasy Genetics," shows how three authors tried to hybridize real-world taxonomies with (mostly) fantastical creatures (Table 7.2).[68] Therein, goblins are classified as part of the genus *Australopithecus*, a group of early primates based in Africa millions of years ago with a close genetic relationship to humans. Unlike the variations of the genus *Homo*, which had additional fantasy descriptors (i.e., *sylvanus*) added to them, the goblin races here are presented as pre-human primates. Moore, the author of this portion of the article and an eventual magazine editor for TSR, Inc., elaborates on this choice:

> The general description of all the goblin races, as to sloping brows, receding chins and flattened noses, corresponds strongly to skull specimens of *Australopithecus* … Had the australopithenes evolved in a separate area of the planet rather than in the same general area as hominids, they might well have toughened up and survived into recorded times, as appears to have

Table 7.2 Taxonomies from the "Fantasy Genetics" series

- Genus *Homo*
  - Men (*Homo sapiens sapiens*)
  - Elves (*Homo sapiens sylvanus*)
  - Orcs (*Homo sapiens orc*)
  - Cavemen (*Homo sapiens neanderthalensis*)
  - Dwarves (*Homo faber*)
  - Sasquatch (*Homo sasquatch*)
- Genus *Australopithecus*
  - Kobold (*Australopithecus boisei*)
  - Goblin (*Australopithecus africanus*)
  - Hobgoblin (*Australopithecus robustus*)
  - Bugbear (*Australopithecus giganticus*)

Writers for *Dragon* speculated about real-world analogs to goblins and other monstrous humanoids, placing the former as *Australopithecus africanus*

[68] Gregory G.H. Rihn, "Humanoid Races in Review," *Dragon* V, no. 6 (December 1980): 16–17; Roger E. Moore, "Half-Orcs in a Variety of Styles," *Dragon* V, no. 6 (December 1980): 17–18; John S. Olson, "What Do You Get When You Cross...?," *Dragon* V, no. 6 (December 1980): 19.

happened in the world of *Dungeons & Dragons*. They have been driven by *Homo sapiens* and his allies into the most wild and desolate places, and underground, for which reason they harbor an understandable grudge against humankind.[69]

To Moore, the fossil record provides a "logical basis" for the existence of goblins and other monstrous humanoids, which in turn could allow DMs to make more concrete rules about (among other issues) the kind of genetic hybrids that could exist in a fantasy world. The importance of race to this framing of fantasy is hard to overstate. Moore presents goblins as a race of creatures outmaneuvered by genetically superior humanoids, driven underground, and forever resentful of their place on the edges of civilized society. Irrelevant are cosmic clashes of good and evil, the will of *AD&D*'s many gods, or the existence of multiple planes of existence. Conflict between humanoids ultimately boils down to the brutality of natural selection. This idea of applying real-world scientific ideas to the races of *AD&D* extended to language, too.[70] A.D. Rogan crafted a speculative diagram based on the idea that humanoids of low or average intelligence spoke "obviously related and probably fairly simple" languages that were distinct from more complex ones of, say, elves and dwarves.

Articles about the classification of goblins and their kin speak to a desire that DMs had to craft believable worlds for their players by applying real-world science to the fantastic. Not content with the vague idea of goblin and their "cousins" in *AD&D* rulebooks, authors applied what they knew about evolutionary biology and linguistics to make sense of them. These ideas had little bearing on the outcome of combat within *AD&D* but were instead crucial to building worlds for players with clear and predictable natural laws. Accordingly, goblins were relatively weak, stupid, and under-developed compared to races like humans and elves. Their dark skin reflected the dark environments that they called home, and their evolutionary inferiority made them eternally resentful of the success of other races. Even as these authors debated the kind of fantasy they wanted to see in their games of *AD&D*, they tended not to question its underlying racialist framing and elevation of light-skinned creatures over their dark-skinned counterparts. Rather, they

---

[69] Moore, "Half-Orcs in a Variety of Styles." Moore was a contributor when he wrote this article, and he eventually joined TSR, Inc. in 1983.

[70] A.D. Rogan, "Language Rules Leave Lots of Room for Creativity in Your Campaign," *Dragon* VII, no. 5 (October 1982): 46–49.

transposed knowledge about our world onto this fantasy system to more clearly articulate the logic behind worlds divided along racial lines.

CHALLENGING THE TROPES OF *D&D*

The popularity of *D&D* spurred the creation of other fantasy TTRPGs in the late 1970s and 1980s from designers across the United States. Goblins are commonplace in these systems as low-level monsters—including *Tunnels & Trolls* (1975), *Monsters! Monsters!* (1976), and *Adventures in Fantasy* (1979)—and closely resemble those found in both *D&D* and the works of Tolkien.[71] Wargaming systems like *Warhammer* (1983), which see players commanding large fantasy armies on tabletops, also present goblins as "naturally evil creatures" with a tendency for infighting and natural animosity to the nobler races of men, elves, and dwarves.[72] Within some rulesets, however, designers tried to distance themselves from these tropes. Systems like *Arduin* and *Palladium* provided avenues for players to inhabit the bodies of fictional goblins, even as these creatures retained their malevolent and evil associations. *GURPS Fantasy*, conversely, rid goblins of their sinister connotations and instead presented them as cosmopolitan merchants always on the hunt for the next great bargain. These developments show some backlash to the Tolkien-inspired goblins of *D&D*, even as the motifs of Middle-earth remained central to TTRPGs of the 1980s.

As early as 1976's *Bunnies and Burrows: Fantasy Adventure & Role-Play in a World of Intelligent Rabbits*, which was inspired by Adams' *Watership Down*, designers were thinking about ways to allow players to create different kinds of fantastical characters.[73] Some explicitly sought to

[71] The community for TTRPGs was still quite small in the late 1970s, so many of these games were designed and playtested by an overlapping group of gamers (some with direct ties to *D&D*'s developers). Ken St. Andre, *Monsters! Monsters!* (Austin: Metagaming Concepts, 1976); David L. Arneson and Richard Snider, *Adventures in Fantasy: Book of Adventure* (TSR, Inc., 1979); Ken St. Andre, *Tunnels & Trolls: 1st Edition Reprint* (Phoenix: Cosmic Circle, 2013). The prevalence of Tolkien is such that "orcs have escaped from the legendarium into the broader fantasy genre: invading one three-decker fantasy series after another, marching across board games, rampaging through cyberspace." Stuart, *Tolkien, Race, and Racism in Middle-earth*, 125.

[72] Rick Priestley and Bryan Ansell, *Warhammer: Forces of Fantasy*, vol. I (Games Workshop, 1983), 27.

[73] B. Dennis Sustare and Scott Robinson, *Bunnies and Burrows: Fantasy Adventure & Role-Play in a World of Intelligent Rabbits* (Roslyn: Fantasy Games Unlimited, Inc., 1976).

undermine the Tolkien-centric mythology of *D&D* and the brutality that it entailed. The rules for *Arduin* by David A. Hargrave, for example, encourage players to look beyond the tropes of Middle-earth:

> The classical fantasy game almost always uses a Tolkeinian type cast of character types to a greater or lesser extent. This is not in itself bad, but it does tend to limit the scope of a game if they are all that are in the game. The people who put out D&D have put much more than that into the game, but it has been my experience that most players all highly reluctant to utilize unconventional characters. So to all of you who always seem to use elven mages or white anglo saxon protestant paladins, this paragraph is dedicated … Do not be a small player from a small world … I think you will find that the world your game is in will become a lot more fun if you do.[74]

The rules of *Arduin* fittingly allow players to create characters from a wide range of creatures, including goblins. Early editions of *Arduin* are essentially rules supplements for *D&D*, however, and did not differentiate their goblins in meaningful ways. They are described as small, chaotic evil creatures with a general temperament of "cunning, sadistic" that is not quite as bad as "nastier" hobgoblins. Goblins are distinct from orcs and have some kind of internal competition with them, as goblins are "always trying to be 'better than damn Orcs.'" Players can inhabit these creatures as, for example, a goblin cleric or a hobgoblin thief, but the attributes of this species reflect that of *AD&D* and are most suitable for those wanting to play an evil character.

When Hargrave fully separated *Arduin* from the system of *D&D* in the earlier 1980s, he reverted goblins back to the role of unplayable monsters but minimized their evil characteristics. He describes them as "smallish humanoids" with "over-large heads with bulging yellow or orange eyes and huge, pointed ears." They have a dark complexion ("dusty brown to hot chocolate"), dislike daylight, have comparable intelligence to orcs, and hate "Hobbitts."[75] Retaining their taxonomic distinction from

---

[74] David A. Hargrave, the California-based designer of this system, initially self-published *Arduin* supplements based on the rules of *D&D* in the 1970s. Appelcline, *Designers & Dragons: The '70s*, 315–31. The publication of the standalone rules for *Arduin* in the early 1980s removed this invective language. David A. Hargrave, *The Arduin Adventure* (Berkeley: Grimoire Games, 1980). *Arduin* also introduces the hybrid "Knoblin," a monster that is a "weird combination of a little goblin, a bit of kobold, and a smidgen of bat."

[75] Hargrave, *The Arduin Adventure*, 37.

koboldings and orcs, they nonetheless are stripped of their inherent evil and fondness for destruction. This change in perspective is likely a reflection of the morality system in *Arduin*, which is restricted to player characters and eliminates the binary of good/evil. Although Hargrave was critical of Tolkien-centric fantasy and its tired tropes, he only made modest efforts to redesign the goblin within early editions of his rulesets.

Malevolence and evil are central to the goblins in 1983's *Palladium Fantasy Role-Playing Game*, which features them as one of thirteen playable races.[76] Players making goblin characters are given carte blanche to indulge in all kinds of villainous acts:

> Goblins, hob-goblins, kobolds, and orcs are the malicious, ugly inhabitants of the faerie folk. These villains are thieves and bushwackers lurking in shadows and dark places to attack the unsuspecting. The descendants of a swarthy mining race, much like the dwarves, recent generations have forsaken the pick and shovel for the sword and dagger in pursuit of easy treasure. They are disagreeable, vindictive, stupid creatures with a passion for precious metals and gems. Goblins hate the larger and more handsome races, particularly elves and humans.[77]

Palladium goblins bear many of the hallmarks of the malevolent goblins of Tolkien and earlier TTRPGs, though they are infused with the folkloresque categorization of the "faerie folk." Goblins feud with kobolds, who are their "uglier cousins." Hobgoblins, meanwhile, are taller than goblins—but slower, without night vision, and much less common (such that their "days in this world seem numbered"). Orcs are "not related in any way" to goblins, though they share their proclivity for violence and chaos. Sometimes, these races unite under the command of a Wolfen leader (an anthropomorphized wolf) that can repel even the combined forces of humans and their dwarf, elven, and gnome allies. Explicit in the world of *Palladium* are feuding races reminiscent of both Tolkien and *D&D*. Accompanying images of goblins and monsters often associated with them (even if not genetically related) are united by their dark skin, large ears, and wide mouths (Fig. 7.1).

---

[76] On *Palladium*, see Appelcline, *Designers & Dragons: The '80s*, 151–73.

[77] This description is slightly complicated by a passing mention of goblins early in the rulebook as being "extremely agile" and with "high physical prowess." Kevin Siembieda, *The Palladium Role-Playing Game* (Taylor: Palladium Books, Inc., 1983), 4, 195–99.

Fig. 7.1 Artwork from *Palladium*. (Clockwise from top-left): goblin, hobgoblin, orc, and kobold depictions from the *Palladium Fantasy RPG*. (All art by Kevin Siembieda. © Palladium Books, Inc.)

Although *Arduin* and *Palladium* provide instructions for how players can construct characters out of goblins, the underlying descriptions of these creatures remain firmly attached to the tradition of Tolkien and *D&D*. Going further than these systems in reframing goblins is Steve Jackson's *GURPS Fantasy* (1986).[78] Goblins are not presented as sadistic cave-dwellers but instead as "great traders and merchants" that travel everywhere peddling their goods. This impulse for commerce means there are no goblin nations or cities. Instead, goblins are nomadic, always on the move looking for the next great bargain. These goblins also "like magic and respect mages," have bonuses to their IQ, harbor no animosity to other species, and have night vision (presumably because they travel at night). Goblins retain their traditional appearance ("green skin, pointed ears, and sharp white teeth") but lose their association with barbaric tribalism. Instead, that trope falls to hobgoblins, the "large brutish, savage ancestors of goblins" that are antagonistic to all other races and prey on those who cross their path. Orcs are similarly disparaged as the most common "cannon fodder" of fantasy worlds and considered to be "stupid, dirty, and aggressive." In these descriptions, *GURPS Fantasy* elevates the goblin into the role of enterprising trader and thrusts their historic baggage onto orcs and hobgoblins.[79]

It is unclear what precise inspirations were behind this unique description of goblins within TTRPGs. Jackson was familiar with the work of Tolkien and saw the orcs therein as the most fitting creature to fulfill the "cannon fodder" archetype; he also drew on *D&D* when depicting the larger and more brutish hobgoblin.[80] The mercantile emphasis on goblins themselves, though, elevated their industrious characteristics that had hitherto been a vehicle for evil. I briefly corresponded with Jackson about his recollection of designing them, and he wrote that their depiction was "whole cloth, a reaction to the unsympathetic depictions of goblins in other games."[81] Jackson replaced this inherent evil with commercial ambition, which was likely based on goblins' associations with mining and

---

[78] The *Generic Universal RolePlaying System (GURPS)* was designed to be playable without a specific fantasy setting or environment in mind. Supplements like *GURPS Fantasy* added magical flavors to this system. Appelcline, *Designers & Dragons: The '80s*, 27–58.

[79] Steve Jackson, *GURPS Fantasy* (Austin: Steve Jackson Games, 1986), 82.

[80] One of the first adventure scenarios for *GURPS* was Orcslayer, which fittingly features no shortage of slaying orcs as well as a few hobgoblins. Warren Spector and Steve Jackson, *Orcslayer: A Combat Supplement for Man to Man* (Austin: Steve Jackson Games, 1985).

[81] Steve Jackson, "Goblin Inspirations," November 5, 2024.

cleverness—attributes that would serve them well if they sought to barter their underground wares rather than fight with them. Jackson was not the only creator of fantasy media in the 1980s to deviate from the tropes associated with the goblins of Middle-earth and *D&D*; literature and multimedia that follow a similar path are considered in the next chapter.

The innovations of *GURPS Fantasy* continued into the 1990s with *GURPS Goblins* (1996), which takes place in a fantastical Georgian London. Written by two New Zealand designers, this system imagines "that people might enjoy roleplaying goblins rather than chopping them up."[82] Replete with pantomime-inspired imagery and comical adventures more likely to result in injury than death, *GURPS Goblins* roundly rejects depictions of these creatures stemming from the pens of MacDonald, Tolkien, and Gygax. Instead, goblins are diverse in "shape, size and colour"—and these attributes morph based on individualized adaptations to the environment rather than an ill-defined genetic lineage.[83] This fictionalized London is also blissfully peaceful and suitable for "bold, healthy, hearty fun. Pure, open, honest fun. Elegant and cultured fun. Civilised fun." Instead of trudging deep within the mountains to root out ancient evils, players of *GURPS Goblins* are more likely to find adventure by helping a hungover cabbie go about his daily duties or tracking down the cause of a ghost at a theater (Fig. 7.2).

Although *GURPS* has not reached the same level of popularity as *D&D*, this ruleset shows that goblins were translatable to other fantasy

---

[82] This setting was published twice in the 1980s by Circle Games, though its eventual publication in *GURPS* led to a much-expanded rulebook. Malcolm Dale and Klaude Thomas, "Designer's Notes: GURPS Goblins," Steve Jackson Games, September 1, 1996, https://www.sjgames.com/pyramid/sample.html?id=4704

[83] The birth and early years of goblins are unique, too. "At birth they have an unformed, foetal appearance, exactly 12 inches long and weighing exactly 3 lbs., with a coffee-and-cream complexion and no distinguishing features—not even sex. Goblins have no gender until they reach the age of 14, at which time they choose, based on individual whim or the hope of gain, whether to be male or female. Because baby Goblins are all the same they are not given names, but instead are all known as Prole. From the moment of birth, however, individual Proles start adapting to their environments: growing tall if food is found in high places; becoming tiny if safety is found in small nooks and crannies. Those brought up in dark places develop keen night vision, while those raised near the sea become sleek-bodied and proficient swimmers. By the age of six, the Proles have been stretched and warped into every conceivable shape and size by their unique histories and environments, and although they share local traits with others raised under the same circumstances, it is difficult to find two who are exactly alike." Malcolm Dale and Klaude Thomas, *GURPS Goblins* (Austin: Steve Jackson Games, 2020), 7.

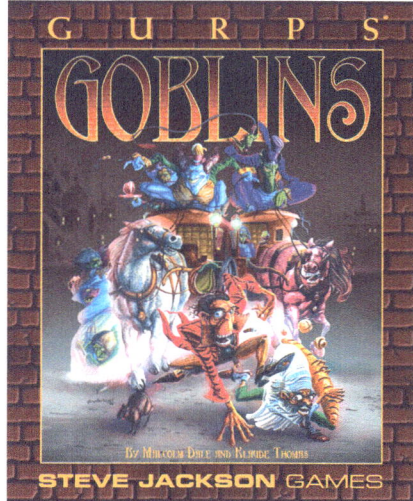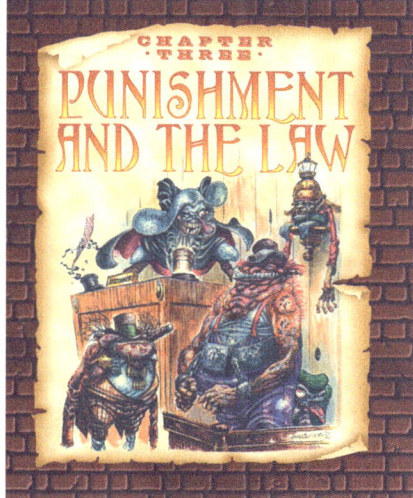

Fig. 7.2   Artwork from *GURPS Goblins*. Illustrations for the cover of the second edition of *GURPS Goblins* (left) and cover page for chapter 3 (right). The cover design was by Jeff Koke based on an original painting by Guy Burwell. The image for chapter 3 was illustrated by Guy Burwell. This edition was written by Malcolm Dale and Klaude Thomas; it was edited by Sean Punch and Susan Pinsonneault. (Images courtesy of Steve Jackson Games. Accessible here: https://www.sjgames. com/gurps/books/goblins/)

settings based on the willingness of designers to part with established high-fantasy tropes.[84] Reviewers praised the innovations of *GURPS Goblins* and welcomed the reinterpretation of goblins from their usual lairs deep within mountains.[85] The critical success that came of this rulebook,

[84] Another 2003 sourcebook, *GURPS Faerie*, immerses readers in folkloric and folklor-esque traditions. It describes the hobgoblin as one of several "British domestic fairies" as opposed to the "hobgoblin of most fantasy games." A handful of other creatures from out-side of the British tradition are described as "goblin-like," including the *duende* and *bake-mono*. Later, though, the author groups together the Seelie Court ("elves, dwarves, and other fair and just races") against the Unseelie Court ("goblins, orcs, imps, and other dark and evil races") based on divisions in Tolkien. The book also categorizes folkloric creatures across geographical traditions into broad headings like "Domestic Faeries" and "Little People." Graeme Davis, *GURPS Faerie* (Austin: Steve Jackson Games, 2003), 19–21, 65–70.

[85] See, for example, Steve Faragher, "GURPS Goblins Review," *Arcane Magazine* 6 (May 1996): 60–61; Rick Swan, "Review of GURPS Goblins and GURPS Alternate Earths," *Dragon* XXI, no. 7 (December 1996): 113–14.

though, did not lead to changes in the goblins of *D&D* (at least immediately). It took a larger cultural reckoning in the twenty-first century for designers of the most popular TTRPG system to re-evaluate their portrayal of this ubiquitous troglodyte.

Goblins Beyond *AD&D*

Since the publication of *AD&D* and a lightly revised second edition of its rules, *D&D* has undergone several major revisions: a fully-fledged third edition (*3e*), updated third edition (*3.5e*), fourth edition (*4e*), and fifth edition (*5e*). Wizards of the Coast released the core rulebooks for a revised fifth edition (*5r*) in late 2024 and early 2025, which I was only able to briefly consult because of their date of printing relative to my research timeline. That said, the core rulebooks for *3e*, *3.5e*, *4e*, and *5e* present goblins largely as they had been in *AD&D*.[86] They are low-level monsters that live in dismal locations in the dark corners of the world, organized into crude tribes, and prone to attacking whomever they can for plunder. The art style for these creatures evolved in keeping with the artistic visions for each of the editions of *D&D*, from the epic fantasy of *3e* to the more cartoony *4e*. So too did the expanded scope of these systems afford designers the opportunity to create more types of goblin soldiers, delve into the details of in-game mythologies, and detail regional variations of these creatures. Developers also made minor changes to the classification and language of goblins as part of the "goblinoid" family alongside hobgoblins and bugbears.

As far back as the 1980s, designers of *D&D* released supplementary rulebooks and campaign scenarios to broaden the content of each edition's core rules. Within some of these texts, players were provided with guidelines for how to create goblin characters. Up to *4e*, these rules assumed that most players would create goblins with a preference for violence, thievery, and evil. Supplements for *4e* and *5e*, however, moved away from these malicious characterizations and instead depicted goblins as underdogs with a knack for overcoming creatures larger than them. One of *D&D*'s most popular competitors, *Pathfinder*, took a similar approach in its second edition and made goblins one of the default ancestries that players could use to create characters. The fantasy goblin, which had so long been relegated to the status of puny and eminently killable monster,

---

[86] Shannon Appelcline, *Designers & Dragons: The '90s* (Silver Spring: Maryland, 2014), 125–204.

has thus seen a considerable rehabilitation within two of the most popular TTRPG systems of the twenty-first century.

The designers of *3e* and beyond worked to clarify some of the classificatory ambiguities of earlier editions of *D&D*. By noting the functional (though not necessarily genetic) relationship of monsters to one another, designers provide DMs with distinct groupings that can be inserted into game situations. *3e* and *3.5e* introduce the "goblinoid" class, which comprises bugbears, goblins, and hobgoblins. Creatures previously grouped with goblins like kobolds, orcs, and ogres are sorted into their own subtypes.[87] The same division persists into *4e*, in which designers note that "there are goblins, and then there are *goblins*," meaning both the broad, folkloresque category of the "small, ill-tempered humanoid" and the more specific "family of creatures that include bugbears, hobgoblins, and regular goblins."[88] Among goblinoids are specific types of soldiers like the Bugbear Strangler, Goblin Blackblade, and Hobgoblin Archer—militaristic divisions that reflect the emphasis on tactical combat within this edition.[89] The *Monster Manual* for *5e* uses the same classification system, though with fewer soldier archetypes. Instead, designers emphasize distinct characteristics for each race. Hobgoblins organize themselves into armies with clear hierarchies and discipline; bugbears are powerful tribal raiders that do not hesitate to enslave goblins and bully hobgoblins; and lowly goblins seek whatever treasure they can find in the "dismal settings" of the world.[90] Across these editions, the native tongue of goblinoids is goblin, which simplifies the creature-specific and alignment-dependent linguistic system of *AD&D*.

Later editions of *D&D* also see more explicit references to goblin mythology and its place in the game's multiverse. The 1980 supplement

[87] Skip Williams et al., *3.5e Monster Manual* (Renton: Wizards of the Coast, 2003), 29, 133, 153.

[88] According to in-game lore, bugbears were potentially the creation of hobgoblins because of the brutality of their "magical traditions." Mike Mearls, Stephen Schubert, and James Wyatt, *4e Monster Manual* (Renton: Wizards of the Coast, 2008), 135–41.

[89] Designers of *4e* wanted to make the game more balanced at all levels, ensure that all classes (not just magic users) had exciting tactical abilities, and to differentiate character classes based on the roles they performed in combat. Appelcline, *Designers & Dragons: The '90s*, 181–82.

[90] This perspective is summarized in an embedded note from a Slave Lord: "If you want soldiers or thugs, hire hobgoblins. If you want someone clubbed to death in their sleep, hire bugbears. If you want mean little fools, hire goblins." Christopher Perkins, Mike Mearls, and Jeremy Crawford, *5e Monster Manual* (Renton: Wizards of the Coast, 2014), 33, 165, 185.

Deities & Demigods introduces the deity Maglubiyet, who is worshipped by goblins and hobgoblins.[91] One of the first deities crafted for *D&D* and not based on real-world belief systems, Maglubiyet commands goblin armies in Hell against the orcish armies of Gruumsh in an eternal war that (according to the goblins) Maglubiyet always wins.[92] Details on goblin worship are provided in the core rulebooks of later editions of *D&D*. The *3.5e Monster Manual* notes that Maglubiyet has given goblins a mandate to "expand their numbers and overwhelm their competition."[93] This pantheon of goblin worship is expanded in *4e* to include the god Bane and his two goblin exarchs, Maglubiyet and Hruggek.[94] In potential anticipation of a later reframing of goblins as more sympathetic characters, the *5e Monster Manual* presents the relationship between goblins and Maglubiyet (described as "an eleven-foot-tall battle-scarred goblin with black skin and fire erupting from his eyes") as one based on fear rather than adoration. Goblins "dread" the prospect of fighting in his eternal conflict in Acheron (not Hell), as opposed to the warrior-like hobgoblins that do not fear death and are honored to serve in Maglubiyet's army.[95]

Depictions of goblins in *D&D* reflect both goblinoid hierarchies and the artistic vision for each game. In *3e* and *3.5e*, illustrators opted for a dark, mature style of artwork to appeal to an aging audience that grew up with *AD&D*. This stylistic trend was reversed in *4e*, which introduced a more cartoony art style reminiscent of some contemporary fantasy RPGs. The art of *5e* is somewhere between these two previous artistic styles. Although these iterations of goblinoids reflect the artistic direction of a given edition of *D&D*, they have remarkable consistencies. Most depictions are of male (or male-coded) goblins, though the artwork of *4e* is

[91] James M. Ward and Robert J. Kuntz, *Deities & Demigods: Cyclopedia of Gods and Heroes from Myth and Legend* (Lake Geneva: TSR Games, 1980), 109.

[92] This iteration of Hell is grounded in a cosmology with unique planes of existence that reflect its inhabitants (i.e., Elysium populated with neutral good creatures and the Nine Hells filled with "absolute lawful evil"). Ward and Kuntz, *Deities & Demigods: Cyclopedia of Gods and Heroes from Myth and Legend*, 129. Gitzen and Gershon call this embedding of folklore within works of fiction "fictitious folklore." Timothy Gitzen and Ilana Gershon, "Fictitious Folklore and World Making in Popular Culture," in *Möbius Media: Popular Culture, Folklore, and the Folkloresque*, ed. Jeffrey A. Tolbert and Michael Dylan Foster (Logan: Utah State University Press, 2024), 137–54.

[93] Williams et al., *3.5e Monster Manual*, 134. Despite being part of the goblinoid family, bugbears worship their own species-specific deity, Hruggek.

[94] Mearls, Schubert, and Wyatt, *4e Monster Manual*, 135.

[95] Perkins, Mearls, and Crawford, *5e Monster Manual*, 165, 186.

notable for its inclusion of feminine goblinoids. These creatures have dark complexions that range in color from gray to green to brown to deep red. Hobgoblins are militarized creatures, depicted in full plate armor and more-or-less bearing the proportions of a human. Bugbears are the largest and most muscular of these creatures, their barbarity reflected in their hirsute frame, spiked leather armor, and the giant maces that they wield. Goblins pale in comparison. They are small in stature with disproportionately large heads and have less protective armor. These depictions align with the accompanying descriptions of these creatures across editions of the game, which see goblins bullied or enslaved by their more formidable brethren and statistically inferior to them. The "Challenge Rating" system of *5e*, which assigns monsters difficulty levels based on their threat to characters, gives a sense of their relative difficulties: bugbears have a rating of 1, hobgoblins ½, and goblins ¼. Though goblinoids together are relatively low on the hierarchy of enemies, goblins are clearly inferior to their bugbear and hobgoblin cousins.

This presentation of goblins in recent editions of the core rulebooks of *D&D* does not tell the whole story. Supplementary rulebooks beginning in the late 1980s provided avenues for players to create goblin characters in their games. *The Orcs of Thar* (1988) takes place in a universe dominated by orcs, bugbears, hobgoblins, goblins, and various subspecies that bear scientific names like *Goblinus hyborianus* and *Ursus bipedis vulgaris*. Players are thus able to play "the puny kobolds, the cowardly goblins," and other creatures such that the real "monsters" are elves, dwarves, and humans.[96] These rules do not do much to alter common tropes associated with fantasy goblins—but they provide an avenue through which players can embrace their barbarous, even evil tendencies. The *Monster Manuals* for *3e* and *3.5e* provide brief notes on how players can create goblin characters, and supplementary materials detail many variations on them, including Dekanter goblins and snow goblins.[97] Though uniformly inclined toward evil, each variation has distinct abilities and characteristics based on the environment that they inhabit.

[96] Bruce Heard, *The Orcs of Thar* (Lake Geneva: TSR, Inc., 1988), 14.

[97] Williams et al., *3.5e Monster Manual*, 133–34; James Wyatt and Rob Heinsoo, *Monster Compendium: Monsters of Faerûn* (Renton: Wizards of the Coast, 2001), 53; Wolfgang Baur, James Jacobs, and George Strayton, *Frostburn: Mastering the Perils of Ice and Snow* (Renton: Wizards of the Coast, 2004), 136.

In supplemental materials for *D&D 4e*, however, designers begin to encourage players to think about goblins as more than just vile troglodytes. The sourcebook *Into the Unknown: The Dungeon Survival Handbook* (2012), for example, notes that some goblins are "pint-sized rascals" rather than ruthless raiders. They inhabit dungeons and dark places around the world not because of megalomania, but because they are "endlessly curious." The opening paragraph about the characteristics of goblins provides a sense of this perspective:

> The image of puny, nose-picking, knife-wielding goblins is common throughout the world. Most adventurers believe in a keen sword and room to swing as the best way to deal with them. Goblins might be the most numerous humanoids in the world, with a reputation for infesting every dank hole and tormenting the countryside with never-ending raids, violence, and maniacal scheming. The majority of them are rapacious and vile, but some have the intellect and attitude to join the ranks of heroes. Though they might face prejudice, goblins can be independent, cunning, and crafty adventurers.[98]

Though some goblins live up to their historical reputation, those that players create can be more palatable "social scoundrel[s]" from an underappreciated culture. This inversion of goblins from slave-taking raiders to cunning rascals, which reflects larger trends in fantasy media during the late twentieth and early twenty-first centuries (considered in the next chapter), enables players to create heroic versions of these creatures. Supplemental materials for *5e* further expanded on this idea as part of an overdue reckoning on the part of its publisher, Wizards of the Coast, with problematic content from earlier editions. Released in 2014, *5e* brought in a new generation of diverse players, many of whom questioned the racist and sexist tropes from previous iterations of the game.[99] Critiques of Wizards' content surged around 2020, spurred by the popularity of the

---

[98] Logan Booner, Matt Sernett, and Jeff Morgenroth, *Into the Unknown: The Dungeon Survival Handbook* (Renton: Wizards of the Coast, 2012), 34.

[99] Andrew Limbong, "'Dungeons & Dragons' Tries To Banish Racist Stereotypes," *NPR: All Things Considered*, June 29, 2020, https://www.npr.org/sections/live-updates-protests-for-racial-justice/2020/06/29/884824236/dungeons-dragons-tries-to-banish-racist-stereotypes; Cass Marshall, "Wizards of the Coast Is Addressing Racist Stereotypes in Dungeons & Dragons," *Polygon*, June 23, 2020, https://www.polygon.com/2020/6/23/21300653/dungeons-dragons-racial-stereotypes-wizards-of-the-coast-drow-orcs-curse-of-strahd

game during Covid lockdowns and heightened awareness of systemic racism in the United States following the murder of George Floyd. *5e* books published since then have changed some of the game's core rules, removed historical tropes with troubling modern associations, and introduced content from underrepresented fantasy media across the globe.[100]

Goblins are part of this reimagining of *5e*.[101] The original *Monster Manual* for this edition reflects the traditional view of fantasy goblins and frames them as vile monsters:

> Goblins are small, black-hearted, selfish humanoids that lair in caves, abandoned mines, despoiled dungeons, and other dismal settings. Individually weak, goblins gather in large—sometimes overwhelming—numbers. They crave power and regularly abuse whatever authority they obtain.[102]

This perception of goblins is reinforced in the 2016 sourcebook, *Volo's Guide to Monsters*, which adds "more distinctive race options" for player characters. The descriptions and mechanics assigned to goblins have the same thematic similarities as previous interpretations of them, though with additional details about their culture:

> Goblins occupy an uneasy place in a dangerous world, and they react by lashing out at any creatures they believe they can bully. Cunning in battle and cruel in victory, goblins are fawning and servile in defeat, just as in their own society lower castes must scrape before those of greater status and as goblin tribes bow before other goblinoids …
>
> Goblins know they are a weak, unsophisticated race that can be easily dominated by bigger, smarter, more organized, more ferocious, or more

---

[100] Charlie Hall, "Dungeons & Dragons' next Anthology Is Written Entirely by Black and Brown Authors," *Polygon*, March 22, 2022, https://www.polygon.com/22989321/dnd-journeys-through-the-radiant-citadel-release-date-price; Ajit George et al., *Journeys Through the Radiant Citadel* (Renton: Wizards of the Coast, 2022).

[101] Carpenter argues that these attempts to address racism within *5e* were "superficial" because they did not address the "racialising logics" embedded within the system. Importantly, this article was published before the first books for *5r* were published, and Carpenter acknowledges that they aim to tackle these systemic issues. Benjamin J.J. Carpenter, "'Monstrous Adventurers': The Racecraft of the Dungeons and Dragons Imaginary," *Howard Journal of Communications* 35, no. 1 (2024): 16.

[102] Perkins, Mearls, and Crawford, *5e Monster Manual*, 165. Additional details from this entry include goblins' laziness, greed, trap-ridden lairs, delight in tormenting other creatures, propensity for organizing under a goblin king or queen, and affinity with certain animals.

magical creatures. Their god was conquered by Maglubiyet, after all, and now when the Mighty One calls for it, even their souls are forfeit. It is this realization that drives them to dominate other creatures whenever they can — for goblins, life is short.

Goblins seek to trap and enslave any creatures they encounter, but they flee from opposition that seems too daunting. For miles around their lair, they employ pit traps, snares, and nets to catch the unwary, and when their hunting patrols encounter other beings, they always look for ways to capture their foes instead of killing them. Goblins that run up against the fringes of a society first test its defenses by stealing objects, and if these crimes go unpunished, they begin stealing people ...

A goblin tribe is organized in a four-tiered caste system made up of lashers, hunters, gatherers, and pariahs. The status of every family in the tribe is based on its importance to the tribe's survival. Families that belong to the higher-ranking castes keep their status by not sharing their knowledge and skills with other families, while those in the lower castes have little hope of escaping their plight ... Outsiders who don't understand the goblins' social system are sometimes surprised by how different castes interact with them.[103]

Other goblinoids are presented along the same lines. Bugbears are sneaky barbarians that attack wandering travelers; hobgoblins are warriors that thrive in organized armies and enslave those they subjugate. Guidelines for playing these villainous goblinoids draw on these backgrounds. Goblins, for example, receive bonuses to their dexterity and charisma, can see in the dark, and are particularly skilled at hiding and retreating from combat.

The goblins of *5e* underwent even more extensive revisions in 2022's *Mordenkainen Presents: Monsters of the Multiverse*. Therein, designers entirely eliminate the inherent evil from goblins and other humanoid monsters, effectively undermining the racially determinist tropes of earlier editions. Goblins in this sourcebook are nearly unrecognizable compared to earlier descriptions:

A subterranean folk, goblins can be found in every corner of the multiverse, often beside their bugbear and hobgoblin kin. Long before the god Maglubiyet conquered them, early goblins served in the court of the Queen

---

[103] Revising previous iterations of *D&D* cosmology, this edition sees Maglubiyet destroying many of the goblins' previous gods, leaving only the cruel Khurgorbaeyag as his lieutenant. Mike Mearls and Jeremy Crawford, *Volo's Guide to Monsters* (Renton: Wizards of the Coast, 2016), 40–52, 119–20.

of Air and Darkness, one of the Feywild's archfey. Goblins thrived in her dangerous domain thanks to a special boon from her—a supernatural knack for finding the weak spots in foes larger than themselves and for getting out of trouble. Goblins brought this fey boon with them to worlds across the Material Plane, even if they don't remember the fey realm they inhabited before Maglubiyet's rise. Now many goblins pursue their own destinies, escaping the plots of both archfey and gods.[104]

Removed in this description are references to goblins' propensity for slavery and tribal organization. Instead, they have their origins in the Feywild (the "Plane of Faeries"), a knack for finding vulnerable points in larger enemies, and skills to get themselves out of sticky situations.[105] They are victims of Maglubiyet's conquest, rather than mindless drones in his armies. Significant, too, is the illustration of a heroic female goblin alongside this description, which is a departure from the overwhelmingly masculine goblins depicted in previous editions. She has a dark brown/gray complexion as well, indicating to players that they can and should create heroes with non-white skin. Hobgoblins receive a similar overhaul. They are creatures driven from the Feywild by Maglubiyet, and their connection to this land leads them to channel its "rule of reciprocity, which creates a mystical bond between the giver and the receiver of a gift." Hobgoblins in some places have formed huge armies with "ranks of devoted soldiers famed for their unity," while others have formed peaceful communities "with deep ties to one another." Bugbears, too, are linked to the Feywild, though they are more likely to be "quiet skulkers" than soldiers.[106]

This revised image of goblinoids is part of a larger project that Wizards of the Coast has undertaken since 2020 to minimize the racialist framing of their fantasy worlds and, in doing so, to make monstrous races more approachable and appealing to an increasingly diverse playerbase.[107] No longer should dark-skinned goblins only be piddling enemies for low-level heroes or vessels through which players can vicariously conduct acts of

---

[104] Jeremy Crawford, *Mordenkainen Presents: Monsters of the Multiverse* (Renton: Wizards of the Coast, 2021), 20.

[105] The Feywild is one of the planes of existence in the *D&D* multiverse. It is the plane of fairies, inhabited with a host of creatures inspired by Fairyland and other belief systems. Christopher Perkins et al., *The Wild Beyond the Witchlight* (Renton: Wizards of the Coast, 2021).

[106] Crawford, *Mordenkainen Presents: Monsters of the Multiverse*, 8, 23.

[107] Jeremy Crawford, *Tasha's Cauldron of Everything* (Renton: Wizards of the Coast, 2020).

evil. Instead, this design philosophy turns some of the tropes associated with fantasy goblins (small, cowardly, weak) into assets. They are underdogs that use their size, stealthiness, and knack for magic to defeat their foes. Their connection to fairies (the Feywild) is emphasized over their dismal lairs, a return to a folkloresque motif often minimized in high fantasy. Make no mistake, goblins still can be the evil raiders within these rules, and they remain staples of campaign settings as introductory encounters.[108] But goblins are no longer so bound by this particular trope. Wizards of the Coast has thus provided players with explicit license to experiment with different kinds of goblins in their campaign settings.

Perhaps predictably, these changes to *D&D* have led to discontent among some players, who have decried it stripping certain monsters of their historic characteristics.[109] Wizards of the Coast remains committed to this new approach, though, as seen in the verbiage of its latest iteration of the system, *5r*, which removes character "races" and replaces them with "species."[110] Other rule changes elevate the importance of a character's background and gives flexibility to the bonuses provided by being part of a given species. Executives hope that this push for diversity (both within the game and in the people who design it) will bring in new players and, alongside new monetization efforts through digital systems like *D&DBeyond*, increase revenues.[111]

Mirroring this reinterpretation of goblins is the *Pathfinder* system of Paizo Publishing. Initially designed as a modified version of *3.5e*, this system has grown to become one of the most popular TTRPG alternatives to

[108] Amanda Hamon et al., *Phandelver and Below: The Shattered Obelisk* (Renton: Wizards of the Coast, 2023).

[109] Charlie Hall, "Tasha's Cauldron Makes D&D a Better Game, but Whiffs on Race Changes," Polygon, November 16, 2020, https://www.polygon.com/reviews/2020/11/16/21569738/dungeons-dragons-tashas-cauldron-of-everything-review; Corey Plante, "D&D Book Tasha's Cauldron of Everything Shatters Expectations, for Better or Worse," Inverse, November 19, 2020, https://www.inverse.com/gaming/dungeons-dragons-tashas-cauldron-of-everything-review

[110] Jeremy Crawford et al., *OneD&D Player's Handbook* (Renton: Wizards of the Coast, 2024).

[111] Mason argues that this monetization scheme is not just about strengthening *D&D* as a brand, but about marketing it as a lifestyle. Kelsey Paige Mason, "Just Make-Believe: Assumed Neutrality, Archetypical Exceptionalism, and Performative Progressivism in Dungeons and Dragons," *Vector*, February 15, 2023, https://vector-bsfa.com/2023/02/15/just-make-believe-assumed-neutrality-archetypical-exceptionalism-and-performative-progressivism-in-dungeons-and-dragons/

D&D.[112] The first edition of *Pathfinder* (2009) features goblins as the kind of lowly monster typical of TTRPGs, though with some unique variations, in its *Bestiary*:

> Goblins prefer to dwell in caves, amid large and dense thickets of thistles and brambles, or in structures built and then abandoned by others. Very few goblins have the drive to build structures of their own. Coastlines are favored, as goblins are quite fond of sifting through junk and flotsam in an unending quest to find treasures among the refuse of more civilized races. Goblin hatred runs deep, and few things inspire their wrath more than gnomes (who have long fought against goblins), horses (who frighten goblins tremendously), and regular dogs (whom goblins regard as pale imitations of goblin dogs) ... Goblins are voracious and can eat their body weight in food daily without growing fat. Goblin lairs always have numerous storerooms and larders. While they prefer human and gnome flesh, a goblin won't turn down any food—except, perhaps, vegetables.[113]

Within the goblinoid family, hobgoblins are more powerful goblinoids and presented as "the most civilized of goblinkind." Bugbears are the largest of this triumvirate, though they prefer a life of solitary barbarism than one in a large community. Taken together, these goblinoids "each represent a different face of evil." Goblins are a primal evil; hobgoblins are an ordered and militaristic evil; bugbears are perhaps the most terrifying, for they seek "to inflict pain and suffering in the most destructive ways possible." The first edition of *Pathfinder* uses some unique language to describe goblinoids, though it is largely reflective of *D&D*.

The second edition of *Pathfinder* (2019) is a substantial overhaul of the system.[114] Most notable for this history is the inclusion of goblins as one of the six default "Ancestries" for player characters in its *Core Rulebook*

---

[112] Shannon Appelcline, *Designers & Dragons: The '00s* (Silver Spring: Maryland, 2014), 205–29. It is difficult to compare the sales of *D&D* and *Pathfinder* in the late 2000s/early 2010s, though Paizo claims that *Pathfinder* was outselling *D&D* by 2012.

[113] The bestiary for *Pathfinder* has guidelines for having players inhabit monstrous characters, though it emphasizes that "monsters are not designed with the rules for players in mind." Jason Bulmahn and James Jacobs, *1e Pathfinder Bestiary* (Redmond: Paizo Publishing, LLC, 2009), 156, 313–14.

[114] *Symbaroum*, released in Swedish in 2014 and translated into English in 2016, also features goblins as one of five playable races (two human variations, changelings, and ogres are the others) in its core rulebook. It is accessible here: https://freeleaguepublishing.com/shop/symbaroum/core-rulebook/

(alongside dwarves, elves, gnomes, halflings, and humans). Although a brief entry in the *Bestiary* notes that goblins can be adversarial monsters in-game, the *Core Rulebook* shows that these creatures are designed with player agency in mind:

> The convoluted histories other people cling to don't interest goblins. These small folk live in the moment, and they prefer tall tales over factual records. The wars of a few decades ago might as well be from the ancient past. Misunderstood by other people, goblins are happy how they are. Goblin virtues are about being present, creative, and honest. They strive to lead fulfilled lives, rather than worrying about how their journeys will end. To tell stories, not nitpick the facts. To be small, but dream big.
>
> Goblins have a reputation as simple creatures who love songs, fire, and eating disgusting things and who hate reading, dogs, and horses—and there are a great many for whom this description fits perfectly. However, great changes have come to goblinkind, and more and more goblins resist conformity to these stereotypes …
>
> If you want a character who is eccentric, enthusiastic, and fun-loving, you should play a goblin.[115]

The designers of *Pathfinder* mention stereotypes about fantasy goblins to highlight how radically their own goblins depart from them. Instead of being vindictive slave owners, goblins have settlements that "erupt with songs and laughter." Instead of having a natural antagonism with other groups, they are instead learning to trust taller races, colloquially called "longshanks." Instead of trending toward the "chaotic evil" portion of the alignment chart, they instead "have trouble following the rules" but tend to gravitate toward "chaotic neutral" or "chaotic good" morals. This vision of goblins, which predates that of *Mordenkainen Presents: Monsters of the Multiverse* by several years, encourages players to valorize these small, dark-skinned creatures as heroes alongside the likes of humans, elves, and dwarves. Goblins' love of "tall tales," too, is a nod to their folkloric origins and (perhaps) a subtle jab at the Tolkienian literary tradition that depicts goblins as inherently evil and capable only of barbaric malevolence.

---

[115] Logan Bonner et al., *2e Pathfinder Core Rulebook* (Redmond: Paizo Inc., 2019), 46–49. The *Bestiary* provides a less charitable description of goblins, acknowledging both their propensity for evil and ability to break free from it: "While some goblins are civilized and have worked hard to be considered upstanding members of humanoid communities, most are impetuous and vicious creatures who delight in wreaking havoc." Logan Bonner et al., *2e Pathfinder Bestiary* (Redmond: Paizo Inc., 2019), 180.

CONCLUSION

This overview of goblins in TTRPGs, especially *D&D*, has shown both the persistence of certain negative tropes associated with goblins and the recent movement of game designers to challenge them.[116] Goblins have been ubiquitous creatures in medieval-inspired fantasy universes since the first iterations of *D&D* in the 1970s as dark-skinned, lowly antagonists living in dark crevices of the world that prey on the weak for plunder. They are a natural foil for morally righteous, light-skinned heroes whose appearance reflected the ideals of the games' creators. Beginning in the 1980s, some game designers undermined these stereotypes by allowing players to inhabit goblins as player characters—whether as unlikely protagonists or vessels through which players could act out their more wicked impulses. It is not until the 2010s that *D&D* and *Pathfinder*, however, have seriously challenged this paradigm. Spurred by a broader movement to make fantasy gaming more accessible, designers have reframed goblins as plucky underdogs, often misunderstood within their own worlds, and freed from the evil and sadistic tropes to which they had long been tethered. In doing so, these systems actively encourage players to create heroes out of these diminutive, dark-skinned creatures.

TTRPGs were one of many kinds of fantasy media since the mid-twentieth century that has challenged Tolkienian conceptions of these creatures. This breadth of interpretation in the world of fantasy, alongside other folkloric and cultural contexts, is the subject of our final body chapter.

REFERENCES

Andre, Ken St. 1976. *Monsters! Monsters!* Austin: Metagaming Concepts.
Appelcline, Shannon. 2013. *Designers & Dragons: The '70s.* Maryland: Silver Spring.
Appelcline, Shannon. 2014a. *Designers & Dragons: The '80s.* Maryland: Silver Spring.

---

[116] Worth noting, too, is the proliferation of indie TTRPGs that draw on themes from heroic fantasy but emphasize more playful aspects of the genre. In *Goblin Errands*, players undertake "comical (mis)adventures trying to complete seemingly mundane tasks as you struggle with a world not designed for you." *Goblin Quest* is similarly framed as a TTRPG about "slapstick violence" and "violent ineptitude." Perhaps most absurd is *Stacks of Goblins*, which features players working together as a stack of goblins impersonating a human from beneath a trench coat, in search of treasure for the Goblin King.

Appelcline, Shannon. 2014b. *Designers & Dragons: The '90s.* Maryland: Silver Spring.

Appelcline, Shannon. 2014c. *Designers & Dragons: The '00s.* Maryland: Silver Spring.

Arenas, Daniel Luccas, Anna Viduani, and Renata Brasil Araujo. 2022. Therapeutic Use of Role-Playing Game (RPG) in Mental Health: A Scoping Review. *Simulation & Gaming* 53 (3): 285–311. https://doi.org/10.1177/10468 781211073720.

Armstrong, Tom. 1981. The Best DMs Will Look Further than the Book. *Dragon* VI (2): 62.

Arneson, David L., and Richard Snider. 1979. *Adventures in Fantasy: Book of Adventure.* TSR, Inc.

"At Last, The Real Thing…". 1986. *Dragon* X (9, February): 75.

Baur, Wolfgang, James Jacobs, and George Strayton. 2004. *Frostburn: Mastering the Perils of Ice and Snow.* Renton: Wizards of the Coast.

Bebergal, Peter, ed. 2021. *Appendix N: The Eldritch Roots of Dungeons and Dragons.* London: Strange Attractor Press.

Bogost, Ian. 2006. *Unit Operations: An Approach to Videogame Criticism.* Cambridge: MIT Press.

Bogost, Ian. 2009. Videogames Are a Mess: My DiGRA 2009 Keynote, on Videogames and Ontology. *Writing* (blog), September 3.

Bonner, Logan, Jason Bulmahn, Stephen Radney-MacFarland, and Mark Seifter. 2019a. *2e Pathfinder Bestiary.* Redmond: Paizo Inc.

Bonner, Logan, Jason Bulmahn, Stephen Radney-MacFarland, and Mark Seifter. 2019b. *2e Pathfinder Core Rulebook.* Redmond: Paizo Inc.

Booner, Logan, Matt Sernett, and Jeff Morgenroth. 2012. *Into the Unknown: The Dungeon Survival Handbook.* Renton: Wizards of the Coast.

Bruner, Scott M. 2017. *Constructing a Canon for 'Dungeons & Dragons': A Generative Analysis of Gary Gygax's Appendix N.* Master's Thesis, San Diego State University.

Bulmahn, Jason, and James Jacobs. 2009. *1e Pathfinder Bestiary.* Redmond: Paizo Publishing, LLC.

de Camp, L. Sprague. 1963. *Swords and Sorcery.* New York: Pyramid Books.

der Camp, L. Sprague. 1983. *The Goblin Tower.* New York: Del Rey.

Carpenter, Benjamin J. J. 2024. 'Monstrous Adventurers': The Racecraft of the Dungeons and Dragons Imaginary. *Howard Journal of Communications* 35 (1): 15–32.

Charlton, Coleman. 1984. *Middle-Earth Role Playing.* Charlottesville: Iron Crown Enterprises.

Clay, Joseph. 1989. Hey, Wanna Be a Kobold? Humanoids as Player Characters in AD&D® Games. *Dragon* XIII (8): 38–43.

Collins, Arthur. 1989. Boulder-Throwers and Humanoid Hordes. *Dragon* XIII (8): 34–36.

Crawford, Jeremy. 2020. *Tasha's Cauldron of Everything*. Renton: Wizards of the Coast.

Crawford, Jeremy. 2021. *Mordenkainen Presents: Monsters of the Multiverse*. Renton: Wizards of the Coast.

Crawford, Jeremy, Christopher Perkins, Ben Petrisor, F. Wesley Schneider, Ray Winninger, and James Wyatt. 2024. *OneD&D Player's Handbook*. Renton: Wizards of the Coast.

Dale, Malcolm, and Klaude Thomas. 1996. Designer's Notes: GURPS Goblins. *Steve Jackson Games*, September 1. https://www.sjgames.com/pyramid/sample.html?id=4704. Accessed December 1, 2024.

Dale, Malcolm, and Klaude Thomas. 2020. *GURPS Goblins*. Austin: Steve Jackson Games.

Dashiell, Steven L. 2022. Chasing the Dragon (Magazine): Gender Erasure Through Discourse in Dragon Magazine, 1978–2005. *Cultural Studies ↔ Critical Methodologies* 22 (6): 620–630.

Davis, Graeme. 2003. *GURPS Faerie*. Austin: Steve Jackson Games.

Ewalt, David M. 2013. *Of Dice and Men: The Story of Dungeons & Dragons and The People Who Play It*. New York: Scribner.

Faragher, Steve. 1996. GURPS Goblins Review. *Arcane Magazine* 6:60–61.

Fine, Gary Alan. 1983. *Shared Fantasy: Role Playing Games as Social Worlds*. Chicago: University of Chicago Press.

Fitzgerald, Lyle. 1978. It's a Good Day to Die (Death Statistics of D & D Players). *Dragon* III (6): 26–27.

Francis, I. V., and W. Edgar. 1984. The Forum: Opinions and Observations. *Dragon* IX (4): 6.

Frankfurter, David. 2006. *Evil Incarnate: Rumors of Demonic Conspiracy and Satanic Abuse in History*. Princeton: Princeton University Press.

Garcia, Antero. 2017. Privilege, Power, and Dungeons & Dragons: How Systems Shape Racial and Gender Identities in Tabletop Role-Playing Games. *Mind, Culture, and Activity* 24 (3): 232–246.

George, Ajit, Justice Ramin Arman, Dominique Dickey, Basheer Ghouse, Alastor Guzman, D. Fox Harrell, T. K. Johnson, et al. 2022. *Journeys Through the Radiant Citadel*. Renton: Wizards of the Coast.

Gitzen, Timothy, and Ilana Gershon. 2024. Fictitious Folklore and World Making in Popular Culture. In *Möbius Media: Popular Culture, Folklore, and the Folkloresque*, ed. Jeffrey A. Tolbert and Michael Dylan Foster, 137–154. Logan: Utah State University Press.

Greenwood, Ed. 1984. Nine Hells Revisited: More 'Facts' about Devildom. *Dragon* IX (6): 18–34.

Gygax, Gary. 1975. Women and Wargaming. *Europa* 10 (11): 86–94.

Gygax, Gary. 1977. *AD&D Monster Manual*. Lake Geneva: TSR, Inc.

Gygax, Gary. 1978. *AD&D Players Handbook*. Lake Geneva: TSR, Inc.

Gygax, Gary. 1979a. *AD&D Dungeon Masters Guide*. Lake Geneva: TSR, Inc.

Gygax, Gary. 1979b. The Half-Ogre, Smiting Him Hip and Thigh. *Dragon* IV (3): 12.

Gygax, Gary. 2002a. Q&A with Gary Gygax, Part VI. *Dragonsfoot Forums*, May 20. https://www.dragonsfoot.org/forums/viewtopic.php?p=328256. Accessed December 1, 2024.

Gygax, Gary. 2002b. Q&A with Gary Gygax, Part VIII. *Dragonsfoot Forums*, May 20. https://www.dragonsfoot.org/forums/viewtopic.php?p=351833. Accessed December 1, 2024.

Gygax, Gary, and Dave Arneson. 1974. *Dungeons & Dragons: Rules for Fantastic Medieval Wargames Campaigns Playable with Paper and Pencil and Miniature Figures*. Lake Geneva: TSR, Inc.

Gygax, Gary, and Dave Arneson. 1983. *Dungeons & Dragons Players Manual*. Edited by Frank Mentzer. Lake Geneva: TSR, Inc.

Gygax, Gary, and Rob Kuntz. 1975. *Supplement I: Greyhawk*. Lake Geneva: TSR, Inc.

Gygax, Gary, and Jeff Perren. 1972. *Chainmail: Rules for Medieval Miniatures*. 2nd ed. Maine: Guidon Games.

Gygax, Gary, and Jeff Perren. 1975. *Chainmail: Rules for Medieval Miniatures*. 3rd ed. Lake Geneva: TSR, Inc.

Gygax, Gary, Dave Arneson, and Tom Moldvay. 1981. *Dungeons & Dragons Fantasy Adventure Game Basic Rulebook*. Lake Geneva: TSR, Inc.

Hall, Charlie. 2020. Tasha's Cauldron Makes D&D a Better Game, but Whiffs on Race Changes. *Polygon*, November 16. https://www.polygon.com/reviews/2020/11/16/21569738/dungeons-dragons-tashas-cauldron-of-everything-review. Accessed December 1, 2024.

Hall, Charlie. 2022. Dungeons & Dragons' next Anthology Is Written Entirely by Black and Brown Authors. *Polygon*, March 22. https://www.polygon.com/22989321/dnd-journeys-through-the-radiant-citadel-release-date-price. Accessed December 1, 2024.

Hamon, Amanda, Richard Baker, Eytan Bernstein, Makenzie De Armas, Ron Lundeen, and Christopher Perkins. 2023. *Phandelver and Below: The Shattered Obelisk*. Renton: Wizards of the Coast.

Hargrave, David A. 1980. *The Arduin Adventure*. Berkeley: Grimoire Games.

Harrop, Lance. 1979. Would the Real Orc Please Step Forward? Dealing with the Proliferation of Orcish Miniatures. *Dragon* III (11): 18–19.

Heard, Bruce. 1988. *The Orcs of Thar*. Lake Geneva: TSR, Inc.

Henrich, Sören, and Rachel Worthington. 2021. Let Your Clients Fight Dragons: A Rapid Evidence Assessment Regarding the Therapeutic Utility of 'Dungeons & Dragons'. *Journal of Creativity in Mental Health*. https://doi.org/10.1080/15401383.2021.1987367.

Howery, David. 1987. Falcon's Peak. *Dungeon* 3:4–10.

Jackson, Steve. 1986. *GURPS Fantasy*. Austin: Steve Jackson Games.

James, Edward. 2012. Tolkien, Lewis and the Explosion of Genre Fantasy. In *The Cambridge Companion to Fantasy Literature*, ed. Edward James and Farah Mendlesohn, 62–78. New York: Cambridge University Press.

James, Edward, and Farah Mendlesohn. 2012. Unending Romance: Science Fiction and Fantasy in the Twentieth Century. In *The Cambridge History of the English Novel*, ed. Robert L. Caserio and Clement Hawes, 872–886. New York: Cambridge University Press.

Johnson, Jeffro. 2017. *Appendix N*. Zug: Castalia House.

Kelk, Robert. 1988. They Also Serve… Who Misappropriate. *Dungeon* 2 (4): 12–22.

Laycock, Joseph P. 2015. *Dangerous Games: What the Moral Panic Over Role-Playing Games Says About Play, Religion, and Imagined Worlds*. Oakland: University of California Press.

Limbong, Andrew. 2020. 'Dungeons & Dragons' Tries To Banish Racist Stereotypes. *NPR: All Things Considered*, June 29. https://www.npr.org/sections/live-updates-protests-for-racial-justice/2020/06/29/884824236/dungeons-dragons-tries-to-banish-racist-stereotypes. Accessed December 1, 2024.

Marshall, Cass. 2020. Wizards of the Coast Is Addressing Racist Stereotypes in Dungeons & Dragons. *Polygon*, June 23. https://www.polygon.com/2020/6/23/21300653/dungeons-dragons-racial-stereotypes-wizards-of-the-coast-drow-orcs-curse-of-strahd. Accessed December 1, 2024.

Martin, Daniel, and Gary Alen Fine. 2017. Satanic Cults, Satanic Play: Is 'Dungeons and Dragons' a Breeding Ground for the Devil? In *The Satanism Scare*, ed. James T. Richardson, Joel Best, and David G. Bromley, 107–125. New York: Routledge.

Mason, Kelsey Paige. 2023. Just Make-Believe: Assumed Neutrality, Archetypical Exceptionalism, and Performative Progressivism in Dungeons and Dragons. *Vector*, February 15. https://vector-bsfa.com/2023/02/15/just-make-believe-assumed-neutrality-archetypical-exceptionalism-and-performative-progressivism-in-dungeons-and-dragons/. Accessed December 1, 2024.

McManus, Amy, and Andrew Hale Feinstein. 2006. Narratology and Ludology: Competing Paradigms or Complementary Theories in Simulation. *Developments in Business Simulation and Experiential Learning* 33:363–372.

Mearls, Mike, and Jeremy Crawford. 2016. *Volo's Guide to Monsters*. Renton: Wizards of the Coast.

Mearls, Mike, Stephen Schubert, and James Wyatt. 2008. *4e Monster Manual*. Renton: Wizards of the Coast.

Moore, Roger E. 1980a. Half-Orcs in a Variety of Styles. *Dragon* V (6): 17–18.

Moore, Roger E. 1980b. Hate Orcs? You'll Love This Campaign. *Dragon* V (5): 56.

Moore, Roger E. 1982. Giants in the Earth: Classic Heroes from Fiction & Literature. *Dragon* VII (2): 15–18.

Moore, Roger E. 1986. Out of the Dungeon, Into the Fire. *Dungeon* 1:1.

Olson, John S. 1980. What Do You Get When You Cross…? *Dragon* V (6): 19.

Perkins, Christopher, Mike Mearls, and Jeremy Crawford. 2014. *5e Monster Manual*. Renton: Wizards of the Coast.

Perkins, Christopher, Stacey Allan, Will Doyle, and Ari Levitch. 2021. *The Wild Beyond the Witchlight*. Renton: Wizards of the Coast.

Peterson, Jon. 2012. *Playing at the World: A History of Simulating Wars, People and Fantastic Adventures, from Chess to Role-Playing Games*. 2nd ed. San Diego: Unreason Press.

Peterson, Jon. 2016. A Game Out of All Proportions: How a Hobby Miniaturized War. In *Zones of Control: Perspectives on Wargaming*, ed. Pat Harrigan and Matthew G. Kirschenbaum, 3–32. Cambridge: The MIT Press.

Peterson, Jon. 2021. *Game Wizards: The Epic Battle for Dungeons & Dragons*. Cambridge: Massachusetts Institute of Technology.

Plante, Corey. 2020. D&D Book Tasha's Cauldron of Everything Shatters Expectations, for Better or Worse. *Inverse*, November 19. https://www.inverse.com/gaming/dungeons-dragons-tashas-cauldron-of-everything-review. Accessed December 1, 2024.

Priestley, Rick, and Bryan Ansell. 1983. *Warhammer: Forces of Fantasy*. Vol. III. Games Workshop.

Rahman, Glenn. 1981. The History of Zorn and the Goblins. *Dragon* V (12): 44–47.

Riggs, Ben. 2022. *Slaying the Dragon: A Secret History of Dungeons and Dragons*. New York: JABberwocky Literary Agency, Inc.

Riggs, Ben. 2024. D&D Co-Creator Gary Gygax Was Sexist. Talking About It Is Key to Preserving His Legacy. *Ben Riggs's Blog*, July 7. https://www.writerben-riggs.com/blog/4h8ich5klfw83ehgcxamqko6u1yrg7.   Accessed December 1, 2024.

Rihn, Gregory G. H. 1980. Humanoid Races in Review. *Dragon* V (6): 16–17.

Rogan, A. D. 1982. Language Rules Leave Lots of Room for Creativity in Your Campaign. *Dragon* VII (5): 46–49.

Sagui, Charles. 1978. A Short History of Adamanite. *Dragon* III (3): 31–33.

Sagui, Charles. 1979. Hirelings Have Feelings Too. *Dragon* III (12): 26–27.

Salen, Katie, and Eric Zimmerman. 2003. *Rules of Play: Game Design Fundamentals*. Cambridge: The MIT Press.

Siembieda, Kevin. 1983. *The Palladium Role-Playing Game*. Taylor: Palladium Books, Inc.

Smith, Carl. 1984. *The Forest Oracle*. Lake Geneva: TSR, Inc.

Spector, Warren, and Steve Jackson. 1985. *Orcslayer: A Combat Supplement for Man to Man*. Austin: Steve Jackson Games.

St. Andre, Ken. 2013. *Tunnels & Trolls: 1st Edition Reprint.* Phoenix: Cosmic Circle.

Stang, Sarah, and Aaron Trammell. 2020. The Ludic Bestiary: Misogynistic Tropes of Female Monstrosity in Dungeons & Dragons. *Games and Culture* 15 (6): https://doi.org/10.1177/1555412019850059.

Stuart, Robert. 2022. *Tolkien, Race, and Racism in Middle-Earth.* Cham: Palgrave Macmillan.

Sustare, B. Dennis, and Scott Robinson. 1976. *Bunnies and Burrows: Fantasy Adventure & Role-Play in a World of Intelligent Rabbits.* Roslyn: Fantasy Games Unlimited, Inc.

Švelch, Jaroslav. 2013. Monsters by the Numbers: Controlling Montrosity in Video Games. In *Monster Culture in the 21st Century: A Reader*, ed. Marina Levina and Diem-My T. Bui, 193–208. New York: Bloomsbury.

Švelch, Jaroslav. 2018. Encoding Monsters: 'Ontology of the Enemy' and Containment of the Unknown in Role-Playing Games. In *The Philosophy of Computer Games Conference.* Copenhagen.

Swan, Rick. 1996. Review of GURPS Goblins and GURPS Alternate Earths. *Dragon* XXI (7): 113–114.

Trammell, Aaron. 2014. Misogyny and the Female Body in Dungeons & Dragons. *Analog Game Studies* I (III). https://analoggamestudies.org/2014/10/constructing-the-female-body-in-role-playing-games/. Accessed December 1, 2024.

Trammell, Aaron. 2016. How Dungeons & Dragons Appropriated the Orient. *Analog Game Studies* III (I). https://analoggamestudies.org/2016/01/how-dungeons-dragons-appropriated-the-orient/. Accessed December 1, 2024.

Trammell, Aaron. 2018. Militarism and Masculinity in Dungeons & Dragons. In *Masculinities in Play*, ed. Nicholas Taylor and Gerald Voorhees, 129–148. New York: Palgrave Macmillan.

Trammell, Aaron. 2021. The Rules for Race: Dungeons & Dragons in the Suburbs. *Gamers with Glasses.* https://www.gamerswithglasses.com/features/the-rules-for-race-dungeons-amp-dragons-in-the-suburbs. Accessed December 1, 2024.

Ward, James M., and Robert J. Kuntz. 1980. *Deities & Demigods: Cyclopedia of Gods and Heroes from Myth and Legend.* Lake Geneva: TSR Games.

White, William J. 2020. *Tabletop RPG Design in Theory and Practice at the Forge, 2001–2012: Designs and Discussions.* New York: Palgrave Macmillan.

Williams, Skip, Monte Cook, Jonathan Tweet, and Skip Williams. 2003. *3.5e Monster Manual.* Renton: Wizards of the Coast.

Williamson, Jamie. 2009. *The Evolution of Modern Fantasy: From Antiquarianism to the Ballantine Adult Fantasy Series.* New York: Palgrave Macmillan.

Witwer, Michael, Kyle Newman, Jon Peterson, and Sam Witwer. 2018. *Dungeons & Dragons Art & Arcana: A Visual History.* New York: Clarkson Potter/Ten Speed.

Wyatt, James, and Rob Heinsoo. 2001. *Monster Compendium: Monsters of Faerûn*. Renton: Wizards of the Coast.

Zagal, José P., and Sebastian Deterding. 2018. Definitions of 'Role-Playing Games.'. In *Role-Playing Game Studies: Transmedia Foundations*, ed. José P. Zagal and Sebastian Deterding, 19–52. New York: Routledge.

Zambrano, J. R. 2024. D&D History Book Mentions Sexism and the Internet Has Big Feelings About It. *Bell of the Souls*, July 10. https://www.belloflost-souls.net/2024/07/dd-history-book-mentions-sexism-and-the-internet-has-big-feelings-about-it.html. Accessed December 1, 2024.

CHAPTER 8

Goblin Modes

Tabletop games were far from the only form of fantasy media to modify Tolkienian motifs associated with the goblin. A corpus of literature, movies, television shows, and videogames since the mid-twentieth century has downplayed goblins' malevolence in favor of attributes loosely connected to folkloric or folkloresque precedent. Televised adaptations of MacDonald's *The Princess and the Goblin* of the 1960s culminated not in the goblins' wholesale destruction, but rather (depending on the program) their comedic expulsion to their cavernous homes or their agreement to live in peace with their human neighbors. The goblins of *Labyrinth* (1986) kidnapped human children, though the eclectic style and operatic sensibilities of their king (played by David Bowie) were a clear departure from earlier traditions. Other works of fiction from Edith Blyton's fairy tales to the animated *Ghostbusters* series provided sympathetic portrayals of goblins as creatures misunderstood by others. Antagonistic goblins nonetheless persisted across all forms of fantasy media, the Green Goblin of Marvel Comics prominent among them, though they were now paralleled by various iterations of these creatures without the same level of underlying malevolence.

The explosion of fantasy media in the late twentieth and early twenty-first centuries, inspired in part by the success of J.K. Rowling's *Harry Potter* (1997–2007) series, brought with it a more widespread reappraisal of goblins. Within Rowling's books, goblins serve as bankers and skilled

347

M. King, *A History of Goblins*,
https://doi.org/10.1007/978-3-032-01063-6_8

metalsmiths with a fraught relationship to human wizards. Relegated to the margins of society by centuries of conflict, they are simultaneously crude, oppressed, malicious, and misunderstood. Authors since Rowling have embraced similar complexities in their fantasy worlds, including Terry Pratchett in *Snuff* (2011) and Katherine Addison in *The Goblin Emperor* (2014). Authors of children's literature, too, have didactically used negative identifiers of goblins, so long viewed as ugly and evil, to examine the perils of stereotyping others. Some fantasy videogames have likewise moved away from uniformly coding goblins as enemies fit only for slaughter. Depending on the game, players can befriend misunderstood goblins, command their own goblin armies (complete with experimental explosives), or become goblins defending their homes from invading adventurers.

Goblins are not constrained to the realm of fantasy media in the twenty-first century. Strands of modern paganism encourage individuals to cultivate deeply personal and spiritual relationships with these beings. Some pagans depict goblins as helpers from Fairyland that can provide assistance to discerning believers. Others see them as malevolent beings that harass fairies and humans. Still others do not recognize their existence (physical or spiritual) at all. When incorporated into pagan belief systems, goblins are frequently framed with a nostalgic eye toward a time when people lived closer to the earth (and its spirits)—one that is far removed from the technological and environmental destruction associated with modernity. This pre-industrial yearning represents an inversion of folkloric stereotypes present throughout much of this book. Instead of urban elites disparaging the beliefs of uneducated rural folk, many pagans see these folk as having a largely forgotten connection to the earth.

These sympathetic interpretations of goblins facilitated the arrival of two Internet-driven phenomena in the early 2020s: Goblincore and Goblin Mode. The former is an eclectic celebration of natural phenomena typically considered to be ugly, which dovetails into support of environmentally sustainable living and non-binary gender identities. Goblins exist as the namesake for this aesthetic not because they feature prominently in its imagery. Rather, they embody this kind of underappreciated beauty. Such naturalistic associations are less apparent in the idea of Goblin Mode, which had its moment of viral fame in 2022 as Covid-era lockdowns eased and the rhythm of daily life resumed. Though commentators have offered many definitions of what it means to enter Goblin Mode, they typically revolve around atypical or antisocial behavior, framed (depending on the circumstances) anywhere from slovenly laziness to productive self-care.

Though these two movements are distinct from each other, they are thematically united by using the goblin as an avatar for non-conformity and the rejection of airbrushed lifestyles curated on social media.

SYMPATHETIC GOBLINS OF THE TWENTIETH CENTURY

Much of the fairy-centric children's literature to emerge in the United States and United Kingdom in the early to mid-twentieth century echoed the themes of earlier decades. Adaptations of classic fairy tales that replaced dated moral messaging with contemporary ones were common, and they circulated in an increasingly globalized world driven by multinational corporations (especially American ones).[1] Original fairy stories, too, often feature goblins whose appearance and behaviors resemble those of decades past.[2] In *The Little Green Goblin* (1907) by James Ball Naylor, a young boy is whisked away by the titular Fitz, the "oddest, most grotesque figure the boy had ever beheld," to Goblinville, where he learns to appreciate his original life in Yankeeland.[3] Some of Enid Blyton's original stories feature

---

[1] Indeed, per Ó Giolláin, "Americanization is a form of globalization, and both are products of the transformations in communications which are central to the experience of modernity." Ó Giolláin, *Locating Irish Folklore: Tradition, Modernity, Identity*, 171. In this context, Disney has had outsized significance. Cristina Bacchilega, *Fairy Tales Transformed? Twenty-First-Century Adaptations and the Politics of Wonder* (Detroit: Wayne State University Press, 2013), 13–16.

[2] Reinterpretations of children's stories serve to induct "its audience into the social, ethical and aesthetic values of the producing culture." The original text (or "pre-text") is refashioned over time in keeping with contemporary preoccupations and genre conventions. John Stephens, "Retelling Stories across Time and Cultures," in *The Cambridge Companion to Children's Literature*, ed. M.O. Grenby and Andrea Immel (New York: Cambridge University Press, 2010), 91–92. These fantasies "recontextualize myths, placing them back into history and reminding us of their social and political power. By telling stories about, around, and upon mythic stories, we put ourselves onto the same stage with the gods and heroes and monsters and thus are forced to confront our godlike, heroic, and monstrous selves." Brian Attebery, *Stories about Stories: Fantasy and the Remaking of Myth* (New York: Oxford University Press, 2014), 4. In the movie adaptation of *The Wizard of Oz* (which, in book form, some have argued is the first American fairy tale), a song includes a passing mention of goblins as the people of Emerald City rejoice at the death of the Wicked Witch: "She's gone where the goblins go / Below, below, below."

[3] The distinction between human and goblin is blurred in this story. Fitz initially jokes to the protagonist, Bob, that "a man's a man, and a goblin's a goblin. Understand? It's all as clear as muddy water, when you think it over." The "green" of Fitz, too, is a reference to his clothing, but not his skin (which is pale in illustrations). James Ball Naylor, *The Little Green Goblin* (New York: The Saalfield Publishing Company, 1907).

more malevolent goblins whose actions lead to their righteous comeuppance (or the comeuppance of an even less scrupulous character), including "The Goblin's Toyshop," "The Goblin Aeroplane," "The Enchanted Button," "The Goblins and the Ice Cream," and "Boody the Great Goblin."[4] The more generic category of goblin, too, persists in these stories as a marker of the supernatural.

Enid Blyton was also among the first, however, to turn goblins into more relatable protagonists. *The Green Goblin Book* (1935) begins with a sobbing goblin, Tuppany, explaining that he was kicked out of his cave because he prefers gardening and the outdoors to mining. Tuppany then works with two other goblins, Feefo and Jinks, to open a shop. Their ensuing adventures culminate in a fight against a group of evil witches and imps, followed by happy goblin marriages to human princesses with the blessing of the King of Fairyland. Illustrations accompanying this story show the goblins as pale-skinned young boys with pointy ears and long noses. Their greenness reflects their clothing, not their skin, and any kind of grotesque visage is minimized—passed off instead to the more villainous inhabitants of Fairyland.[5] The adventures of Tuppany, Feefo, and Jinks continue in *The Second Green Goblin Book*, which sees them embark on a royal quest to capture an enchanter and free his prisoners.

Blyton's tales of these three goblins are outliers in a sea of children's literature that emphasizes goblins' tricky and malevolent deeds. As the century progressed, however, a handful of writers made goblins more likable and relatable characters. A fairy tale embedded in 1961's *Little Bear's Visit* tells of a terrified goblin chased through the forest by a mysterious entity, which is eventually revealed to be his misplaced shoes.[6] Geraldine Grimm's trilogy from the early 1970s follows a benevolent King Goblin who helps relocate a group of frogs to a parcel of his kingdom with abundant water.[7] A 1973 comic, *Dilly Duckling and the Goblins*, details the "land of the friendly Goblins" and their peaceful life in the forest.[8] These

---

[4] Enid Blyton, *The Goblin Aeroplane and Other Stories* (London: Red Fox, 1990); Enid Blyton, *The Goblin's Toyshop and Other Stories* (London: Award Publications Limited, 1994); Enid Blyton, *The Goblin Hat and Other Stories* (London: Award Publications Limited, 1997).

[5] This text was retitled in Enid Blyton, "The First Green Goblin Book," in *An Enid Blyton Omnibus* (London: Cresset Editions, 1994), 159–264.

[6] Else Holmelund Minarik, *Little Bear's Visit* (New York: HarperCollins, 1961), 42–55.

[7] Geraldine Grimm, *King Goblin and His Forest Friends* (London: Ward Lock Limited, 1972).

[8] Matagne Peyo, *Dilly Duckling and the Goblins* (London: Rylee Limited, 1973).

creatures were eventually rebranded as Smurfs, a closer reflection of the original French *Schtroumpfs*.[9] Brian Froud's *Goblins* (1983) uses pop-up illustrations to comically show the disguised presence of goblins despite a young girl's insistence that they do not exist.[10] Illustrations that accompany these texts show considerable variation, reflecting to some degree the intended audience of the text, from the pale gnome of *Little Bear's Visit* to the camouflaged lurkers of Froud. Uniting these works, though, is the minimization of goblins as agents of fear or markers of a harmful supernatural force. Goblins look strange and usually have magical powers, but they do not possess the malevolence of (say) those in Middle-earth.

This dampening of the more malevolent tendencies of goblins in the mid-twentieth century extended to on-screen adaptations of fairy stories, too. A 1961 episode of *Fractured Fairy Tales* in *The Adventures of Rocky and Bullwinkle and Friends*, for example, condenses MacDonald's *The Princess and the Goblin* into a six-minute animated sketch with goblins equal parts comical and inept.[11] Their weak feet and aversion to poetry becomes the stuff of slapstick. An apparent inability to distinguish between humans leads to an attempted shotgun wedding between Curdie (mistakenly believed to be Irene) and a goblin. When defeated, the goblins are not massacred in a flood beneath a mountain but instead driven back to their cavernous homes forevermore. Neither the gleeful slaughter of these creatures nor MacDonald's Christian messaging has any place in this

---

[9] Two short stories in Denan's *Goblin Tales* (1980) adapt the stories of Hans Christian Andersen and tell of a goblin learning to love poetry and an impoverished human winning the love of a goblin. Corinne Denan, *Goblin Tales* (Troll Associates, 1980).

[10] Brian Froud, *Goblins* (New York: Macmillan, 1983).

[11] "The Princess and the Goblins." *Fractured Fairy Tales: The Adventures of Rocky and Bullwinkle and Friends*, directed by Gerard Baldwin, 2.45 (ABC, April 23, 1961). This episode shows that MacDonald was "important and recognizable enough to fracture in the first place" even if much of the plot and themes of his original were abandoned. Ginger Stelle, North Wind: A Journal of George MacDonald Studies Volume 26 Article 6 1-1-2007 "Fracturing MacDonald: The Princess and the Goblin and 'Fractured Fairy Tales,'" *North Wind: A Journal of George MacDonald Studies* 26, no. 6 (2007): 124. Scholars have broadly rejected the importance of "authenticity" in on-screen adaptations of literature in favor of "hypertextual" or "intertextual" approaches that examine the intent and context of these interpretations. Such adaptations are not a reduction of the literary original, but an addition to it. Deborah Carmell and Imelda Whelehan, "Literature on Screen: A Synoptic View," in *The Cambridge Companion to Literature on Screen*, ed. Deborah Cartmell and Imelda Whelehan (New York: Cambridge University Press, 2007), 2–5.

adaptation, which elevates the slapstick comedy that made *Rocky and Bullwinkle* popular among both children and adults (Fig. 8.1).

One year later, a more moralizing version of *The Princess and the Goblin* aired in a 1961 episode of *Shirley Temple's Storybook*.[12] In this live-action retelling, the goblins are introduced as "a little lopsided," for they "frowned too much, and they rarely smiled. They quarreled too much, and they never made up. They loved to hate but they hated to love." Such attitudes lead to their banishment underground, whence they unsuccessfully plot to kidnap Princess Irene. After their scheme is thwarted, the goblins realize that they are happier living in the fresh air and agree to co-exist peacefully with the humans. Though squabbles between the goblins provide some comic relief, this reinterpretation of *The Princess and the Goblin* emphasizes forgiveness and coexistence, a moral center that (to some critics) was lacking in children's television programing of the era.[13] This retelling further minimizes any language of devolution found in MacDonald (the theory of evolution was still controversial in the United States) and instead attributes the poor attitude of the goblins to their appearance and home.

The popularity of Rossetti's *Goblin Market*, too, resulted in numerous editions during the twentieth century. Illustrations by Arthur Rackham, an artist renowned for his depictions of Fairyland, were most frequently reprinted. His goblins retain some of the animalistic features of those depicted in the original woodcuts of Dante Rossetti, though they are shorter in stature, and many have the long noses, pointed ears, sneering

[12] "The Princess and the Goblins." *Shirley Temple's Storybook*, directed by Robert Ellis Miller, 2.24 (NBC, March 19, 1961). Both this episode and the one from *Fractured Fairy Tales* alter MacDonald's title by pluralizing "goblin." Sylvia Plath took inspiration from MacDonald in a poem of her own, which reframes the story around sexual awakening and the questioning of "the power of romance and fantasy." Jessica Hritz McCort, "Getting out of Wonderland: Elizabeth Bishop, Sylvia Plath, Adrienne Rich, and Anne Sexton" (St. Louis, Washington University in St. Louis, 2009), 134.

[13] Approximately 87% of American households had televisions by 1960. Most parents thought that children were better off with television than without it, though they were wary of advertisements and violent imagery. Newton N. Minow, chair of the Federal Communications Commission, hyperbolically referred to television in a 1961 speech as a "vast wasteland" that includes violence, cartoons, endless commercials, and boredom. Robert W. Morrow, *Sesame Street and the Reform of Children's Television* (Baltimore: The Johns Hopkins University Press, 2006), 7–29.

Fig. 8.1 A shotgun wedding in *Fractured Fairy Tales*. Curdie is led to a literal shotgun wedding by a pair of goblins in *Fractured Fairy Tales* (restored) in *The Adventures of Rocky and Bullwinkle and Friends* (season 2, episode 45)

grins, and spindly limbs characteristic of Rackham's other illustrations.[14] The antagonists of *Goblin Market* were seen as versatile enough, however, to appeal to very different audiences, as seen in two printings of the poem from the 1970s. Ellen Raskin's 1970 adaptation for children renders these creatures as comical cartoons rather than animalistic predators. They are age-appropriate threats to sisters Laura and Lizzie and, fittingly, portions of the poem with sexual or violent overtones are removed.[15] An entirely

[14] Christina Rossetti, *Goblin Market* (Philadelphia: J.B. Lippincott & Co., 1933). This 1933 edition of *Goblin Market* "assured its status" as a children's classic. Lorraine Janzen Kooistra, *Christina Rossetti and Illustration: A Publishing History* (Athens: Ohio University Press, 2002), 207. See also James Hamilton, *Arthur Rackham: A Life with Illustration* (London: Pavilion Books Limited, 1995), 139–66.

[15] Christina Rossetti and Ellen Raskin, *Goblin Market* (New York: E.P. Dutton, 1970).

different interpretation is found in a 1973 reprinting of *Goblin Market* in *Playboy*, which introduced the poem as "the all-time hard-core pornographic classic for tiny tots." Accompanying artwork by Kinuko Y. Craft emphasizes its sexual undertones (while echoing the style of Rackham). Laura's succumbing to the goblins becomes an erotic encounter; her nude figure is swarmed by these creatures in a Bacchic frenzy. When Lizzie is tempted by the goblins' fruit, they tear off her clothes and ply her with their phallic and yonic wares.[16] The thematic complexity of *Goblin Market* was such that it could be repackaged in such different venues without issue. Its titular antagonists could be depicted as either cartoonish villains or grotesque-yet-erotic tempters.[17]

Operating alongside some of these cartoonish or sympathetic goblins were new iterations of more villainous creatures. Works of children's literature, including *The Rainbow Goblins* (1978) and Maurice Sendak's *Outside Over There* (1981), provide colorful depictions of goblins scheming to steal the colors of the rainbow and neglected children (respectively).[18] High fantasy novels and (later) TTRPG campaign books across the second half of the twentieth century are full of the kind of lowly, troglodytic, killable-en-masse goblins that echo the depictions of Tolkien and Gygax. It was the so-called Silver Age of Comic Books (roughly 1956–70), however, that produced perhaps the most famous goblin of all time: the Green Goblin.[19] He first appears in a 1963 issue of *The Amazing Spider-Man*, titled "The Grotesque Adventure of 'the Green Goblin,'" equipped with

[16] Christina Rossetti and Kinuko Y. Craft, "Goblin Market," *Playboy* 20, no. 9 (September 1973): 115–19.

[17] The 1988 science-fiction novel *Goblin Market* has only a passing resemblance to Rossetti's poem. As part of the *Warchild* series, it tells of a human rebellion to end the rule of tyrannical goblins, who have expansive slave markets and pose the "greatest threat of all time." Richard Bowes, *Goblin Market* (New York: Warner Books, 1988).

[18] Ul De Rico, *The Rainbow Goblins* (London: Thames & Hudson, 1978); Maurice Sendak, *Outside Over There* (New York: Ursula Nordstrom, 1981). Sendak's narrative was inspired by the Lindbergh baby kidnapping.

[19] This era of comics was "primarily an American phenomenon" in which established heroes "were revamped" and "more 'realistic' characters and storytelling became the standard." Such narratives were constrained by the Comics Code Authority, which self-policed content to avoid censorship by the United States government. In these comics, women were typically relegated to minor roles (romantic interests and/or damsels in distress), heroes were overwhelmingly white, and contemporary events like the Vietnam War or Civil Rights Movement were avoided. Jim Casey, "Silver Age Comics," in *The Routledge Companion to Science Fiction*, ed. Mark Bould, Andrew M. Butler, and Sherryl Vint (New York: Routledge, 2009), 123–33.

a rocket-powered broomstick and bag full of explosives. A cover blurb encourages readers to discard any cutesy or charitable interpretations they have of these creatures: "Does the Green Goblin look cute to you? Does he make you want to smile? Well, forget it! He's the most sinister, most dangerous foe Spidey's ever fought!"[20] Stan Lee, writer of this issue, acknowledges the warm feelings his readers might have had toward goblins but introduces this villain as drawing on their most malevolent form.

Foregrounded in this 1963 issue as a human in a green-and-purple costume (complete with pointed ears, long nose, and maniacal grin), the Green Goblin is an inventor who subdues his foes with his crafty gadgets and trickery. Perhaps hearkening back to the goblins of *The Hobbit*, this villain makes "no beautiful things," but he does craft "clever ones."[21] He uses the promise of a blockbuster movie to lure Spider-Man into a trap that culminates in the Green Goblin's defeat and inevitable escape "like the rat he is." Defeated the first time of many, the Green Goblin became one of Spider-Man's archvillains—a rivalry only intensified when his identity is revealed to be Norman Osborn, the father of Spider-Man's best friend. Osborn's descent into villainy is framed around a desire for power and wealth stemming from the business failures of his father. He steals inventions and recklessly modifies them, causing a chemical explosion that gives him superhuman intelligence and strength at the expense of his sanity. Ceaselessly tinkering away at new gadgets to destroy Spider-Man, the Green Goblin is not a mining, ore-seeking goblin in a neo-medieval fantasy world. Instead, he is a product of the Cold War: a merciless capitalist and mad scientist willing to construct and use unstable technologies as it suited him.[22] The malevolence with which he deploys these weapons inspires his villainous visage, though these contemporary anxieties are crucial to his identity.[23]

[20] Stan Lee and Steve Ditko, "The Grotesque Adventure of 'the Green Goblin,'" *The Amazing Spider-Man*, 1963.

[21] Tolkien, *The Hobbit, or There and Back Again*, 2001, 60–62.

[22] This is one of many "inverted-superhero supervillains" whose powers reflect and magnify their pre-transformation flaws. Peter Coogan, "The Supervillain," in *The Supervillain Reader*, ed. Robert Moses Peaslee and Robert G. Weiner (Jackson: University Press of Mississippi, 2019), 47–48.

[23] Later interpretations of the Green Goblin are likewise reflective of the circumstances of their creation. Sam Raimi's *Spider-Man* (2002) frames the villain as the result of an intentional gambit by Norman Osborn to secure a military contract for his company. Marc Webb's *The Amazing Spider-Man 2* (2014) depicts the transformation of Norman's son, Harry, as the Green Goblin while he desperately seeks a cure for a terminal disease. Bryn Upton,

Villainous goblins reared their heads in television and film, too, as fantasy media surged in popularity (and controversy) during the 1980s.[24] Although the Smurfs were briefly rendered as Goblins in the 1970s, this designation was given to another group of villainous creatures in a handful of episodes from the 1980s animated series. These goblins work in the service of evil imps and have many forms. Some tear through the sky as the "fiercest creatures in the air," while water-dwelling swamp goblins harass Smurfs that venture into the Brackish Bog.[25] In the 1980s animated series *The Real Ghostbusters*, goblins are usually associated with malevolence. Samhain, the Ghost of Halloween, has two goblin minions that assist him in his evil plans. A group of goblins also accompanies a demoness who kidnaps the descendants of those who wronged her. More sympathetic, though, is a shape-shifting goblin named Drool. Mistakenly perceived to be a threat, Drool ultimately sacrifices himself to save a crowd of onlookers—a heroic deed that undermines an earlier truism from one of the Ghostbusters that "Harmless and Goblin are mutually exclusive terms."[26]

On the big screen, Brian Froud adapted elements of his 1983 pop-up book in *Labyrinth* (1986), for which he served as conceptual designer.[27] Therein, David Bowie takes on the role of Jareth, king of the goblins, who (traditionally) kidnaps children from their homes and (less traditionally) operatically sings about his exploits and emotions. Froud, reflecting on his inspirations for Jareth, notes his "romantic" yet "adversarial" character, which is part of the "inner life" of the movie's adolescent protagonist, Sarah (Jennifer Connelly). His eclectic aesthetic was inspired by *Wuthering Heights* (Heathcliff), Kabuki theater, the Brothers Grimm, and

Hollywood and the End of the Cold War: Signs of Cinematic Change (New York: Rowman & Littlefield, 2014), 87.

[24] Since the success of *Star Wars* (1977), fantasy has been the "dominant genre of Hollywood blockbusters." I.Q. Hunter, "Post-Classical Fantasy Cinema: The Lord of the Rings," in *The Cambridge Companion to Literature on Screen*, ed. Deborah Cartmell and Imelda Whelehan (New York: Cambridge University Press, 2007), 154.

[25] "Papa's Family Album." *The Smurfs*, directed by Ray Patterson, 5.17 (NBC, October 26, 1985); "Calling Doctor Smurf." *The Smurfs*, directed by Ray Patterson, 6.15, (NBC, October 10, 1986).

[26] "When Halloween Was Forever." *The Real Ghostbusters*, directed by Richard Raynis, 1.8, (ABC, November 1, 1986); "Drool, the Dog-Faced Goblin." *The Real Ghostbusters*, directed by Richard Raynis, 2.34 (ABC, October 29, 1987).

[27] *Labyrinth*, directed by Jim Henson (Tri-Star Pictures, 1986). The narrative of *Labyrinth* resembles to some degree that of Sendak's *Outside Over There*, which is credited as an inspiration in the film's credits.

contemporary ballet.[28] In some scenes, Bowie was even given a codpiece to represent "male sexual aggression" directed at our protagonist, an energy intended to be both scary and attractive.[29] Although goblin kings had long served as antagonistic figures in folkloresque narratives, the aesthetic and presentation of Jareth made this iteration more endearing than many of his predecessors. Surrounding Jareth, too, is an eclectic ensemble of goblin puppets and animatronics, no two quite alike. Froud and Terry Jones (screenwriter) note that they are, generally, "small, grotesque creatures" that are "malevolent and cantankerous to humans—even when they are on their best behavior."[30]

A different folkloresque tradition inspired Blix, the "most loathsome" of the goblins working for the villain Darkness in 1985's fantasy-adventure *Legend*.[31] The diminutive creature has green skin, long ears, a hooked nose, and a high-pitched voice that renders his gender somewhat ambiguous (he has generally male-coded features, masculine pronouns, but is played by a woman, Alice Playten). Blix is an unmistakable antagonist within a high-fantasy heroic quest. His heart is "black as midnight, black as pitch, blacker than the foulest witch." As lowly servant to Darkness, Blix stalks the movie's protagonists, slays a unicorn, and ransacks a house, all while bickering with his fellow goblins and not realizing the substantial power of the magic unicorn horn in his possession. Though Blix's fate is unresolved after his defeat at the hands of our heroes, the movie culminates in a characteristic triumph of the forces of light/good over dark/evil.[32] Both Blix and Jareth, then, take on antagonistic roles in their respective fantasy films. Their appearance and actions, however, hearken back to different traditions associated with goblins. Blix fulfills the role of the

---

[28] Froud's discussion of Jareth's inspirations comes from audio commentary (time stamp 12:17–13:15).

[29] Russ Burlingame, "Brian Henson Confirms David Bowie's Codpiece in Labyrinth Was Intentional (Exclusive)," ComicBook, February 19, 2024, https://comicbook.com/movies/news/brian-henson-confirms-david-bowies-codpiece-in-labyrinth-was-intentional-exclusive/

[30] Brian Froud and Terry Jones, *The Goblins of Labyrinth* (London: Pavilion Books Limited, 1986), dust jacket. Similar in tone and presentation is 1994's *The Goblin Companion*, which frames the goblin world around the discoveries made by "eccentric piscepodiastrist" Brian Froud in Africa. Brian Froud and Terry Jones, *The Goblin Companion* (Atlanta: Turner Publishing, Inc., 1996).

[31] *Legend*, directed by Ridley Scott (Universal Pictures, 1985).

[32] Gene Siskel, "'Legend' May Become One, but for All the Wrong Reasons," *Chicago Tribune*, April 18, 1986, N7.

lowly antagonist in a high fantasy world; Jareth is an innovative rendering of the folkloresque goblin that kidnaps children, albeit imbued with some of the sexual imagery reminiscent of Rossetti's *Goblin Market*. These goblins firmly belong in the genre of the fantasy adventure, though their divergent forms therein showcase variability within this tradition.

The rise in popularity of videogames during the 1980s provided additional venues in which people could encounter goblins. Even more rigid in rulesets than TTRPGs, videogames provide a multimedia experience through thousands of lines of code that create an immersive narrative to players—a persuasive "procedural rhetoric" within virtual worlds.[33] Player agency exists within the confines of this code, but the ability to transgress these rules is virtually impossible, unlike in TTRPGs, where house rules and the judgment of a DM can result in different rulesets across (and even within) campaigns. Someone playing *Pac-Man*, for example, can control the movements of its hero based on the location of walls, dots, and hostile ghosts. They cannot, however, speak to the ghosts in an attempt to understand the root of their conflict or leave the endless maze in which Pac-Man exists. When goblins were coded into videogames of the 1980s, players often had little choice but to slaughter them if they wished to progress in-game. Take, for example, the 1985 arcade game *Ghosts 'n Goblins*. Players inhabit the virtual body of Sir Arthur, a knight who must slay legions of monsters to rescue a kidnapped princess.[34] The only way to advance in the game is to destroy hordes of fairy-inspired monsters, relegating them to the dubious role of enemies whose destruction is the only way for players to progress.

Early videogame RPGs drew heavily on the setting and mechanics of *D&D*, which led to developers coding goblins into neo-medieval settings as punching bags for low-level heroes.[35] *Ultima III: Exodus* (1983) uses a

---

[33] Ian Bogost, *Persuasive Games: The Expressive Power of Videogames* (Cambridge: The MIT Press, 2007); Ian Bogost, "The Rhetoric of Video Games," in *The Ecology of Games: Connecting Youth, Games, and Learning*, ed. Katie Salen (Cambridge: The MIT Press, 2008), 117–40.

[34] The original Japanese title of this game was "Demon World Village," and the game became an arcade hit in both Japan and the United States. *Ghosts 'n Goblins*, Capcom, released 1985, Arcade.

[35] Such settings "gleefully combine medieval tropes, plots, characters, settings and situations … into pixilated, interactive gaming environments that no longer seek any mooring in the actual Middle Ages." Daniel T. Kline, "Contemporary Neo-Medieval Digital Gaming: An Overview of Genre," in *Medieval Afterlives in Contemporary Culture*, ed. Gail Ashton (New York: Bloomsbury Academic, 2015), 93–102. Not all games require this kind of

single sprite for orcs, goblins, and trolls: a triumvirate of evil forged by a magical mutation.[36] Goblins are hardly fearsome enemies, though, as they have the lowest hit points and experience granted of any monster in the game. In *Might and Magic Book One: The Secret of the Inner Sanctum* (1986), goblins are among the weakest of enemies, tied with the likes of the *kobold* and battle rat for experienced granted upon death.[37] Even in games where Goblin Princes and Goblin Shamans provide slightly more dangerous challenges to players, like *Wizardry III: Legacy of Llylgamyn* (1983), they are creatures that exist to be killed.[38]

The designers of *Ultima*, *Might and Magic*, and *Wizardry* series were American men with a deep appreciation for *D&D* and related fantasy media.[39] Their pathfinding games proved influential for the team of Japanese developers responsible for the acclaimed *Final Fantasy* (1987) series.[40] Goblins are among the first enemies encountered in the game and pose little threat to players. Significant, too, is the word used to label this enemy, ゴブリン, a Japanese rendering of "goblin" that transliterates to "*goburin*."[41] Japanese folklore and belief systems have no shortage of creatures that could conceivably replace the goblin in a high fantasy story: *tengu*, *oni*, and *yōkai* come to mind. Michael Dylan Foster, too, characterizes Japan in the 1980s as experiencing a "*yōkai* boom" based on their proliferation in visual media, but the developers of *Final Fantasy* chose to render this creature as part of the Anglophone tradition of *Ultima*, *D&D*,

destruction, however, especially those outside of the RPG tradition. *Transylvania*, a 1982 adventure game, sees players encounter a lone goblin in a forest holding the key that they need to progress in the game. The only way to force the creature to drop the key is to say "IJNID," which causes the goblin to inexplicably drop the key and run away. *Transylvania*, Penguin Software, released 1982, Apple II.

[36] *Ultima III: Exodus*, Origin Systems, released 1983, Apple II.

[37] *Might and Magic Book One: The Secret of the Inner Sanctum*, New World Computing, released 1986, Apple II.

[38] *Wizardry III: Legacy of Llylgamyn*, Sir-Tech, released 1983, Apple II.

[39] Richard Garriott, for example, grew up with a fondness for Tolkien and Lewis. He recalls the moment he thought to fuse these books with modern technology: "I was suddenly introduced to *D&D*, fantasy and computers, and something went 'click, bang!'—that's when I realized I'd found something I considered fun, that I'd found my own thing to do." Shay Addams, *The Official Book of Ultima*, 2nd ed. (Greensboro: Compute Books, 1992), 4–5.

[40] *Final Fantasy*, Square, released 1987, NES.

[41] I would like to thank Mako Nozu for her helpful comments on the *goburin*.

and Tolkien.[42] When *Final Fantasy* was ported to North America in 1990, this creature was unsurprisingly translated back to "goblin."

The Japanese developers of *The Legend of Zelda* (1986) showed a similar admiration for high fantasy stories from the Anglophone world, though their game-design philosophy departed from the RPGs considered above.[43] Games like *Might and Magic* and *Final Fantasy* were designed around turn-based combat reminiscent of *D&D* and other TTRPGs. Movement and combat in *The Legend of Zelda* takes place in real-time, meaning that players have to rely on dexterous fingers and quick reaction times to contend with enemies. Among the least threatening of these monsters is the Molblin (モリブリン): a mean, forest-dwelling, "bulldog-like goblin."[44] A portmanteau of "*goburin*" with the Japanese "*mori*" (モリ, meaning "forest,"), these creatures are pig-faced humanoids, some orange and some blue, that throw a seemingly endless supply of spears at our hero.[45] The antagonistic, lowly Anglophone goblin of this high fantasy tradition was thus imported into Japan by developers and encoded into their videogames.

Low-pixel-count graphics of the 1980s restricted how goblins could be rendered within videogames. Only certain machines running *Ultima III* had the ability to render color graphics, for example, which meant that users (depending on their machine) might encounter white or green goblins. When color graphics became more widespread, designers still only had limited colors available to use from preset color palettes. Given these restrictions, designers chose which physical aspects of goblins were most important to render: ears, horns, red eyes, and/or weapons (depending on the game). Important, too, in these depictions was the camera angle of the game, which ranged from the first-person perspective of *Might and*

---

[42] Foster clarifies that *yōkai* is "an umbrella signifier for things we generally translate with terms such as *monster, spirit, goblin, demon, phantom, specter, fantastic being, lower-order deity*, or *unexplainable occurrence.*" Foster, *The Book of Yokai: Mysterious Creatures of Japanese Folklore*, 37, 96.

[43] *The Legend of Zelda*, Nintendo, released 1986, Family Computer Disk System and NES.

[44] The spelling of this enemy morphed in the early 1990s to "Moblin," which remains the Standard English spelling in the series. *The Legend of Zelda Instruction Booklet* (Nintendo, 1987), 30.

[45] The goblin was ubiquitous enough in the Japanese fantasy sphere that the developers of *Digital Devil Story: Megami Tensei* (1987), a game based on Japanese sci-fi novels, labeled one of its "demons" as "*goburin.*" *Digital Devil Story: Megami Tensei*, Atlus, released 1987, Famicom.

Fig. 8.2   Videogame goblins of the 1980s. The sprites for a Blue Molblin from *The Legend of Zelda* (left) and a goblin from *Final Fantasy* (right). (These images were reconstructed from game screenshots by the author in *Aseprite*)

Magic to the removed, top-down perspective of *The Legend of Zelda* (Fig. 8.2).

The fictional goblins detailed in this chapter were meant to evoke a range of responses for their respective audiences. Conspicuously absent in such depictions, however, is an emphasis on fear or horror. This represents a departure from the genres of Gothic and weird fiction, wherein authors like Walter Scott and Clark Ashton Smith provided monstrous descriptions of goblins to invoke such emotions or set the stage for eerie supernatural encounters.[46] Goblins could certainly be scary in the contexts described above, but they are noticeably absent from mainstream horror films of the 1970s and 1980s. Many of their monsters could conceivably

---

[46] Some scholars, like S.S. Prawer, see a distinction between "fantasy terror" (which better describes Shelley and Scott) and "horror" itself, the latter of which involves "a *painful* emotion composed of repugnance and fear, a shudder of *loathing*, as well as terror." I follow the lead of Grixti, however, in seeing horror fiction cutting across such distinctions. Joseph Grixti, *Terrors of Uncertainty: The Cultural Contexts of Horror Fiction* (New York: Routledge, 1989), ix–x. The editors of *The Cambridge Companion to American Horror* also acknowledge that its essays "share no consensus as to what horror actual is" even as they describe a "definable cultural object" from Gothic fiction to body horror. Mark Storey and Stephen Shapiro, "American Horror: Genre and History," in *The Cambridge Companion to American Horror*, ed. Stephen Shapiro and Mark Storey (New York: Cambridge University Press, 2022), 1–2.

have been called goblins based on precedents in fantasy media and definitions provided by folklorists—but they were not.[47] The categorical ambiguities that defined such monsters had, after all, long been associated with
goblins as a generic catch-all term.[48] However, goblins had apparently
become so thoroughly connected to fairy tales, children's literature, and
high fantasy media that screenwriters did not see them as suitable for elic-
iting the fear-based emotional response they sought out of audiences.[49]

When goblins do feature in less-mainstream horror movies, the results
have been laughable. *Hobgoblins* (1988) and *Troll 2* (1990) share the
dubious distinction of being regarded as two of the worst movies ever
made.[50] The goblins in both are so decidedly unscary that the films have
reached cult status for their poor production quality and unintentional
hilarity.[51] Goblins' lack of suitability for horror is further seen in a parody
commercial within the psychological horror film *Mandy* (2018), wherein
the green mascot of Cheddar Goblin Macaroni spews cheesy vomit onto a
pair of children.[52] Within a movie featuring ritualized cannibalism and
demon worship, goblins are only deployed to provide a moment of levity
for audiences.[53] Broadly taken, then, depictions of goblins in the mid- to
late twentieth century minimized previous associations with horror and

---

[47] In *Don't Be Afraid of the Dark*, both the 1973 original and 2010 remake, a house is
haunted by small, evil, diminutive creatures. At no point in either film are they called goblins—the simple "creature" conveys their horrifying ambiguity. *Don't Be Afraid of the Dark*,
directed by John Newland (Lorimar Productions, 1973); *Don't Be Afraid of the Dark*,
directed by Troy Nixey (Miramax, 2010).

[48] Noel Carroll, *The Philosophy of Horror: Or, Paradoxes of the Heart* (New York: Routledge,
1990), 31–50.

[49] Hart, indeed, sees horror cinema as "defined by the way it engaged with its audience—
by styles and forms that are designed to elicit emotional responses." Adam Charles Hart,
Monstrous Forms: Moving Image Horror Across Media (New York: Oxford University Press,
2019), 8.

[50] *Troll 2*, directed by Claudio Fragasso (Filmirage, 1990); "The Beauty Of The 'Best
Worst Movie,'" *Talk of the Nation* (NPR, June 15, 2009).

[51] *Best Worst Movie*, directed by Michael Stephenson (Magicstone Productions, 2009). The
only other goblin-centric horror movie I could locate (not situated in the parody tradition)
is a 2010 SyFy original movie called *Goblin*, which involved a nineteenth-century cleansing
ritual in a rural village. It, too, receiving scathing reviews. *Goblin*, directed by Jeffrey Scott
Lando (SyFy, 2010).

[52] *Mandy*, directed by Panos Cosmatos (RLJE Films, 2018).

[53] In 2023's *Unwelcome*, too, the creatures in question are Red Caps. The script mentions
goblins in stage directions, but the word is not used in the movie itself. *Unwelcome*, directed
by Jon Wright (Warner Bros. Pictures, 2023).

fear. Instead, while their appearance could be surprising and scary, they were not intended to frighten or unsettle audiences like some monsters in the horror tradition.

Harry Potter and Fantasy Goblins in the Twenty-First Century

The explosion of popular interest in fantasy media at the beginning of the twenty-first century prompted a further re-evaluation of tropes associated with the goblin and the continued rehabilitation of its image. J.K. Rowling's *Harry Potter* series (1997–2007), initially marketed toward children but now commonly classified as young adult literature, stands out for its monumental popularity and influence.[54] Therein, Rowling describes goblins as short in stature, spindly-fingered, and with pointy ears and long noses. Their native tongue, called Gobbledegook by wizards, is a "rough and unmelodious tongue, a string of rattling, guttural noises."[55] Their skin tone varies. One of the first goblins introduced in *Harry Potter and the Philosopher's Stone* is described as "swarthy," though later descriptions indicate lighter skin.[56] Female goblins might exist in the *Harry Potter* universe, though they are absent from the books, as readers encounter only male (or male-coded) goblins. Some of these physical characteristics of goblins, particularly those presented in the *Harry Potter* film series, have led to accusations of antisemitism among commentators (more on that shortly).

In *Harry Potter*, goblins are best known as bankers who operate Gringotts Wizarding Bank, an occupation that does little to calm their complicated relationship with human wizards. Goblin rebellions and

[54] Judith Rosen, "Middle Grade and YA: Where to Draw the Line?," Publishers Weekly, July 18, 2014, https://www.publishersweekly.com/pw/by-topic/childrens/childrens-industry-news/article/63358-middle-grade-and-ya-where-to-draw-the-line.html. In the 1980s, publishers recognized a "developing teen market" distinct from children's fantasy—though this division has been complicated by the fact that "there has never been a time when teens and adults did not continue to read fantasy written for children." Levy and Mendlesohn, *Children's Fantasy Literature: An Introduction*, 161.

[55] J.K. Rowling, *Harry Potter and the Deathly Hallows* (London: Bloomsbury, 2007), chapter 15. The characterizations in this paragraph are based on the original seven books in the series and not the sprawling corpus of media and merchandise that has developed around them.

[56] In the movie series, too, most goblins have white skin. J.K. Rowling, *Harry Potter and the Philosopher's Stone* (London: Bloomsbury, 1997), chapter 5.

unsatisfactory treaties resolving them are frequently referenced in History of Magic classes. One character summarizes the relationship between the two species as "fraught for centuries."[57] However pervasive these tensions, even wizards cannot deny the technical skill with which goblins forge magical equipment and build intricate vaults deep underground—characteristics that broadly align with those of Tolkien's dwarves. Outside of the banking system, goblins act as creditors and can be seen hounding a delinquent wizard for his debts. A "Goblin Liaison Office" and "Department for the Regulation and Control of Magical Creatures" within the Ministry of Magic give some indication of hierarchies between these groups and the impulse wizards have for controlling nonhuman beings.[58] Indeed, when Hermione charitably speculates that a dispute between humans and goblins could be the result of the latter's poor English, Ron mocks her and proposes she start up an activist organization, the "Society for the Protection of Ugly Goblins."[59]

The goblin Griphook is explicit about the subservient status of goblins to humans, proclaiming that "your race is set still more firmly above mine! Gringotts falls under Wizarding rule, house-elves are slaughtered, and who amongst the wand-carriers protests?"[60] However marginalized, goblins take great pride in their work. When negotiating a price for his cooperation, Griphook is adamant that an ancient sword, crafted expertly by goblins, ought to be returned to its rightful place among its creators. Some goblins also choose to abandon Gringotts rather than work for the evil lord Voldemort, who brought the institution under his control and

[57] Rowling, *Harry Potter and the Deathly Hallows*, chapter 25. Even the lowly house-elf Winky disparages goblins by comparing the actions of her friend Dobby to their work: "And next thing I hear you's up in front of the Department for the Regulation and Control of Magical Creatures, like some common goblin." J.K. Rowling, *Harry Potter and the Goblet of Fire* (London: Bloomsbury, 2000), chapter 8.

[58] Sridevi Rao and Preethi Gorecki, "Is Dobby a Free Elf?," in *Harry Potter and the Other: Race, Justice, and Difference in the Wizarding World*, ed. Sarah Park Dahlen and Emily Elizabeth Thomas (Jackson: University Press of Mississippi, 2002), 276–86.

[59] Rowling, *Harry Potter and the Goblet of Fire*, chapter 24. See also Keridiana Chez, "Sorry, Not Sorry: The Limits of Empathy for Nonhuman Creatures," in *Open at the Close: Literary Essays on Harry Potter*, ed. Cecilia Konchar Farr (Jackson: University Press of Mississippi, 2022), 166–77.

[60] Rowling, *Harry Potter and the Deathly Hallows*, chapter 24. See also Juliana Valadão Lopes, "'All Was Well'? The Sociopolitical Struggles of House-Elves, Goblins, and Centaurs," in *Open at the Close: Literary Essays on Harry Potter*, ed. Cecilia Konchar Farr (Jackson: University Press of Mississippi, 2022), 178–87.

asked goblins to perform "duties ill-befitting the dignity of [their] race."[61] This pride notwithstanding, goblins occupy a lowly position in *Harry Potter*'s social hierarchy.

Harry Potter was one of a handful of fantasy media franchises of the late 1990s and early 2000s that spurred additional interest in the genre. *His Dark Materials* by Philip Pullman, *Twilight* by Stephanie Meyer, and *Artemis Fowl* are among the most popular. Today, fantasy literature "makes up a considerable proportion of the market for popular fiction" across numerous subgenres that, taken in their totality, reimagine the folklore and fantasy on which they are based.[62] The success of Peter Jackson's *The Lord of the Rings* film adaptations also inspired a wave of renewed interest in its source material, another movie trilogy based on *The Hobbit*, and a streaming series based on the appendices of *The Return of the King*.[63] High fantasy videogames, many of which adopted mechanics and tropes from tabletop games, have gone mainstream as well. *EverQuest* was among the first online RPGs to gain widespread popularity, though it was eventually eclipsed in popularity by *World of Warcraft*, which reached a peak of 12 million monthly subscribers in 2010.[64] These franchises and countless others without the same level of fame have provided new interpretations of goblins, some of which reject them as an unambiguous and irredeemable evil (Fig. 8.3).[65]

Fantasy literature for children of all ages has seen a slew of books that elevate goblins' comedic mischief and sympathetic lowly status. The second edition of Froud's *Goblins! A Survival Guide and Fiasco in Four*

---

[61] Rowling, *Harry Potter and the Deathly Hallows*, chapter 15.

[62] James, "Tolkien, Lewis and the Explosion of Genre Fantasy," 76–77. Children's fantasy literature has had an enormous influence in shaping discourse around "Celtic" history and mythology, too. The motifs of druidic priests, megaliths, and associated rituals in particular are linked to modern Celtic identity. Dimitra Fimi, *Celtic Myth in Contemporary Children's Fantasy: Idealization, Identity, Ideology* (New York: Palgrave Macmillan, 2017).

[63] Tolkien scholars had a more muted reaction to Jackson's original trilogy. Jane Chance, "'In the Company of Orcs': Peter Jackson's Queer Tolkien," in *Queer Movie Medievalisms*, ed. Kathleen Coyne Kelly and Tison Pugh (New York: Taylor & Francis, 2016), 79.

[64] Rebekah Valentine, "World of Warcraft Subscription Numbers Are Higher Now Than at Expansion Launch in a Franchise First," IGN, March 25, 2024, https://www.ign.com/articles/world-of-warcraft-subscription-numbers-are-higher-now-than-at-expansion-launch-in-a-franchise-first

[65] On these trends in the Francophone tradition, see Noémie Budin, "La Représentation du Petit Peuple dans la littérature francophone contemporaine pour adolescents: tradition et renouvellement féeriques depuis 1992" (Doctoral Dissertation, Université de Lorraine, 2016).

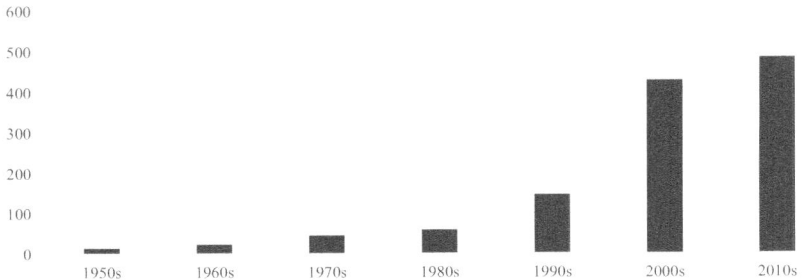

Fig. 8.3 Instances of "Goblin" and "Hobgoblin" in the Children's Literature Comprehensive Database. (Instances of goblins in children's literature are quite low in the mid- to late twentieth century, slightly increasing in the 1990s before shooting up in popularity during the 2000s and 2010s.) (This data was taken from the Children's Literature Comprehensive Database in November 2024 and is accessible at https://www.clcd.com/. The search used to gather this data sorted texts by first publication date and included references to goblin(s) and hobgoblin(s) within title, series, subjects, and blurbs. When standardized based on the total number of texts within this database per decade, the proportions of this graph remain similar. Namely, there is a substantial jump in references to goblins and hobgoblins between the 1990s (0.107%) and 2000s (0.232%))

Parts (2004) merges the imagery of the original with a folkloresque anthropology of goblins by Ari Berk. Its narrative is framed around the authors' ill-fated endeavors to understand the goblin world as these creatures take over Froud's house. Berk embraces the role of goblins as comical troublemakers. They are "untidy authors of more of our everyday accidents and annoyance, troubles and travails, calamities and catastrophes." Their neo-medieval society (complete with scribes and guilds) has a hierarchy determined by a goblin's ability to cause problems for humans. For readers worried about these goblins taking over their house, fear not, for the authors include in each copy an Elvish Talisman of Catastrophic Containment to keep them away. Although the creatures of *Goblins!* cause endless trouble, the tone, absurdist framing, and illustrations of the book elevate their comedic antics.[66]

---

[66] Brian Froud and Ari Berk, *Goblins! A Survival Guide and Fiasco in Four Parts* (London: Pavilion Books, 2004).

Other reappraisals of goblins have used their traditionally grotesque appearance and mischievous character to various ends. *Goblin Secrets*, a 2012 National Book Award winner, includes misunderstood goblins (the result of unfair human stereotypes) that live within the town clock tower as non-citizens, putting on theatrical productions despite a ban on act-ing.[67] The graphic novel *Mighty Jack and the Goblin King* (2017) sees the abduction of a human (Lily) by a group of goblins that had been relegated to a sewer after being displaced by the giants. The goblin king plans to marry and then eat her, but Lilly manages to rally disaffected goblins to her side. She defeats the goblin king and inspires a goblin rebellion against the oppressive giants—restoring in the process a verdant link between castle and sewer.[68] Even in situations where goblins retain their associa-tions with mischief, their malevolence is minimized. *Hobgoblins Just Wanna Have Fun* (2019), for example, sees a band of these creatures breaking into houses, causing a mess, and stealing food from houses. The young hero of the story, Mitch, manages to befriend these hobgoblins after gifting them musical instruments.[69] In *Goblin Magic* (2021), mean-while, historical antagonism between humans and goblins (with "batlike ears, long hooked noses, short torsos, and large glowing eyes") has led to the latter to lose their magical powers. But the goblins of Hobsgrove are not as evil as they seem. A unified force of humans and goblins eventually win the day, reinforcing that there are "plenty of good goblins" in the world and that standing up for what is right is not always easy.[70]

Examples abound in children's literature for all reading levels of goblins acting as unlikely heroes, misunderstood outcasts, or comedic sidekicks: *The Goblin Wood* (2003), *The Seeing Stone* (2003), *Goblin on the Reef* (2003), the *Jig the Goblin* series (2004–11), *The Unseen World of Poppy Malone: A Gaggle of Goblins* (2012), the *Goblins* trilogy (2012–14), *Goblins on the Prowl* (2016), *Nobody Likes a Goblin* (2016), *The Goblin Princess: The Grand Goblin Ball* (2017), *Hobgoblin and the Seven Stinkers of Rancidia* (2019), *Unicorns are the Worst!* (2020), *Goblin* (2021), and *There's a Goblin on the Ark!* (2023) are a few of them.[71] This is not to say that children's literature has abandoned the role of goblins as antagonists,

[67] William Alexander, *Goblin Secrets* (New York: Margaret K. McElderry Books. 2012).

[68] Ben Hatke, *Mighty Jack and the Goblin King* (New York: First Second, 2017).

[69] Baron Specter, *Hobgoblins Just Wanna Have Fun* (North Mankato: Magic Wagon, 2019).

[70] Jordan Quinn, *Goblin Magic* (New York: Little Simon, 2021).

[71] *Unicorns are the Worst!* was even the subject of controversy when a representative of Moms for Liberty complained to a Florida school district about an illustration showing a

but rather that a growing number of authors see the goblin as an appropriate vessel to show the importance of sympathy, perseverance, and understanding.[72] The general absence of goblins from the long-running series *Goosebumps*, too, indicates that they are seen as inappropriate creatures through which to inspire fear, even in children and young adults.[73] The historical stereotyping of goblins as malevolent monsters has thus become a foundation on which to build stories that tend to have an underlying message about the pervasive harm that comes from unfairly judging those who are different. These works encourage readers to have compassion for goblins and perhaps even to empathize with them.[74]

Many authors of fantasy literature for adults have similarly rejected the antagonistic goblins of Tolkien and Gygax in favor of more complicated creatures. Although Jackson's adaptation of *The Lord of the Rings* was a

---

"goblin's bare bottom." Nicholas Kristof, "The School Issues We're Battling Over Aren't the Ones That Matter," *The New York Times*, March 6, 2024.

[72] This is part of a trend of children's authors since the late twentieth century deliberately "disordering" gender identities. Such books act "as a kind of fairy tale of adolescence, enabling children to satisfy an urge to experiment with gender without the need to destabilise their real-life identities." Judy Simons, "Gender Roles in Children's Fiction," in *The Cambridge Companion to Children's Literature*, ed. M.O. Grenby and Andrea Immel (New York: Cambridge University Press, 2010), 157.

[73] In the original series of sixty-two books, only one mentions a goblin, and this is in the context of Halloween decorations. In the twenty-five books of *Goosebumps Series 2000*, the only mention of goblins comes from a description of Halloween costumes. A more monstrous example comes from "The Goblin's Glare," a short story featuring a papier-mâché goblin used to scare trick-or-treaters. For R.L. Stine, goblins bear a clear association with Halloween but are not suitable for inspiring fear. It is only with the publication of *Goblin Monday* in 2024 that we see goblins featuring as antagonists in a *Goosebumps* book—and here they are presented as folkloric haunters rather than creatures of Halloween. R.L. Stine, *Attack of the Jack-O'-Lanterns*, Goosebumps (New York: Scholastic, 1996); R.L. Stine, *Full Moon Fever*, Goosebumps Series 2000 (New York: Scholastic, 1999); R.L. Stine, *Still More Tales to Give You Goosebumps* (New York: Scholastic, 1996); R.L. Stine, *Goblin Monday*, Goosebumps House of Shivers (New York: Scholastic, 2024).

[74] This is a common theme in children's literature of the twenty-first century. Authors frequently "ensure that encounters with the fantastic precipitate significant emotional growth, if not life-defining change, in their protagonists." Catherine Butler, "Modern Children's Fantasy," in *The Cambridge Companion to Fantasy Literature*, ed. Edward James and Farah Mendlesohn (New York: Cambridge University Press, 2012), 255. Even within this list, considerable variability exists. *The Seeing Stone*, for example, features goblins that are villainous, but a hobgoblin prisoner is crucial in helping our heroes escape from imprisonment. Tony DiTerlizzi and Holly Black, *The Seeing Stone* (New York: Simon & Schuster Children's, 2011).

commercial success, its portrayal of orcs reignited debates about their real-world inspirations and the visual portrayal of forces of light/white destroying hordes of dark/evil creatures.[75] Racially determinist framings of high fantasy, which had initially been one of the selling points of the genre, have increasingly been replaced with more dynamic approaches to world-building. Terry Pratchett's *Snuff* (2011), for example, details a cartel of corrupt leaders that traffic in drugs and enslaved goblins.[76] When these injustices are brought to light, our heroes arrange for a concert showcasing the talent of a local goblin, which inspires a team of ambassadors to codify the rights of much-maligned goblins. This book was part of a larger trend in the latter half of Pratchett's career to complicate the narratives presented in early works of the *Discworld* series and minimize the "easy 'speciesism'" of protagonist Sam Vimes.[77] Books like *Feet of Clay* and *Unseen Academicals*, for example, complicate earlier tropes associated with golems and orcs (respectively).[78]

Other works of high fantasy in the twenty-first century have similarly reimagined the tropes associated with goblins. In *The War of the Flowers* (2004), a goblin revolution against oppressive fairy overlords is led by a creature that one commentator describes as "a kind of cross between Nelson Mandela and Leon Trotsky."[79] *Dance of the Goblins* (2005) tells of a friendship between a goblin and human despite their species being constantly at odds. Though these goblins live in a parallel world below ground, they are defined less by their lust for precious metals and more for "The Dance," a spiritual testament to their way of life.[80] In *Orconomics: A Satire* (2014), goblins and other historically unsavory creatures must apply to be "Noncombatant Paper Carriers" (cheekily, NPCs) so that they do not

---

[75] N.K. Jemisin writes that "I have a problem with orcs. I'm orc-averse, you might say; even orcophobic" because they are a "warped mirror of humanity" that exists only to be mowed down, usually on sight and sans negotiation, by Our Heroes." N.K. Jemisin, "The Unbearable Baggage of Orcing," *On Writing* (blog), February 13, 2013, https://nkjemisin.com/2013/02/from-the-mailbag-the-unbearable-baggage-of-orcing/

[76] Terry Pratchett, *Snuff* (New York: Harper, 2011).

[77] A.S. Byatt, "Snuff by Terry Pratchett - Review," *The Guardian*, October 21, 2011, https://www.theguardian.com/books/2011/oct/21/snuff-terry-pratchett-review

[78] Terry Pratchett, *Feet of Clay* (New York: Harper, 2001); Terry Pratchett, *Unseen Academicals* (New York: Harper, 2010).

[79] Tad Williams, *The War of the Flowers* (New York: DAW Books, 2004). See also Andrew Leonard, "'The War of the Flowers' by Tad Williams," *Salon*, June 12, 2003, https://www.salon.com/2003/06/12/williams_14/

[80] Jaq D. Hawkins, *Dance of the Goblins* (Independently Published, 2005).

incur the wrath of violent adventurers.[81] Katherine Addison's *The Goblin Emperor*, winner of the 2015 Locus Award for Best Fantasy Novel, details the unexpected ascent of Maia, a half-goblin, half-elf leader. The heritage of Maia matters less, however, than the court intrigue and political machinations around her that transcend any stereotype about troglodytic goblins or forest-dwelling elves.[82] The list goes on (Fig. 8.4).

Videogame designers, too, have broadened the kinds of goblins present in their games. The motifs of Tolkien and Gygax dominated videogames in the 1980s and early 1990s such that it was rare for goblins to receive sympathetic treatments therein. The occasional comical goblin, like those of the French puzzle series *Gobliiins* (1991) and its sequels, are outliers in a sea of role-playing games (especially) in which goblins exist to be killed for experience and treasure.[83] Strengthening sales of videogames in the 1990s, paired with increased processing power with which to design them, encouraged developers to adopt fantasy themes to new genres. Real-time strategy games, for example, require players to build up entire settlements

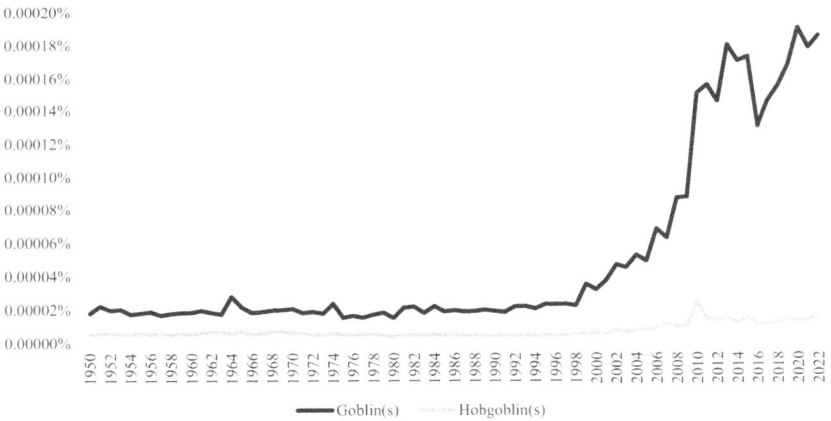

Fig. 8.4 Frequency of "Goblin" and "Hobgoblin" in Google Books. (Data from Google Books [via Ngrams] since the 1950s show that the relative instances of "goblin" and "hobgoblin" have increased substantially since the year 2000)

[81] J. Zachary Pike, *Orconomics: A Satire* (New Hampshire: Gnomish Press LLC, 2014).

[82] Katherine Addison, *The Goblin Emperor* (New York: Tor, 2014).

[83] *Gobliiins*, Coktel Vision, released 1991, DOS.

and armies with which to defeat their foes: a digital spin on tabletop wargames. In *Warcraft II: Tides of Darkness* (1995), players can unleash armies of the Alliance (good-ish) or Horde (evil-ish).[84] Goblins are part of the latter faction as sappers, zeppelin pilots, and alchemists with an appetite for destruction. This fusion of a high-fantasy medievalism with steampunk retrofuturism, reflecting to some degree *The Hobbit*, the Green Goblin, and the "Goblin Balloon Brigade" of *Magic: The Gathering*, has since become a staple of the *Warcraft* series.[85]

The political affiliation of goblins is minimized in *Warcraft III: Reign of Chaos*, wherein they have a similar appetite for explosives but are willing to sell their wares to anyone who desires it.[86] This emphasis on profit and trade is also central to their identity in *World of Warcraft*, which revolves around conflict between Alliance and Horde—framed predictably around warring races of light and dark in a world of "biological essentialism."[87] Goblins are one of seven core "races" of the Horde (introduced as playable characters in the 2009 expansion, *Cataclysm*), though they are less involved in this faction's conflict with the Alliance than others. Many goblins work as independent merchants; others are members of trade groups or cartels; others are employed as mercenaries. More important than their involvement in geopolitical conflict is their ability to create new

---

[84] *Warcraft II: Tides of Darkness*, Blizzard Entertainment, released 1995, MS-DOS. The original *Warcraft: Orcs & Humans* (1994) does not include goblins. Travis Fahs, "IGN Presents the History of Warcraft," IGN, August 18, 2009, https://www.ign.com/articles/2009/08/18/ign-presents-the-history-of-warcraft

[85] One of the first trading card games, *Magic: The Gathering*, borrowed some of its high fantasy motifs from *D&D*. The "Goblin King" and "Goblin Balloon Brigade" cards (part of the red/mountainous deck) are featured in its earliest alpha- and beta-tests. This Balloon Brigade does not have quite the level of technological sophistication as *Warcraft* goblins, as seen in the quotation on the card, "'From up here we can drop rocks and arrows and more rocks!' 'Uh, yeah boss, but how do we get down?'" Titus Chalk, *Generation Decks: The Unofficial History of Gaming Phenomenon Magic: The Gathering* (Oxford: Solaris, 2017).

[86] *Warcraft III: Reign of Chaos*, Blizzard Entertainment, released 2002, Windows.

[87] Melissa J. Monson, "Race-Based Fantasy Realm: Essentialism in the World of Warcraft," *Games and Culture* 7, no. 1 (January 2012): 48–71. Despite some degree of player agency, the overall framing of Alliance (good and light) against Horde (evil and dark) is the result of Tolkien and Gygax's influences on the designers of *World of Warcraft*. Resulting divisions between players permanently splits them into "warring, racially divided factions." Although this is a "simulation of a racist war," players of the game have tried to circumvent this categorization by framing conflict as one of nations instead. Christopher Jonas Ritter, "Why the Humans Are White: Fantasy, Modernity, and the Rhetorics of Racism in World of Warcraft" (Doctoral Dissertation, Pullman, Washington State University, 2010), iv.

technologies (often explosives) and sell them for immense profits. Such preoccupations are embedded within goblins' in-game history. They served for thousands of years as slaves to trolls, laboring deep within mines. Eventually, though, the goblins (intellectually awakened by a magical mineral) rebelled against the trolls and established themselves as independent inventors and traders.[88]

Keen to avoid oppression at the hands of other species, goblins use their potions on members of their own kind, creating fearsome hobgoblin sentries with enhanced strength but diminished intelligence. Goblins respect profit as an ideology. Funerals for goblins reflect the wealth of the dead: the richer the goblin, the bigger the funeral—and those with the greatest wealth might be invited to join the Everlasting Party in the afterlife. When players of *World of Warcraft* create goblin characters, they are fittingly given access to rocket belts, discounts at merchants, and enhanced alchemy skills. Players can also customize some aspects of their goblins' physical appearance. Goblins are uniformly short in stature with disproportionately long arms and ears, though their skin tones can range from green to brown (the former being the most common in media advertising the game). Other features like nose length, eye color, shape of teeth, hair color, and gender are left to the discretion of players. Like the physical customizability of these creatures, players can take actions as goblins based on their own preferences. They can use the expansive digital landscape of *World of Warcraft* to act out heroic fantasies, build unimaginable wealth, and fight endlessly against other players.[89]

Another bestselling RPG series, *The Elder Scrolls*, has acknowledged these rehabilitating fantasy tropes without changing goblins' in-game behaviors. In *Arena* (1994), goblins are typical antagonists that exist to be killed: vile, nasty, stupid, and "almost rodent-like in their frenzy to feed."[90] *Morrowind: Tribunal* (2002) also sees goblins lurking in the sewers beneath the city of Mournhold. One city guard calls them "little vermin" and would like "to get my hands on some of their scrawny little necks."[91]

---

[88] *World of Warcraft*, Blizzard Entertainment, released 2004, Windows. See also Chris Metzen, Matt Burns, and Robert Brooks, *World of Warcraft: Chronicle* (Milwaukie: Dark Horse books, 2016).

[89] Such actions (and their implications) are considered in Garry Young, *Ethics in the Virtual World: The Morality and Psychology of Gaming* (London: Routledge, 2014).

[90] *The Elder Scrolls: Arena*, Bethesda Softworks, released 1994, MS-DOS.

[91] *The Elder Scrolls III: Morrowind—Tribunal Expansion*, Bethesda Game Studios, released 2002, Windows.

They occupy a similar role in *Oblivion* (2006), though players can fight eight different goblin clans that reside within complex cave systems complete with domesticated rats and prison cells.[92] Within *The Elder Scrolls Online* (2014), goblins are still hostile creatures, though one quest reveals that in-game scholar (and closeted goblinophile) Nellic Sterone is trying to correct misperceptions about them. His comical studies reveal cultural activities of the Stonechewer Tribe, a group "so misunderstood. Like us, yet unlike. The Goblins live in a world apart, one I may never enter. I can only dream." Upon completing a quest on his behalf, Sterone reminisces: "If only more people were aware of the Goblins' rich cultural heritage, perhaps they wouldn't be so persecuted. Plus, the females are kind of cute. In a way."[93] Sterone, seemingly motivated by less-than-academic objectives, fared better than another researcher documenting the Toad-Tongue Goblins, who was killed while conducting her fieldwork. The in-game work of both scholars is unappreciated in their time, as a letter from the editor of the *Species and Speculation Journal* rejects an anonymous manuscript for its "ridiculous" and "insupportable" claims that goblins can domesticate certain species.[94] Developers of *The Elder Scrolls Online* thus acknowledge the trend of reframing the goblin in other fantasy worlds but choose to retain goblins' antagonistic core in their game.[95]

Other developers have selectively drawn from goblin traditions in games across genres. *Goblin Commander: Unleash the Horde* (2003) allows players to command goblin armies, equipped with neo-medieval weapons

[92] *The Elder Scrolls IV: Oblivion*, Bethesda Game Studios, released 2006, Windows. Goblins are not present in the base game of *Skyrim* (2011). In a downloadable quest through the game's "Creation Club," players encounter a group of misguided goblins who think they are worshipping the deity Malacath, though it is actually just an orc in blue body paint. Upon freeing the goblins from this orcish tyranny, players have the option of recruiting a goblin named Gogh as their follower.

[93] *The Elder Scrolls Online*, Bethesda Softworks, released 2015, Windows. Sterone, to be fair, makes a seemingly important connection between "Muluk" of the goblins and the Deadrich Prince, Mauloch, which he hopes will win him tenure at the College of Wayrest.

[94] These examples are from the in-game texts "Researcher's Notes" (from the "Goblin Research" quest) and "Academy's Rejection Letter."

[95] A similar tension is found in a 2011 episode of the NBC sitcom, *Community*. Therein, a group of college misfits play a game of *AD&D*, the first encounter of which is an ambush from six goblins. The sometimes-activist-minded character, Britta (Gillian Jacobs), asks "Why are these goblins attacking us? Maybe these woods are their rightful land and from their perspective ..." before being drowned out by a chorus of groans from the rest of the group, who then slaughter three of the goblins and cause the rest to flee. "Advanced Dungeons & Dragons." *Community*, directed by Joe Russo, 2.14, (NBC, February 3, 2011).

and armor, in a civil war between five clans.[96] Humans are the unjust persecutors of orcs and goblins in the 2012 action game *Of Orcs and Men*, which spawned two prequel games in which players operate as a cunning goblin thief/assassin, more intelligent and versed in magic than his kin.[97] The free-to-play *Clash of Clans* (2012) includes goblin infantry soldiers that carry bags of loot on their backs and are programmed to prioritize resource-rich buildings instead of enemy soldiers.[98] *Goblins & Grottos*, a 2016 platformer, sees the lowly goblin finally get revenge on the "greedy powerleveling adventurers" who have so long antagonized them; a similar inversion of the dungeon crawler is found in *Looterkings* (2017), in which players take on the role of a goblin fighting up to the surface to loot the palace of the Elven Queen.[99] Part of the quirky cast of characters encountered in the point-and-click adventure game *Lost in Play* (2022) are goblins inhabiting a floating village, including a bard-turned-heavy-metal enthusiast and a fisherman trying to catch metallic loot from a perch on the sky.[100] Players can even take on the role of a goblin shopkeeper in *Trash Goblin* (2024), finding and cleaning trinkets to upsell to customers.[101] Like works of fantasy literature, these games tend to either emphasize non-violent characteristics of goblins or reframe their violence as a sympathetic response to aggression against them.

As with child-centric literature, videogames and works of fantasy literature for adults do not supplant those in which goblins are vermin designed to be slaughtered. Tolkien remains immensely popular and influential. High-fantasy series of the twenty-first century like *Goblin Slayer* (both an anime and a manga) delight in the episodic destruction of these creatures. Jackson's *The Lord of the Rings* trilogy inspired a predictable slew of licensed videogames that saw players destroy orcs/goblins in great numbers for experience and treasure.[102] No developers have attempted to make a Middle-earth game portraying goblins in a sympathetic light, and the abysmal failure of *The Lord of the Rings: Gollum* (2023) is unlikely to spur

[96] *Goblin Commander: Unleash the Horde*, Jaleco Entertainment, released 2003, Xbox.

[97] *Of Orcs and Men*, Cyanide and Spiders, released 2012, PlayStation 3.

[98] *Clash of Clans*, Supercell, released 2012, iOS.

[99] *Goblins & Grottos*, Psychic Software and Goblin Portal, released 2016, PC; *Looterkings*, Headup Games, released 2017, PC.

[100] *Lost in Play*, Happy Juice Games, released 2022, PC.

[101] *Trash Goblin*, Spilt Milk Studios Ltd., released 2024, PC.

[102] In videogame adaptations set in Middle-earth, it is common for goblins to be distinct from orcs (in ways that make the former weaker and less threatening).

confidence in the possibility of inverting Tolkienian tropes within his own universe. Outside of licensed videogames are ones that delight for the destruction of goblins and their kin across genres: *Runescape* (2001), *Dwarf Fortress* (2006), the *Orcs Must Die!* series (2011–22), *Dragon's Dogma* (2012), *Sword Slinger* (2020), *Pawnbarian* (2021), and *Wytchwood* (2021) are a few. Even as many authors and developers saw the goblin as an apt subject for a high-fantasy reappraisal, others chose to retain this evil, antagonistic core.

The goblin is not the only monster to have received a reappraisal in fantasy media. Since the mid-twentieth century, the "overall trend in monstrous representation" has been "toward not just sympathizing but empathizing with—and ultimately aspiring to be—the monster."[103] *Grendel*, *Wicked*, *Shrek*, *Vampire Chronicles*, *Monsters, Inc.*, *Twilight*, *Hellboy*, and *True Blood* operate in this tradition in which behaviors define monstrosity, not appearance. The reframing of goblins has taken place alongside them, using the classificatory ambiguities of monsters to make larger claims about how societal expectations force people into ill-fitting categories. The ugliness of goblins, too, so long a marker of sin and moral depravity, becomes a vehicle through which audiences can examine prejudices engrained within us. More important than issues of taxonomy and classification, then, is the use of goblins and other monsters to make larger points about the normative values of the cultures that create them.

BELIEF IN GOBLINS PERSISTS

A recurrent theme in this history has been the idea of the perpetual recession of the fairies, in which commentators lament how fairy belief has declined in their time and only persists among certain groups (usually the superstitious and uneducated). The rise of modern paganism, however, has seen a rhetorical reversal in this trend. Members of some pagan groups actively seek out spiritual experiences from fairies, goblins included, as part of a larger goal of exploring oneself and one's relationship to the earth.

---

[103] Jeffrey Andrew Weinstock, "Invisible Monsters: Vision, Horror, and Contemporary Culture," in *The Ashgate Research Companion to Monsters and the Monstrous*, ed. Asa Simon Mittman and Peter J. Dendle (New York: Routledge, 2012), 277. Asma similarly argues that "the liberal lesson of monsters is one of tolerance: we must overcome our innate scapegoating, our xenophobic tendencies." Stephen T. Asma, "Monsters and the Moral Imagination," in *The Monster Theory Reader*, ed. Jeffrey Andrew Weinstock (Minneapolis: University of Minnesota Press, 2020), 289.

Built into this spirituality is a narrative about the perils of modernity, which has separated humans from the environment in destructive ways and severed an ancient bond that once existed between us and nature spirits.[104] Fairy belief also persists outside of modern paganism. Simon Young's *Fairy Census* has documented people's perceived interactions with fairies over the last several decades. It is rare for people to describe these creatures as goblins, though when this happens, they retain some elements common in folkloric and folkloresque interpretations: short, dark-skinned, masculine, and/or tricksy. Self-reported belief in fairies and goblins thus persists into the present.

The origins of modern paganism in the Anglophone world are in the ancient religious practices of Europe and the Mediterranean.[105] This pagan revival began in earnest in the nineteenth century, spurred by a combination of Romantic-era nostalgia for classical antiquity, nationalism, and the folklore. Interest in paganism surged in the first half of the twentieth century through the leadership of Gerald Gardner, whose fusion of Freemasonry, spiritualism, Buddhism, Malay folklore, Classical history, and "tribal magical practices" inspired the Wicca movement.[106] His writings in the 1940s and 1950s brought international attention to Wicca and provided a corpus of texts around which his followers framed their beliefs. In the United States, members of the counterculture movement of the

---

[104] Recent academic studies of modern paganism can be found in Hutton, *The Triumph of the Moon: A History of Modern Pagan Witchcraft*; Susan Greenwood, *Magic, Witchcraft and the Otherworld: An Anthropology* (New York: Routledge, 2000); Michael York, *Pagan Theology: Paganism as a World Religion* (NYU Press, 2003); Magliocco, *Witching Culture: Folklore and Neo-Paganism in America*; Chas Clifton, *Her Hidden Children: The Rise of Wicca and Paganism in America* (Lanham: Rowman & Littlefield, 2006); Nevill Drury, *Stealing Fire from Heaven: The Rise of Modern Western Magic* (New York: Oxford University Press, 2011); Robin Douglas and Francis Young, *Paganism Persisting: A History of European Paganisms since Antiquity* (Exeter: University of Exeter Press, 2024).

[105] Hutton argues that learned magic in Europe went through five phases of development: ancient, medieval (beginning in the twelfth century), early modern, Enlightenment, and modern. Ronald Hutton, *The Triumph of the Moon: A History of Modern Pagan Witchcraft* (New York: Oxford University Press, 1999), 66–67. When Hutton published *The Triumph of the Moon*, "the study of Wicca was widely disparaged, and Hutton endured some professional embarrassment because of the subject matter of the book, which only began to be rectified post-2010." Ethan Doyle White and Shai Feraro, "Twenty Years On: An Introduction," in *Magic and Witchery in the Modern West: Celebrating the Twentieth Anniversary of "The Triumph of the Moon,"* ed. Shai Feraro and Ethan Doyle White (New York: Palgrave Macmillan, 2019), 8–9.

[106] Hutton, *The Triumph of the Moon: A History of Modern Pagan Witchcraft*, 204–40.

1960s fused these pagan ideas with (especially) the sexual revolution and environmentalism. Less secretive and more outwardly feminist in framing, American paganism has since flourished in decentralized groups organized around various aspects of pagan tradition.[107] Controversially embedded in some of these practices, too, are components of belief systems from American Indians—which have led to accusations of appropriation for a religion that largely stems from European traditions.[108]

Modern paganism is such a disparate and diverse movement, often practiced individually by "solitaires," that even broad generalizations like those in the above paragraph run the risk of being oversimplistic.[109] The breadth of perspectives found in pagan-centric publishing houses (including Llewellyn, Avalonia, and Inner Traditions) alongside self-published works gives some sense of this variation. Sabina Magliocco's synthesis of modern paganism provides as useful a summary as any for unifying threads across this patchwork of beliefs and practices:

> This group of religions is broad and eclectic. … Neopagans share a desire to reconnect with nature, community, and the sacred, a view of the divine as immanent, and a search for religious experience that is personal, direct, and embodied. They generally lack a single codified sacred text or charismatic leader. Drawing heavily from traditional folklore in their creation of rituals,

---

[107] See, for example, Jone Salomonsen, *Enchanted Feminism: Ritual, Gender and Divinity Among the Reclaiming Witches of San Francisco* (New York: Routledge, 2002).

[108] Barbara Jane Davy, *Introduction to Pagan Studies* (New York: AltaMira Press, 2007), 96–97. Indeed, Berger argues that the process of adaptation and appropriation of disparate rituals was central to the development of this movement (Wicca particularly) in late modernity. Its "pastiche of rituals from diverse cultures" is skeptical of the Enlightenment "to rationalism itself." Helen A. Berger, *A Community of Witches: Contemporary Neo-Paganism and Witchcraft in the United States* (Columbia: University of South Carolina Press, 1999), 123–24. See also Eduardo Viveiros de Castro, *The Relative Native: Essays on Indigenous Conceptual Worlds* (Chicago: Chicago University Press, 2015).

[109] Llewellyn marketers estimated in the late 1990s that around 70% of self-reported pagans were "solitary practitioners." Clifton, *Her Hidden Children: The Rise of Wicca and Paganism in America*, 12. This number has increased since then in the United States. The Pagan Census Revisited, which collected data in 2009 and 2010, estimated around 78% of American pagans were solitary practitioners. Helen A. Berger, *Solitary Pagans: Contemporary Witches, Wiccans, and Others Who Practice Alone* (Columbia: University of South Carolina Press, 2019), 1–2.

their goal is the re-enchantment of the world and the creation of a personal-ized relationship with divinity.[110]

Fairies play an important role in some strands of modern paganism. In one survey, Magliocco finds that 56% of pagan respondents say fairies are important to their practice.[111] Variations in interpretations of fairies are explicit in the world of pagan publishing, wherein authors describe tech-niques for finding, summoning, and interacting with fairies. They often begin with a history of how technological progress has severed a once-prominent connection between humans and fairies. Buck Young of EarthSpirit sees the destruction of forests as shrinking the habitable space for "gnomes and elves, fauns and faeries, goblins, ogres, trolls and bogies, nymphs, sprites, and dryads" such that they changed form. Some went to their own world, which humans can contact under the right circumstances, while others send their souls to our world as human babies.[112] Ted Andrews, best known for his book *Animal Speak*, similarly notes that humans have "grown insensitive to the nuances of nature" and its fair-ies.[113] Cassandra Eason, who claims a broad base of experience in psychic and spiritual phenomena, presents our world as a "plastic fairyland" in which modernization has minimized human's ability to interface with fair-ies.[114] The emphasis of connection between humans and fairies—which here can perhaps be identified as "more-than-human" creatures, to use David Abram's term—shows a desire for connectivity across all life.[115]

[110] Sabina Magliocco, "Neopaganism," in *The Cambridge Companion to New Religious Movements*, ed. Olav Hammer and Mikael Rothstein (New York: Cambridge University Press, 2012), 150. The use of the term "neopagan" is controversial, as some groups prefer not to be seen as a "new" version of an ancient belief, but rather as practitioners of this ancient belief itself.

[111] Sabina Magliocco, "The Taming of the Fae: Literary and Folkloric Fairies in Modern Paganisms," in *Magic and Witchery in the Modern West: Celebrating the Twentieth Anniversary of "The Triumph of the Moon,"* ed. Shai Feraro and Ethan Doyle White (New York: Palgrave Macmillan, 2019), 109–10.

[112] Young Buck, "An Historical Overview of the Whereabouts of Gnomes and Elves, Fauns and Faeries, Goblins, Ogres, Trolls and Bogies, Nymphs, Sprites and Dryads, Past and Present," *FireHeart* 6 (1991): 8–10.

[113] Ted Andrews, *Enchantment of the Faerie Realm: Communicate with Nature Spirits & Elementals* (Saint Paul, MN: Llewellyn Publications, 1993), 1–2.

[114] Cassandra Eason, *A Complete Guide to Fairies and Magical Beings* (London: Judy Piatkus Publishers, 2001), 216.

[115] Abram, *The Spell of the Sensuous: Perception and Language in a More-Than-Human World*. Pike shows, however, that pagan authors sometimes hold competing ideas of nature,

Pagans see humans and fairies as part of a "plurispecies community" (per Bird-David) partially severed by modernity but accessible to those who seek it.[116]

Broadly taken, these fairies are much sanitized from their medieval and early modern iterations, a process of "taming" that reflects the eclectic combination of folkloric scholarship, literature (especially Victorian and Edwardian), and fantasy media that informs them.[117] Goblins, though, sometimes maintain their tricky or malevolent nature from centuries past. John Kruse, for example, views goblins as having a spectrum of pre-dispositions from helpful to malicious and distinct from hags, bogles, and boggarts within the larger category of fairy "land beasts."[118] D.J. Conway is less charitable, arguing that goblins are inherently antagonistic to earth spirits because of their "malicious mischief and evil cunning."[119] They enjoy frightening and terrorizing humans, and if they infiltrate one's home, it is difficult to get rid of them. Echoing a different tradition,

presenting "the earth as nurturing Mother who takes care of her human children and wild nature as unknowable and unconstrained by human categories, a nature unconcerned about human life." Sarah M. Pike, "'Wild Nature' and the Lure of the Past: The Legacy of Romanticism Among Young Pagan Environmentalists," in *Magic and Witchery in the Modern West: Celebrating the Twentieth Anniversary of "The Triumph of the Moon"* ed. Shai Feraro and Ethan Doyle White (New York: Palgrave Macmillan, 2019), 133.

[116] Nurit Bird-David, "Size Matters! The Scalability of Modern Hunter-Gatherer Animism," *Quaternary International* 464 (2018): 305–14. Most pagan texts that I encountered created a fairly rigid binary between humans and fairies. Such divisions are complicated, though, by those who see themselves as having souls or parts of fairies within them. Miguel Astor-Aguilera and Graham Harvey, *Rethinking Relations and Animism: Personhood and Materiality* (New York: Routledge, 2020); Nurit Bird-David, "A Peer-to-Peer Connected Cosmos: Beyond Egalitarian/Hierarchical Hunter-Gatherer Societies," *L'Homme* 236 (2020): 77–106. These scholarly ideas owe much to the work of Philippe Descola, who argues for an ethnographic approach to the environment framed "from the standpoint of the dynamic interactions between the techniques used in socializing nature and the symbolic systems that organize them." Philippe Descola, *In the Society of Nature: A Native Ecology in Amazonia*, trans. Nora Scott (New York: Cambridge University Press, 1994), 2–3.

[117] Magliocco, "The Taming of the Fae: Literary and Folkloric Fairies in Modern Paganisms," 107–8.

[118] John T. Kruse, *Beyond Faery: Exploring the World of Mermaids, Kelpies, Goblins & Other Faery Beasts* (Woodbury: Llewellyn Publications, 2020), 129–54.

[119] D.J. Conway, *The Ancient Art of Faery Magick* (Berkeley: The Crossing Press, 2005). McCoy similarly states that "goblin is a generic term for a malicious, dark, ugly faery, one who is generally disliked and unwelcome even by other faery folk." Edain McCoy, *A Witch's Guide to Faery Folk: How to Work with the Elemental World* (Saint Paul, MN: Llewellyn Publications, 1994), 173.

Nancy Arrowsmith sees helpful household brownies as the equivalent to hobgoblins (which are almost extinct) and leaves the term "goblin" unexamined.[120] These distinctions are sometimes framed, too, around broader categories like Seelie and Unseelie to distinguish between benevolent and malevolent fairies.[121] Such associations need not necessarily be tied to belief at all. The EarthSpirit community, for example, holds an annual "Goblin Market" fair that invokes fond associations of fey beings and the craftsmanship of goblins without ritualistically interfacing with them.

More important than the specifics of these categorizations, though, is the belief that these fairies can exist on this earth and interact with humans physically, psychologically, and/or spiritually. No longer are fairies the product of rural ignorance. Instead, rural people of centuries past possessed a connection to the earth that was lost on educated elites and the technologies that surrounded them. This argumentation flips the centuries-old trope of urban academics disparaging rural people and elevates the latter as having a timeless connection to nature and its spirits. Pagans seek to re-enchant a world dominated by industrialization and capitalism; they embrace immanence (the presence of the divine in the material world) and encourage others to do so.[122]Accordingly, many pagan authors describe their own experiences with fairies or in Fairyland in the hopes that others can follow in their footsteps; such phenomena are likewise documented among anthropologists who have embedded themselves in these communities.[123]

---

[120] Nancy Arrowsmith, *Field Guide to the Little People* (Hill and Wang: New York, 1977), 120–22.

[121] Tara Sanchez, *Urban Faery Magick: Connecting to the Fae in the Modern World* (Woodbury: Llewellyn Publications, 2021), 8.

[122] Marshall Sahlins, *The New Science of the Enchanted Universe: An Anthropology of Most of Humanity* (Princeton: Princeton University Press, 2022).

[123] See, especially, Magliocco, *Witching Culture: Folklore and Neo-Paganism in America*, 1–19. Goulet and Miller argue that ethnographers must acknowledge and embrace extraordinary experiences within their work: "In our field experience, transformative events lived with others in their world cannot be wished away. Our hosts know this and we do too. They expect us to take seriously what we have lived with them and have learned from them. In other words, the expectation is that we rise to the challenge of effective and respectful cross-cultural communication. We are called to transcend our own ethnocentrism and to explore forms of knowledge production and knowledge dissemination that serve the best interests of our hosts and our profession." Jean-Guy A. Goulet and Bruce Granville Miller, "Embodied Knowledge: Steps toward a Radical Anthropology of Cross-Cultural Encounters," in *Extraordinary Anthropology: Transformations in the Field*, ed. Jean-Guy A. Goulet and Bruce Granville Miller (Lincoln: University of Nebraska Press, 2007), 7. This discourse resembles

Within this rich corpus of pagan beliefs, folkloric and fantastical tropes often merge. Cassandra Eason, for example, sees the works of Tolkien and Lewis as expressing larger truths about spiritual dissatisfaction with modernity. Their worlds, which see "no real divisions between magic and spirituality, Fairyland, religion and the Otherworld," might reflect the reality of our distant ancestors. Eason's consideration of goblins thus draws on some of the tropes found in Middle-earth alongside those more associated with folklore:

> Another fairy foe that is as inimical to other fairies as to humans is the goblin or orc of Germanic and Scandinavian origin. Goblins are small, strong, black and ugly, with eyes like glowing coals. These spiteful creatures of the night shun daylight, roam in bands, live in dark, underground places or deep forests and are often regarded as the antithesis of the elves. In Tolkien's *The Hobbit* the Goblin King captured and enslaved the dwarves and Bilbo for a time in the mines of the Misty Mountains. Goblins are notorious in folklore for capturing other fairy people and forcing them to work as slaves in their mines.
>
> Goblins are great shape-shifters but, true to kind, turn into wild animals, bats or owls. They terrify and harass travelers and children. ... Goblins are also associated with the darker side of Halloween, their special festival when they roam unchecked over the Earth.[124]

Eason rejects the classification of hobgoblins as sinister variations of their kin. Instead, they are "harmless" domestic spirits that resemble brownies of Scotland, and authors who assert otherwise have erroneously absorbed the "dark image" of hobgoblins from fantasy media. Not all agree with Eason. The solitary worship of pagans, combined with the ease of self-publishing in the digital age, has resulted in the production of texts from authors with claimed personal experiences dealing with goblins. J.D. Wizard, apparently well-versed in summoning them, sees goblins as defined by "honesty" and as "stubborn, opinionated, outspoken, pranky people who delight in handing out justice to people who think they're

---

to some degree the debate in media studies on the relationship between academics who enjoy a certain kind of media and the groups about which they write—hence the coining of the term "acafan." Henry Jenkins, "The Origins of 'Acafan,'" *Pop Junctions: Reflections on Entertainment, Pop Culture, Activism, Media Literacy, Fandom and More* (blog), June 20, 2011, http://henryjenkins.org/blog/2011/06/acafandom_and_beyond_week_two.html

[124] Eason, *A Complete Guide to Fairies and Magical Beings*, 93–95, 166–67.

clever enough to get away with intentionally causing malice."[125] S. Rob Invictus provides descriptions of spells that channel goblins (via Hermes) to give strength, power, money, and health to its casters.[126] More detailed, still, is the *Goblin Grimoire* of Jake Edward Bretherick, which seeks to move beyond the "regurgitated Christian propaganda" surrounding goblins and to see them for what they really are: a "shadow of the human psyche" that (while certainly an actual creature) also invites humans to consider "what is ugly or undesirable in ourselves." Bretherick considers the many species within the goblin genus (itself part of the Fey family), both historical and personal, as well as the spells and magical formulas brought to him by goblins.[127]

Looking for some continuity or coherence in this sea of perspectives, I reached out to a handful of pagan organizations in 2024 to see what their leaders thought about goblins. Their responses highlight the diversity of perspectives within modern paganism. Some see them as outside their belief system. Selena Fox of the Circle Sanctuary writes that "we connect with the Divine and spiritual dimensions in many forms and many ways, but work with Goblins is not part of our spiritual tradition and practices."[128] Similarly, George Franklin of Reclaiming Quarterly notes that, although he could not speak for all in his community, "I haven't heard people talk about goblins. Some speak of 'faeries' or 'the fey.'"[129] These perspectives are by no means universal, however. The Director of Records at Spirit Haven, Riven Lake, writes that "in modern Paganism … Goblins are considered spirit guides and magical entities that can be reconnected with through stories, spells, and ritual."[130] Ben Kowalsky-Grahek, President of The Troth, acknowledges that "for the most part we don't believe in goblins" in so far as many think of them. Instead, he tentatively equates the goblin with the "vætt" or "wight" as a "general term for some sort of

[125] J.D. Wizard, *Goblin*, 2022.

[126] S. Rob Invictus, *Goblin Magick for Strength and Power*, 2017.

[127] The historical groupings are hobgoblin, bugbear, clurichaun, dokkaebi, fear dearg, kappa, and redcap. His personal groupings are betwixter, bloodlin(g), copper, eye, mask, night tribe, pookie, remnant, spider, snatcher, and unclassified. Jake Edward Bretherick, *Goblin Grimoire*, 2024.

[128] Selena Fox, "Query on Goblins," November 10, 2024, https://www.circlesanctuary.org/

[129] George Franklin, "Query on Goblins," November 11, 2024, https://www.weaveandspin.org/

[130] Riven Lake, "Query on Goblins," November 11, 2024, https://spirit-haven.org/

'spirit' out there in the world around us" that ought to be engaged kindly, truthfully, and with "generosity and care."[131] Morgan Daimler, a prolific author on pagan topics and priest of Na Daoine Maithe, is similarly open to their existence. Although she has no personal experiences with them, she prefers "to believe they at least potentially exist" based on the "wide body of folk belief" surrounding them. Because some pagans believe in them, they "do exist spiritually," even if their physical presence on earth is uncertain. The characteristics of goblins are difficult to parse because of their frequent conflation with other preternatural creatures, but Daimler sees hobgoblins as a "less malicious and more helpful" subtype of goblins writ large.[132] Taken together, these responses give some sense of the diversity of goblin-related beliefs among pagans.[133]

Fairy belief today is not restricted to pagan communities. Simon Young's two-volume *Fairy Census* contains one thousand self-reported encounters that individuals had with fairies, collected from 2014 to 2023.[134] Those who contributed to this collection come from diverse backgrounds, including various Christian denominations, and represent only a fraction of those sympathetic to fairy beliefs.[135] That said, goblins

[131] Ben Kowalsky-Grahek, "Query on Goblins," November 8, 2024, https://thetroth.org/

[132] Morgan Daimler, "Query on Goblins," November 15, 2024, https://lairbhan.blogspot.com/

[133] The conspiracy-minded Frederick William Holiday posthumously published a treatise on the unexplainable particularities of the universe and the follies of science in Frederick William Holiday, *The Goblin Universe*, ed. Colin Wilson (Saint Paul, MN: Llewellyn Publications, 1986).

[134] Details on the *Fairy Census* can be found here: https://www.fairyist.com/survey/. Citations for this work will be simplified as Young, *Fairy Census*, [volume]:[entry]. I have used the PDFs made publicly available by Young for the following analysis. This project is an extension of earlier projects, especially *Seeing Fairies*, which reports fairy encounters in the early twentieth century. One entry from Leeds in 1926–27 mentions the presence of "a little creature of the goblin type" with "blue-and-white pantaloons and a little jacket, and he had a curious small, mischievous face." This creature appeared to Muriel M. Golding, who had insomnia after a bout of the flu. After kicking up the blankets of her bed, he put his face on a pillow, winked, and then disappeared. Golding reflects: "If he came to cheer me … he certainly succeeded." Marjorie T. Johnson, *Seeing Fairies: From the Lost Archives of the Fairy Investigation Society, Authentic Reports of Fairies in Modern Times* (San Antonio: Anomalist Books, 2014).

[135] It is impossible to precisely quantify belief in fairies (however "belief" is defined), though a 2017 survey from the Pew Research Center reported that around two-thirds of Americans "hold supernatural or paranormal beliefs of some kind, including beliefs in reincarnation, spiritual energy and psychic powers." This number is lower in the United Kingdom

are uncommon within this census (named in less than twenty of them), but their appearances show a continuation of ideas expressed in earlier chapters of this history. One respondent from Somerset (England) describes "tribal" dancing from two otherworldly female figures and "a small dwarf or goblin, covered in leaves and branches." The females "seemed delighted he had made an appearance," and he was soon followed by a vaguely humanoid mass of soil, mud, and rock.[136] Another encounter from Cork in Ireland involves "little gobliny type men running in and out of bushes … about two-feet tall, very dark skinned, swarthy with big noses," and one entry from the midwestern United States details an ongoing psychic relationship with Robin Goodfellow.[137] Some encounters were more hostile. One person reports goblins creating a sense of "crippling fear, dread, uneasiness," and another notes the presence of "frightening neon goblins" in their room as a sick child.[138]

Perhaps as important as the naming of goblins within these encounters is the use of them to denote a particular preternatural aesthetic. The above entry from Cork shows that the reporter envisioned a certain "gobliny" archetype that broadly applied to creatures of a certain appearance. Another encounter features creatures "like beautiful little goblins," and one late-night meeting involves "what I can only describe as a goblin."[139] When one respondent sees "dark hairless creatures with long skinny limbs," they speculate that they had encountered "goblins maybe."[140] A tiny creature hunched by a tree is likewise what one person "would expect a goblin to look like."[141] Because of the amorphous boundaries of the fairies and the fleeting nature of their appearances, respondents are not always comfortable saying that a particular entity was a goblin. Instead, they bear

(approximately 43%). Clay Routledge, "Don't Believe in God? Maybe You'll Try U.F.O.s," *The New York Times*, July 21, 2017; Grant Bailey, "Top 10 Unconventional Beliefs Held by People in Britain Confirmed in New Study," *The Independent*, January 5, 2023, https://www.the-independent.com/news/uk/ghost-aliens-paranormal-beliefs-b2256483.html

[136] Young, *Fairy Census*, I:118.

[137] Young, *Fairy Census*, I:144 and II:783.

[138] Young, *Fairy Census*, II:590B and 680.

[139] Young, *Fairy Census*, I:189 and II:533A. In a different survey, a respondent answered the question, "What was a boggart for you?" with "At first, probably a nameless horror, but as I read fairy stories and saw illustrations in them, I think my idea of a boggart developed into a goblin or troll type of creature." Young, *The Boggart: Folklore, History, Place-Names and Dialect*, 159.

[140] Young, *Fairy Census*, II:590B.

[141] Young, *Fairy Census*, II:714.

a resemblance to the idea of a goblin that already existed in their minds. These categorical ambiguities are sometimes even explicitly addressed. A respondent from Ohio notes how their house was home to goblins that sometimes stole their belongings, though they understood "that the Fae are known by many names."[142] Another, borrowing a historically Scottish term, defines fairies broadly as encompassing "Goblins, Brownies, Boggarts and a lot of other unseelie creatures."[143]

Young's *Fairy Census* does not aim to make definitive claims about the existence of fairies, which is a meaningful departure from the goals of earlier compendia from Walter Evans-Wentz and Marjorie T. Johnson. Nor do I. In describing contemporary claims of fairy interactions, I hope to show the persistence of certain themes common in earlier iterations of goblins from folklore and literature. Goblins are likely to be short, dark-skinned, and masculine, though exceptions can be found for even these basic descriptors. They can be associated with natural environments or domesticity, and they can have dispositions that range from friendly to hostile—though the most malevolent characteristics of folkloric goblins have largely evaporated in these modern interpretations. In the case of modern paganism, encounters with goblins and their fairy kin are often framed as an explicit attempt to return to an enchanted time before the onslaughts of Christianity, science, and industrialization pushed the fairies away. These attempts to reverse the perpetual recession of the fairies hearken back to an idealized time when humans and more-than-humans peacefully co-existed.

THE UNDERAPPRECIATED BEAUTY OF GOBLINCORE

During the COVID-19 pandemic, Internet communities dedicated to shared aesthetic preferences exploded in popularity. As people sought reprieve from the claustrophobia and tedium of social distancing, they congregated on digital platforms like Tumblr, Pinterest, and Reddit, united by algorithms designed to create continuous engagement among users, to discuss and share their takes on Dark Academia, Acid Pixie, Feralcore, Preppy, and Cottagecore (among many others).[144] Although

---

[142] Young, *Fairy Census*, I:348.

[143] Young, *Fairy Census*, I:428.

[144] Guro Flinterud, "'Folk' in the Age of Algorithms: Theorizing Folklore on Social Media Platforms," *Folklore* 134, no. 4 (2023): 493–461.

these aesthetics might have a titular connection to a historical group or era, they represent a contemporary vision of a style based on a collective and contested memory.[145] As such, members of the Punk aesthetic are not necessarily fond of the lifestyle of actual participants in the Punk-rock movement. Instead, they distill this movement into an aesthetic essence (mohawks, leather jackets, piercings). The people who congregate in aesthetic forums are experiencing a taste of a particular style, though without the in-person community that it once entailed.[146]

One such aesthetic is Goblincore, which is first attested in the late 2010s but surged during the summer and fall of 2020. This style, as defined by its subreddit of over 158,000 members (as of November 2024), is "inspired by the folklore of goblins, centered on the celebration of natural ecosystems usually considered less beautiful by conventional norms."[147] The ugliness of goblins is central to this aesthetic, whose members find natural beauty in wildlife that is not appreciated as such. A similar framing is found on its Aesthetics Wiki page:

> Goblincore is an aesthetic based on the appreciation of aspects of nature that are not typically regarded as beautiful. These aspects can range from animals such as frogs and snails to materials such as moss, mud, plants, and fungi such as mushrooms. A part of this beloved "ugliness" is the Goblin itself, a malevolent thieving creature in European folklore, but in Goblincore a carefree representation of one's infatuation with nature's "ugliness" and general unpredictability.[148]

Goblincore uses its preternatural inspiration as an avatar for underappreciated beauty in the environment and a reclamation of lifeforms often

---

[145] Anthony Bak Buccitelli, "Fairytale as Fuck: Antimodern Media, Sensory Experience, and the Folkloresque," in *Möbius Media: Popular Culture, Folklore, and the Folkloresque*, ed. Jeffrey A. Tolbert and Michael Dylan Foster (Logan: Utah State University Press, 2024), 86–112.

[146] Kaitlyn Tiffany, "Cottagecore Was Just the Beginning," The Atlantic, February 5, 2021; Terry Nguyen, "Trends Are Dead," Vox, May 11, 2022, https://www.vox.com/the-goods/23065462/trends-death-subcultures-style; Mireille Silcoff, "Teen Subcultures Are Fading. Pity the Poor Kids.," *The New York Times*, February 21, 2024, https://www.nytimes.com/2024/02/21/magazine/aesthetics-tiktok-teens.html

[147] As of December 2024, this subreddit has over 162,000 members: https://www.reddit.com/r/goblincore/

[148] "Goblincore," Aesthetics Wiki, December 1, 2024, https://aesthetics.fandom.com/wiki/Goblincore

considered to be ugly. It has an additional emphasis on sustainability, seen in the reuse of household objects and the hoarding of discarded items (especially shiny ones) found in nature. This aesthetic centrally locates the goblin as representative of a particular style—and it is one of many creatures from Fairyland subject to this aesthetic reappraisal. Fairycore prioritizes the parts of nature more commonly regarded as beautiful and feminine. Elfcore is its more masculine counterpart. Pixiecore, meanwhile, emphasizes "more tunics and t-shirts" as well as indoor gardening and baths. These aesthetics distill preternatural creatures into a style informed by an amorphous combination of folklore, literature, multimedia, and other cultural associations. Although they celebrate the beauty and diversity of nature (often paired with rejections of modern consumerism), its communities primarily congregate in online spaces.

Goblincore pages are filled with imagery of mushrooms, snails, frogs, old jewelry, bugs, moss, worms, hoarded trinkets, dreary forests, and living spaces with recycled furniture. Goblincore media, as listed on its Aesthetics Wiki page, includes *Where the Wild Things Are*, *The Hobbit*, the *Frog and Toad* series, *Labyrinth*, *Gremlins*, *Princess Mononoke*, *Over the Garden Wall*, and *Stardew Valley*. As of December 2024, the highest scoring posts of all time on r/goblincore are pictures of wooden birdhouses with faces hand-carved into them; wooden fungi called "Booty-ful Mushrooms" with the expected voluptuousness suggested by their title; toilet paper dispensers shaped like toads; and a cross-section of a purple cabbage that looks like an "enchanted fairy path leading to a glowing doorway." Gone in this subreddit are any references to the malevolent deeds of folkloric or fantastical goblins. Instead, quirky nature and art inspired by them are dominant.

Some on Goblincore forums call themselves "practicing Goblins," and this aesthetic's emphasis on non-traditional beauty has contributed to its popularity among the LGBTQ+ community. A subgroup calls themselves "Enby Goblins" in reference to their non-binary identities. One community member elaborates: "For me, as an autistic nonbinary individual, I find goblincore as a safe community. … I identify as a goblin since to me, goblins are little sneaky critters with no real sense of gender identity."[149] User overlap between subreddits shows the prominence of non-binary

---

[149] Mary Frances Knapp, "The Essentials of Goblincore, a Digital Community of Faeries, Frogs, and Nonbinary Folks," Vice, March 24, 2021, https://www.vice.com/en/article/goblincore-aesthetic-essentials/

members in the Goblincore community. Posters in r/goblincore are seventy-eight times more likely than an average user to post in r/nonbinary and fifty-nine times more likely to post in r/witchesvspatriarchy (the two highest correlations).[150] Other demographic trends on online forums are difficult to parse because of user anonymity, though these spaces seem to cater to American and British users with reliable Internet access. For those that actively post, too, proximity to forests or wooded areas is a clear benefit.[151]

Alongside this pro-LGBTQ+ dynamic is a decidedly anti-capitalist one. Goblincore's embrace of nature and thrifting has inspired countless posts about the excesses of modern capitalism and consumerism. One user fantasizes, "[I]magine u r living inside a tiny mushroom house … with a tiny chimney. … deep in the woods. … no one knows u exist. … u make soup in a tiny pot … u are free."[152] Another shows an image of an anthropomorphic mole drinking tea beneath a giant mushroom in the rain with the caption: "stop glamorising The Hustle and start glamorising whatever lifestyle this is."[153] Posts' titles like "No more capitalism only foraging and friendship" and "Reject Capitalism, embrace the Goblin" are representative of this kind of thought, which yearns for a bucolic and ahistorical time when humans were peacefully surrounded by nature and free from the societal burdens of the twenty-first century. Discussion of this lifestyle ironically takes place on the most modern of technologies, the Internet, and is more of an escapist fantasy than a concerted movement to abandon

---

[150] The data used from these statistics comes from https://subredditstats.com, which reflects traffic on Reddit through 2023 (when API changes to the site restricted access to data from third-party platforms).

[151] The association of goblins with gender non-conformity has seeped outside of Internet spaces, too. In season three of HBO's hit dramedy, *The White Lotus*, finance bro Saxon (played by Patrick Schwarzenegger) mocks his more liberal sister Piper (played by Sarah Catherine Hook) for telling him that women are not attracted to "super jacked" guys. His response: "Really? What are they into, Piper? Gender goblins that tuck their dicks between their legs?" "Hide or Seek." *The White Lotus*, directed by Mike White, 3.4 (HBO, March 9, 2025).

[152] Originally from Twitter, this quotation was reposted in meowstash321, "Bliss," *Goblincore Subreddit*, April 14, 2022, https://www.reddit.com/r/goblincore/comments/u3mqi0/bliss/

[153] lucillegooseberry, "Seeeeeriously," *Goblincore Subreddit*, April 24, 2002, https://www.reddit.com/r/goblincore/comments/ub2i79/seeeeeriously/. Image is from Wallace Tripp, *A Great Big Ugly Man Came Up and Tied His Worse to Me: A Book of Nonsense Verse* (Boston: Little, Brown and Company, 1973), 37.

the comforts of modernity. Perhaps inevitably, too, the popularity of Goblincore has resulted in a cottage industry of related products. Some vendors attempt to square this capitalistic circle with rhetoric about sustainability; others simply list Goblincore alongside a slew of other aesthetics to increase search engine optimization for nature-themed jewelry, occult paraphernalia, and earth-toned clothing.[154]

The Goblincore aesthetic uses the ugliness of goblins as a theme around which community members can reframe the beauty of nature and the lifestyle that should accompany it. In a rejection of the historically masculine presentation of goblins, the framing of this aesthetic is often explicitly feminine and non-binary. For many, it is an online trend that occupies a portion of their social media feeds. Others have built more holistic approaches to living based loosely on its ideas. McKayla Coyle's *Goblin Mode: How to Get Cozy, Embrace Imperfection, and Thrive in the Muck* provides the most detailed guide to how people can move these Internet discussions into the real world to live their happiest goblin life. To Coyle, the unifying feature of goblins is their weirdness, which practicing goblins should proudly wear on their sleeve as they practice the tenets of the Goblin Code: to see beauty everywhere, embrace your weirdness, get cozy, celebrate clutter, be a good community member, and honor nature. She concludes that "honoring our goblin selves means celebrating our passions, asserting our right to green spaces, listening to our bodies, watching the world with curiosity, and prioritizing comfort."[155] Coyle distills the aesthetic preferences of Goblincore forums into a guide for better living, using the goblin as an embodiment of a certain kind of anti-conformist lifestyle.

To some, the desired inclusivity of this movement is undermined by its titular subject matter. Indeed, perhaps the most striking feature of the Goblincore Aesthetic Wiki is a "Sensitivity Content Notice" at the top of the page, which notes that it "may be seen as racist (specifically as antisemetic [sic], stereotyping, bigotry, and the issue of people not being able

---

[154] *The Guardian* reports a 652% increase in Goblincore-related items between July 2020 and July 2021. Ellie Violet Bramley, "Goblincore: The Fashion Trend That Embraces 'Chaos, Dirt and Mud,'" *The Guardian*, July 30, 2021, https://www.theguardian.com/fashion/2021/jul/30/goblincore-fashion-trend-embraces-chaos-dirt-mud

[155] To Coyle (a "lesbian writer" who uses they/them pronouns), the one idea unifying goblins—from Puck to the Green Goblin—is that they "are all weirdos." McKayla Coyle, *Goblin Mode: How to Get Cozy, Embrace Imperfection, and Thrive in the Muck* (Philadelphia: Quirk Books, 2023), 16, 21–26, 207.

to distinguish between ancient folkloric traditions and more recent anti-Jewish propaganda)."[156] Discussion about antisemitism in Goblincore is traceable to 2019 as the movement gained traction on Internet forums but escalated in December 2021 when Jon Stewart noted the antisemitic tropes embedded in goblins from the *Harry Potter* film series and compared them to depictions of Jews in *The Protocols of the Elders of Zion* (1903).[157]

Discourse about various forms of antisemitic goblins surged into 2022, including a blog post titled "The Antisemitic History of Goblins," which ties folkloric goblins to antisemitic stereotypes dating back to the Middle Ages. The author speculates that "goblins as a whole do seem to have dubious origins," though she acknowledges depictions of them may or may not be antisemitic depending on the context.[158] Another post quoted at length on Aesthetics Wiki cautions readers to avoid warted, hooked noses on their goblins and the stereotype of the "greedy little goblin," both of which (to the author) veer into the realm of antisemitism.[159] Some even advocated for a change of the community's title to Gremlincore, reflecting a perceived underlying similarity between gremlins and goblins (though without the historical baggage).[160] Defenders of Goblincore, seeking to circumvent this controversy, urge community members to envision goblins as fey creatures that operate outside of these fraught historical contexts.

This debate about the antisemitism of goblins has had the dual effect of elevating discussions about the intersection of folklore and anti-Jewish

---

[156] This notice was posted in December 2023, though the section on antisemitism in the main body of the page was added in August 2020 (initially under a "Discourse" heading that was later edited to "Criticism"). The apparent impetus for this section was a (now deleted) post on Tumblr: "I'm Jewish, and I can guarantee you it's far from a consensus that goblins are inherently anti-Semitic. Also, not in favor of brigading a kid on Tumblr for making mistakes in the way they responded to something."

[157] Jon Stewart, "The Problem With Goblins: J. K. Rowling, Harry Potter, & Jews," The Problem with Jon Stewart, December 16, 2021, https://www.youtube.com/watch?v=DzffpeYnv-w&list=PL4RaSiGWHbPKMpVO5ILO-ocOnd-_Rday1&index=71

[158] Evelyn Frick, "The Antisemitic History of Goblins," heyalma, February 23, 2023, https://www.heyalma.com/the-antisemitic-history-of-goblins/

[159] This post admittedly pre-dates the flurry of discussion in 2022. "The Two Types of Goblincore," *Just Some Guy* (blog), July 3, 2019, https://the-kazoo-kid.tumblr.com/post/186034379297/the-two-types-of-goblincore

[160] Gremlins were a creation of members of the Royal Air Force in the early twentieth century to explain mechanical malfunctions on aircrafts.

sentiment while minimizing other unsavory tropes historically associated with goblins. The question of whether goblins are antisemitic is tied to the one's definition of the creature, which is so varied (and often so broad) as to make the question an impossibility to answer with any kind of totality. Some goblins or creatures often categorized as them have clear ties to antisemitic tropes, including later iterations of the "knockers" of Cornwall.[161] G.K. Chesterton, an English writer of the early twentieth century (quoted earlier in relation to Dickens), likely used the template of the grotesque goblin when he wrote about the unnatural appearance and corrupting influence of Jews.[162] One modern scholar argued, too, that the antagonists of *Goblin Market* were encoded in antisemitic language to create a "lush theological fantasy of Jewish erasure."[163] Goblins in the *Harry Potter* film series also have antisemitic characteristics (greedy, disfigured, hooked-nosed bankers), regardless of underlying authorial or directorial intent.[164]

Other visual correlations between goblins and Jewish caricatures are more difficult to parse, as similarities in appearance do not necessarily show antisemitic causation. As I discussed in Chap. 2, as early as the

---

[161] Manning shows that the changing face of capitalism was a central preoccupation surrounding beliefs in the knocker, including the development of it as "ghosts of Jewish miners who were also fairies." Paul Manning, "Jewish Ghosts, Knackers, Tommyknockers, and Other Sprites of Capitalism in the Cornish Mines," *Cornish Studies* 13, no. 1 (2005): 217. James argues, too, that the "Jewish association of the knockers is yet another unique Cornish fingerprint in the realm of European folklore. That said, it is important to place this motif in perspective: the Jewish origin of the knockers was conjecture applied at a later date. The knockers began as underground fairies, and people, as they did throughout Europe, blended these sorts of supernatural beings with ghosts and other traditions." James, *The Folklore of Cornwall: The Oral Tradition of a Celtic Nation*, 143.

[162] Simon Mayers, *Chesterton's Jews: Stereotypes and Caricatures in the Literature and Journalism of G.K. Chesterton* (Independently Published, 2013), 56–64.

[163] Scheinberg, *Women's Poetry and Religion in Victorian England: Jewish Identity and Christian Culture*, 126.

[164] Critics were divided on whether such correlations indicate antisemitic causation. Shira Hanau, "Jon Stewart Says J.K. Rowling's 'Harry Potter' Goblin Characters Clearly Antisemitic," *The Times of Israel*, January 5, 2022, https://www.timesofisrael.com/jon-stewart-says-the-harry-potter-goblin-characters-are-clearly-antisemitic/; Eliya Smith, "I Am Begging You All to Please Shut up about the Harry Potter Jew-Goblins," Forward, January 5, 2022, https://forward.com/culture/480388/please-shut-up-about-the-harry-potter-jew-goblins-antisemitism-jk-rowling/; "Goblins, Jews, and Antisemitism," *Jewitches* (blog), accessed December 1, 2024, https://jewitches.com/blogs/blog/goblins-jews-and-anti-semitism-1?srsltid=AfmBOorp3uNrp2cCC9l5ifsvK2X4iChnYd542qEPtDh rA7lYB0_nw4PS

Middle Ages, some non-Christians were seen as "literally ugly as sin." Latin Christians commonly depicted Jews, Muslims, Africans, and Mongols as "monstrous races" with grotesque features similar to demons.[165] Bodily distortions (including long noses and ears) that rendered goblins and Jews occasionally similar in caricatured appearance were the result of Christian prejudice well into the twentieth century more than any underlying folkloric connection. The presence of a handful of children's books written by Jewish authors about Judaism featuring goblins (including *Hershel and the Hanukkah Goblins*, which received a Caldecott Honor in 1990) undermines the idea that the goblin itself is antisemitic—even if some examples cherry-picked from its history do fall into this category.[166]

What is most striking about this discussion of goblins and antisemitism, however, is the extent to which it has minimized other historical tropes related to these creatures that would be seemingly unpalatable to modern audiences. I have not seen any discussions on Goblincore forums about the historical association of goblins with "freakery" and disability. Nor have I encountered any conversations about the racist and racialist theories surrounding the relationship of fairies and goblins to the pygmies of Central Africa. Such concerns take a back seat to discussions of antisemitism, I expect, because of the popularity of *Harry Potter* (and to a lesser extension *The Lord of the Rings*) among those in the Goblincore community, which caused people to project concerns about modern antisemitism onto earlier historical iterations. The amplifying effect of outrage within Internet algorithms resulted in a brief flurry of activity about this topic in 2021 and 2022, though it has since died down. Forums dedicated to Goblincore today are mostly devoid of this controversy and instead filled with the peculiar beauty that its members enjoy.

---

[165] Strickland, *Saracens, Demons, & Jews: Making Monsters in Medieval Art*, 29.

[166] *Hershel and the Hannukah Goblins* details how the Jewish folk hero, Hershel of Ostopol, deals with goblins that haunt his synagogue during Hanukkah. Hershel plays tricks on the goblins (some small and winged, others large and reptilian) and stops them from interfering with the lighting of the menorah. The king of the goblins, batlike and demonic, destroys Hershel's synagogue but has no power over the candles of the menorah. Eric Kimmel, *Hershel and the Hanukkah Goblins* (New York: Holiday House, 1989). *There's a Goblin on the Ark* narrates how the animals that aboard Noah's Ark come to accept the presence of two goblins aboard the ship—a story designed to help Jewish families celebrate differences and gender fluidity. Susan Tarcov, *There's a Goblin on the Ark!* (Millburn: Apples & Honey Press, 2023). See also Zoe Klein, *The Goblins of Knottingham: A History of Challah* (Millburn: Apples & Honey Press, 2017).

ENTERING AND EXITING GOBLIN MODE

Aesthetic communities based on the inhabitants of Fairyland allow members to construct styles that conform to their preconception of a given creature. Goblincore forums provide a place for people to both share their love for an underappreciated kind of nature and critique prevailing standards of beauty. This latter preoccupation is pertinent to the second goblin-related phenomenon to emerge in the twenty-first century: Goblin Mode. Though first attested via social media in 2009, the term surged in popularity in 2022 as restrictions on social distancing eased and people began to return to their pre-Covid lifestyles. Like any grassroots Internet phenomenon, the idea of entering Goblin Mode has numerous interpretations, but they gravitate around an embodiment of appearances and behaviors that defy societal expectations—especially with regard to the glamor of social media.

In the early 2000s, the term "goblin mode" was used in isolated contexts and without the underlying mentality that defined its later usage. In 2000, the Cincinnati Zoo went into "goblin mode" for its annual Halloween festivities.[167] Willem Dafoe distinguished between his character in *Spider-Man* (2002) being in "Norman mode" and "Goblin mode."[168] A 2007 review of an Edmonton-based production of *The Enchantment* (inspired by *Goblin Market*) notes how its creatures go into "full goblin-cavort mode" when harassing the sisters—an attempt at chaos that is unfortunately undermined by their "silly" appearance and maneuvers that resemble "a class in modern dance."[169] In February 2009, a Twitter user anticipated the eventual use of the term as a kind of mentality when she posted that someone "was in full hyperactive goblin mode last night. it was as if she ate a bag of sugar-coated candy, then washed it down with a few red bulls."[170]

It would take more than a decade, however, for Goblin Mode to go viral on social media. In the intervening years, the closest trend I could

---

[167] "Pumpkin Pursuits," *The Cincinnati Post*, October 19, 2000.

[168] Susan Wloszczyna, "Willem Dafoe Finds Depth in Green Goblin Role," *Battle Creek Enquirer*, November 8, 2001.

[169] Liz Nicholls, "Refugees from the Great Repression," *Edmonton Journal*, March 14, 2007, sec. D.

[170] @jenniferdujour, Twitter, February 10, 2009: https://x.com/jenniferdujour/status/1194850359

find resembling it was the "party goblin" as described by Iliza Shlesinger in a 2016 Netflix special:

> I feel a lot of people are wired this way. I get a sip of liquor. It sends a message to my party goblin that it's time to do it. Everybody's got a party goblin. Some people have party goblins that have lost their ability to walk from partying too much. My party goblin sleeps on a bunk bed. She sleeps on the top bunk; my dignity sleeps on the bottom bunk. He is not invited. The second I taste liquor, it wakes her up. She smells it in my brains. She is sitting there, grrrr, dreaming of eating frozen pizza 'cause she is a monster.

Her party goblin then goes to the megaphone inside Shlesinger's brain and takes charge. Cue a low, monstrous voice that takes over:

> 'You need to raaaaaage! Find the door guy! Ask him if he has drugs! Do not specify. See what he comes up with! Do it! Fucking go … Go outside. Take a picture. Put it on Instagram. Take it down 10 minutes later 'cause, oops, we can see your nipple.' Like, that's what party goblins do.[171]

Shlesinger describes the party goblin lurking within us, ready to be unleashed with a sip of liquor. This bit does not quite conform with the antisocial attitude that defined entering Goblin Mode (as popularized a few years later), though it still shows an underlying impulse to associate irregular behavior with an erratic (and hilarious) goblin living within us. The idea of people entering "goblin mode" specifically began to circulate on social media in 2020. A user on Urban Dictionary defined the term as "when you lose yourself so you resort to becoming a goblin."[172] Selfies taken without makeup and animals behaving erratically could qualify as a kind of Goblin Mode. So too could certain sexual acts, as seen in a 2021 Tweet that garnered some 39,000 likes, "thinkin about how someone i used to hook up with called cowgirl position 'goblin mode.'" It took a photoshopped headline, however, for Goblin Mode to go viral, when a Twitter user misquoted Julia Fox as saying that ex-boyfriend Kanye West

---

[171] "Confirmed Kills." *Netflix Stand-Up*, directed by Iliza Shlesinger (Netflix, September 23, 2016).

[172] The posts referenced in this chapter, some of which have since been deleted, have been preserved via "Goblin Mode," KnowYourMeme, accessed December 1, 2024, https://knowyourmeme.com/memes/goblin-mode#fn1

disliked when she "went goblin mode." Interest in Goblin Mode surged for a few months as the headline circulated and, later, was debunked.

Veracity aside, Internet commentators detailed their own ideas about what it meant to enter Goblin Mode before the term became the Oxford Word of the Year in December 2022. Kari Paul of *The Guardian* writes that Goblin Mode "embraces the comforts of depravity" like simultaneously watching reality TV, scrolling through social media, and eating junk food in bed.[173] Dave McNamee, quoted in Paul's article, considers Goblin Mode a "frame of mind" that rejects the importance of visual appearance "because why would a goblin care what they look like? Why would a goblin care about presentation?" This attitude is an explicit rejection of unrealistic beauty standards on social media (especially #thatgirl) and curated pages devoted to beauty trends. One commentator describes it as the "ultimate anti-aesthetic" that is "giving the finger to the self-improvement movement," especially those advocating for a certain kind of feminine beauty.[174] Merrill Kaplan, a scholar of medieval literature and folklore, speculates that the unifying theme for people going Goblin Mode is a delightful kind of "antisocial" behavior in the sense that people entering it are "violating the norms of society."[175]

Goblin Mode is not an all-encompassing lifestyle, but rather a mindset—sometimes healthy, sometimes destructive—that one can enter and exit based on their current circumstances. Elon Musk even used the term jokingly (or maybe not, as his humor is hard to parse even with the benefit of hindsight) as an excuse for his erratic behavior. In a since-deleted tweet, Musk posted an image of Saul Goodman (*Breaking Bad* and *Better Call Saul*) with the caption, "In all fairness your honor, my client was in 'goblin mode'" in reference to his weeklong venture of buying 9% of Twitter, pondering turning its headquarters into a homeless shelter, and then

[173] Kari Paul, "Slobbing out and Giving up: Why Are so Many People Going 'Goblin Mode'?," *The Guardian*, March 14, 2022, https://www.theguardian.com/technology/2022/mar/14/slobbing-out-and-giving-up-why-are-so-many-people-going-goblin-mode

[174] Jade Wickes, "Goblin Mode Is the Spiritual Rejection of 'That Girl' Aesthetic," The Face, March 16, 2022, https://theface.com/life/goblin-mode-rejects-that-girl-aesthetic-tiktok-social-media-girlboss-culture-wellness-health-feral-girl-summer

[175] Heather Schwedel, "How Defamatory Is 'Goblin Mode' to Real Goblins?," Slate, March 23, 2022, https://slate.com/human-interest/2022/03/goblin-mode-explained-history-professor-tolkien.html

abandoning his board seat.[176] Other iterations of Goblin Mode, which uniformly have less economic significance, revolve around the ability to exit it when the time comes to enter the civilized world, only to return to this indulgent mindset when able.

In December 2022, Oxford Languages announced that "Goblin Mode" had been selected as the Oxford Word of the Year over "Metaverse" and "#IStandWith" after it garnered 318,956 votes (93% of all cast) from the public. Intended to reflect "the ethos, mood or preoccupations" of the year, Goblin Mode received the following definition:

> A slang term, often used in the expressions "in goblin mode" or "to go goblin mode"—is "a type of behaviour which is unapologetically self-indulgent, lazy, slovenly, or greedy, typically in a way that rejects social norms or expectations."[177]

Oxford Languages saw Goblin Mode as a reflection of the times, as "people are looking at social norms in new ways" and have a "license to ditch social norms and embrace new ones." This announcement sparked a flurry of headlines about Goblin Mode, including pushback about the perceived negativity of the definition from Oxford Languages. Some authors considered Goblin Mode as an appropriate rejection of unrealistic societal standards and the constant pressure for self-improvement. It is an "embrace [of] the comforts of lethargy" and, when undertaken in moderation, a way to reduce stress.[178] Psychology Today, Massachusetts General Hospital, and the Cleveland Clinic even published guidelines for ways to healthily and responsibly enter Goblin Mode.[179] This more

[176] Felix Salmon, "Elon Musk Goes into Full Goblin Mode," Axios, April 14, 2022, https://www.axios.com/2022/04/14/elon-musk-goes-into-full-goblin-mode
[177] "Oxford Word of the Year 2022," Oxford Languages, December 4, 2022, https://languages.oup.com/word-of-the-year/2022/. This was the first ever public vote for Oxford Word of the Year. The dominance of "Goblin Mode" in this electoral process was likely the result of a grassroots advocacy campaign from the forums of PC Gamer. Jennifer Schuessler, "The Word of the Year Goes Goblin Mode," *The New York Times*, December 4, 2022, https://www.nytimes.com/2022/12/04/arts/goblin-mode-oxford-word.html
[178] Sofia Phillips, "Goblin Mode: A Rejection of the Self-Improvement Movement," Medium, March 25, 2022, https://medium.com/@Sofia_Phillips/goblin-mode-a-rejection-of-the-self-improvement-movement-3c4c53565a6
[179] "Why Goblin Mode Is the New Self-Care Routine," The Cleveland Clinic, December 29, 2022, https://health.clevelandclinic.org/goblin-mode-and-your-health; Daniel Fryer, "Using 'Goblin Mode' to Reduce Stress," December 19, 2022, https://www.psychologytoday.com/us/blog/keeping-an-even-keel/202212/using-goblin-mode-to-reduce-stress;

optimistic spin on Goblin Mode is reflected in its entry from the *Cambridge Dictionary*: "[T]he behavior of someone who wants to feel comfortable and do and eat whatever they want, not caring about trying to be clean, healthy, or attractive, or about pleasing or impressing other people."[180]

Some saw more sinister undertones to this phenomenon. Disability advocates claim its lethargy is able-bodied people "cosplaying disabled life," particularly for people with chronic illnesses, for whom "goblin mode is survival mode."[181] One commentator argues that "to me, and within the crip communities I reside in, goblin mode is a natural state of being."[182] The choice of wearing the same clothes for a week, rarely leaving one's bed, and not bathing is not the same, she argues, as being restricted to these realities because of chronic disabilities. This critique inadvertently echoes some of the discourse around goblins from the nineteenth century, when humans with (perceived) atypical appearance were given the label of goblin. Such associations had been so minimized in subsequent decades, however, that these commentators did not invoke this historical precedent. Indeed, the closest comparison I have found to goblins as freaks in the twenty-first century is the musical number, "A Freak Like Me Needs Company" from the musical *Spider-Man: Turn Off the Dark*, which sees the Green Goblin fantasize about genetically manipulating others so that they are like him—a far cry from the discourse here.[183]

Others perceived a gendered double-standard at the heart of Goblin Mode. Lurking beneath the term, they argue, is the assumption that men "can behave as disgustingly as they want to without being labelled goblins, but this is not the case for women."[184] Goblin Mode is a version of

"What Is 'Goblin Mode'?—Oxford's Word of 2022," Massachusetts General Hospital, January 26, 2023, https://www.massgeneral.org/psychiatry/news/goblin-mode

[180] "Goblin Mode," *Cambridge Dictionary*, accessed December 1, 2024, https://dictionary.cambridge.org/us/dictionary/english/goblin-mode

[181] @unwellunlimitedly, Instagram, December 5, 2022: https://www.instagram.com/unwellunlimitedly/p/ClzZbR9u8CT/

[182] Hannah Turner, "As A Disabled Woman, The Goblin Mode Trend Doesn't Sit Right With Me," Refinery29, March 22, 2022, https://www.refinery29.com/en-us/goblin-mode-offensive

[183] Samuel Yates, "Spider-Man's Designer Genes: Hypercapacity and Transhumanism in a 'DIY World,'" in *The Matter of Disability: Materiality, Biopolitics, Crip Affect* (Ann Arbor: University of Michigan Press, 2019), 143–59.

[184] Morgan Lucy, "Oxford Dictionary Has Chosen 'Goblin Mode' as Its Word of the Year—What Does the Viral Term Actually Mean?," *Glamour*, December 5, 2022, https://www.glamourmagazine.co.uk/article/goblin-mode

oneself "unfit for public consumption, and for women especially, that version often involves time and money" and unending self-scrutiny.[185] Here, the perceived ugliness of the goblin takes center stage as a grotesque projection forced onto women—a marked departure from the appropriation of ugliness among some in Goblincore forums. Critiques of Goblin Mode, whether approached from ableist or gendered angles, speak to a perceived depth of societal inequalities even for a term that supposedly encouraging the rejection of contemporary mores. The goblin itself is not the subject of critique (unlike discussions around antisemitism in Goblincore), but rather the underlying motivations of humans that entered into it.

Whether spun as a destructive streak of slovenly indulgence or an act of self-care, Goblin Mode had specific resonance near the end of the most acute phase of the COVID-19 pandemic. The absurdities of certain societal expectations, particularly with regard to appearance and hygiene, were readily apparent to those wallowing in the enforced isolation of lockdowns. Interest in Goblin Mode was correspondingly fleeting—spiking in early 2022 followed by a brief surge when Oxford Libraries announced it as Word of the Year.[186] However short-lived, the popularity of Goblin Mode indicates the suitability of the goblin to embody this kind of socially subversive behavior. Commentators had a panoply of creatures onto which they could project a broader rejection of societal norms. The goblin was the creature most apt for such a designation—not a troll, gremlin, fairy, ghoul, dwarf, or anything else. It was ubiquitous and, whether visualized from readings of *Harry Potter* or folkloric compendia, had an underlying reputation for weirdness, ugliness, and erratic behaviors suitable for this mentality among humans.

[185] Marianna Manson, "Goblin Mode: Does It Have To Be A Dirty Secret That Women Don't Wear Makeup And Heels At Home?," *Grazia*, March 18, 2022, https://graziadaily.co.uk/life/opinion/goblin-mode/. See also Hayley Peppin, "Goblin Mode: Why It's Okay to Get Cozy at Home and Eat Last Night's Cheeseboard by Yourself," Bazaar, accessed December 1, 2024, https://harpersbazaar.com.au/goblin-mode-is-a-good-thing/

[186] Data from Google Trends shows a small spike in interest in "goblin mode" after the doctored headline about Julia Fox and Kanye West, followed by a substantially larger surge when the word was announced as the 2022 Oxford Word of the Year.

Conclusion

For most of this history, associating someone with a goblin dehumanized them and painted them as atypical, grotesque, or ugly. Depending on the context, it could be disparagingly applicable to sycophantic bishops, misled politicians, or entire groups of people. A much less common phenomenon was calling oneself a goblin or using it as a tongue-in-cheek nickname, which is attested only a handful of times in the nineteenth and early twentieth centuries.[187] Such isolated instances, however, pale in comparison to the rehabilitation of the goblin across genres since the 1980s and, more recently, the trend of certain groups identifying with these creatures. This chapter has provided a number of examples of the ways in which authors, directors, and game developers have minimized the malevolent tropes associated with goblins and elevated other aspects of their character. Media within this tradition has varied considerably, from the comical pranksters of Brian Froud to the multilayered half-goblin royal of Katherine Addison to the ambitious traders of *World of Warcraft*. Outside of these fantasy contexts, many modern pagans frame their beliefs in goblins and other spirits as attempts to re-connect with an enchanted world fractured by technology and environmental destruction.

The ascendency of more sympathetic goblins has made people more willing to relate to these creatures, to empathize with them, and, in some cases, to identify as them. Role-playing games provide outlets for people to inhabit these creatures within fantastical worlds, both on screens and atop tables. The Internet phenomena of Goblincore and Goblin Mode are less restrained to the confines of ludic rulesets. Instead, they speak to countercultural impulses for which goblins are fitting avatars. The former uses a selective library of folkloric and folkloresque sources to emphasize underappreciated natural beauty and a nostalgic yearning for simpler, bucolic days. The latter is a frame of mind. It rejects contemporary

---

[187] An early satirical magazine, *The Black Dwarf* (1817–1824), for example, featured a host of fictionalized correspondents operating on behalf of the eponymous Black Dwarf, including the Yellow Bonze (Japan), Blue Devil (St. James, London), and Green Goblin (Ireland). This nickname was bestowed upon Sir Israel Gollancz by one of his friends, who congratulated him "on becoming Sir Goblin" after obtaining his knighthood in 1919. Richard Hendrix, "Popular Humor and 'The Black Dwarf,'" *Journal of British Studies*, no. 1 (Autumn 1976): 124; Gordon McMullan, "Goblin's Market: Commemoration, Anti-Semitism and the Invention of 'Global Shakespeare' in 1916," in *Celebrating Shakespeare Commemoration and Cultural Memory*, ed. Clara Calvo and Coppélia Kahn (New York: Cambridge University Press, 2015), 182.

standards of beauty and socialization in favor of slovenly excess, an ugly goblin lurking within all of us that does not seek the approval of others. Both phenomena use the grotesqueness of goblins as a banner under which people can mobilize against normative perceptions of proper appearance and conduct.

REFERENCES

"Goblincore." *Aesthetics Wiki*. https://aesthetics.fandom.com/wiki/Goblincore. Accessed December 1, 2024.

"The Beauty of the 'Best Worst Movie.'" 2009. *Talk of the Nation*. NPR, June 15.

Abram, David. 1996. *The Spell of the Sensuous: Perception and Language in a More-Than-Human World*. New York: Vintage Books.

Addams, Shay. 1992. *The Official Book of Ultima*. 2nd ed. Greensboro: Compute Books.

Addison, Katherine. 2014. *The Goblin Emperor*. New York: Tor.

Alexander, William. 2012. *Goblin Secrets*. New York: Margaret K. McElderry Books.

Andrews, Ted. 1993. *Enchantment of the Faerie Realm: Communicate with Nature Spirits & Elementals*. Saint Paul, MN: Llewellyn Publications.

Arrowsmith, Nancy. 1977. *Field Guide to the Little People*. New York: Hill and Wang.

Asma, Stephen T. 2020. Monsters and the Moral Imagination. In *The Monster Theory Reader*, ed. Jeffrey Andrew Weinstock, 289–294. Minneapolis: University of Minnesota Press.

Astor-Aguilera, Miguel, and Graham Harvey. 2020. *Rethinking Relations and Animism: Personhood and Materiality*. New York: Routledge.

Attebery, Brian. 2014. *Stories about Stories: Fantasy and the Remaking of Myth*. New York: Oxford University Press.

Bacchilega, Cristina. 2013. *Fairy Tales Transformed? Twenty-First-Century Adaptations and the Politics of Wonder*. Detroit: Wayne State University Press.

Bailey, Grant. 2023. Top 10 Unconventional Beliefs Held by People in Britain Confirmed in New Study. *The Independent*, January 5. https://www.the-independent.com/news/uk/ghost-aliens-paranormal-beliefs-b2256483.html. Accessed December 1, 2024.

Baldwin, Gerard, director. 1961. The Princess and the Goblins. *Fractured Fairy Tales: The Adventures of Rocky and Bullwinkle and Friends* 2 (45). ABC, April 23.

Berger, Helen A. 1999. *A Community of Witches: Contemporary Neo-Paganism and Witchcraft in the United States*. Columbia: University of South Carolina Press.

Berger, Helen A. 2019. *Solitary Pagans: Contemporary Witches, Wiccans, and Others Who Practice Alone*. Columbia: University of South Carolina Press.

Bird-David, Nurit. 2018. Size Matters! The Scalability of Modern Hunter-Gatherer Animism. *Quaternary International* 464:305–314.

Bird-David, Nurit. 2020. A Peer-to-Peer Connected Cosmos: Beyond Egalitarian/ Hierarchical Hunter-Gatherer Societies. *L'Homme* 236:77–105.

Blyton, Enid. 1990. *The Goblin Aeroplane and Other Stories*. London: Red Fox.

Blyton, Enid. 1994a. The First Green Goblin Book. In *An Enid Blyton Omnibus*, 159–264. London: Cresset Editions.

Blyton, Enid. 1994b. *The Goblin's Toyshop and Other Stories*. London: Award Publications Limited.

Blyton, Enid. 1997. *The Goblin Hat and Other Stories*. London: Award Publications Limited.

Bogost, Ian. 2007. *Persuasive Games: The Expressive Power of Videogames*. Cambridge: The MIT Press.

Bogost, Ian. 2008. The Rhetoric of Video Games. In *The Ecology of Games: Connecting Youth, Games, and Learning*, ed. Katie Salen, 117–140. Cambridge: The MIT Press.

Bowes, Richard. 1988. *Goblin Market*. New York: Warner Books.

Bramley, Ellie Violet. 2021. Goblincore: The Fashion Trend That Embraces 'Chaos, Dirt and Mud.' *The Guardian*, July 30. https://www.theguardian. com/fashion/2021/jul/30/goblincore-fashion-trend-embraces-chaos-dirt-mud. Accessed December 1, 2024.

Bretherick, Jake Edward. 2024. *Goblin Grimoire: Magick & Lore from the Outcast Fey*.

Buccitelli, Anthony Bak. 2024. Fairytale as Fuck: Antimodern Media, Sensory Experience, and the Folkloresque. In *Möbius Media: Popular Culture, Folklore, and the Folkloresque*, ed. Jeffrey A. Tolbert and Michael Dylan Foster. 86–112. Logan: Utah State University Press.

Buck, Young. 1991. An Historical Overview of the Whereabouts of Gnomes and Elves, Fauns and Faeries, Goblins, Ogres, Trolls and Bogies, Nymphs, Sprites and Dryads, Past and Present. *FireHeart* 6:8–10.

Budin, Noémie. 2016. *La Représentation du Petit Peuple dans la littérature francophone contemporaine pour adolescents: tradition et renouvellement féeriques depuis 1992*. Doctoral Dissertation, Université de Lorraine.

Burlingame, Russ. 2024. Brian Henson Confirms David Bowie's Codpiece in Labyrinth Was Intentional (Exclusive). *ComicBook*, February 19. https://comicbook.com/movies/news/brian-henson-confirms-david-bowies-codpiece-in-labyrinth-was-intentional-exclusive/. Accessed December 1, 2024.

Butler, Catherine. 2012. Modern Children's Fantasy. In *The Cambridge Companion to Fantasy Literature*, ed. Edward James and Farah Mendlesohn, 224–235. New York: Cambridge University Press.

Byatt, A. S. 2011 Snuff by Terry Pratchett - Review. *The Guardian*, October 21. https://www.theguardian.com/books/2011/oct/21/snuff-terry-pratchett-review. Accessed December 1, 2024.

Cambridge Dictionary. 2024. *Goblin Mode*, December 1. https://dictionary.cambridge.org/us/dictionary/english/goblin-mode. Accessed December 1, 2024.

Carmell, Deborah, and Imelda Whelehan. 2007. Literature on Screen: A Synoptic View. In *The Cambridge Companion to Literature on Screen*, ed. Deborah Cartmell and Imelda Whelehan, 1–12. New York: Cambridge University Press.

Carroll, Noel. 1990. *The Philosophy of Horror: Or, Paradoxes of the Heart*. New York: Routledge.

Casey, Jim. 2009. Silver Age Comics. In *The Routledge Companion to Science Fiction*, ed. Mark Bould, Andrew M. Butler, and Sherryl Vint, 123–133. New York: Routledge.

de Castro, Eduardo Viveiros. 2015. *The Relative Native: Essays on Indigenous Conceptual Worlds*. Chicago: Chicago University Press.

Chalk, Titus. 2017. *Generation Decks: The Unofficial History of Gaming Phenomenon Magic: The Gathering*. Oxford: Solaris.

Chance, Jane. 2016. 'In the Company of Orcs': Peter Jackson's Queer Tolkien. In *Queer Movie Medievalisms*, ed. Kathleen Coyne Kelly and Tison Pugh, 79–96. New York: Taylor & Francis.

Chez, Keridiana. 2022. Sorry, Not Sorry: The Limits of Empathy for Nonhuman Creatures. In *Open at the Close: Literary Essays on Harry Potter*, ed. Cecilia Konchar Farr, 166–177. Jackson: University Press of Mississippi.

Clifton, Chas. 2006. *Her Hidden Children: The Rise of Wicca and Paganism in America*. Lanham: Rowman & Littlefield.

Conway, D. J. 2005. *The Ancient Art of Faery Magick*. Berkeley: The Crossing Press.

Coogan, Peter. 2019. The Supervillain. In *The Supervillain Reader*, ed. Robert Moses Peaslee and Robert G. Weiner, 36–61. Jackson: University Press of Mississippi.

Cosmatos, Panos, director. 2018. *Mandy*. RLJE Films.

Coyle, Mc Kayla. 2023. *Goblin Mode: How to Get Cozy, Embrace Imperfection, and Thrive in the Muck*. Philadelphia: Quirk Books.

Davy, Barbara Jane. 2007. *Introduction to Pagan Studies*. New York: AltaMira Press.

De Rico, Ul. 1978. *The Rainbow Goblins*. London: Thames & Hudson.

Denan, Corinne. 1980. *Goblin Tales*. Troll Associates.

Descola, Philippe. 1994. *In the Society of Nature: A Native Ecology in Amazonia*. Translated by Nora Scott. New York: Cambridge University Press.

DiTerlizzi, Tony, and Holly Black. 2011. *The Seeing Stone*. New York: Simon & Schuster Children's.

Douglas, Robin, and Francis Young. 2024. *Paganism Persisting: A History of European Paganisms since Antiquity*. Exeter: University of Exeter Press.

Drury, Nevill. 2011. *Stealing Fire from Heaven: The Rise of Modern Western Magic*. New York: Oxford University Press.

Eason, Cassandra. 2001. *A Complete Guide to Fairies and Magical Beings*. London: Judy Piatkus Publishers.

Fahs, Travis. 2009. IGN Presents the History of Warcraft. *IGN*, August 18. https://www.ign.com/articles/2009/08/18/ign-presents-the-history-of-warcraft. Accessed December 1, 2024.

Fimi, Dimitra. 2017. *Celtic Myth in Contemporary Children's Fantasy: Idealization, Identity, Ideology*. New York: Palgrave Macmillan.

Flinterud, Guro. 2023. 'Folk' in the Age of Algorithms: Theorizing Folklore on Social Media Platforms. *Folklore* 134 (4): 493–461.

Fragasso, Claudio, director. 1990. *Troll 2*. Filmirage.

Frick, Evelyn. 2023. The Antisemitic History of Goblins. *heyalma*, February 23. https://www.heyalma.com/the-antisemitic-history-of-goblins/. Accessed December 1, 2024.

Froud, Brian, and Ari Berk. 1983. *Goblins*. New York: Macmillan.

Froud, Brian, and Ari Berk. 2004. *Goblins! A Survival Guide and Fiasco in Four Parts*. London: Pavilion Books.

Froud, Brian, and Terry Jones. 1986. *The Goblins of Labyrinth*. London: Pavilion Books Limited.

Froud, Brian, and Terry Jones. 1996. *The Goblin Companion*. Atlanta: Turner Publishing, Inc.

Fryer, Daniel. 2022. *Using 'Goblin Mode' to Reduce Stress*, December 19. https://www.psychologytoday.com/us/blog/keeping-an-even-keel/202212/using-goblin-mode-to-reduce-stress. Accessed December 1, 2024.

Goulet, Jean-Guy A., and Bruce Granville Miller. 2007. Embodied Knowledge: Steps toward a Radical Anthropology of Cross-Cultural Encounters. In *Extraordinary Anthropology: Transformations in the Field*, ed. Jean-Guy A. Goulet and Bruce Granville Miller, 1–13. Lincoln: University of Nebraska Press.

Greenwood, Susan. 2000. *Magic, Witchcraft and the Otherworld: An Anthropology*. New York: Routledge.

Grimm, Geraldine. 1972. *King Goblin and His Forest Friends*. London: Ward Lock Limited.

Grixti, Joseph. 1989. *Terrors of Uncertainty: The Cultural Contexts of Horror Fiction*. New York: Routledge.

Hamilton, James. 1995. *Arthur Rackham: A Life with Illustration*. London: Pavilion Books Limited.

Hanau, Shira. 2022. Jon Stewart Says J.K. Rowling's 'Harry Potter' Goblin Characters Clearly Antisemitic. *The Times of Israel*, January 5. https://www.timesofisrael.com/jon-stewart-says-the-harry-potter-goblin-characters-are-clearly-antisemitic/. Accessed December 1, 2024.

Hart, Adam Charles. 2019. *Monstrous Forms: Moving Image Horror Across Media*. New York: Oxford University Press.

Hatke, Ben. 2017. *Mighty Jack and the Goblin King*. New York: First Second.

Hawkins, Jaq D. 2005. *Dance of the Goblins*. Independently Published.

Hendrix, Richard. 1976. Popular Humor and 'The Black Dwarf'. *Journal of British Studies* 1 (Autumn): 108–128.

Henson, Jim, director. 1986. *Labyrinth*. Tri-Star Pictures.

Holiday, Frederick William. *The Goblin Universe*. Edited by Colin Wilson. Saint Paul, MN: Llewellyn Publications, 1986.

Hunter, I. Q. 2007. Post-Classical Fantasy Cinema: The Lord of the Rings. In *The Cambridge Companion to Literature on Screen*, ed. Deborah Cartmell and Imelda Whelehan, 154–166. New York: Cambridge University Press.

Hutton, Ronald. 1999. *The Triumph of the Moon: A History of Modern Pagan Witchcraft*. New York: Oxford University Press.

Invictus, S. Rob. 2017. *Goblin Magick for Strength and Power*.

James, Edward. 2012. Tolkien, Lewis and the Explosion of Genre Fantasy. In *The Cambridge Companion to Fantasy Literature*, ed. Edward James and Farah Mendlesohn, 62–78. New York: Cambridge University Press.

James, Ronald M. 2018. *The Folklore of Cornwall: The Oral Tradition of a Celtic Nation*. Exeter: University of Exeter Press.

Jemisin, N. K. 2013 The Unbearable Baggage of Orcing. *On Writing* (blog), February 13. https://nkjemisin.com/2013/02/from-the-mailbag-the-unbearable-baggage-of-orcing/. Accessed December 1, 2024.

Jenkins, Henry. 2011. The Origins of 'Acafan.' *Pop Junctions: Reflections on Entertainment, Pop Culture, Activism, Media Literacy, Fandom and More* (blog), June 20. http://henryjenkins.org/blog/2011/06/acafandom_and_beyond_week_two.html. Accessed December 1, 2024.

Jewitches. 2024. Goblins, Jews, and Antisemitism. Accessed December 1. https://jewitches.com/blogs/blog/goblins-jews-and-antisemitism-1?srsltid=AfmBOorp3uNrp2cCC9l5ifsvK2X4iChnYd542qEPtDhrA7lYB0_nw4PS. Accessed December 1, 2024.

Johnson, Marjorie T. 2014. *Seeing Fairies: From the Lost Archives of the Fairy Investigation Society, Authentic Reports of Fairies in Modern Times*. San Antonio: Anomalist Books.

Just Some Guy. 2019. *The Two Types of Goblincore*, July 3. https://the-kazoo-kid. tumblr.com/post/186034379297/the-two-types-of-goblincore. Accessed December 1, 2024.

Kimmel, Eric. 1989. *Hershel and the Hanukkah Goblins*. New York: Holiday House.

Klein, Zoe. 2017. *The Goblins of Knottingham: A History of Challah*. Millburn: Apples & Honey Press.

Kline, Daniel T. 2015. Contemporary Neo-Medieval Digital Gaming: An Overview of Genre. In *Medieval Afterlives in Contemporary Culture*, ed. Gail Ashton, 93–102. New York: Bloomsbury Academic.

Knapp, Mary Frances. 2021. The Essentials of Goblincore, a Digital Community of Faeries, Frogs, and Nonbinary Folks. *Vice*, March 24. https://www.vice. com/en/article/goblincore-aesthetic-essentials/. Accessed December 1, 2024.

KnowYourMeme. 2024. Goblin Mode, December 1. https://knowyourmeme. com/memes/goblin-mode#fn1. Accessed December 1, 2024.

Kooistra, Lorraine Janzen. 2002. *Christina Rossetti and Illustration: A Publishing History*. Athens: Ohio University Press.

Kristof, Nicholas. 2024. The School Issues We're Battling Over Aren't the Ones That Matter. *The New York Times*, March 6.

Kruse, John T. 2020. *Beyond Faery: Exploring the World of Mermaids, Kelpies, Goblins & Other Faery Beasts*. Woodbury: Llewellyn Publications.

Lando, Jeffrey Scott, director. 2010. *Goblin*. SyFy.

Lee, Stan, and Steve Ditko. 1963. The Grotesque Adventure of 'the Green Goblin'. *The Amazing Spider-Man*.

Leonard, Andrew. 2003. 'The War of the Flowers' by Tad Williams. *Salon*, June 12. https://www.salon.com/2003/06/12/williams_14/. Accessed December 1, 2024.

Levy, Michael, and Farah Mendlesohn. 2016. *Children's Fantasy Literature: An Introduction*. New York: Cambridge University Press.

Lopes, Juliana Valadão. 2022. 'All Was Well'? The Sociopolitical Struggles of House-Elves, Goblins, and Centaurs. In *Open at the Close: Literary Essays on Harry Potter*, ed. Cecilia Konchar Farr, 178–187. Jackson: University Press of Mississippi.

lucillegooseberry. 2002. Seeeeriously. *Goblincore Subreddit*, April 24. https:// www.reddit.com/r/goblincore/comments/ub2i79/seeeeriously/. Accessed December 1, 2024.

Lucy, Morgan. 2022. Oxford Dictionary Has Chosen 'Goblin Mode' as Its Word of the Year—What Does the Viral Term Actually Mean? *Glamour*, December 5. https://www.glamourmagazine.co.uk/article/goblin-mode. Accessed December 1, 2024.

Magliocco, Sabina. 2004. *Witching Culture: Folklore and Neo-Paganism in America*. Pennsylvania: University of Pennsylvania Press.

Magliocco, Sabina. 2012. Neopaganism. In *The Cambridge Companion to New Religious Movements*, ed. Olav Hammer and Mikael Rothstein, 150–166. New York: Cambridge University Press.

Magliocco, Sabina. 2019. The Taming of the Fae: Literary and Folkloric Fairies in Modern Paganisms. In *Magic and Witchery in the Modern West: Celebrating the Twentieth Anniversary of "The Triumph of the Moon"*, ed. Shai Feraro and Ethan Doyle White, 107–130. New York: Palgrave Macmillan.

Manning, Paul. 2005. Jewish Ghosts, Knackers, Tommyknockers, and Other Sprites of Capitalism in the Cornish Mines. *Cornish Studies* 13 (1): 216–255.

Manson, Marianna. 2022. Goblin Mode: Does It Have To Be A Dirty Secret That Women Don't Wear Makeup And Heels At Home? *Grazia*, March 18. https://graziadaily.co.uk/life/opinion/goblin-mode/. Accessed December 1, 2024.

Massachusetts General Hospital. 2023. *What Is 'Goblin Mode'?—Oxford's Word of 2022*, January 26. https://www.massgeneral.org/psychiatry/news/goblin-mode. Accessed December 1, 2024.

Mayers, Simon. 2013. *Chesterton's Jews: Stereotypes and Caricatures in the Literature and Journalism of G.K. Chesterton*. Independently Published.

McCort, Jessica Hritz. 2009. *Getting out of Wonderland: Elizabeth Bishop, Sylvia Plath, Adrienne Rich, and Anne Sexton*. Washington University in St. Louis.

McCoy, Edain. 1994. *A Witch's Guide to Faery Folk: How to Work with the Elemental World*. Saint Paul, MN: Llewellyn Publications.

McMullan, Gordon. 2015. Goblin's Market: Commemoration, Anti-Semitism and the Invention of 'Global Shakespeare' in 1916. In *Celebrating Shakespeare Commemoration and Cultural Memory*, ed. Clara Calvo and Coppélia Kahn. New York: Cambridge University Press.

meowstash321. 2022. Bliss. *Goblincore Subreddit*, April 14. https://www.reddit.com/r/goblincore/comments/u3mqi0/bliss/. Accessed December 1, 2024.

Metzen, Chris, Matt Burns, and Robert Brooks. 2016. *World of Warcraft: Chronicle*. Milwaukie: Dark Horse books.

Miller, Robert Ellis, director. 1961. The Princess and the Goblins. *Shirley Temple's Storybook*, 2.24. NBC, March 19.

Minarik, Else Holmelund. 1961. *Little Bear's Visit*. New York: HarperCollins.

Monson, Melissa J. 2012. Race-Based Fantasy Realm: Essentialism in the World of Warcraft. *Games and Culture* 7 (1): 48–71.

Morrow, Robert W. 2006. *Sesame Street and the Reform of Children's Television*. Baltimore: The Johns Hopkins University Press.

Naylor, James Ball. 1907. *The Little Green Goblin*. New York: The Saalfield Publishing Company.

Newland, John, director. 1973. *Don't Be Afraid of the Dark*. Lorimar Productions.

Nguyen, Terry. 2022. Trends Are Dead. Vox, May 11. https://www.vox.com/the-goods/23065462/trends-death-subcultures-style.   Accessed December 1, 2024.

Nicholls, Liz. 2007. Refugees from the Great Repression. *Edmonton Journal*, March 14, sec. D.

Nixey, Troy, director. 2010. *Don't Be Afraid of the Dark*. Miramax.

Ó Giolláin, Diarmuid. 2000. *Locating Irish Folklore: Tradition, Modernity, Identity*. Cork: Cork University Press.

Oxford Languages. 2022. Oxford Word of the Year 2022, December 4. https://languages.oup.com/word-of-the-year/2022/. Accessed December 1, 2024.

Patterson, Ray, director. 1985. Papa's Family Album. *The Smurfs*, 5.17. NBC, October 26.

Patterson, Ray, director. 1986. Calling Doctor Smurf. *The Smurfs*, 6.15. NBC, October 10.

Paul, Kari. 2022. Slobbing out and Giving up: Why Are so Many People Going 'Goblin Mode'? *The Guardian*, March 14. https://www.theguardian.com/technology/2022/mar/14/slobbing-out-and-giving-up-why-are-so-many-people-going-goblin-mode. Accessed December 1, 2024.

Peppin, Hayley. 2024. Goblin Mode: Why It's Okay to Get Cozy at Home and Eat Last Night's Cheeseboard by Yourself. *Bazaar*, December 1. https://harpersbazaar.com.au/goblin-mode-is-a-good-thing/. Accessed December 1, 2024.

Peyo, Matagne. 1973. *Dilly Duckling and the Goblins*. London: Rylee Limited.

Phillips, Sofia. 2022. Goblin Mode: A Rejection of the Self-Improvement Movement. *Medium*, March 25. https://medium.com/@Sofia_Phillips/goblin-mode-a-rejection-of-the-self-improvement-movement-3c4c53565a6. Accessed December 1, 2024.

Pike, J. Zachary. 2014. *Orconomics: A Satire*. New Hampshire: Gnomish Press LLC.

Pike, Sarah M. 2019. 'Wild Nature' and the Lure of the Past: The Legacy of Romanticism Among Young Pagan Environmentalists. In *Magic and Witchery in the Modern West: Celebrating the Twentieth Anniversary of "The Triumph of the Moon"*, ed. Shai Feraro and Ethan Doyle White, 131–152. New York: Palgrave Macmillan.

Pratchett, Terry. 2001. *Feet of Clay*. New York: Harper.

Pratchett, Terry. 2010. *Unseen Academicals*. New York: Harper.

Pratchett, Terry. 2011. *Snuff*. New York: Harper.

Quinn, Jordan. 2021. *Goblin Magic*. New York: Little Simon.

Rao, Sridevi, and Preethi Gorecki. 2002. Is Dobby a Free Elf? In *Harry Potter and the Other: Race, Justice, and Difference in the Wizarding World*, ed. Sarah Park Dahlen and Emily Elizabeth Thomas, 276–286. Jackson: University Press of Mississippi.

Raynis, Richard, director. 1986. When Halloween Was Forever. *The Real Ghostbusters* 1 (8). ABC, November 1.

Raynis, Richard, director. 1987. Drool, the Dog-Faced Goblin. *The Real Ghostbusters* 2 (34). ABC, October 29.

Ritter, Christopher Jonas. 2010. *Why the Humans Are White: Fantasy, Modernity, and the Rhetorics of Racism in World of Warcraft*. Doctoral Dissertation, Washington State University.

Rosen, Judith. 2014. Middle Grade and YA: Where to Draw the Line? *Publishers Weekly*, July 18. https://www.publishersweekly.com/pw/by-topic/childrens/childrens-industry-news/article/63358-middle-grade-and-ya-where-to-draw-the-line.html. Accessed December 1, 2024.

Rossetti, Christina. 1933. *Goblin Market*. Philadelphia: J.B. Lippincott & Co.

Rossetti, Christina, and Kinuko Y. Craft. 1973. Goblin Market. *Playboy* 20 (9): 115–119.

Rossetti, Christina, and Ellen Raskin. 1970. *Goblin Market*. New York: E.P. Dutton.

Routledge, Clay. 2017. Don't Believe in God? Maybe You'll Try U.F.O.s. *The New York Times*, July 21.

Rowling, J. K. 1997. *Harry Potter and the Philosopher's Stone*. London: Bloomsbury.

Rowling, J. K. 2000. *Harry Potter and the Goblet of Fire*. London: Bloomsbury.

Rowling, J. K. 2007. *Harry Potter and the Deathly Hallows*. London: Bloomsbury.

Russo, Joe, director. 2011. Advanced Dungeons & Dragons. *Community* 2 (14). NBC, February 3.

Sahlins, Marshall. 2022. *The New Science of the Enchanted Universe: An Anthropology of Most of Humanity*. Princeton: Princeton University Press.

Salmon, Felix. 2022. Elon Musk Goes into Full Goblin Mode. Axios, April 14. https://www.axios.com/2022/04/14/elon-musk-goes-into-full-goblin-mode. Accessed December 1, 2024.

Salomonsen, Jone. 2002. *Enchanted Feminism: Ritual, Gender and Divinity among the Reclaiming Witches of San Francisco*. New York: Routledge.

Sanchez, Tara. 2021. *Urban Faery Magick: Connecting to the Fae in the Modern World*. Woodbury: Llewellyn Publications.

Scheinberg, Cynthia. 2002. *Women's Poetry and Religion in Victorian England: Jewish Identity and Christian Culture*. New York: Cambridge University Press.

Schuessler, Jennifer. 2022. The Word of the Year Goes Goblin Mode. *The New York Times*, December 4. https://www.nytimes.com/2022/12/04/arts/goblin-mode-oxford-word.html. Accessed December 1, 2024.

Schwedel, Heather. 2022. How Defamatory Is 'Goblin Mode' to Real Goblins? *Slate*, March 23. https://slate.com/human-interest/2022/03/goblin-mode-explained-history-professor-tolkien.html. Accessed December 1, 2024.

Scott, Ridley, director. 1985. *Legend*. Universal Pictures.

Sendak, Maurice. 1981. *Outside Over There*. New York: Ursula Nordstrom.

Shlesinger, Iliza, director. 2016. "Confirmed Kills." *Netflix Stand-Up*. Netflix, September 23.

Silcoff, Mireille. 2024. Teen Subcultures Are Fading. Pity the Poor Kids. *The New York Times*, February 21. https://www.nytimes.com/2024/02/21/magazine/aesthetics-tiktok-teens.html. Accessed December 1, 2024.

Simons, Judy. 2010. Gender Roles in Children's Fiction. In *The Cambridge Companion to Children's Literature*, ed. M. O. Grenby and Andrea Immel, 143–158. New York: Cambridge University Press.

Siskel, Gene. 1986. 'Legend' May Become One, but for All the Wrong Reasons. *Chicago Tribune* N7.

Smith, Eliya. 2022. I Am Begging You All to Please Shut up about the Harry Potter Jew-Goblins. *Forward*, January 5. https://forward.com/culture/480388/please-shut-up-about-the-harry-potter-jew-goblins-antisemitism-jk-rowling/. Accessed December 1, 2024.

Specter, Baron. 2019. *Hobgoblins Just Wanna Have Fun*. North Mankato: Magic Wagon.

Stelle, Ginger. 2007. "Fracturing MacDonald: The Princess and the Goblin and 'Fractured Fairy Tales.'" *North Wind: A Journal of George MacDonald Studies* 26 (6): 121–125.

Stephens, John. 2010. Retelling Stories across Time and Cultures. In *The Cambridge Companion to Children's Literature*, ed. M. O. Grenby and Andrea Immel, 91–107. New York: Cambridge University Press.

Stephenson, Michael, director. 2009. *Best Worst Movie*. Magicstone Productions.

Stewart, Jon. 2021. The Problem With Goblins: J. K. Rowling, Harry Potter, & Jews. *The Problem with Jon Stewart*, December 16. https://www.youtube.com/watch?v=DzffpeYnv-w&list=PL4RaSiGWHbPKMpVO5ILO-ocOnd-_Rday1&index=71. Accessed December 1, 2024.

Stine, R. L. 1996a. *Attack of the Jack-O'-Lanterns*. Goosebumps. New York: Scholastic.

Stine, R. L. 1996b. *Still More Tales to Give You Goosebumps*. New York: Scholastic.

Stine, R. L. 1999. *Full Moon Fever*. Goosebumps Series 2000. New York: Scholastic.

Stine, R. L. 2024. *Goblin Monday*. Goosebumps House of Shivers. New York: Scholastic.

Storey, Mark, and Stephen Shapiro. 2022. American Horror: Genre and History. In *The Cambridge Companion to American Horror*, ed. Stephen Shapiro and Mark Storey, 1–12. New York: Cambridge University Press.

Strickland, Debra Higgs. 2003. *Saracens, Demons, & Jews: Making Monsters in Medieval Art*. Princeton: Princeton University Press.

Tarcov, Susan. 2023. *There's a Goblin on the Ark!* Millburn: Apples & Honey Press.

The Cincinnati Post. 2000. Pumpkin Pursuits. October 19.

The Cleveland Clinic. 2022. Why Goblin Mode Is the New Self-Care Routine, December 29. https://health.clevelandclinic.org/goblin-mode-and-your-health. Accessed December 1, 2024.

The Legend of Zelda Instruction Booklet. 1987. Nintendo.

Tiffany, Kaitlyn. 2021. Cottagecore Was Just the Beginning. *The Atlantic*, February 5.

Tolkien, J. R. R. 2001. *The Hobbit, or There and Back Again*. New York: Ballantine Books.

Tripp, Wallace. 1973. *A Great Big Ugly Man Came Up and Tied His Worse to Me: A Book of Nonsense Verse*. Boston: Little, Brown and Company.

Turner, Hannah. 2022. As A Disabled Woman, The Goblin Mode Trend Doesn't Sit Right With Me. *Refinery29*, March 22. https://www.refinery29.com/en-us/goblin-mode-offensive. Accessed December 1, 2024.

Upton, Bryn. 2014. *Hollywood and the End of the Cold War: Signs of Cinematic Change*. New York: Rowman & Littlefield.

Valentine, Rebekah. 2024. World of Warcraft Subscription Numbers Are Higher Now Than at Expansion Launch in a Franchise First. *IGN*, March 25. https://www.ign.com/articles/world-of-warcraft-subscription-numbers-are-higher-now-than-at-expansion-launch-in-a-franchise-first. Accessed December 1, 2024.

Weinstock, Jeffrey Andrew. 2012. Invisible Monsters: Vision, Horror, and Contemporary Culture. In *The Ashgate Research Companion to Monsters and the Monstrous*, ed. Asa Simon Mittman and Peter J. Dendle, 275–289. New York: Routledge.

White, Mike, director. 2025. Hide or Seek. *The White Lotus* 3 (4). HBO, March 9.

White, Ethan Doyle, and Shai Feraro. 2019. Twenty Years On: An Introduction. In *Magic and Witchery in the Modern West: Celebrating the Twentieth Anniversary of "The Triumph of the Moon"*, ed. Shai Feraro and Ethan Doyle White, 1–20. New York: Palgrave Macmillan.

Wickes, Jade. 2022. Goblin Mode Is the Spiritual Rejection of 'That Girl' Aesthetic. *The Face*, March 16. https://theface.com/life/goblin-mode-rejects-that-girl-aesthetic-tiktok-social-media-girlboss-culture-wellness-health-feral-girl-summer. Accessed December 1, 2024.

Williams, Tad. 2004. *The War of the Flowers*. New York: DAW Books.

Wizard, J. D. 2022. *Goblin*.

Wloszczyna, Susan. 2001. Willem Dafoe Finds Depth in Green Goblin Role. *Battle Creek Enquirer*, November 8.

Wright, Jon, director. 2023. *Unwelcome*. Warner Bros. Pictures.

Yates, Samuel. 2019. Spider-Man's Designer Genes: Hypercapacity and Transhumanism in a 'DIY World'. In *The Matter of Disability: Materiality, Biopolitics, Crip Affect*, 143–159. Ann Arbor: University of Michigan Press.

York, Michael. 2003. *Pagan Theology: Paganism as a World Religion*. NYU Press.

Young, Garry. 2014. *Ethics in the Virtual World: The Morality and Psychology of Gaming*. London: Routledge.

Young, Simon. 2022. *The Boggart: Folklore, History, Place-Names and Dialect*. Exeter: Exeter University Press.

CHAPTER 9

A Goblin Conclusion

At a deeply spiritual level, I empathize with Dianne Purkiss' self-assessment of *At the Bottom of the Garden* as an "imperfect and limping creature."[1] While I hope that my history has a fraction of the utility of her wonderful book, I am aware that it has limitations—both those on my radar and those joyful unknown unknowns that have evaded detection despite my best efforts. This conclusion seems as good a place as any to discuss these (known) shortcomings alongside themes in the book that broadly cut across chapters but have been given less attention than I would have liked. I approach this conclusion, then, as a frank discussion about the contents of this book, some underdeveloped trends therein, methodological issues that arose when writing it, and potential avenues for future research. I hope that this approach provides an accessible-yet-informative denouement for a history that has catapulted readers through close to 1000 years of history in around 150,000 words.

---

[1] Purkiss, *At the Bottom of the Garden: A Dark History of Fairies, Hobgoblins, Nymphs, and Other Troublesome Things*, xi.

© The Author(s), under exclusive license to Springer Nature Switzerland AG 2026
M. King, *A History of Goblins*,
https://doi.org/10.1007/978-3-032-01063-6_9

A THEMATIC SUMMATION

This history has provided a sweeping historical overview of the many ways that people have encountered and envisioned goblins since the Middle Ages. I chose to organize this book chronologically, which has the benefit of grounding my analysis of a given topic in its historical context. A drawback to this approach, though, is that some trends with temporal breadth have been choppily considered over the course of multiple chapters. This summation attempts to address this shortcoming by foregrounding major ideas of this book across historical eras—even if it results in a minor case of chronological whiplash for readers.

Although the origins of the word "goblin" are unclear, its earliest written attestation comes from the monk Orderic Vitalis in the twelfth century. He testifies to popular belief in a creature called *gobelinus*, which he claims is the neutered remnant of the demon Zabulon. Like Orderic, many clerics of the medieval and early modern periods interpreted goblins either as a type of devil or as a named devil in the service of Satan. They were creatures of darkness, ugliness, and sin that posed a threat to Christians. They could physically stalk this earth, implant themselves in the mind of the vulnerable, or stand guard over the depths of Hell. Not all clerics, however, were convinced of these satanic threats. During the English Reformation and subsequent witch trials, elite Christians questioned whether demons (goblins included) existed or were only present in the minds of corrupt Catholics and the uneducated masses. Such skepticism toward demons became the dominant perspective by the eighteenth century and, since then, it has been rare for goblins to be seen as agents of Satan.

Goblins undoubtedly circulated as the objects of oral tradition in northern France long before the twelfth century. They were part of a vibrant but poorly documented tapestry of beliefs that existed alongside Christian practice (much to the horror of ecclesiastical officials) and formed a crucial part of how the laity perceived the world. As migration across the English Channel increased during the Central Middle Ages, the goblin and other folkloric creatures from the continent found their way to Britain, where they were absorbed into the amalgamation of folk beliefs already present there. Stories about folkloric goblins, which reach us primarily through skeptical written accounts recorded across the centuries, are substantial. Goblins might do chores for families that appropriately honor them, replace neglected babies with changelings, lead nighttime travelers astray, or cause a general ruckus in the dark spaces of human dwellings. Some believed goblins and their kin were physically present on this earth and, under the right circumstances, could lead humans to the mystical Fairyland. Others might honor the traditions associated with these creatures and tell stories of them (for entertainment or moralizing purposes) even if they were skeptical of their existence. Goblins were frequently, though not universally, conflated with other entities of Fairyland. They could also indicate an entire category of preternatural beings—often those with mischievous or malicious intent. Though belief in the existence of goblins (and fairies more broadly) is undoubtedly less widespread today than it was in the Elizabethan era, it remains in some circles, especially modern pagan communities. Lamentations about the seemingly endless retreat of these creatures from this earth, which are documented as early as Chaucer, ironically attest to the persistence of traditions and beliefs surrounding them.

Intertwined with these folkloric goblins are folkloresque depictions of them in literature and theater, which often present them as expressly fictional creatures but could also be used to make audiences question their understandings of reality. The court of Fairyland was an especially popular subject in early modern England, and its inhabitants were the subjects of fairy tales and fiction in later centuries. The character of Hobgoblin (also known as Puck or Robin Goodfellow) might be a member of this court or a preternatural entity outside of it. Goblins, too, might be mischievous pranksters tethered to a particular place, malicious fiends that preyed on the unwary, or ultimately benevolent entities that used magic to scare humans into living more moral lives. Their appearance could bring about fear, laughter, repulsion, joy, and any number of other emotions. Ubiquitous and adaptable, these creatures were easily inserted into works across genres that touched on the preternatural. The rise of Anglophone fairy tales and book-length stories in the mid-nineteenth century provided a particularly influential niche for goblins that, in some cases, saw them as masculine antagonists under a goblin king oppositional to benevolent fairies ruled by a fairy queen/godmother. Such characterizations were far from universal, though they were numerous enough to inspire many works of fantasy in which goblins are short, monstrous, cave-dwelling humanoids with malicious intent that must be defeated for the triumph of good.

The impulse to categorize the goblin as a particular type of demon or preternatural creature stretched back to the Middle Ages—and however compelling some of these attempts, they were all futile efforts to impose taxonomic structures on disparate oral traditions with little interest in classificatory specifics. Folklore scholars of the nineteenth century were especially keen on comparing oral traditions across borders to make larger claims about the supposed natures of peoples and their nations. Therein, the goblin often served as an umbrella term for supernatural creatures, though it was sometimes identified as a more specific entity of English folk traditions. Authors of fantasy literature, meanwhile, were untethered from the classificatory impossibilities of folklore and able to craft worlds in which goblins were a specific type or "race" of creature. Tolkien influentially depicted goblins/orcs as devolutions of nobler races and as irredeemable forces of evil destined for slaughter. When Gary Gygax and his co-authors developed *Dungeons & Dragons*, they borrowed heavily from Tolkien but encoded goblins into a rigid ruleset that made these creatures mechanically distinct from their monstrous brethren. The dominance of these tropes from Tolkien and Gygax gradually led to backlash from producers of fantasy media in the late twentieth century. Reflecting a broader cultural reevaluation of the nature of monstrosity, these creators have reframed certain folkloric and folkloresque characteristics of goblins to make them sympathetic outsiders, quirky sidekicks, and underdog heroes.

The association of goblins with darkness, ugliness, and strange behaviors led to people using the word as an abstraction stretching back to the early modern period. Harmful ideas or pieces of legislation could be given the goblin label. So too could hideous works of art or gnarled trees. Even people judged to have peculiar appearances, per an author's normative eye, might be called a goblin or goblin-like. These pejorative uses directed at humans often intersected with anxieties about race and physical disability (especially in the nineteenth century). Some scholars theorized that the pygmies of Central Africa were the distant descendants of folkloric fairies—and their dark skin and behaviors resembled goblins. Those with recognizable disabilities, from crossed-eyes to dwarfism, might also be insultingly called or compared to goblins. It is only in the twenty-first century that the ugliness, deformity, and atypical behaviors of goblins have been reframed as nonconformist assets in an age of absurd societal norms. The internet phenomena of Goblincore and Goblin Mode speak to the broad applicability of the goblin to represent the rejection of unrealistic beauty standards and social conventions.

WHY ARE SO MANY GOBLINS GREEN?

The book is an incredible piece of technology for conveying complex ideas and synthesizing the discourse surrounding them. It is much less ideal, especially in the case of academic publishing, for presenting and analyzing

Fig. 9.1 "Goblin" according to Microsoft Copilot based on a June 2025 query. (Generated by AI)

visual media. I have provided a number of images of goblins in this book, but far fewer than I would have liked—a reality informed by a combination of copyright woes (i.e., Wizards of the Coast) and editorial practicalities. The goblins you have seen in this book have therefore been an uneven corpus of public domain images and those kindly provided by indie game developers, supplemented with my written descriptions of other media. I imagine that many of these depictions have not aligned with the mental image of goblins among many readers, which, if I had to guess, would look more like the creature in Fig. 9.1.

The inevitable pivot to AI is here. In the summer of 2025, I put the prompt of "goblin" into a number of image generators (Adobe Firefly, Nightcafe, Ideogram, Stable Diffusion, ChatGPT/Dall-E, and Microsoft CoPilot) to see what synthetic horrors would arise. If AI is going to scrape my writing without credit and tempt my students with the promise of vacuous-yet-grammatically-correct writing, then I am going to use this technology as a framing mechanism. These large language models (LLMs) returned images of goblins that are remarkably similar. All of them are green humanoids with large ears, pronounced noses, and wide mouths (typically smiling and emphasizing wrinkles in their skin). Their heads are disproportionately large compared to their short bodies, and if they have hair, it is gray or white. Most have tattered clothing/armor and crude medieval weaponry. Some of them are placed in caves, others in forests, others without any scenic backdrop at all. These depictions roughly conformed to the image in my mind: an archetypal fantasy goblin that could easily slot into a game of *D&D*.[2]

I have spent much of this book showing the many ways that people have envisioned and interpreted goblins. What these AI models indicate, though, is that the pool of visual media (accessible on the internet) related to the word "goblin" is so skewed toward neo-medieval high fantasy that these LLMs, despite scraping different corners of the internet, have produced similar synthetic renderings. The black-skinned, fire-breathing *gobelinus* is nowhere to be found. Nor is the goblin king of "The Story of the Goblins Who Stole a Sexton." Nor is an abstract visualization of a goblin idea or goblin forest. Instead, fantasy tropes for a specific creature are dominant, and the prevalent use of AI art will only reinforce this imagery, which in turn will feed future LLMs, which in turn will reinforce this imagery. The cycle of enshittification continues.

How, then, did this particular iteration of the fantasy goblin become so dominant? Some components are fairly straightforward. The pipeline of George MacDonald to J.R.R. Tolkien to Gary Gygax informed the neo-medieval worlds in which goblins are frequent antagonists. Their potential for cunning, malevolence, trickery, and mischief is displayed in pointy-toothed smiles accompanied by raggedy clothing and weapons. I have lost track, too, of the number of goblins described as short or diminutive, a

---

[2] When I tried "folkloric goblin" on these same LLMs, the goblins were quite similar in appearance but had magical staffs instead of swords, cute tunics instead of raggedy armor, and less menacing smiles.

trend that stretches back to the early modern period. Often accompanying this stature is a disproportionately large head, which was informed in part by dwarfism among humans (see Walter Scott).

The question of green skin is a bit trickier. Goblins have been associated with darkness since the Middle Ages, and when depicted in mass-produced illustrations or woodcuts, they tend to be black or cross-hatched with black lines. MacDonald, Tolkien, and Gygax do not frequently describe the skin of their goblins as green—instead gravitating toward gray, yellow, and orange. Animated iterations of goblins and orcs from *The Hobbit* (1977) and *The Lord of the Rings* (1978) also have dark skin ranging from gray to brown to black.[3] Such coloration is reminiscent of many creatures illustrated by Arthur Rackham, whose goblins were prominently featured in the 1933 edition of *Goblin Market*.

For the tradition of the green-skinned goblin, then, we have to turn elsewhere. Folkloric and fairy tale compilations from the nineteenth century associated certain fairies with the color green, especially with regard to the color of their clothing.[4] A handful of fairy tales in the early-mid twentieth century also describe goblins in green clothing, including *The Little Green Goblin* (1907) by Naylor and *The First Green Goblin Book* (1935) by Blyton, both of which I briefly considered in Chap. 8.[5] Even though these goblins were pale-skinned, the labeling of them as green goblins influenced a later generation of authors and artists. When Stan Lee and Steve Ditko crafted the villainous Green Goblin, his costume was green and skin-tight, thus giving the appearance of green skin even though the human beneath it (Norman Osborn) was white. Likely informing the coloration of this villain, too, was alliteration, a common trend in the world of Peter Parker, J. Jonah Jameson, and Otto Octavius. Opting for a green goblin instead of a gray or gold goblin, though, reflected the folkloric and fairy tale precedents set above, which Lee obliquely referenced in the cover blurb and title for the first comic book featuring this villain in 1963.

---

[3] *The Hobbit*, directed by Jules Bass and Arthur Rankin Jr. (NBC, 1977); *The Lord of the Rings*, directed by Ralph Bakshi (United Artists, 1978).

[4] See, for example, Sikes, *British Goblins: Welsh Folk-Lore, Fairy Mythology, Legends and Traditions*, 132. Daimler speculates that the color has "layered symbolism of death, life, and immortality." Morgan Daimler, *Fairies: A Guide to the Celtic Fair Folk* (Lanham: John Hunt Publishing, 2017), chapter 2.

[5] Relevant, too, is Tudor Jenks, "The Spelling-Match," *St. Nicholas*, November 1921.

Other fantasy goblins drifted toward green coloration in the 1970s and 1980s. Some of the art inspired by *The Lord of the Rings* and *D&D* depicted green orcs, which could be conflated with or related to goblins in these respective universes.[6] Peripheral, too, is the creature Yoda from *The Empire Strikes Back* (1980), whom director George Lucas described as a combination of a "leprechaun and a troll and a gnome."[7] Yoda is diminutive, green, wrinkly, had long ears, did tricksy things, and spoke in a strange voice—so it is easy to see how he might have been compared to a goblin even though he is not called one in the film.[8] The developers of *Ultima III* and *Wizardry III* made their goblins green, too, and the antagonistic Blix from *Legend* has green-gray skin as well. When the designers of *Warhammer* described goblins in the second edition of the game (1984/1985), they noted that their skin color "varies a great deal, some are pallid and greenish; others are dark skinned or almost black."[9] By the 1990s, though, designers grouped goblins and orcs under the banner of "Greenskins" to reflect a homogenization of their skin tone.[10] I suspect that this choice was partially inspired by the need for armies to have some degree of coherence in presentation for a tabletop wargame. A swarm of multi-colored figurines is more confusing than a more visually consistent, green-skinned horde.

The green-skinned goblin was then adopted for the *Warcraft* series, which some developers had initially wanted to be set within the universe of *Warhammer*.[11] Green goblins play a minor role in *Warcraft II* and

[6] Tim Kirk, *The J.R.R. Tolkien Calendar 1975* (New York City: Ballantine Books, 1974), September; "The Treasure of Tardos." *Dungeons & Dragons*, directed by John Gibbs, 2.2 (CBS, September 15, 1984). The cover art for *AD&D Figure Set* #2011: Orc's Lair (produced in 1980) also features green orcs. See also Doug Stewart, *2e Monstrous Manual* (Lake Geneva: TSR, Inc., 1993), 281.

[7] J.W. Rinzler, *The Making of Star Wars: The Empire Strikes Back* (New York: Random House Worlds, 2010), 34.

[8] Yoda is even called a goblin in Cavan Scott, *Dooku: Jedi Lost* (Random House Audio, 2019).

[9] Richard Halliwell, Bryan Ansell, and Rick Priestley, *Warhammer: Battle Bestiary* (Games Workshop, 1984), 16. See, also, the green-skinned orcs on the cover of Ian Page, Gary Chalk, and Joe Dever, *Blood Bath at Orc's Drift* (Games Workshop, 1985).

[10] Rick Priestley, William Donald Ælian King, and John Blanche, *Warhammer Armies: Orcs & Goblins* (Games Workshop, 1993).

[11] Luke Plunkett, "How Warcraft Was Almost a Warhammer Game (and How That Saved WoW)," Kotaku, July 26, 2012, https://kotaku.com/how-warcraft-was-almost-a-warhammer-game-and-how-that-5929161

Warcraft III, but they have been part of *World of Warcraft* since its release in 2004 and were made a playable race in 2009's *Cataclysm*. The default skin tone of goblins in this universe and related media is green, though it can be modified in-game based on player preferences.[12] In my estimation, the monumental popularity and longevity of *World of Warcraft*, combined with the above iterations of green goblins (especially the Spider-Man villain), solidified green as the predominant skin tone for goblins writ large. To be clear, goblins continue to have non-green skin in many circumstances (the *Harry Potter* universe especially), but *World of Warcraft* seems to be a tipping point in the ubiquity of green goblins for visual media circulating on the internet.

One parting note on the realm of skin tone and appearance. AI models provide much more diverse iterations when given the prompt of "hobgoblin." The culled materials from ChatGPT produce a demonic creature with deep red skin, menacing tusks, and bearing a formidable blade. Microsoft Copilot (Fig. 9.2) draws on the soldier hobgoblin of *D&D*. Stable Diffusion appears to have absorbed a combination of high fantasy traditions with the villainous Hobgoblin from Spider-Man (first introduced in 1983). Adobe Firefly goes in another direction entirely that embraces a cuter, more hirsute hobgoblin potentially derived from children's fantasy media. Due to copyright restrictions, I am unable to provide all of these depictions in this book, and the unclear corpus of culled materials from these LLMs might render your goblin/hobgoblin searches to be quite different. In any case, the high fantasy tradition is not quite as ubiquitous for the hobgoblin, which has led LLMs to elevate other contexts in which they have been invoked.

GERIATRIC GOBLINS

Before leaving the realm of visual representation, I want to address the issue of age. Descriptions of goblins in folklore usually do not emphasize their age—after all, the life cycles of these preternatural beings are unclear. Instead, the ugliness of goblins can manifest in grotesque smiles, bulging eyes, and/or other disproportionate facial features that emphasize wrinkles. Thus, an 1891 song proclaims "Go, you gaunt and grisly goblin, / Wrinkled-skinned and bacon-hued" and a 1925 compilation of children's

---

[12] See, for example, http://worldofwarcraft.blizzard.com/en-us/game/races/goblin

Fig. 9.2 "Hobgoblin" according to Microsoft Copilot based on a June 2025 query. (Generated by AI)

stories tells of a goblin with a "face wrinkled into a cheerful smile."[13] These characteristics could be true of masculine characters more broadly— and were striking in juxtaposition to young women or feminine fairies that radiated beauty, as exemplified by the work of Arthur Rackham (Fig. 9.3).

[13] Oscar E. Young, *Seaside Songs and Woodland Whispers* (Buffalo: Charles Wells Moulton, 1891), 236; Walter Taylor Field, *The Fourth Field Reader* (Boston: Ginn and Company, 1925), 320.

Fig. 9.3 Two illustrations by Arthur Rackham. Arthur Rackham's illustrations from "Snow White and the Seven Dwarfs" in *The Fairy Tales of the Brothers Grimm* (1909, left) and *Goblin Market* (1933, right). Images courtesy of Wikimedia. (Mrs. Edgar Lucas, *The Fairy Tales of the Brothers Grimm* (New York: Doubleday, Page & Co., 1909), 161–70; Rossetti, *Goblin Market*, cover. Accessible here: https://commons.wikimedia.org/wiki/File:Arthur_Rackham_Snow_White.jpg and https://commons.wikimedia.org/wiki/File:Goblin_Market_032.jpg)

The prominence of the wrinkly goblin was such that Lewis Spence, a Scottish journalist and folklorist, wrote of goblins as embodying old age, sickness, and mortality itself in 1946's *British Fairy Origins*:

> I refer to the appearance which the goblin tribe, and indeed male fairies in general, present. Whence comes the inspiration which depicts the masculine fairy in art and illustration with enormous eye sockets, in which roll large and "goggling" eyes? From what model is drawn the emaciated face, prominently revealing the bony structure, the skinny frame, the wasted hands? To anyone whose avocation has at any time brought him into touch with the wards of great hospitals, the origin of the goblin face and form is only too clear. It represents humanity sick unto death, on the verge of mor-

tality. The goblin or male fairy is, outwardly, artistically, a reminiscence of the dying man; he is a replica of the manner in which generations of artists have sought to depict either the dead soul, or the dead body returned from the grave.[14]

The appearance of dying humans is so similar to the distorted physical characteristics of goblins (and male fairies more broadly) that Spence sees the latter as symbolically reflective of the former. This particular take is, of course, overly simplistic and could never encompass the variety of creatures and the motifs associated with them in this history. It does, however, show another avenue through which the grotesque appearance of goblins could be projected onto a group of people. We have seen this in the cases of non-Christians bearing physical similarities to hideous demons and people with disabilities or certain skin tones being compared to goblins. In this case, the goblins' spindly hands, wrinkles, and pronounced facial features, which broadly resemble the signs of aging in humans, charted onto Spence's broader assessment of male fairies.

That said, I struggled to find specific references to goblins as old aged. They are regularly described as "wrinkled" in the nineteenth and early twentieth centuries, but I could not detect an underlying emphasis on age, which makes sense given the unclear life cycles of creatures in folklore and fairy tales. In fantasy media, goblins are presumed to have similar life cycles as humans (albeit on a condensed timeline), but the trope of old goblins is not particularly common in this genre. If anything, goblins are frequently killed before they are able to reach old age. The characterization of goblins as reflections of old age or as uniformly old creatures is thus rare, especially in comparison to associations with the dark, grotesque, and ugly.

Masculine, Feminine, and Nonbinary Goblins

For much of this history, goblins have been coded as male creatures, though this gendered characterization has been far from uniform. When Christian theologians wrote of goblins as demons, they presumed a transcendence of gender binaries. Demons, after all, were fallen angels and did not have material bodies. They could take male and female forms at will, and medieval art often showed them with both masculine and feminine features. When authors of the early modern period discussed folkloric

---

[14] Spence, *British Fairy Origins*, 82.

goblins, they often used the term as a broad designator that enveloped creatures of all shapes, sizes, and genders. More specific creatures, like Hobgoblin, were coded as masculine—both in illustrations from broadside ballads and folkloresque interpretations (especially Shakespeare). Milton, in his pastoral poem "L'Allegro," also mentions the drudging goblin that seeks to earn "his" cream for performing chores. The occasional mention of a "she-goblin" in early modern texts further presumes a default masculine association for the goblin.[15] I am uncertain of the root cause of this phenomenon, as the dialectic of folklore and the folkloresque is impossible to tease out with precision in the medieval and early modern periods. It is possible that the fairy queens of Spenser and Shakespeare inspired a masculine counterpart that only becomes apparent later. Maybe the masculine Hobgoblin, too, influenced other iterations of the goblin.

In any case, the masculine coding of goblins was crystallized in the nineteenth century. The separation of goblins from fairies (united respectively under a king or queen) in folkloresque works became more pronounced as the century progressed. This gendered division was especially prevalent in fairy tales and solidified the trope of villainous, masculine, and antagonistic goblins that worked in opposition to more benevolent forces. The frequent portrayal of dark-skinned goblin kings seeking to abduct and forcibly marry young, white girls speaks in particular to Victorian anxieties about the formation of proper households. Works of enduring popularity by Dickens and Rossetti, too, depicted masculine and grotesque goblins, though they were deployed to different ends in their narratives. George MacDonald admittedly wrote about goblin families (including a goblin queen) in *The Princess and the Goblin*, but Tolkien thoroughly undermined any scrap of goblin femininity among the creatures of Middle-earth. His goblins—evil, mortal, ugly, barbaric, masculine, and crude reflections of superior races—became the archetype for later fantasy portrayals and have been dominant since the second half of the twentieth century. In early iterations of *D&D*, too, goblins have life cycles that broadly mimic humans and presume some kind of female presence, but depictions of them are uniformly masculine.

As I detailed in Chaps. 7 and 8, creators of fantasy media have pushed back on Tolkienian tropes since the 1980s and drawn on other folkloresque tropes to craft new kinds of goblins. The *Harry Potter* series was certainly important in this context. So was the cult following of *Labyrinth*.

---

[15] Mason, *The Turke A Worthie Tragedie*, 13.

So were later iterations of *D&D*. So was the *Warcraft* universe. Fan-driven internet forums allowed people to discuss these (and other) goblins, which drove sympathy for these monsters alongside many others. This is consistent with broader trends in monstrous media of the twenty-first century, which has reframed monsters as sympathetic and misunderstood—often in a way that casts humans as the real villains. Thus, the inherent evil of fantasy goblins was minimized across contexts. Elevated in its stead was goblins' mischievous nature and ugly appearance, both of which were sympathetically reframed. Members of the LGBTQ+ community, especially nonbinary people, gravitated toward the Goblincore aesthetic, which celebrates non-traditional beauty. The idea of going Goblin Mode also recasts the underground lurking and mischief of the goblin as a state of being that all humans could enter as they wished, alternatively framed as slovenly or self-care. Even though the word "goblin" long carried a masculine connotation, it was ubiquitous and flexible enough to be adapted for these phenomena that cut across gender boundaries without issue.

This reappraisal of the goblin in the twenty-first century has resulted in new gendered dynamics within fantasy media, too. It has become something of a stereotype for male goblins to be Tolkienian brutes but for female goblins to be cute, domestic, sometimes servile creatures. The best way I can succinctly show this perspective is (maybe embarrassingly) via a Reddit thread. One user on a *D&D* subreddit asked in 2020 "Why are goblin males almost always ugly?" and included an image showing the following dialogue:

Person One: Okay Google find me a picture of a normal looking goblin male
Person Two: Here are some random pics of sexy shortstack female goblins
Person One: I just want one picture of a goblin male for my character reference…
Person Two: Here are some random pics of ugly deformed evil looking goblin males

Commenters on this thread provide a few examples for where this user could find "normal looking" male goblins (an interesting idea in itself).[16]

---

[16] DUCATISLO, "Why Are Goblin Males Almost Always Ugly," *DnD Memes Subreddit*, December 29, 2020, https://www.reddit.com/r/dndmemes/comments/kmnpz2/why_

One even summarizes the three varieties of goblins one could expect to encounter on the internet: "Sexy Bimbo, Spittle encrusted monster, Thinly Veiled Antisemitism." Beneath this humor, though, is a trend in fantasy media that makes masculine humanoids more monstrous and feminine ones more sexual (in ways that neatly map onto prevailing notions of beauty as imagined by straight men). Even as goblins have undergone a reappraisal in fantasy media that sees more female goblins, then, there is a degree of stereotyping nonetheless that makes them less threatening and more sexual than their masculine counterparts. This is by no means universal—recent editions of *D&D* especially reject this portrayal—but it is certainly persistent among certain consumers of fantasy media and speaks to an impulse to conquer masculine monsters and sexualize their feminine counterparts.[17] There is much more to say about this phenomenon, and I am presently envisioning how to mine internet forums to further interrogate these ideas, but for the sake of keeping this book a one-volume affair, I will move on.

GOBLIN EMOTIONS

It is one thing to analyze goblins as depicted by a given creator; it is another to chart how people felt when they encountered them. My own reading of the short stories of Charles Dickens did not see me joyfully giggling as he described the grotesque creatures circling around Gabriel Grub and Trotty. But Dickens' contemporaries found much to laugh at in the portrayal of goblins and the terrified reactions of these characters (especially when adapted for pantomime). Indeed, the line between comical and scary can be thin, overlapping, and context-dependent. For example, the area that would become Goblin Valley State Park was documented in the early 1950s in articles that highlight the "grotesque features" of its

---

are_goblin_males_almost_always_ugly/. See also @MemesDnd, Twitter, March 8, 2022: https://x.com/MemesDnd/status/1501154163056652288

[17] Fantasy creatures seem to be carving out distinctive niches in the realm of erotica, too. Stories about goblins frequently feature feminine goblins that encourage men to indulge in their baser desires without regard for societal norms. When images accompany these texts, the goblins are basically busty human women but with green skin and pointy ears. Male goblins are much rarer in this genre than orcs, which are typically depicted as human men, rippling with muscles, and only noticeable as a monster because of their green skin and (sometimes) fangs.

rocky hoodoos.[18] One reporter called photographs of the location "silent and sullen, and full of sorcery" such that "nightmares are re-created—in sandstone." She writes that "if any wandering sheepherder, cowboy, or Indian has ever spied the valley he's never said a word—maybe scared out by the weird formations of misshapen Goblins."[19]

Overly dramatic? I think so. Written with an eye to sell newspapers? Most likely. But this reporter nonetheless uses the promise of mystery and fear to drive engagement about this creepy location. When Goblin Valley attracted more attention in the 1960s as a state park, however, language about the same goblin rock formations shifted. A 1962 article calls the place an "unusual and little-known" attraction because of its "eerie" rock formations.[20] Another from 1968 describes the "fantastic, ridiculous figures" of Goblin Valley that are difficult not to "laugh out loud" upon seeing.[21] The rocks in Goblin Valley did not change over the course of these decades, but the context of people's visits (i.e., visiting a state park instead of the wilderness) and the emotions inspired by these hoodoos did. This brief case study helps us glimpse the complexities associated with labeling goblins as funny, scary, ugly, grotesque, or any other identifier— since such judgments are ultimately down to individuals.

These difficulties only multiply when trying to read the minds of children—a task already monumentally difficult when one is sitting right in front of you, much less transported back decades or centuries. Take, for example, an adorable review of *Little Orphant Annie* (1918) from a girl at a day nursery in Long Beach, California (Fig. 9.4):

> And [Annie] used to tell them about the gobel-lins'll catch you if you don't watch out, and the gob'llins with the funny faces and such awful eyes were flying around all the time, and I got almost scared... And I think the movies

---

[18] These formations broadly resemble those in Yellowstone in Chap. 4. Another name floated for this space was "Mushroom Valley." Philip W. Tompkins, "Goblin Valley," *National Parks Magazine* 28, no. 119 (December 1954): 157–62. See also "Utahns to See Films of Valley of Goblins," *Salt Lake Telegram*, January 13, 1950.

[19] Marian Crawford, "The Lost Valley of the Goblins," *Deseret News*, January 15, 1950. She does admit, though, that some areas are not ugly—including symmetrical pagodas of rocks and "three colonial ladies" of stone amid the monstrosities.

[20] "Goblin Valley Is Future Park," *The Neighbor*, December 26, 1962.

[21] Maxine Martz, "Goblin Valley Too Big for Words," *Deseret News*, August 3, 1968.

Fig. 9.4   Annie and the Goblins. A still from the 1918 film *Little Orphant Annie* showing the titular protagonist (played by Colleen Moore) surrounded by some of the goblins that terrorize disobedient children. *Little Orphant Annie*, directed by Colin Campbell (Pioneer Film Corporation, 1918. This film is accessible via the Silent Hall of Fame: https://www.youtube.com/watch?v=sduwxYTUPB4)

was almost as nice as the circus, and the birthday party in the park and all those nice things Mr. Mottell takes us to....[22]

We have goblins that are funny, awful, almost scary, and wrapped up in a movie-going excursion that was, overall, pretty great.[23] The same sentiment was even shared by a modern commentator who called the film's goblins "as adorable as they are scary."[24] I do not have the qualifications

[22] "Day Nursery Kiddies See 'Little Orphan Annie,'" *The Long Beach Telegram and The Long Beach Daily News*, October 20, 1919.
[23] Jessica R. McCort, "Introduction: Why Horror? (Or, The Importance of Being Frightened)," in *Reading in the Dark: Horror in Children's Literature and Culture*, ed. Jessica R. McCort (Jackson: University Press of Mississippi, 2016), 3–36.
[24] Robert K. Klepper, *Silent Films, 1877–1996: A Critical Guide to 646 Movies* (Jefferson: McFarland & Company, Inc., 1999), 135–36.

to do a deep dive into the neurological bases of fear, humor, and their intersections. Having struggled through a few academic works on the subject, it certainly seems as though they are closely related. They might even have been evolutionarily programmed into us, which helps explain the popularity of a game like peekaboo, the proliferation of "scare prank" videos on social media, and the rise of the comedy-horror genre.[25] Multiplying this complexity is the spectrum of fear-based emotions from the vaguely scary to the downright horrifying, all of which is contingent on cultural context. This is all to say that, whatever the intention behind the characteristics of a given iteration of a goblin, the reaction of audiences might have been very different. I have touched on this issue of reception in a few cases, but I will be the first to acknowledge that much more can be done with it.

A Few Quantitative Ideas

I have used a handful of digital resources across this book to extrapolate quantitative changes over time and show how my qualitative analyses intersect with them. My toolset for retrieving and processing data has been admittedly basic. I have scraped some online repositories using web-scraper.io and Python scripts. Microsoft Excel has been an asset through virtually every stage of data processing. English Corpora and Voyant Tools have had incredible utility as well (both of which are browser-based and do not require coding). While I am mildly content with the results of this quantitative work, I know that someone with more advanced coding knowledge (and knowledge of linguistics) could push this data and the questions asked of it to another level.[26] Cross-referenced textual data related to places of publication, gender of author, genre, intended reading level, and other qualifiers would likely shine additional light on the ways in which "goblin" and other lexemes were deployed across corpora. The cre-

[25] Ronald C. Simons, *Boo! Culture, Experience, and the Startle Reflex* (New York: Oxford University Press, 1996); Jaak Panksepp and Lucy Biven, *The Archaeology of Mind: Neuroevolutionary Origins of Human Emotion* (New York: W.W. Norton & Company, 2012); Marc Hye-Knudsen et al., "First They Scream, Then They Laugh: The Cognitive Intersections of Humor and Fear," *Evolutionary Psychology* 22, no. 2 (June 2024), https://doi.org/10.1177/14747049241258355

[26] For an informative and technical read on some of these linguistic specifics, see Eric Friginal and Jack A. Hardy, eds., *The Routledge Handbook of Corpus Approaches to Discourse Analysis* (New York: Routledge, 2020).

ation of web tools that aggregate and clean primary source texts relevant to folklore and the folkloresque would also be an invaluable contribution to future studies.

While I anxiously wait for such software to come to light—or try to do it myself, only to quit yet another Python course on Codecademy after learning how to type *print ("Hello, World!")* for the hundredth time—I can offer a few supplemental quantitative notes to complement the ones already presented in this book.[27] The first relates to political discourse. I have provided a few examples of politicians criticizing hostile people or ideas as goblins or hobgoblins. My sense from reading these texts was that this was a phenomenon of the latter half of the nineteenth century, which then faded away as the words became the stuff of fairy tales and fantasy. Data from the UK Parliament and the US Congress indicates that this is partially true.[28] Usages of "goblin" and (much more commonly) "hobgoblin" spike in the UK Parliament during the 1860s and 1970s. Consistent records for the US Congress only stretch back to the 1870s, and we only see relatively frequent deployment of the terms in the 1960s and 1970s (Figs. 9.5 and 9.6) (Table 9.1).

First things first: we should not overstate the reach of the data from these graphs and tables. It is not reflective of the entirety of political

Table 9.1   Collocates for "Goblin" and "Hobgoblin" in the US Congress

Hobgoblin	354	Hobgoblins	222	Goblin	114	Goblins	167
Minds	166	Ghosts	20	Minds	19	Ghosts	49
Consistency	135	Raised	11	Valley	18	Ghouls	10
Little	120			State	17		
Foolish	71			Consistency	15		
Small	54			Park	14		

The first row of this data shows the number of instances of "hobgoblin(s)" and "goblin(s)." Subsequent rows show collocates for each of these four words. Collocates from the US Congress shows that the words "goblin" and "hobgoblin" were most often deployed in reference to Goblin Valley State Park and Emerson's quotation "A foolish consistency is the hobgoblin of little minds, adored by little statesmen and philosophers and divines"

[27] Alan Liu, "N + 1: A Plea for Cross-Domain Data in the Digital Humanities," in *Debates in Digital Humanities*, ed. Matthew K. Gold and Lauren F. Klein (Minneapolis: University of Minnesota Press, 2016), 599–568.

[28] These records are accessible at https://hansard.parliament.uk/ and https://www.congress.gov/congressional-record

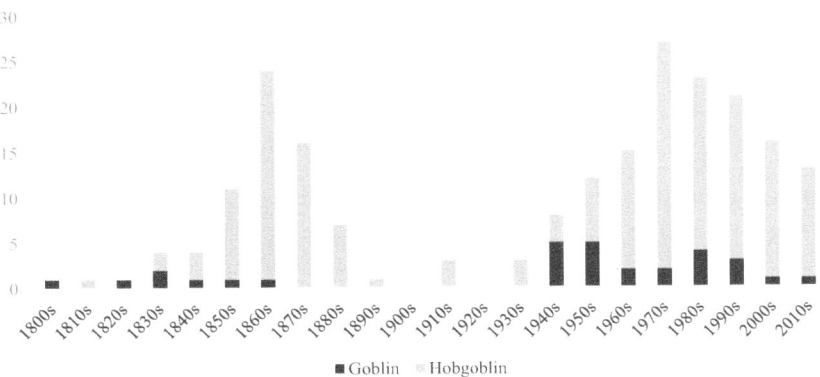

Fig. 9.5 "Goblin" and "Hobgoblin" in the UK Parliament. (Data from the UK Parliament shows a surge of instances of "goblin" and "hobgoblin" in the 1850s–1870s as well as a second peak in the mid-twentieth century that tapers off into the 2010s)

discourse, nor does it consider changing practices in documentation, nor does it consider the relative number of words recorded in each decade. I unfortunately do not have the capacity to obtain this data based on the resources I could locate online. What this data suggests, though, is that a few politicians in the United Kingdom latched onto the hobgoblin as a creature that could be used to label unfavorable people, policies, or ideas in the mid-late nineteenth century. The growing popularity of folklore and fairy tales around this time might have contributed to politicians' willingness to invoke the preternatural. In both the United Kingdom and the United States, deployments of this quotation increased again in the mid-twentieth century, likely the result of renewed interest in Emerson and, perhaps, the growing ubiquity of Tolkien. A broad and often pejorative atmosphere of superstition surrounded the plural forms of "goblins" and "hobgoblins." Such associations have nonetheless fallen since the 1970s, and none of the terms are deployed with any regularity today. While the examples provided earlier in this book show that goblins could be marshaled in the realm of politics to disparage harmful ideas or groups, this appears to be a rare niche in the histories of this lexeme.

Moving toward the twenty-first century, the ascendency of the goblin as a creature overwhelmingly associated with fantasy media, particularly in neo-medieval universes, can be glimpsed in a few ways. Quantitative data

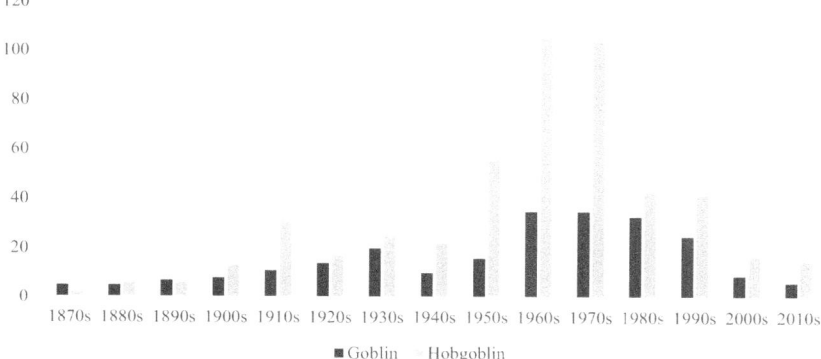

Fig. 9.6 "Goblin" and "Hobgoblin" in the US Congress. (Data from the US Congress dating back to the 1870s shows surging instances of "goblin" and "hobgoblin" in the 1960s and 1970s)

from both Google Books alongside corpora based on movies and TV shows show surging attestations of goblins (far more than hobgoblins) in the early 2000s.[29] This timeline aligns neatly with the renaissance of fantasy literature begun by Rowling, Pullman, and others, which in turn facilitated movies and television series on similar themes (Figs. 9.7 and 9.8).

As I so often tell my students, correlation does not equal causation. To show that these attestations from the 2000s are the result of fantasy media, we need to turn to another dataset. Collocation data from iWeb, a corpus of some 14 billion words scraped from 22 million web pages, confirms that the words most used around "goblin(s)" fit into a tradition of high fantasy.[30] Collocates are overwhelmingly other fantastical creatures and words that fit into narratives of questing and dungeon-diving. The notable exception is the goblin shark, which is mentioned on nature-themed websites. "Hobgoblin(s)" follows a broadly similar pattern with the notable exception of Emerson's quotation about the "hobgoblins of little minds," which is apparent in this data (Table 9.2).

---

[29] These corpora of movies and TV shows were compiled by Mark Davies. They are accessible at https://www.english-corpora.org/movies/ and https://www.english-corpora.org/tv/

[30] Technical details on this corpus can be found at https://www.english-corpora.org/iweb/

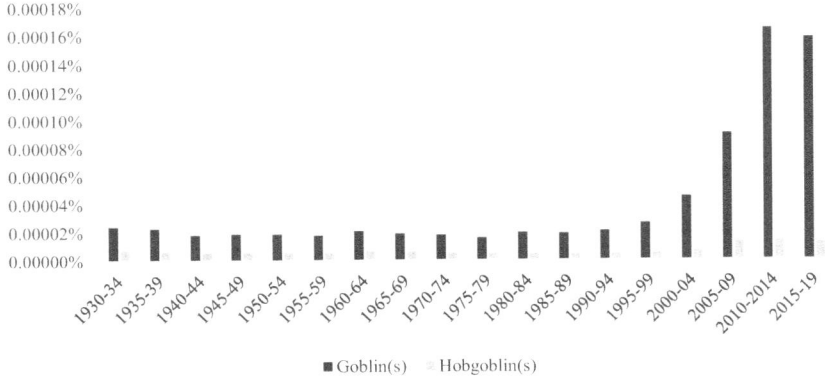

Fig. 9.7 "Goblin" and "Hobgoblin" in Google Books. (Data from Google Books shows the frequency of the word "goblin" remaining relatively low until the early 2000s, when it skyrockets in popularity, as opposed to the use of "hobgoblin," which only increases slightly in the early 2000s)

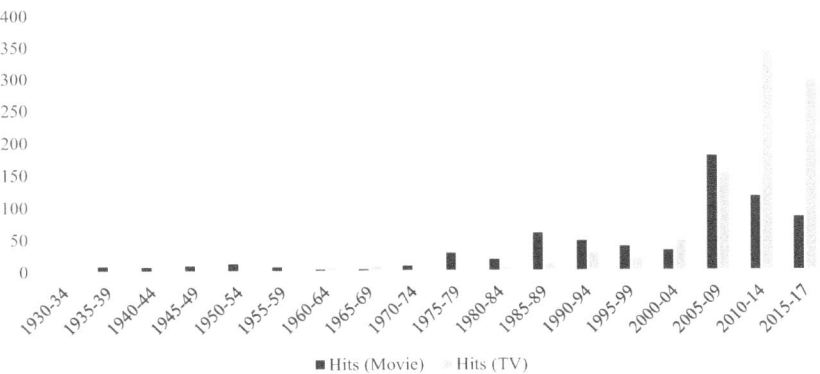

Fig. 9.8 "Goblin" and "Hobgoblin" in movies and TV. (Movie and TV show scripts show increased references to goblins and hobgoblins since 2005)

The increased presence of goblins in fantasy media has even caught the imagination of some scientists. Evocations of goblins in nature during the nineteenth century were colloquial (i.e., a goblin forest or goblin shark) but not embedded into scientific nomenclature. A handful of scientists since 2010, though, have taxonomized new species of small creatures

Table 9.2   iWeb Data for "Goblin" and "Hobgoblin"

Goblins
Collocates (Noun): ghost, orc, ghoul, shark, king, troll, army, witch
Collocates (Verb): kill, fight, attack, defeat, steal, spear, encounter, spawn
Collocates (Adj): green, little, evil, giant, scary, weak, orange, magic
Collocates (Adv): underground, rightfully, single-handedly, maniacally, mortally, stealthily, mercilessly, bravely
Hobgoblins
Collocates (Noun): mind, goblin, consistency, orc, tribe, ghost, bugbear, witch
Collocates (Verb): kill, attack, fight, demand, haunt, inhabit, defend, chase
Collocates (Adj): little, foolish, small, evil, endless, ancient, supernatural, remaining
Collocates (Adv): and, meanwhile, fearfully, abroad, barely, doubt, strictly, utterly

Data from iWeb shows that topics and collocates of "goblin" and "hobgoblin" overwhelmingly revolve around neo-medieval, high fantasy tropes

using the word and Latinized derivations: *Adetomyrma goblin* (ant), *Brachioppiella goblina* (mite), *Eucosma goblinana* (moth), *Goblinia tiane* (spider), and *Orchestina goblin* (spider).[31] The cataloguers of *Adetomyrma goblin* briefly justify their choice because "the males are small and black, and the workers possess long dentition on their masticatory margin."[32] Dark skin and a wide mouth are enough to give this ant a goblin name. The scientists that coined *Brachioppiella goblina* credit the goblins of J.K. Rowling since "long fingers are one of their distinctive features" and the "sensillus" of this species "resembles a long-fingered hand."[33] The two goblin spiders, meanwhile, are part of a larger "Goblin Spider Genus" that has "small size" and "cryptic habits" that make their study difficult.[34] Even if these scientists drew on different goblin traditions, their use of the word in the first place gives some sense of its ubiquity and influence, especially

[31] All of these species can be found at https://www.catalogueoflife.org/

[32] Masashi Yoshimura and Brian L. Fisher, "A Revision of the Malagasy Endemic Genus Adetomyrma (Hymenoptera: Formicidae: Amblyoponinae)," *Zootaxa* 3341, no. 1 (2012): 1–31. The goblin moths, conversely, were named because of their proximity to Goblin Valley: Donald J. Wright, "Nine New Species of Phaneta Stephens (Tortricidae) from Western North America, with Reviews of Ten Related Species," *The Journal of the Lepidopterists' Society* 64, no. 3 (2010): 117–38.

[33] Elizabeth Hugo-Coetzee, "New Oppiidae (Acari: Oribatida) from the Golden Gate Highlands National Park in South Africa," *Zootaxa* 3384, no. 6 (November 2014): 533–52.

[34] Barbara C. Baehr and Darrell Ubick, "A Review of the Asian Goblin Spider Genus Camptoscaphiella (Araneae: Oonopidae)," *American Museum Novitates* 3697 (2010): 1–65.

considering such classifications were exceedingly rare in the twentieth century.[35]

GOBLINS ON THE CUTTING ROOM FLOOR

Michael Ostling cheekily referred to his edited volume, *Fairies, Demons and Nature Spirits: "Small Gods" at the Margins of Christendom* (2017), as an attempt to "create the new scholarly field of 'goblinology' (monster studies, move over and make room!)." This book has provided perhaps the most literal possible interpretation of this field. My restrictive, lexical definition of the goblin has guided me toward a particular history, and even with this narrow focus, I am saddened by those goblins that did not make the cut. I could not find space to detail (among others) the McDonnell XF-85 Goblin prototype aircraft; the 1963 documentary, *Goblin on the Doorstep*, about the need for sophisticated anti-submarine weaponry; the band Nekrogoblicon; John Oliver calling a few conservative media personalities "racial-panic goblins" for demonizing Afghan refugees; the Valley of the Goblins (*Duendes*) at Machu Picchu; the United Kingdom's Goblin Theater; a 1998 performance at Fairy Stone State Park (Virginia) of local youth and American Indians called "Return to Goblin Town"; and the Korean fantasy-romance *Guardian: The Lonely and Great God*, which was previously called *Dokkaebi* and *Goblin*. This is not to say that these goblins are not important, but rather that they did not fit into the underlying trends I thought were most important for this history. I also wince at the thought of the many creatures often considered to be goblins that I could not meaningfully consider. If your favorite goblin did not make the cut, I apologize and can recommend some rituals that might summon one to haunt me (an apt comeuppance).

In any case, I want to mention a few areas that I think could be fruitful sites for further research. The first relates to slang. Our first documented goblin slang arrives in the late nineteenth century with the term, "Jimmy O'Goblin," a rhyming reference to the English sovereign coin.[36] This term surely existed before it was recorded in a slang dictionary, and many others probably did as well without making it into the annals of recorded

---

[35] I could only locate one "goblin" embedded within scientific names from the twentieth century: J.P. Kramer, "Studies of Neotropical Leafhoppers. I. (Homoptera: Cicadellidae)," *Proceedings of the Entomological Society of Washington* 67, no. 2 (1965): 65–74.

[36] *OED*, "Jimmy."

history. More recent slang usages are fortunately easier to locate thanks to the internet. For those brave enough to wade through the morass that is Urban Dictionary, one might find treasures.[37] Slang uses of "goblin" predating Goblin Mode show the term used to describe a number of phenomena. Lil Wayne's 2008 hit "A Milli" asks "what's a goon to a goblin" and places this creature as a gangster to be feared. Some definitions present ill-behaved children as goblins, which anticipates the later phenomenon of the "crotch goblin." Some involve sexual preferences and appetites. Some designate alcoholic and/or disgusting drinks as goblins, including a mixture of vodka and Monster Energy. Some relate to peculiar behavior or appearance: taking too long on a golf course, lurking in a club in the hopes of picking up women, or being a man who is shorter than his female partner (i.e., Tom Cruise).

In reading through a (perhaps excessive) number of these definitions, I can see an underlying trend in unnatural behavior and appearance that is not particularly surprising. But I also notice different spelling conventions and regional references that indicate variations across Anglophone geographies—hence a pejorative definition of goblins as "the locals from the Portsmouth area, the lowest of the low" or the Australian-originated "shitgoblin" to mean a "rude, obnoxious, or contemptible person."[38] The accelerated pace of linguistic change facilitated by the internet is undoubtedly shaping how people invoke goblins and their supernatural kin; broader studies of usage, distribution, and grammatical function over time could be revealing, especially if undertaken by those with expertise in corpus linguistics.[39]

These slang usages, too, speak to a general weakness of this book: the flattening of geographical divisions. With so much history to consider, I was unable to regularly tease out variations between different areas of the

---

[37] Godspeed, dear readers: https://www.urbandictionary.com/define.php?term=goblin

[38] This definition is from https://en.wiktionary.org/wiki/shitgoblin. On Urban Dictionary, the word is sometimes used derogatorily to refer to people from Pakistan and Bangladesh (especially).

[39] Per Blank, "time passes quicker than ever in the digital age; praxis amalgamates as newfangled discursive practices and expressive genres are vernacularly established in rapid-fire succession. And so the recurring cycle of updating and reappropriating the folklorist's mission and purview for studying the Internet is largely a response to the breakneck speed in which digital technologies advance and are then notably adopted by the folk." Trevor J. Blank, *Toward a Conceptual Framework for the Study of Folklore and the Internet* (Logan: Utah State University Press, 2014), 3.

Anglophone sphere. There is a clear precedent for this kind of mapping work. Simon Young, for example, has shown regional geographic distributions that allow for the rough delineation of Boggledom, Dobbiedom, and Boggartdom in northwest England based on naming conventions.[40] I expect that deeper dives into specific geographies could be revealing, especially when the goblin is compared to other preternatural entities across linguistic contexts, from etymological neighbors like the Welsh *coblyn* or French *gobelin* to more distant relatives like the Japanese *tengu*. The issue of geographical precision extends to my source materials, too. I have constructed much of this book off the back of historical sources that have been digitized, which permits quantitative analysis but unfortunately privileges texts deemed important enough by a given group to preserve on the internet. Local historical societies and archives with undigitized sources could shine light on regional variations that I have homogenized for the sake of narrative cohesion. I hope that the arguments I make in this book provide a foundation or point of departure for such studies.

My decision to write this history based on a strict lexical definition of the goblin is bound to rub some readers the wrong way. If it is any consolation, it sometimes rubs me the wrong way. With any broad work of folklore and the folkloresque, we are grappling with words that evolve over time in obscure and uneven ways. Any act of restrictive categorization on the part of an author is bound to be exclusory in some manner, but it is a necessity since our books have to eventually end. I partially chose to focus on the lexeme "goblin" because it facilitated the use of digital tools that could show change over time across genres, but even then, this approach means that I can only capture a narrow window of what is changing. This is all to say that, as I write this conclusion, I see numerous avenues for comparative studies that broaden the ideas under consideration but are more restrictive in geography, chronology, and genre. The colonization of landscapes by deploying familiar supernatural creatures in unfamiliar locations, the regional mapping of goblins and their kin, the deployment of preternatural creatures to describe groups of people, and

---

[40] Young, *The Boggart: Folklore, History, Place-Names and Dialect*, 72. In a different work, Young proposes an alternative to the folkloric bestiary: a "series of different function-based chapters on, say, shape-changers, child-scarers, the social supernatural, water spirits" and the like. These chapters would establish folk taxonomies based on local circumstances and dialects without being restricted to a single location. Simon Young, "Classifying Supernatural Beings: Dialect, Folk Taxonomies and Katharine Briggs' Dictionary of Fairies," *Transactions of the Yorkshire Dialect Society* 23 (2024): 74–75.

the many grassroots internet phenomena that invoke or are inspired by Fairyland are a few possibilities that come to mind. I am sure many more abound.

I began this project as an article-length endeavor that would give me a mental break from the often-brutal history of my area of expertise (the medieval Mediterranean) and allow me to read widely on a topic of personal interest. This was—how to say it—hopelessly naïve. As I was writing this book, I felt a sense of dread at the seemingly endless expanse of scholarship that relates in some way to goblins and fairies and demons and orcs and all of the other things in their general orbit. It was hardly the mental break that I envisioned. It was, though, an immensely useful exercise that inspired me to expand an article into an entire book, which has now exceeded the recommended word count set by my editors by around 50,000 words. I happily exit this project, therefore, with a profound appreciation for how scholars have approached the many faces of Fairyland and a better understanding of the benefits that come from reading scholarship across disciplines. If readers take anything from this book, I hope it is a willingness to venture outside of their academic comfort zone, especially when it comes to folklore and the folkloresque, which cannot be confined to a singular disciplinary silo. This history, then, might be best taken as a humble entry in the ongoing fight against a foolish consistency, that hobgoblin of little minds.

REFERENCES

Baehr, Barbara C., and Darrell Ubick. 2010. A Review of the Asian Goblin Spider Genus Camptoscaphiella (Araneae: Oonopidae). *American Museum Novitates* 3697:1–65.

Bakshi, Ralph, director. 1978. *The Lord of the Rings*. United Artists.

Bass, Jules and Arthur Rankin Jr., directors. 1977. *The Hobbit*. NBC.

Blank, Trevor J. 2014. *Toward a Conceptual Framework for the Study of Folklore and the Internet*. Logan: Utah State University Press.

Campbell, Colin, director. 1918. *Little Orphant Annie*. Pioneer Film Corporation.

Crawford, Marian. 1950. The Lost Valley of the Goblins. *Deseret News*, January 15.

Daimler, Morgan. 2017. *Fairies: A Guide to the Celtic Fair Folk*. Lanham: John Hunt Publishing.

DUCATISLO. 2020. Why Are Goblin Males Almost Always Ugly. *DnD Memes Subreddit*, December 29. https://www.reddit.com/r/dndmemes/comments/kmnpz2/why_are_goblin_males_almost_always_ugly/. Accessed December 1, 2024.

Field, Walter Taylor. 1925. *The Fourth Field Reader*. Boston: Ginn and Company.

Friginal, Eric, and Jack A. Hardy. 2020. *The Routledge Handbook of Corpus Approaches to Discourse Analysis*. New York: Routledge.

Gibbs, John, director. 1984. The Treasure of Tardos. *Dungeons & Dragons* 2 (2). CBS, September 15.

Halliwell, Richard, Bryan Ansell, and Rick Priestley. 1984. *Warhammer: Battle Bestiary*. Games Workshop.

Hendrix, Richard. 1976. Popular Humor and 'The Black Dwarf.'. *Journal of British Studies* 1 (Autumn): 108–128.

Hugo-Coetzee, Elizabeth. 2014. New Oppiidae (Acari: Oribatida) from the Golden Gate Highlands National Park in South Africa. *Zootaxa* 3384 (6): 533–552.

Hye-Knudsen, Marc, Jens Kjeldgaard-Christiansen, Brian B. Boutwell, and Mathias Clasen. 2024. First They Scream, Then They Laugh: The Cognitive Intersections of Humor and Fear. *Evolutionary Psychology* 22 (2): https://doi.org/10.1177/14747049241258355.

Jenks, Tudor. 1921. The Spelling-Match. *St. Nicholas*, November.

Klepper, Robert K. 1999. *Silent Films, 1877–1996: A Critical Guide to 646 Movies*. Jefferson: McFarland & Company, Inc.

Kramer, J. P. 1965. Studies of Neotropical Leafhoppers. I. (Homoptera: Cicadellidae). *Proceedings of the Entomological Society of Washington* 67 (2): 65–74.

Liu, Alan. 2016. N + 1: A Plea for Cross-Domain Data in the Digital Humanities In *Debates in Digital Humanities*, ed. Matthew K. Gold and Lauren F. Klein, 599–568. Minneapolis: University of Minnesota Press.

Lucas, Mrs Edgar. 1909. *The Fairy Tales of the Brothers Grimm*. New York: Doubleday, Page & Co.

Martz, Maxine. 1968. Goblin Valley Too Big for Words. *Deseret News*, August 3.

Mason, John. 1610. *The Turke A Worthie Tragedie*. London: Edward Allde.

McCort, Jessica R. 2016. Introduction: Why Horror? (Or, The Importance of Being Frightened). In *Reading in the Dark: Horror in Children's Literature and Culture*, ed. Jessica R. McCort, 3–36. Jackson: University Press of Mississippi.

Page, Ian, Gary Chalk, and Joe Dever. 1985. *Blood Bath at Orc's Drift*. Games Workshop.

Panksepp, Jaak, and Lucy Biven. 2012. *The Archaeology of Mind: Neuroevolutionary Origins of Human Emotion*. New York: W.W. Norton & Company.

Plunkett, Luke. 2012. How Warcraft Was Almost a Warhammer Game (and How That Saved WoW). *Kotaku*, July 26. https://kotaku.com/how-warcraft-was-almost-a-warhammer-game-and-how-that-5929161.   Accessed December 1, 2024.

Priestley, Rick, William Donald Ælian King, and John Blanche. 1993. *Warhammer Armies: Orcs & Goblins*. Games Workshop.

Purkiss, Diane. 2003. *At the Bottom of the Garden: A Dark History of Fairies, Hobgoblins, Nymphs, and Other Troublesome Things*. New York: NYU Press.

Rinzler, J. W. 2010. *The Making of Star Wars: The Empire Strikes Back*. New York: Random House Worlds.

Rossetti, Christina. 1933. *Goblin Market*. Philadelphia: J.B. Lippincott & Co.

Salt Lake Telegram. 1950. Utahns to See Films of Valley of Goblins. January 13.

Scott, Cavan. 2019. *Dooku: Jedi Lost*. Random House Audio.

Sikes, Wirt. 1880. *British Goblins: Welsh Folk-Lore, Fairy Mythology, Legends and Traditions*. London: Sampson Low, Marston, Searle, & Rivington.

Simons, Ronald C. 1996. Boo! In *Culture, Experience, and the Startle Reflex*. New York: Oxford University Press.

Spence, Lewis. 1946. *British Fairy Origins*. London: Watts & Co.

Stewart, Doug. 1993. *2e Monstrous Manual*. Lake Geneva: TSR, Inc.

The Long Beach Telegram and The Long Beach Daily News. 1919. Day Nursery Kiddies See 'Little Orphan Annie.' October 20.

The Neighbor. 1962. Goblin Valley Is Future Park. December 26.

Tompkins, Philip W. 1954. Goblin Valley. *National Parks Magazine* 28 (119): 157–162.

Wharton, Tom. 1980. New Twists Help Goblin Valley. *The Salt Lake Tribune*, April 10.

Wright, Donald J. 2010. Nine New Species of Phaneta Stephens (Tortricidae) from Western North America, with Reviews of Ten Related Species. *The Journal of the Lepidopterists' Society* 64 (3): 117–138.

Yoshimura, Masashi, and Brian L. Fisher. 2012. A Revision of the Malagasy Endemic Genus Adetomyrma (Hymenoptera: Formicidae: Amblyoponinae). *Zootaxa* 3341 (1): 1–31.

Young, Oscar E. 1891. *Seaside Songs and Woodland Whispers*. Buffalo: Charles Wells Moulton.

Young, Simon. 2022. *The Boggart: Folklore, History, Place-Names and Dialect*. Exeter: Exeter University Press.

Young, Simon. 2024. Classifying Supernatural Beings: Dialect, Folk Taxonomies and Katharine Briggs' Dictionary of Fairies. *Transactions of the Yorkshire Dialect Society* 23:48–80.

INDEX[1]

[1] Note: Page numbers followed by 'n' refer to notes.

© The Editor(s) (if applicable) and The Author(s), under exclusive
license to Springer Nature Switzerland AG 2026
M. King, *A History of Goblins*,
https://doi.org/10.1007/978-3-032-01063-6

The manufacturer's authorised representative in the EU is Springer
Nature Customer Service Centre GmbH, Europaplatz 3, 69115 Heidelberg,
Germany. If you have any concerns regarding our products, please
contact ProductSafety@springernature.com

Printed and bound by CPI Group (UK) Ltd, Croydon, CR0 4YY
29/05/2026
02122042-0001